SLAM DUNK

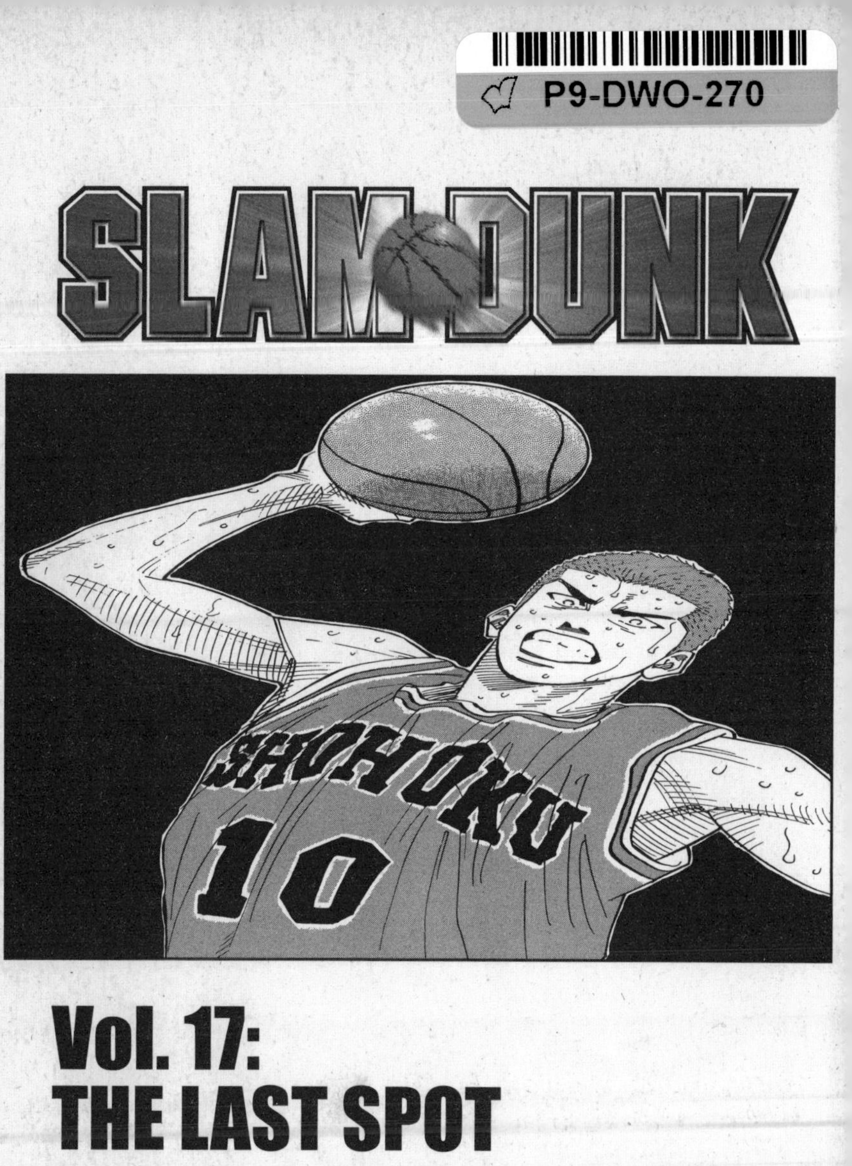
SHOHOKU
10

Vol. 17: THE LAST SPOT

STORY AND ART BY

TAKEHIKO INOUE

Character Introduction

Hanamichi Sakuragi
A first-year at Shohoku High School, Sakuragi is in love with Haruko Akagi.

Haruko Akagi
Also a first-year at Shohoku, Takenori Akagi's little sister has a crush on Kaede Rukawa.

Takenori Akagi
A third-year and the basketball team's captain, Akagi has an intense passion for his sport.

Kaede Rukawa
The object of Haruko's affection (and that of many of Shohoku's female students!), this first-year has been a star player since junior high.

井上雄彦

Takehiko Inoue

1. IT'S BEEN A FEW MONTHS SINCE I MOVED INTO MY NEW WORKSPACE. I SHOULD HAVE A VIEW OF MT. FUJI, BUT SO FAR I'VE ONLY SEEN IT A FEW TIMES.

2. WHEN SHAKING HANDS WITH SOMEBODY I'VE NEVER MET BEFORE, I ALWAYS THINK TO MYSELF, "MY HANDS ARE SO SMALL..."

3. PERHAPS BECAUSE I DID A FOUR-WEEK SERIAL OF "HANG TIME" IN '93, I FELT LIKE I WAS WORKING ALL THE TIME. IT WAS HARD TURNING DOWN INVITATIONS TO GO OUT, BUT I WAS ABLE TO GET SOME GOOD WORK DONE. THANK YOU.

Takehiko Inoue's *Slam Dunk* is one of the most popular manga of all time, having sold over 100 million copies worldwide. He followed that series up with two titles lauded by critics and fans alike—*Vagabond*, a fictional account of the life of Miyamoto Musashi, and *Real*, a manga about wheelchair basketball.

SLAM DUNK
Vol. 17: THE LAST SPOT

SHONEN JUMP Manga Edition

STORY AND ART BY TAKEHIKO INOUE

English Adaptation/Stan!
Translation/Joe Yamazaki
Touch-up Art & Lettering/James Gaubatz
Cover & Graphic Design/Sean Lee, Matt Hinrichs
Editor/Mike Montesa

Printed in Canada

Published by VIZ Media, LLC
P.O. Box 77010
San Francisco, CA 94107

10 9 8 7 6 5 4 3 2 1
First printing, August 2011

Fukuda

Sendoh

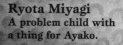

Ryota Miyagi
A problem child with
a thing for Ayako.

Ayako
Basketball Team
Manager

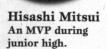

Hisashi Mitsui
An MVP during
junior high.

Our Story Thus Far

Hanamichi Sakuragi is rejected by close to 50 girls during his three years in junior high. He joins the basketball team to get closer to his beloved Haruko Akagi, but the constant fundamental drills cause him endless frustration.

After a good showing in their first exhibition, the team sets its sights on Nationals and ex-problem-child Ryota Miyagi reclaims his position as Point Guard. Not long after Miyagi's return, Hisashi Mitsui—a junior-high-MVP-turned-gang-thug—finds he too misses the game and rejoins the team.

Shohoku advances through the Prefectural Tournament to face Kainan University, but loses by two points. Sakuragi becomes painfully aware of his inability to score points and begins practicing shots from beneath the basket.

Meanwhile, Kainan faces Ryonan in the next round. Thanks to Sendoh and Fukuda's offense, the challengers take the lead, but Maki's leadership helps Kainan rise to the occasion and gradually close the gap.

Vol. 17:
THE LAST SPOT

Table of Contents

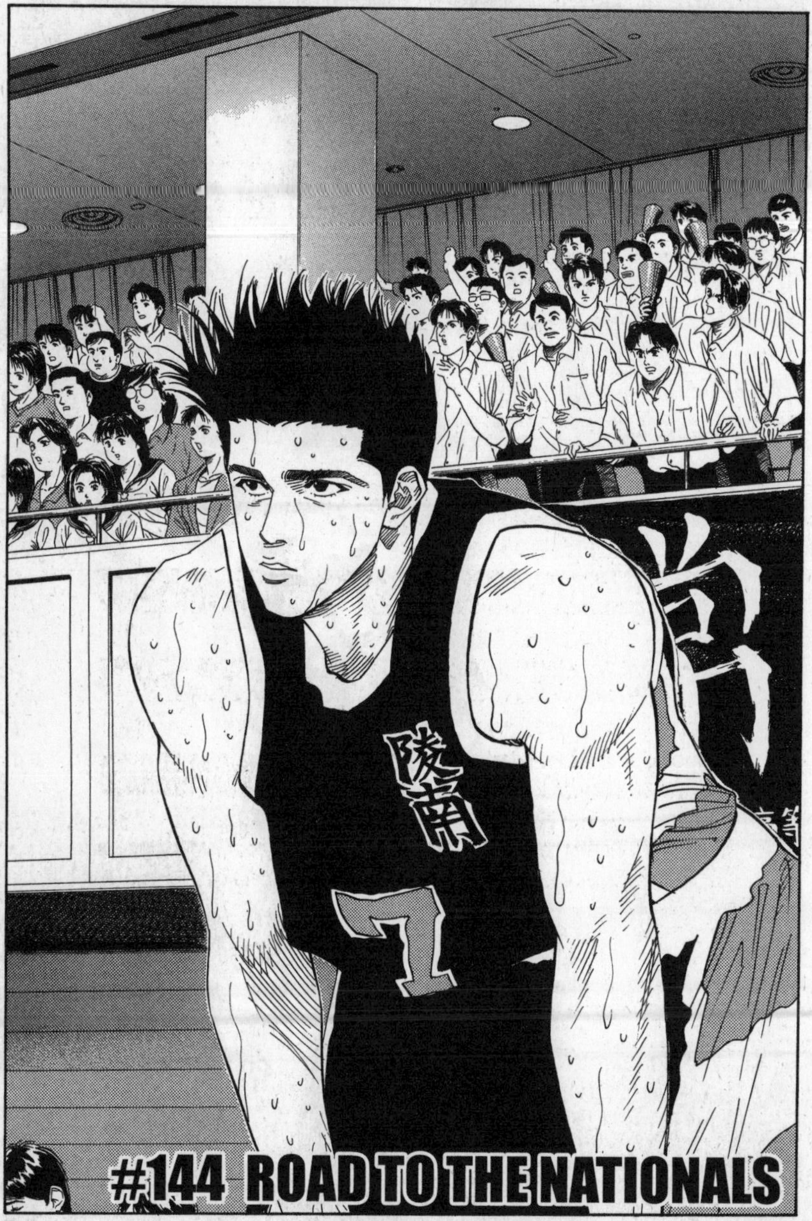
陵南
7
#144 ROAD TO THE NATIONALS

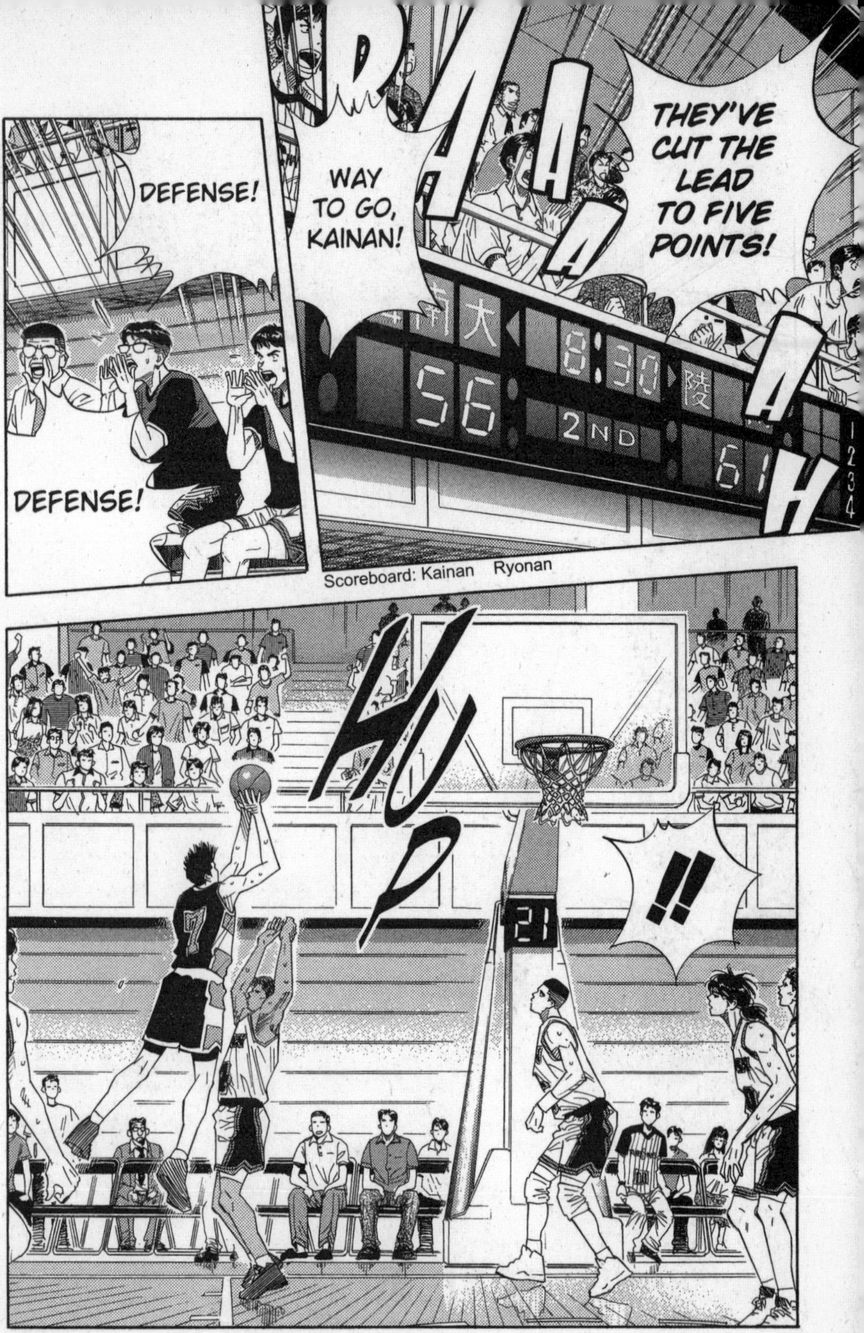
THEY'VE CUT THE LEAD TO FIVE POINTS!
WAY TO GO, KAINAN!
8:30
56
2ND
61
DEFENSE!
DEFENSE!
HUP
!!
Scoreboard: Kainan Ryonan

READ THIS WAY

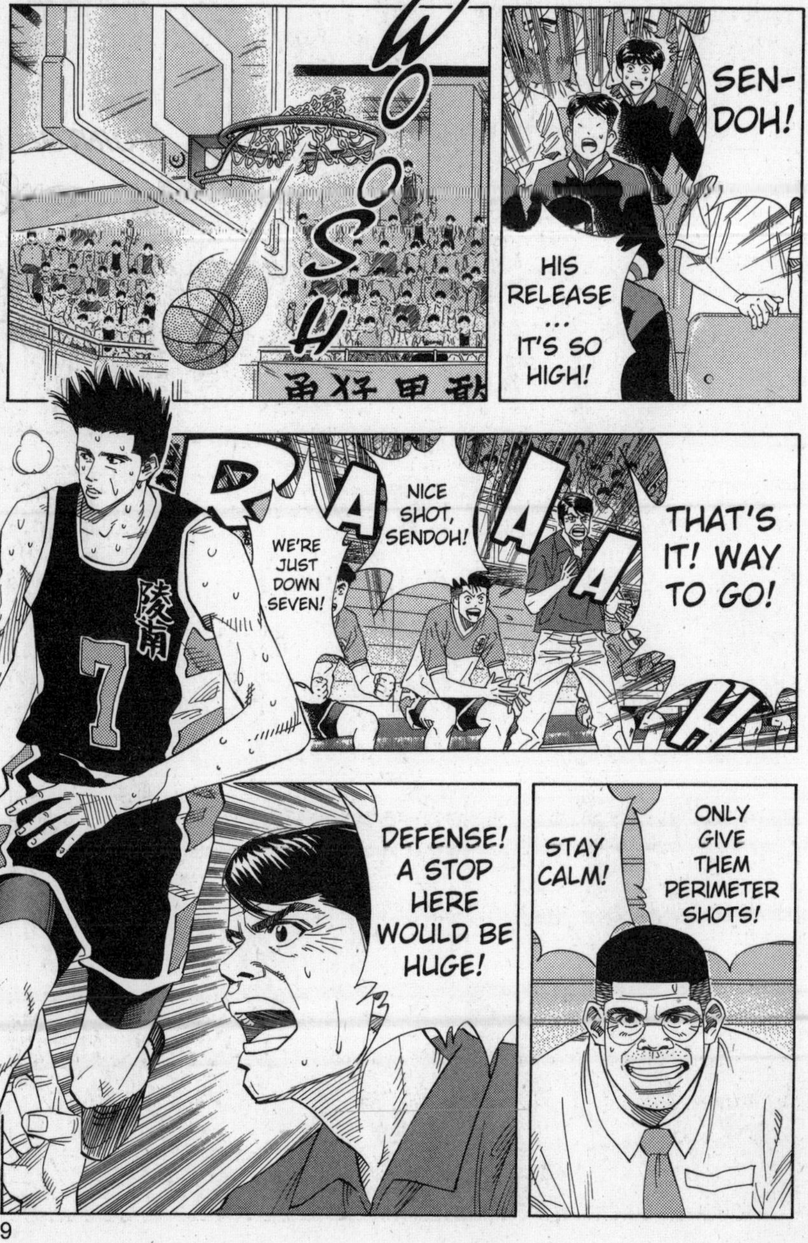
SEN-DOH!
HIS RELEASE ... IT'S SO HIGH!
WOOSH
THAT'S IT! WAY TO GO!
NICE SHOT, SENDOH!
WE'RE JUST DOWN SEVEN!
RAAAAH
陵南
7
ONLY GIVE THEM PERIMETER SHOTS!
STAY CALM!
DEFENSE! A STOP HERE WOULD BE HUGE!

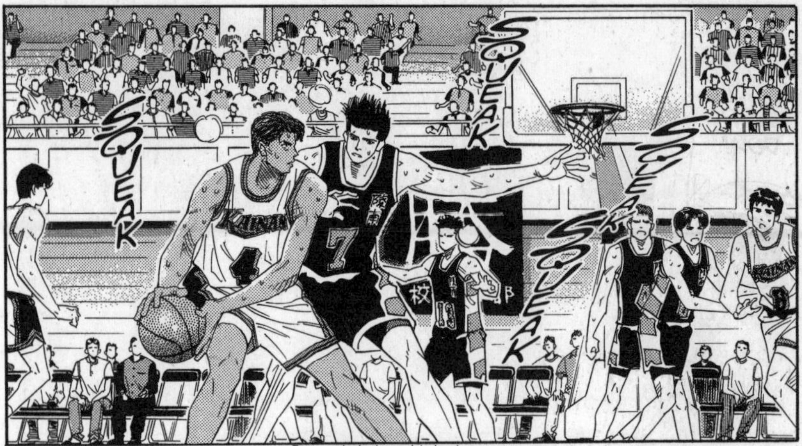
SQUEAK
SQUEAK
SQUEAK
SQUEAK
SQUEAK
Banner: *Josho* (ever victorious)
Kainan Dai Fuzoku High School Basketball Team

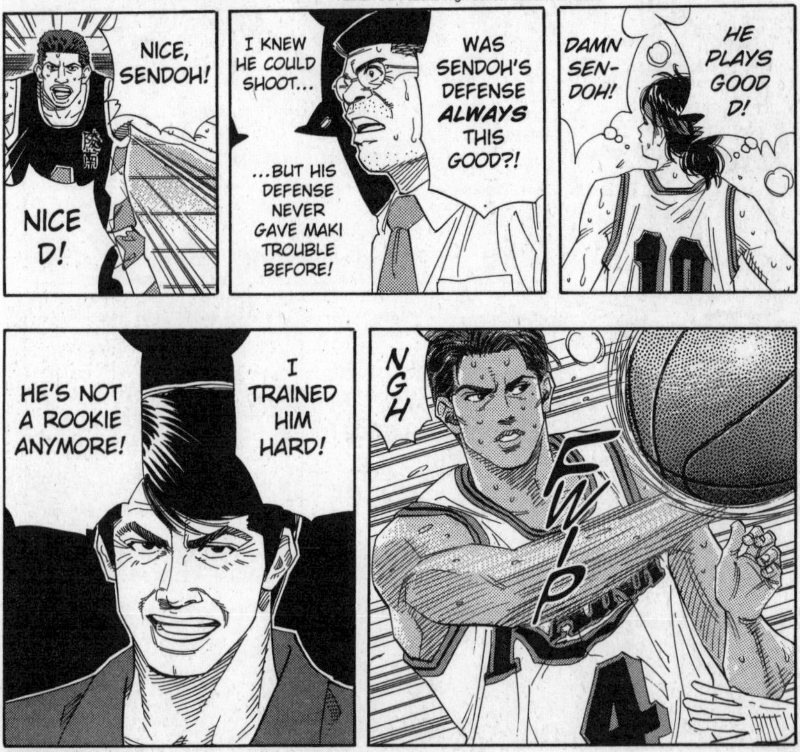
HE PLAYS GOOD D!
DAMN SEN-DOH!
WAS SENDOH'S DEFENSE **ALWAYS** THIS GOOD?!
I KNEW HE COULD SHOOT...
...BUT HIS DEFENSE NEVER GAVE MAKI TROUBLE BEFORE!
NICE, SENDOH!
NICE D!
NGH
FWIP
I TRAINED HIM HARD!
HE'S NOT A ROOKIE ANYMORE!

READ THIS WAY

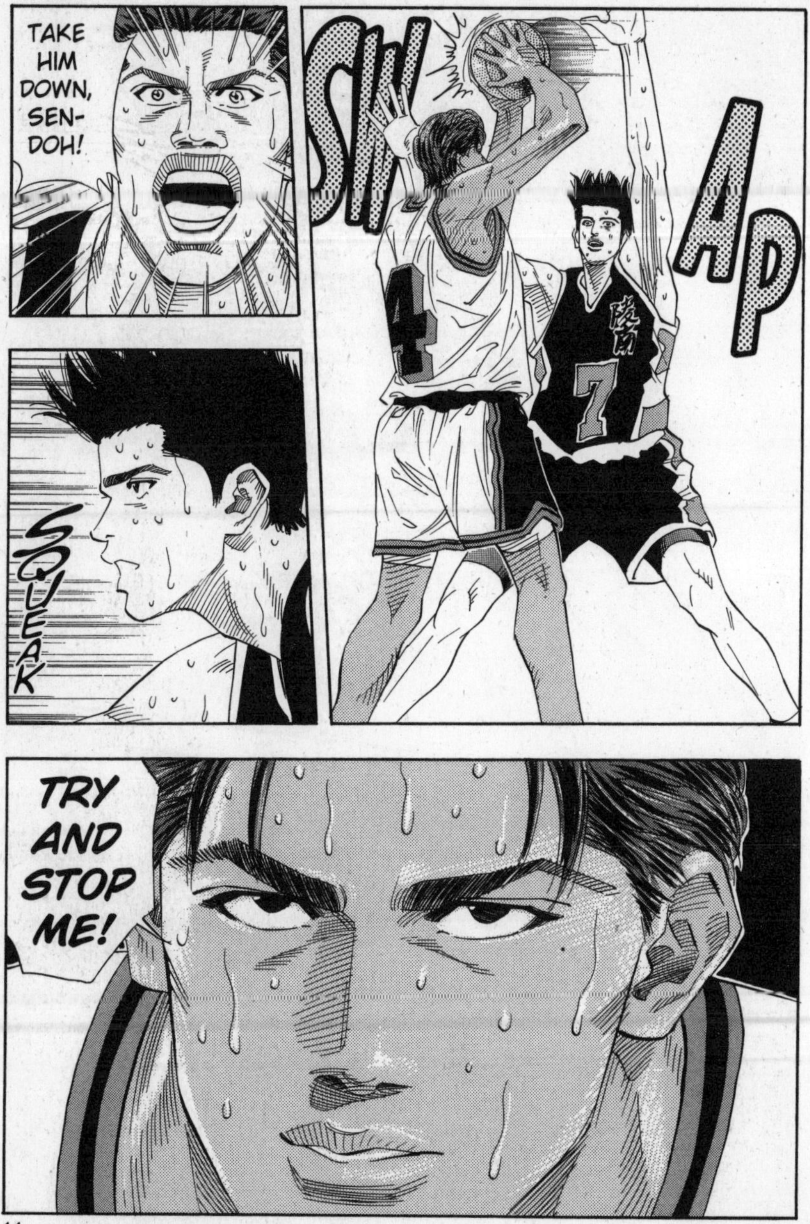
SWAP
TAKE HIM DOWN, SEN-DOH!
SQUEAK
TRY AND STOP ME!

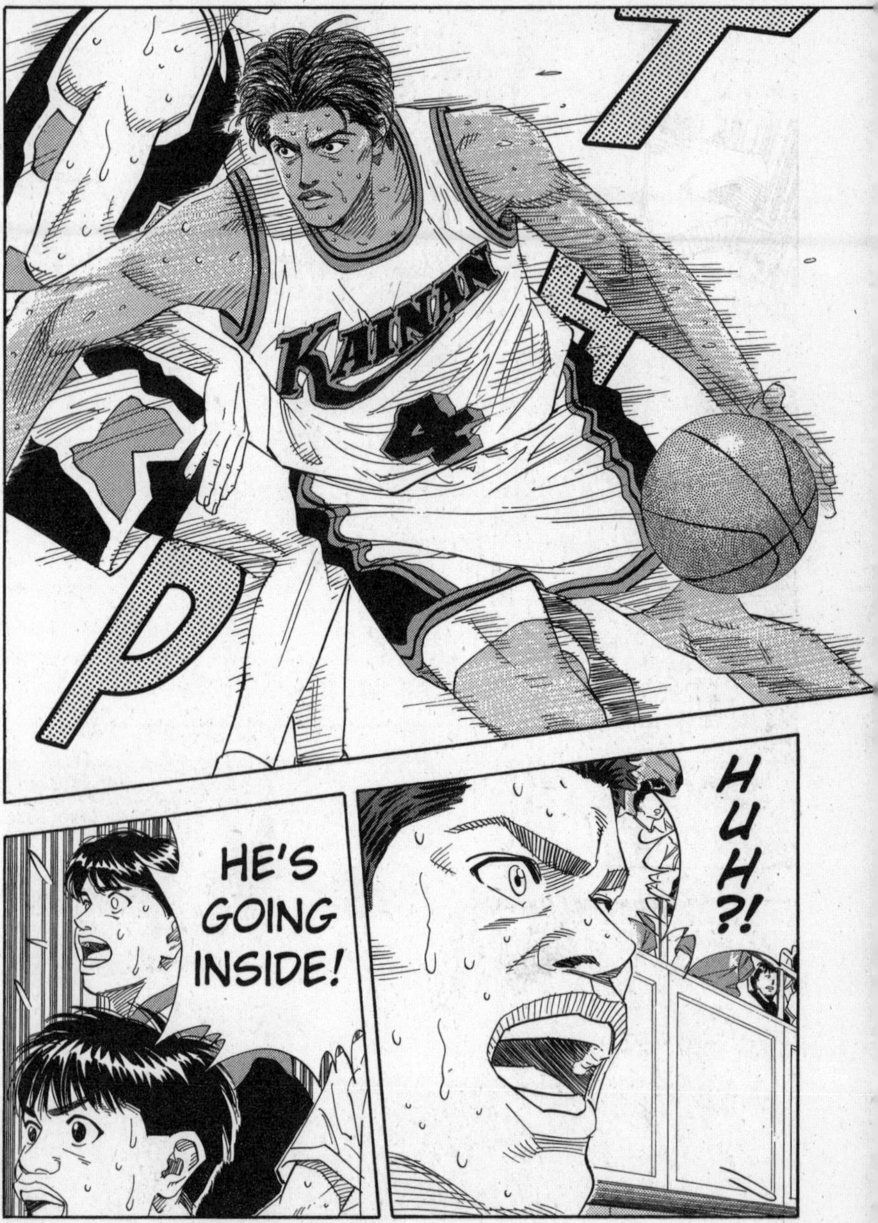
HUH?!
HE'S GOING INSIDE!

READ THIS WAY

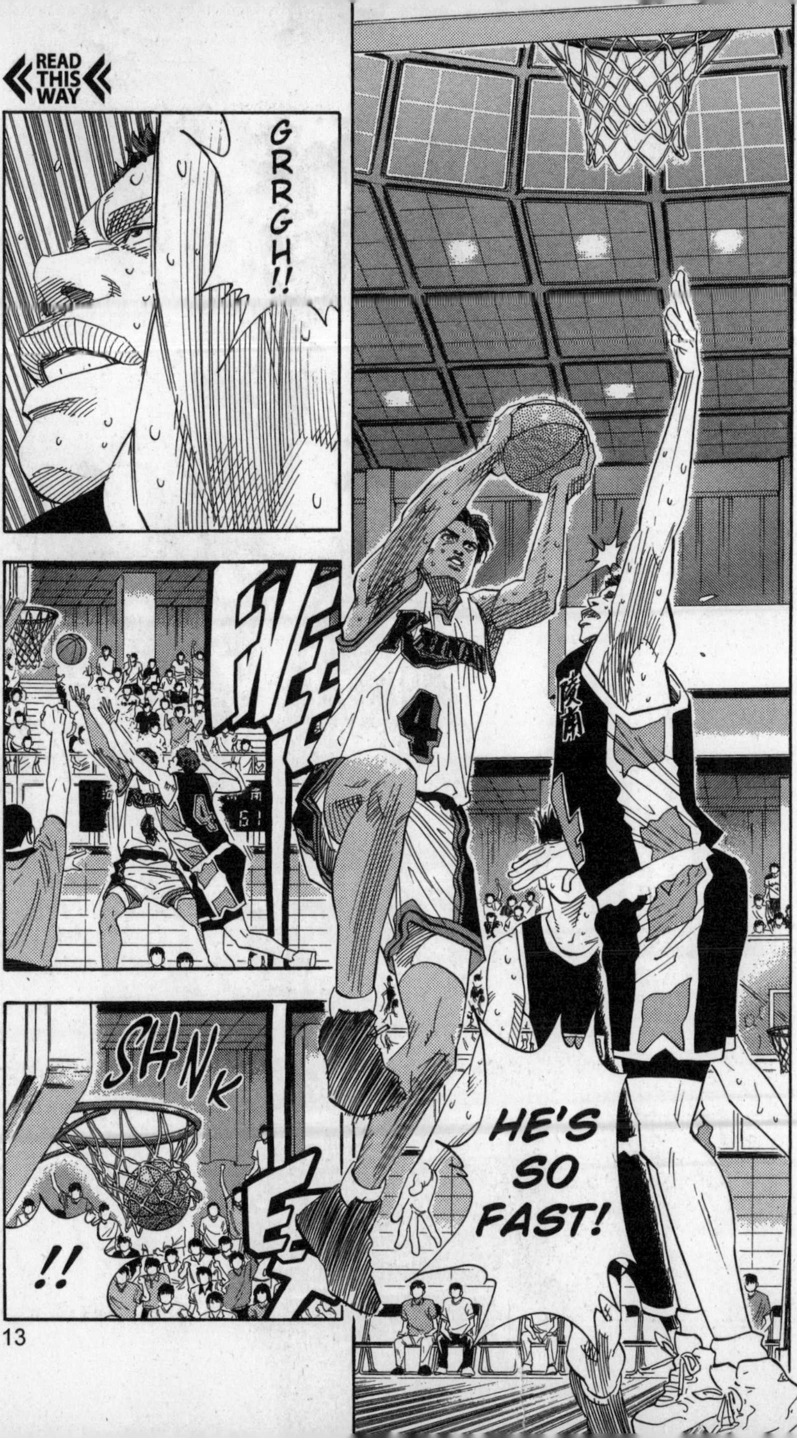
HE'S SO FAST!
GRRGH!!
SHNK
!!

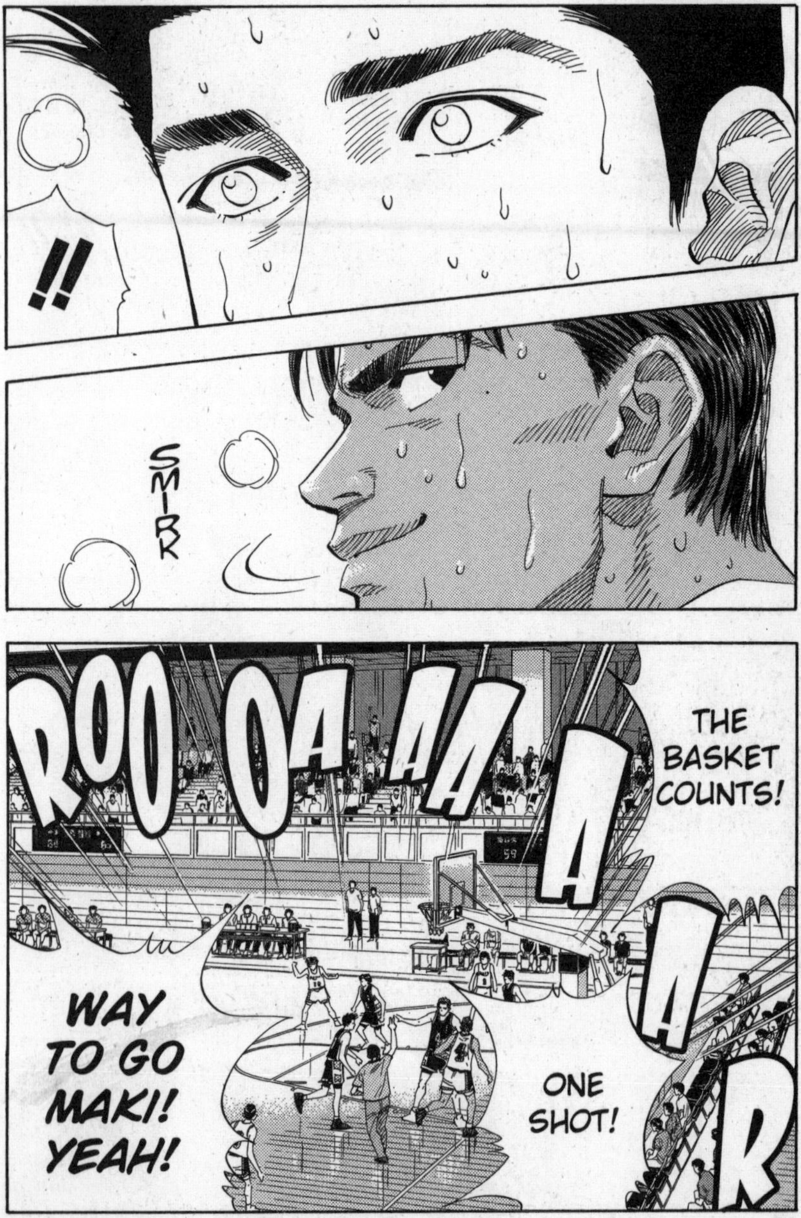
!!
SMIRK
THE BASKET COUNTS!
ROOOAAAAAAR
ONE SHOT!
WAY TO GO MAKI! YEAH!

READ THIS WAY

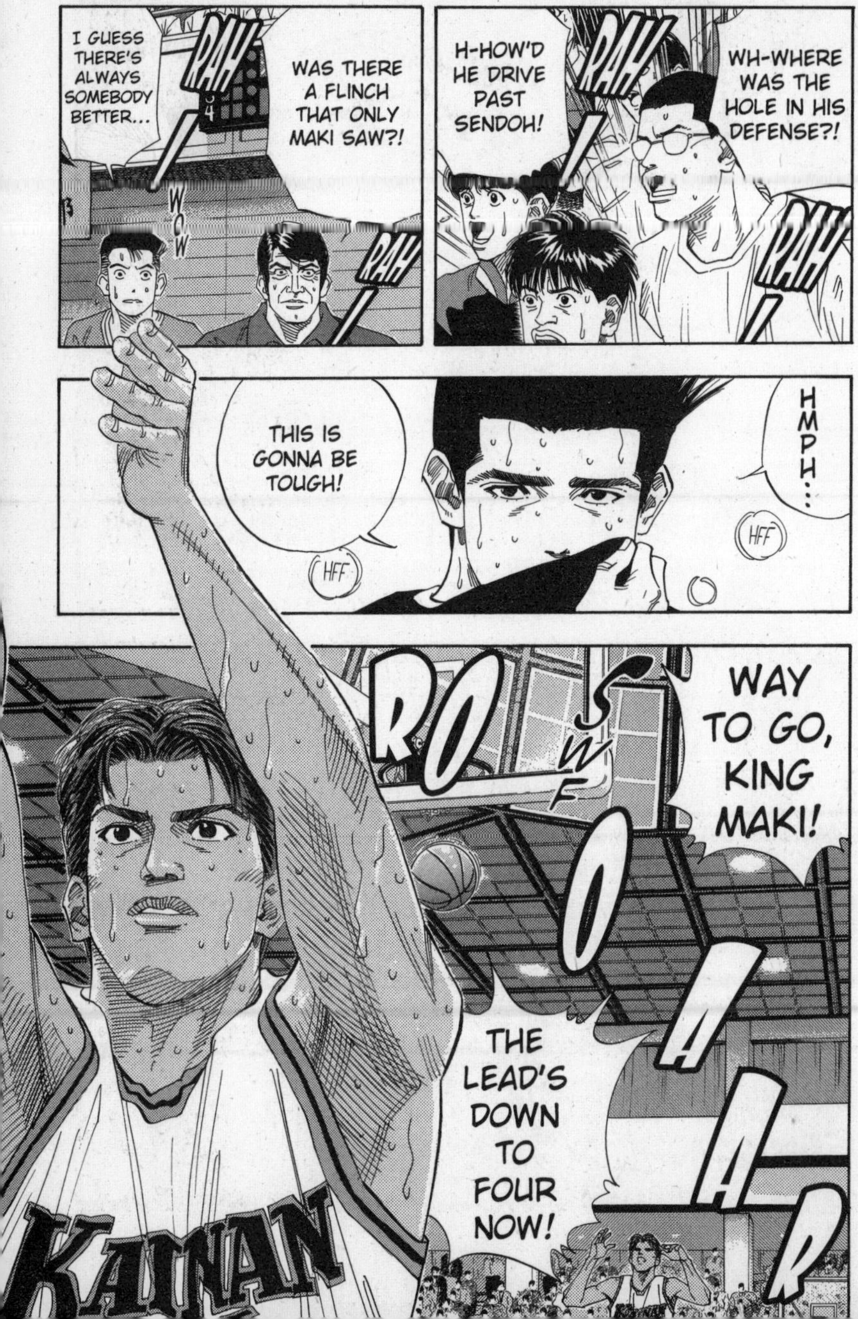
WH-WHERE WAS THE HOLE IN HIS DEFENSE?!
H-HOW'D HE DRIVE PAST SENDOH!
RAH
RAH
WAS THERE A FLINCH THAT ONLY MAKI SAW?!
I GUESS THERE'S ALWAYS SOMEBODY BETTER...
RAH
WOW
RAH
HMPH...
HFF
THIS IS GONNA BE TOUGH!
HFF
WAY TO GO, KING MAKI!
SWF
ROOAAAR
THE LEAD'S DOWN TO FOUR NOW!
KAINAN

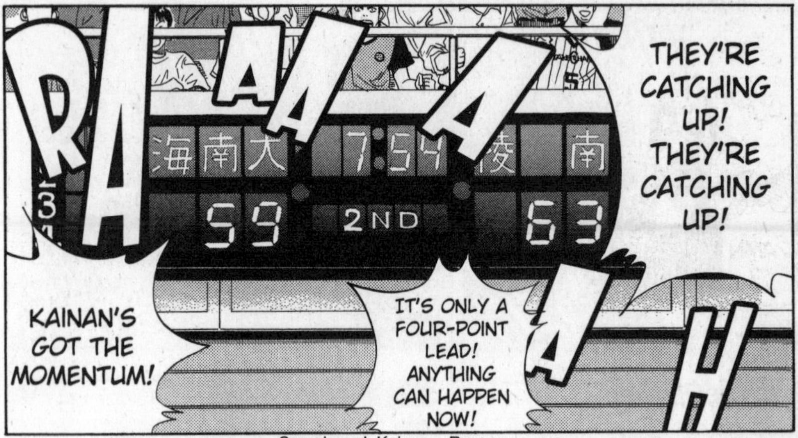
RAAAAAH
THEY'RE CATCHING UP! THEY'RE CATCHING UP!
海南大
7:54
59
2ND
63
IT'S ONLY A FOUR-POINT LEAD! ANYTHING CAN HAPPEN NOW!
KAINAN'S GOT THE MOMENTUM!
Scoreboard: Kainan Ryonan

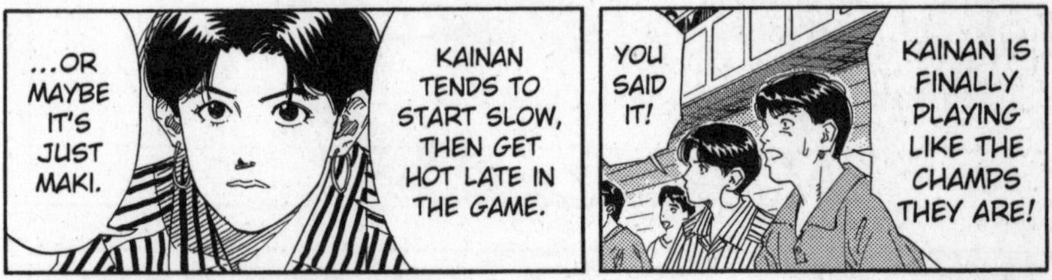
KAINAN IS FINALLY PLAYING LIKE THE CHAMPS THEY ARE!
YOU SAID IT!
KAINAN TENDS TO START SLOW, THEN GET HOT LATE IN THE GAME.
...OR MAYBE IT'S JUST MAKI.

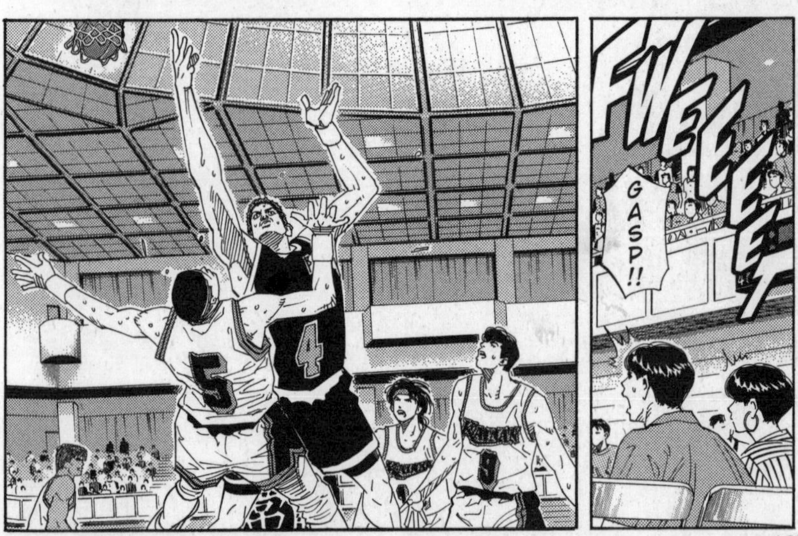
FWEEEET
GASP!!

READ THIS WAY

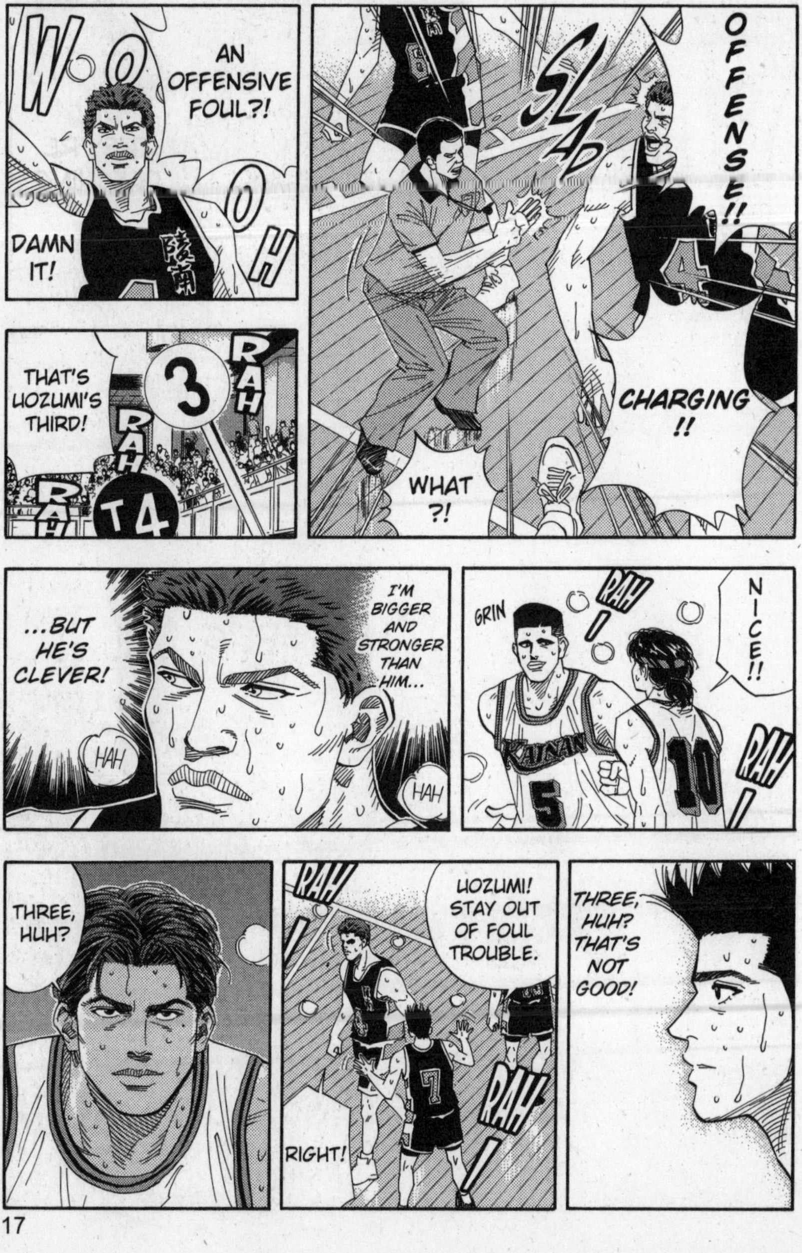

OFFENSE!!
SLAP
CHARGING!!
WHAT?!
WOOOH
AN OFFENSIVE FOUL?!
DAMN IT!
RAH
3
THAT'S UOZUMI'S THIRD!
RAH
RAH
T4
NICE!!
RAH
GRIN
RAH
I'M BIGGER AND STRONGER THAN HIM...
...BUT HE'S CLEVER!
HAH
HAH
THREE, HUH? THAT'S NOT GOOD!
UOZUMI! STAY OUT OF FOUL TROUBLE.
RAH
RAH
RIGHT!
THREE, HUH?

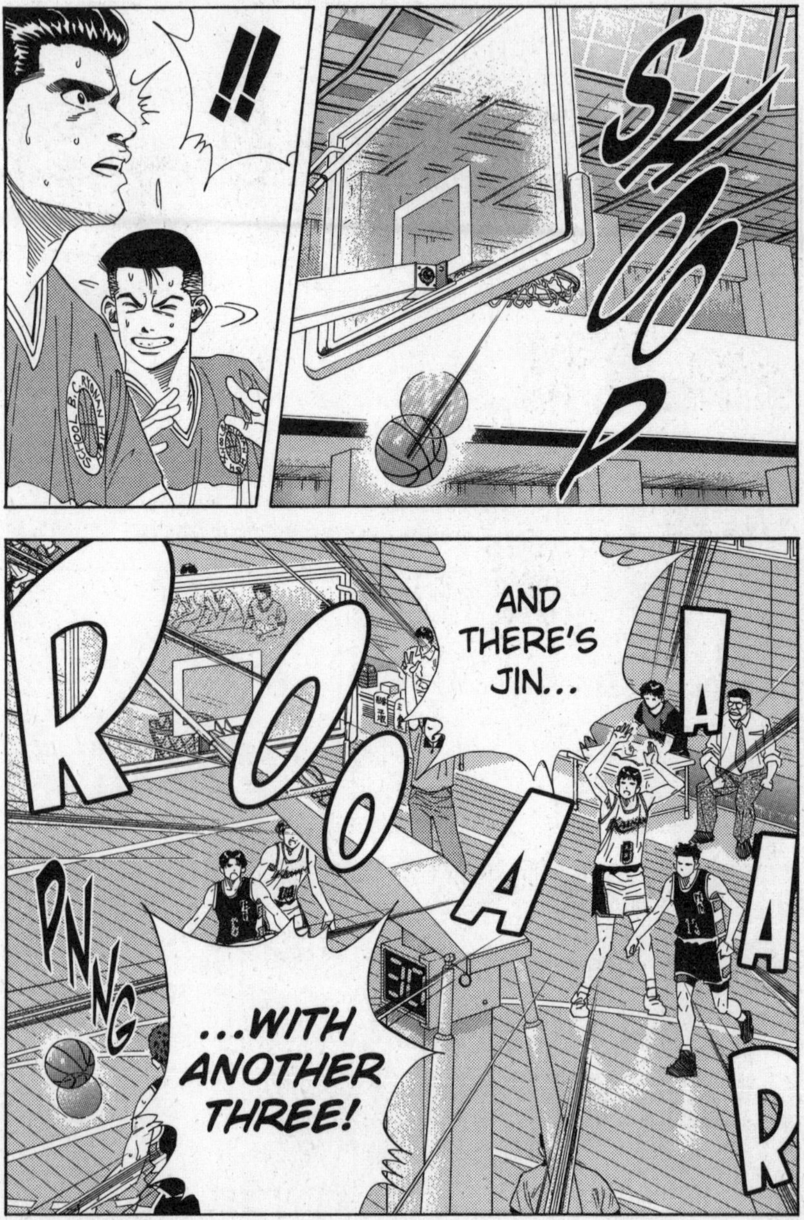
SHOOOP
!!
ROOOAAAR
AND THERE'S JIN...
...WITH ANOTHER THREE!
PNNG

READ THIS WAY

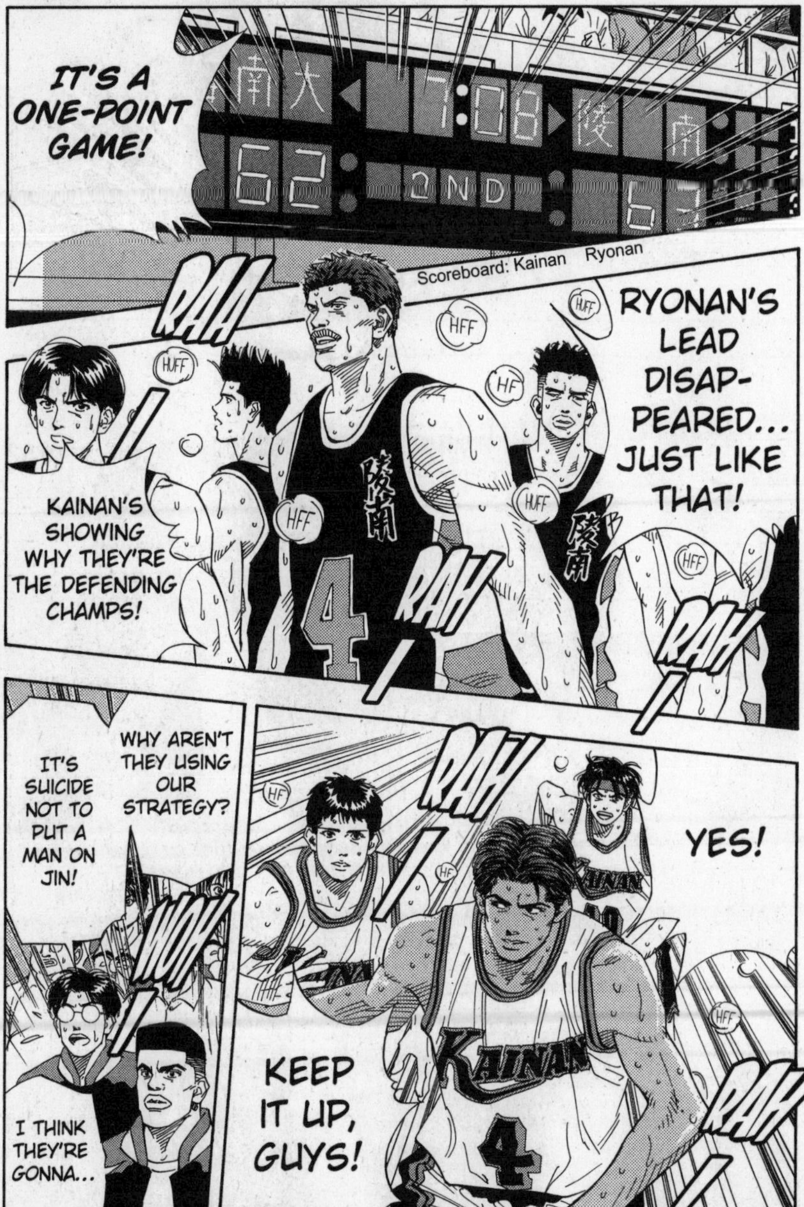
IT'S A ONE-POINT GAME!
7:08
62
2ND
Scoreboard: Kainan Ryonan
RAA
RYONAN'S LEAD DISAPPEARED... JUST LIKE THAT!
HUFF
HFF
HF
HUFF
HFF
HUFF
KAINAN'S SHOWING WHY THEY'RE THE DEFENDING CHAMPS!
RAH
RAH
HFF
YES!
RAH
HF
HF
KEEP IT UP, GUYS!
HFF
RAH
WHY AREN'T THEY USING OUR STRATEGY?
IT'S SUICIDE NOT TO PUT A MAN ON JIN!
WOH
I THINK THEY'RE GONNA...

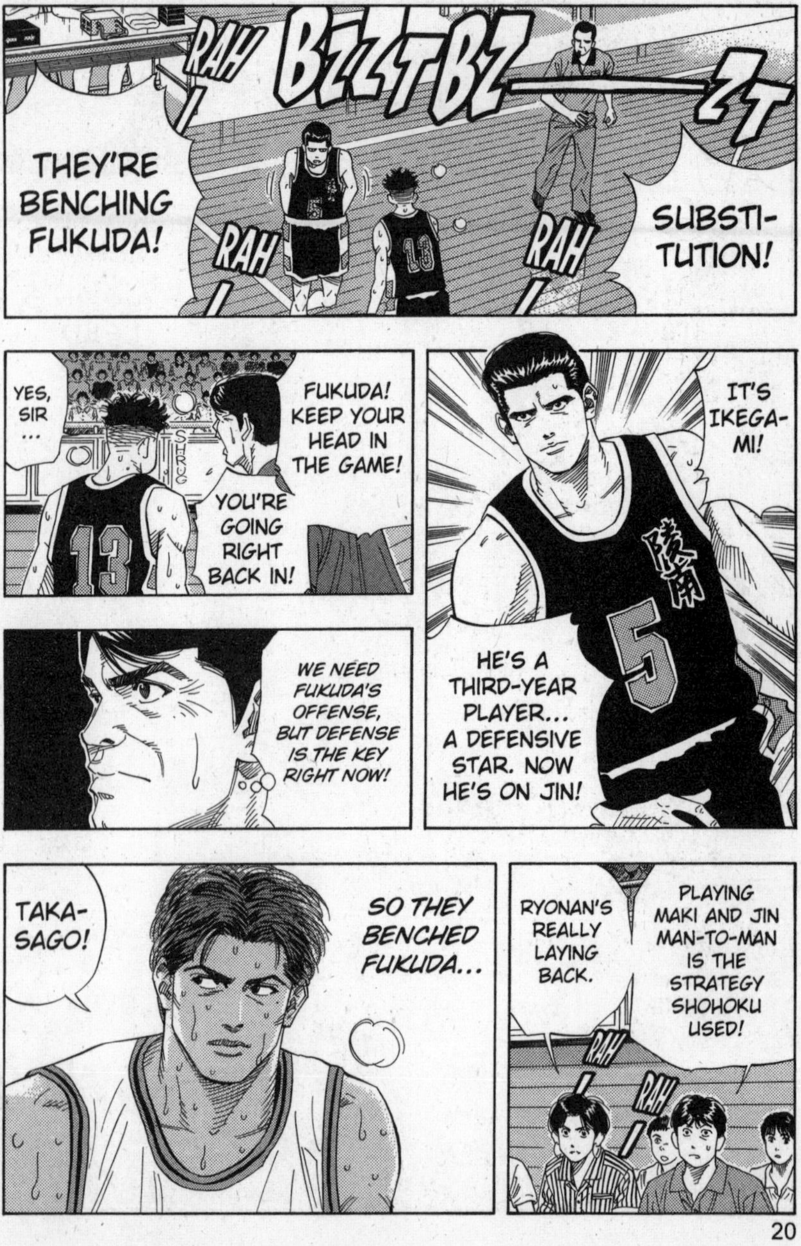
BZZTBZ—ZT
SUBSTI-TUTION!
RAH
RAH
RAH
THEY'RE BENCHING FUKUDA!
IT'S IKEGA-MI!
HE'S A THIRD-YEAR PLAYER... A DEFENSIVE STAR. NOW HE'S ON JIN!
FUKUDA! KEEP YOUR HEAD IN THE GAME!
YOU'RE GOING RIGHT BACK IN!
SHRUG
YES, SIR ...
WE NEED FUKUDA'S OFFENSE, BUT DEFENSE IS THE KEY RIGHT NOW!
PLAYING MAKI AND JIN MAN-TO-MAN IS THE STRATEGY SHOHOKU USED!
RYONAN'S REALLY LAYING BACK.
RAH
RAH
SO THEY BENCHED FUKUDA...
TAKA-SAGO!

READ THIS WAY

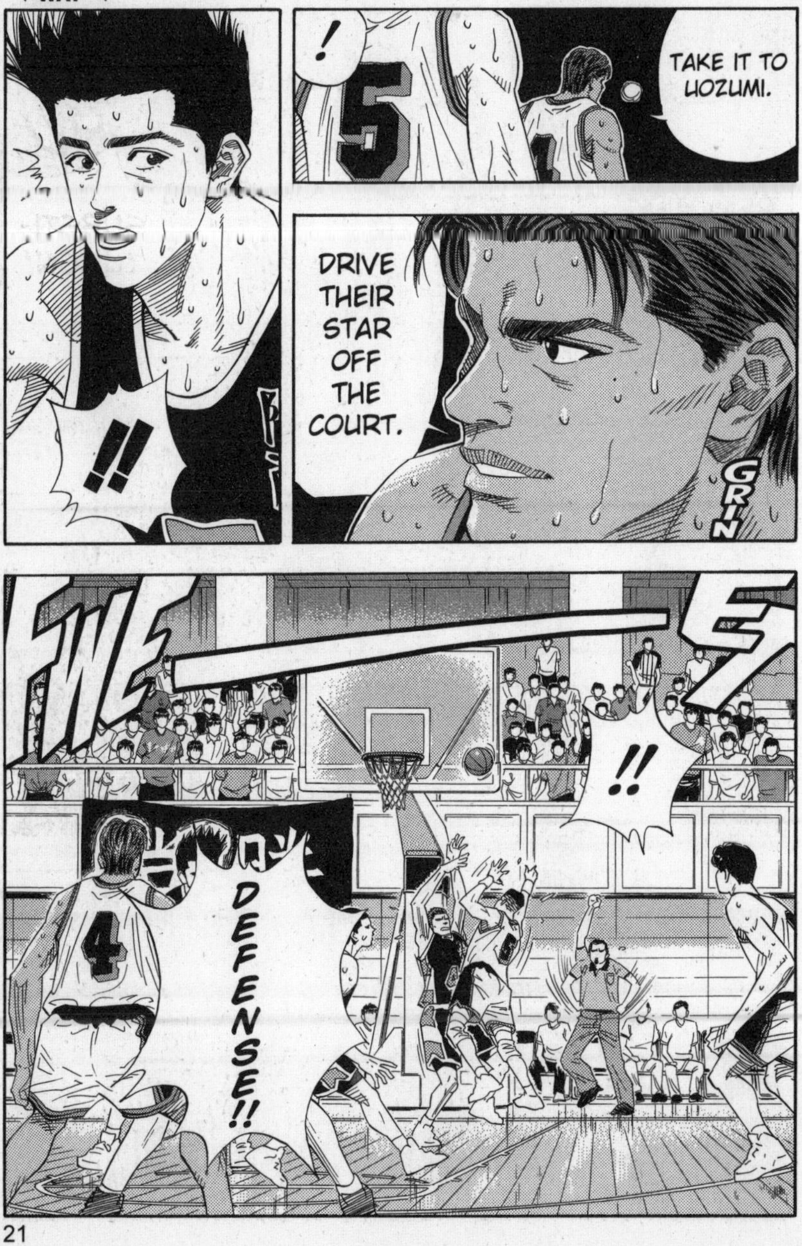
TAKE IT TO UOZUMI.
!
DRIVE THEIR STAR OFF THE COURT.
GRIN
!!
FWEE
!!
DEFENSE!!

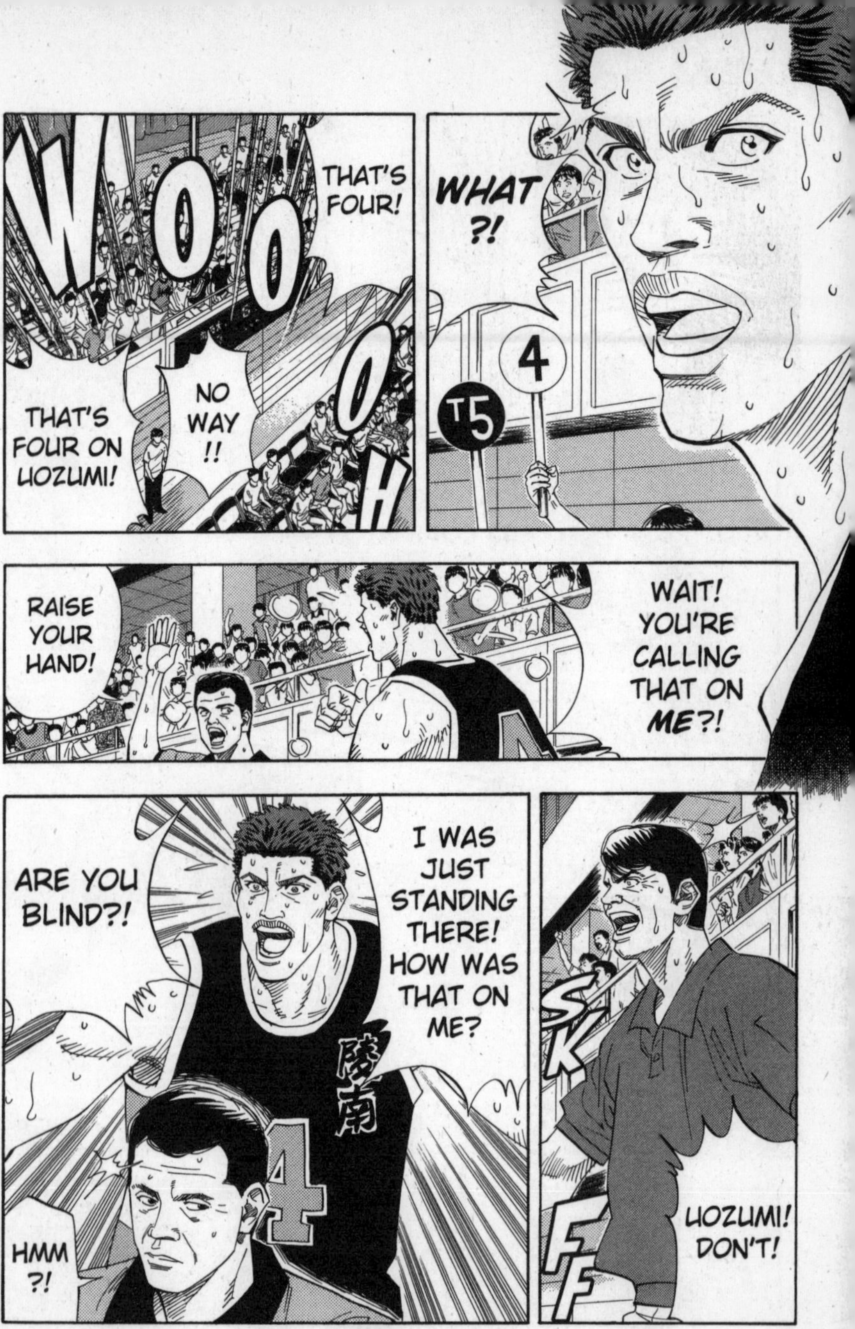
WHAT ?!
WOOOOH
THAT'S FOUR!
NO WAY !!
THAT'S FOUR ON UOZUMI!
WAIT! YOU'RE CALLING THAT ON ME?!
RAISE YOUR HAND!
SKFF
UOZUMI! DON'T!
I WAS JUST STANDING THERE! HOW WAS THAT ON ME?
ARE YOU BLIND?!
HMM ?!

READ THIS WAY

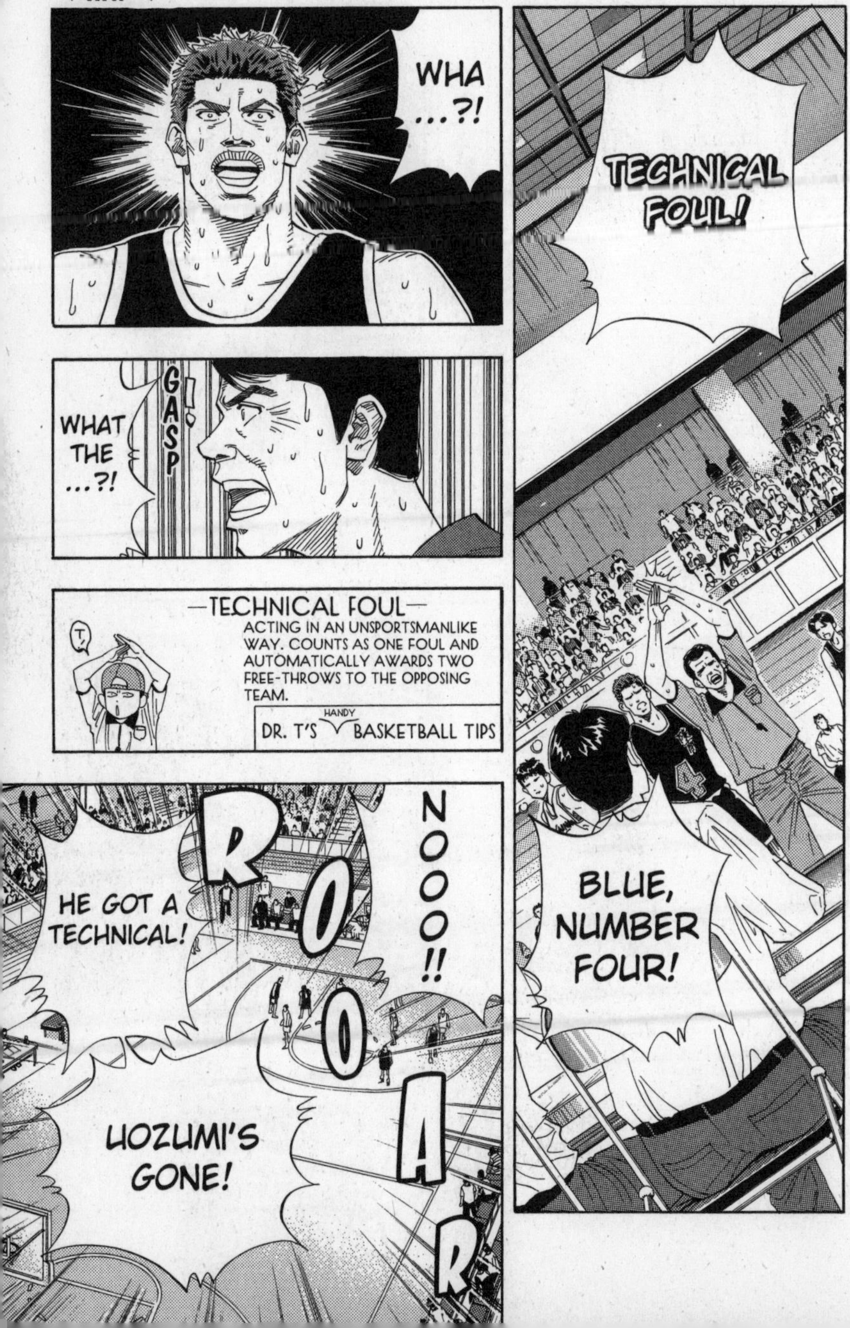
TECHNICAL FOUL!
BLUE, NUMBER FOUR!
WHA ...?!
GASP
WHAT THE ...?!
—TECHNICAL FOUL—
ACTING IN AN UNSPORTSMANLIKE WAY. COUNTS AS ONE FOUL AND AUTOMATICALLY AWARDS TWO FREE-THROWS TO THE OPPOSING TEAM.
T,
DR. T'S HANDY BASKETBALL TIPS
NOOOO!!
ROOOAR
HE GOT A TECHNICAL!
UOZUMI'S GONE!

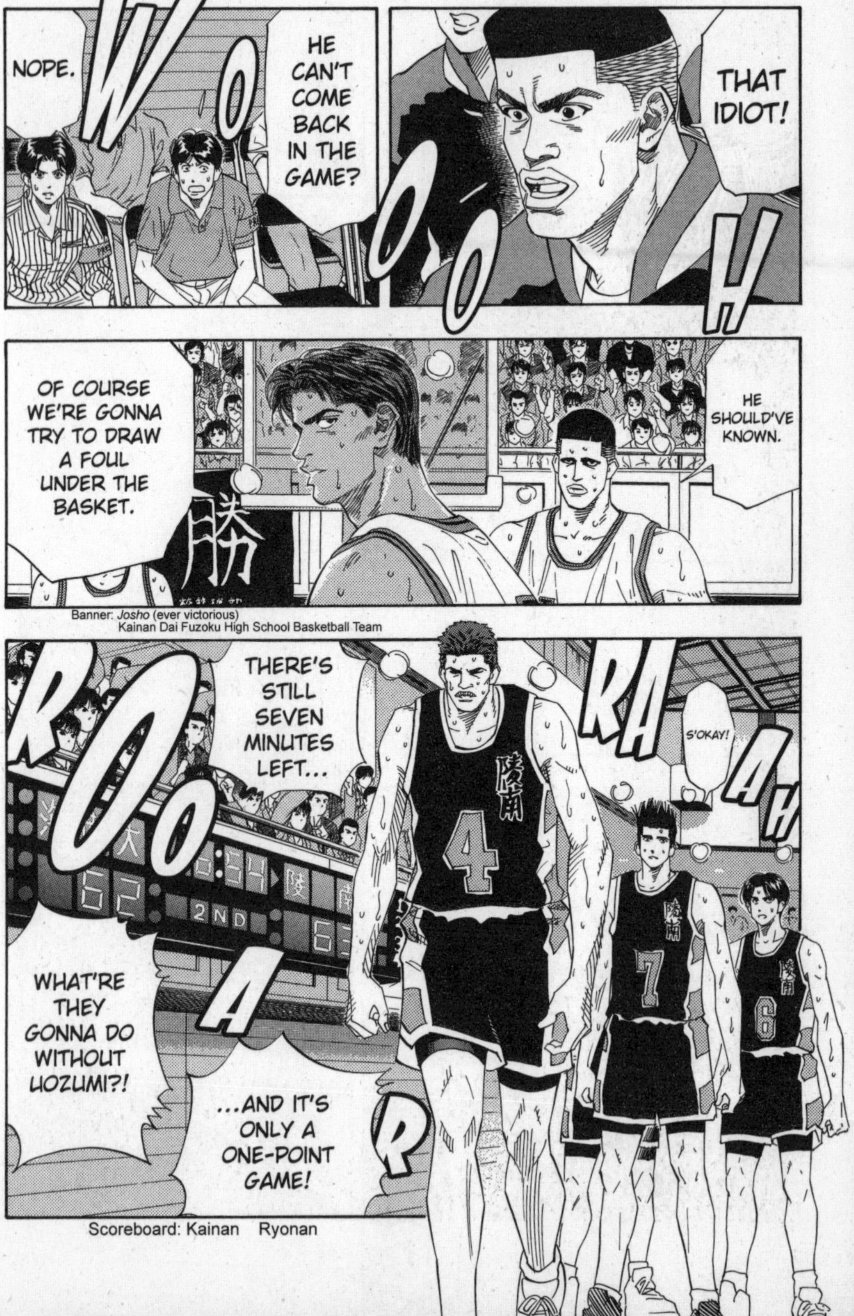
THAT IDIOT!
WOOOOH
HE CAN'T COME BACK IN THE GAME?
NOPE.
HE SHOULD'VE KNOWN.
OF COURSE WE'RE GONNA TRY TO DRAW A FOUL UNDER THE BASKET.
RAAAH
S'OKAY!
THERE'S STILL SEVEN MINUTES LEFT...
ROOOAR
...AND IT'S ONLY A ONE-POINT GAME!
WHAT'RE THEY GONNA DO WITHOUT UOZUMI?!

Banner: *Josho* (ever victorious)
Kainan Dai Fuzoku High School Basketball Team

Scoreboard: Kainan Ryonan

READ THIS WAY

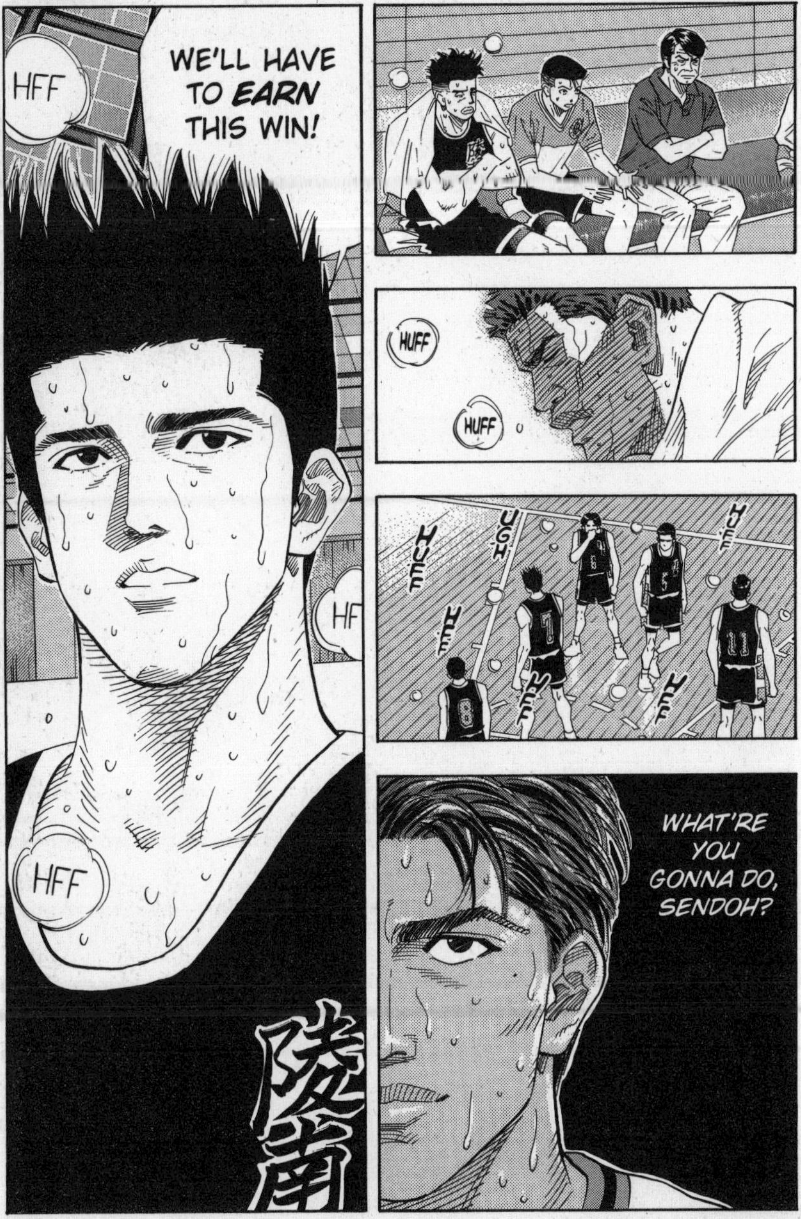
HUFF
HUFF
HUFF
HUFF
UGH
HUFF
HUFF
HUFF
WHAT'RE YOU GONNA DO, SENDOH?
HFF
WE'LL HAVE TO *EARN* THIS WIN!
HFF
HFF

Who cares about Boss Monkey? Show me!
I'm the main character!
MUMBLE
MUMBLE

SLAM DUNK

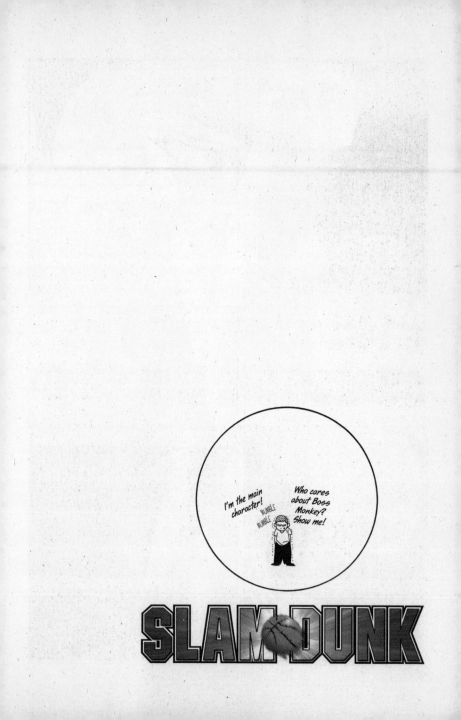

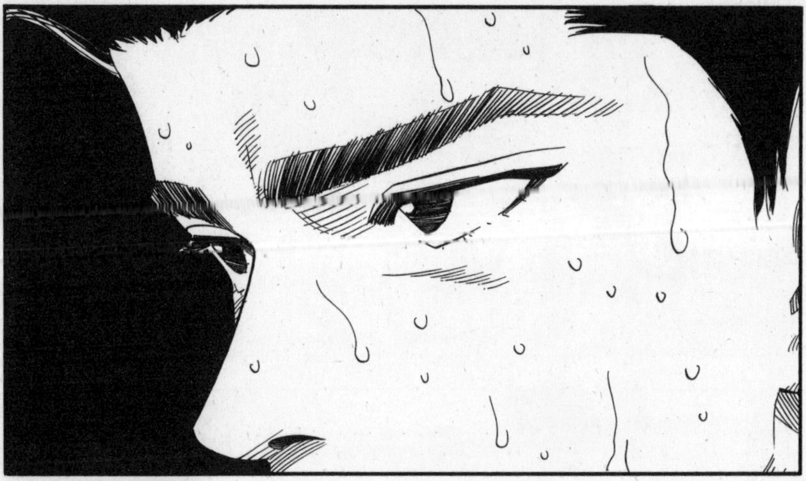

#145 SUPERSTAR MATCHUP

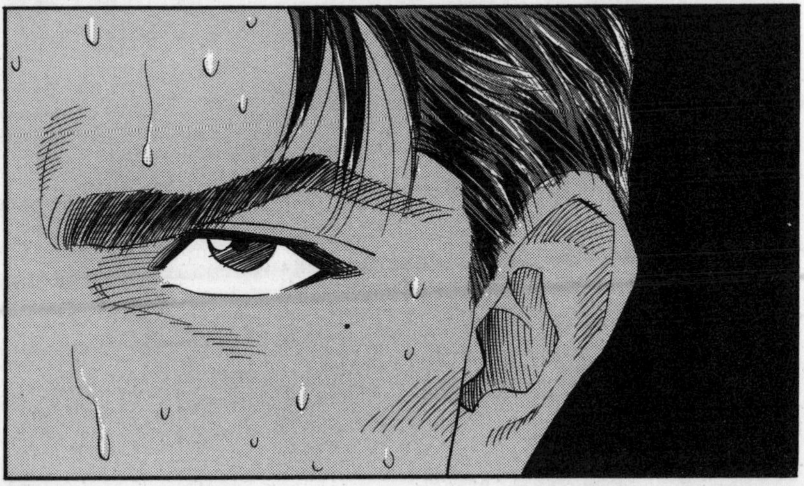

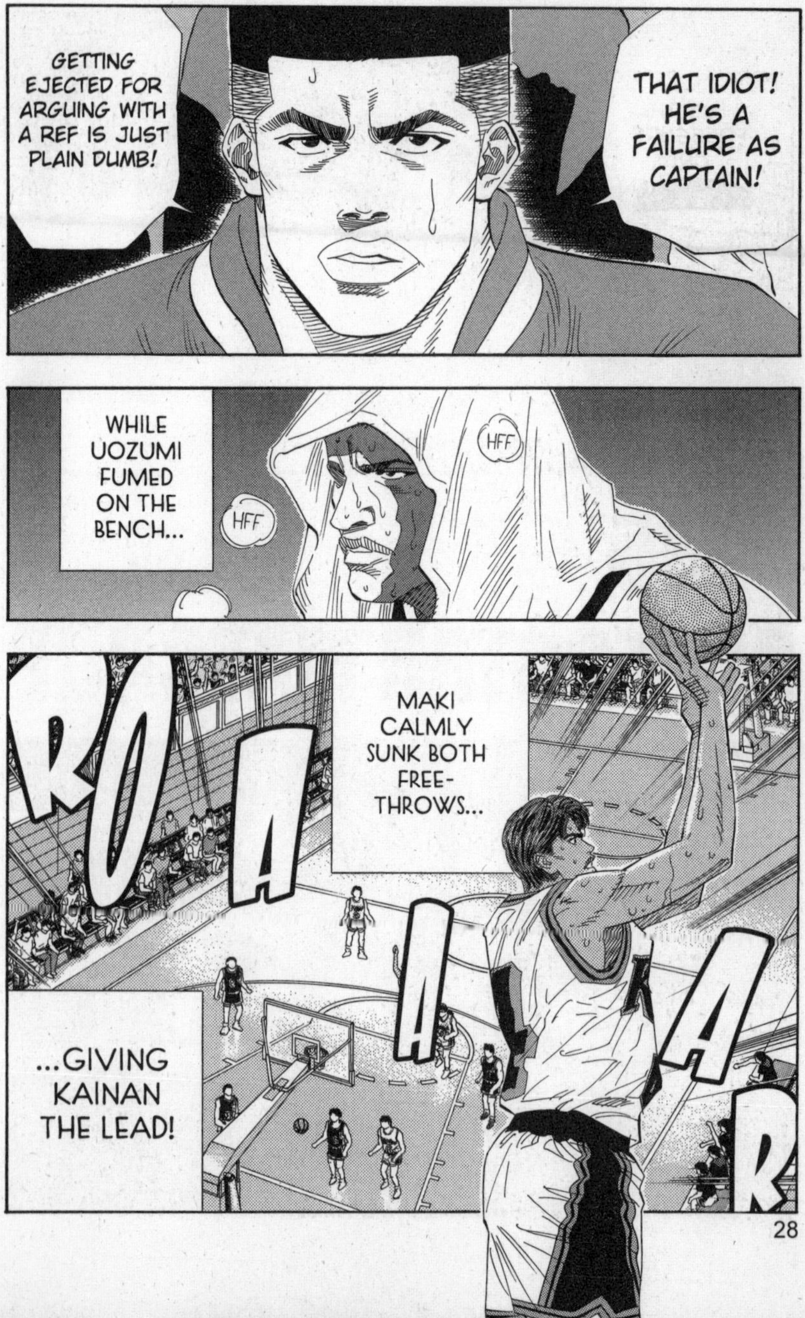
THAT IDIOT! HE'S A FAILURE AS CAPTAIN!
GETTING EJECTED FOR ARGUING WITH A REF IS JUST PLAIN DUMB!
HFF
HFF
WHILE UOZUMI FUMED ON THE BENCH...
MAKI CALMLY SUNK BOTH FREE-THROWS...
ROAAAAR
...GIVING KAINAN THE LEAD!

READ THIS WAY

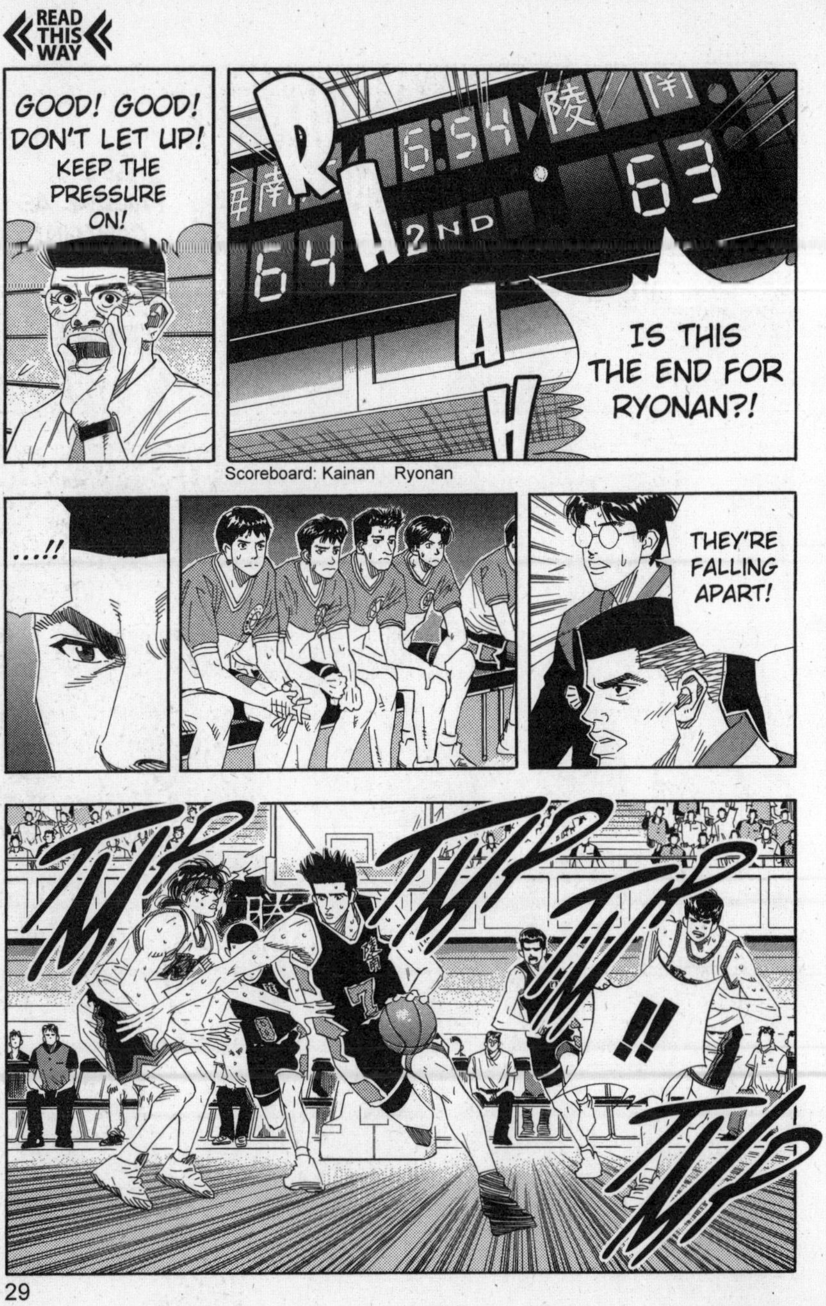
RAAH
IS THIS THE END FOR RYONAN?!
GOOD! GOOD! DON'T LET UP! KEEP THE PRESSURE ON!
THEY'RE FALLING APART!
...!!
TMP TMP TMP TMP
!!
TMP

Scoreboard: Kainan Ryonan

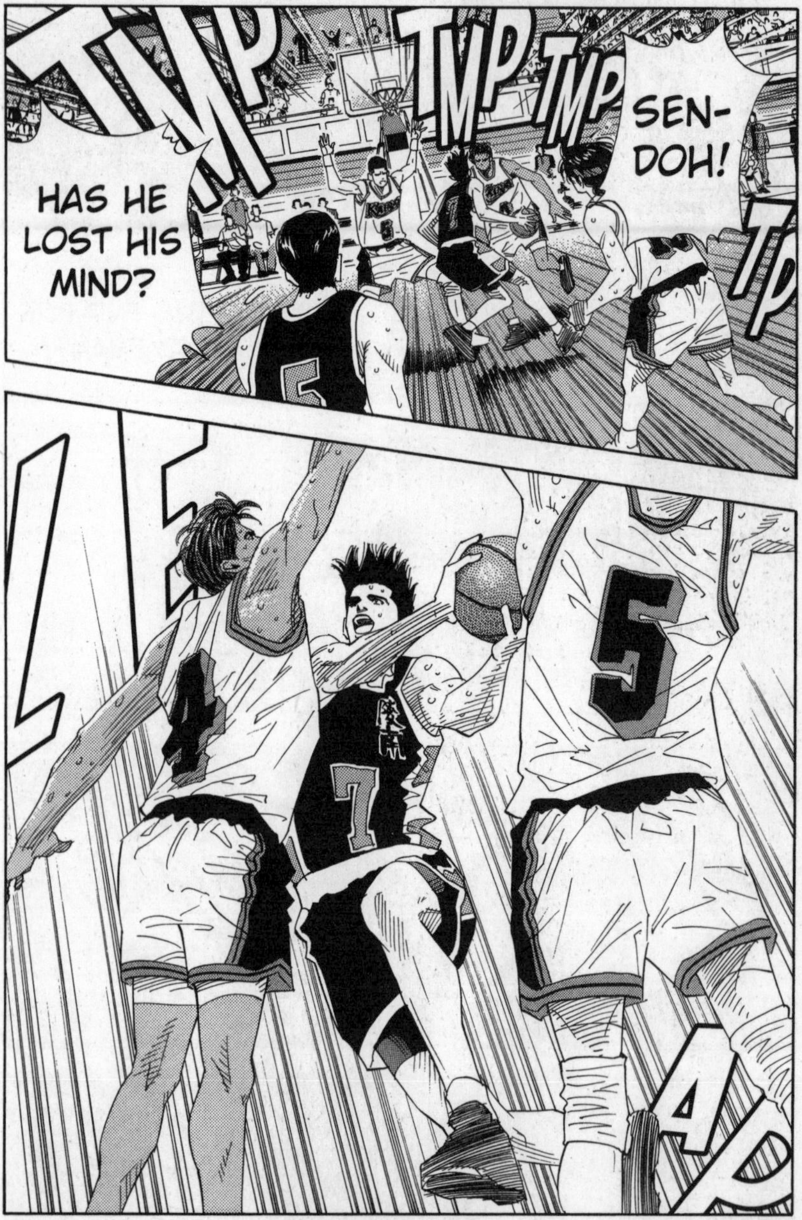
SEN-DOH!
TMP TMP
TMP
HAS HE LOST HIS MIND?
TMP
AP

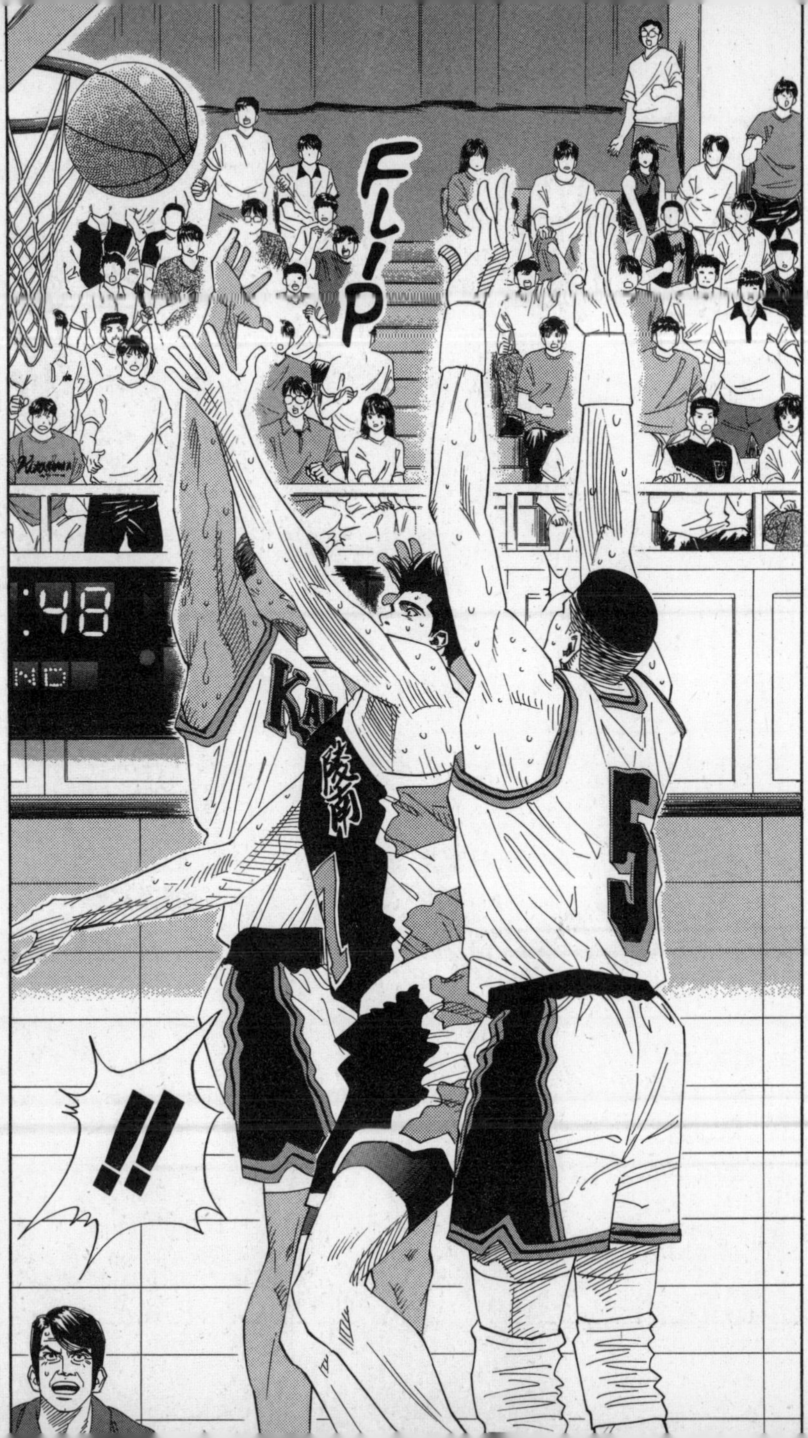
FLIP
!!

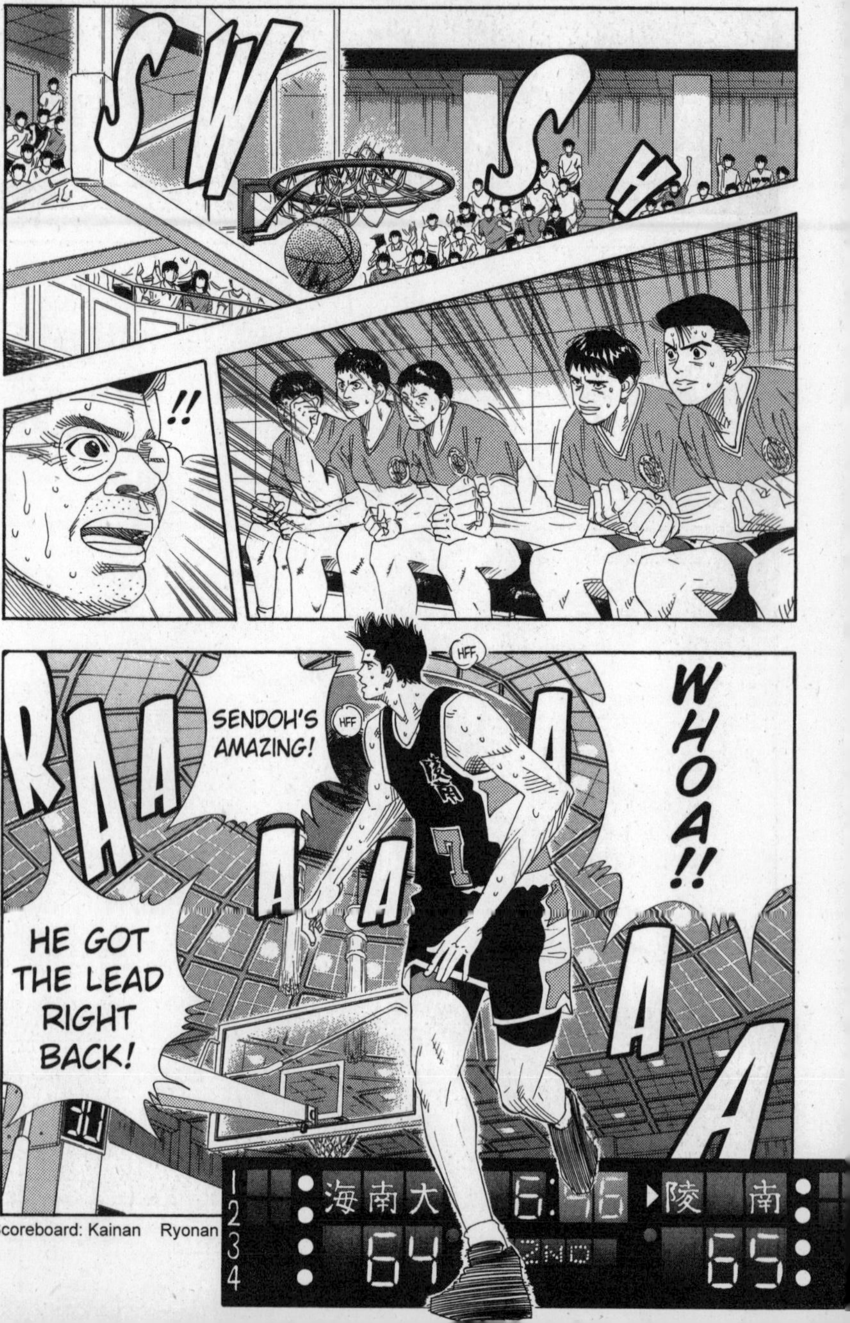
SWISH
!!
WHOA!!
HFF
HFF
SENDOH'S AMAZING!
RAAAAAAAAA
HE GOT THE LEAD RIGHT BACK!
1 2 3 4
海南大
6:46
陵南
64
2ND
65
Scoreboard: Kainan Ryonan

READ THIS WAY

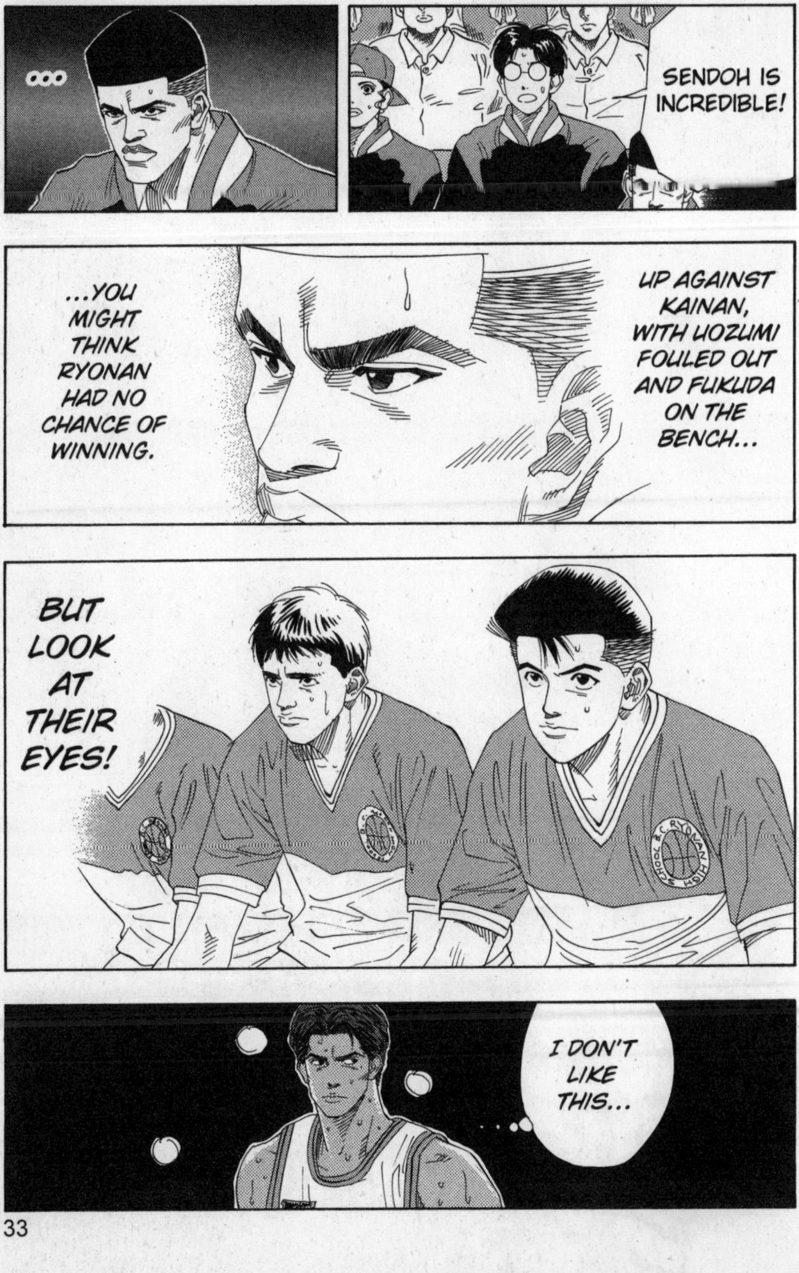
SENDOH IS INCREDIBLE!
...
UP AGAINST KAINAN, WITH UOZUMI FOULED OUT AND FUKUDA ON THE BENCH...
...YOU MIGHT THINK RYONAN HAD NO CHANCE OF WINNING.
BUT LOOK AT THEIR EYES!
I DON'T LIKE THIS...

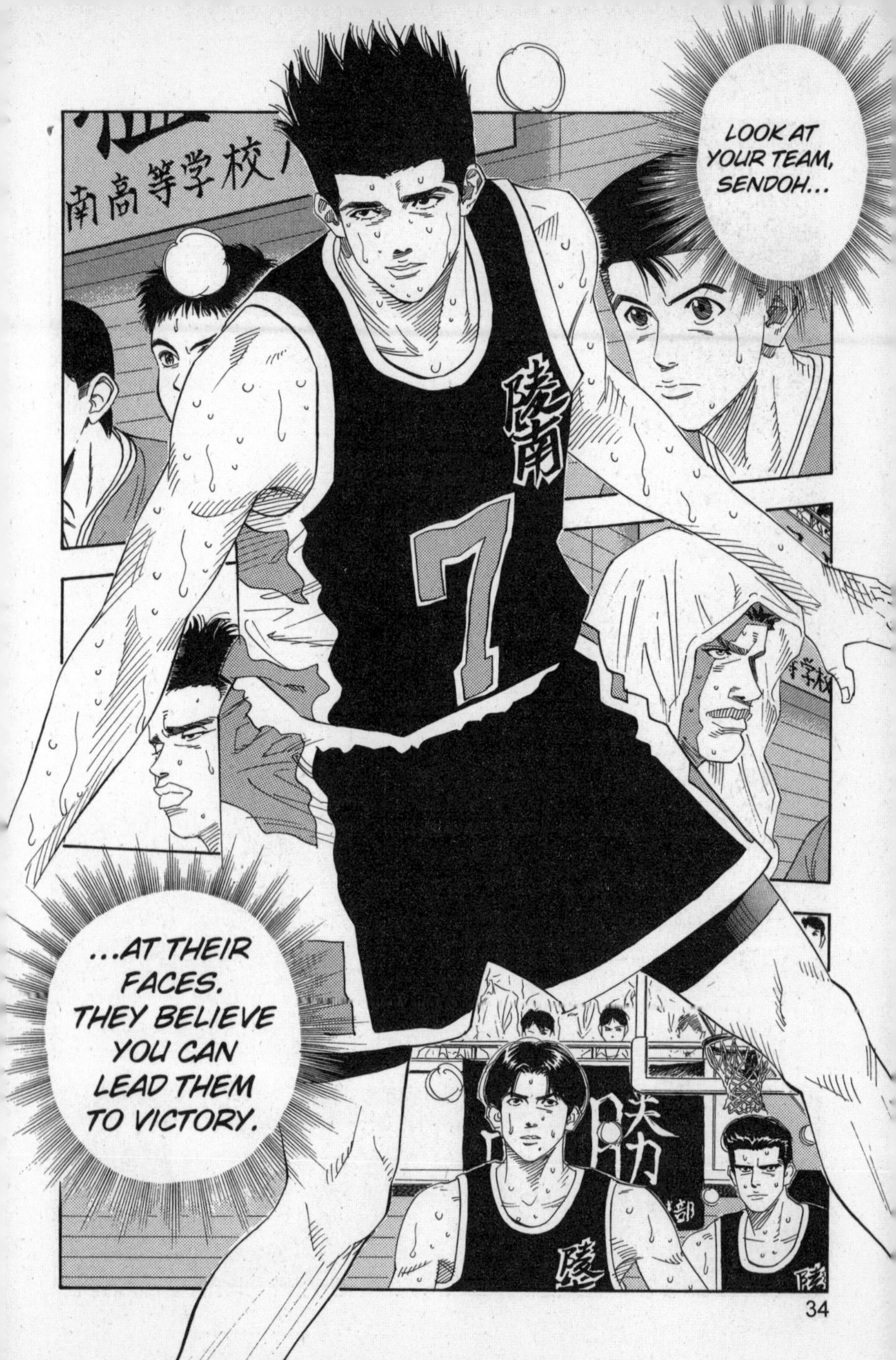
LOOK AT YOUR TEAM, SENDOH...
...AT THEIR FACES. THEY BELIEVE YOU CAN LEAD THEM TO VICTORY.

READ THIS WAY

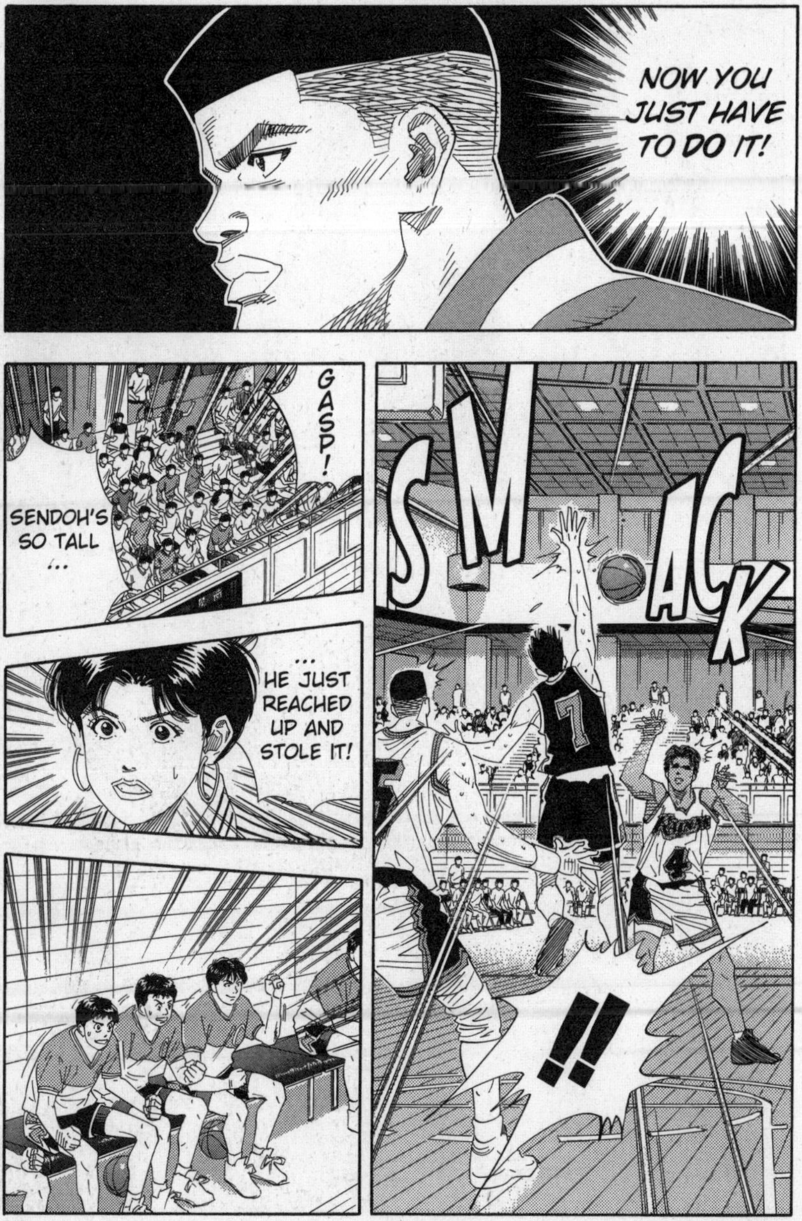

NOW YOU JUST HAVE TO DO IT!
SMACK
!!
GASP!
SENDOH'S SO TALL ...
... HE JUST REACHED UP AND STOLE IT!

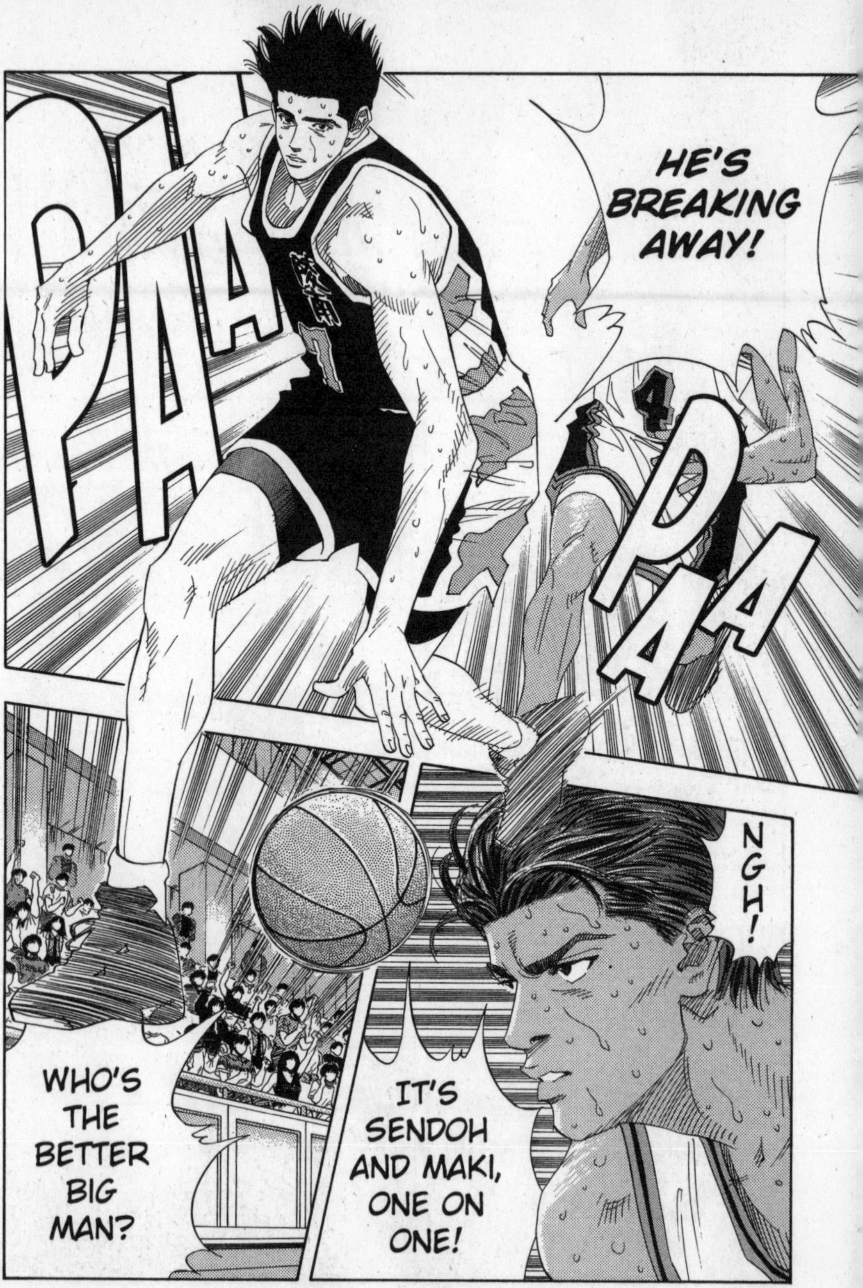
HE'S BREAKING AWAY!
PAA
PA
NGH!
IT'S SENDOH AND MAKI, ONE ON ONE!
WHO'S THE BETTER BIG MAN?

READ THIS WAY

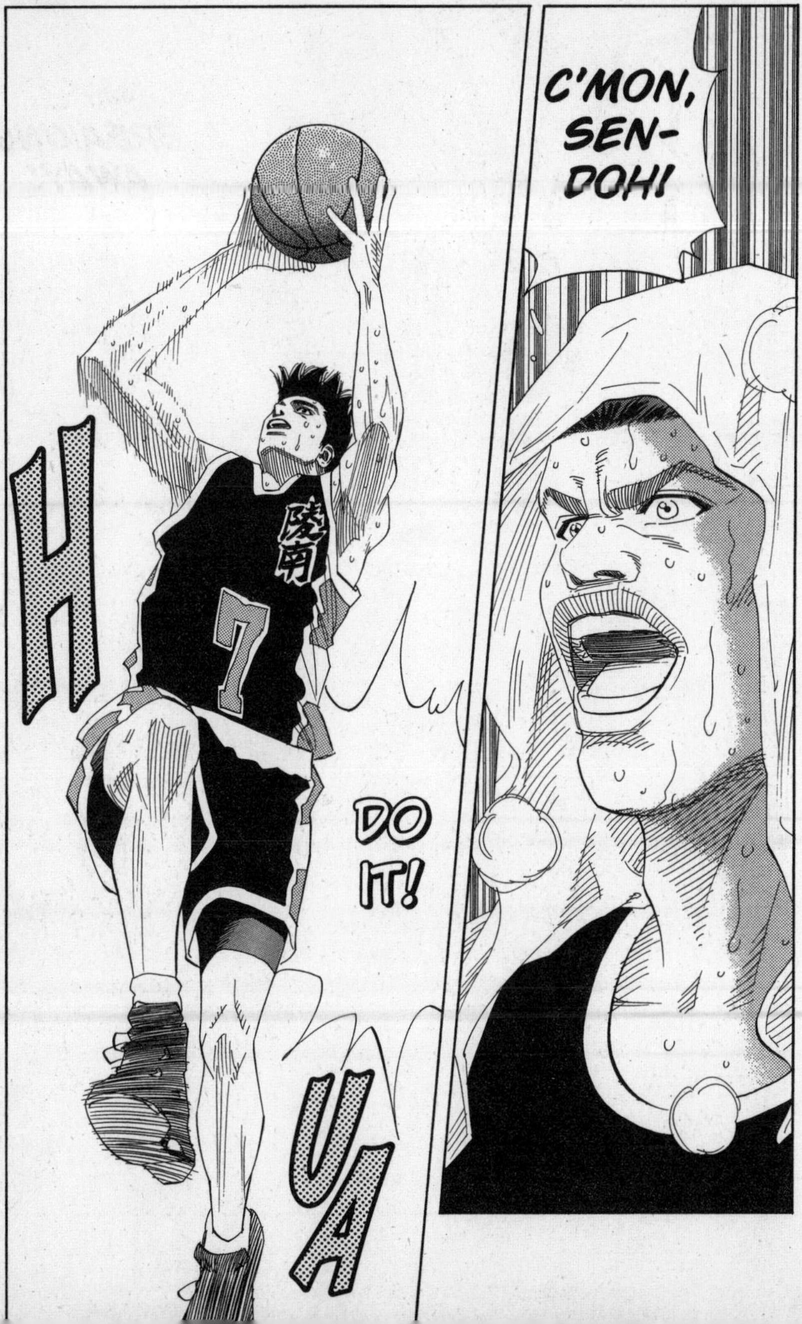
C'MON, SEN-DOH!
DO IT!
H
UA

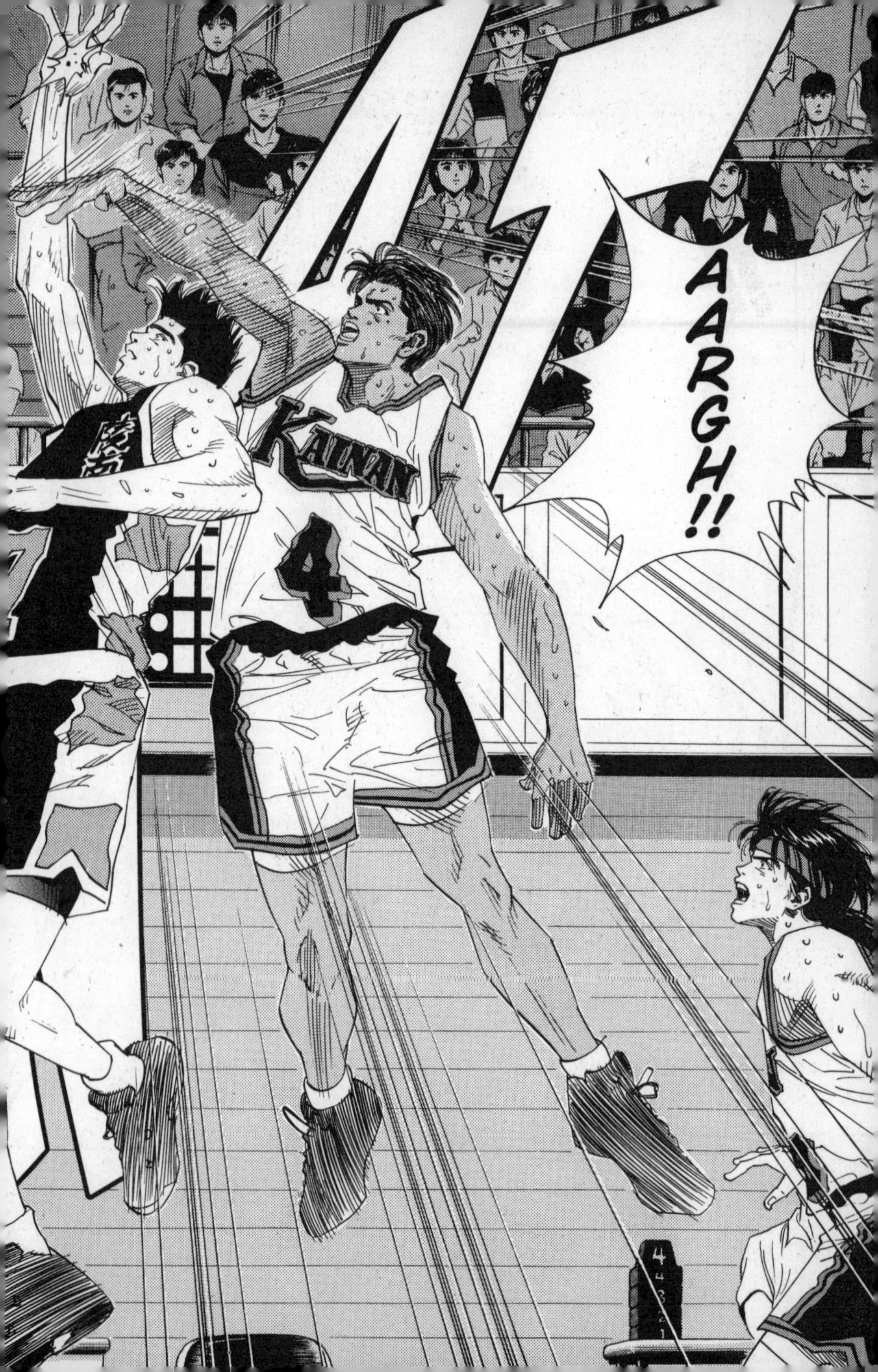
AARGH!!

READ THIS WAY

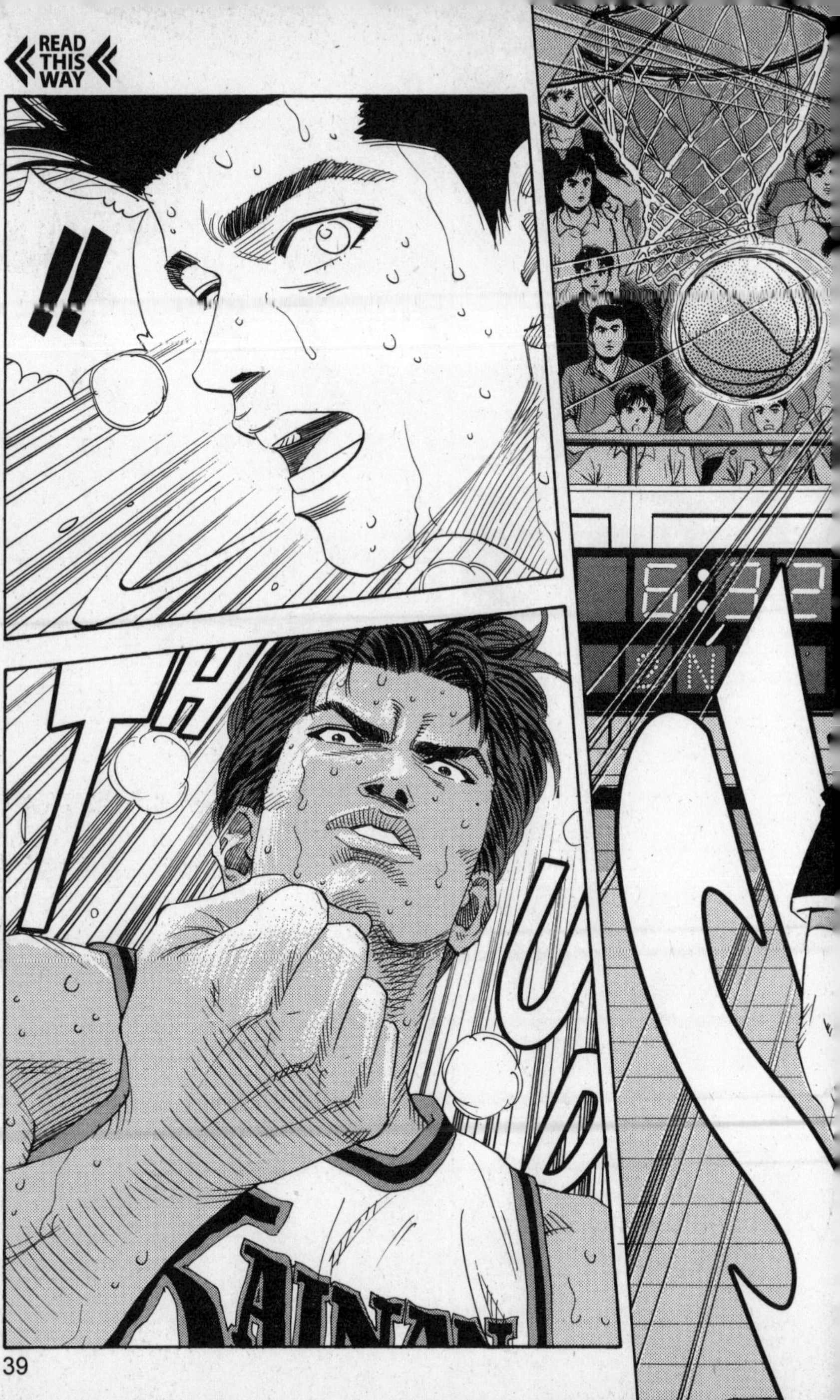

S
!!
THUD

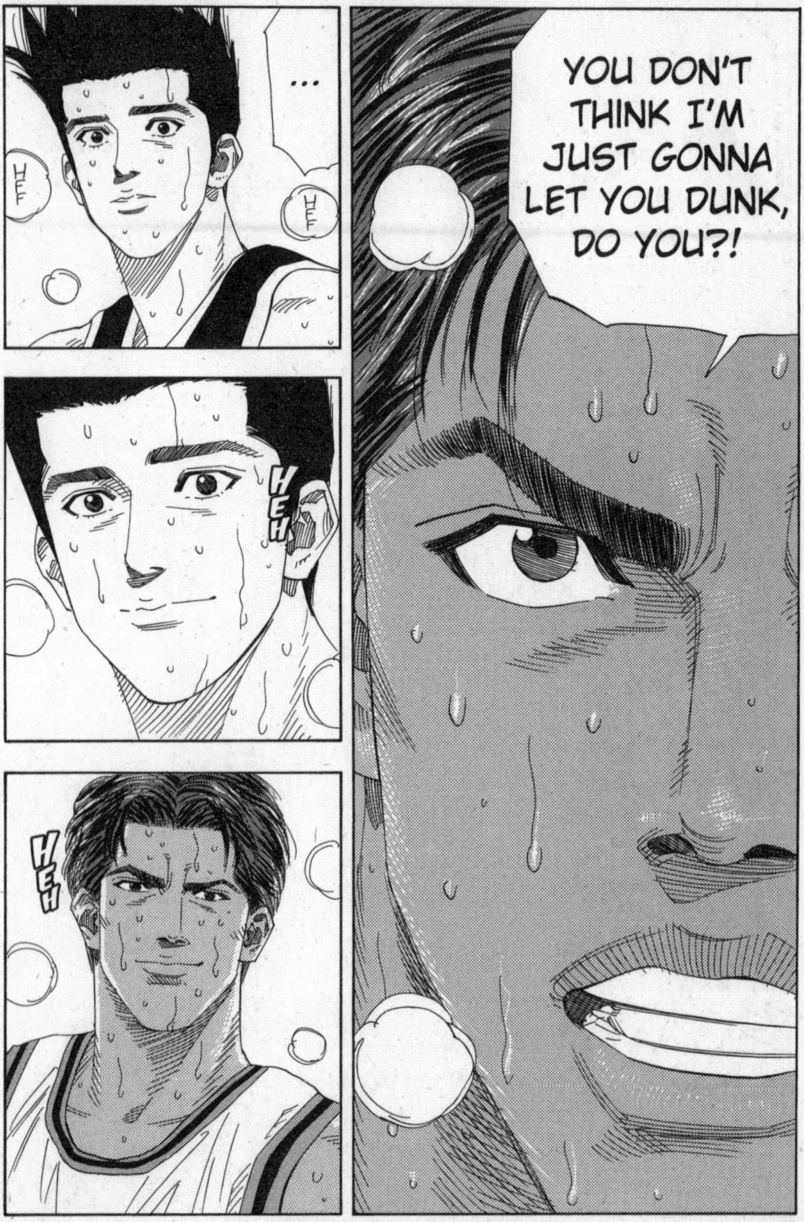
YOU DON'T THINK I'M JUST GONNA LET YOU DUNK, DO YOU?!
...
HEF
HEF
HEH
HEH

READ THIS WAY

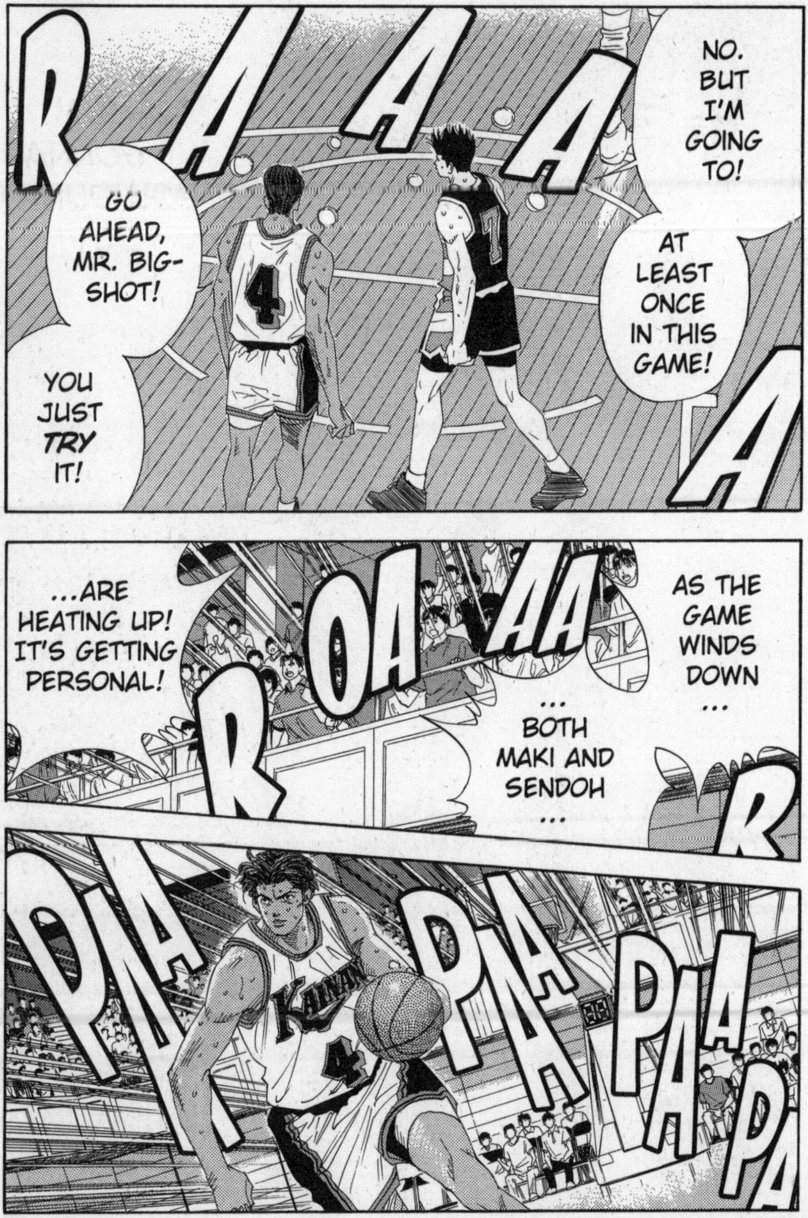

RAAAA
NO. BUT I'M GOING TO!
AT LEAST ONCE IN THIS GAME!
GO AHEAD, MR. BIG-SHOT!
YOU JUST TRY IT!
AA
AS THE GAME WINDS DOWN ...
... BOTH MAKI AND SENDOH ...
...ARE HEATING UP! IT'S GETTING PERSONAL!
ROAAA
R
PAPAPAPAPA
PA
PIA

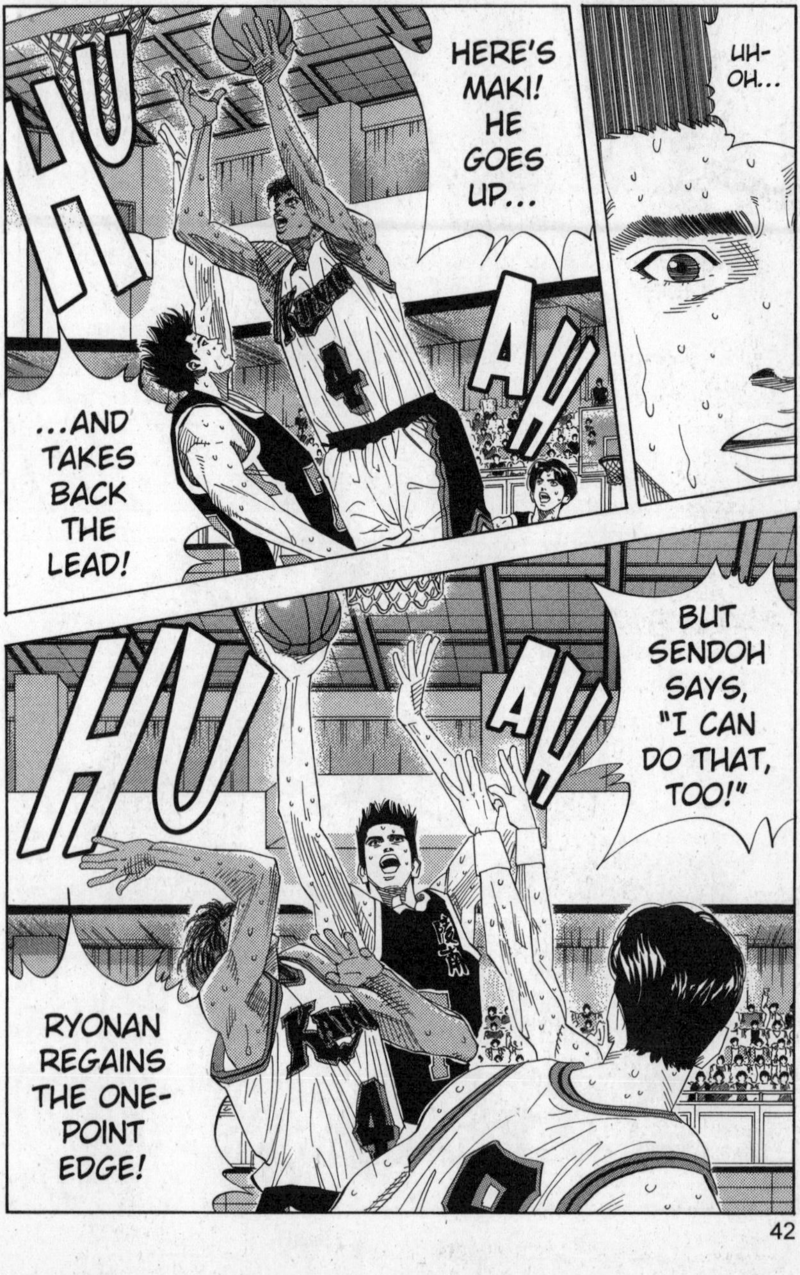
UH-OH...
HERE'S MAKI! HE GOES UP...
...AND TAKES BACK THE LEAD!
BUT SENDOH SAYS, "I CAN DO THAT, TOO!"
RYONAN REGAINS THE ONE-POINT EDGE!

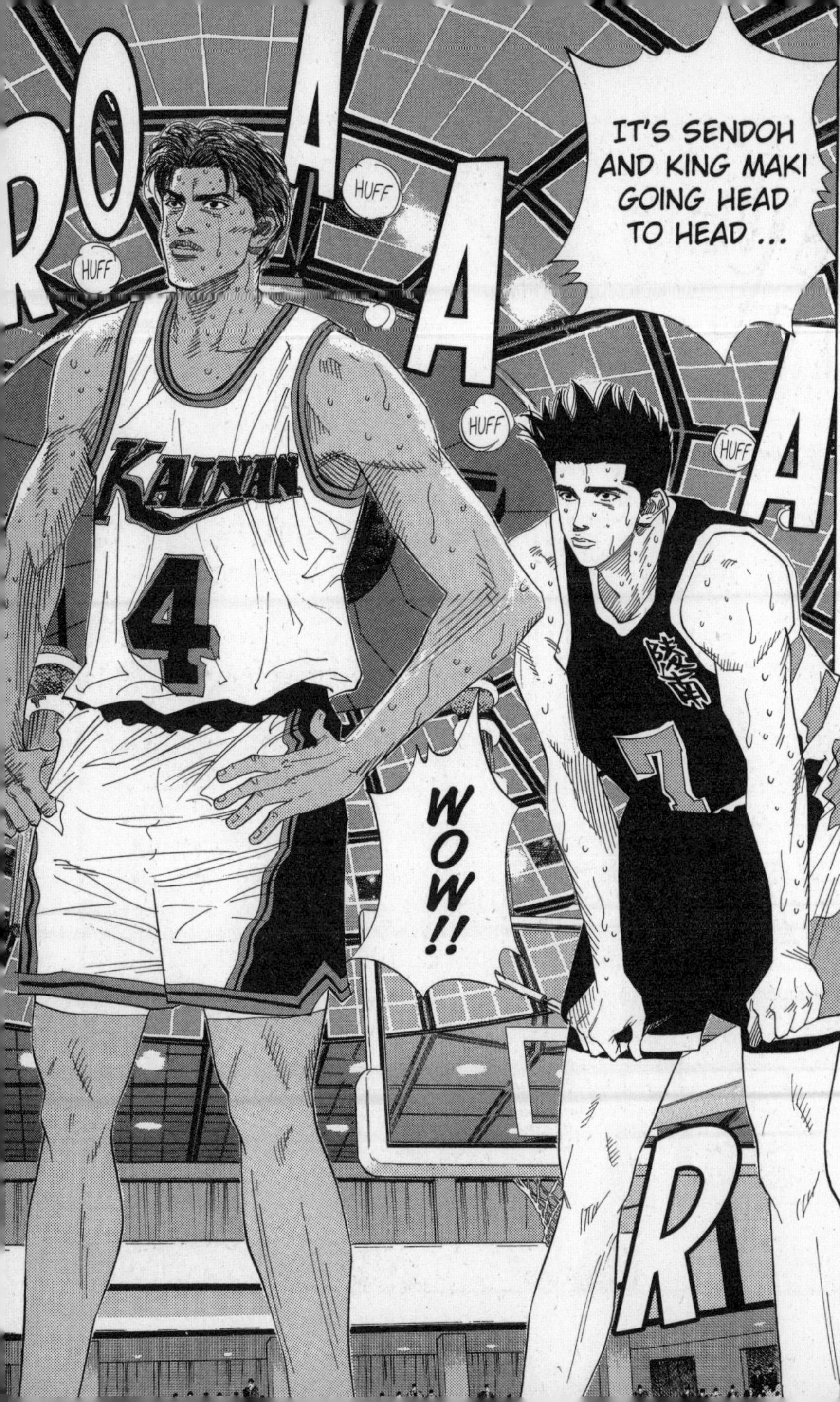
IT'S SENDOH AND KING MAKI GOING HEAD TO HEAD ...
HUFF
HUFF
HUFF
HUFF
ROAAAAR
WOW!!

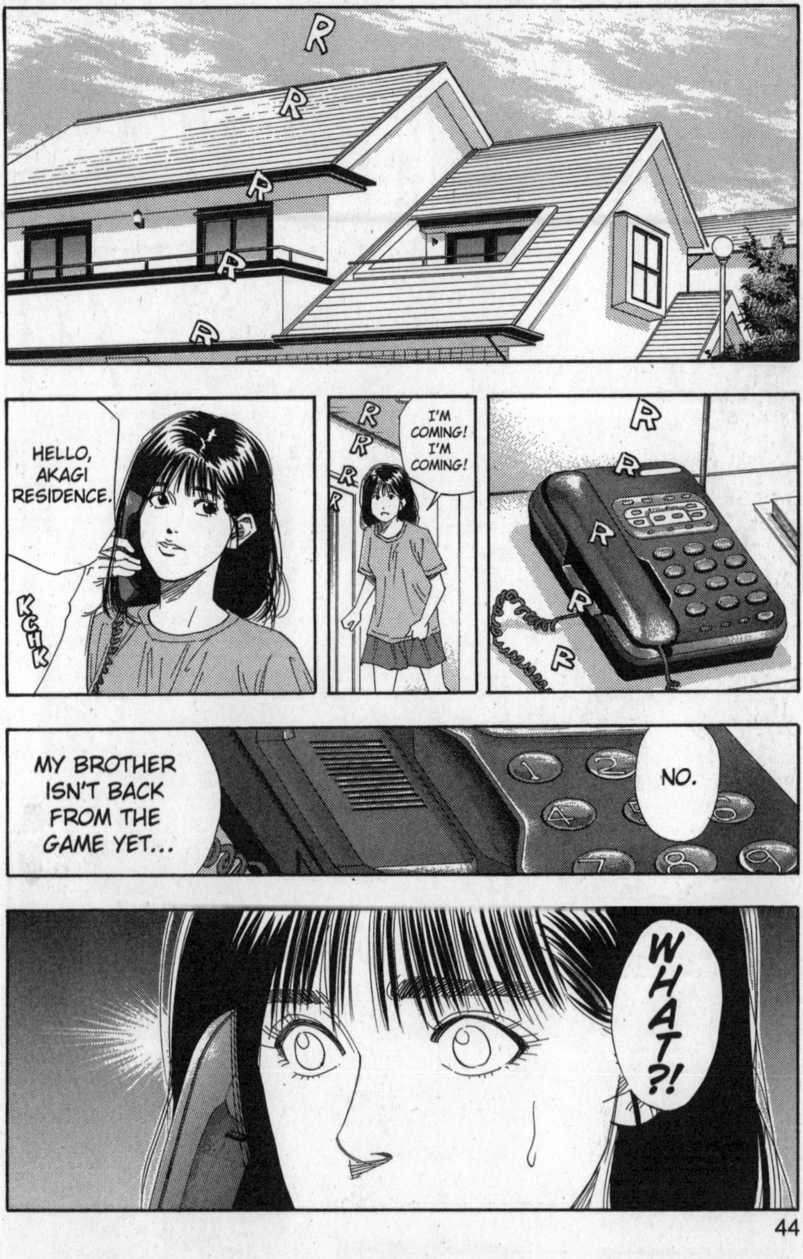
R R R R R
R R R R R R
R R R R
I'M COMING! I'M COMING!
HELLO, AKAGI RESIDENCE.
KCHK
NO.
MY BROTHER ISN'T BACK FROM THE GAME YET...
WHAT?!

READ THIS WAY

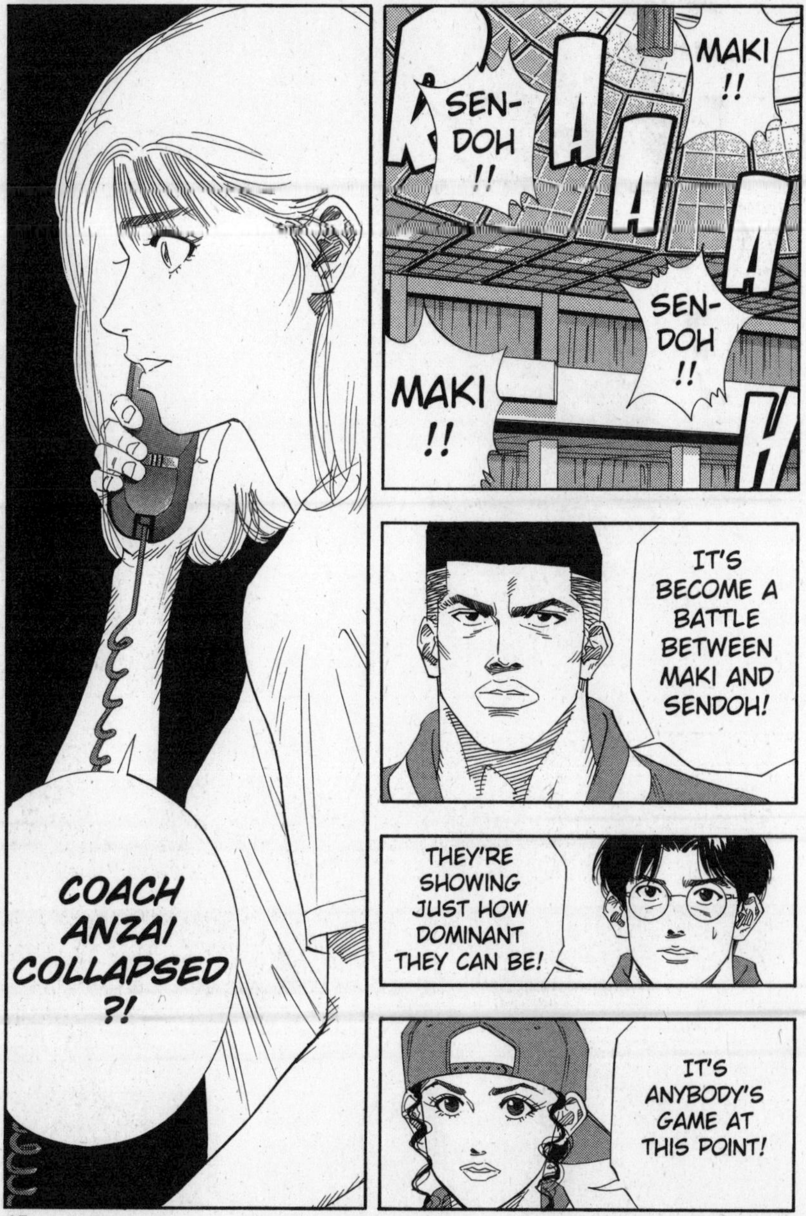

MAKI !!
SEN-DOH !!
SEN-DOH !!
MAKI !!
IT'S BECOME A BATTLE BETWEEN MAKI AND SENDOH!
THEY'RE SHOWING JUST HOW DOMINANT THEY CAN BE!
IT'S ANYBODY'S GAME AT THIS POINT!
COACH ANZAI COLLAPSED ?!

Not even one frame in two chapters!
QUAKE
SHIVER
What's going on?!
SHAKE

SLAM DUNK

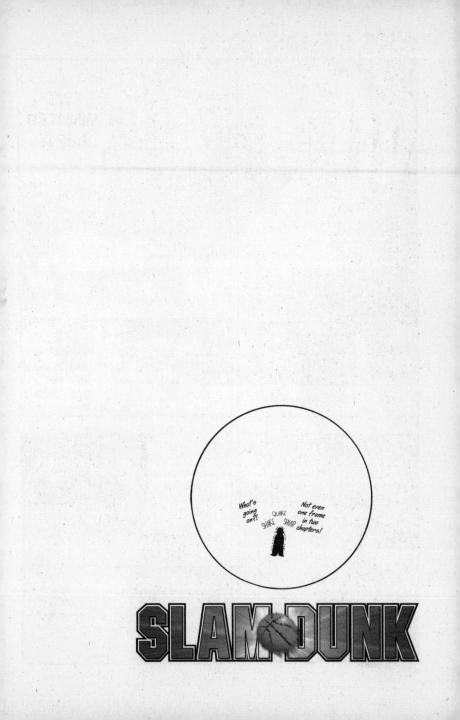

#146 ONE LAST PUSH

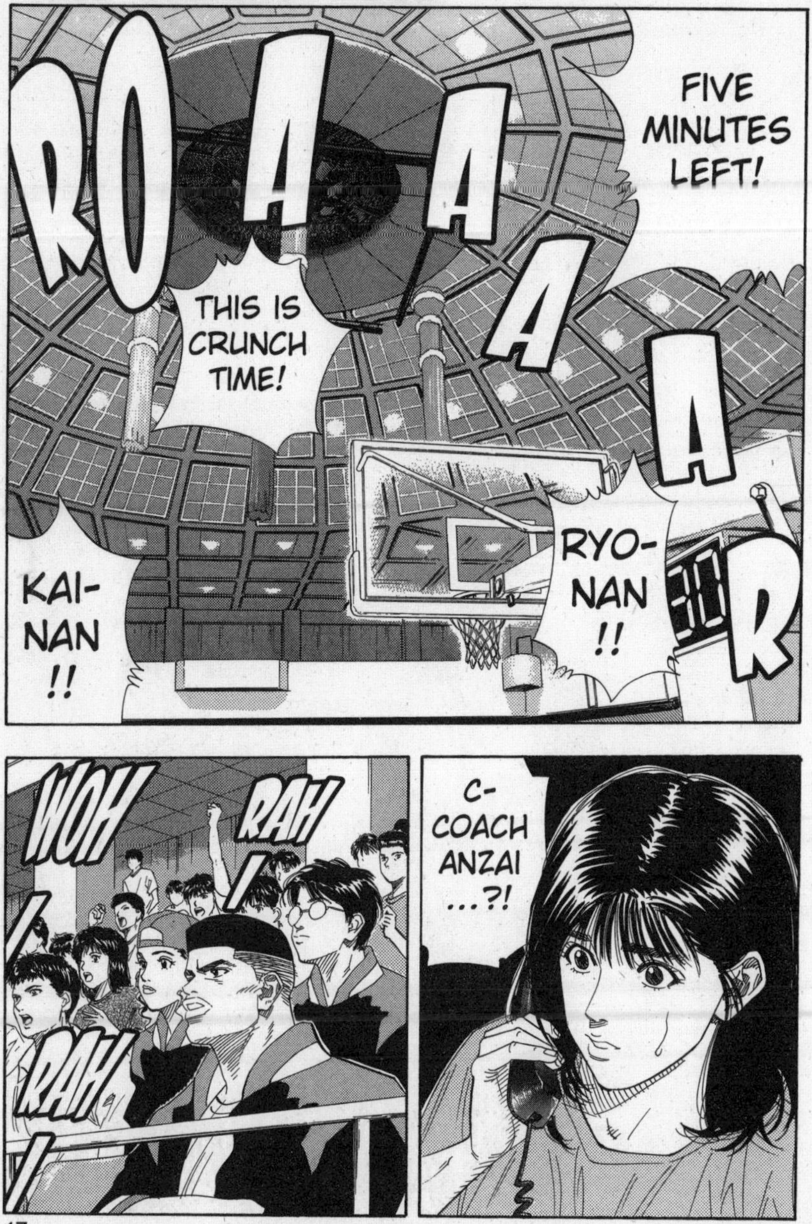
ROAAAAAR
FIVE MINUTES LEFT!
THIS IS CRUNCH TIME!
RYO-NAN!!
KAI-NAN!!
C-COACH ANZAI...?!
RAH!
WOH!
RAH!

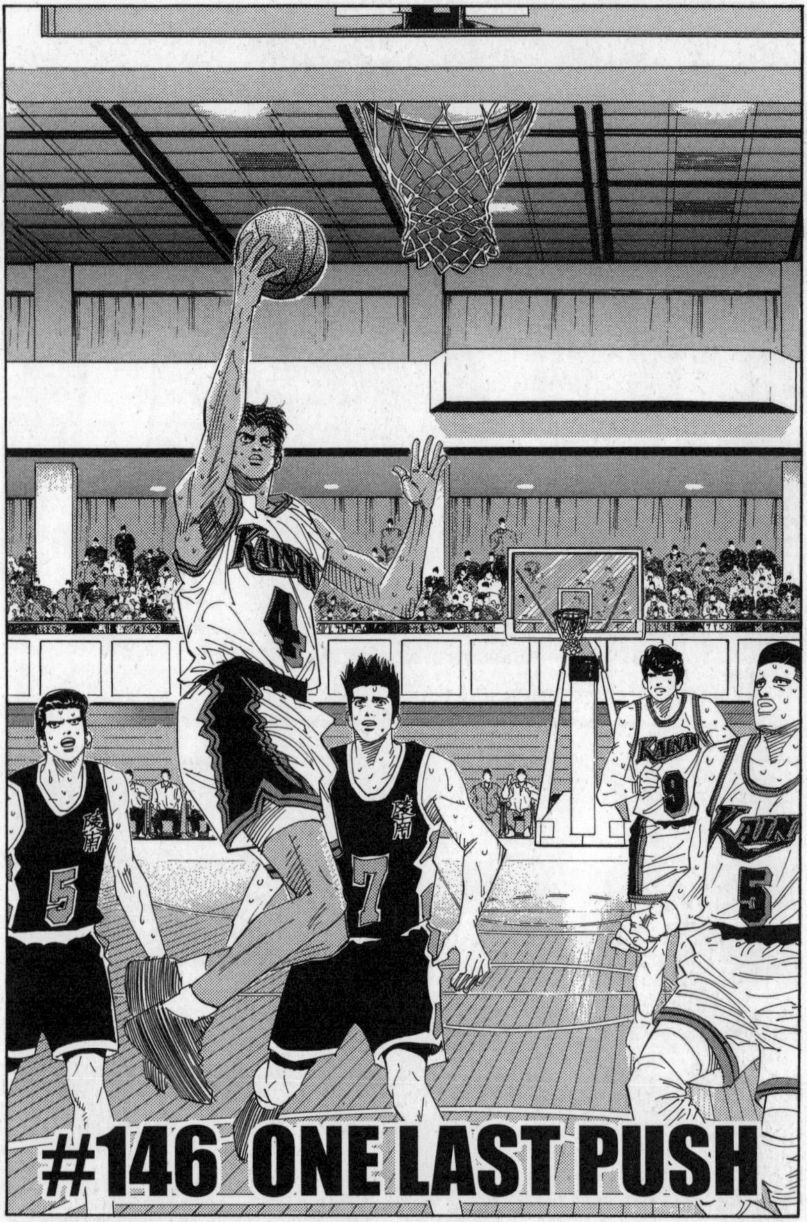
#146 ONE LAST PUSH

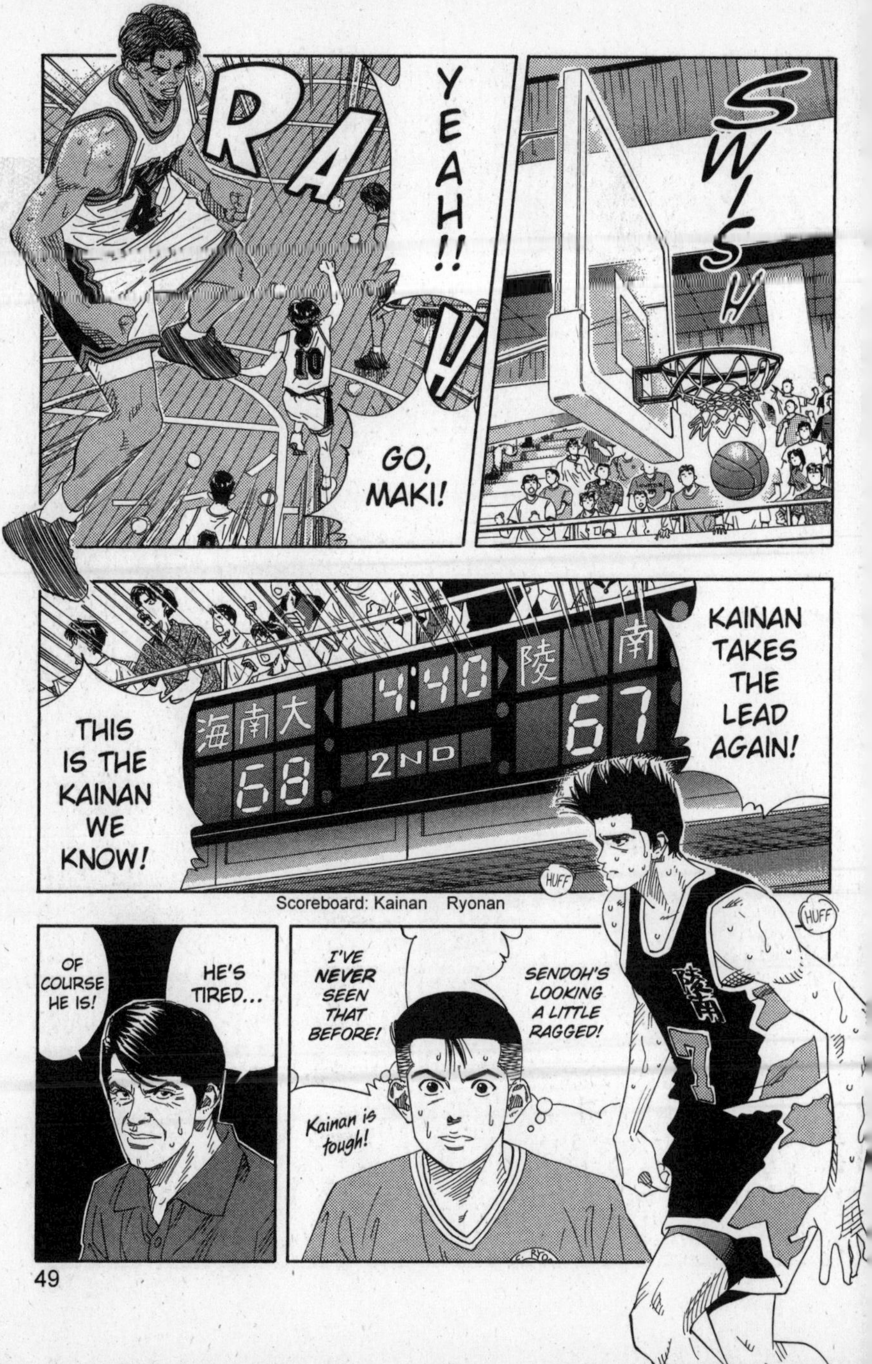
SWISH
RAH
YEAH!!
GO, MAKI!
KAINAN TAKES THE LEAD AGAIN!
陵南
4:40
67
2ND
海南大
68
THIS IS THE KAINAN WE KNOW!
Scoreboard: Kainan Ryonan
HUFF
HUFF
SENDOH'S LOOKING A LITTLE RAGGED!
I'VE NEVER SEEN THAT BEFORE!
Kainan is tough!
HE'S TIRED...
OF COURSE HE IS!

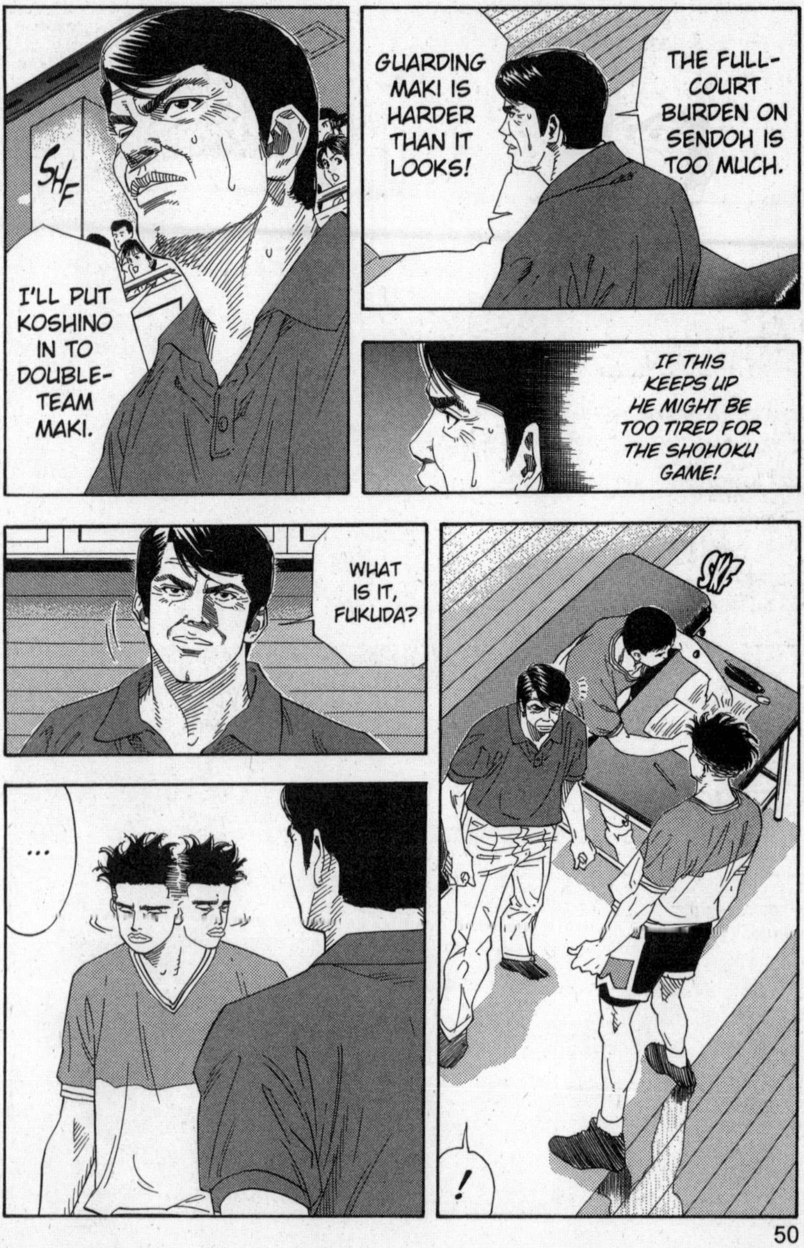
THE FULL-COURT BURDEN ON SENDOH IS TOO MUCH.
GUARDING MAKI IS HARDER THAN IT LOOKS!
IF THIS KEEPS UP HE MIGHT BE TOO TIRED FOR THE SHOHOKU GAME!
SHF
I'LL PUT KOSHINO IN TO DOUBLE-TEAM MAKI.
SKF
!
WHAT IS IT, FUKUDA?
...

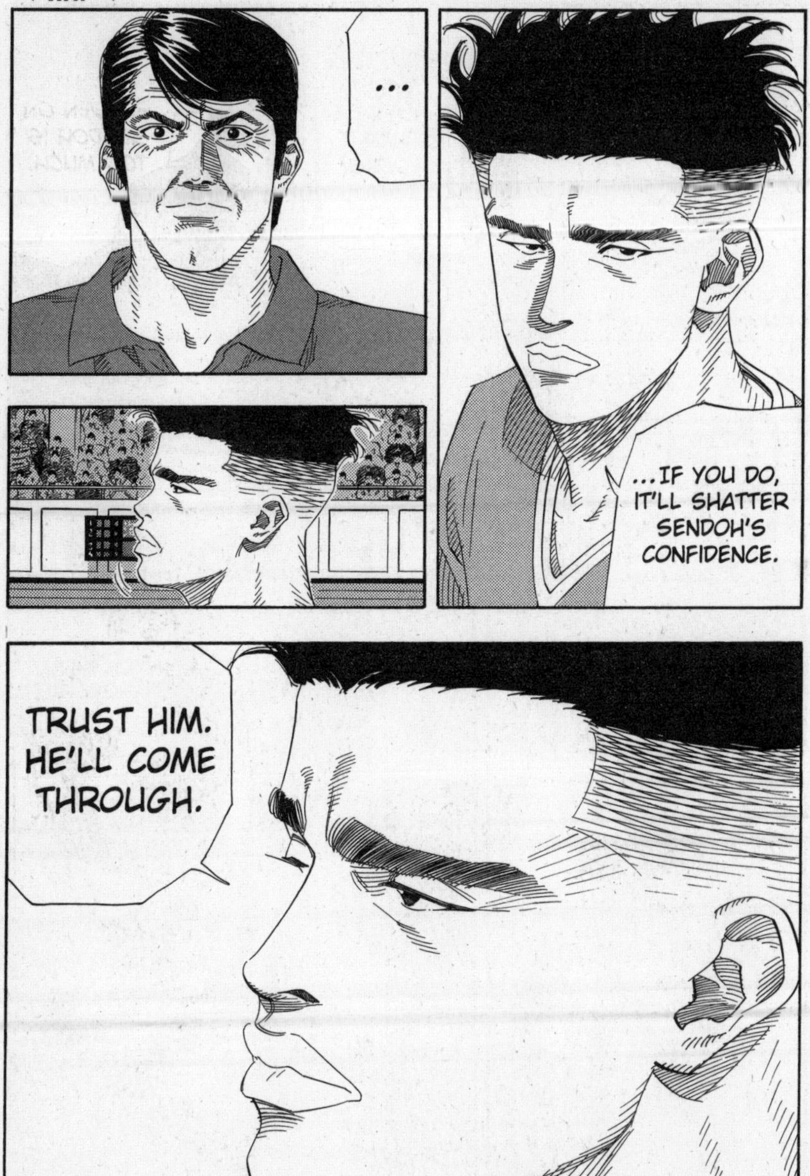
...IF YOU DO, IT'LL SHATTER SENDOH'S CONFIDENCE.
...
TRUST HIM. HE'LL COME THROUGH.

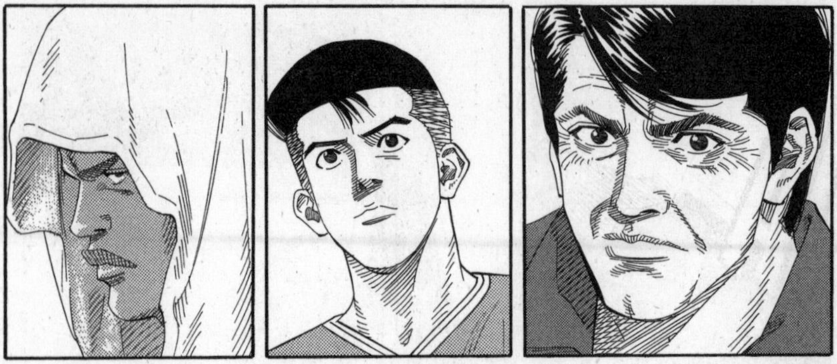

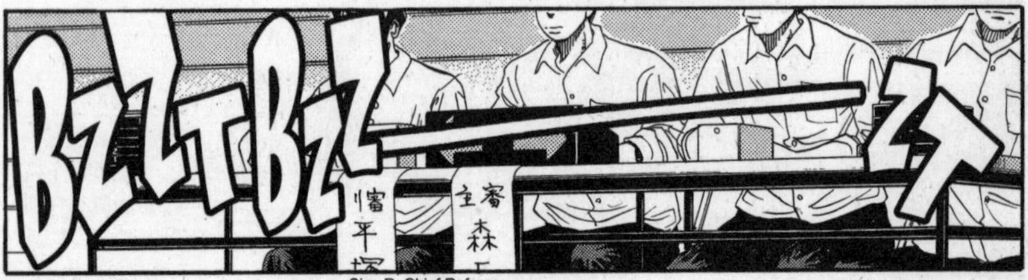
BZZT BZZZT

Sign R: Chief Referee
Sign L: Assistant Referee

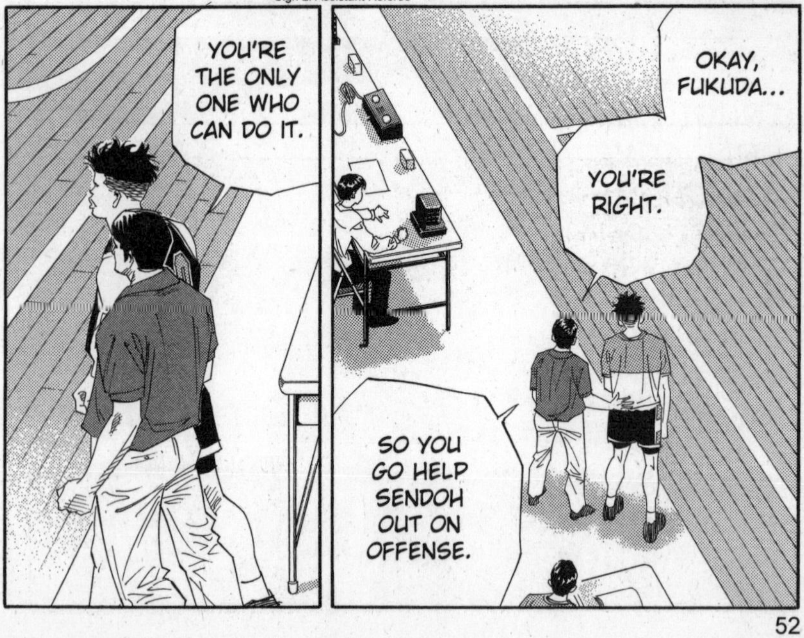
OKAY, FUKUDA...
YOU'RE RIGHT.
SO YOU GO HELP SENDOH OUT ON OFFENSE.
YOU'RE THE ONLY ONE WHO CAN DO IT.

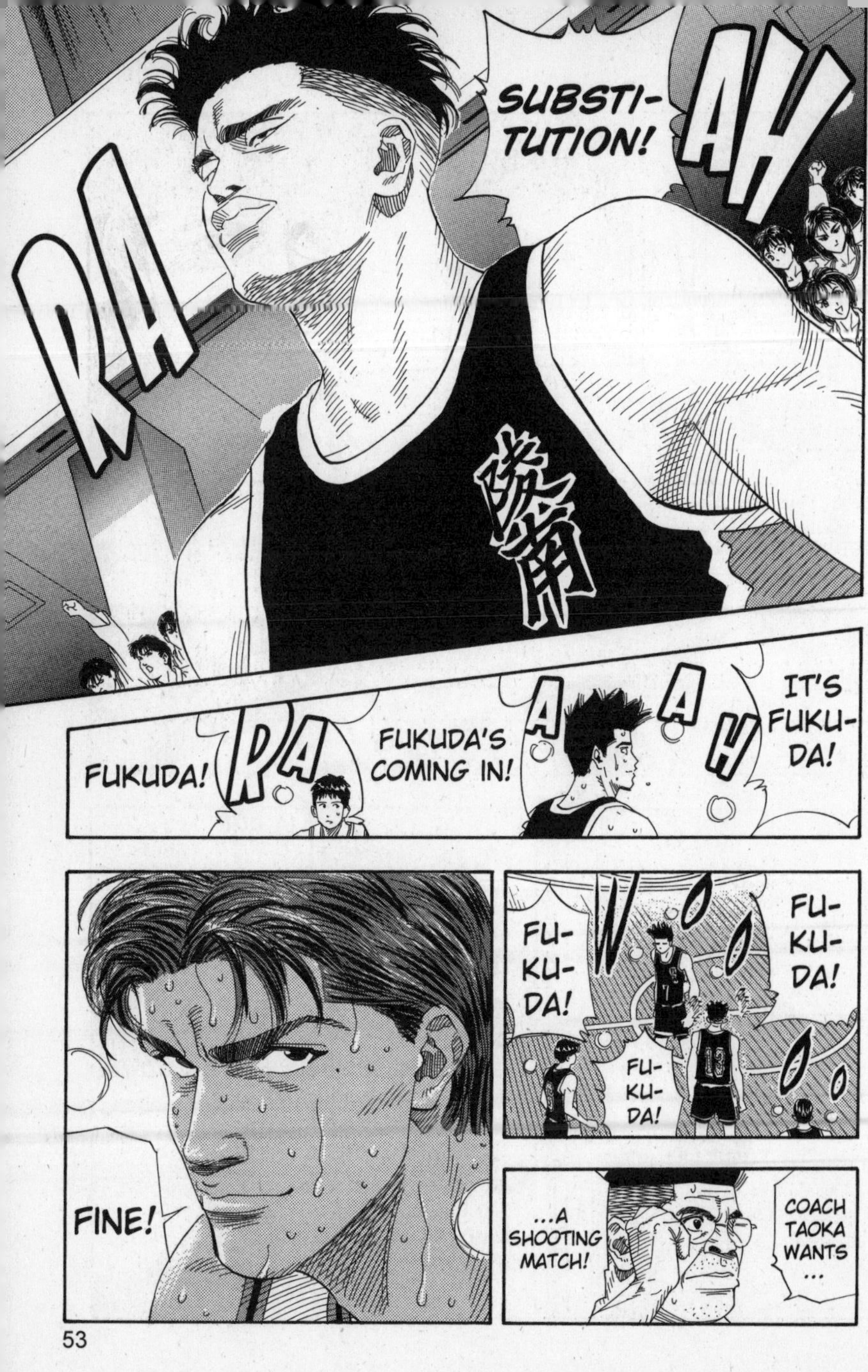
AH
SUBSTI-TUTION!
RA
IT'S FUKU-DA!
AAH
FUKUDA'S COMING IN!
RA
FUKUDA!
FU-KU-DA!
WOOOO
FU-KU-DA!
FU-KU-DA!
COACH TAOKA WANTS ...
...A SHOOTING MATCH!
FINE!

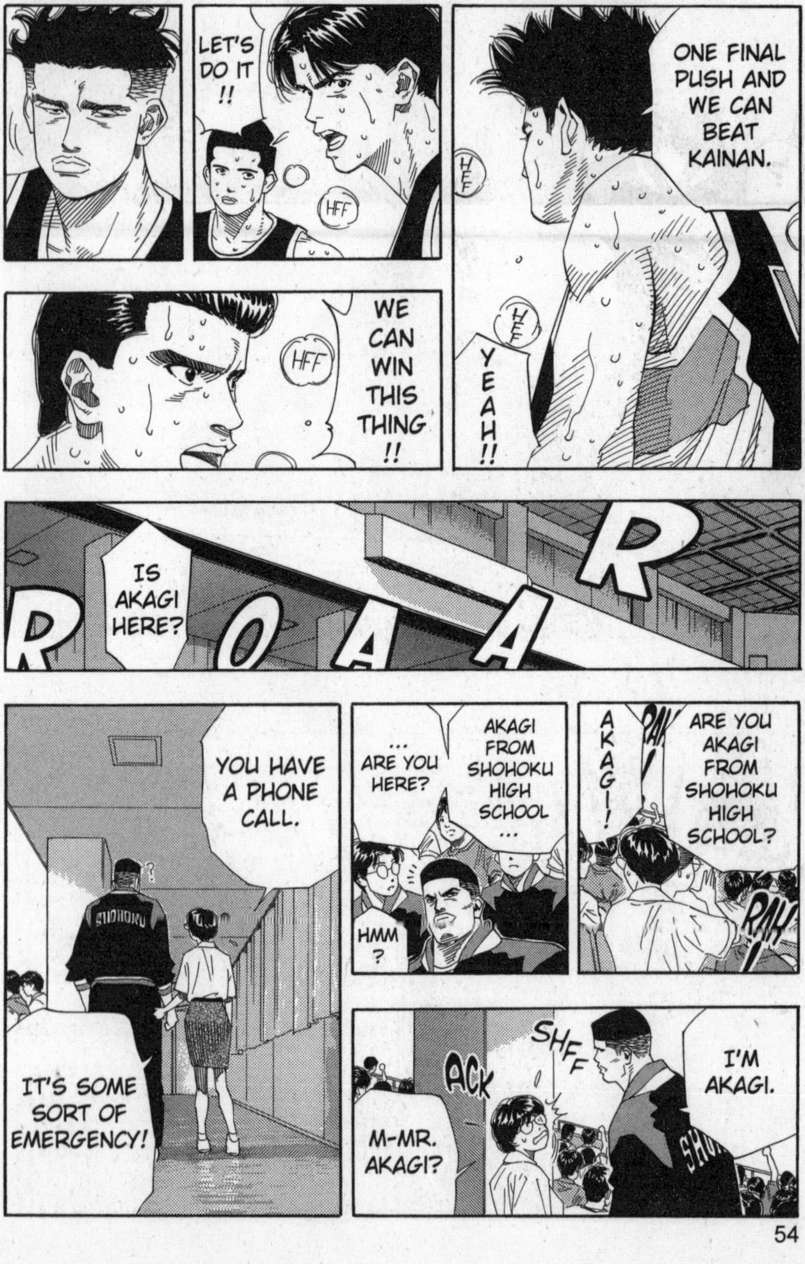
ONE FINAL PUSH AND WE CAN BEAT KAINAN.
HFF
HFF
YEAH!!
LET'S DO IT!!
HFF
WE CAN WIN THIS THING!!
HFF
IS AKAGI HERE?
ROAR
AKAGI!
RAH!
ARE YOU AKAGI FROM SHOHOKU HIGH SCHOOL?
RAH!
AKAGI FROM SHOHOKU HIGH SCHOOL...
...ARE YOU HERE?
HMM?
I'M AKAGI.
SHFF
ACK
M-MR. AKAGI?
YOU HAVE A PHONE CALL.
IT'S SOME SORT OF EMERGENCY!

READ THIS WAY

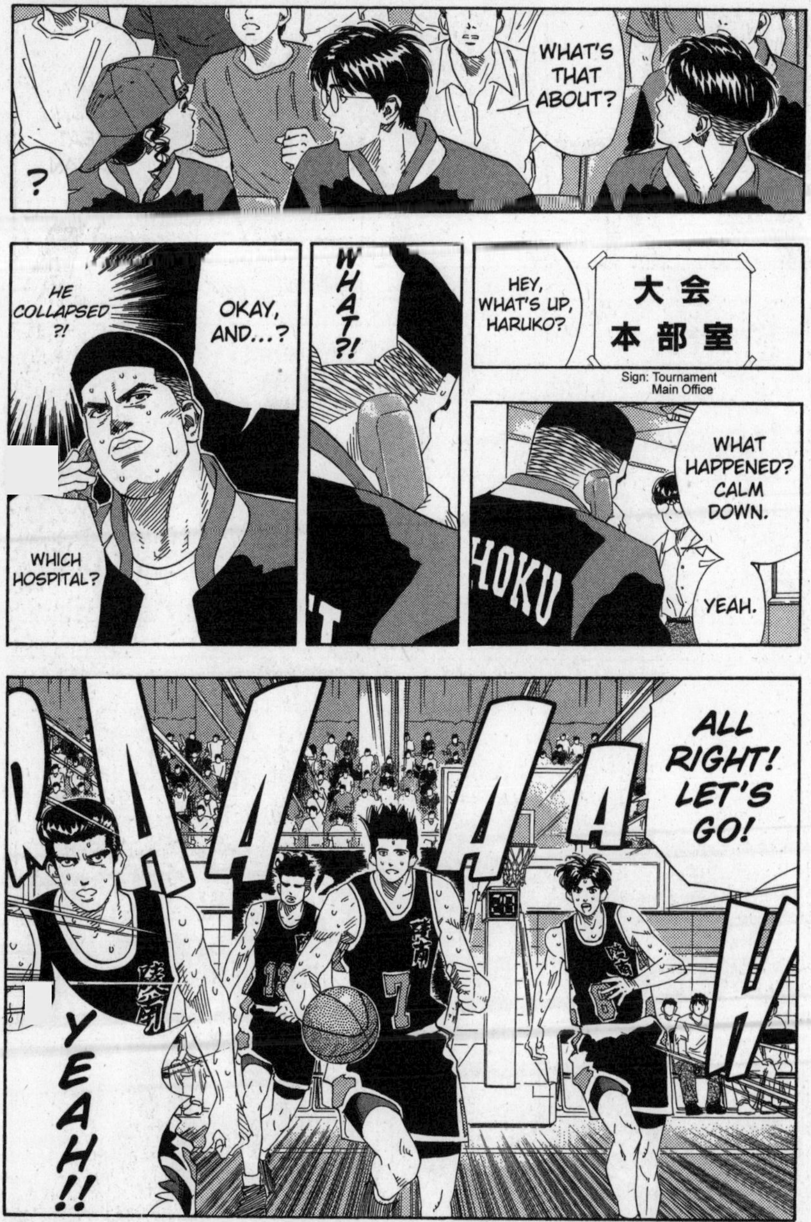
WHAT'S THAT ABOUT?
?
HEY, WHAT'S UP, HARUKO?
大会
本部室
WHAT HAPPENED? CALM DOWN.
YEAH.
WHAT?!
OKAY, AND...?
HE COLLAPSED?!
WHICH HOSPITAL?
ALL RIGHT! LET'S GO!
RAAAAH
YEAH!!
Sign: Tournament Main Office

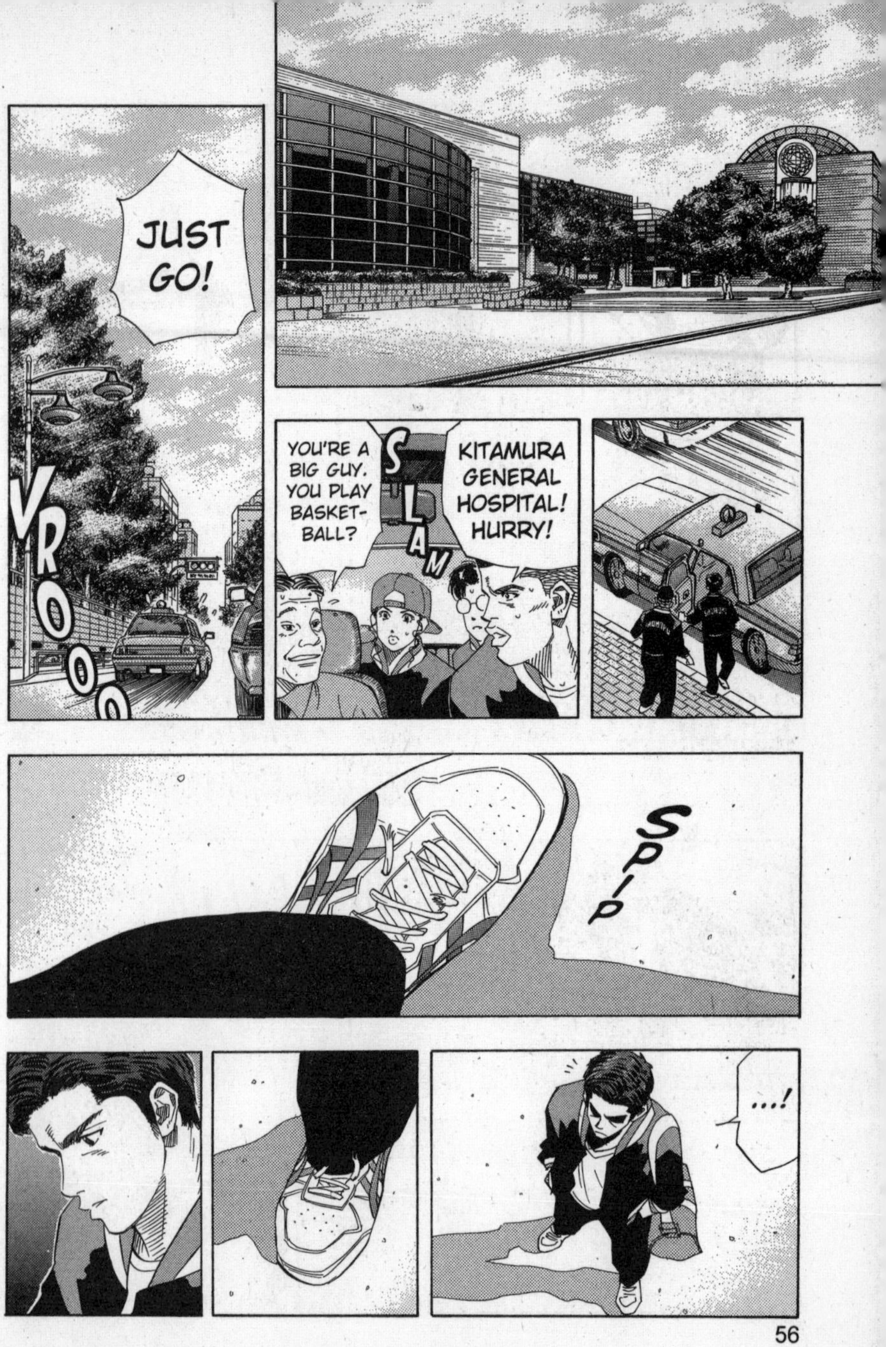
KITAMURA GENERAL HOSPITAL! HURRY!
SLAM
YOU'RE A BIG GUY. YOU PLAY BASKET-BALL?
JUST GO!
VROOOO
SPIP
...!

READ THIS WAY

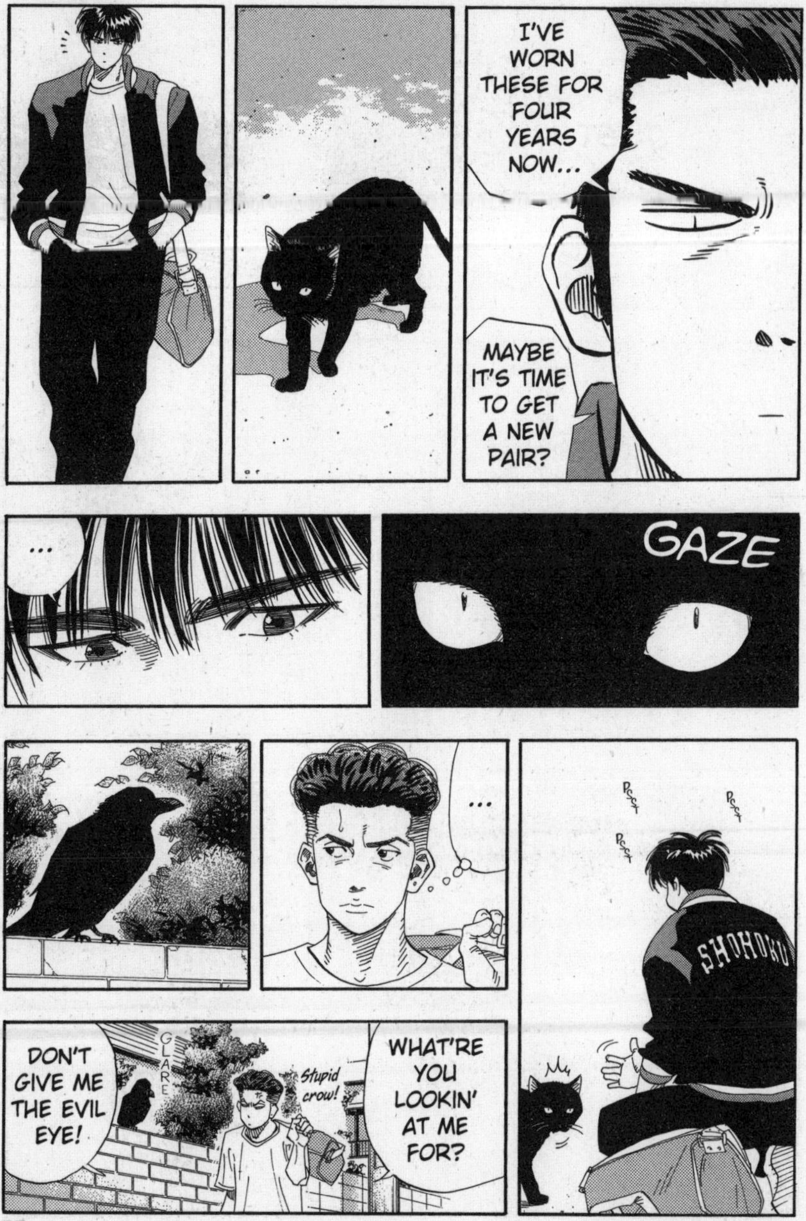
I'VE WORN THESE FOR FOUR YEARS NOW...
MAYBE IT'S TIME TO GET A NEW PAIR?
GAZE
...
Pssst
Pssst
Pssst
...
WHAT'RE YOU LOOKIN' AT ME FOR?
Stupid crow!
GLARE
DON'T GIVE ME THE EVIL EYE!

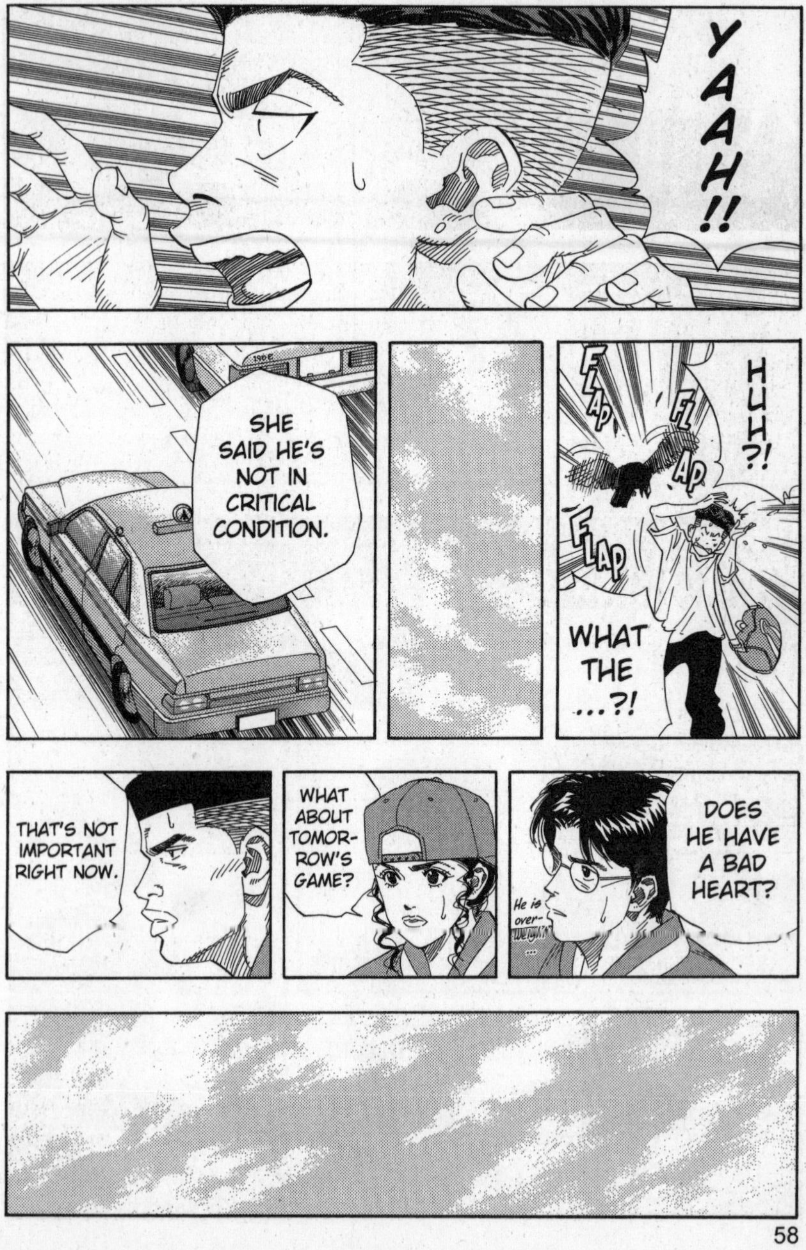
YAAH!!
HUH?!
FLAP
FL AP
FLAP
WHAT THE ...?!
SHE SAID HE'S NOT IN CRITICAL CONDITION.
DOES HE HAVE A BAD HEART?
He is over-weight ...
WHAT ABOUT TOMORROW'S GAME?
THAT'S NOT IMPORTANT RIGHT NOW.

READ THIS WAY

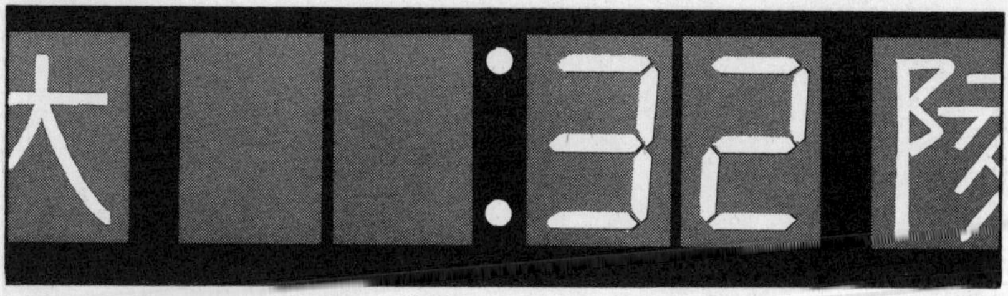
大
:32

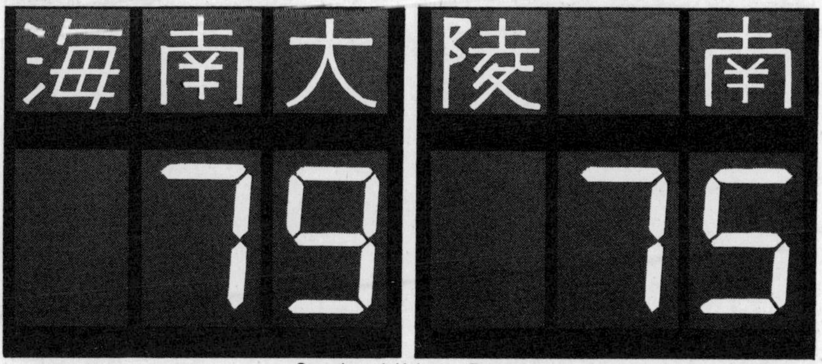
海南大
陵南
79
75

Scoreboard: Kainan Ryonan

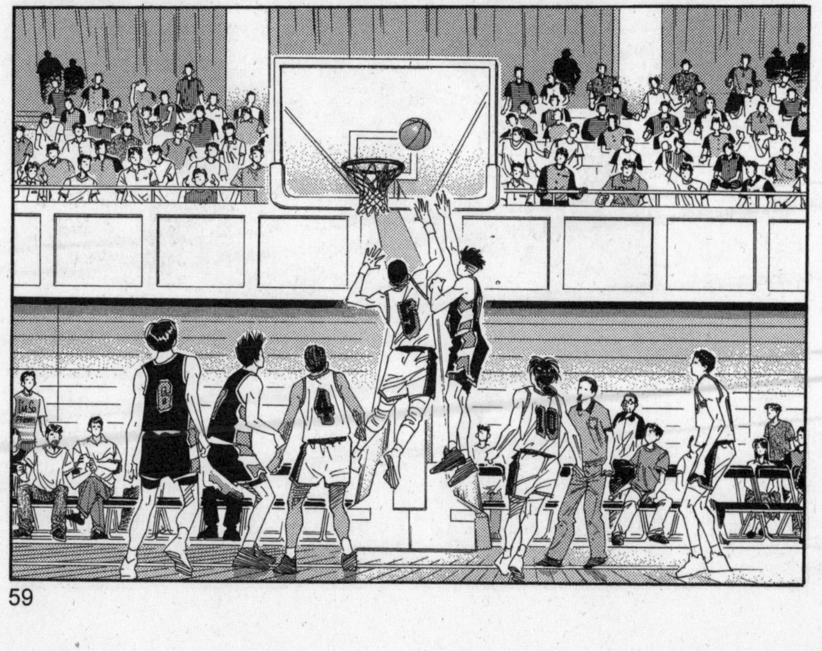

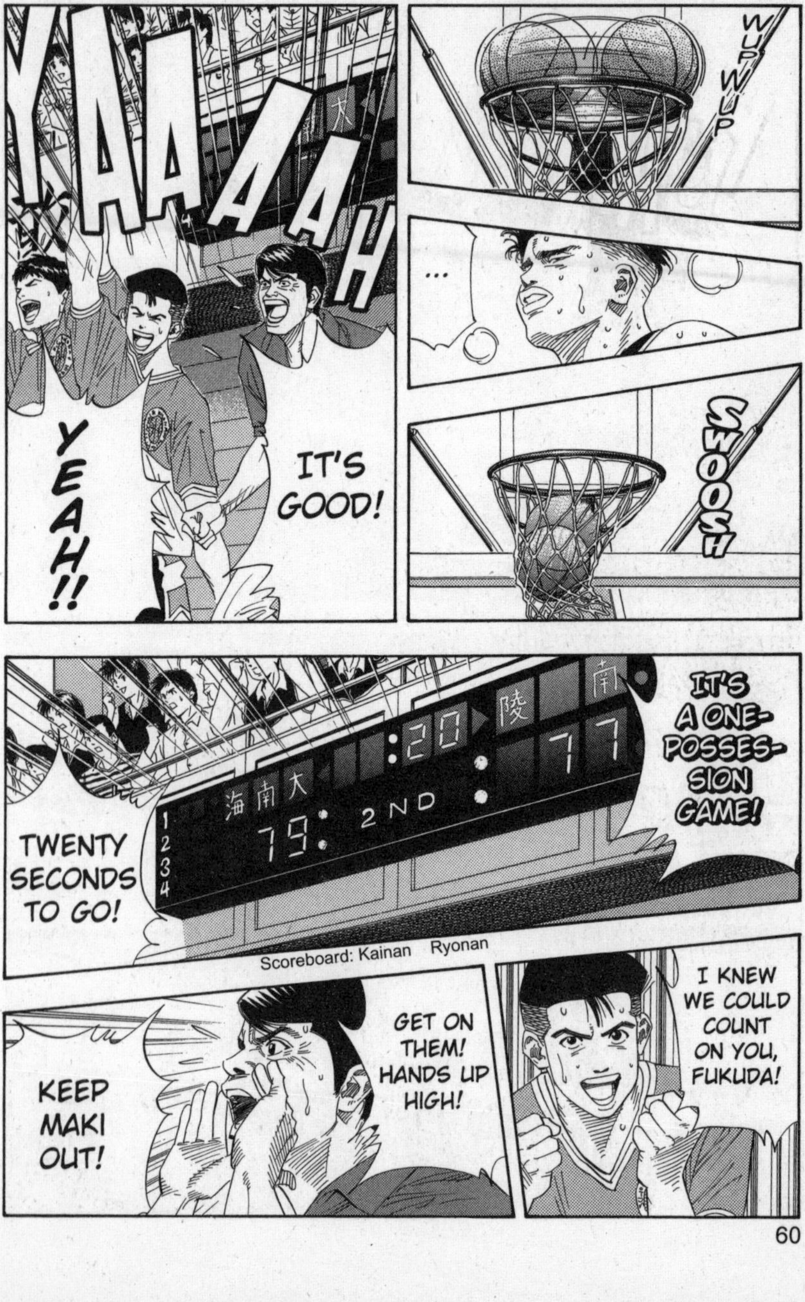
WUPWUPWUP
...
SWOOSH
YAAAAAH
IT'S GOOD!
YEAH!!
IT'S A ONE-POSSESSION GAME!
陵南 77
:20
海南大 79
2ND
TWENTY SECONDS TO GO!
Scoreboard: Kainan Ryonan
I KNEW WE COULD COUNT ON YOU, FUKUDA!
GET ON THEM! HANDS UP HIGH!
KEEP MAKI OUT!

READ THIS WAY

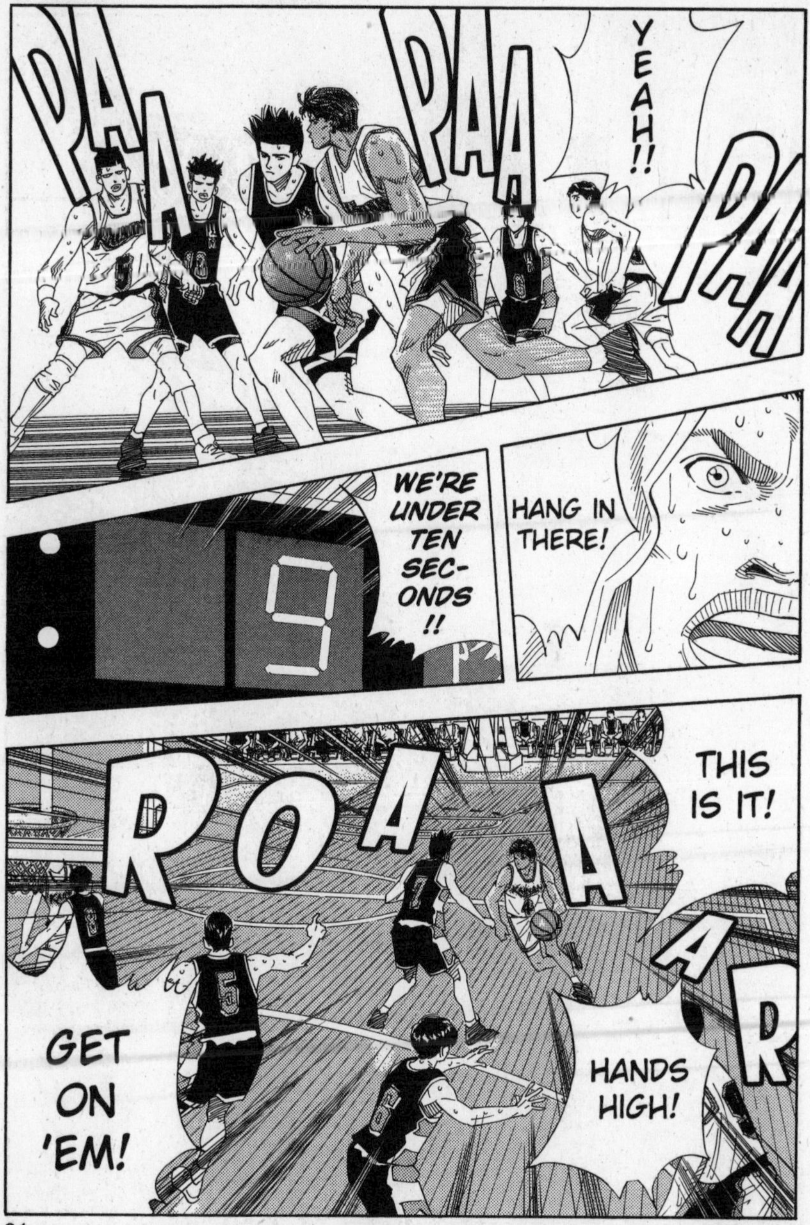

YEAH!!
PAPA
PAA
PAA
HANG IN THERE!
WE'RE UNDER TEN SEC- ONDS!!
THIS IS IT!
ROAAAR
HANDS HIGH!
GET ON 'EM!

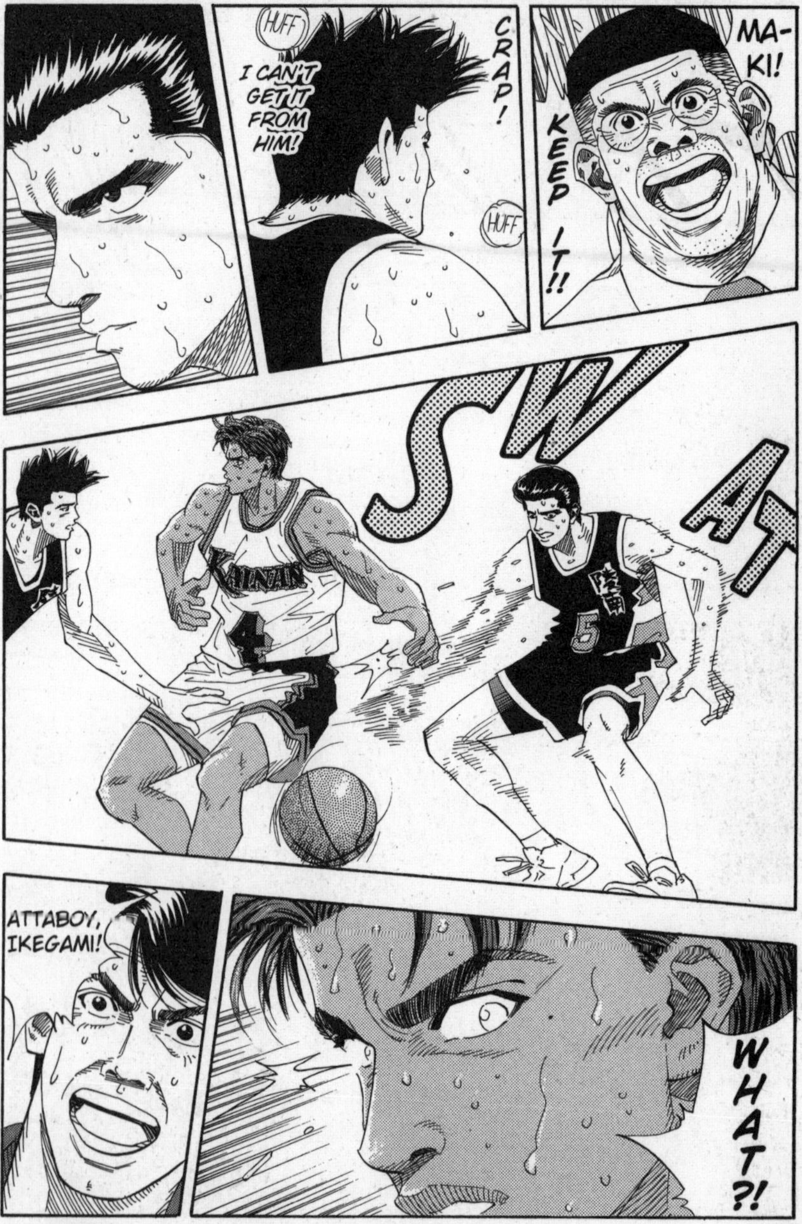
MA-KI!
KEEP IT!!
CRAP!
HUFF
I CAN'T GET IT FROM HIM!
HUFF
SWAT
WHAT?!
ATTABOY, IKEGAMI!

READ THIS WAY

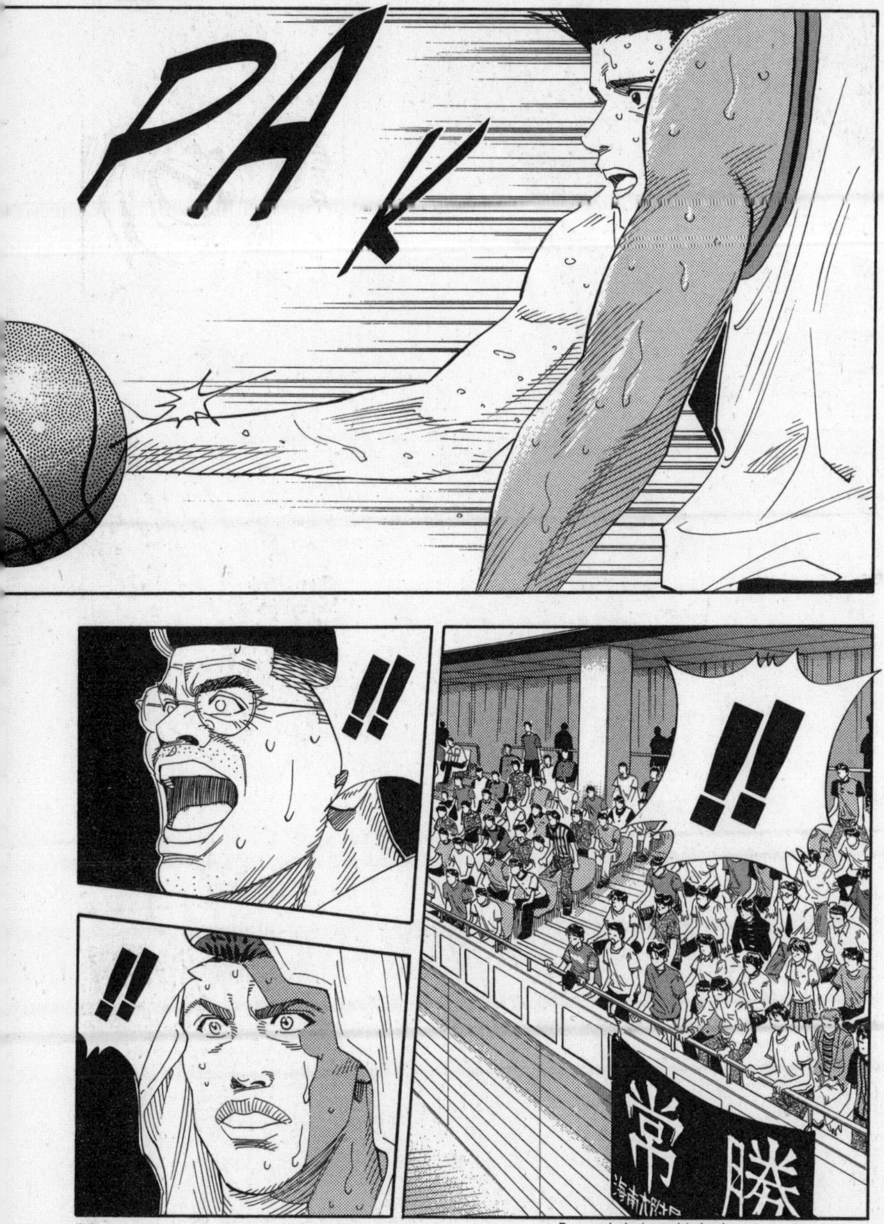
PAK
!!
常勝
!!
!!

Banner: *Josho* (ever victorious)
Kainan Dai Fuzoku High School Basketball Team

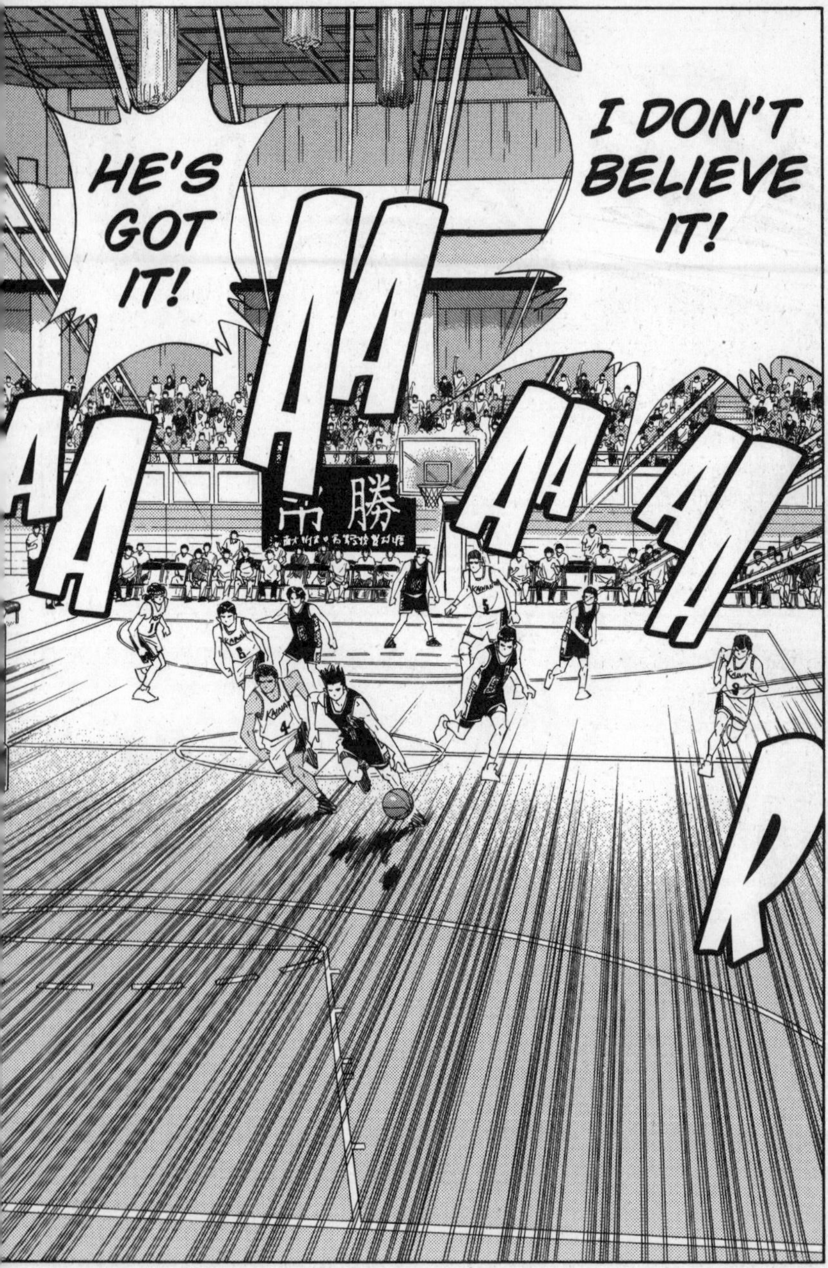
I DON'T BELIEVE IT!
HE'S GOT IT!
AAAAAAAAR

READ THIS WAY

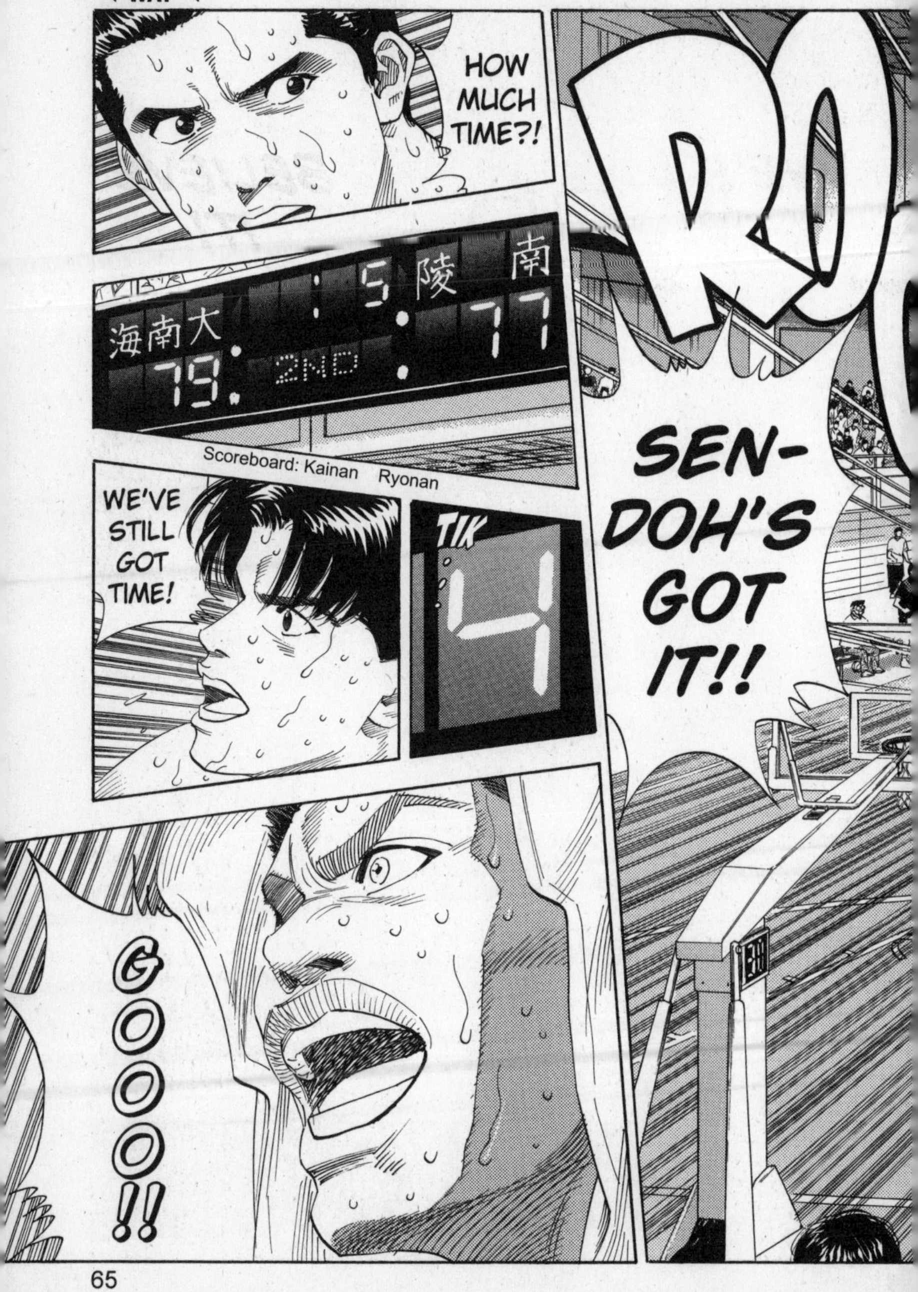

RO
SEN-DOH'S GOT IT!!
HOW MUCH TIME?!
陵南 77
海南大 79
2ND
5
Scoreboard: Kainan Ryonan
TIK
4
WE'VE STILL GOT TIME!
GOOOO!!

That's three weeks in a row now!
TWITCH
QUAKE
SHIVER
QUAKE
SHAKE
TWITCH

SLAM DUNK

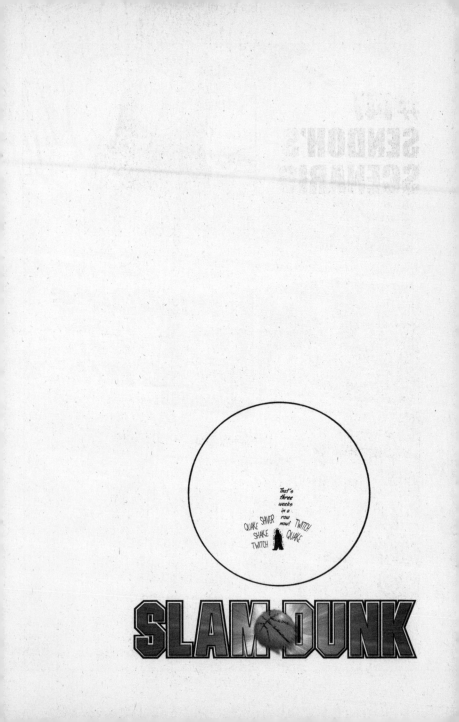

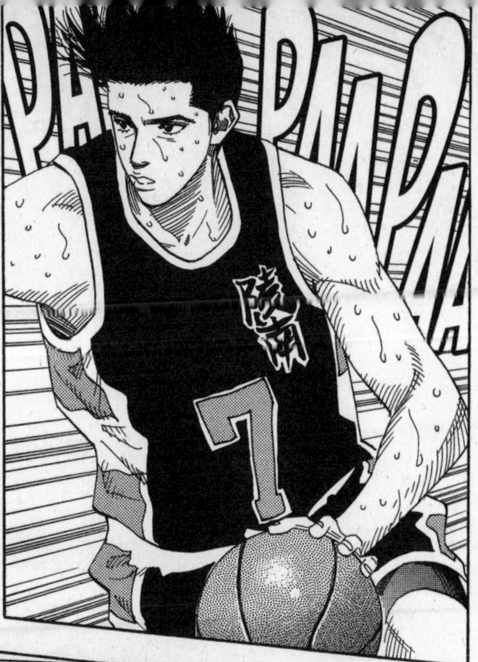
PA
PAPAPA

#147 SENDOH'S SCENARIO

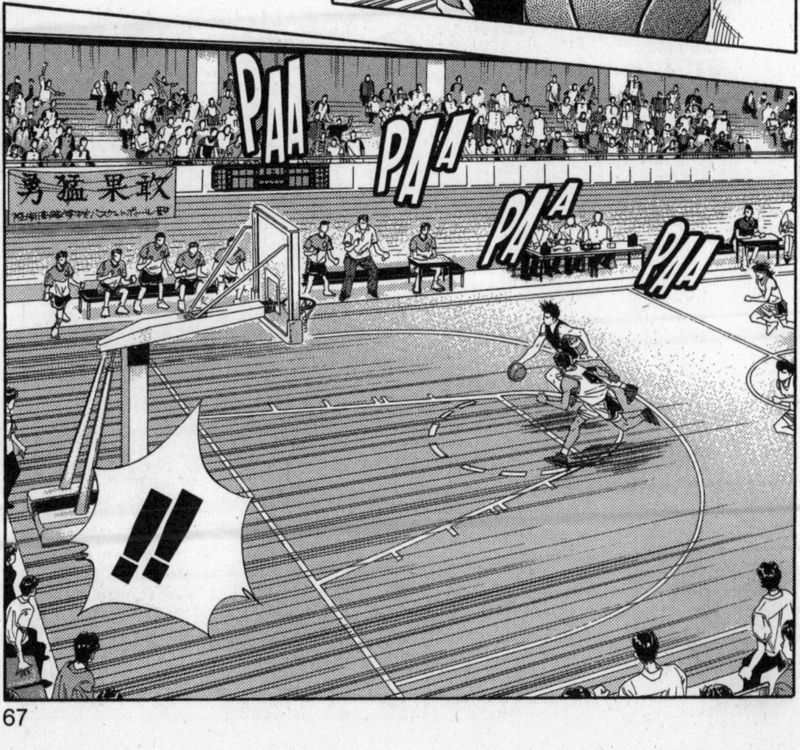
PAA
PAA
PAA
PAA
勇猛果敢
!!

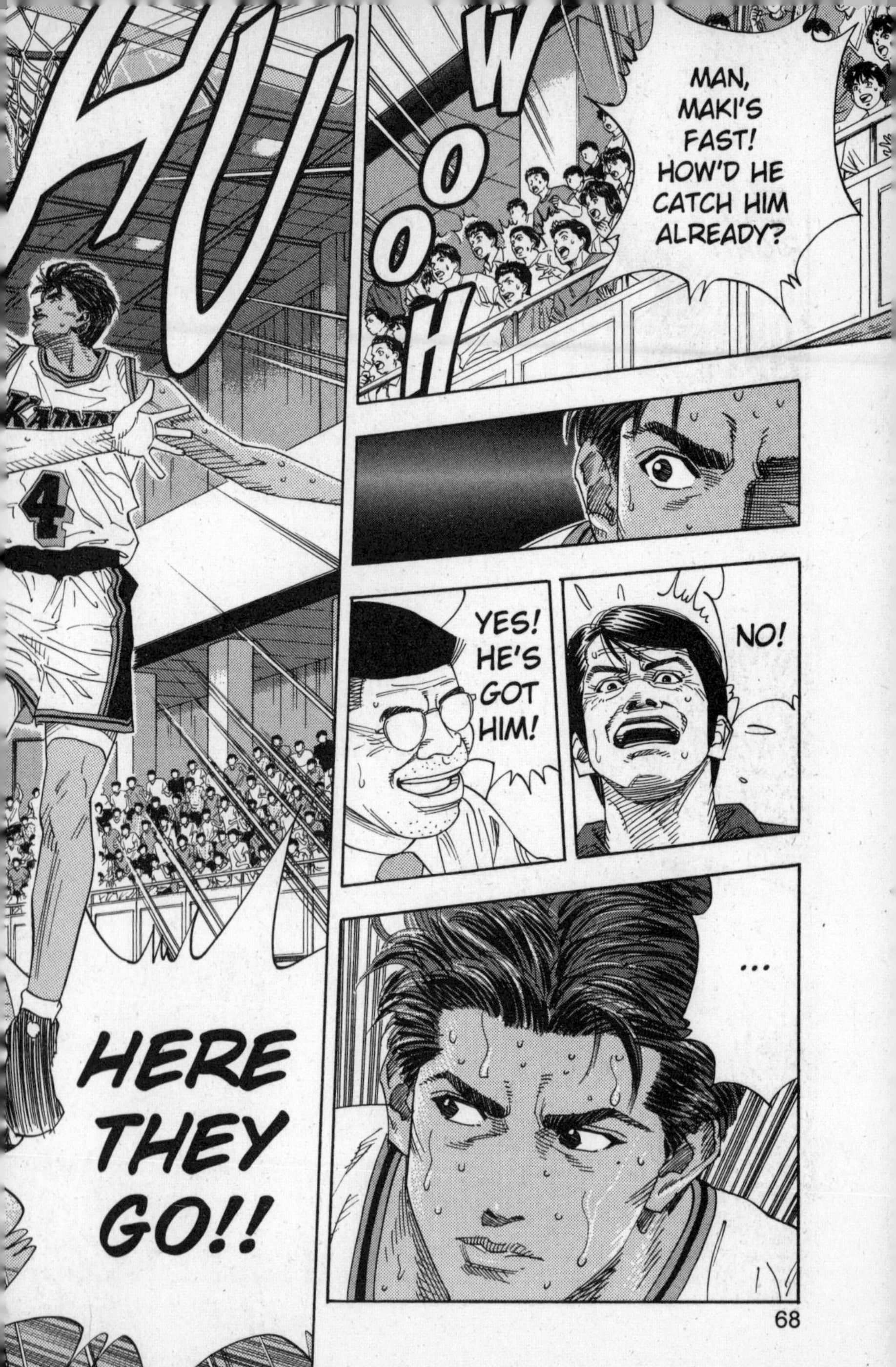
MAN, MAKI'S FAST! HOW'D HE CATCH HIM ALREADY?
WOOOH
NO!
YES! HE'S GOT HIM!
...
HERE THEY GO!!

READ THIS WAY

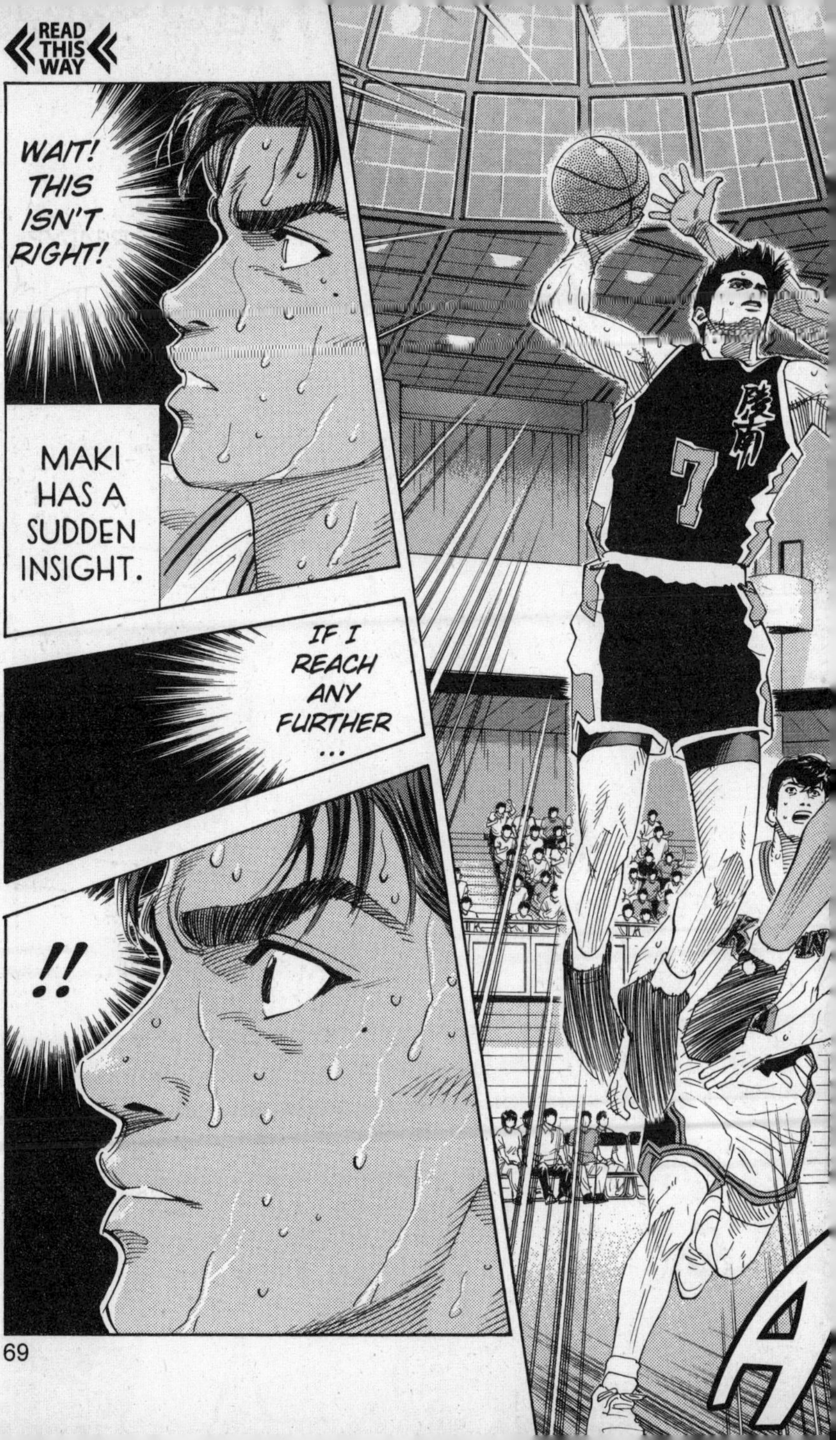
A
WAIT! THIS ISN'T RIGHT!
MAKI HAS A SUDDEN INSIGHT.
IF I REACH ANY FURTHER ...
!!

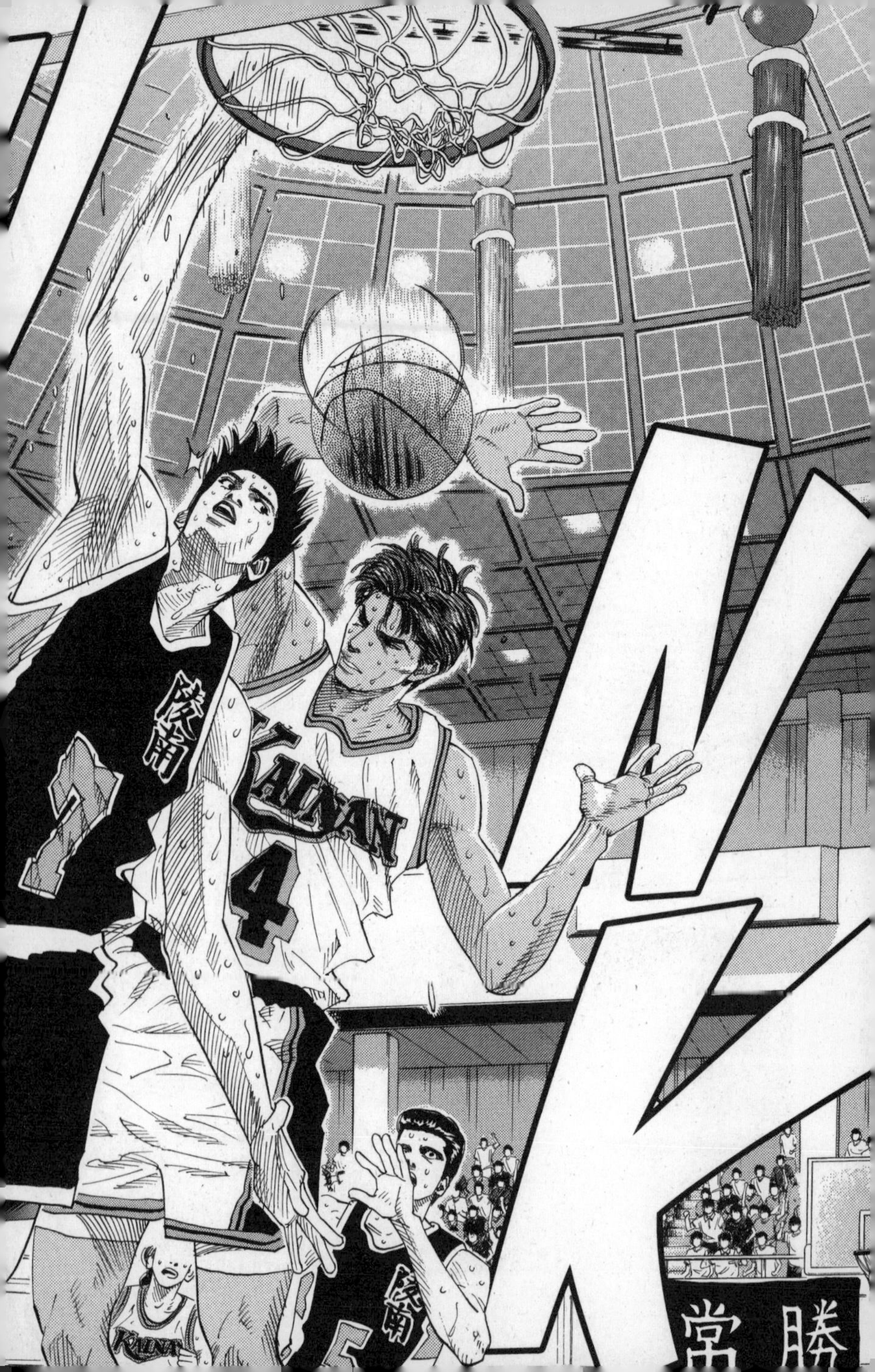
陵南
常勝

READ THIS WAY

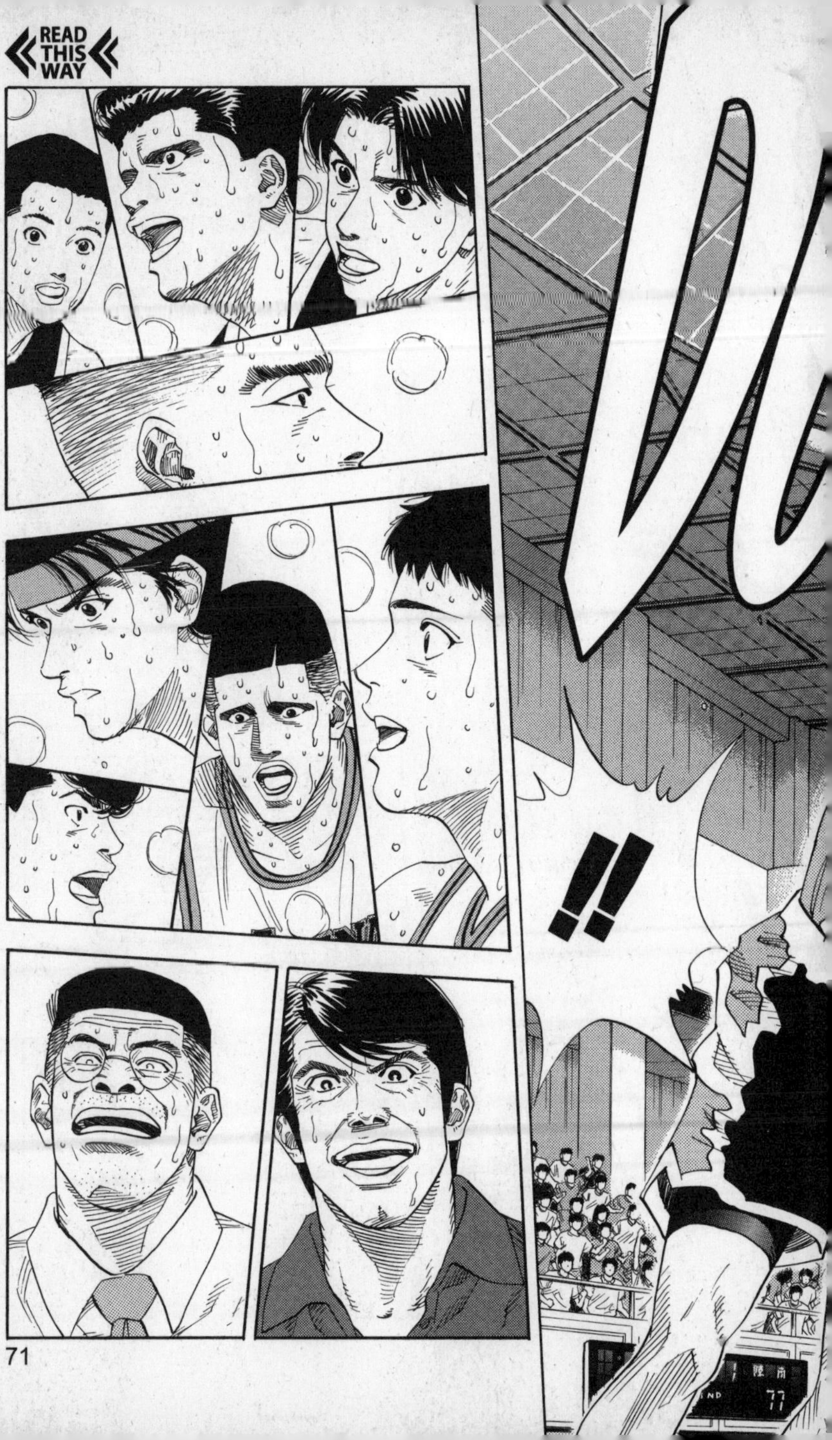
!!
陵南
77

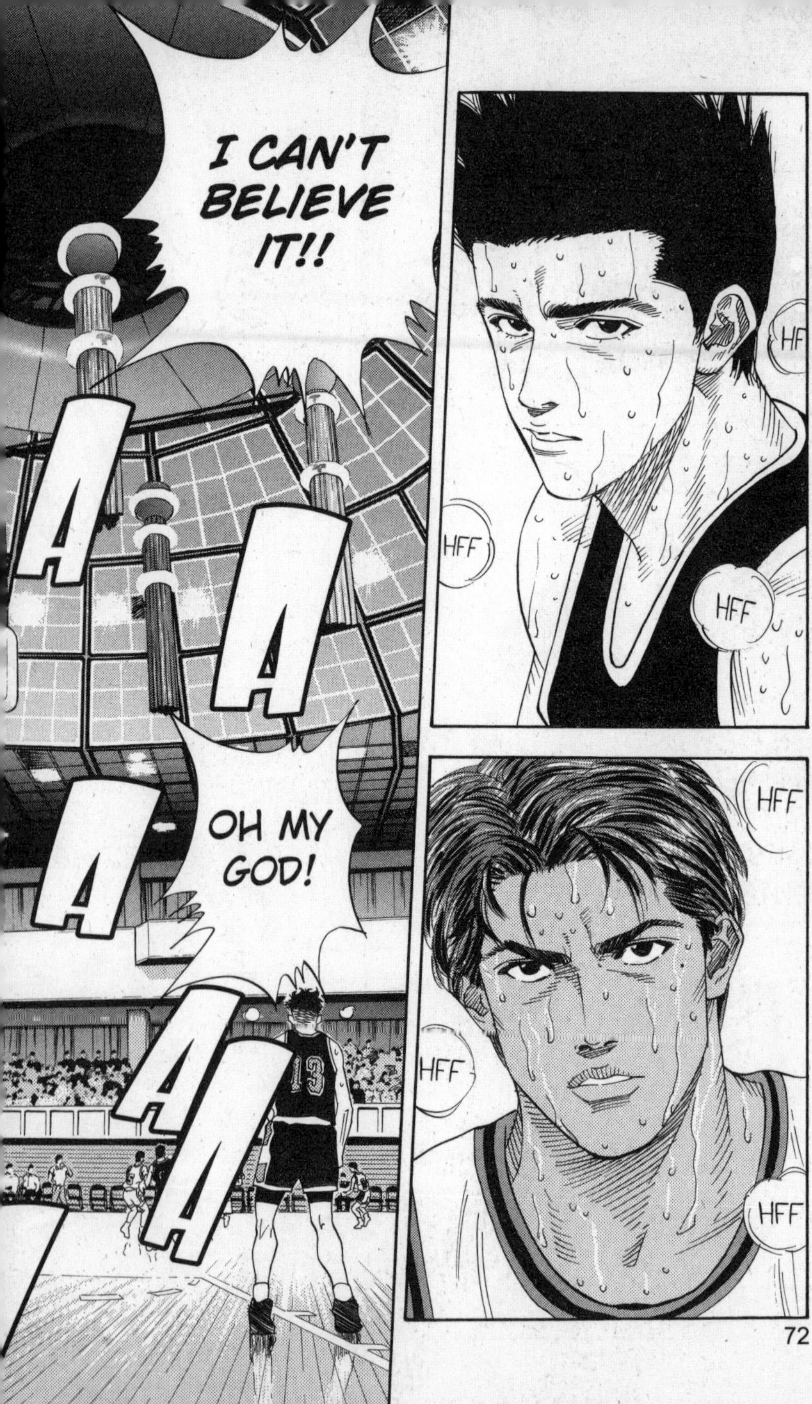
HF
HFF
HFF
HFF
HFF
HFF
I CAN'T BELIEVE IT!!
AAAAA
OH MY GOD!

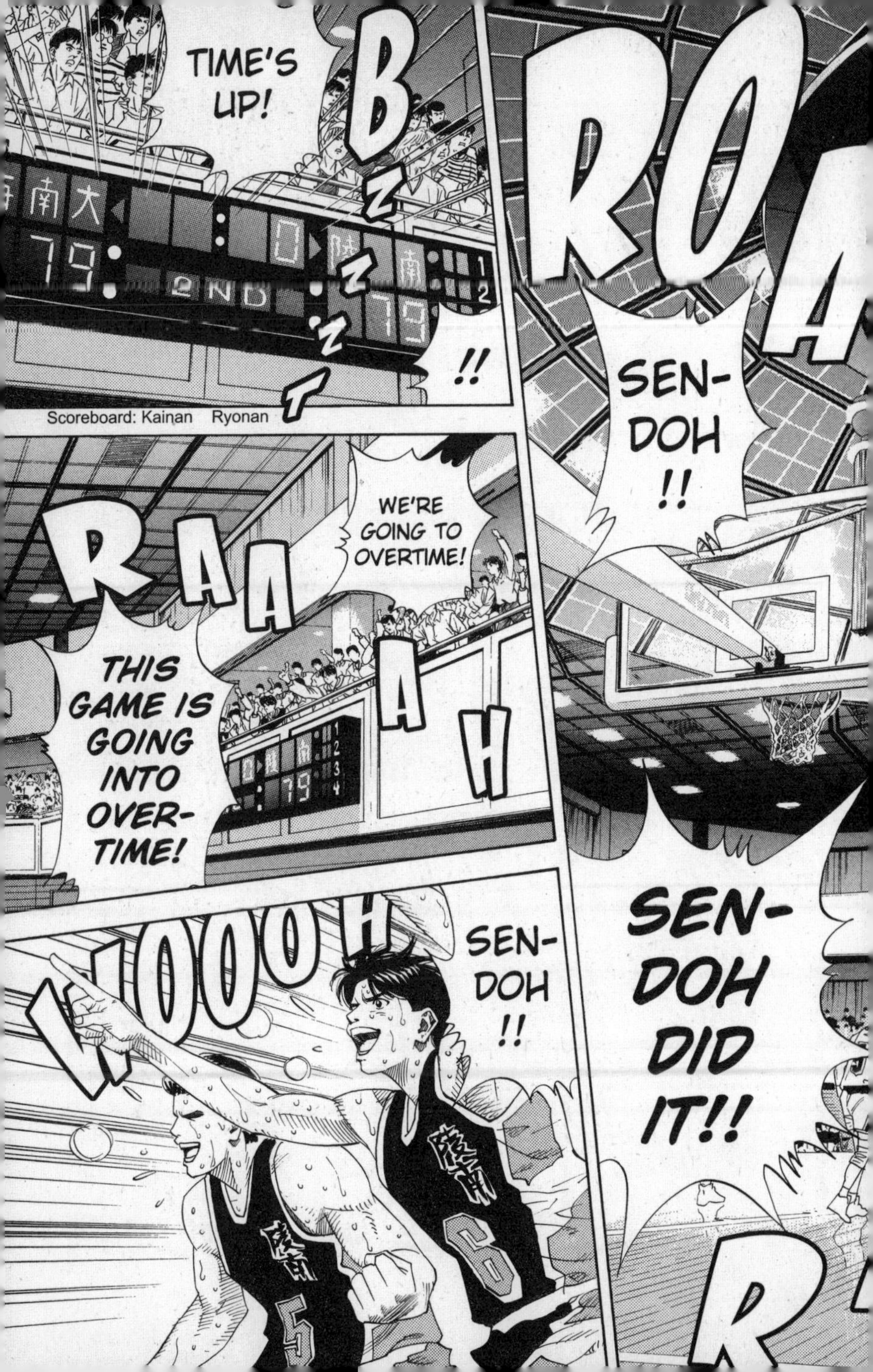
ROA
SEN-DOH!!
SEN-DOH DID IT!!
R
TIME'S UP!
BZZZT
!!
Scoreboard: Kainan Ryonan
RAAAAH
WE'RE GOING TO OVERTIME!
THIS GAME IS GOING INTO OVER-TIME!
WOOOOH
SEN-DOH!!

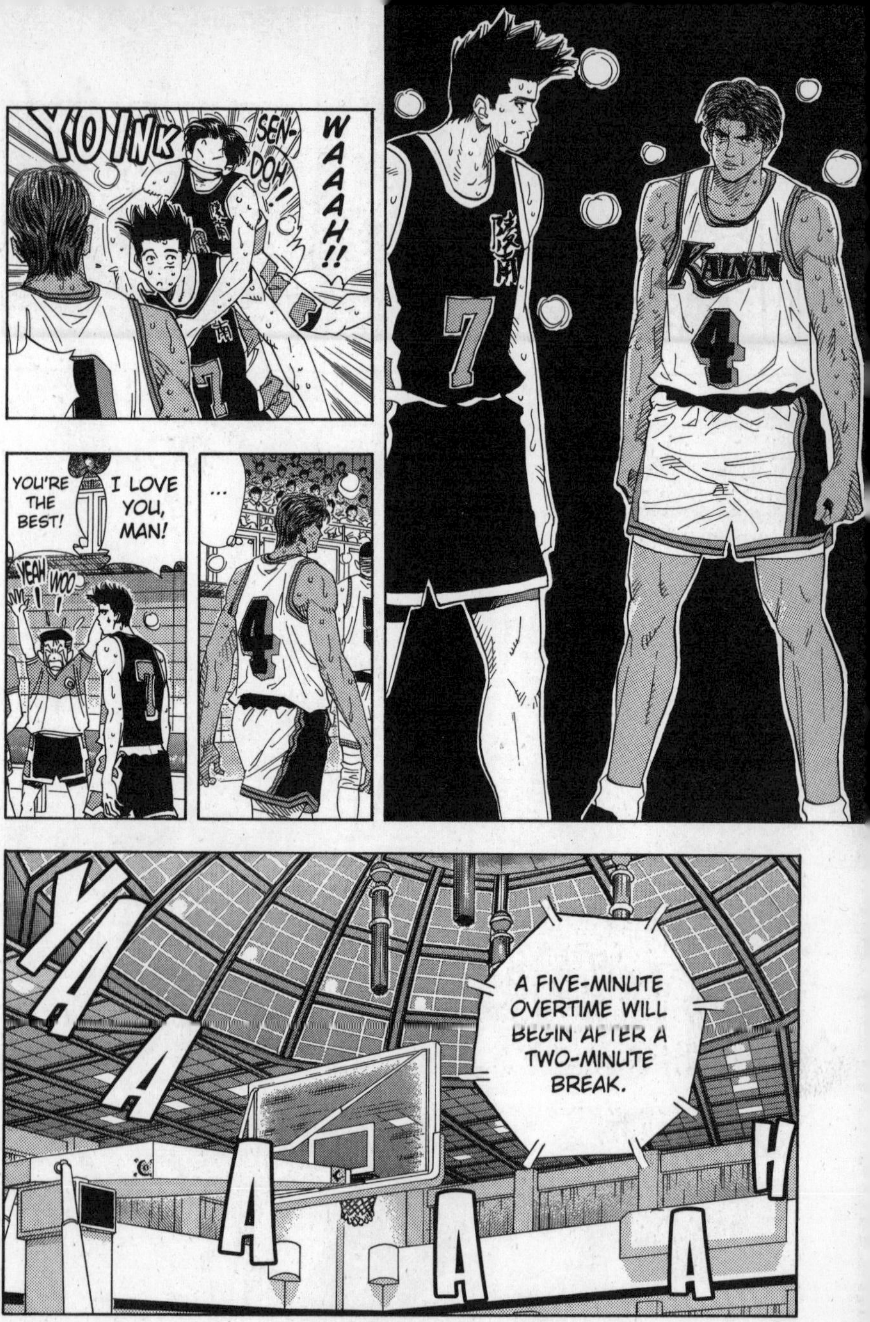
WAAAAAH!!
SEN-DOH!
YOINK
...
I LOVE YOU, MAN!
YOU'RE THE BEST!
WOO!
YEAH!
YAAAAAH
A FIVE-MINUTE OVERTIME WILL BEGIN AFTER A TWO-MINUTE BREAK.

READ THIS WAY

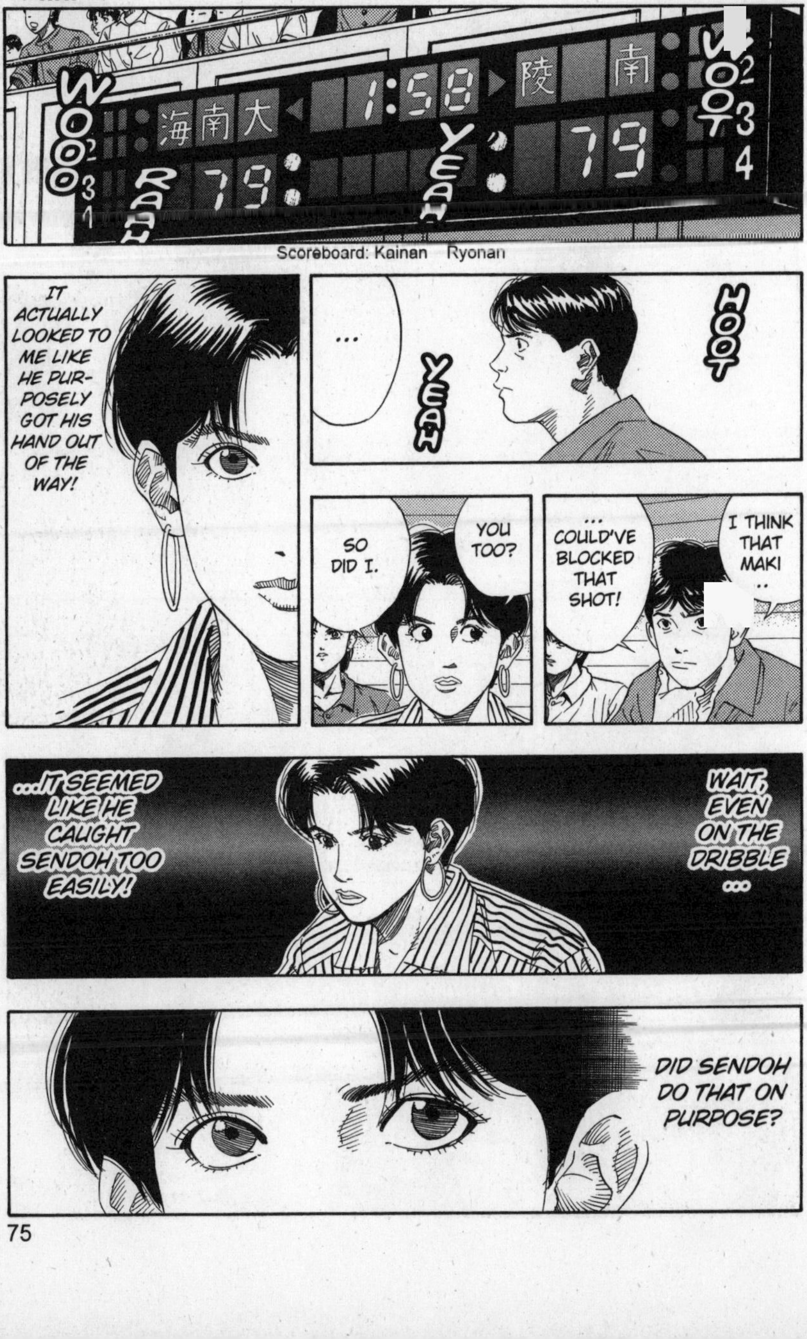
WOOT
陵南
1:58
79
YEAH
海南大
79
RAAH
WOOO
HOOT
YEAH
...
I THINK THAT MAKI ...
... COULD'VE BLOCKED THAT SHOT!
YOU TOO?
SO DID I.
IT ACTUALLY LOOKED TO ME LIKE HE PURPOSELY GOT HIS HAND OUT OF THE WAY!
WAIT, EVEN ON THE DRIBBLE ...
...IT SEEMED LIKE HE CAUGHT SENDOH TOO EASILY!
DID SENDOH DO THAT ON PURPOSE?

Scoreboard: Kainan Ryonan

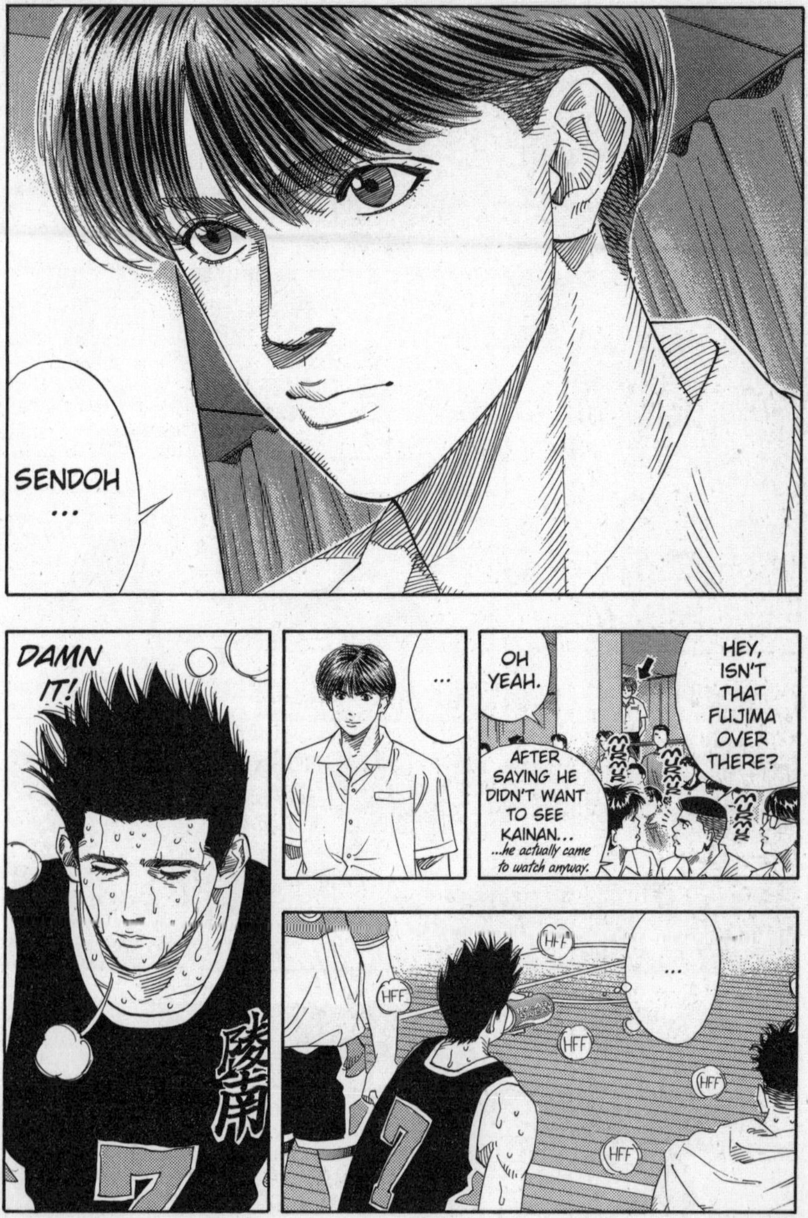
SENDOH ...
HEY, ISN'T THAT FUJIMA OVER THERE?
OH YEAH.
MURMUR
MURMUR
MURMUR
AFTER SAYING HE DIDN'T WANT TO SEE KAINAN...
...he actually came to watch anyway.
...
HFF
HFF
HFF
HFF
HFF
...
DAMN IT!

READ THIS WAY

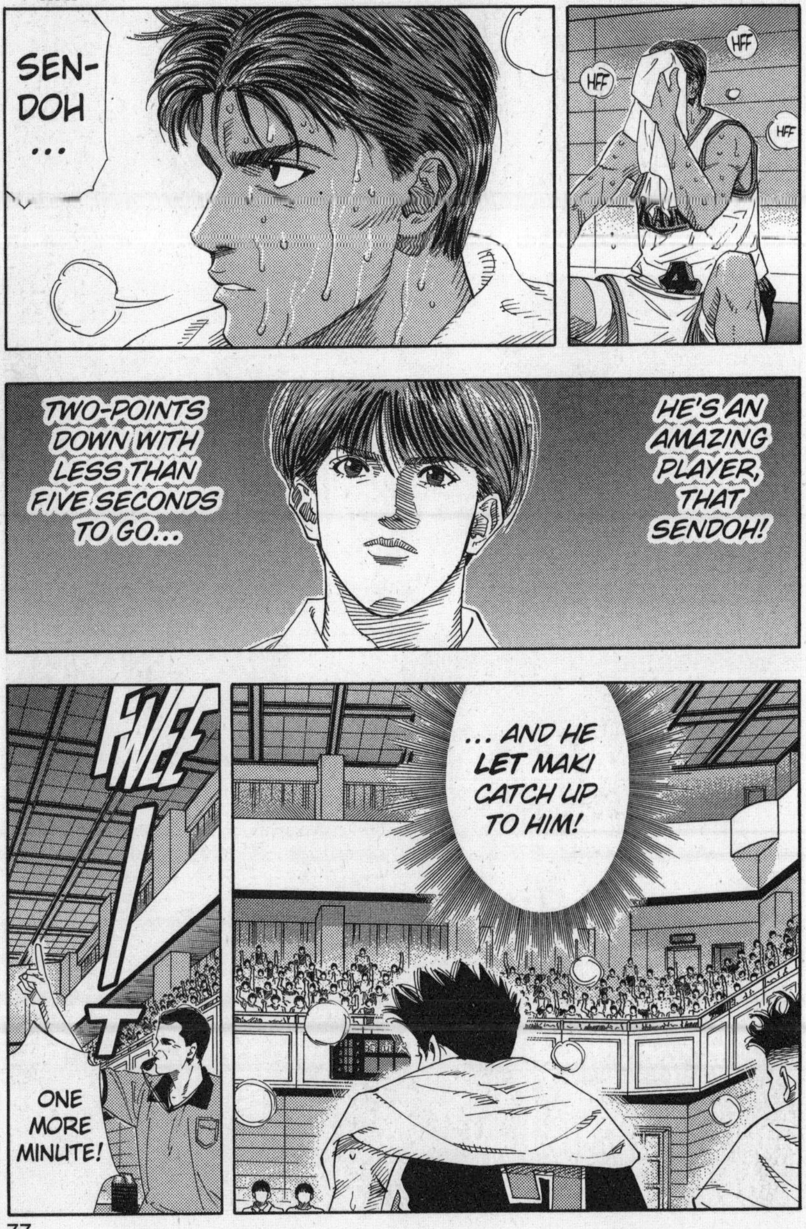
HFF
HFF
HFF
SEN-DOH ...
HE'S AN AMAZING PLAYER, THAT SENDOH!
TWO-POINTS DOWN WITH LESS THAN FIVE SECONDS TO GO...
... AND HE LET MAKI CATCH UP TO HIM!
FWEE
T
ONE MORE MINUTE!

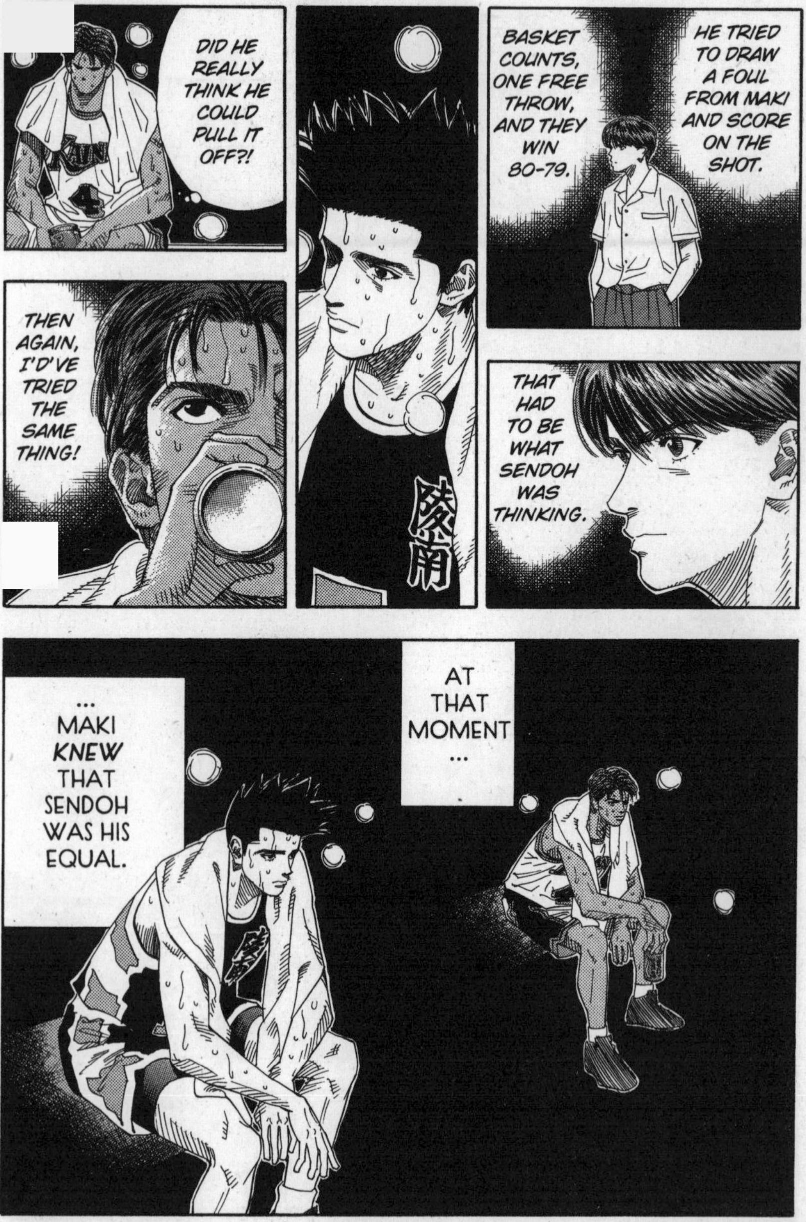
BASKET COUNTS, ONE FREE THROW, AND THEY WIN 80-79.
HE TRIED TO DRAW A FOUL FROM MAKI AND SCORE ON THE SHOT.
THAT HAD TO BE WHAT SENDOH WAS THINKING.
DID HE REALLY THINK HE COULD PULL IT OFF?!
THEN AGAIN, I'D'VE TRIED THE SAME THING!
AT THAT MOMENT...
...MAKI KNEW THAT SENDOH WAS HIS EQUAL.

READ THIS WAY

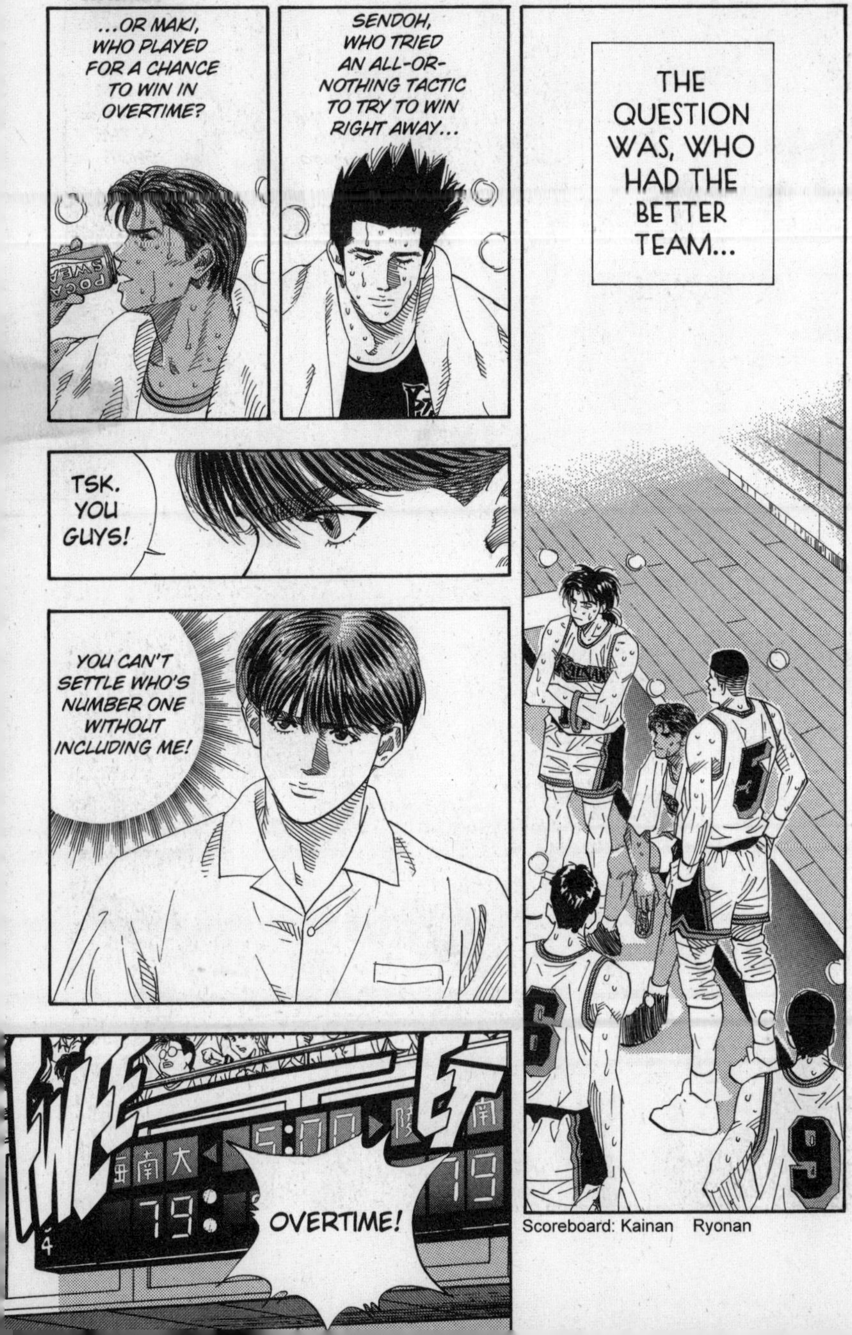
THE QUESTION WAS, WHO HAD THE BETTER TEAM...
SENDOH, WHO TRIED AN ALL-OR-NOTHING TACTIC TO TRY TO WIN RIGHT AWAY...
...OR MAKI, WHO PLAYED FOR A CHANCE TO WIN IN OVERTIME?
TSK. YOU GUYS!
YOU CAN'T SETTLE WHO'S NUMBER ONE WITHOUT INCLUDING ME!
5:00
79
79
OVERTIME!

Scoreboard: Kainan Ryonan

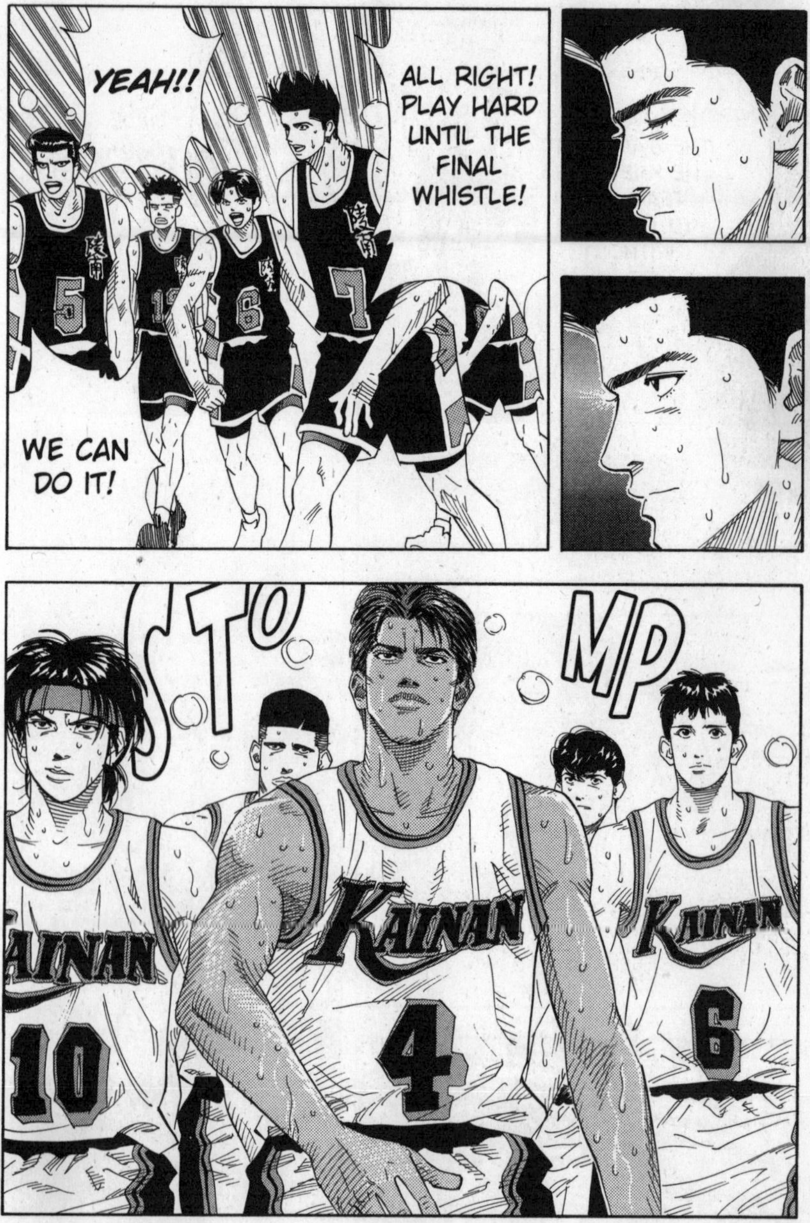
ALL RIGHT! PLAY HARD UNTIL THE FINAL WHISTLE!
YEAH!!
WE CAN DO IT!
STOMP

READ THIS WAY

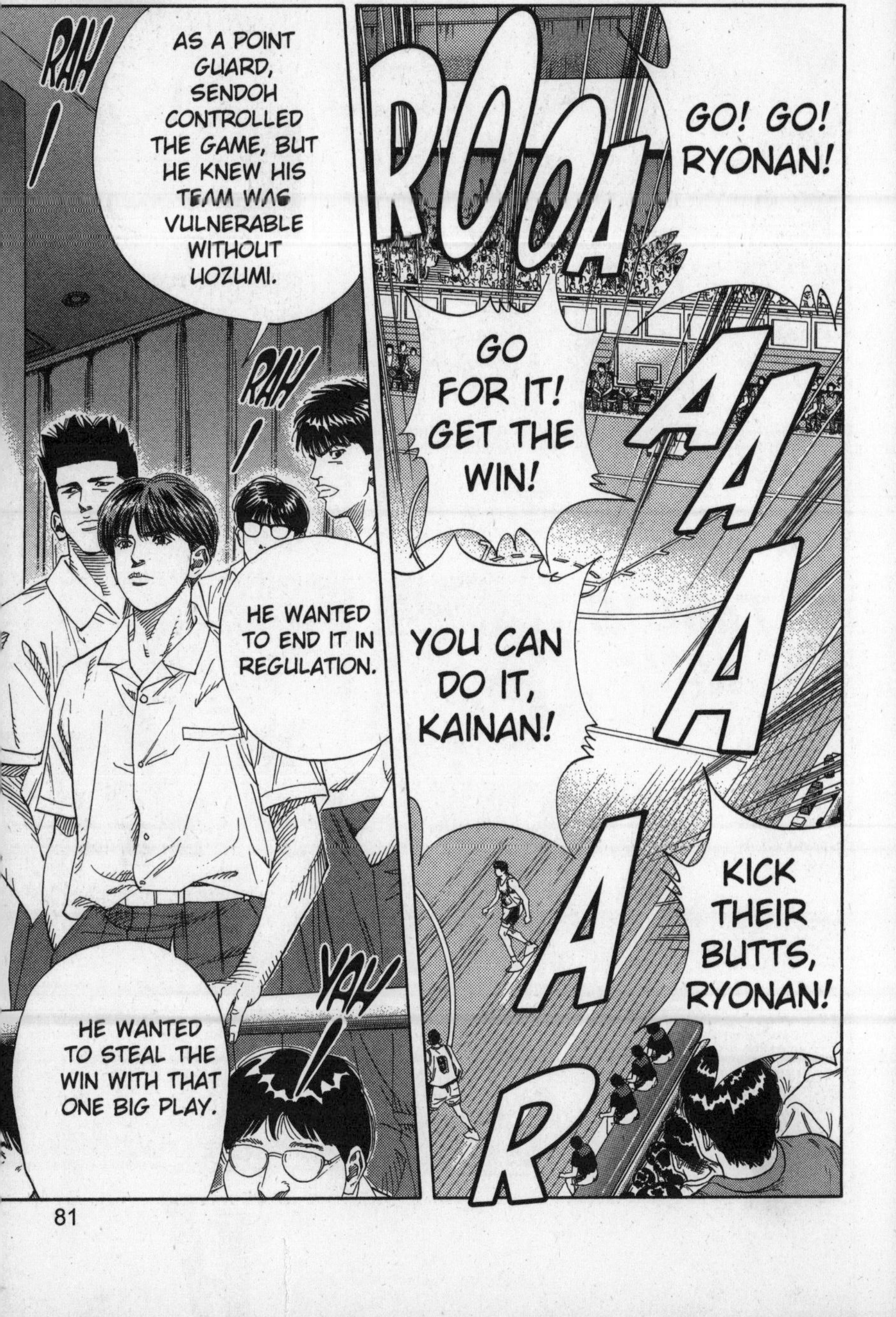
GO! GO! RYONAN!
ROOAAAAR
GO FOR IT! GET THE WIN!
YOU CAN DO IT, KAINAN!
KICK THEIR BUTTS, RYONAN!
RAH!
AS A POINT GUARD, SENDOH CONTROLLED THE GAME, BUT HE KNEW HIS TEAM WAS VULNERABLE WITHOUT UOZUMI.
RAH!
HE WANTED TO END IT IN REGULATION.
YAH!
HE WANTED TO STEAL THE WIN WITH THAT ONE BIG PLAY.

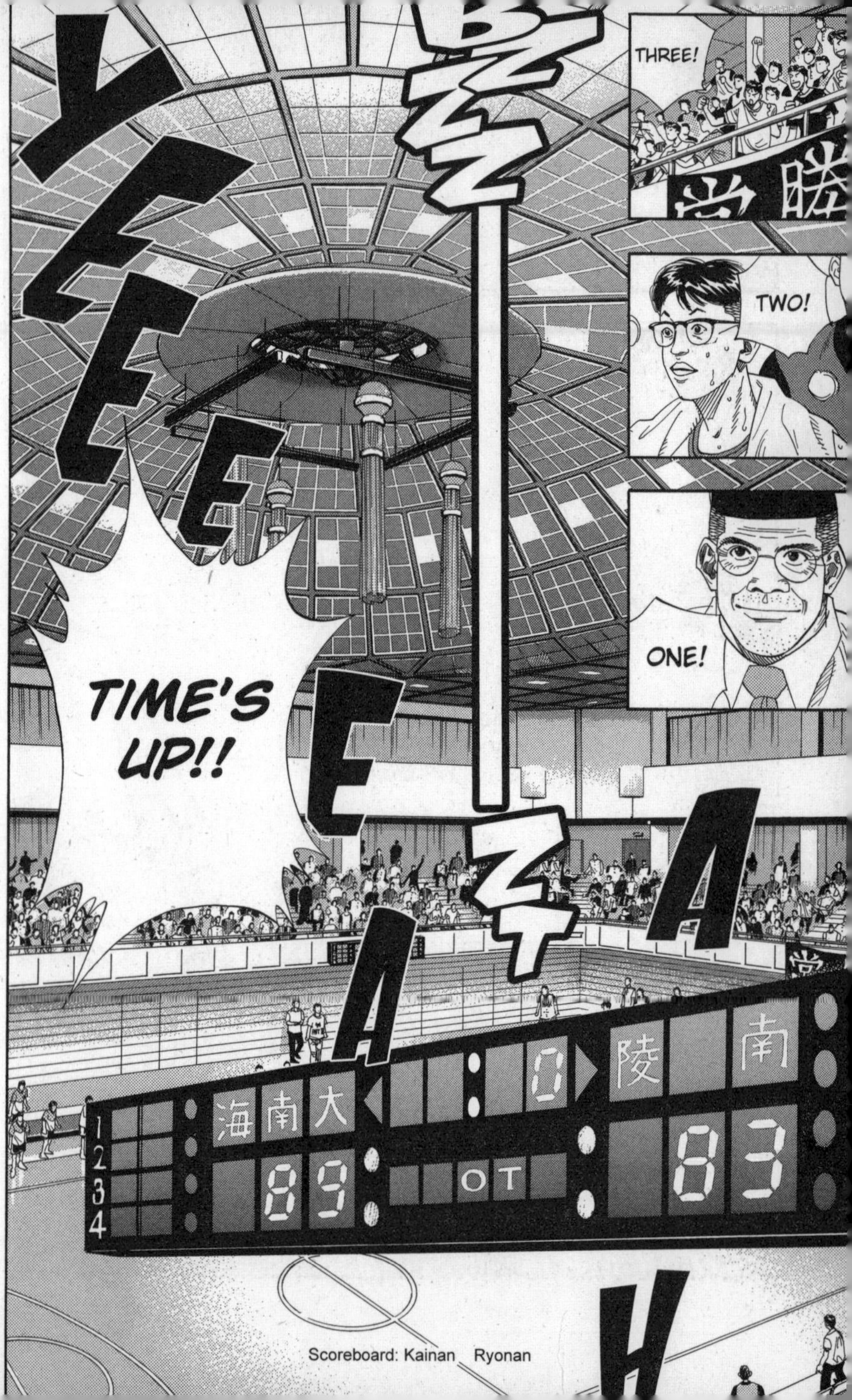
THREE!
TWO!
ONE!
BZZZ
ZT
YEEEE
EAAH
TIME'S UP!!
海南大
陵南
0
89
OT
83
1
2
3
4
Scoreboard: Kainan Ryonan

READ THIS WAY

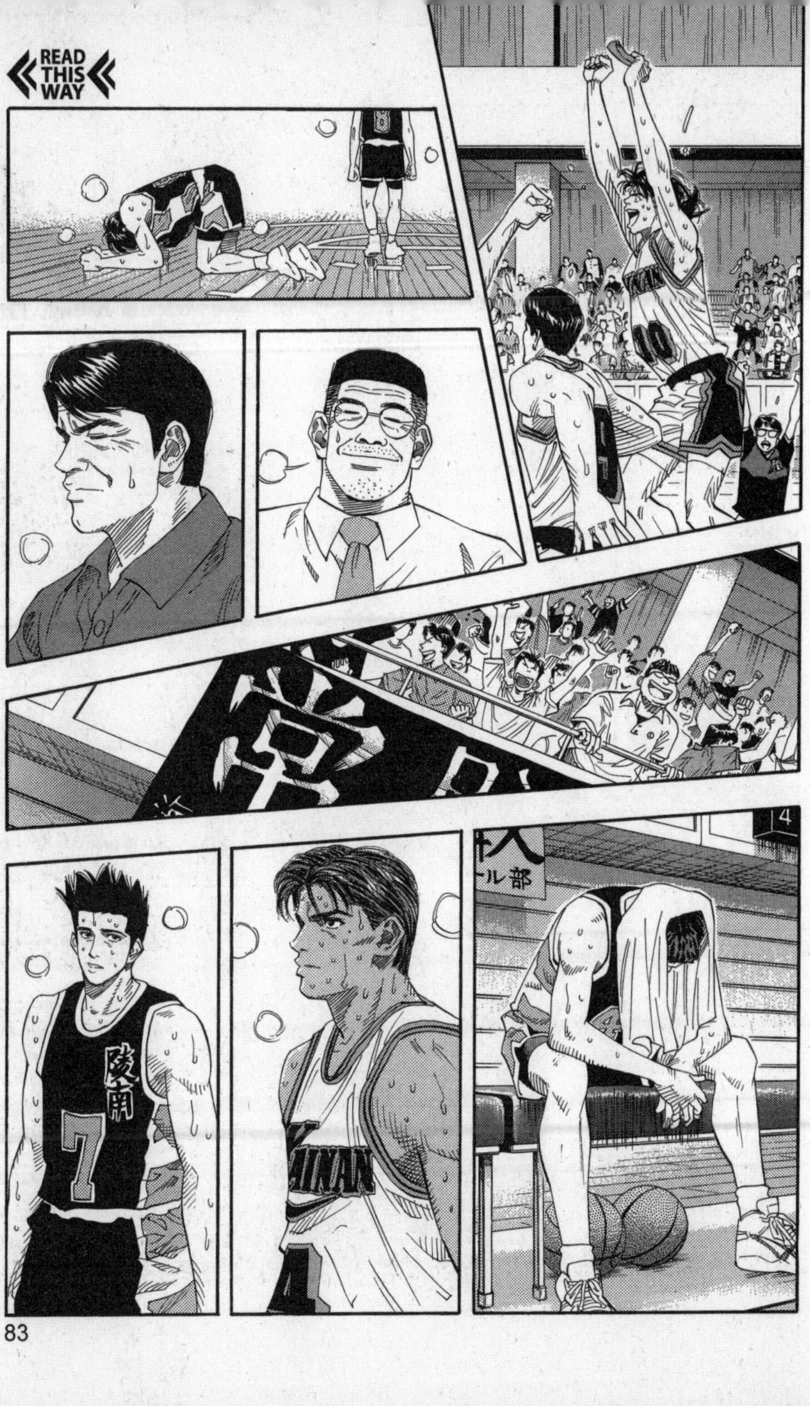
陵南

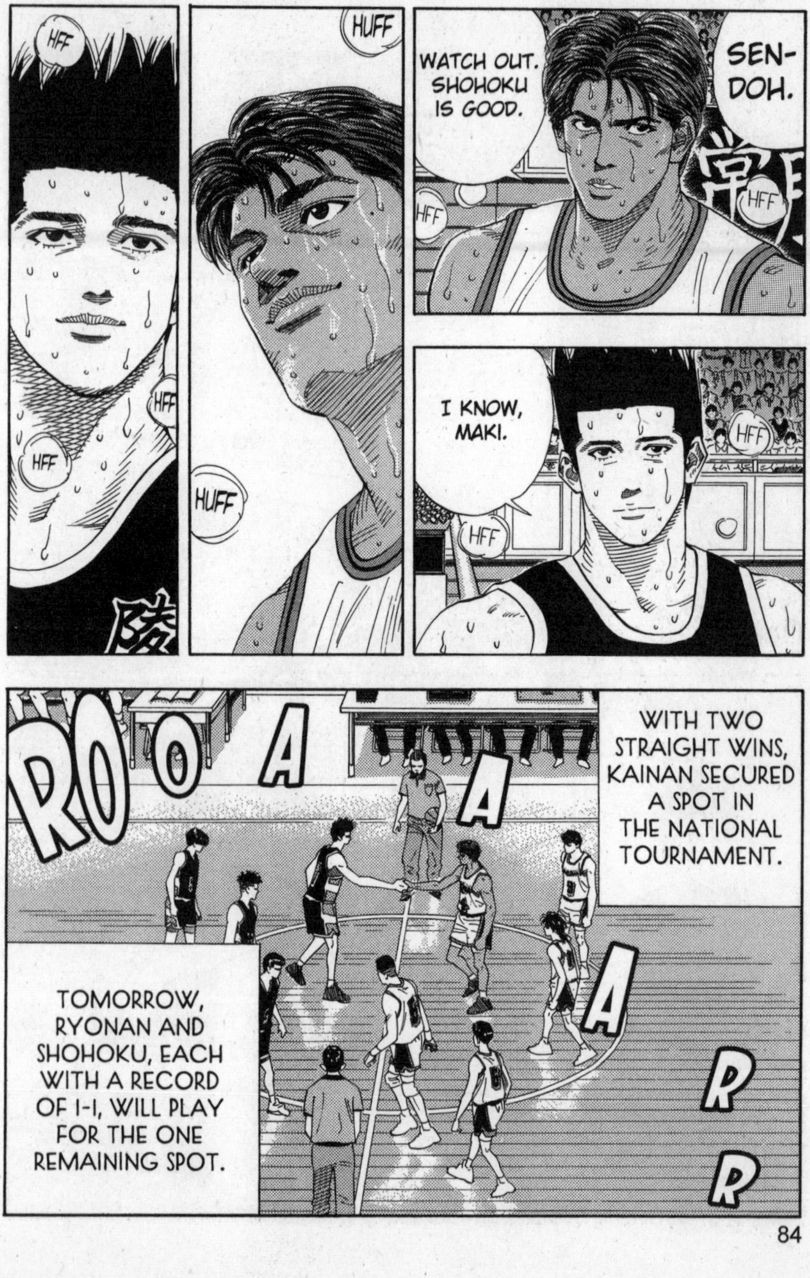
SEN-DOH.
WATCH OUT. SHOHOKU IS GOOD.
HFF
HFF
I KNOW, MAKI.
HFF
HFF
HUFF
HUFF
HFF
HFF
HFF
WITH TWO STRAIGHT WINS, KAINAN SECURED A SPOT IN THE NATIONAL TOURNAMENT.
ROOAAAARR
TOMORROW, RYONAN AND SHOHOKU, EACH WITH A RECORD OF 1-1, WILL PLAY FOR THE ONE REMAINING SPOT.

READ THIS WAY

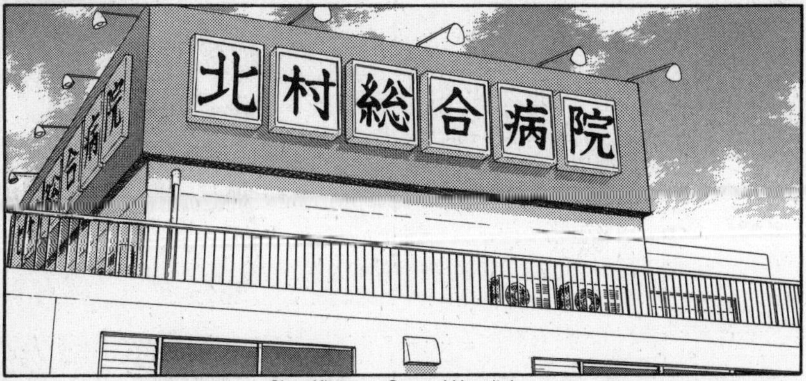
北村総合病院

Sign: Kitamura General Hospital

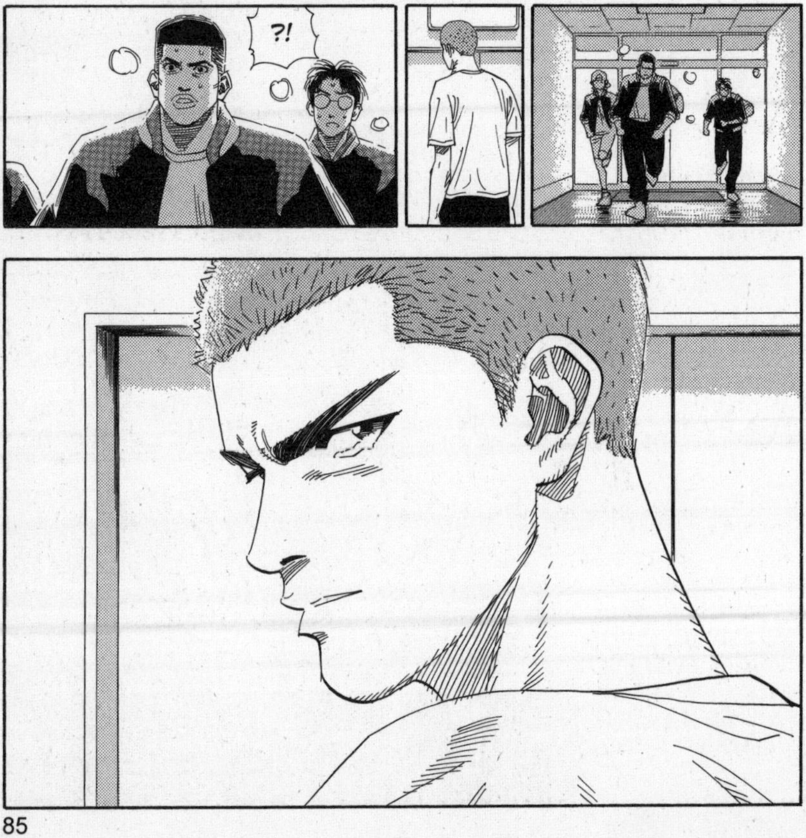
?!

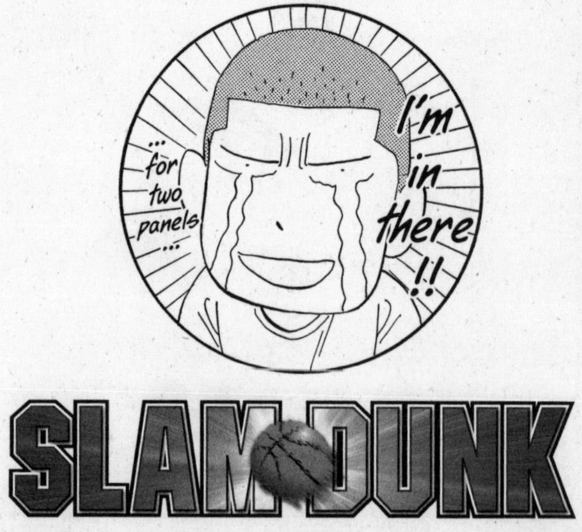
I'm in there!!
...for two panels...

SLAM DUNK

#148 THE OLD MAN

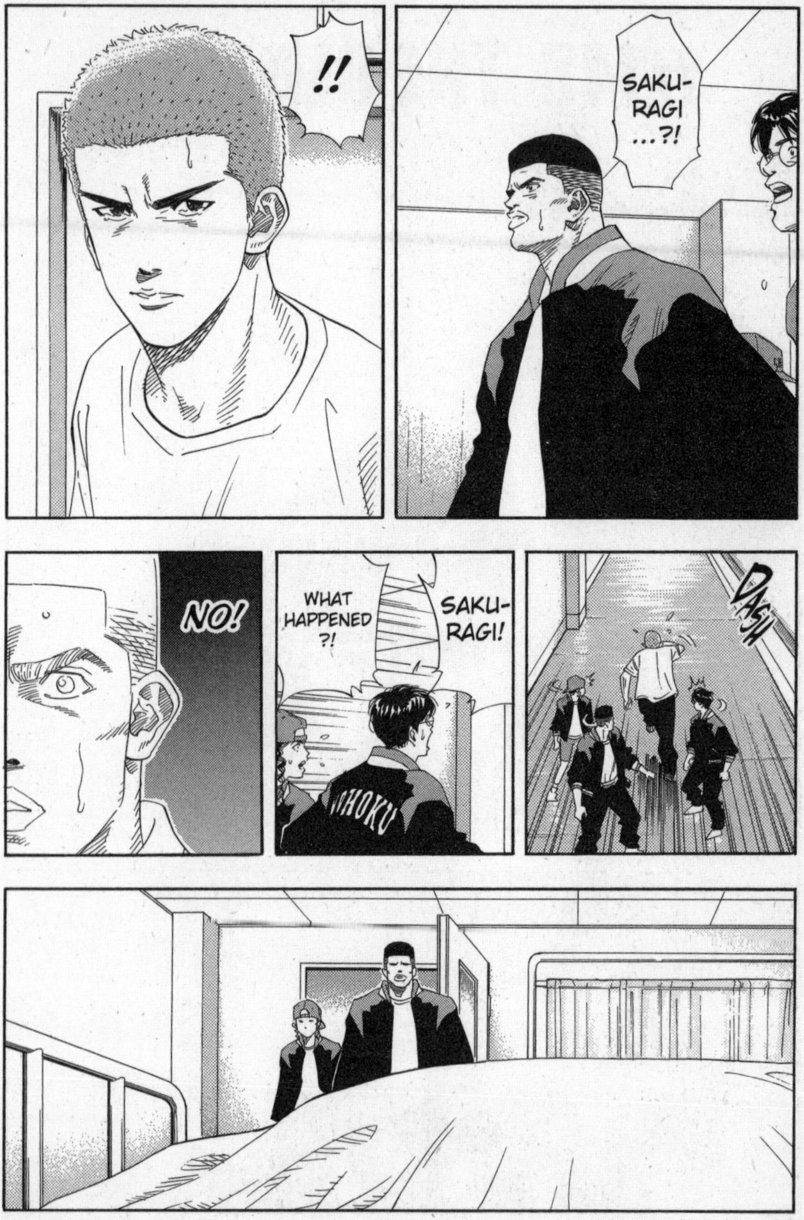
SAKU-
RAGI
...?!
!!
DASH
SAKU-
RAGI!
WHAT
HAPPENED
?!
NO!

READ THIS WAY

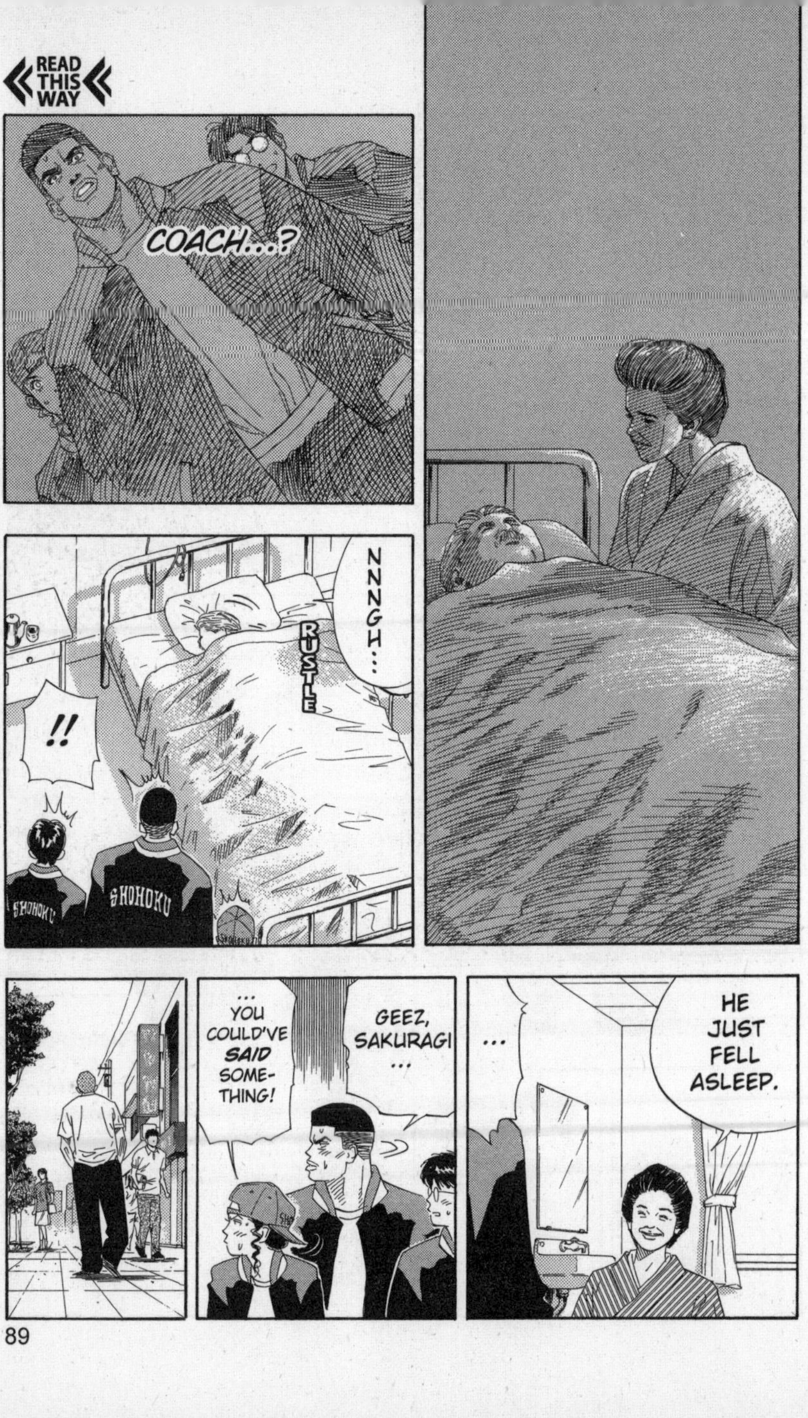
COACH...?
NNNGH...
RUSTLE
!!
HE JUST FELL ASLEEP.
...
GEEZ, SAKURAGI ...
... YOU COULD'VE SAID SOMETHING!

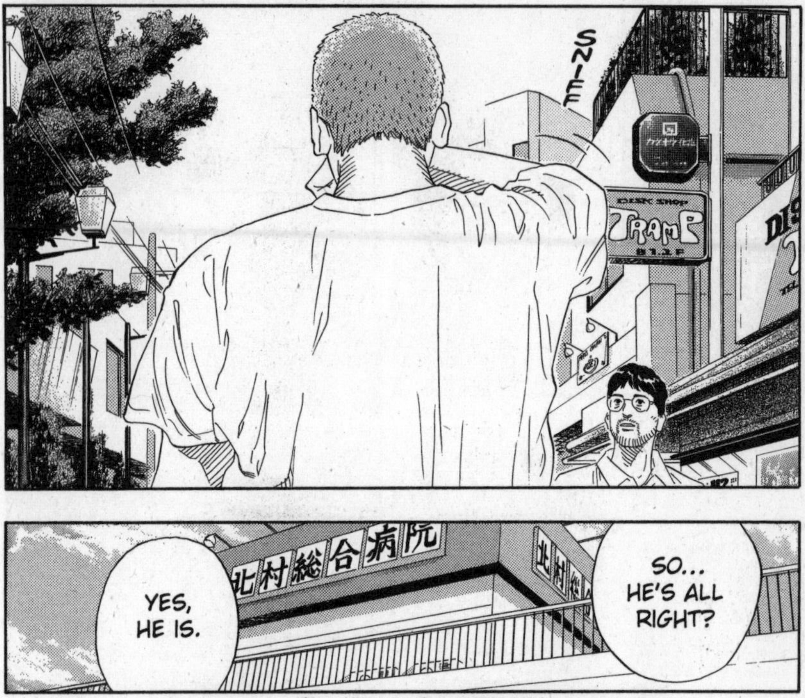
SNIFF
DISK SHOP
TRAMP
SO... HE'S ALL RIGHT?
YES, HE IS.
北村総合病院

Sign: Kitamura General Hospital

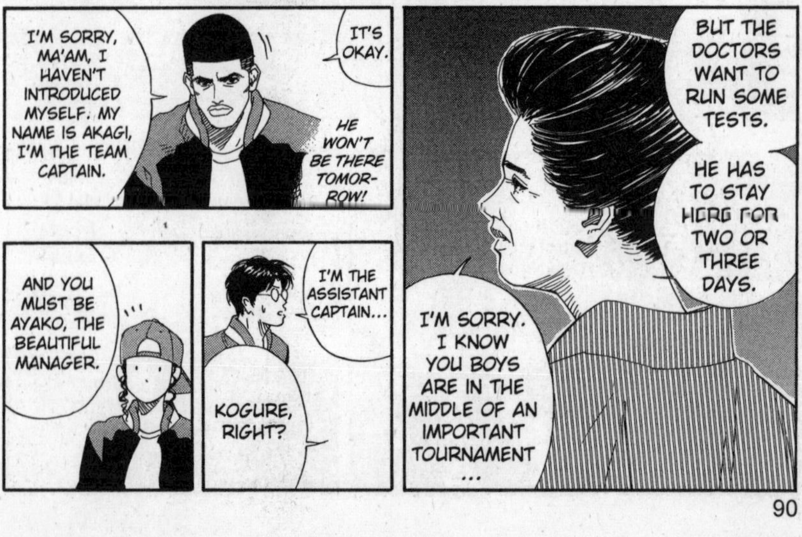
BUT THE DOCTORS WANT TO RUN SOME TESTS.
HE HAS TO STAY HERE FOR TWO OR THREE DAYS.
I'M SORRY. I KNOW YOU BOYS ARE IN THE MIDDLE OF AN IMPORTANT TOURNAMENT ...
IT'S OKAY.
HE WON'T BE THERE TOMORROW!
I'M SORRY, MA'AM, I HAVEN'T INTRODUCED MYSELF. MY NAME IS AKAGI, I'M THE TEAM CAPTAIN.
I'M THE ASSISTANT CAPTAIN...
KOGURE, RIGHT?
AND YOU MUST BE AYAKO, THE BEAUTIFUL MANAGER.
...

READ THIS WAY

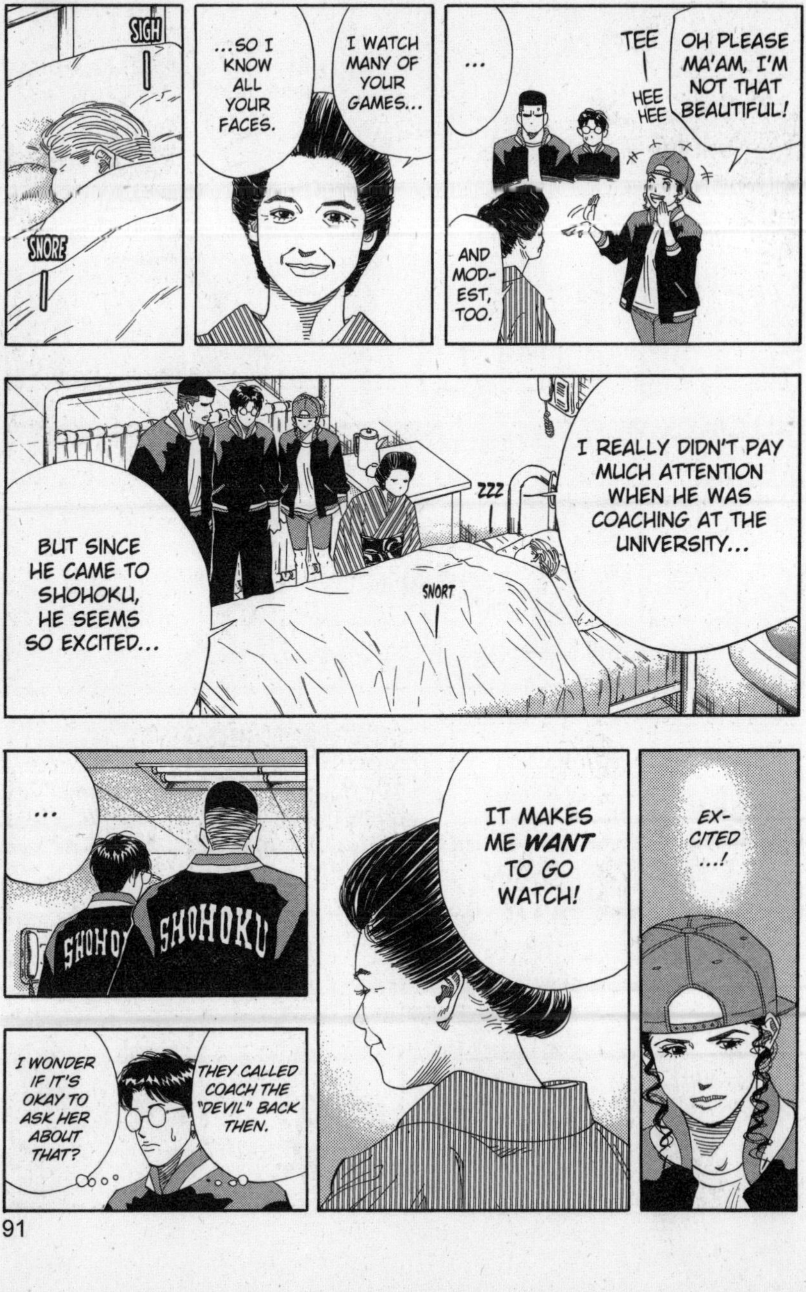
OH PLEASE MA'AM, I'M NOT THAT BEAUTIFUL!
TEE HEE HEE
...
AND MODEST, TOO.
I WATCH MANY OF YOUR GAMES...
...SO I KNOW ALL YOUR FACES.
SIGH
SNORE
I REALLY DIDN'T PAY MUCH ATTENTION WHEN HE WAS COACHING AT THE UNIVERSITY...
ZZZ
SNORT
BUT SINCE HE CAME TO SHOHOKU, HE SEEMS SO EXCITED...
EX-CITED ...!
IT MAKES ME *WANT* TO GO WATCH!
...
SHOHOKU
THEY CALLED COACH THE "DEVIL" BACK THEN.
I WONDER IF IT'S OKAY TO ASK HER ABOUT THAT?

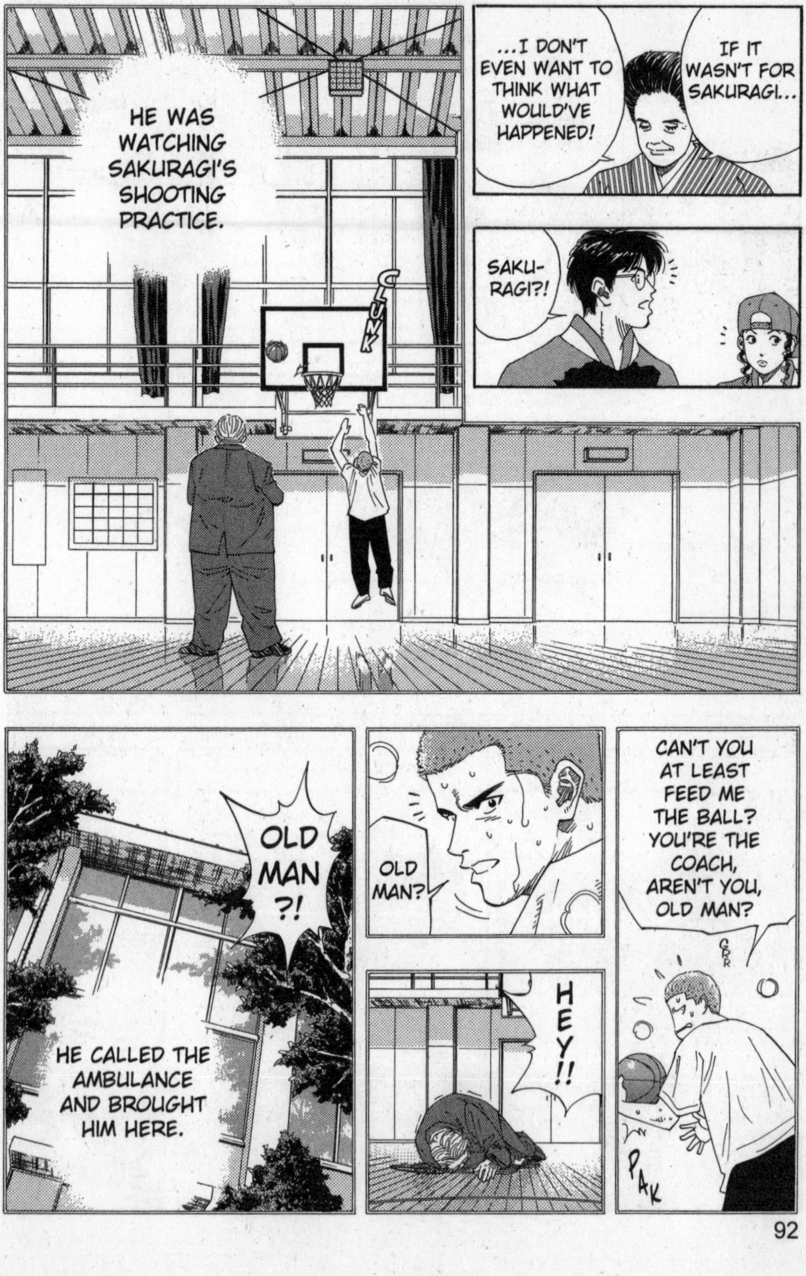
IF IT WASN'T FOR SAKURAGI...
...I DON'T EVEN WANT TO THINK WHAT WOULD'VE HAPPENED!
SAKU-RAGI?!
HE WAS WATCHING SAKURAGI'S SHOOTING PRACTICE.
CLUNK
CAN'T YOU AT LEAST FEED ME THE BALL? YOU'RE THE COACH, AREN'T YOU, OLD MAN?
GRR
PAK
OLD MAN?
HEY!!
OLD MAN ?!
HE CALLED THE AMBULANCE AND BROUGHT HIM HERE.

READ THIS WAY

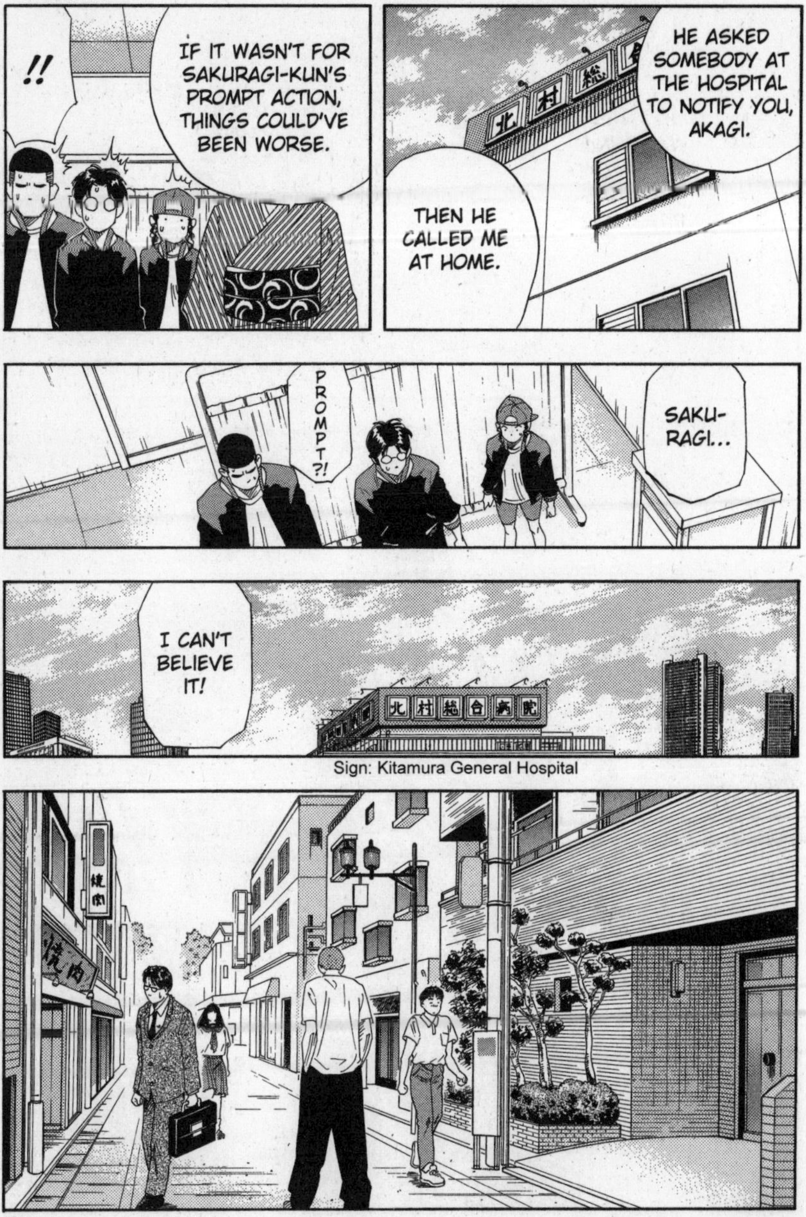
HE ASKED SOMEBODY AT THE HOSPITAL TO NOTIFY YOU, AKAGI.
THEN HE CALLED ME AT HOME.
IF IT WASN'T FOR SAKURAGI-KUN'S PROMPT ACTION, THINGS COULD'VE BEEN WORSE.
!!
SAKU-RAGI...
PROMPT?!
I CAN'T BELIEVE IT!
北村総合病院
Sign: Kitamura General Hospital

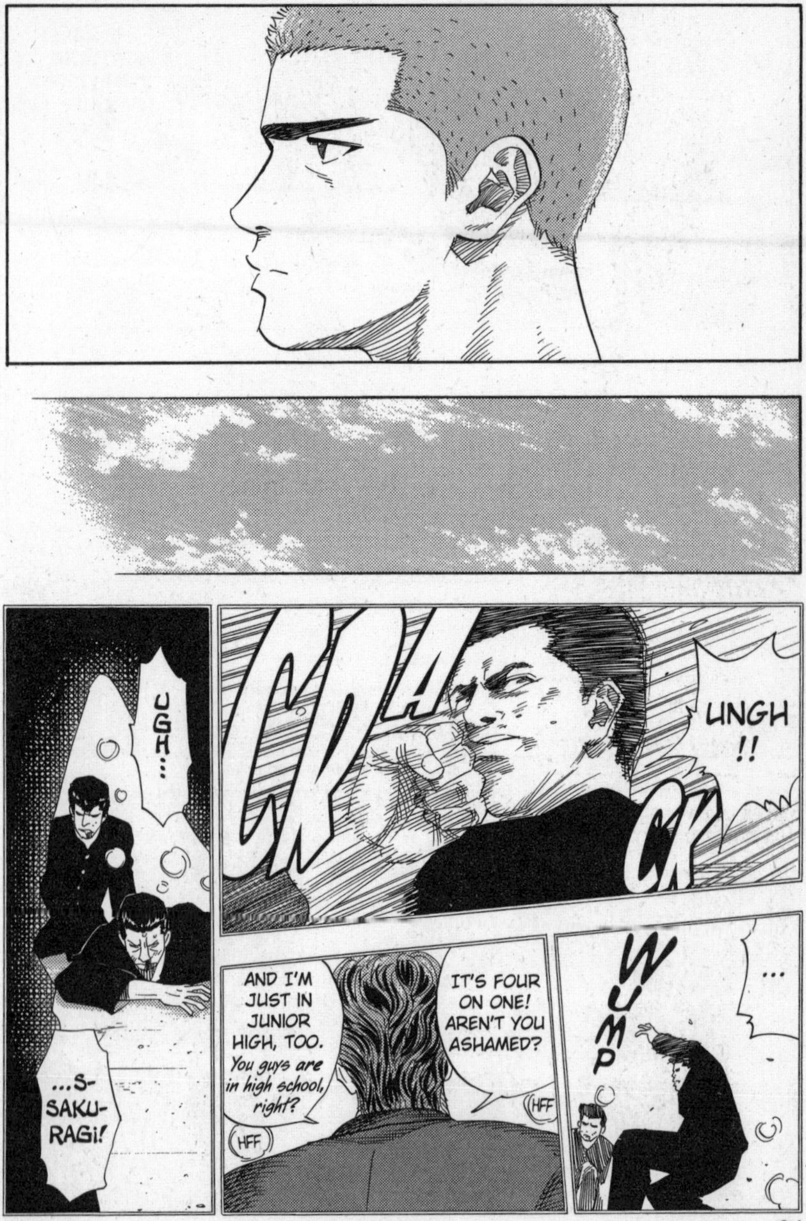
UNGH !!
CRACK
...
WUMP
IT'S FOUR ON ONE! AREN'T YOU ASHAMED?
HFF
AND I'M JUST IN JUNIOR HIGH, TOO. *You guys are in high school, right?*
HFF
UGH...
...S-SAKURAGI!

READ THIS WAY

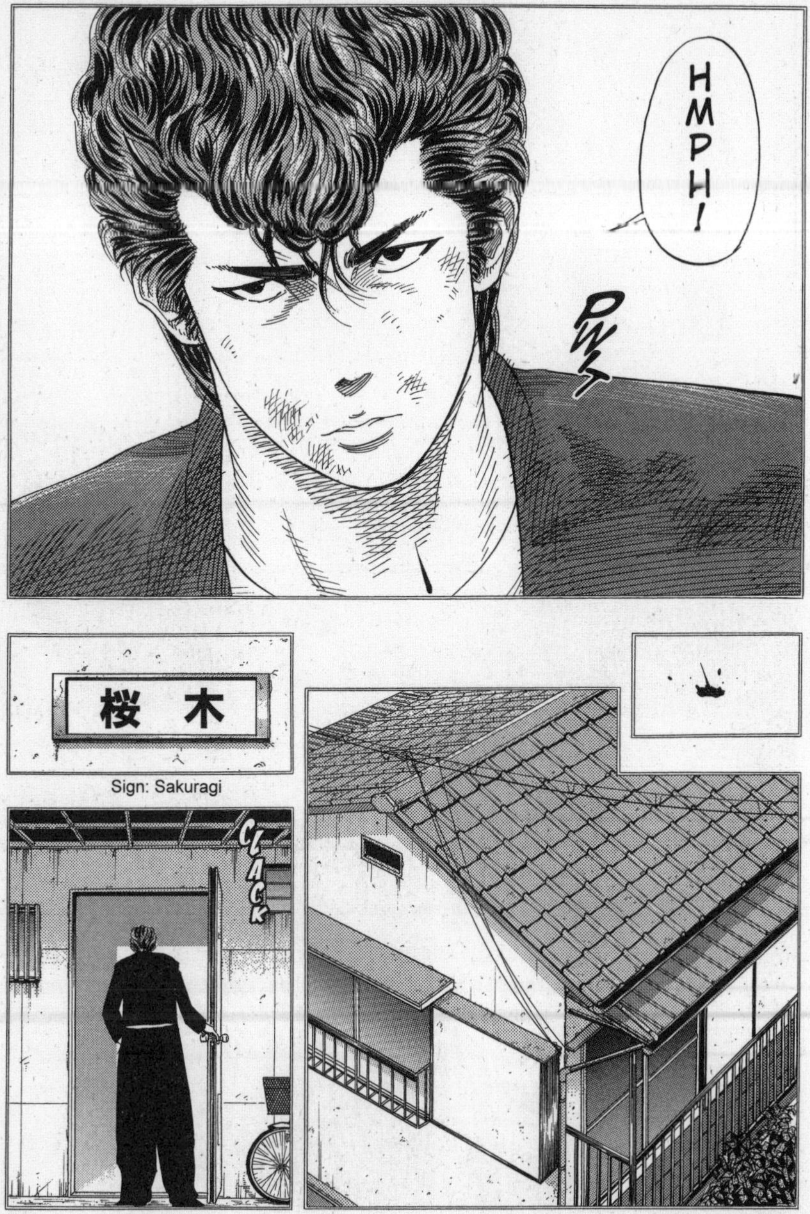
HMPH!
桜木
Sign: Sakuragi
CLACK

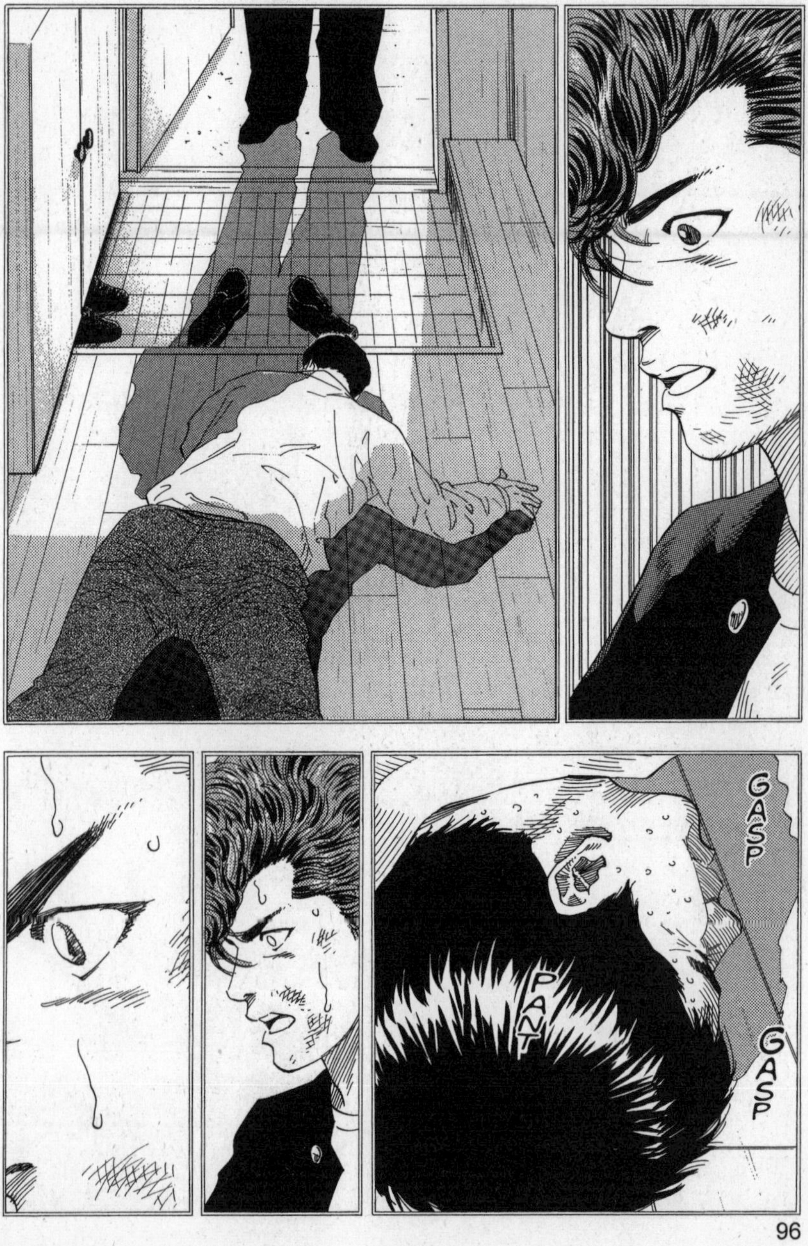
GASP
PANT
GASP

READ THIS WAY

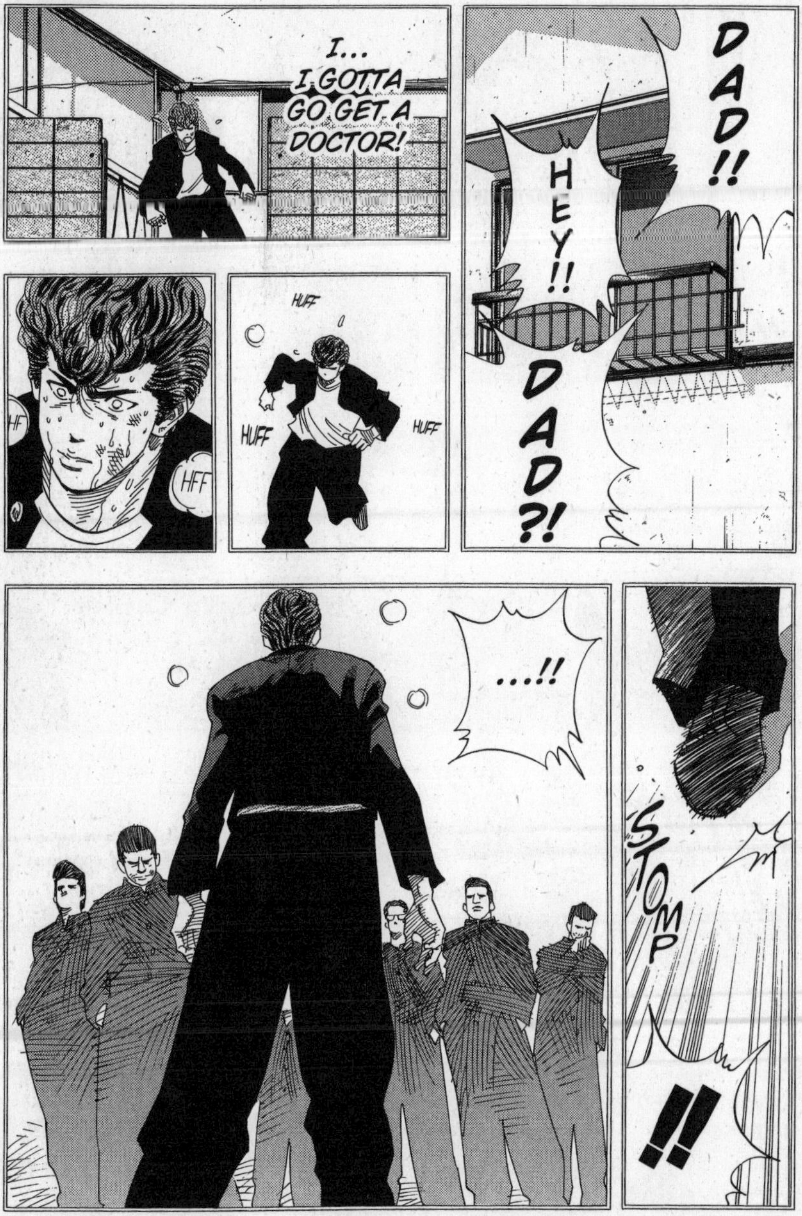

DAD!!
HEY!!
DAD?!
I... I GOTTA GO GET A DOCTOR!
HUFF
HUFF
HUFF
HF
HFF
STOMP
!!
...!!

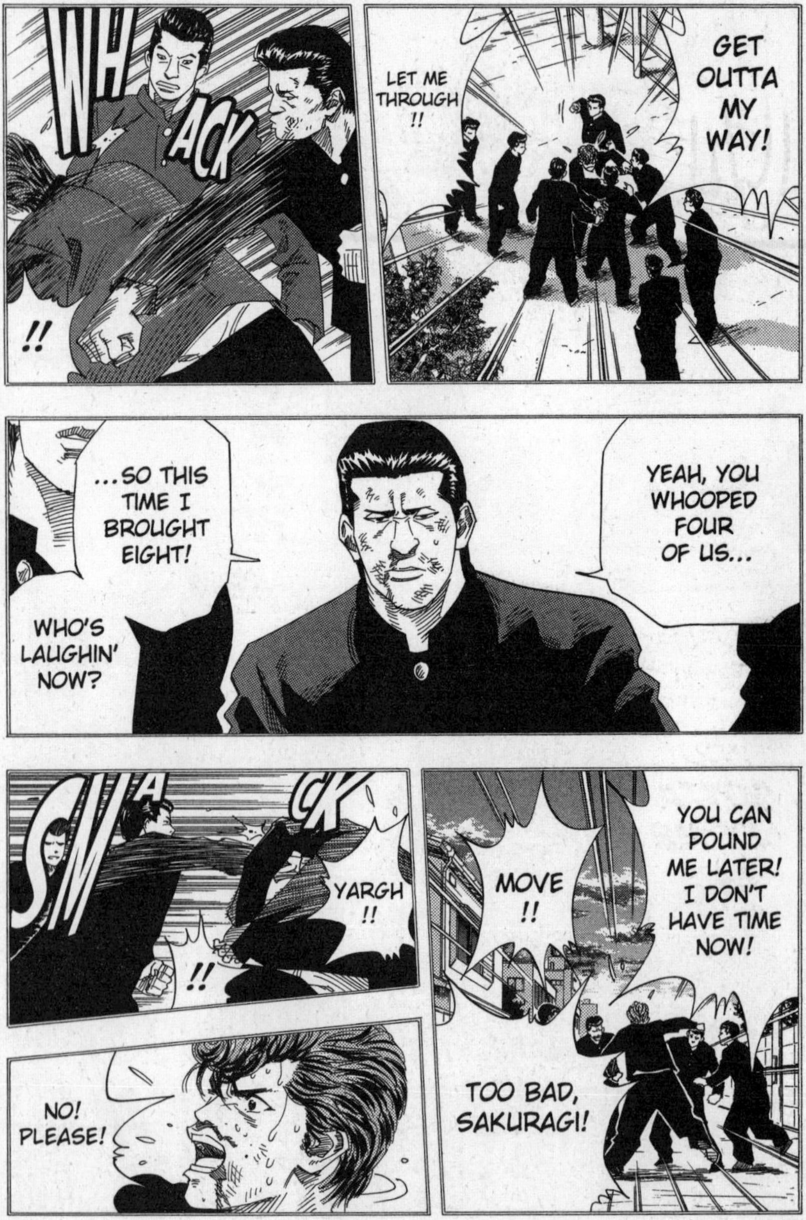
GET OUTTA MY WAY!
LET ME THROUGH !!
WHACK
!!
YEAH, YOU WHOOPED FOUR OF US...
...SO THIS TIME I BROUGHT EIGHT!
WHO'S LAUGHIN' NOW?
YOU CAN POUND ME LATER! I DON'T HAVE TIME NOW!
MOVE !!
TOO BAD, SAKURAGI!
SMACK
YARGH !!
!!
NO! PLEASE!

READ THIS WAY

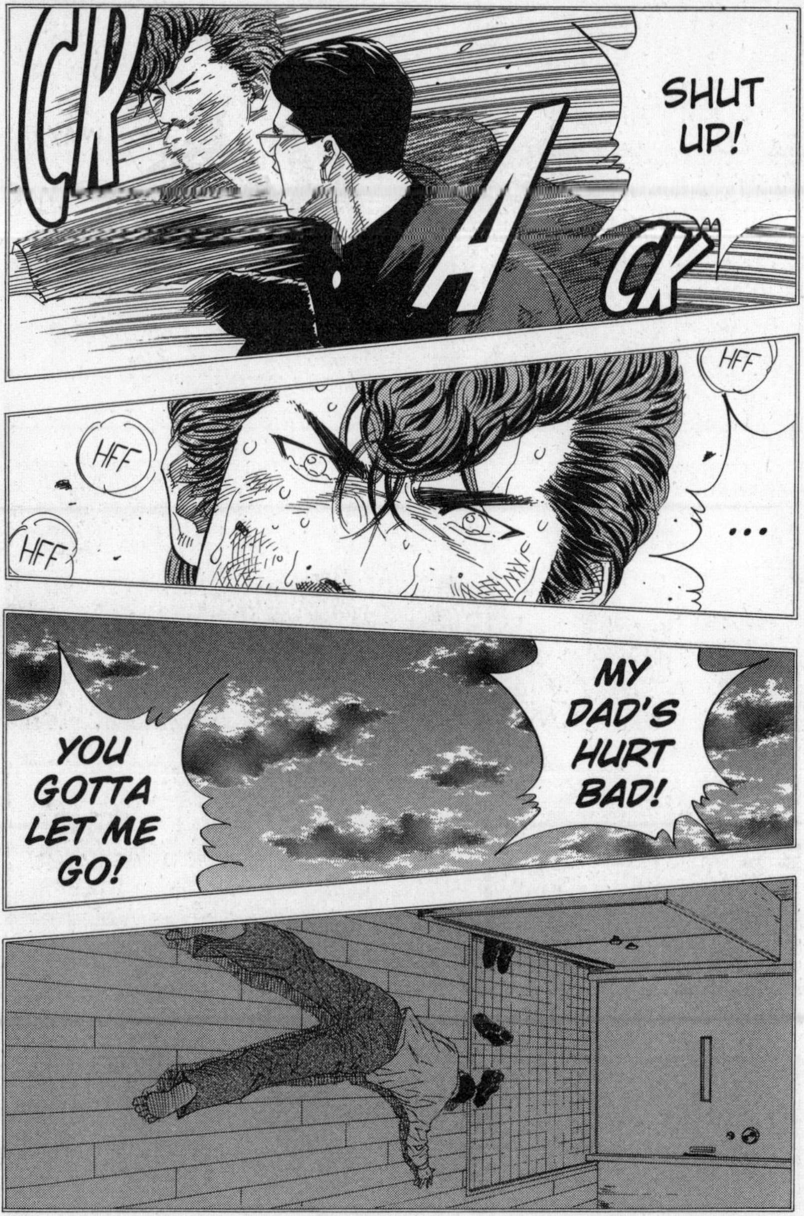
SHUT UP!
CK
A
CK
HFF
...
HFF
HFF
MY DAD'S HURT BAD!
YOU GOTTA LET ME GO!

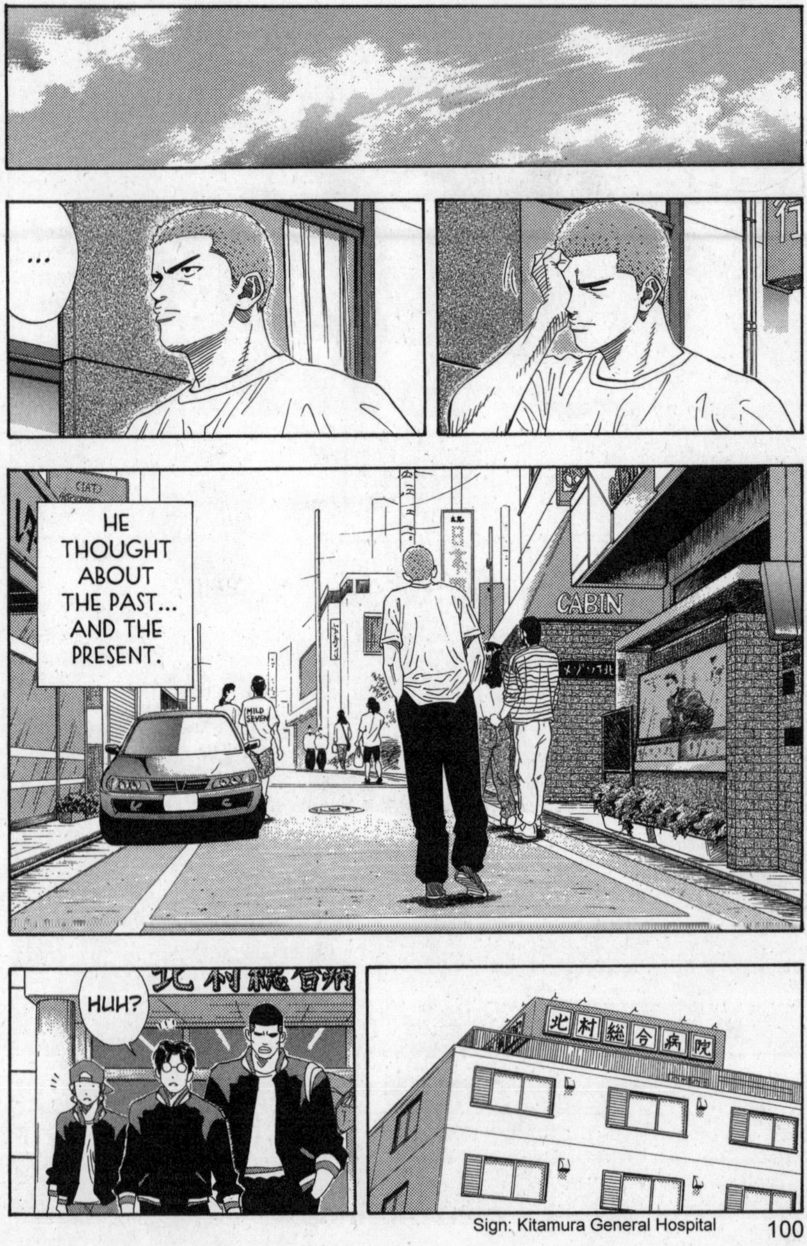
...
HE THOUGHT ABOUT THE PAST... AND THE PRESENT.
CABIN
MILD SEVEN
北村総合病院
HUH?
Sign: Kitamura General Hospital

READ THIS WAY

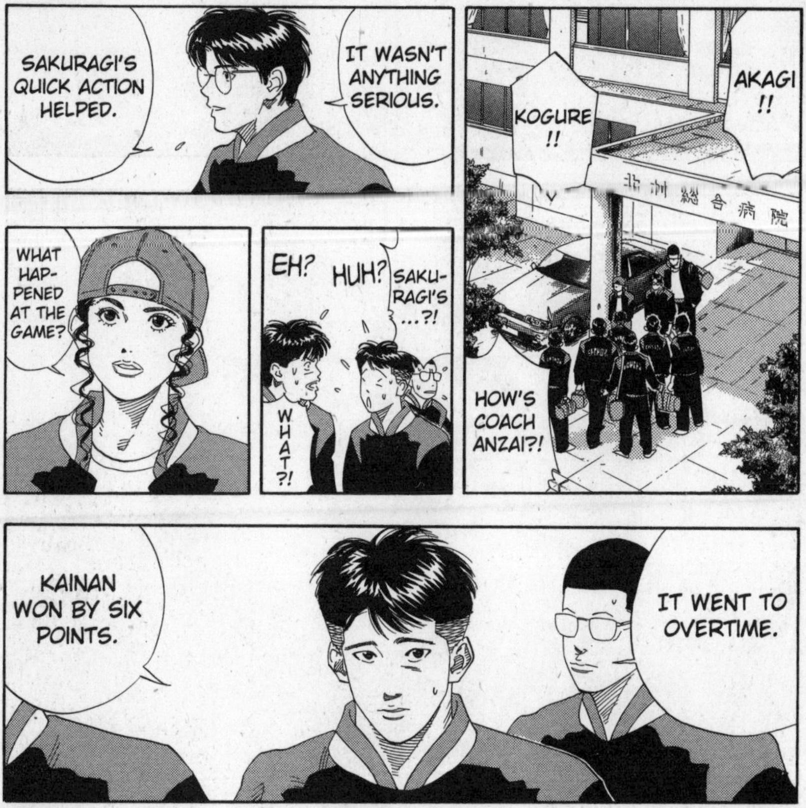
AKAGI !!
KOGURE !!
HOW'S COACH ANZAI?!
IT WASN'T ANYTHING SERIOUS.
SAKURAGI'S QUICK ACTION HELPED.
SAKU-RAGI'S ...?!
HUH?
EH?
WHAT?!
WHAT HAPPENED AT THE GAME?
IT WENT TO OVERTIME.
KAINAN WON BY SIX POINTS.

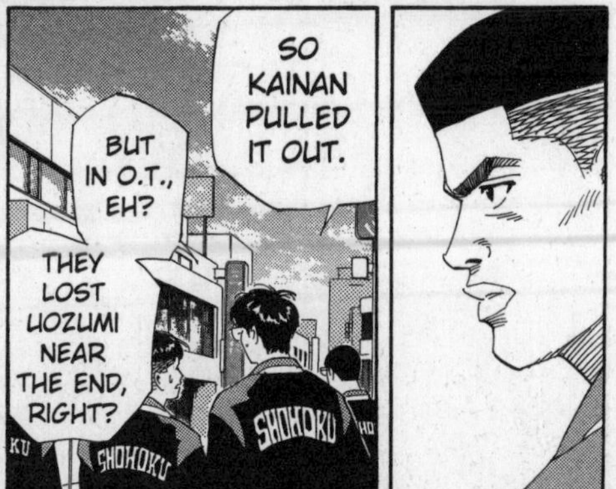
SO KAINAN PULLED IT OUT.
BUT IN O.T., EH?
THEY LOST UOZUMI NEAR THE END, RIGHT?

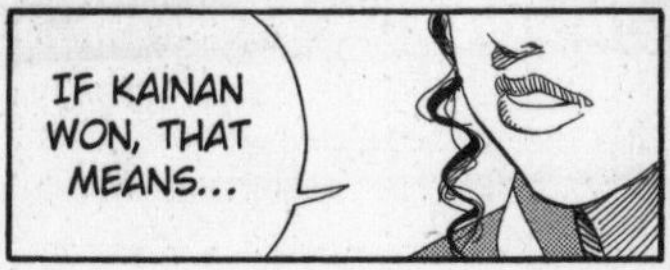
IF KAINAN WON, THAT MEANS...

	Kai	Sho	Ryo	Take
Kainan		○	○	
Shohoku	×			○
Ryonan	×			○
Takezato		×	×	

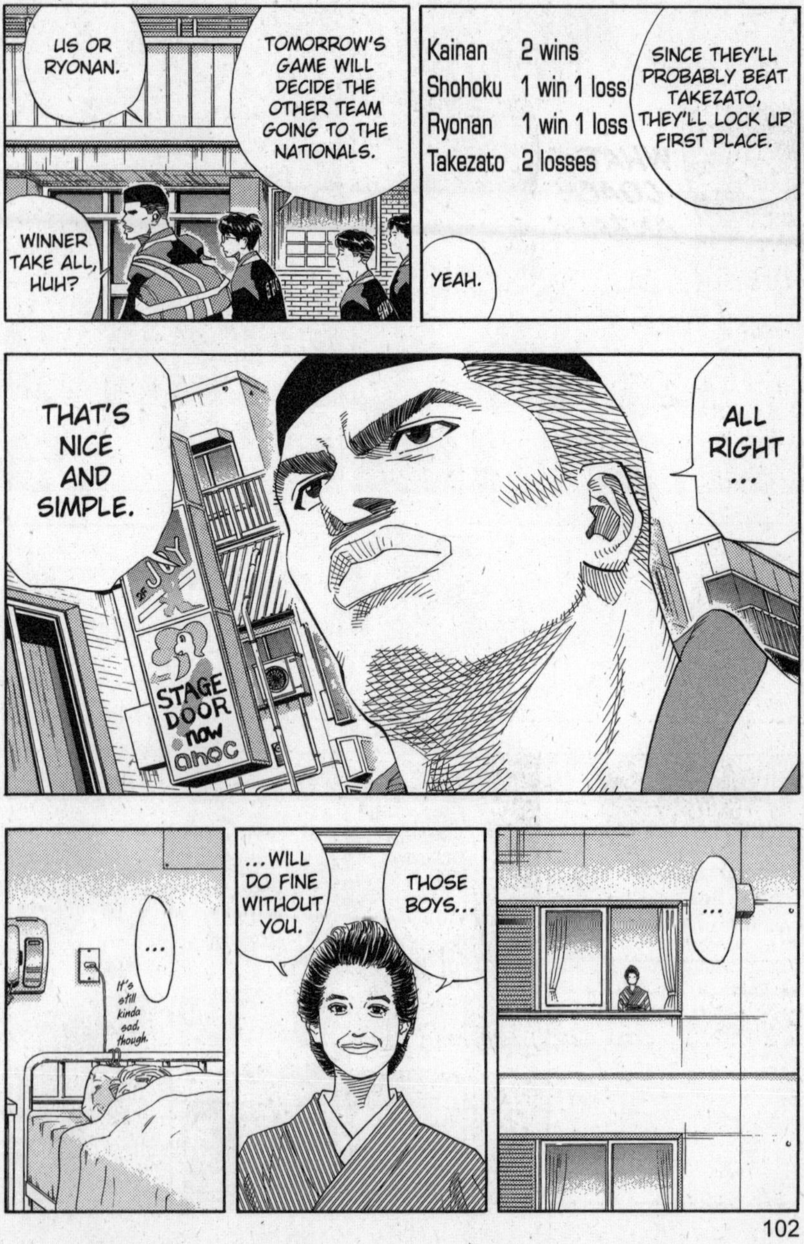
Kainan 2 wins
Shohoku 1 win 1 loss
Ryonan 1 win 1 loss
Takezato 2 losses
SINCE THEY'LL PROBABLY BEAT TAKEZATO, THEY'LL LOCK UP FIRST PLACE.
YEAH.
TOMORROW'S GAME WILL DECIDE THE OTHER TEAM GOING TO THE NATIONALS.
US OR RYONAN.
WINNER TAKE ALL, HUH?
ALL RIGHT...
THAT'S NICE AND SIMPLE.
STAGE DOOR
...
THOSE BOYS...
...WILL DO FINE WITHOUT YOU.
...
It's still kinda sad, though.

READ THIS WAY

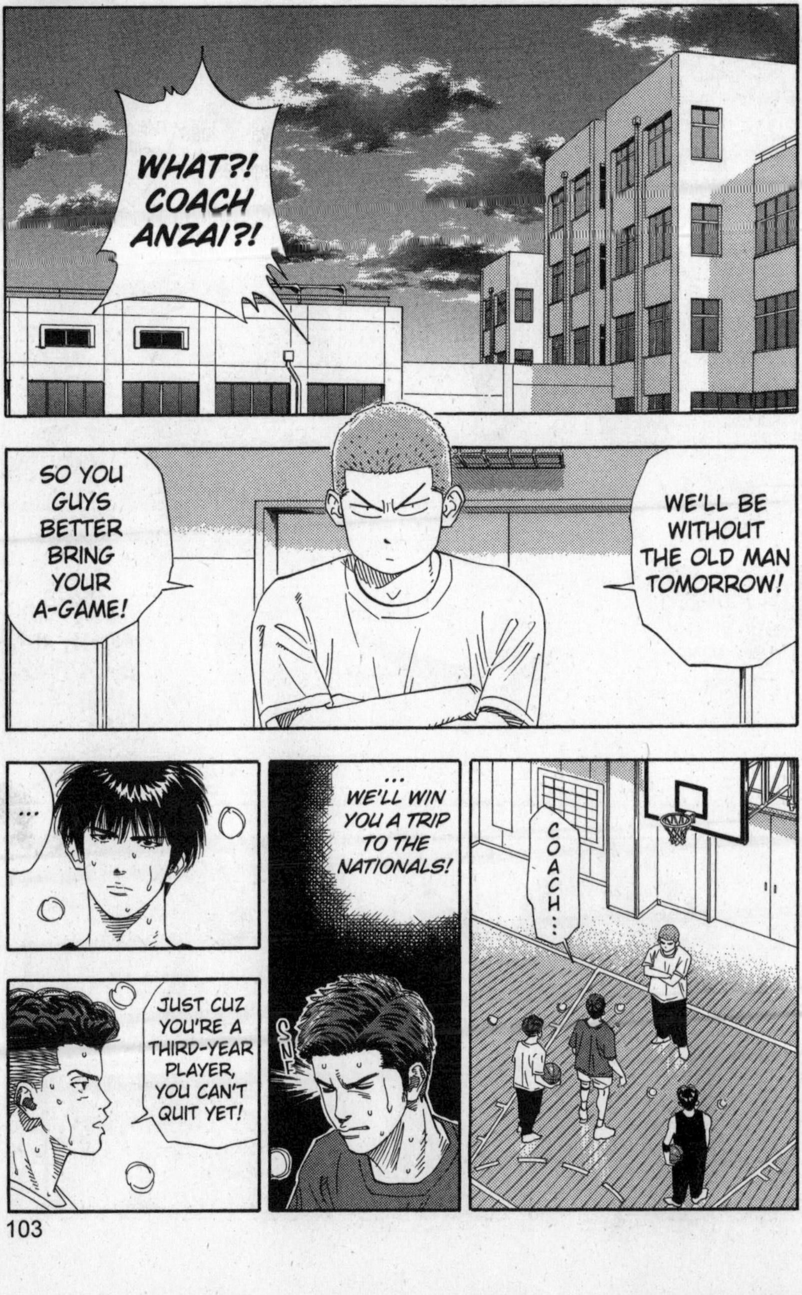

WHAT?! COACH ANZAI?!
WE'LL BE WITHOUT THE OLD MAN TOMORROW!
SO YOU GUYS BETTER BRING YOUR A-GAME!
COACH...
... WE'LL WIN YOU A TRIP TO THE NATIONALS!
SNF
...
JUST CUZ YOU'RE A THIRD-YEAR PLAYER, YOU CAN'T QUIT YET!

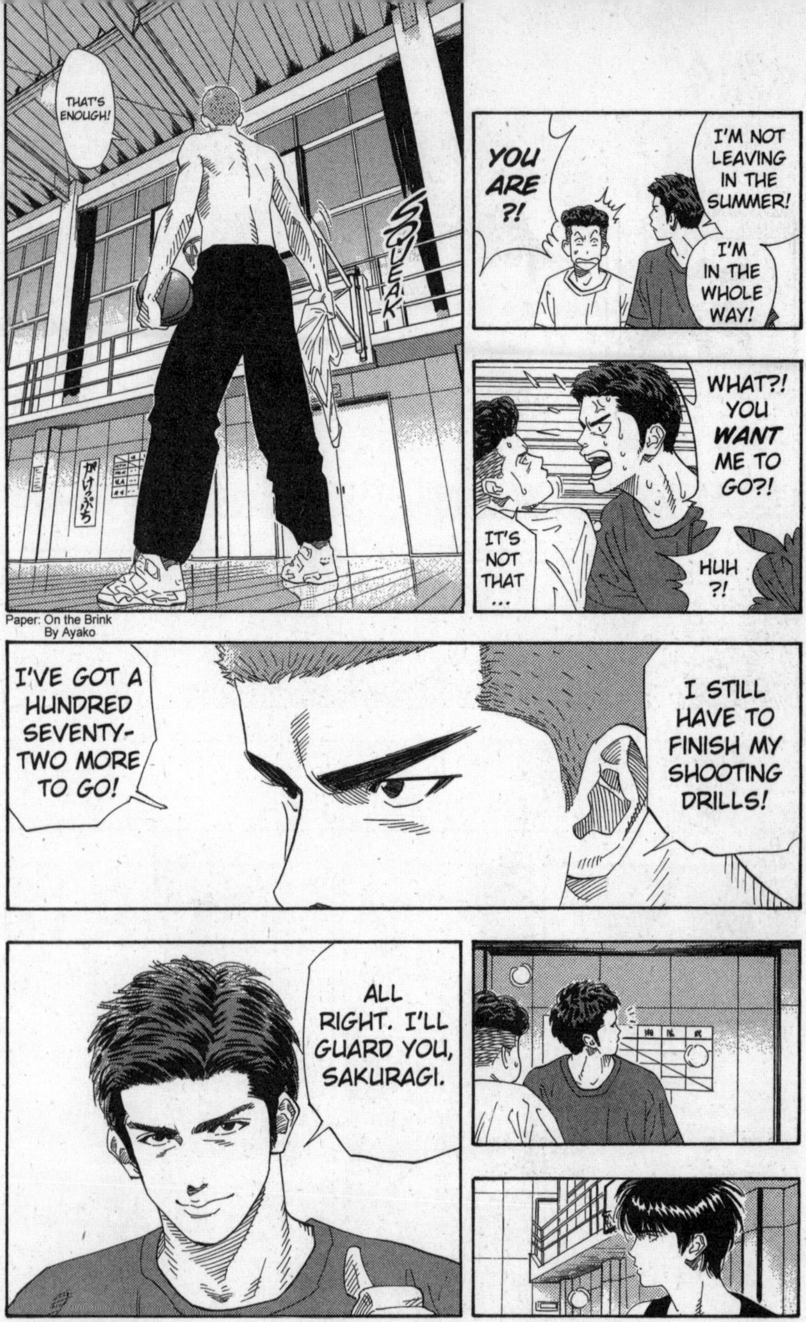
I'M NOT LEAVING IN THE SUMMER!
I'M IN THE WHOLE WAY!
YOU ARE?!
WHAT?! YOU WANT ME TO GO?!
HUH?!
IT'S NOT THAT...
SQUEAK
THAT'S ENOUGH!
がけっぷち
I STILL HAVE TO FINISH MY SHOOTING DRILLS!
I'VE GOT A HUNDRED SEVENTY-TWO MORE TO GO!
ALL RIGHT. I'LL GUARD YOU, SAKURAGI.

Paper: On the Brink
By Ayako

READ THIS WAY

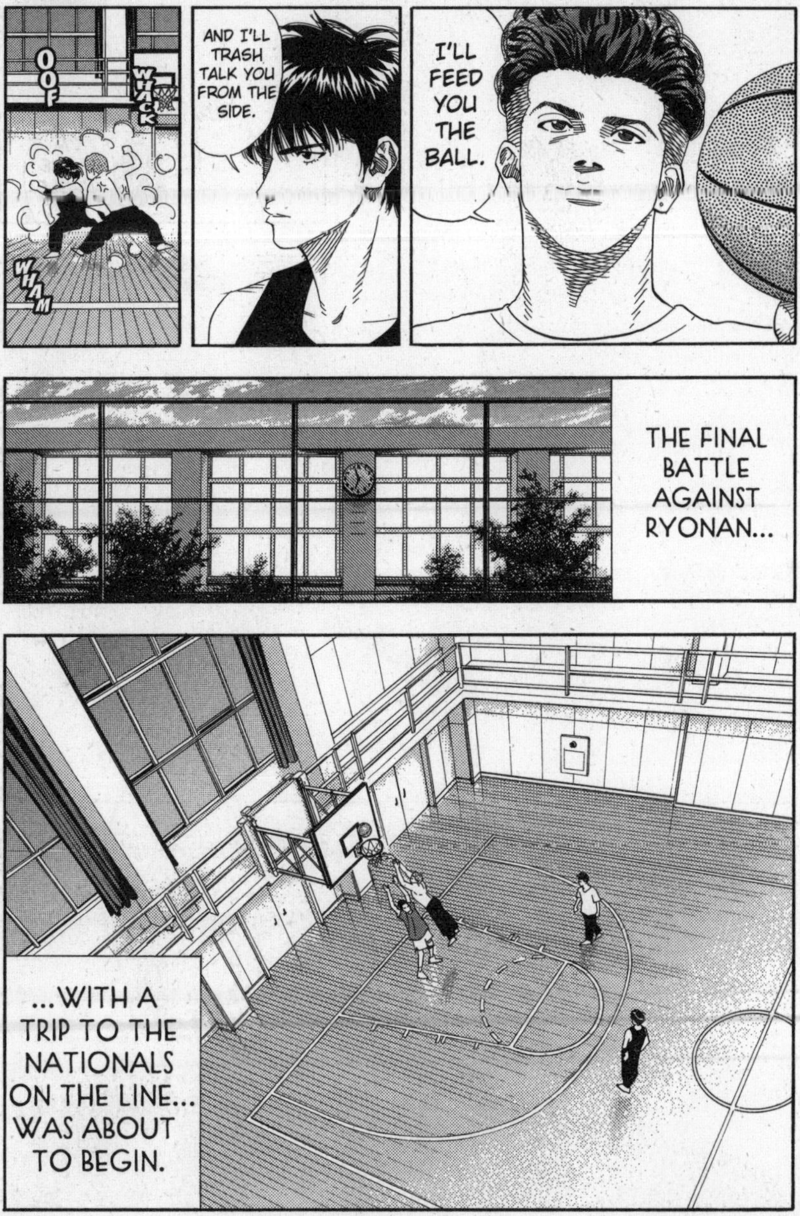
I'LL FEED YOU THE BALL.
AND I'LL TRASH TALK YOU FROM THE SIDE.
WHACK
OOF
WHAM
THE FINAL BATTLE AGAINST RYONAN...
...WITH A TRIP TO THE NATIONALS ON THE LINE... WAS ABOUT TO BEGIN.

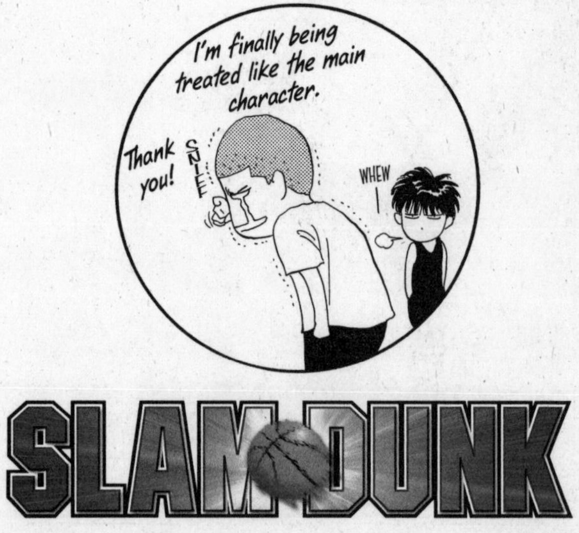
I'm finally being treated like the main character.
WHEW
SNIFF
Thank you!

SLAM DUNK

#149 THE LAST SPOT

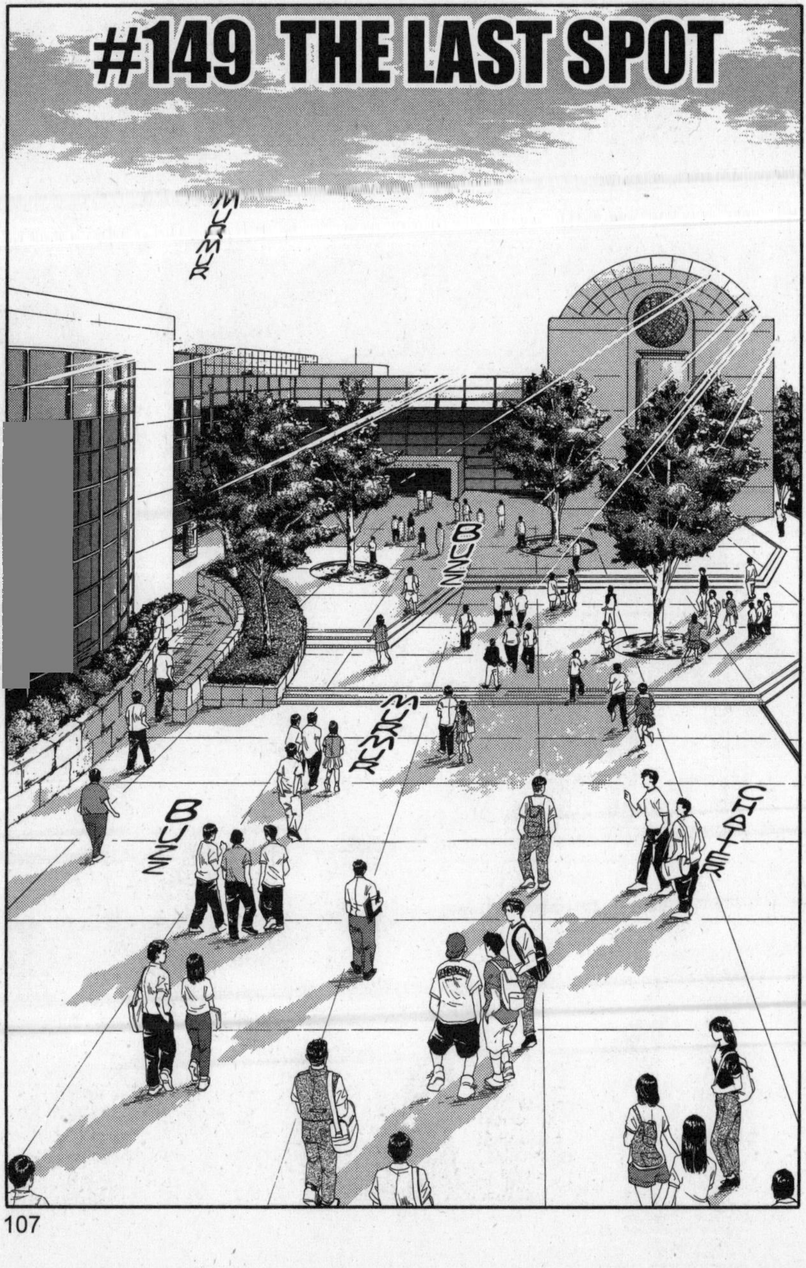
MURMUR
BUZZ
MURMUR
CHATTER
BUZZ

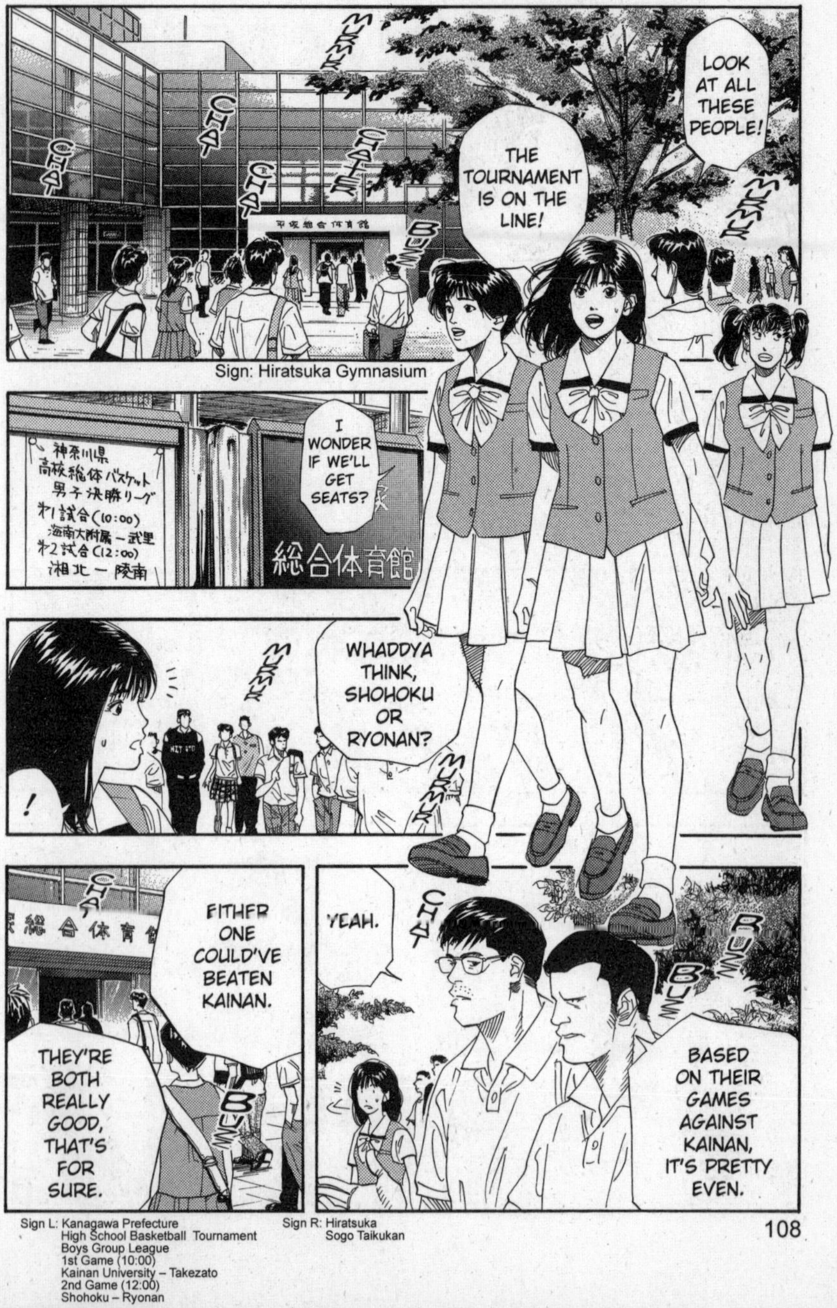
LOOK AT ALL THESE PEOPLE!
MURMUR
THE TOURNAMENT IS ON THE LINE!
BUZZ
CHATTER
CHAT
CHAT
CHAT
MURMUR
平塚総合体育館
Sign: Hiratsuka Gymnasium
I WONDER IF WE'LL GET SEATS?
神奈川県
高校総体バスケット
男子決勝リーグ
第1試合(10:00)
海南大附属－武里
第2試合(12:00)
湘北－陵南
総合体育館
MURMUR
WHADDYA THINK, SHOHOKU OR RYONAN?
MURMUR
!
BUZZ
BUZZ
CHAT
YEAH.
BASED ON THEIR GAMES AGAINST KAINAN, IT'S PRETTY EVEN.
CHAT
EITHER ONE COULD'VE BEATEN KAINAN.
THEY'RE BOTH REALLY GOOD, THAT'S FOR SURE.
BUZZ

Sign L: Kanagawa Prefecture
High School Basketball Tournament
Boys Group League
1st Game (10:00)
Kainan University – Takezato
2nd Game (12:00)
Shohoku – Ryonan

Sign R: Hiratsuka
Sogo Taikukan

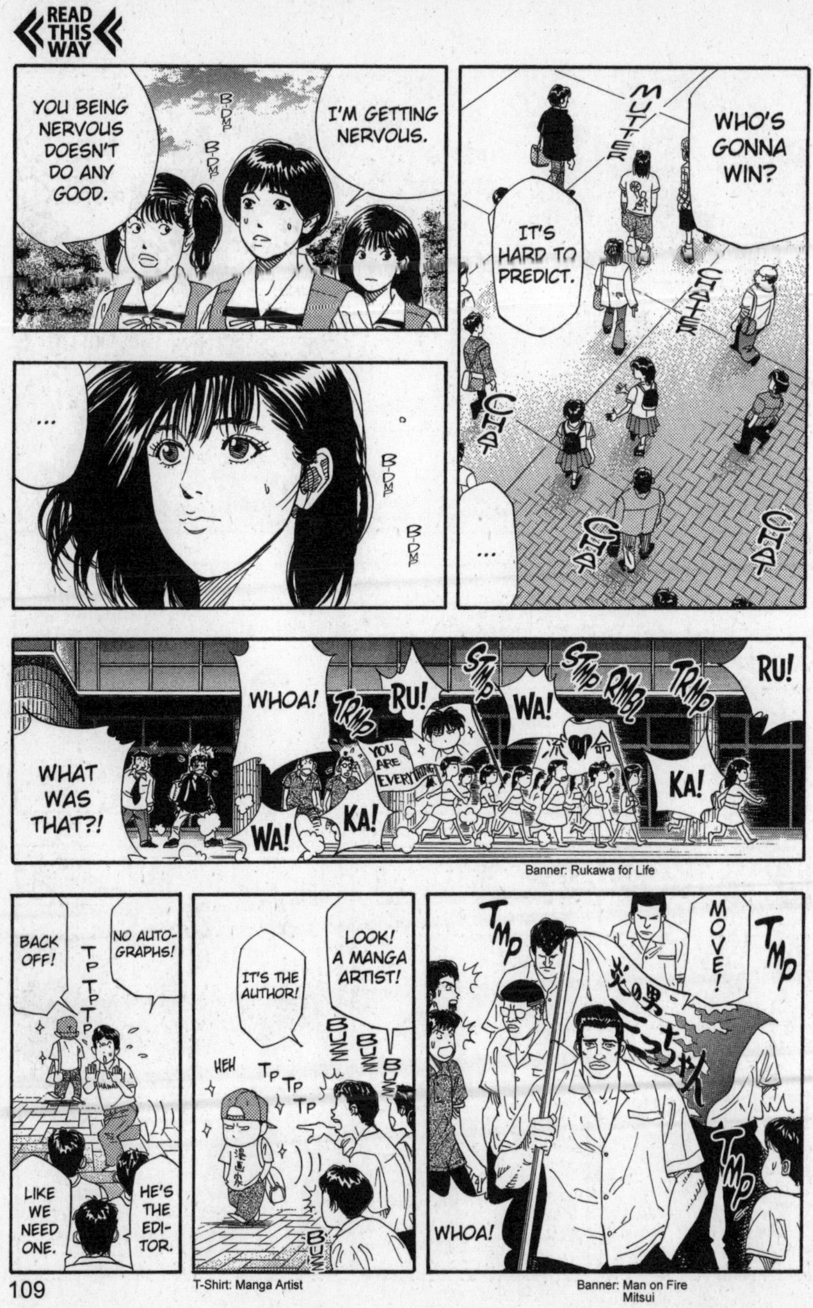
WHO'S GONNA WIN?
MUTTER
IT'S HARD TO PREDICT.
CHATTER
CHAT
CHAT
CHAT
...
I'M GETTING NERVOUS.
B-DMP
B-DMP
YOU BEING NERVOUS DOESN'T DO ANY GOOD.
...
B-DMP
B-DMP
RU!
TRMP
RMBL
STMP
WA!
STMP
RU!
KA!
WHOA!
TRMP
YOU ARE EVERYTHING
KA!
WA!
WHAT WAS THAT?!
MOVE!
TMP
TMP
TMP
WHOA!
LOOK! A MANGA ARTIST!
IT'S THE AUTHOR!
BUZZ
BUZZ
BUZZ
HEH
TP
TP
TP
BUZZ
NO AUTO-GRAPHS!
BACK OFF!
TP
TP
TP
HE'S THE EDI-TOR.
LIKE WE NEED ONE.

Banner: Rukawa for Life

T-Shirt: Manga Artist

Banner: Man on Fire
Mitsui

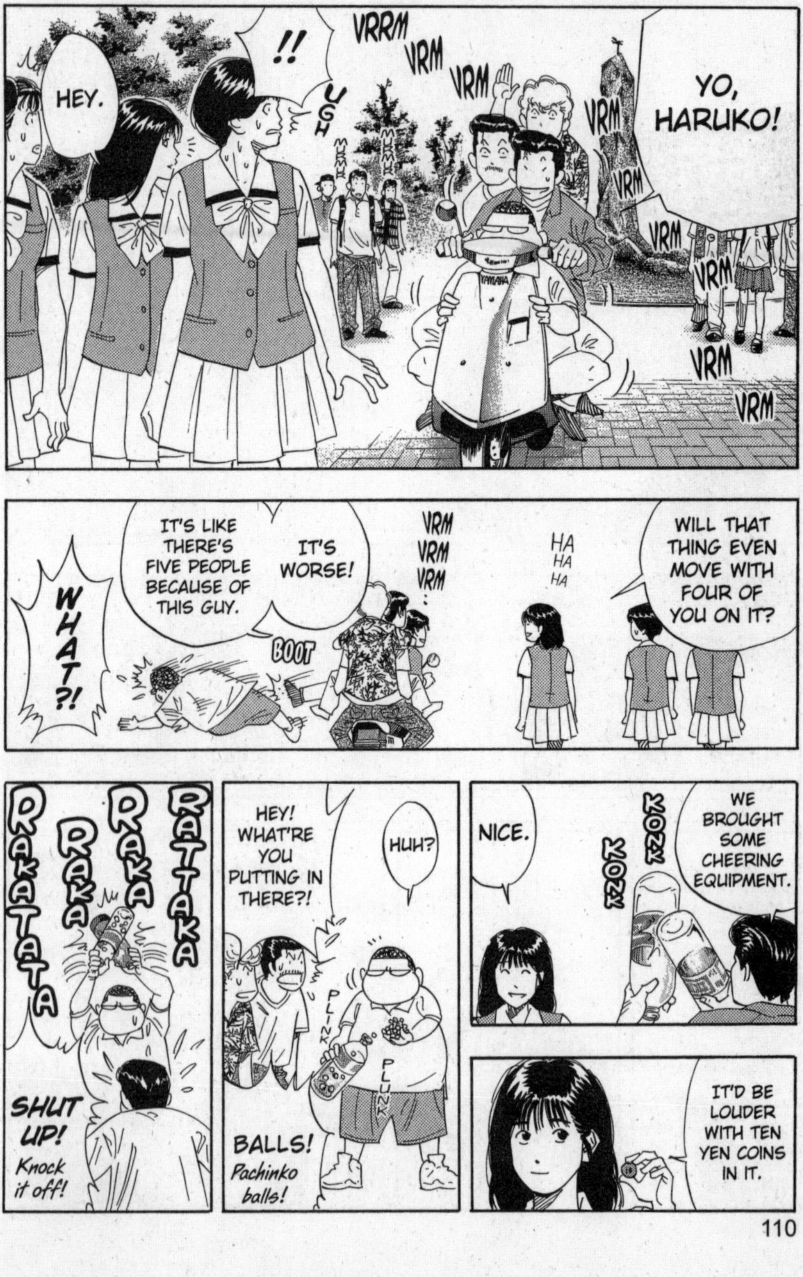
YO, HARUKO!
VRRM
VRM
VRM
VRM
VRM
VRM
VRM
VRM
VRM
!!
UGH
HEY.
WILL THAT THING EVEN MOVE WITH FOUR OF YOU ON IT?
HA HA HA
VRM VRM VRM
IT'S WORSE!
IT'S LIKE THERE'S FIVE PEOPLE BECAUSE OF THIS GUY.
BOOT
WHAT?!
WE BROUGHT SOME CHEERING EQUIPMENT.
KON
KON
NICE.
IT'D BE LOUDER WITH TEN YEN COINS IN IT.
HUH?
HEY! WHAT'RE YOU PUTTING IN THERE?!
PLINK
PLUNK
BALLS!
Pachinko balls!
RATTAKA
RAKA
RAKA
RAKATATA
SHUT UP!
Knock it off!

READ THIS WAY

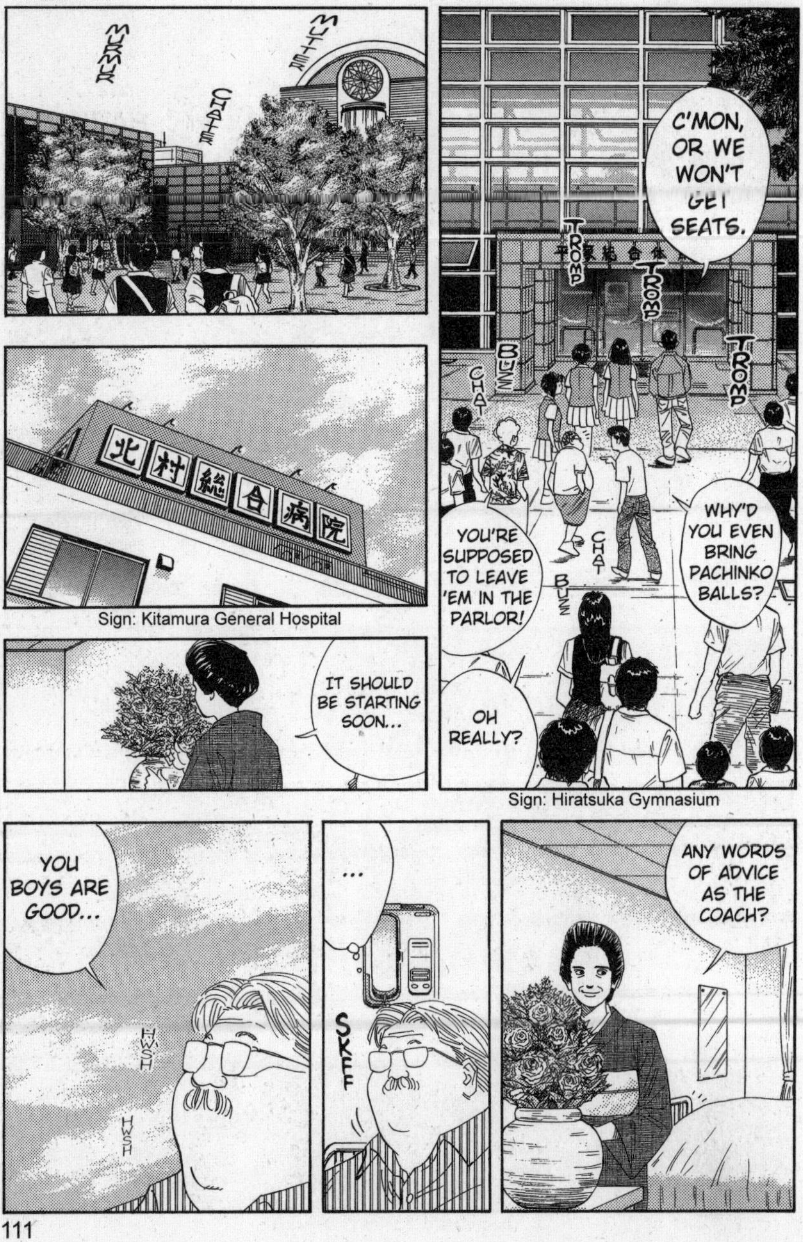
C'MON, OR WE WON'T GET SEATS.
TROMP
TROMP
TROMP
BUZZ
CHAT
WHY'D YOU EVEN BRING PACHINKO BALLS?
YOU'RE SUPPOSED TO LEAVE 'EM IN THE PARLOR!
CHAT
BUZZ
OH REALLY?
Sign: Hiratsuka Gymnasium
MUTTER
CHATTER
MURMUR
北村総合病院
Sign: Kitamura General Hospital
IT SHOULD BE STARTING SOON...
ANY WORDS OF ADVICE AS THE COACH?
...
SKEFF
YOU BOYS ARE GOOD...
HWSH
HWSH

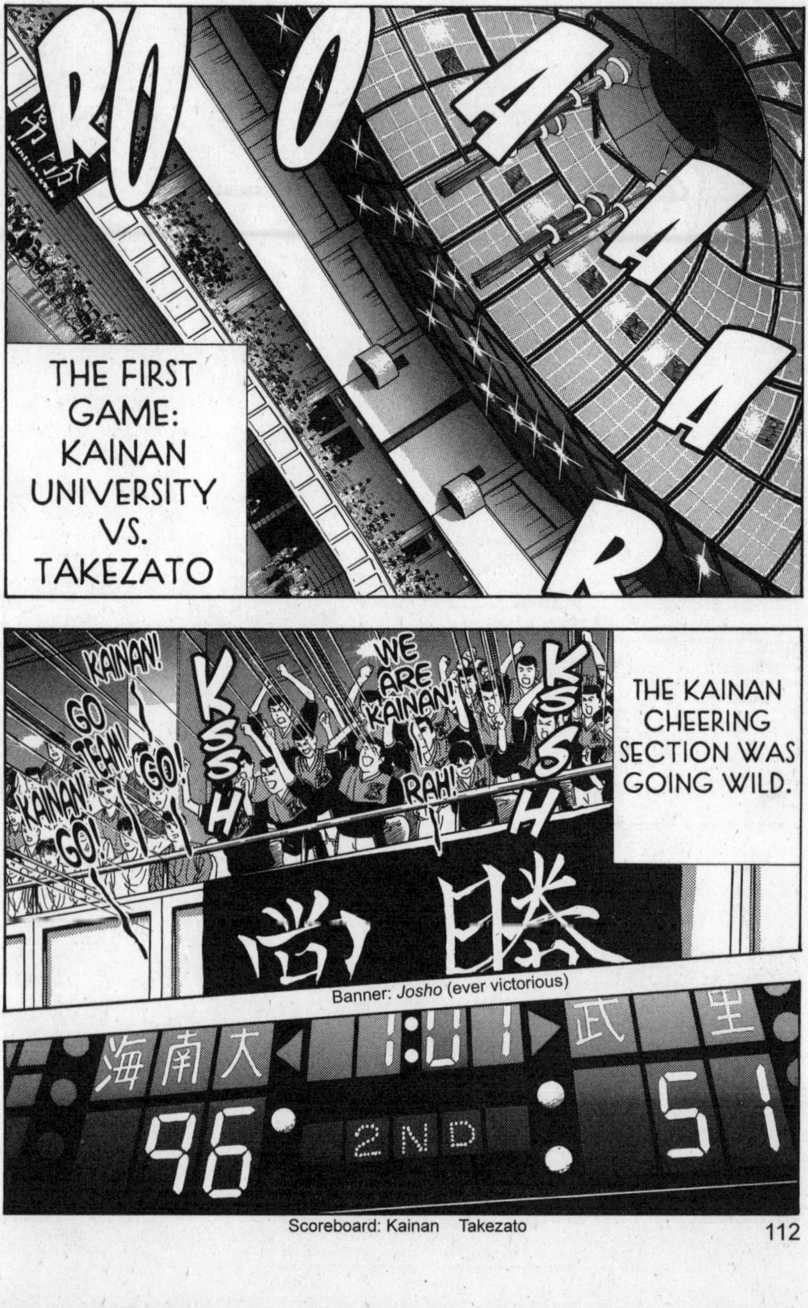
ROOAAAR
THE FIRST GAME: KAINAN UNIVERSITY VS. TAKEZATO
THE KAINAN CHEERING SECTION WAS GOING WILD.
KSSH
WE ARE KAINAN!
RAH!
KSSH
GO!
GO TEAM!
KAINAN!
KAINAN! GO!
Banner: *Josho* (ever victorious)
海南大
1:01
武里
96
2ND
51
Scoreboard: Kainan Takezato

READ THIS WAY

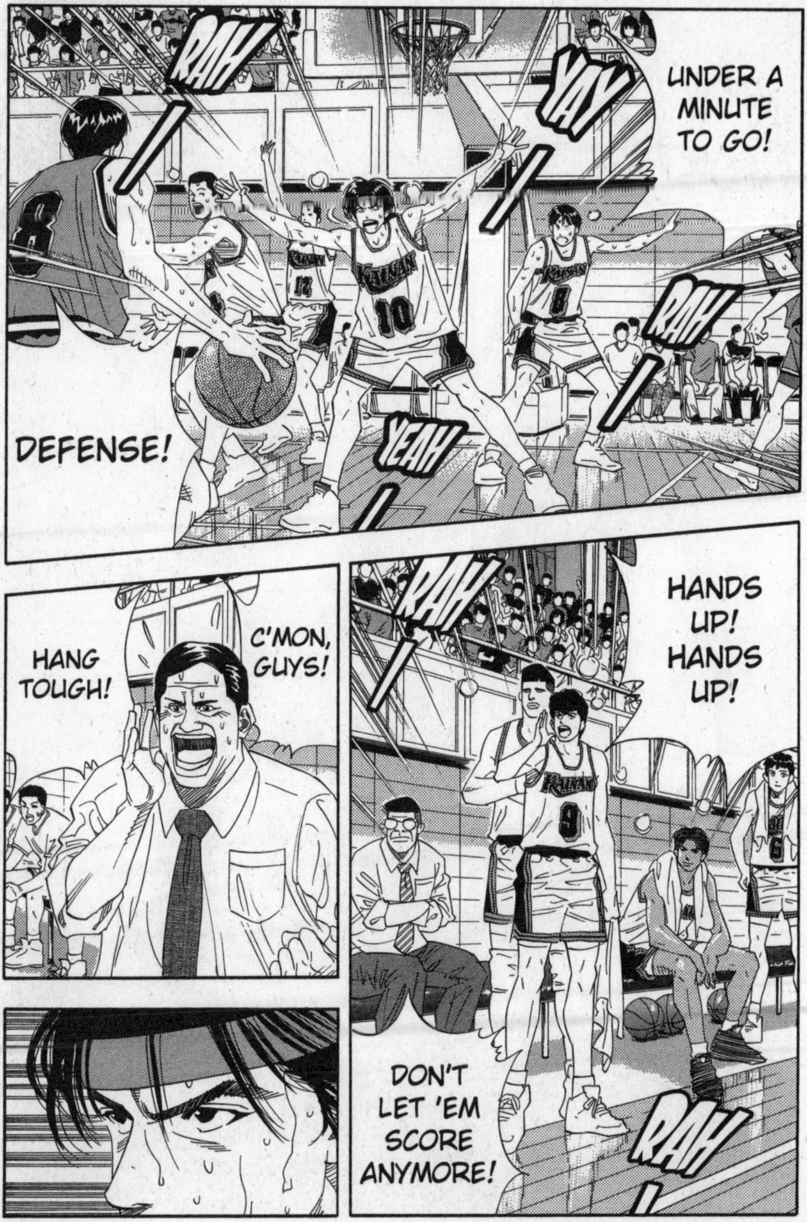

UNDER A MINUTE TO GO!
YAY!
RAH!
RAH!
YEAH!
DEFENSE!
HANDS UP! HANDS UP!
RAH!
DON'T LET 'EM SCORE ANYMORE!
RAH!
C'MON, GUYS!
HANG TOUGH!

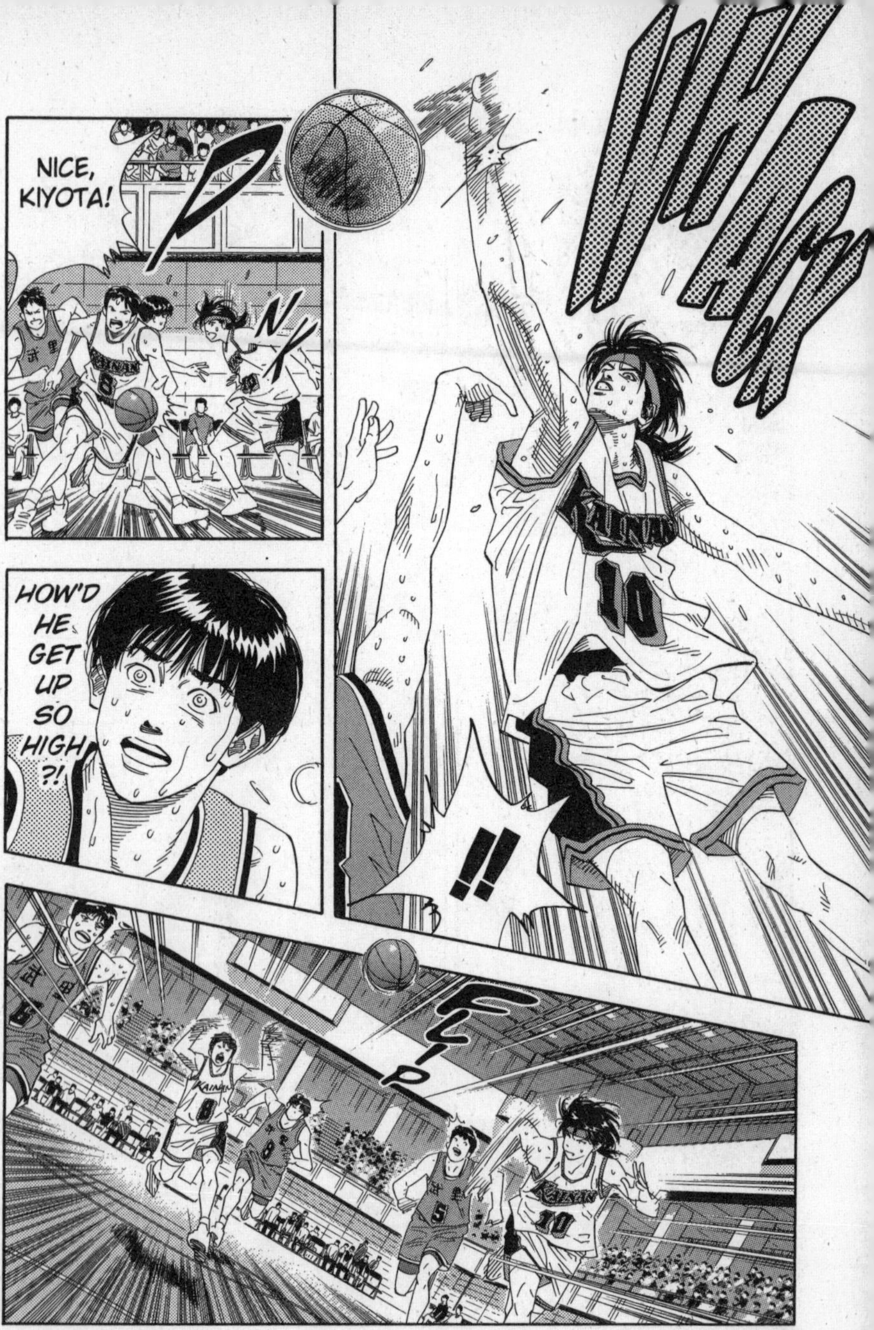
WHAP
!!
NICE, KIYOTA!
HOW'D HE GET UP SO HIGH?!
FLIP

READ THIS WAY

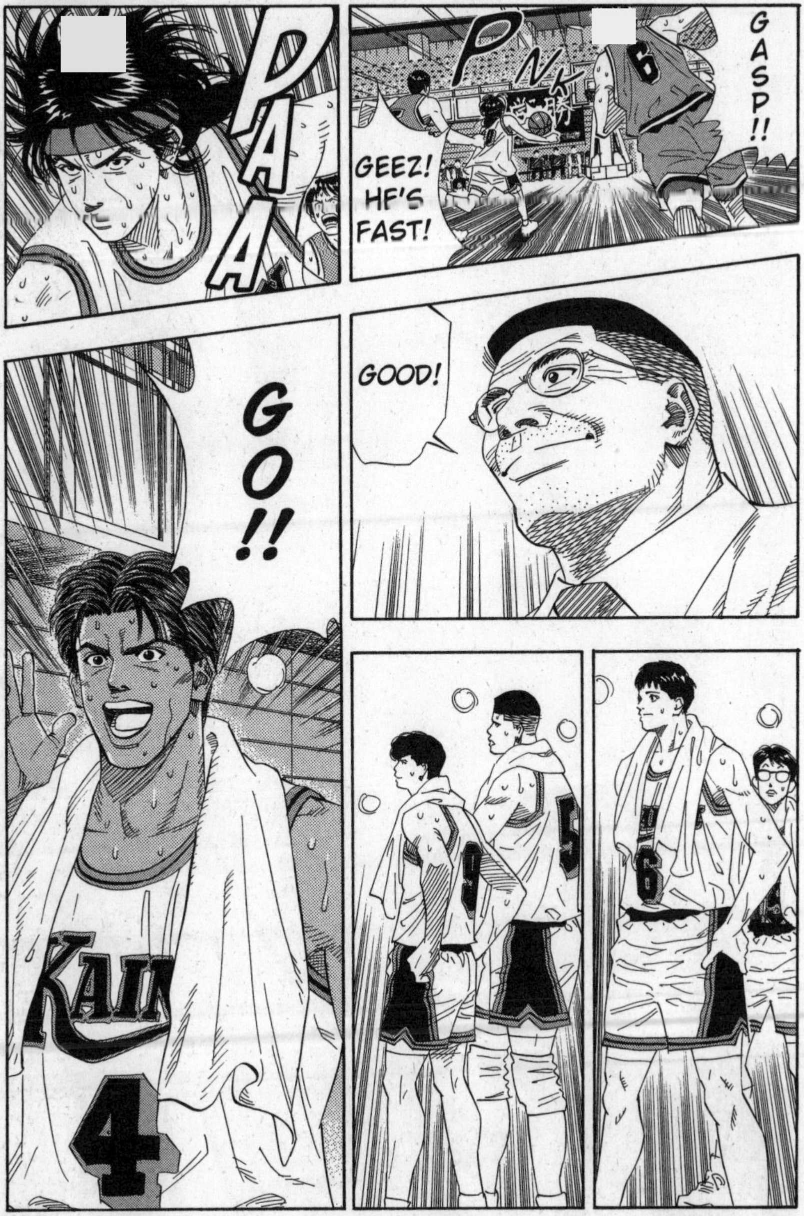
GASP!!
GEEZ! HE'S FAST!
PAA
GOOD!
GO!!

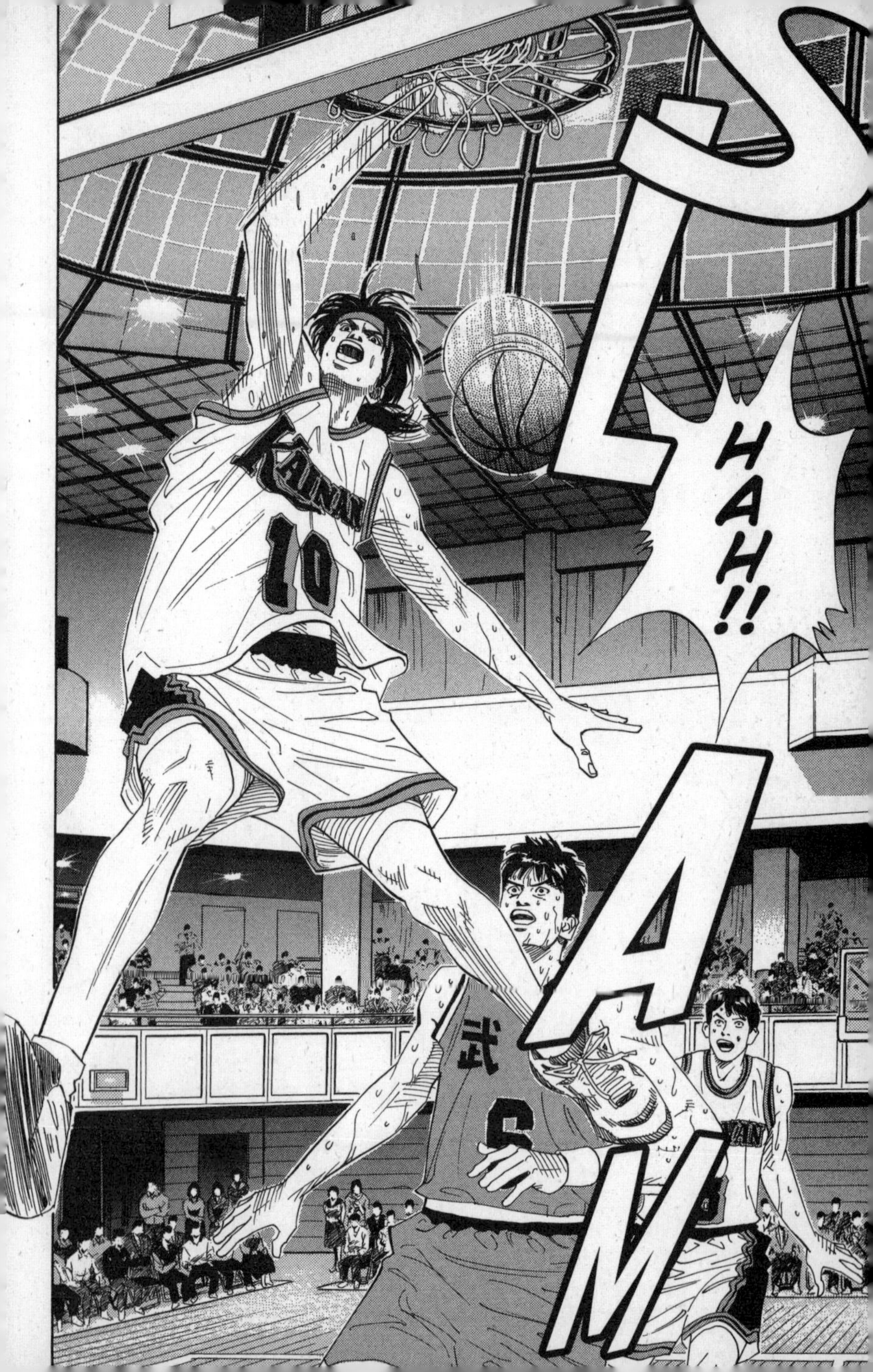
HAH!!
SLAM

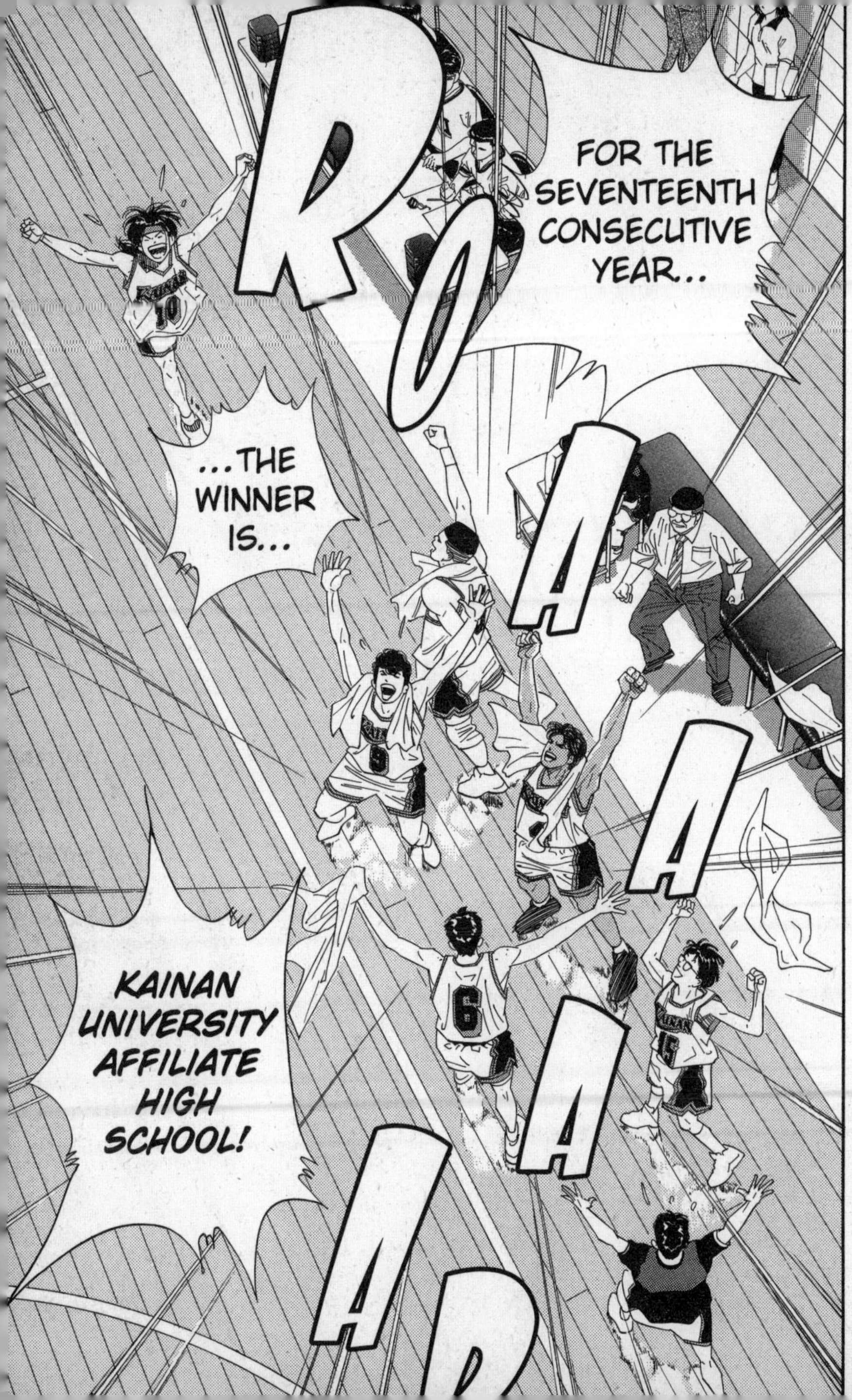
FOR THE SEVENTEENTH CONSECUTIVE YEAR...
ROAAAA
...THE WINNER IS...
KAINAN UNIVERSITY AFFILIATE HIGH SCHOOL!

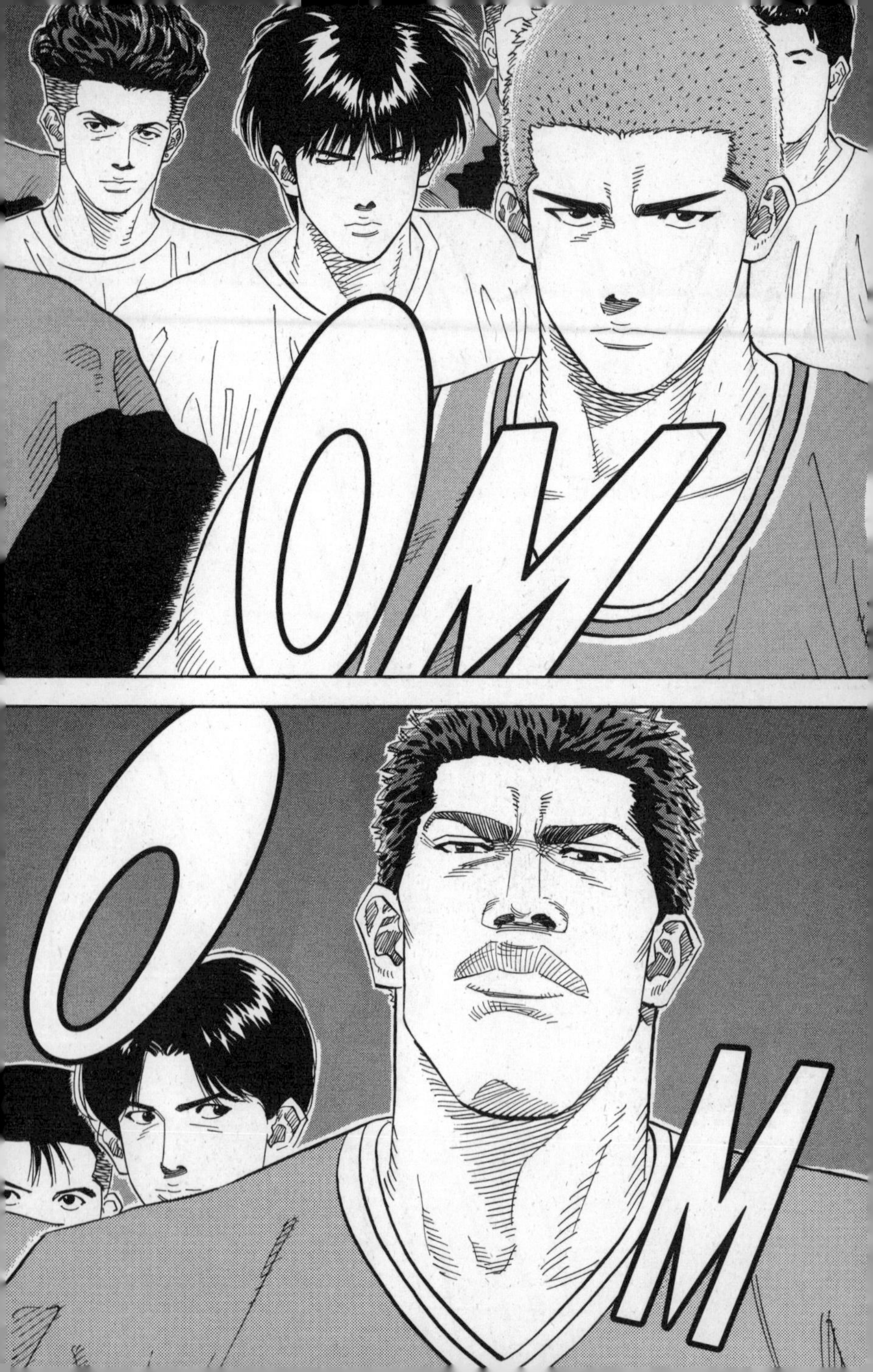
OM
OM

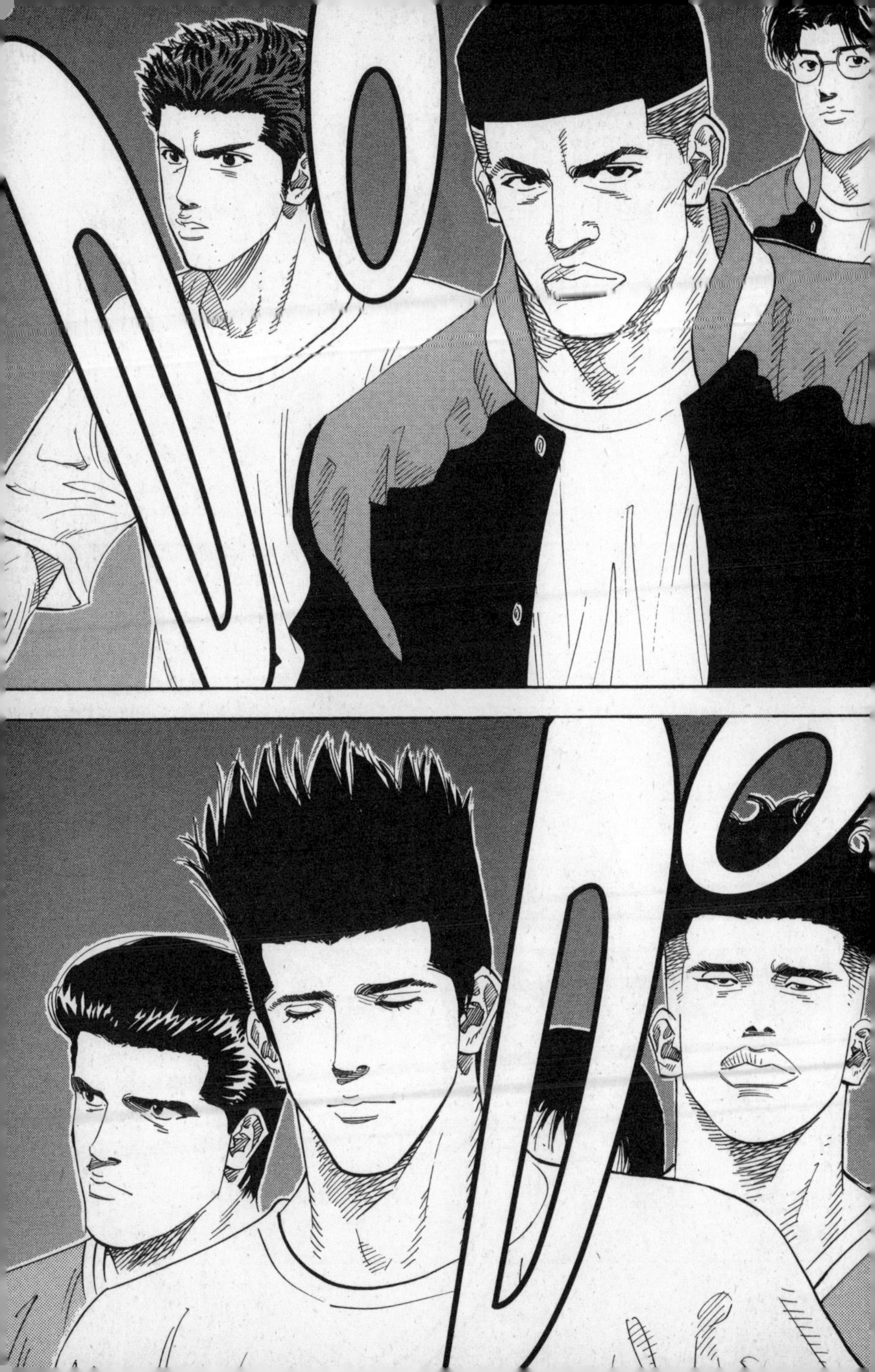

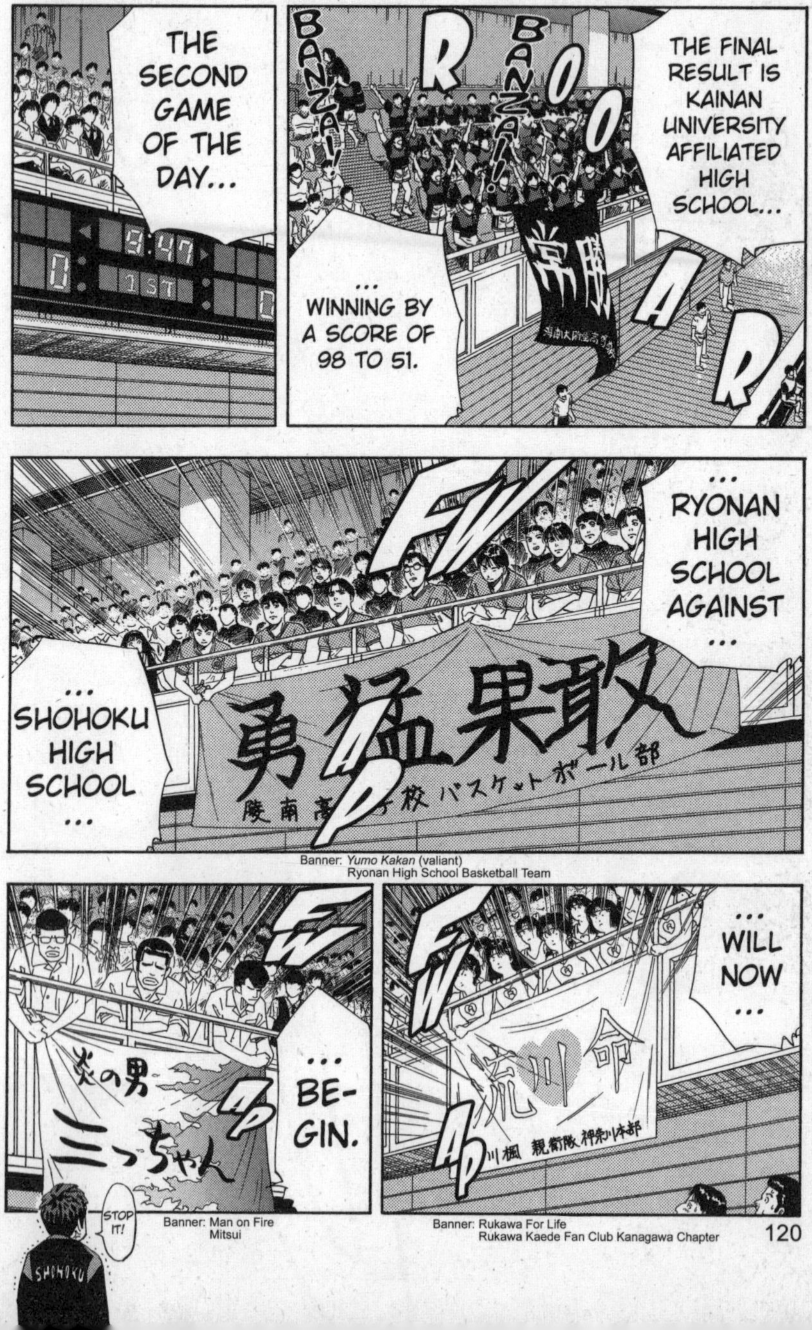
THE FINAL RESULT IS KAINAN UNIVERSITY AFFILIATED HIGH SCHOOL...
ROOAR
BANZAI!
BANZAI!
常勝
海南大附属高等学校
... WINNING BY A SCORE OF 98 TO 51.
THE SECOND GAME OF THE DAY...
... RYONAN HIGH SCHOOL AGAINST ...
FWAP
勇猛果敢
陵南高 校バスケットボール部
... SHOHOKU HIGH SCHOOL ...
Banner: *Yumo Kakan* (valiant)
Ryonan High School Basketball Team
... WILL NOW ...
FWAP
流川命
川楓 親衛隊 神奈川本部
... BE-GIN.
FWAP
炎の男
三っちゃん
STOP IT!
SHOHOKU
Banner: Man on Fire
Mitsui
Banner: Rukawa For Life
Rukawa Kaede Fan Club Kanagawa Chapter

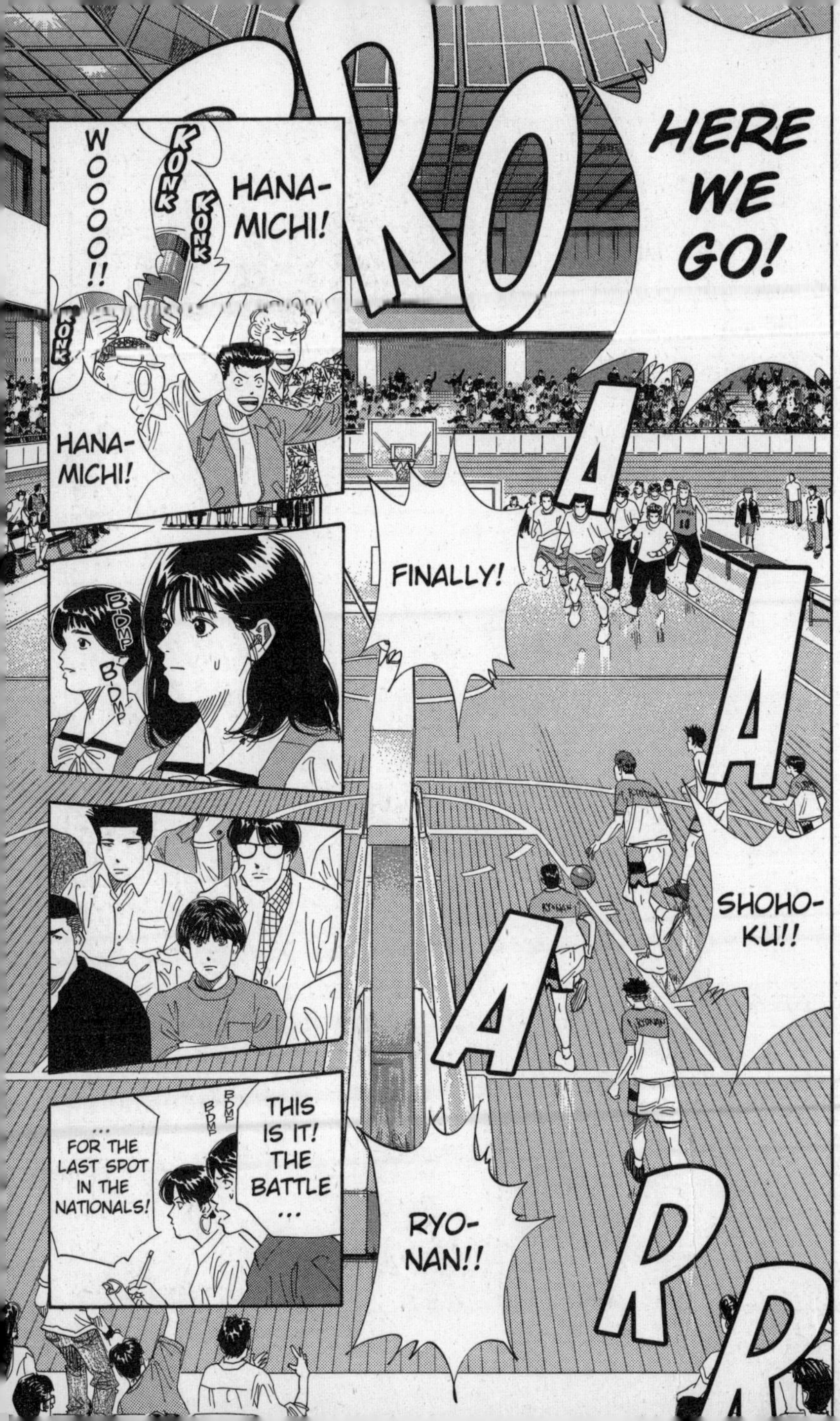
KO
HERE WE GO!
AAAA
FINALLY!
SHOHO-KU!!
RYO-NAN!!
RR
HANA-MICHI!
KONK
KONK
WOOOOO!!
KONK
HANA-MICHI!
B-DMP
B-DMP
BDMP
BDMP
THIS IS IT! THE BATTLE ...
... FOR THE LAST SPOT IN THE NATIONALS!

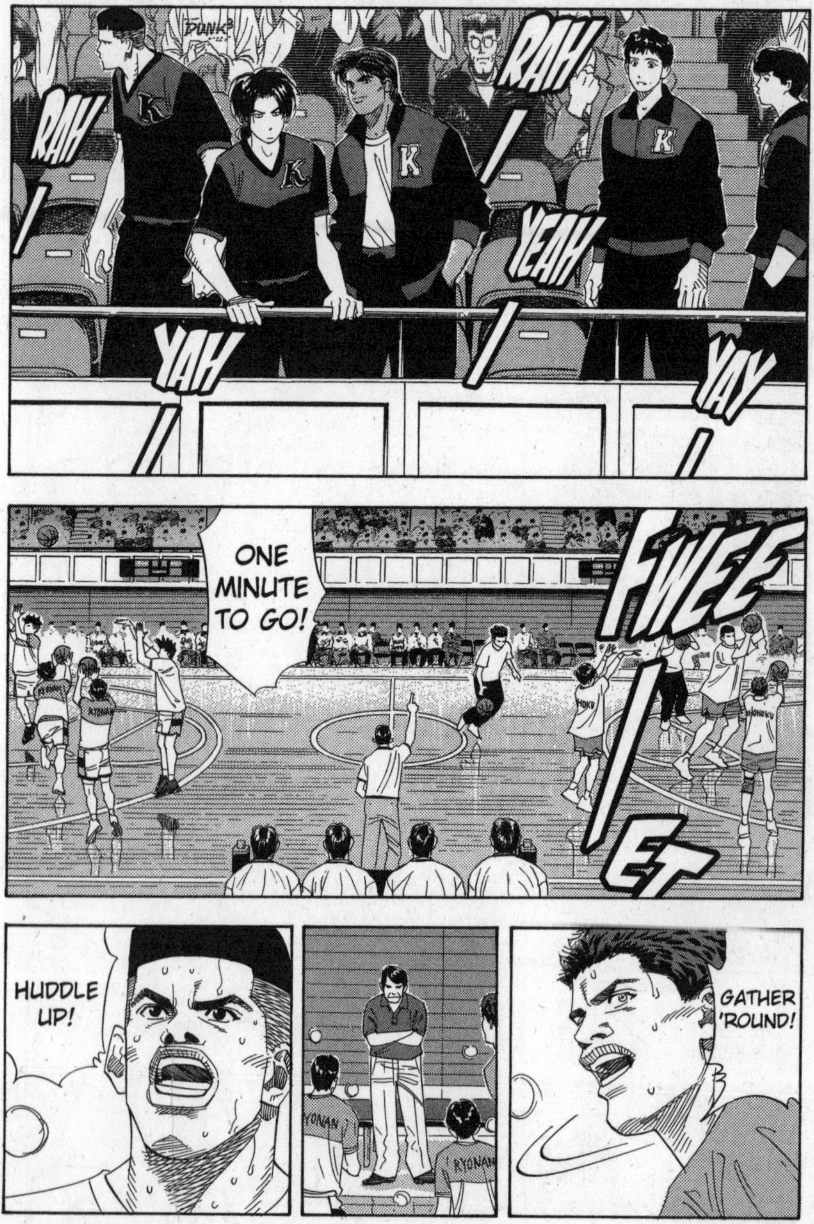
YAY!
RAH!
YEAH!
YAH!
RAH!
FWEE-ET
ONE MINUTE TO GO!
GATHER 'ROUND!
HUDDLE UP!

READ THIS WAY

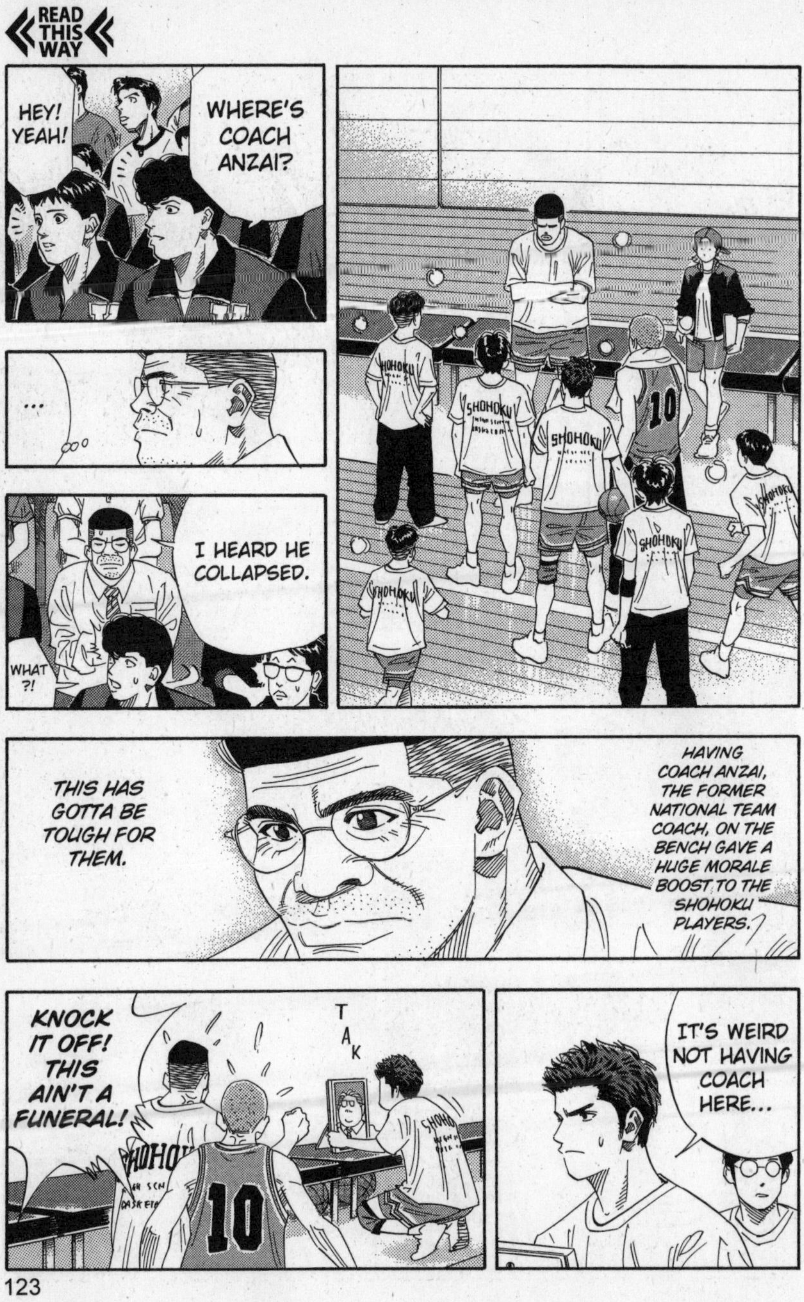
WHERE'S COACH ANZAI?
HEY! YEAH!
...
I HEARD HE COLLAPSED.
WHAT?!
HAVING COACH ANZAI, THE FORMER NATIONAL TEAM COACH, ON THE BENCH GAVE A HUGE MORALE BOOST TO THE SHOHOKU PLAYERS.
THIS HAS GOTTA BE TOUGH FOR THEM.
IT'S WEIRD NOT HAVING COACH HERE...
TAK
KNOCK IT OFF! THIS AIN'T A FUNERAL!

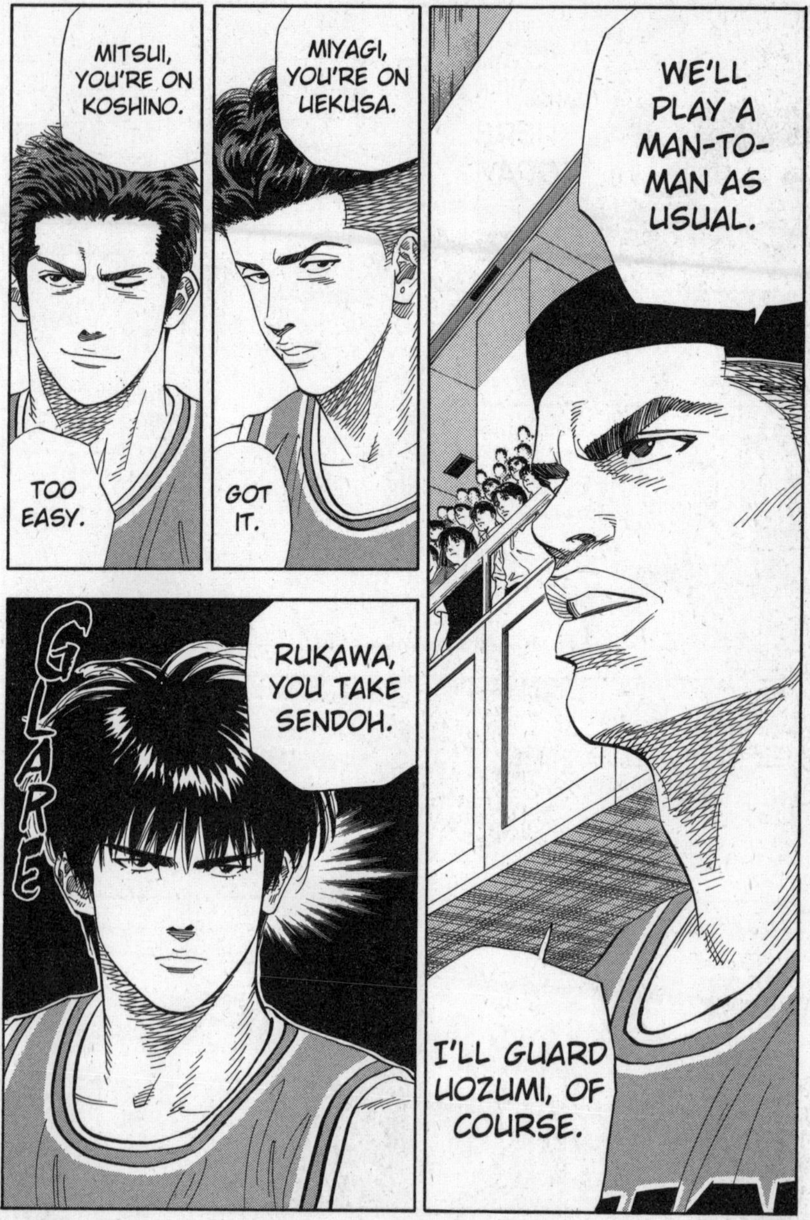
WE'LL PLAY A MAN-TO-MAN AS USUAL.
I'LL GUARD UOZUMI, OF COURSE.
MIYAGI, YOU'RE ON UEKUSA.
GOT IT.
MITSUI, YOU'RE ON KOSHINO.
TOO EASY.
RUKAWA, YOU TAKE SENDOH.
GLARE

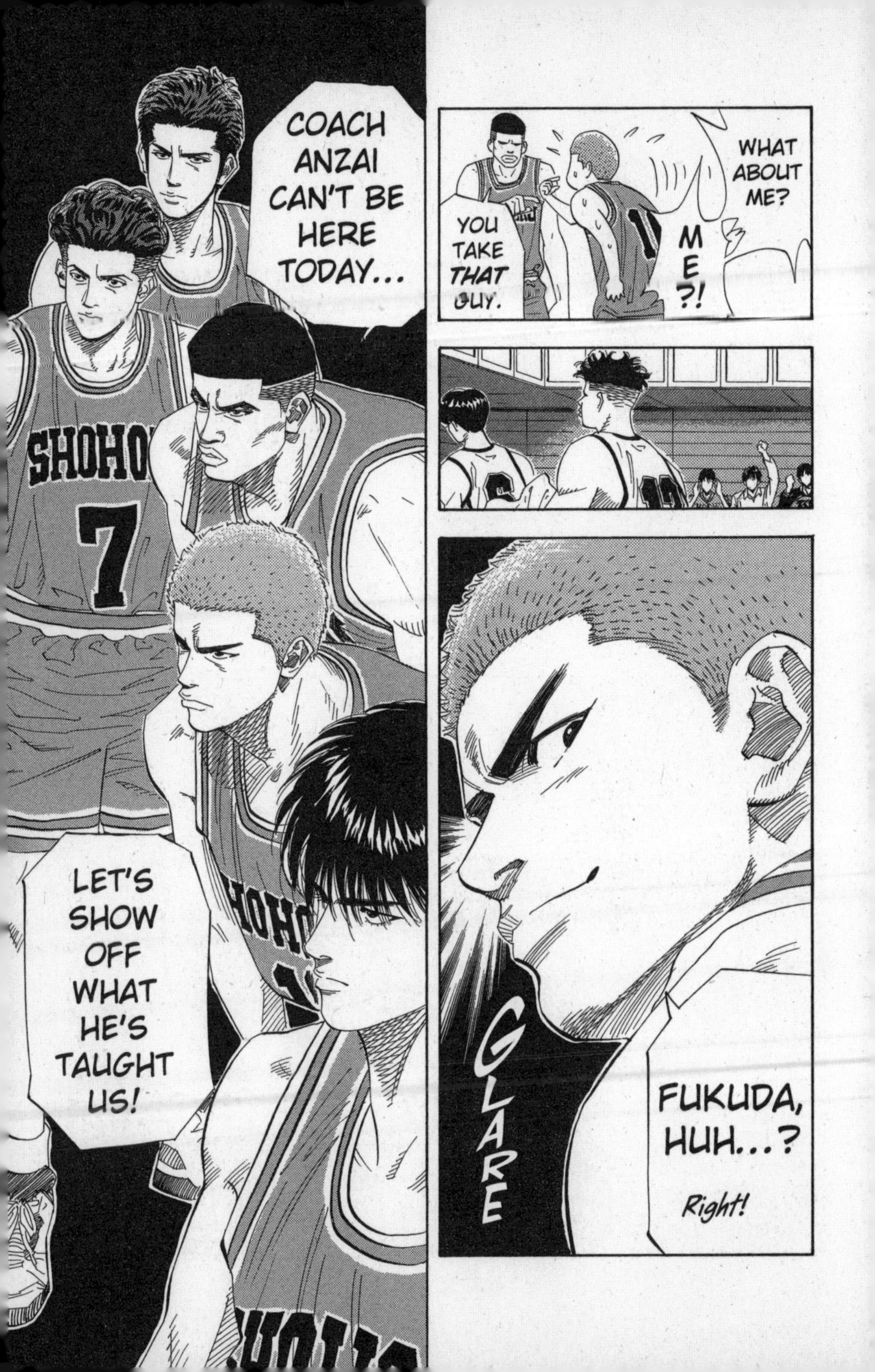
WHAT ABOUT ME?
ME?!
YOU TAKE THAT GUY.
FUKUDA, HUH...?
Right!
GLARE
COACH ANZAI CAN'T BE HERE TODAY...
LET'S SHOW OFF WHAT HE'S TAUGHT US!

MUMBLE
That's better but...
...Wild Monkey's still getting too much attention!

SLAM DUNK

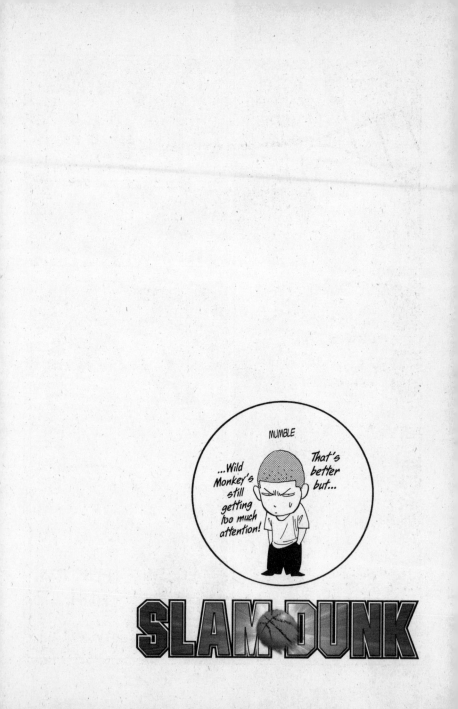

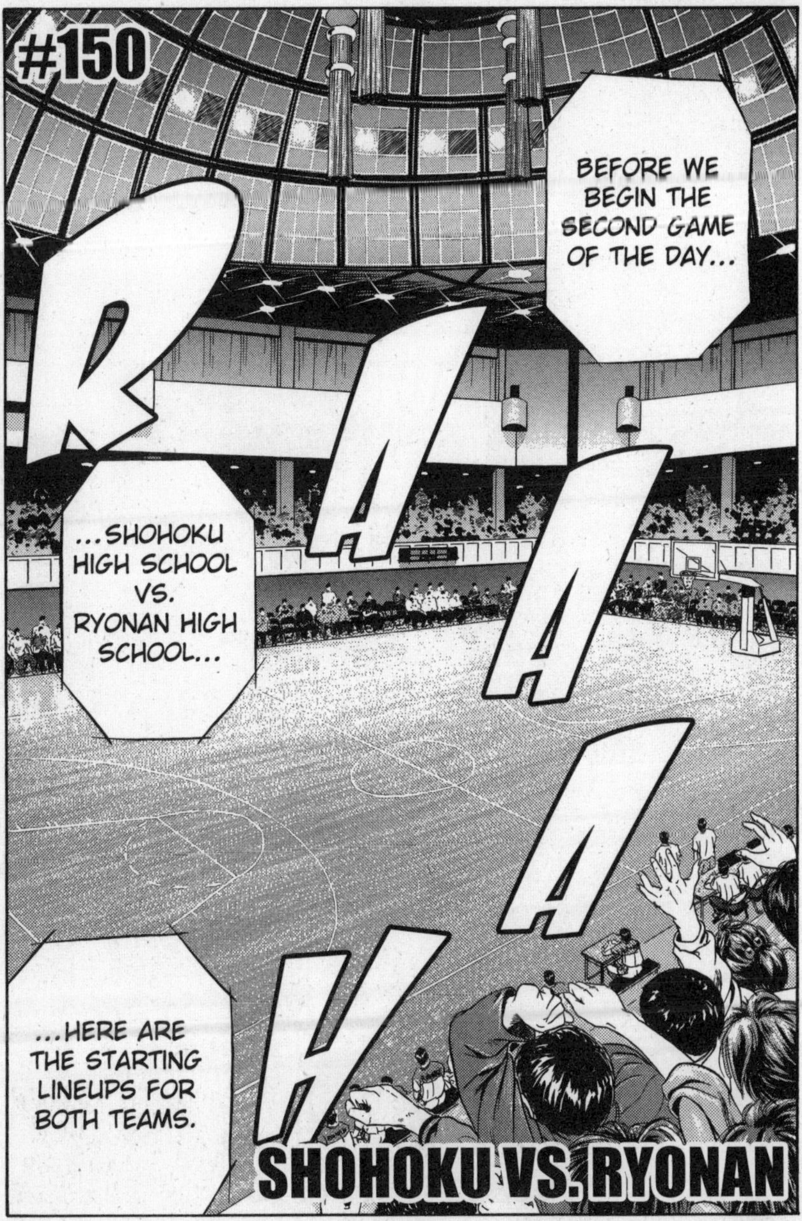
#150
BEFORE WE BEGIN THE SECOND GAME OF THE DAY...
RAAAAH
...SHOHOKU HIGH SCHOOL VS. RYONAN HIGH SCHOOL...
...HERE ARE THE STARTING LINEUPS FOR BOTH TEAMS.
SHOHOKU VS. RYONAN

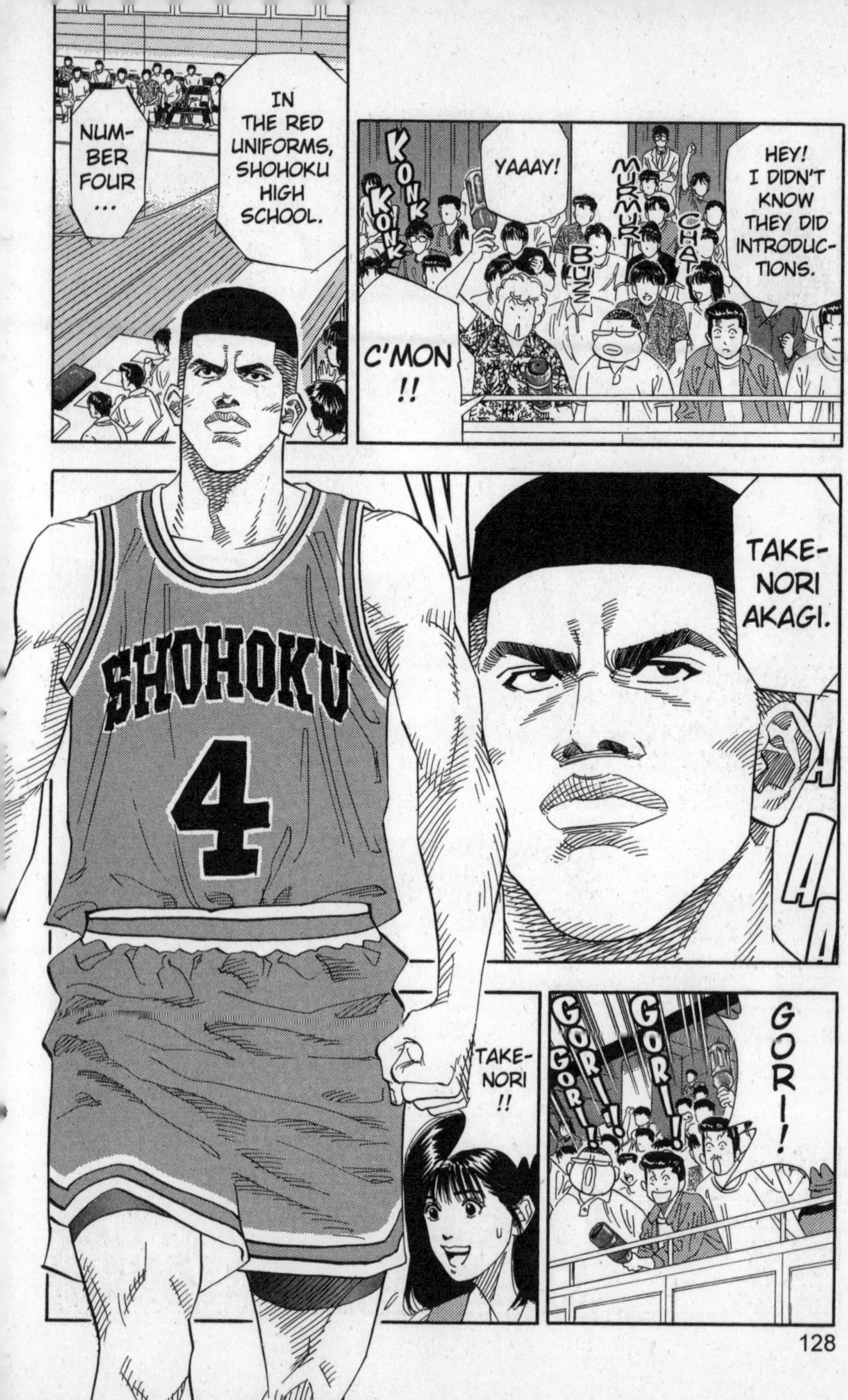
HEY! I DIDN'T KNOW THEY DID INTRODUCTIONS.
CHAT
MURMUR
BUZZ
YAAAY!
KONK
KONK
C'MON!!
IN THE RED UNIFORMS, SHOHOKU HIGH SCHOOL.
NUMBER FOUR...
SHOHOKU
4
TAKENORI AKAGI.
GORI!
GORI!
GORI!
TAKENORI!!

READ THIS WAY

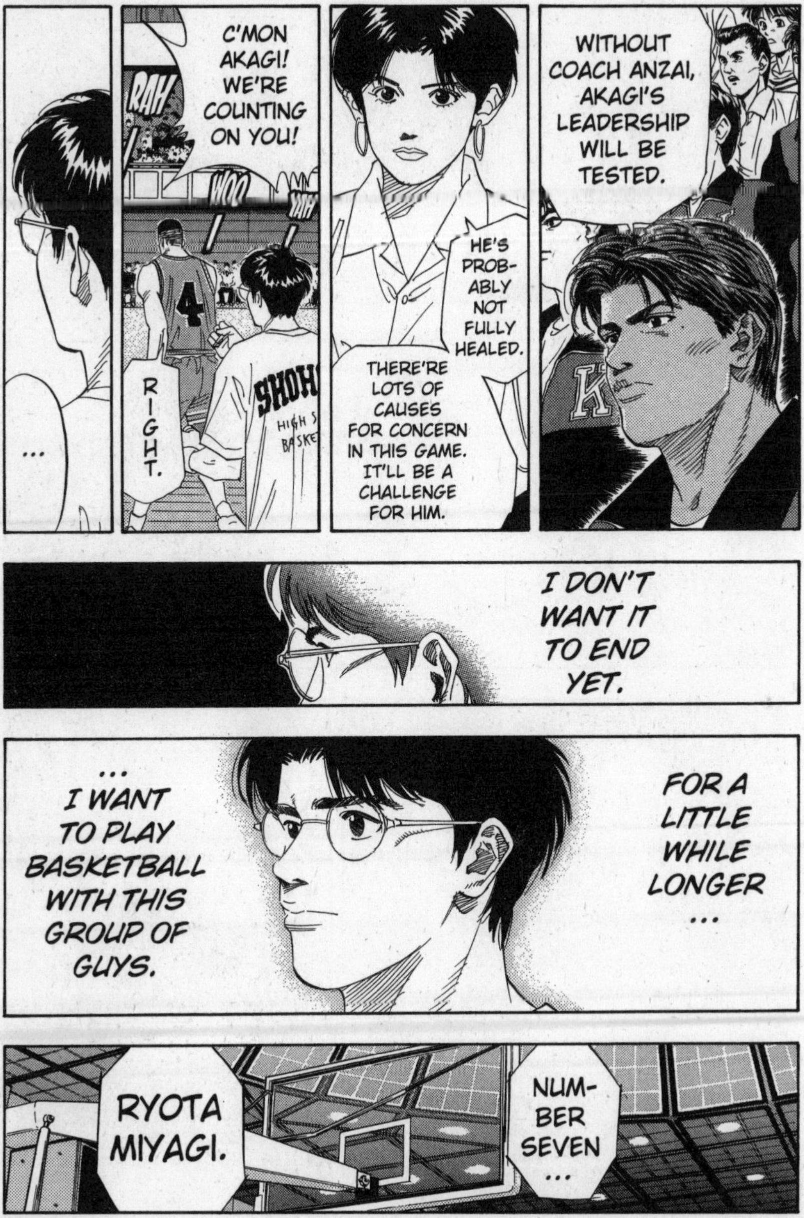

WITHOUT COACH ANZAI, AKAGI'S LEADERSHIP WILL BE TESTED.
HE'S PROB-ABLY NOT FULLY HEALED.
THERE'RE LOTS OF CAUSES FOR CONCERN IN THIS GAME. IT'LL BE A CHALLENGE FOR HIM.
C'MON AKAGI! WE'RE COUNTING ON YOU!
RAH
WOO
YAH
RIGHT.
...
I DON'T WANT IT TO END YET.
FOR A LITTLE WHILE LONGER ...
... I WANT TO PLAY BASKETBALL WITH THIS GROUP OF GUYS.
NUM-BER SEVEN ...
RYOTA MIYAGI.

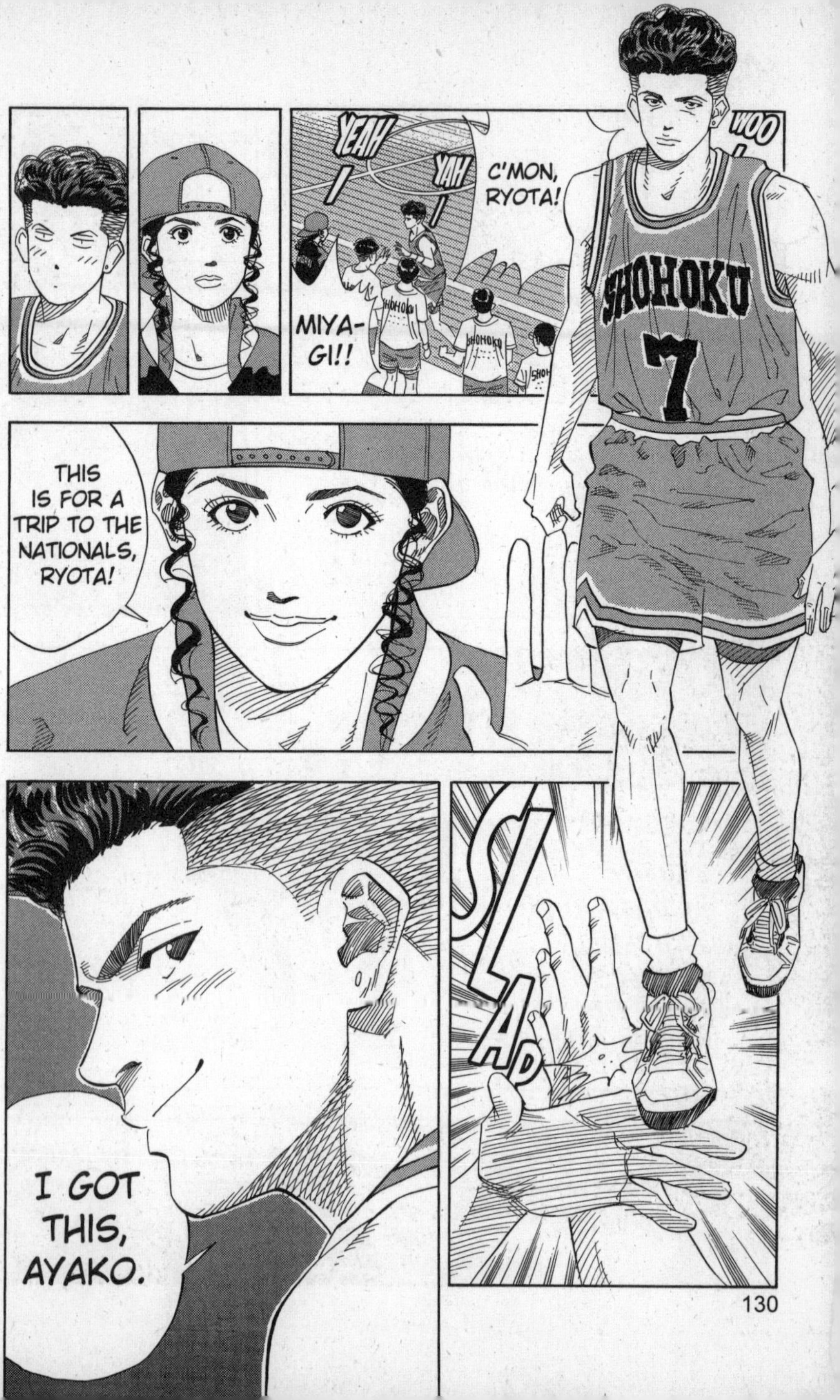
WOO
C'MON, RYOTA!
YEAH
YAH
MIYA-GI!!
SHOHOKU
7
THIS IS FOR A TRIP TO THE NATIONALS, RYOTA!
SLAP
I GOT THIS, AYAKO.

READ THIS WAY

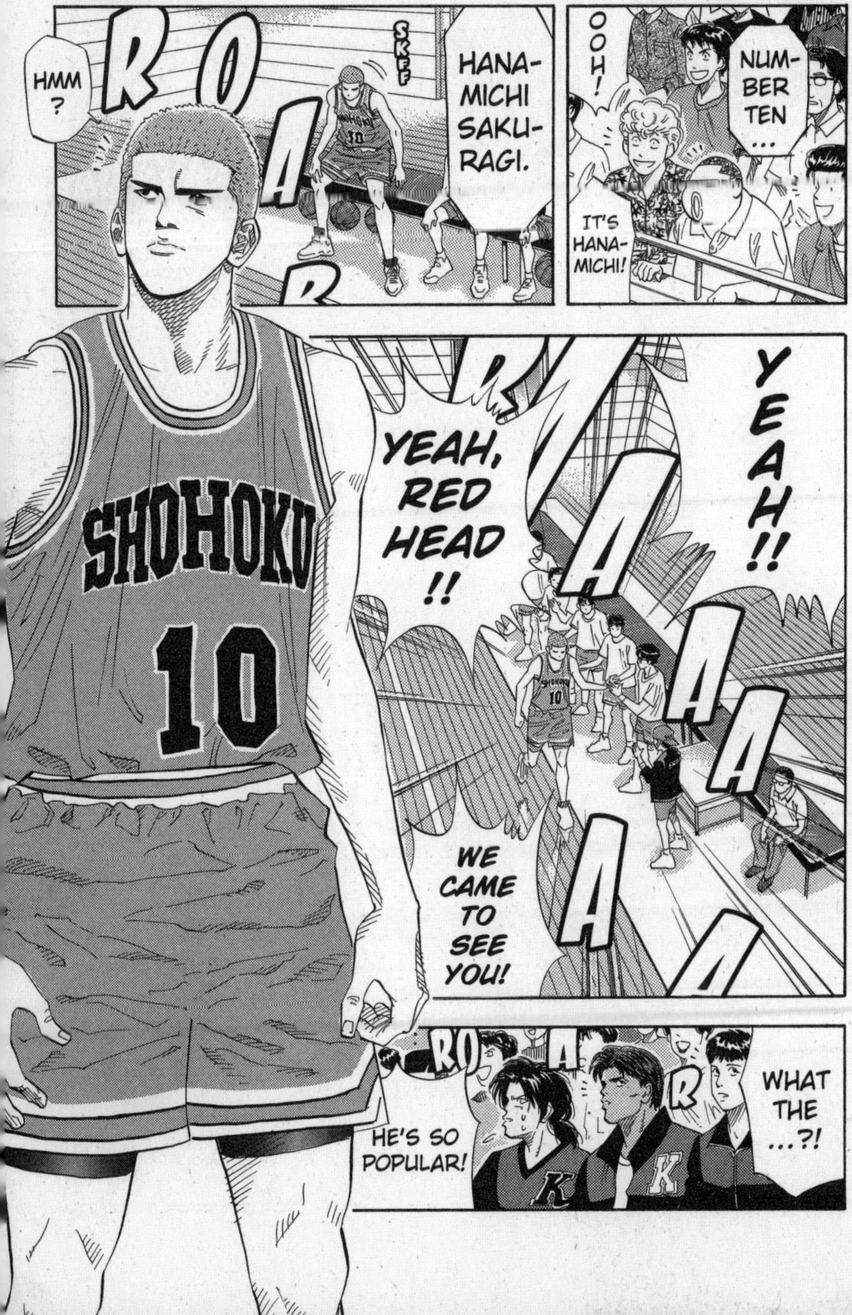
OOH!
NUMBER TEN...
IT'S HANAMICHI!
HANAMICHI SAKURAGI.
SKFF
HMM?
ROAR
YEAH!!
YEAH, RED HEAD!!
WE CAME TO SEE YOU!
WHAT THE...?!
ROAR
HE'S SO POPULAR!

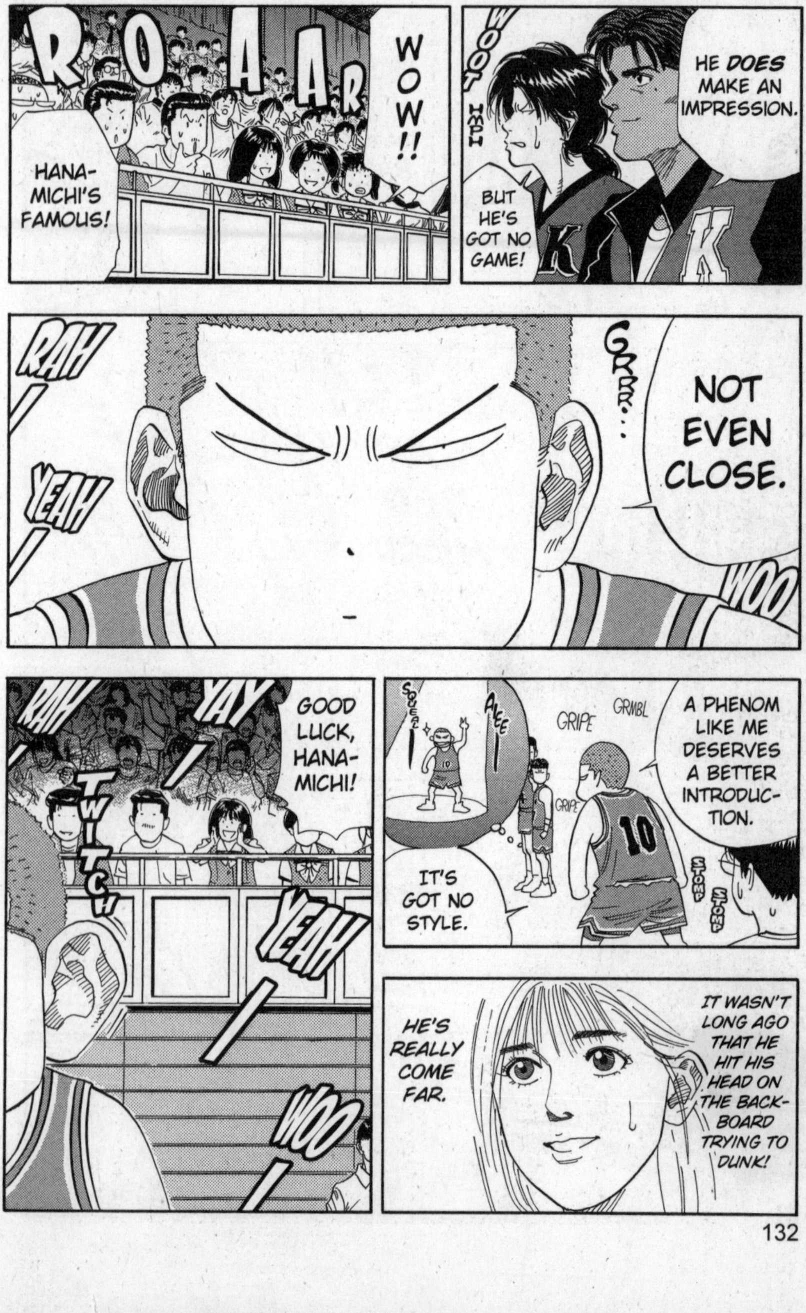
WOOT
HE DOES MAKE AN IMPRESSION.
HMPH
BUT HE'S GOT NO GAME!
ROAAR
WOW!!
HANA-MICHI'S FAMOUS!
GRRR...
NOT EVEN CLOSE.
RAH!
YEAH!
WOO
A PHENOM LIKE ME DESERVES A BETTER INTRODUC-TION.
GRMBL
GRIPE
GRIPE
AIEE!
SQUEAL!
IT'S GOT NO STYLE.
STOMP
STOMP
IT WASN'T LONG AGO THAT HE HIT HIS HEAD ON THE BACK-BOARD TRYING TO DUNK!
HE'S REALLY COME FAR.
GOOD LUCK, HANA-MICHI!
YAY!
RAH!
TWITCH
YEAH!
WOO!

READ THIS WAY

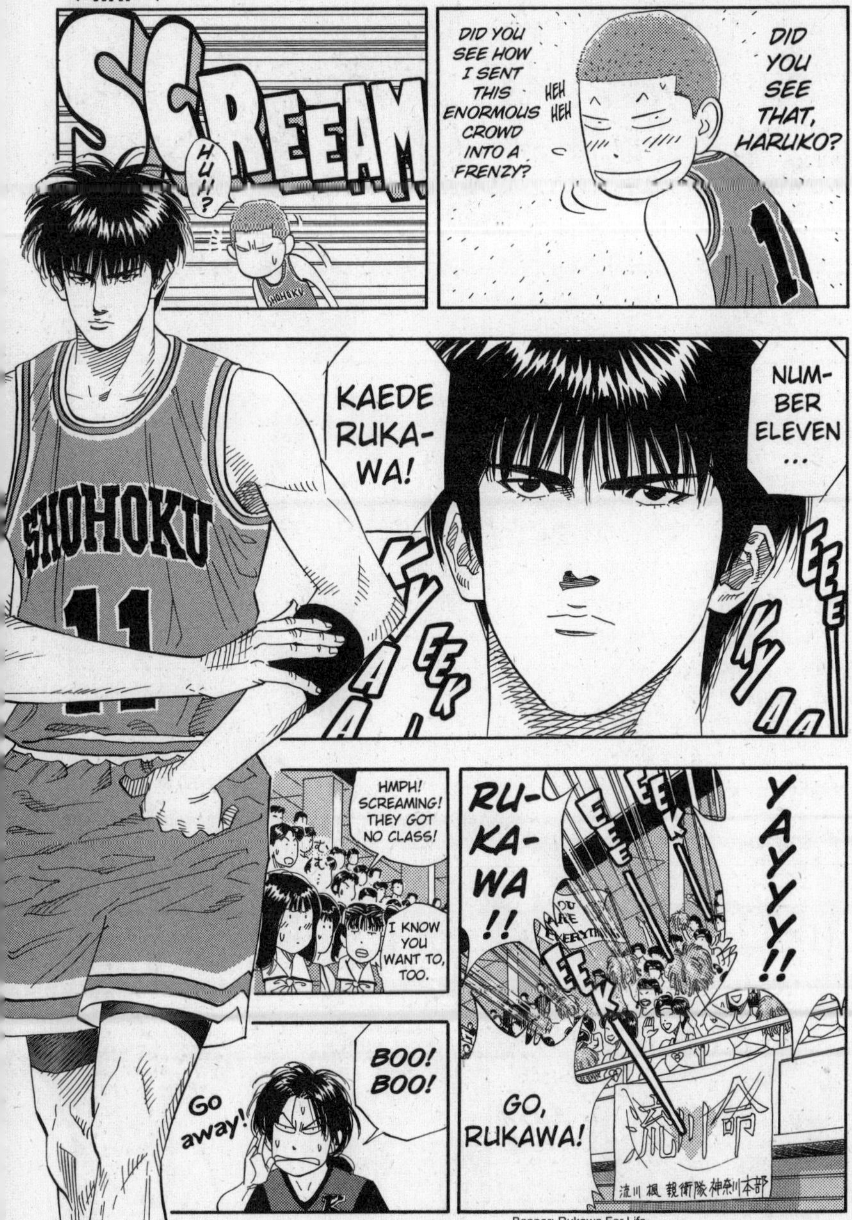
DID YOU SEE THAT, HARUKO?
HEH HEH
DID YOU SEE HOW I SENT THIS ENORMOUS CROWD INTO A FRENZY?
SCREEAM
HUH?
NUMBER ELEVEN...
KAEDE RUKAWA!
KYAAA EEEK
KYAAA EEK
YAYYY!!
RUKAWA!!
EEEK EEEK
GO, RUKAWA!
HMPH! SCREAMING! THEY GOT NO CLASS!
I KNOW YOU WANT TO, TOO.
BOO! BOO!
Go away!

Banner: Rukawa For Life
Rukawa Kaede Fan Club Kanagawa Chapter

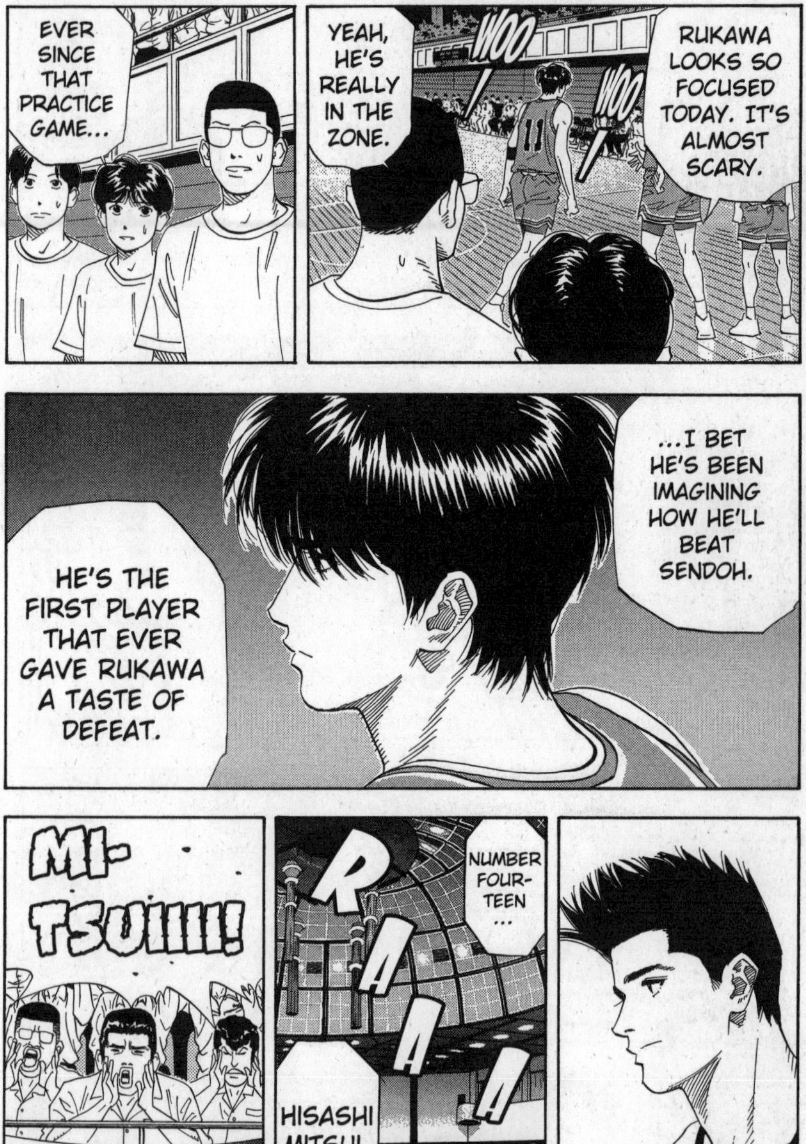
WOO
WOO
RUKAWA LOOKS SO FOCUSED TODAY. IT'S ALMOST SCARY.
YEAH, HE'S REALLY IN THE ZONE.
EVER SINCE THAT PRACTICE GAME...
...I BET HE'S BEEN IMAGINING HOW HE'LL BEAT SENDOH.
HE'S THE FIRST PLAYER THAT EVER GAVE RUKAWA A TASTE OF DEFEAT.
NUMBER FOURTEEN...
RAAAA
HISASHI MITSUI.
MI-TSUIIIII!
炎の男

Banner: Man on Fire

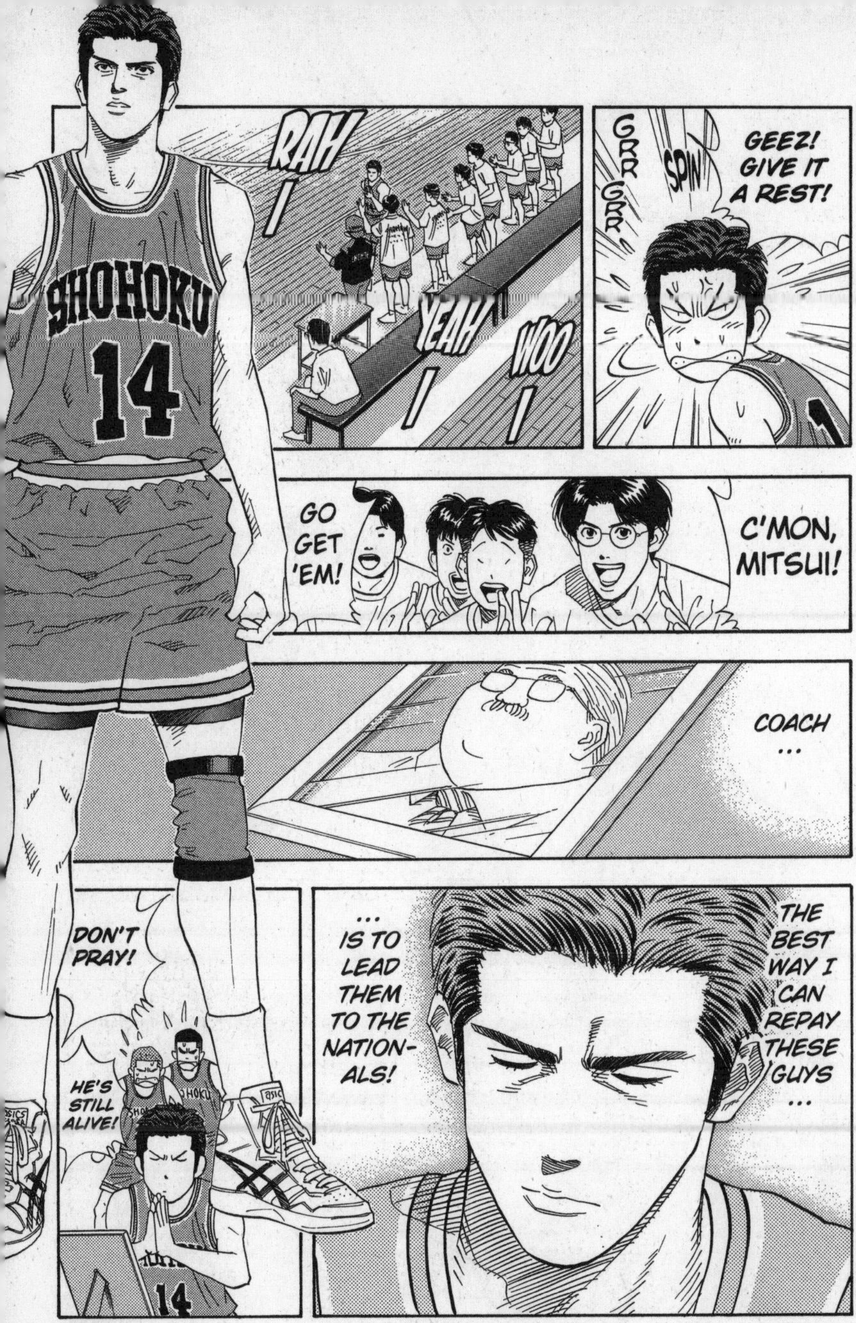
GEEZ! GIVE IT A REST!
SPIN
GRR GRR
RAH
YEAH
WOO
C'MON, MITSUI!
GO GET 'EM!
COACH ...
THE BEST WAY I CAN REPAY THESE GUYS ...
... IS TO LEAD THEM TO THE NATION-ALS!
DON'T PRAY!
HE'S STILL ALIVE!

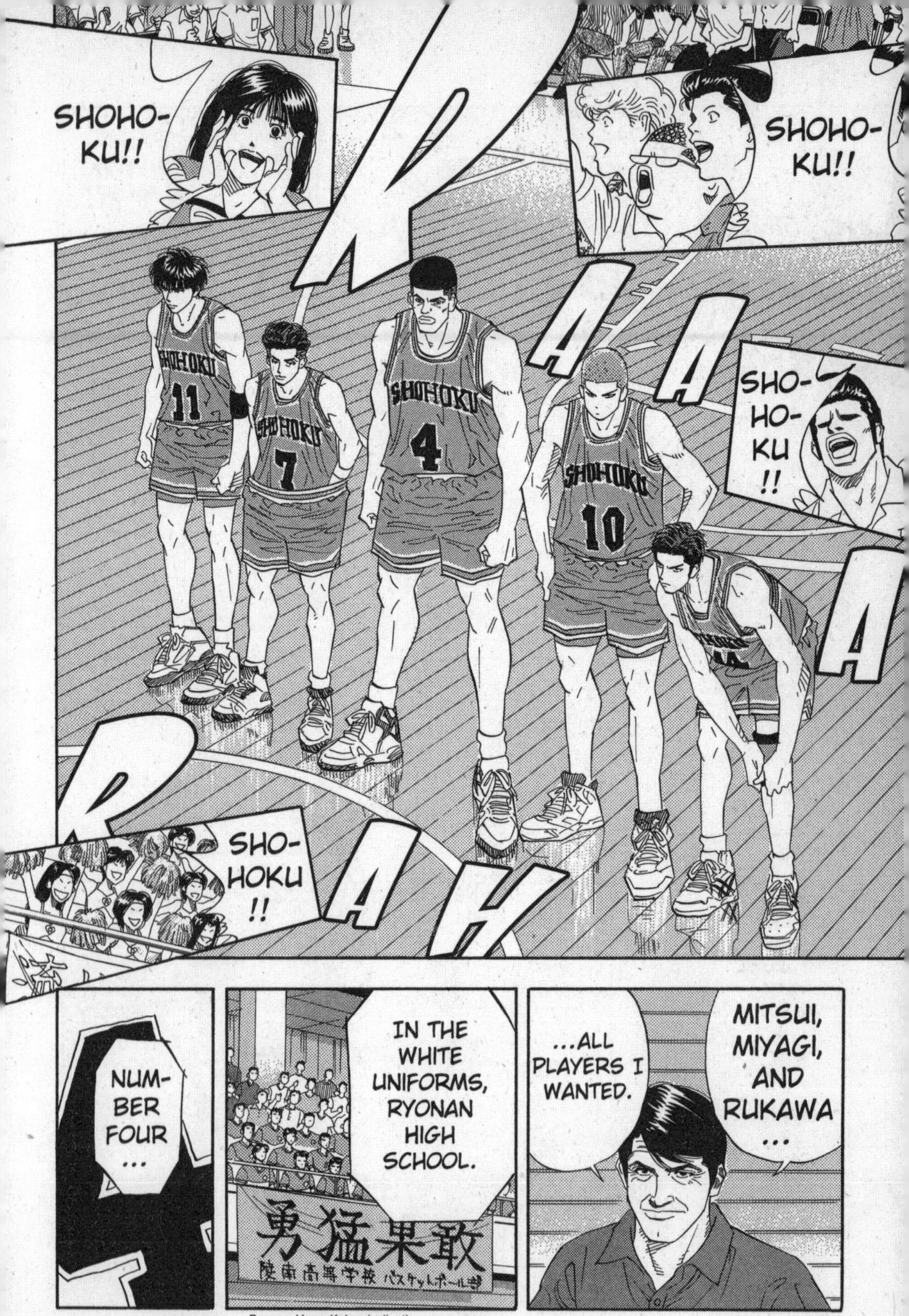
SHOHO-KU!!
SHOHO-KU!!
K
A-A
A
A
SHO-HO-KU!!
R
A
H
SHO-HOKU!!
MITSUI, MIYAGI, AND RUKAWA...
...ALL PLAYERS I WANTED.
IN THE WHITE UNIFORMS, RYONAN HIGH SCHOOL.
勇猛果敢
陵南高等学校 バスケットボール部
NUMBER FOUR...

Banner: *Yumo Kakan* (valiant)
Ryonan High School Basketball Team

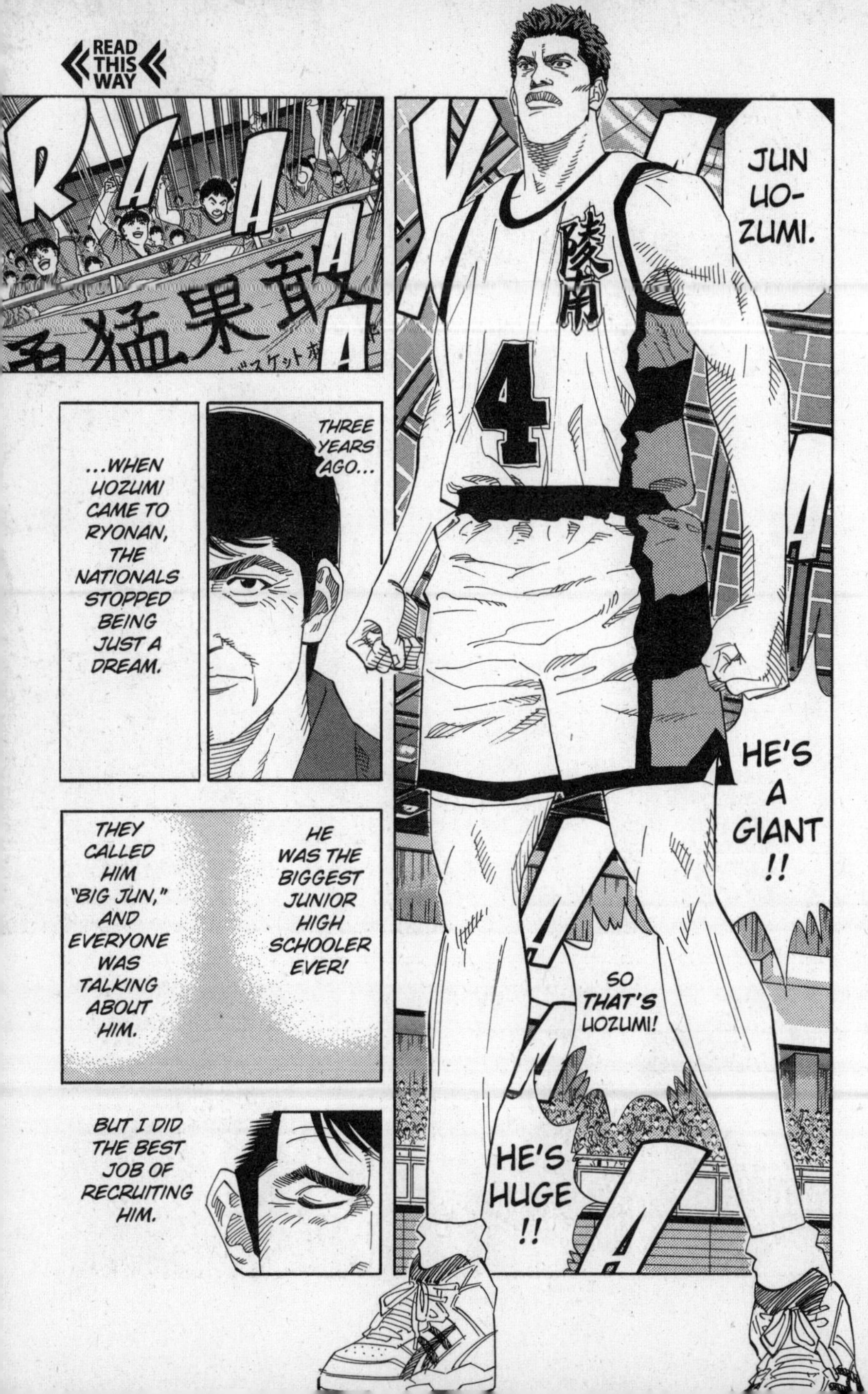
READ THIS WAY
JUN UO-ZUMI.
HE'S A GIANT!!
SO THAT'S UOZUMI!
HE'S HUGE!!
RAAAAA
THREE YEARS AGO...
...WHEN UOZUMI CAME TO RYONAN, THE NATIONALS STOPPED BEING JUST A DREAM.
HE WAS THE BIGGEST JUNIOR HIGH SCHOOLER EVER!
THEY CALLED HIM "BIG JUN," AND EVERYONE WAS TALKING ABOUT HIM.
BUT I DID THE BEST JOB OF RECRUITING HIM.

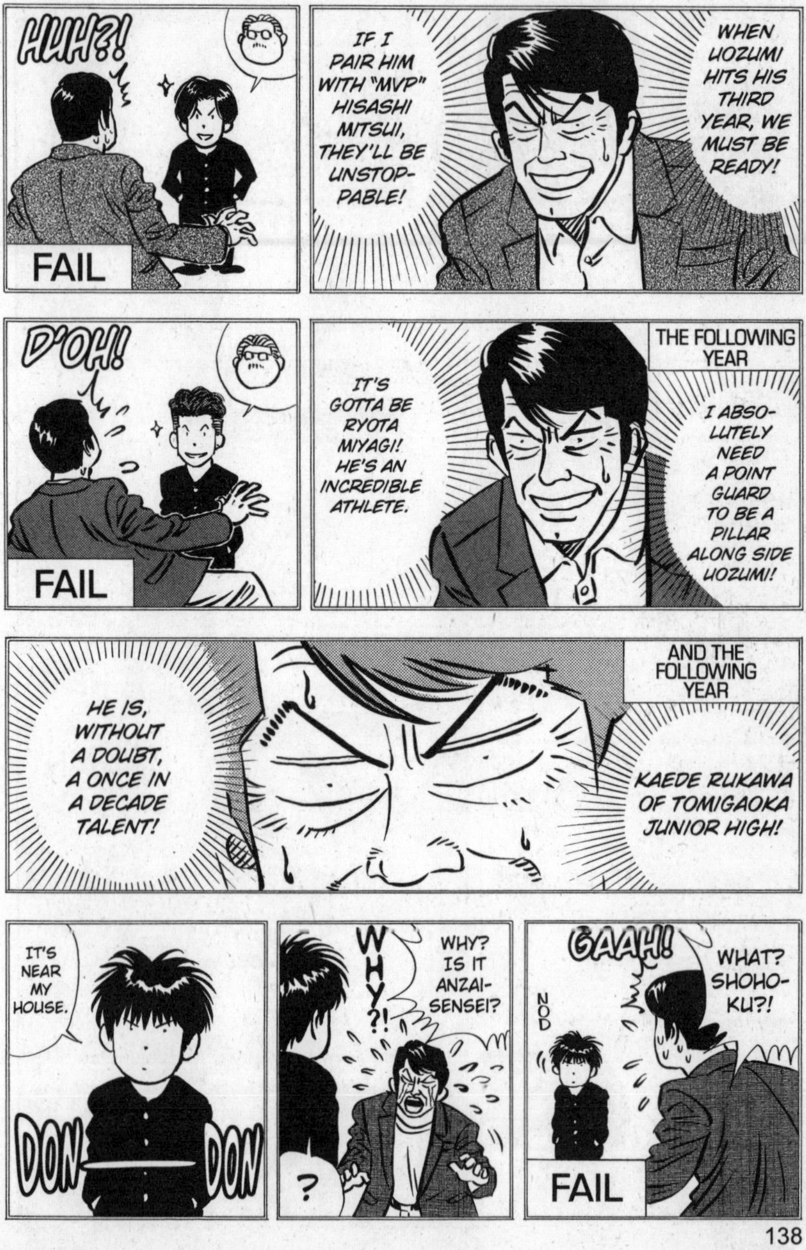
WHEN UOZUMI HITS HIS THIRD YEAR, WE MUST BE READY!
IF I PAIR HIM WITH "MVP" HISASHI MITSUI, THEY'LL BE UNSTOP-PABLE!
HUH?!
FAIL
THE FOLLOWING YEAR
I ABSO-LUTELY NEED A POINT GUARD TO BE A PILLAR ALONG SIDE UOZUMI!
IT'S GOTTA BE RYOTA MIYAGI! HE'S AN INCREDIBLE ATHLETE.
D'OH!
FAIL
AND THE FOLLOWING YEAR
KAEDE RUKAWA OF TOMIGAOKA JUNIOR HIGH!
HE IS, WITHOUT A DOUBT, A ONCE IN A DECADE TALENT!
WHAT? SHOHO-KU?!
GAAH!
NOD
FAIL
WHY? IS IT ANZAI-SENSEI?
WHY?!
?
IT'S NEAR MY HOUSE.
DON
DON

READ THIS WAY

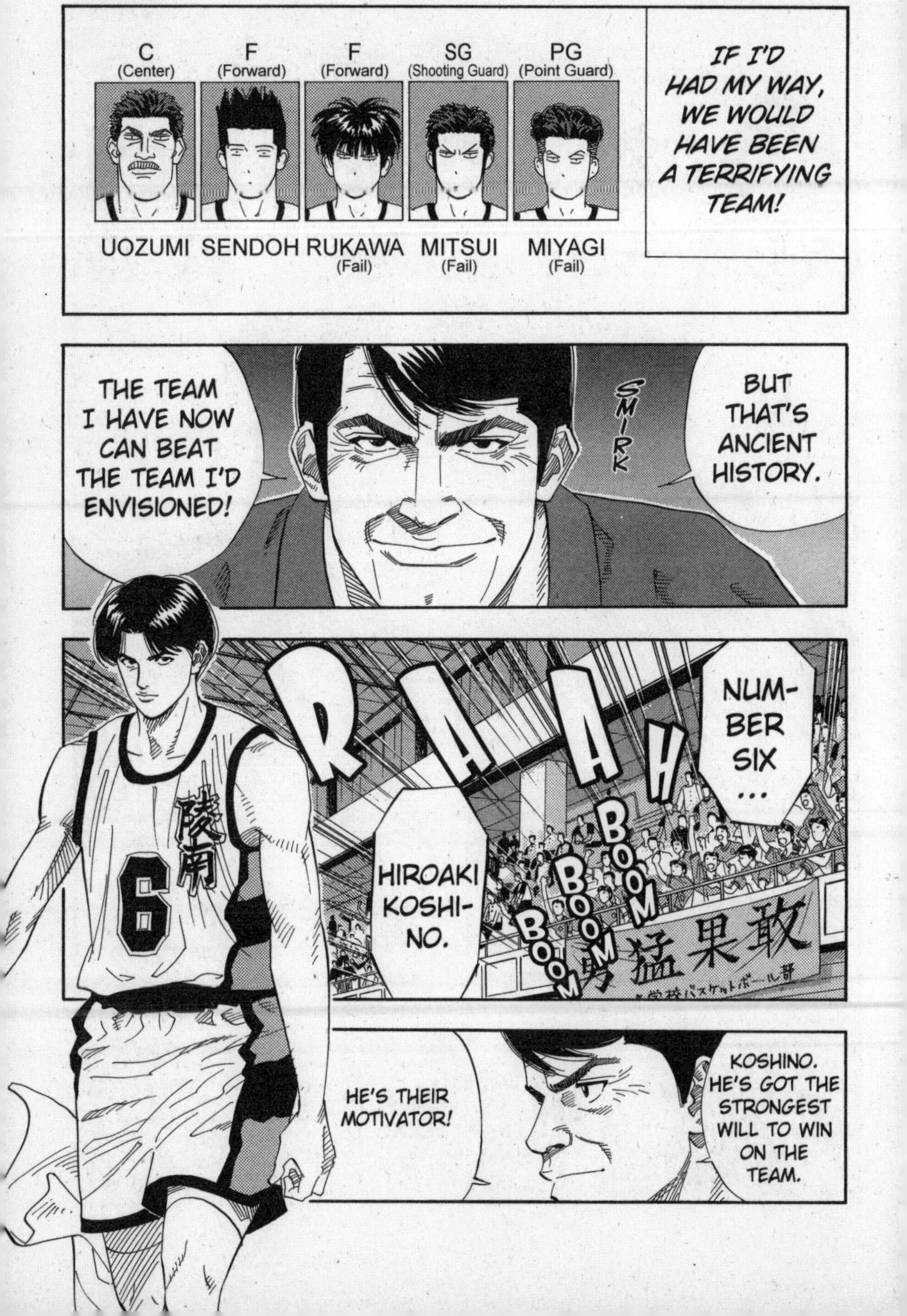
IF I'D HAD MY WAY, WE WOULD HAVE BEEN A TERRIFYING TEAM!
C (Center)
F (Forward)
F (Forward)
SG (Shooting Guard)
PG (Point Guard)
UOZUMI
SENDOH
RUKAWA (Fail)
MITSUI (Fail)
MIYAGI (Fail)
BUT THAT'S ANCIENT HISTORY.
SMIRK
THE TEAM I HAVE NOW CAN BEAT THE TEAM I'D ENVISIONED!
NUMBER SIX...
RAAAH
HIROAKI KOSHINO.
BOOM BOOM BOOM BOOM
KOSHINO. HE'S GOT THE STRONGEST WILL TO WIN ON THE TEAM.
HE'S THEIR MOTIVATOR!

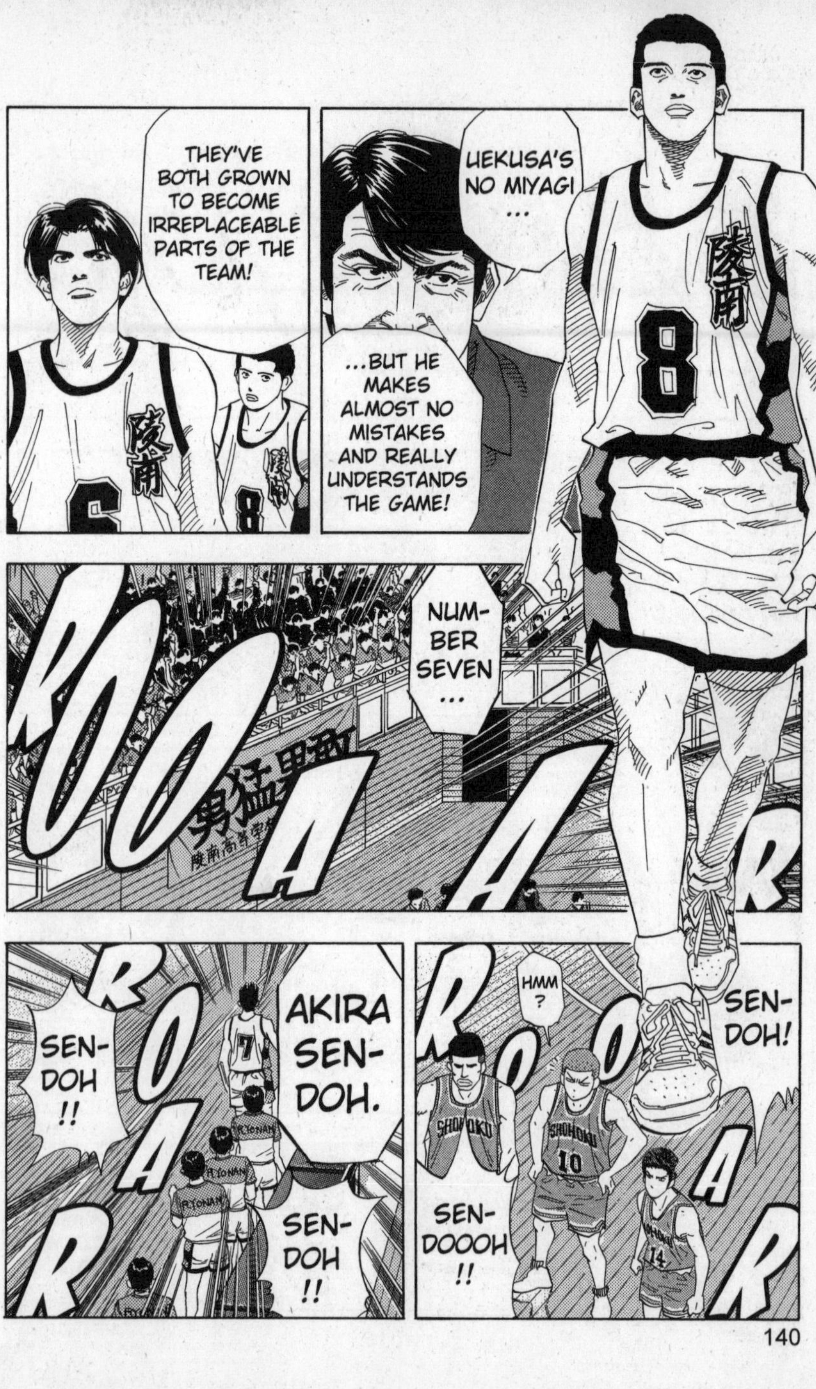
UEKUSA'S NO MIYAGI ...
...BUT HE MAKES ALMOST NO MISTAKES AND REALLY UNDERSTANDS THE GAME!
THEY'VE BOTH GROWN TO BECOME IRREPLACEABLE PARTS OF THE TEAM!
NUM-BER SEVEN ...
WOOAAR
HMM ?
SEN-DOH!
ROOOAR
SEN-DOOOH !!
ROAR
AKIRA SEN-DOH.
SEN-DOH !!
SEN-DOH !!

READ THIS WAY

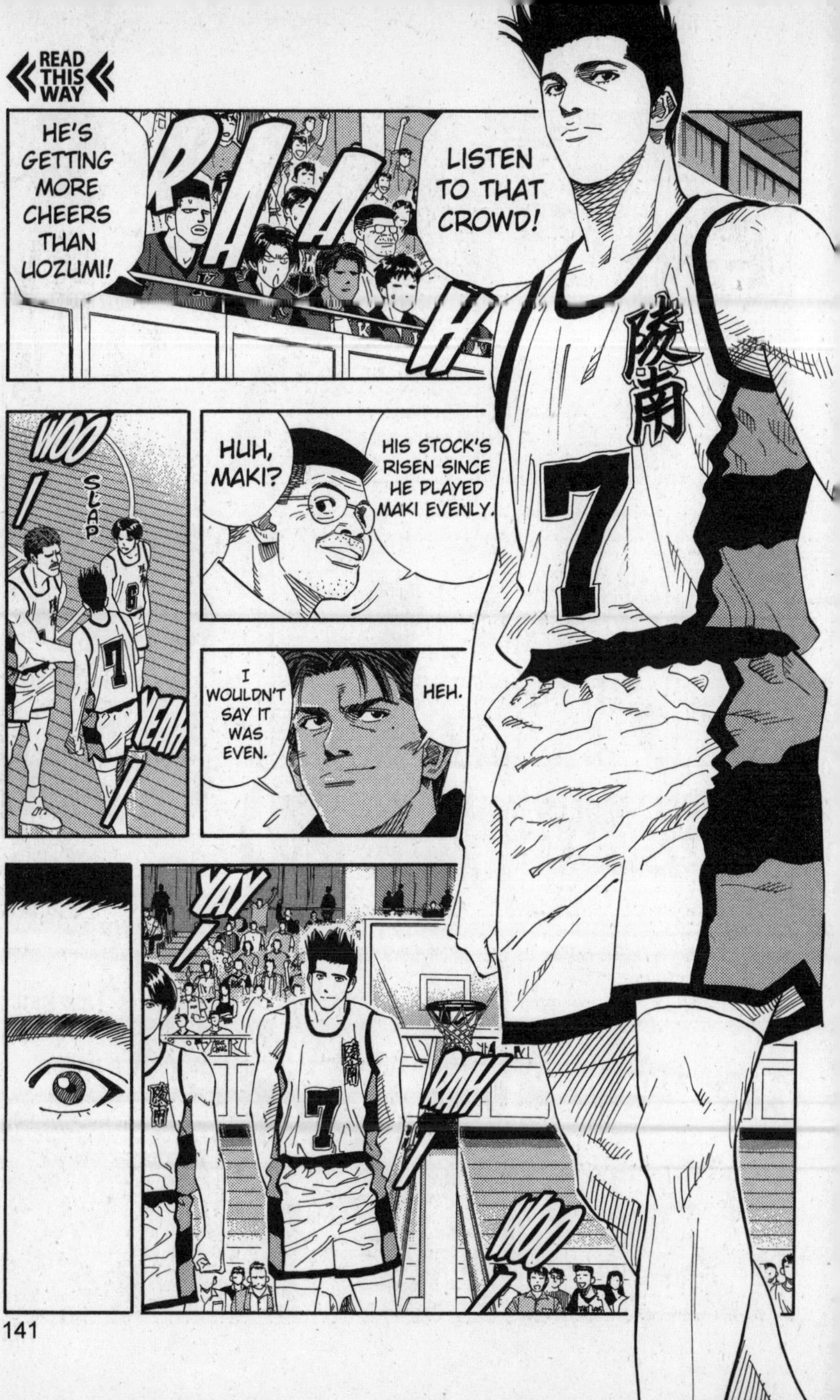
LISTEN TO THAT CROWD!
RAAH
HE'S GETTING MORE CHEERS THAN UOZUMI!
HIS STOCK'S RISEN SINCE HE PLAYED MAKI EVENLY.
HUH, MAKI?
HEH.
I WOULDN'T SAY IT WAS EVEN.
WOO!
SLAP
YEAH!
YAY!
RAH
WOO!

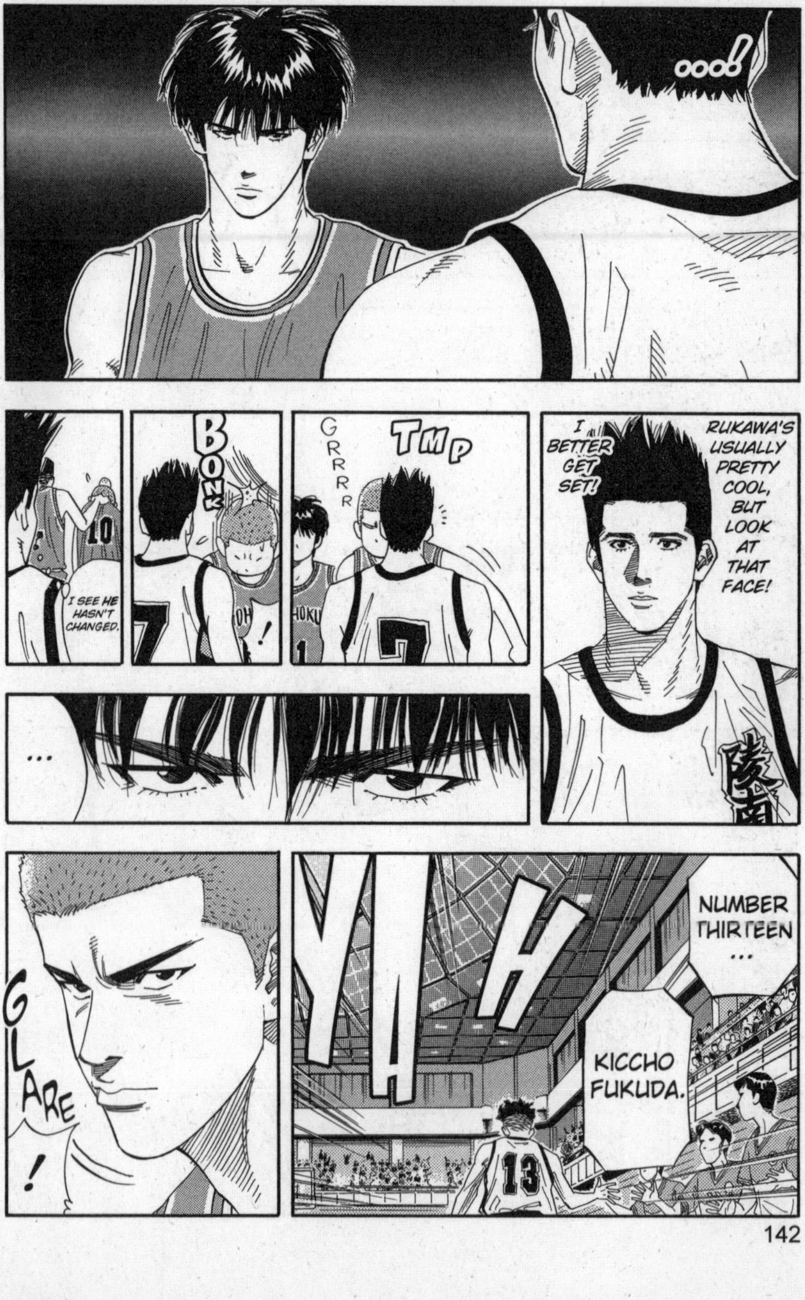
ooo!
RUKAWA'S USUALLY PRETTY COOL, BUT LOOK AT THAT FACE!
I BETTER GET SET!
TMP
GRRRR
BONK
!
I SEE HE HASN'T CHANGED.
...
NUMBER THIRTEEN ...
KICCHO FUKUDA.
YAAH
GLARE
!

READ THIS WAY

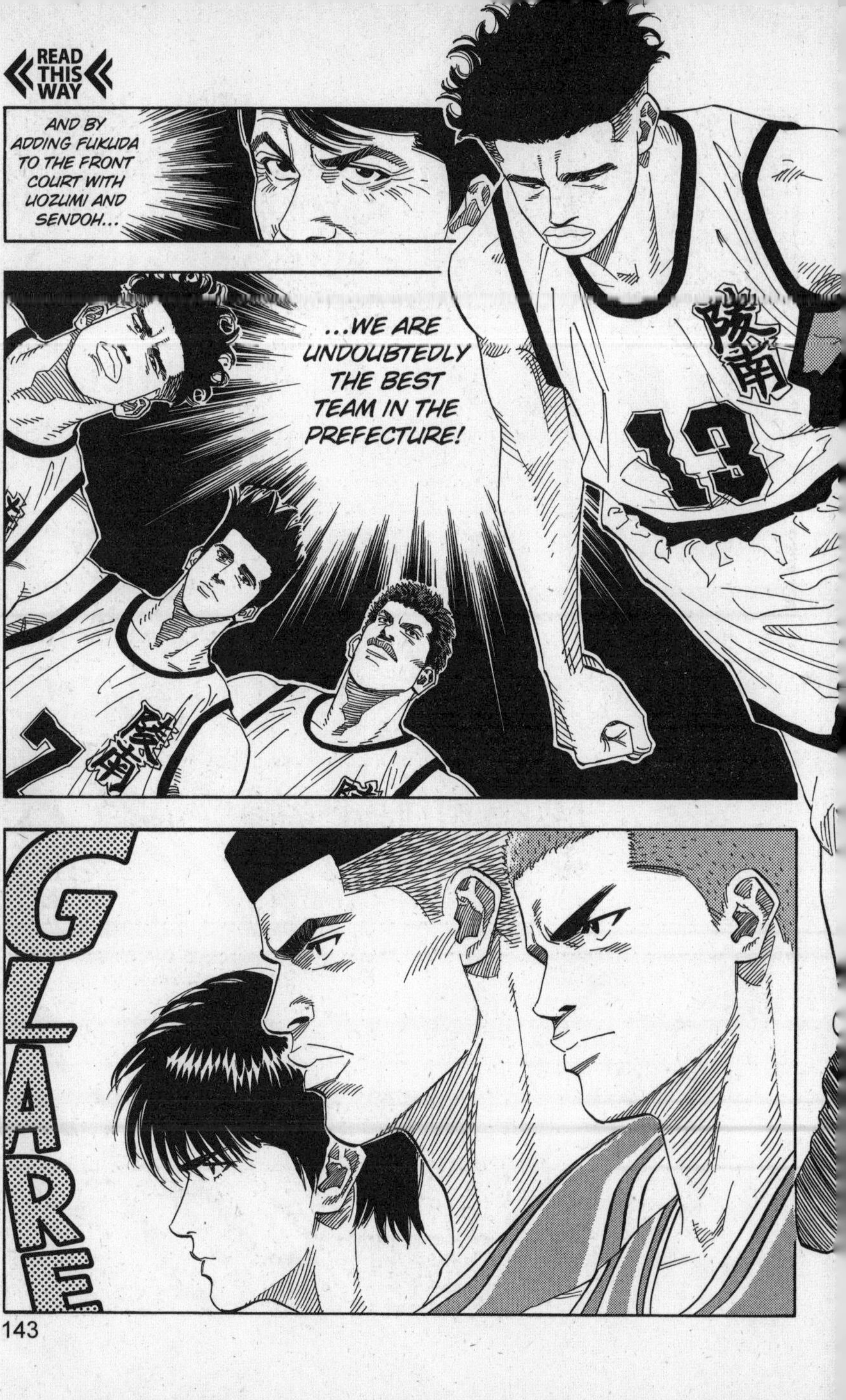
AND BY ADDING FUKUDA TO THE FRONT COURT WITH UOZUMI AND SENDOH...
...WE ARE UNDOUBTEDLY THE BEST TEAM IN THE PREFECTURE!
GLARE

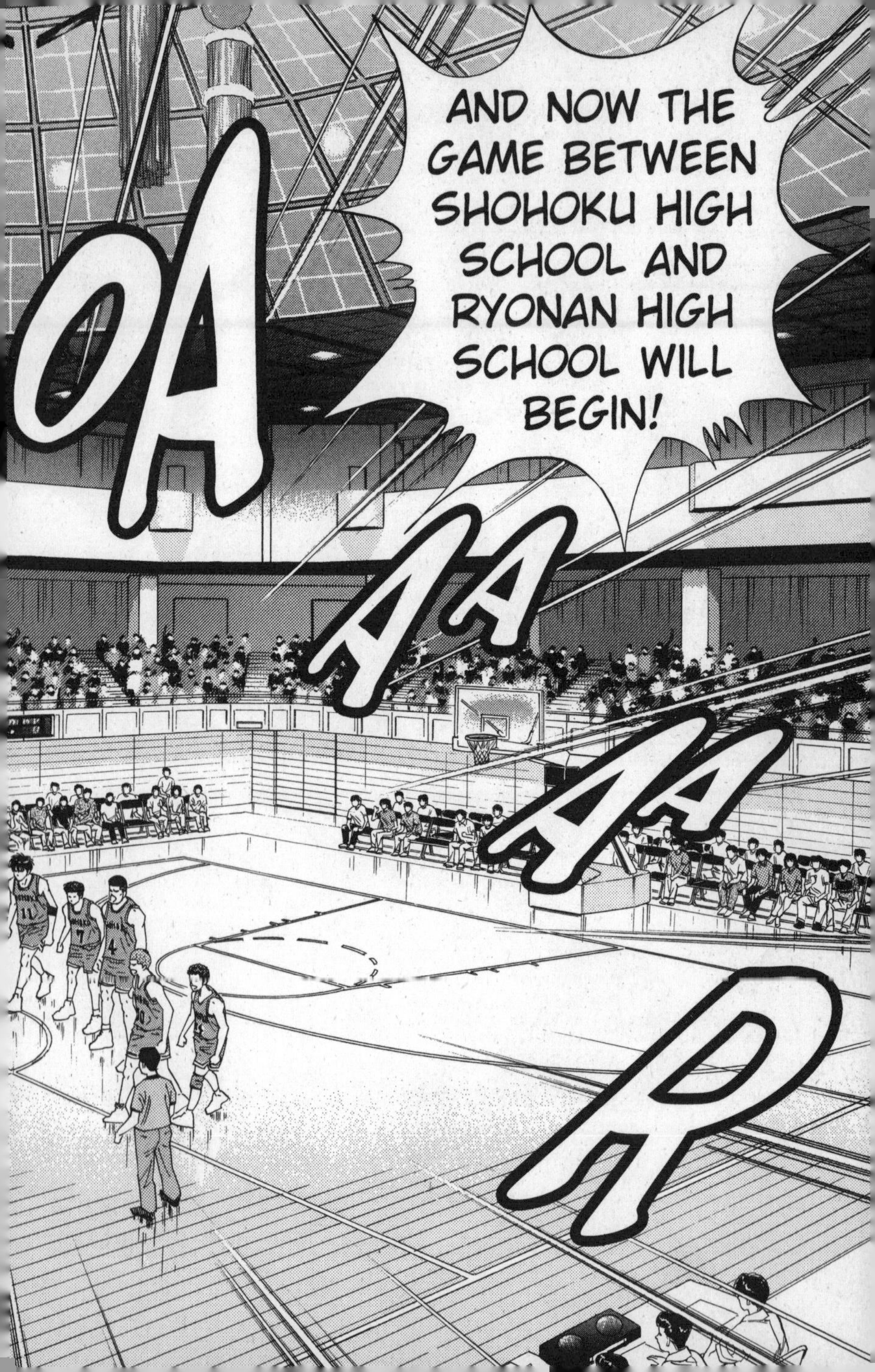
AND NOW THE GAME BETWEEN SHOHOKU HIGH SCHOOL AND RYONAN HIGH SCHOOL WILL BEGIN!
OAAAR

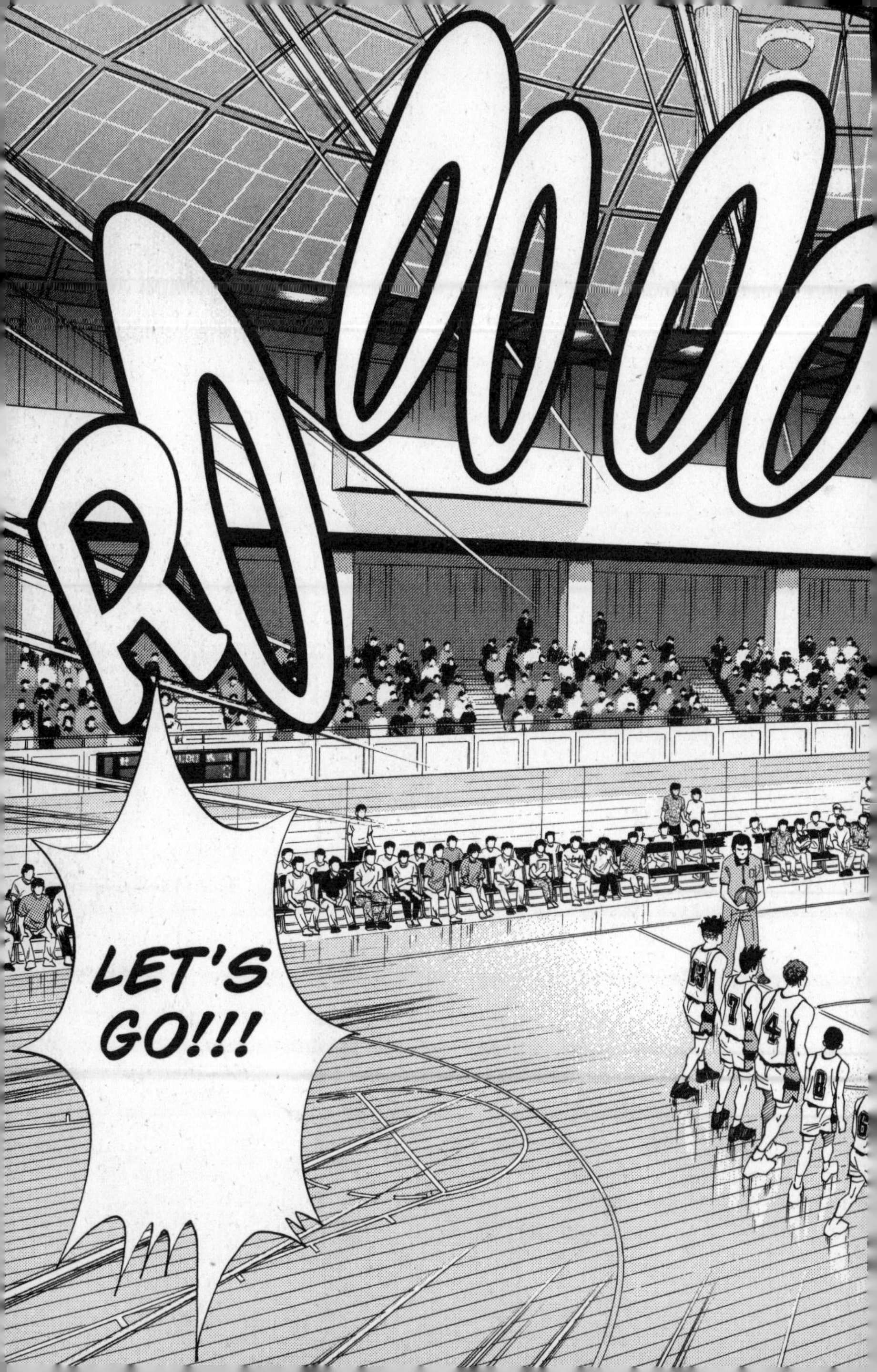
LET'S GO!!!

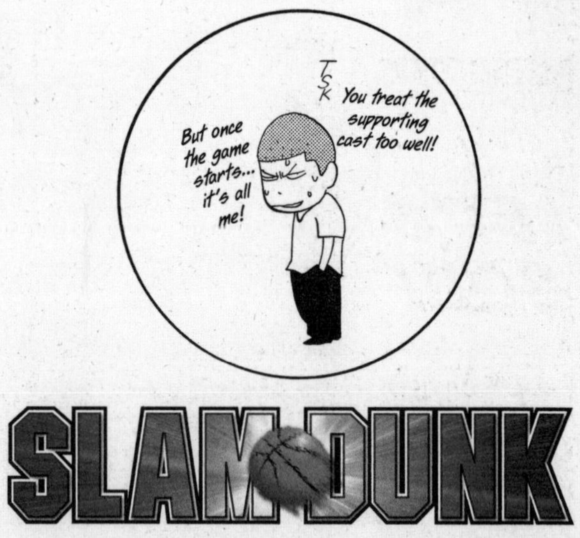
TSK
You treat the supporting cast too well!
But once the game starts... it's all me!

SLAM DUNK

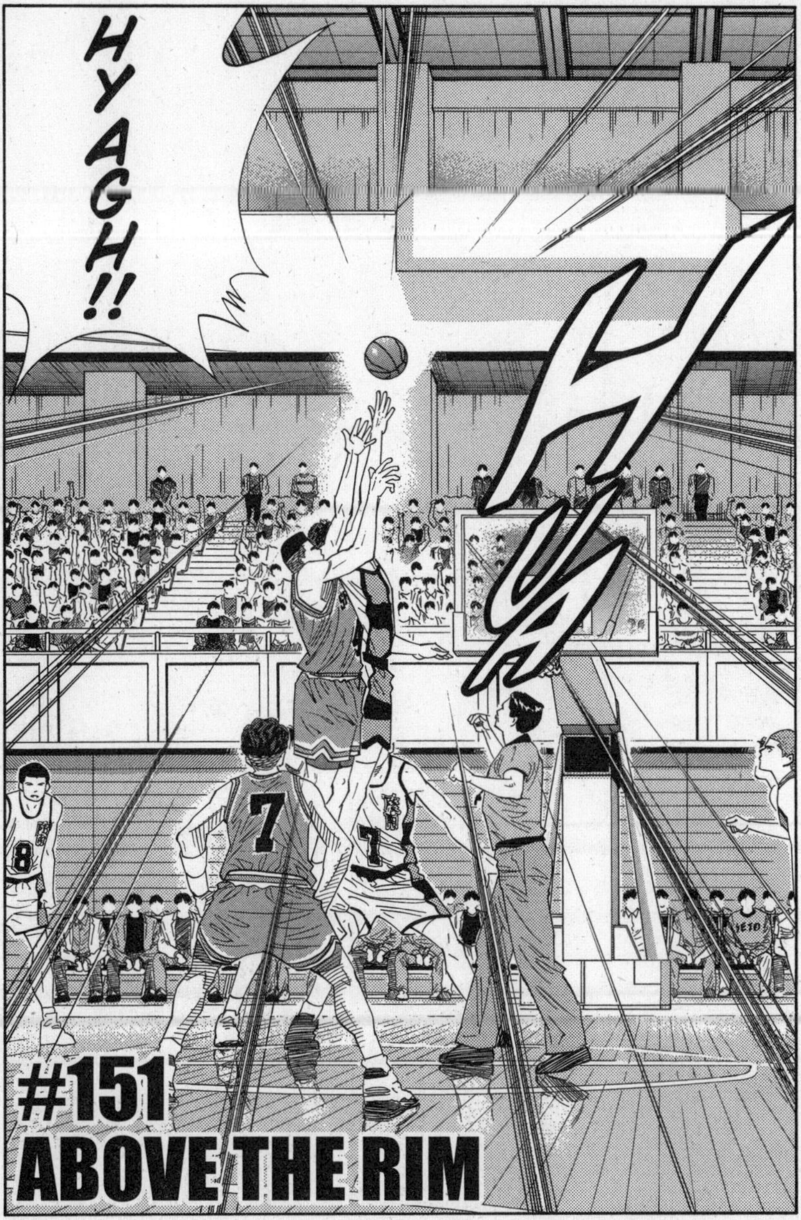
HYAGH!!

#151 ABOVE THE RIM

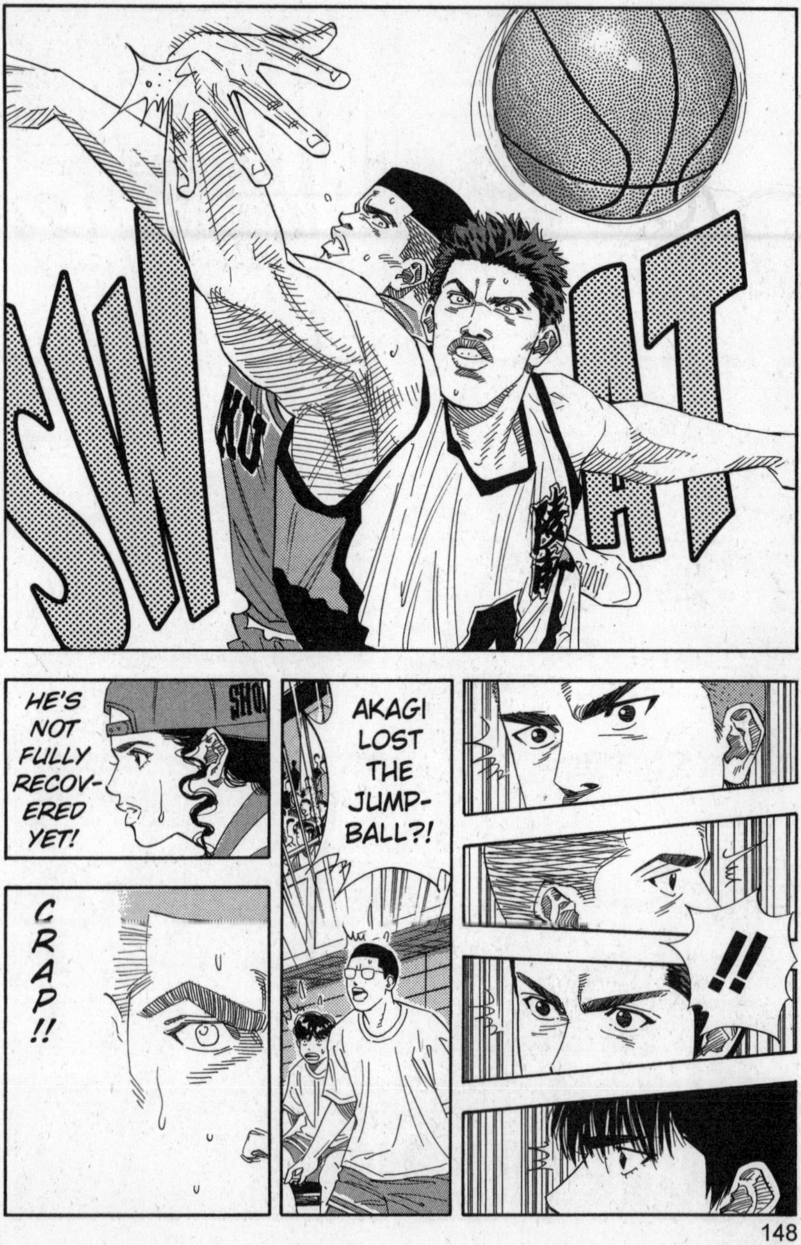
SWAT
!!
AKAGI LOST THE JUMP-BALL?!
HE'S NOT FULLY RECOVERED YET!
CRAP!!

READ THIS WAY

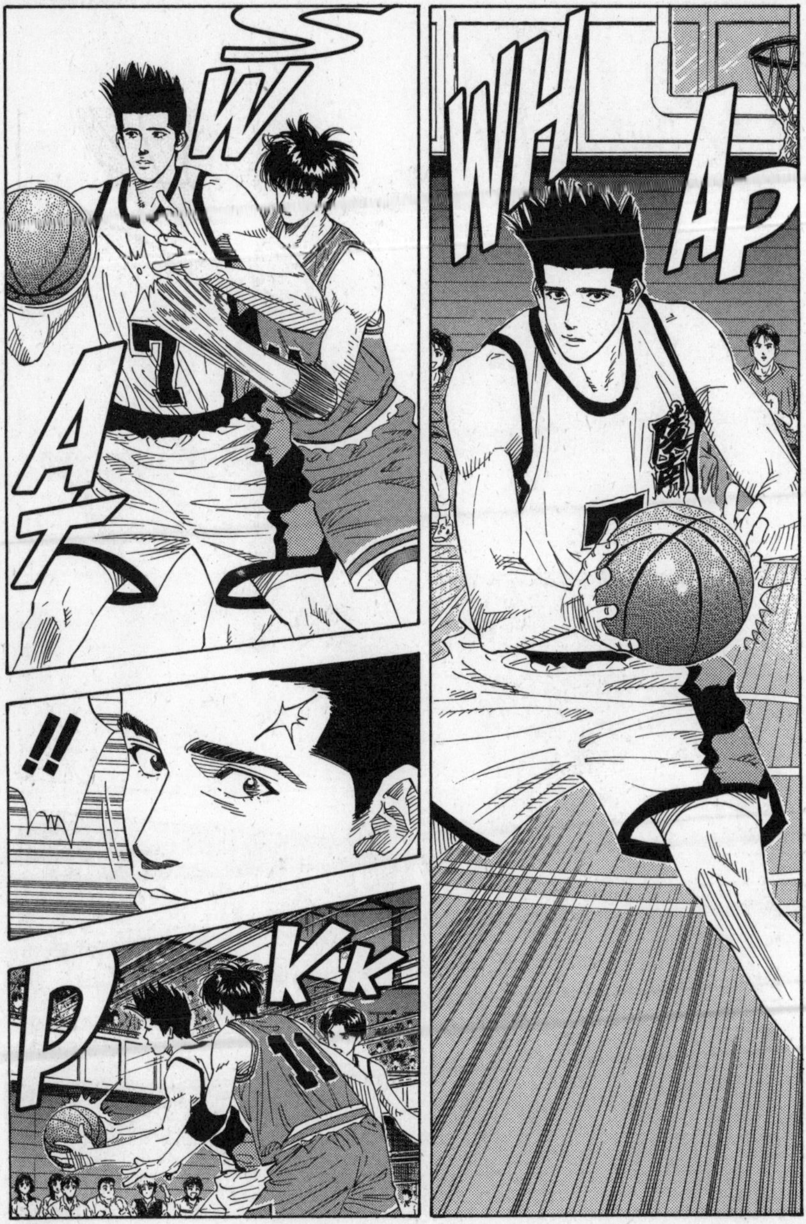

WHAP
SWAT
!!
PKK

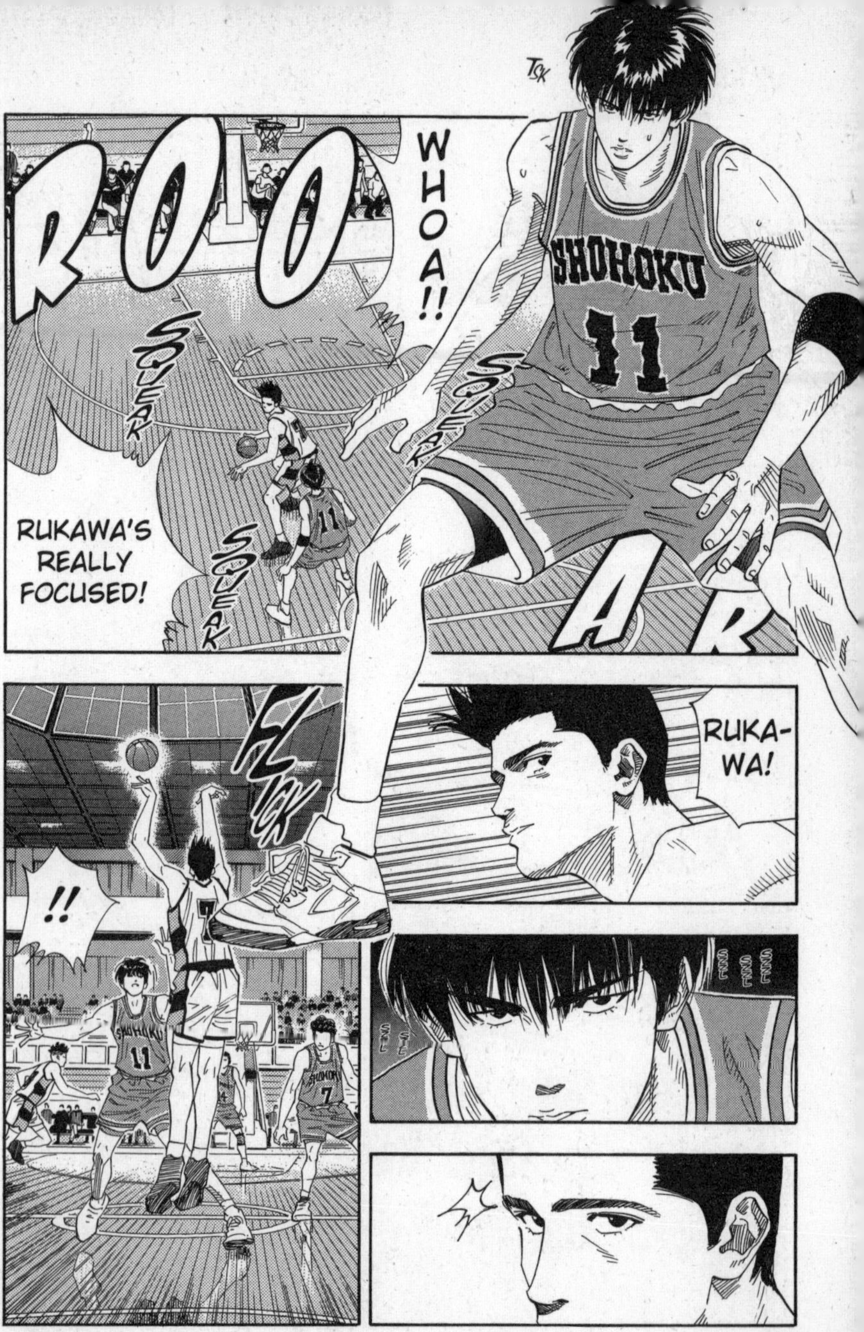
TSK
SQUEAK
AR
ROOO
WHOA!!
SQUEAK
SQUEAK
RUKAWA'S REALLY FOCUSED!
RUKA-WA!
FLICK
!!

READ THIS WAY

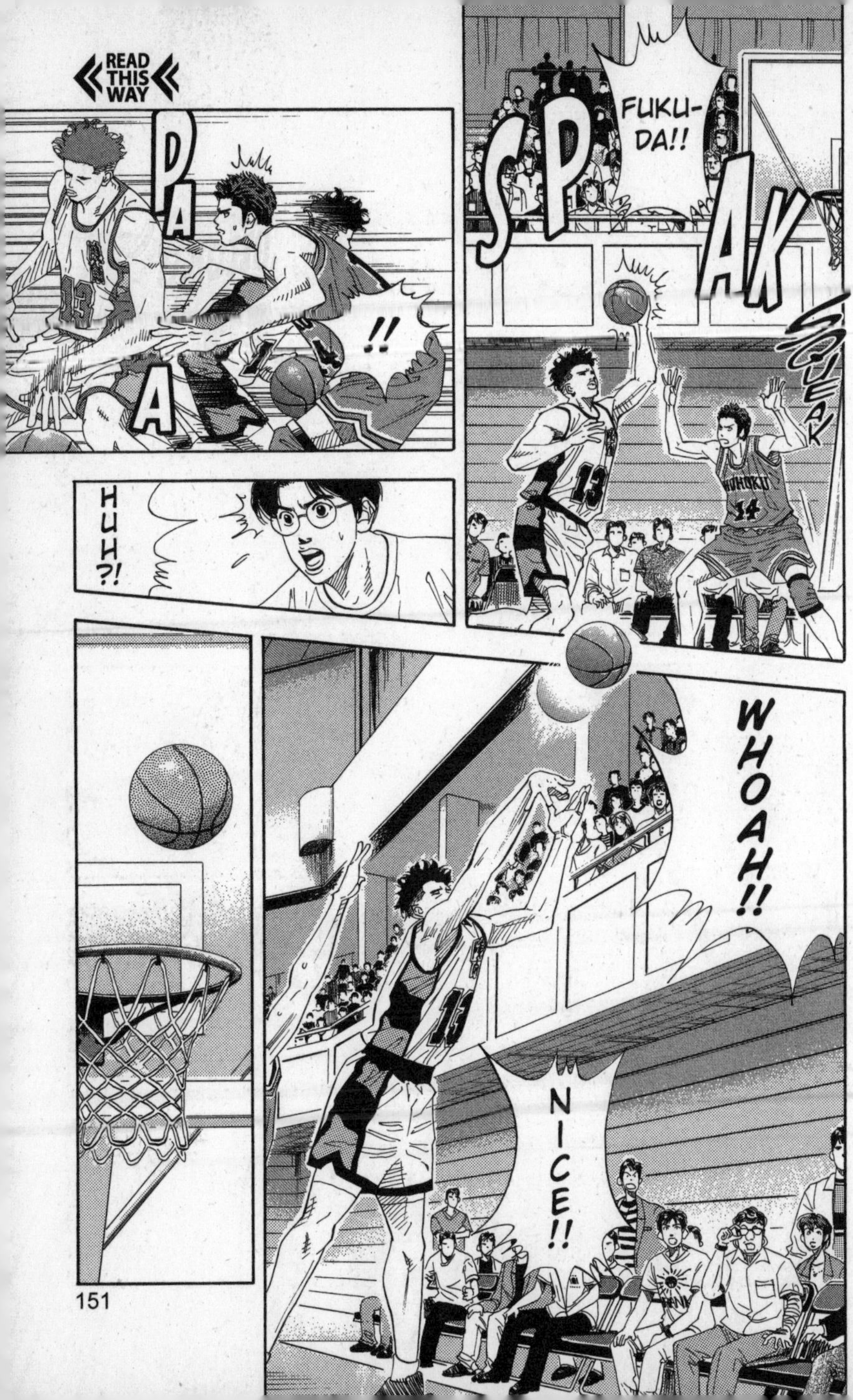

FUKU-DA!!
SPAK
SQUEAK
PA
A
!!
HUH?!
WHOAH!!
NICE!!

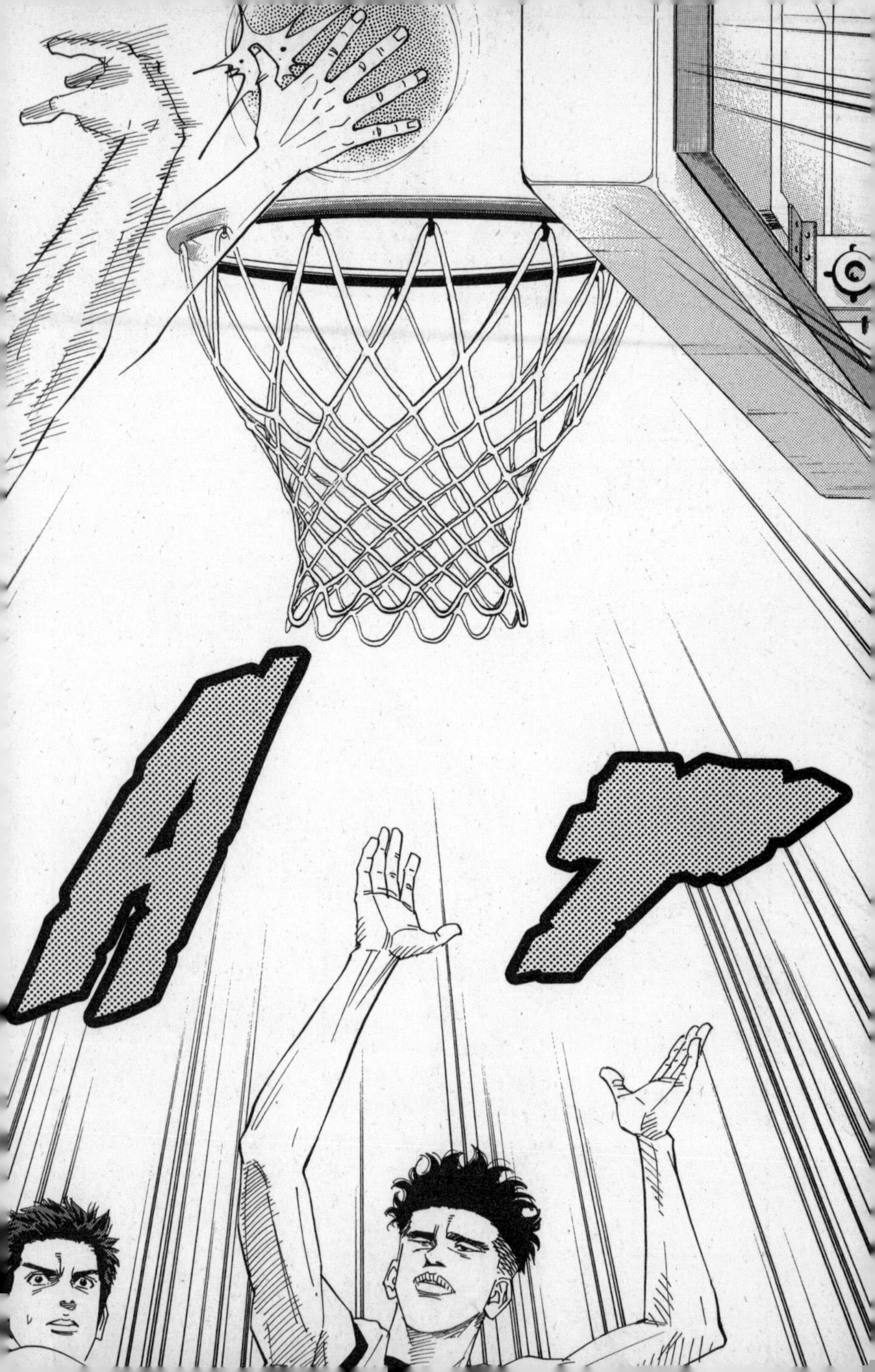

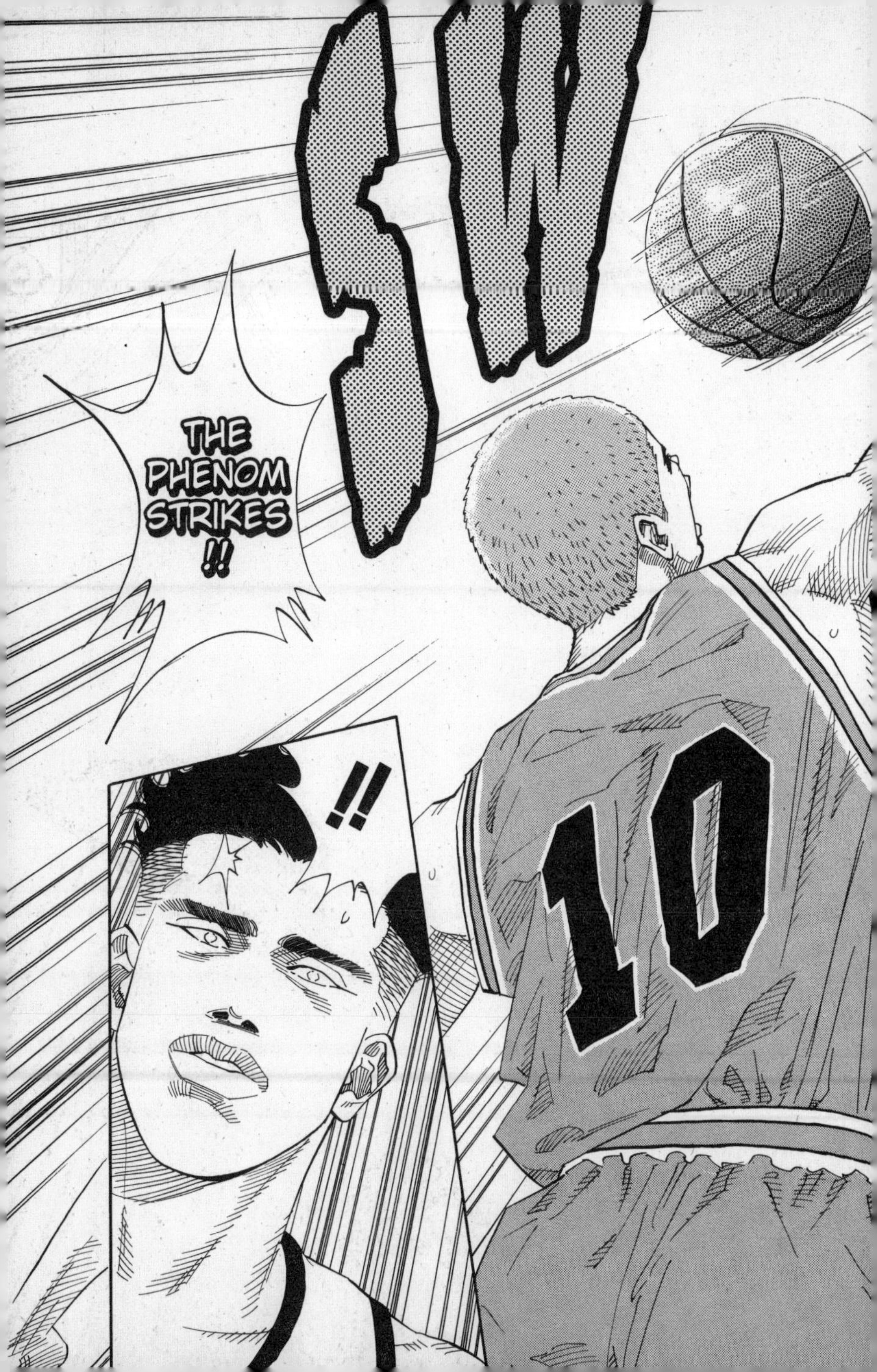
THE PHENOM STRIKES !!
!!

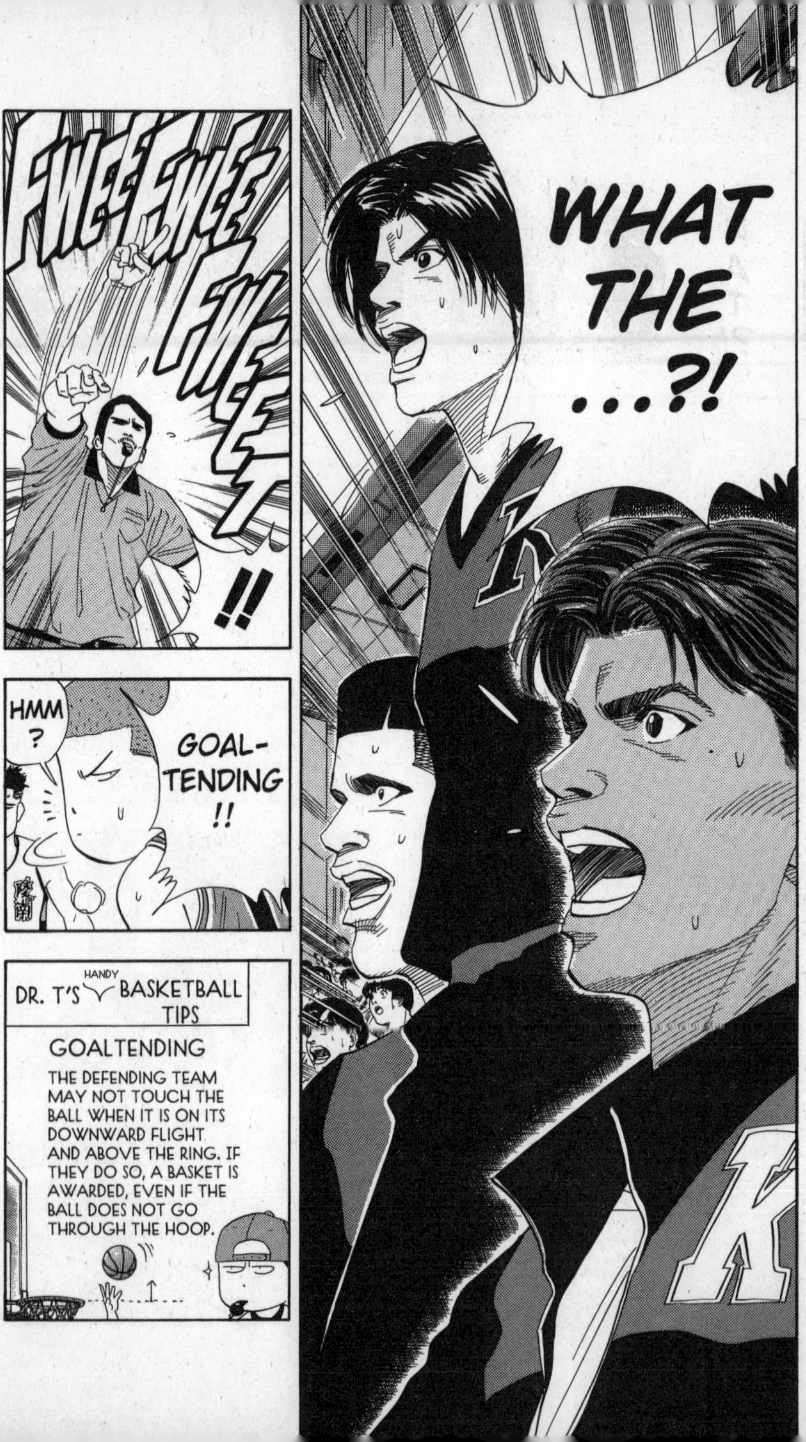
WHAT THE ...?!
FWEE FWEE
FWEET !!
GOAL-TENDING !!
HMM ?
DR. T'S HANDY BASKETBALL TIPS
GOALTENDING
THE DEFENDING TEAM MAY NOT TOUCH THE BALL WHEN IT IS ON ITS DOWNWARD FLIGHT AND ABOVE THE RING. IF THEY DO SO, A BASKET IS AWARDED, EVEN IF THE BALL DOES NOT GO THROUGH THE HOOP.

READ THIS WAY

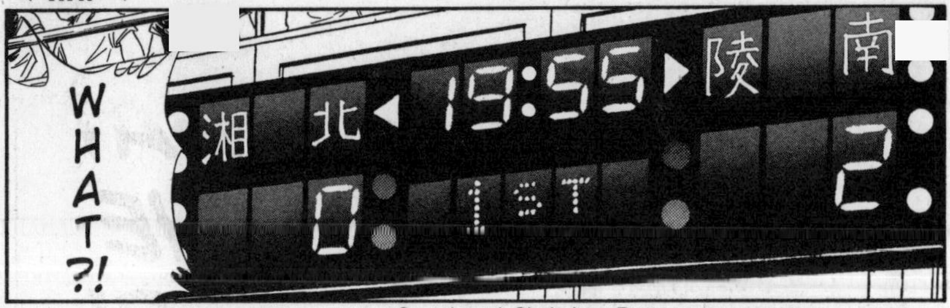
WHAT?!
湘北
19:55
陵南
0
1ST
2

Scoreboard: Shohoku Ryonan

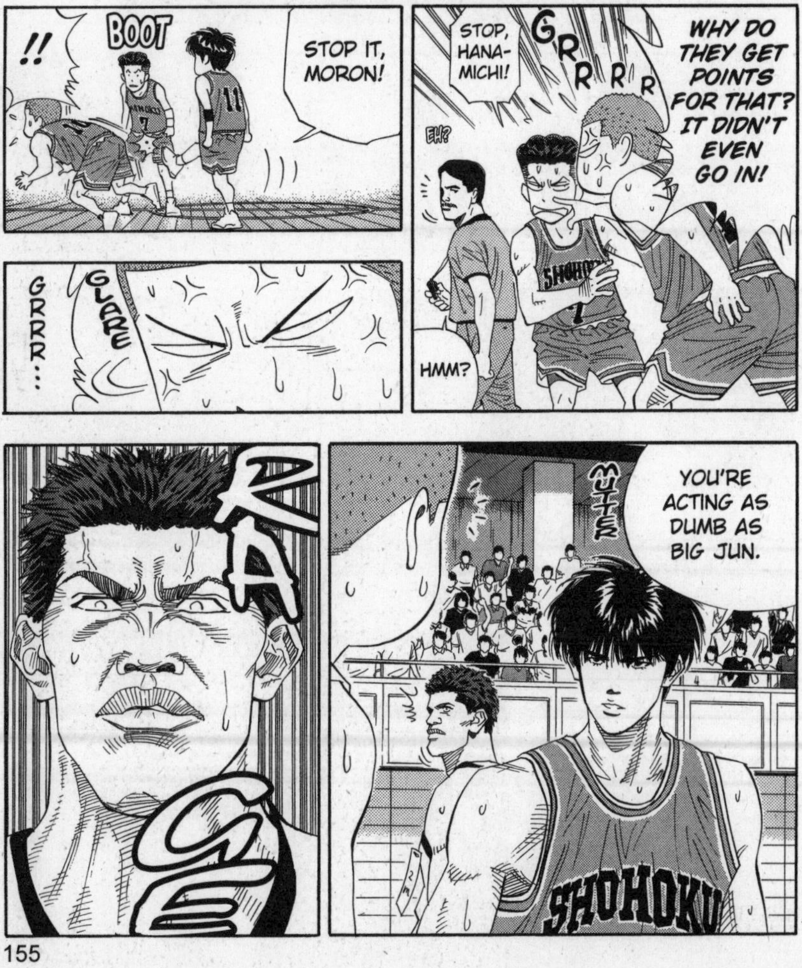
STOP, HANA-MICHI!
GRRRRR
WHY DO THEY GET POINTS FOR THAT? IT DIDN'T EVEN GO IN!
EH?
HMM?
STOP IT, MORON!
BOOT
!!
GLARE
GRRR...
YOU'RE ACTING AS DUMB AS BIG JUN.
MUTTER
RAGE

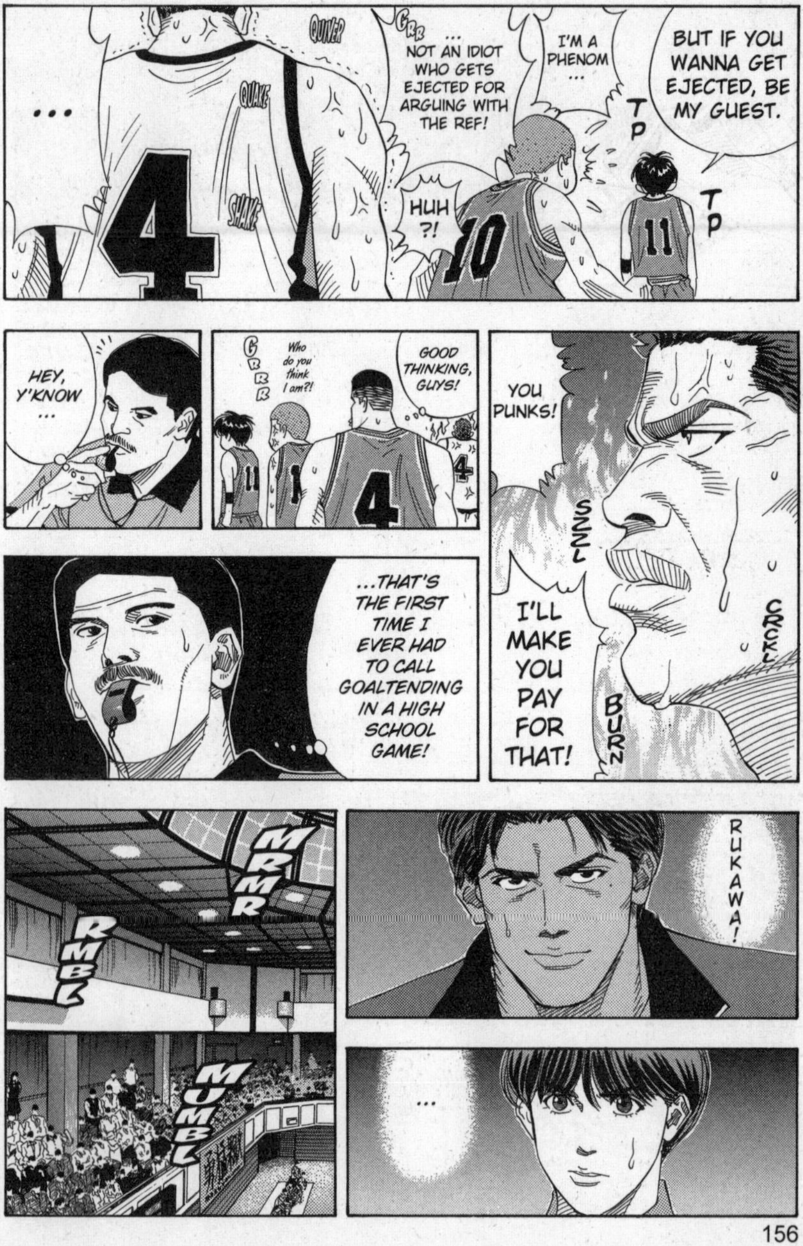
BUT IF YOU WANNA GET EJECTED, BE MY GUEST.
TP
TP
I'M A PHENOM ...
GRR
... NOT AN IDIOT WHO GETS EJECTED FOR ARGUING WITH THE REF!
HUH ?!
QUIVER
QUAKE
SHAKE
...
YOU PUNKS!
SZZL
CRCKL
I'LL MAKE YOU PAY FOR THAT!
BURN
GOOD THINKING, GUYS!
Who do you think I am?!
GRRR
HEY, Y'KNOW ...
...THAT'S THE FIRST TIME I EVER HAD TO CALL GOALTENDING IN A HIGH SCHOOL GAME!
RUKAWA!
...
MRMR
RMBL
MUMBL

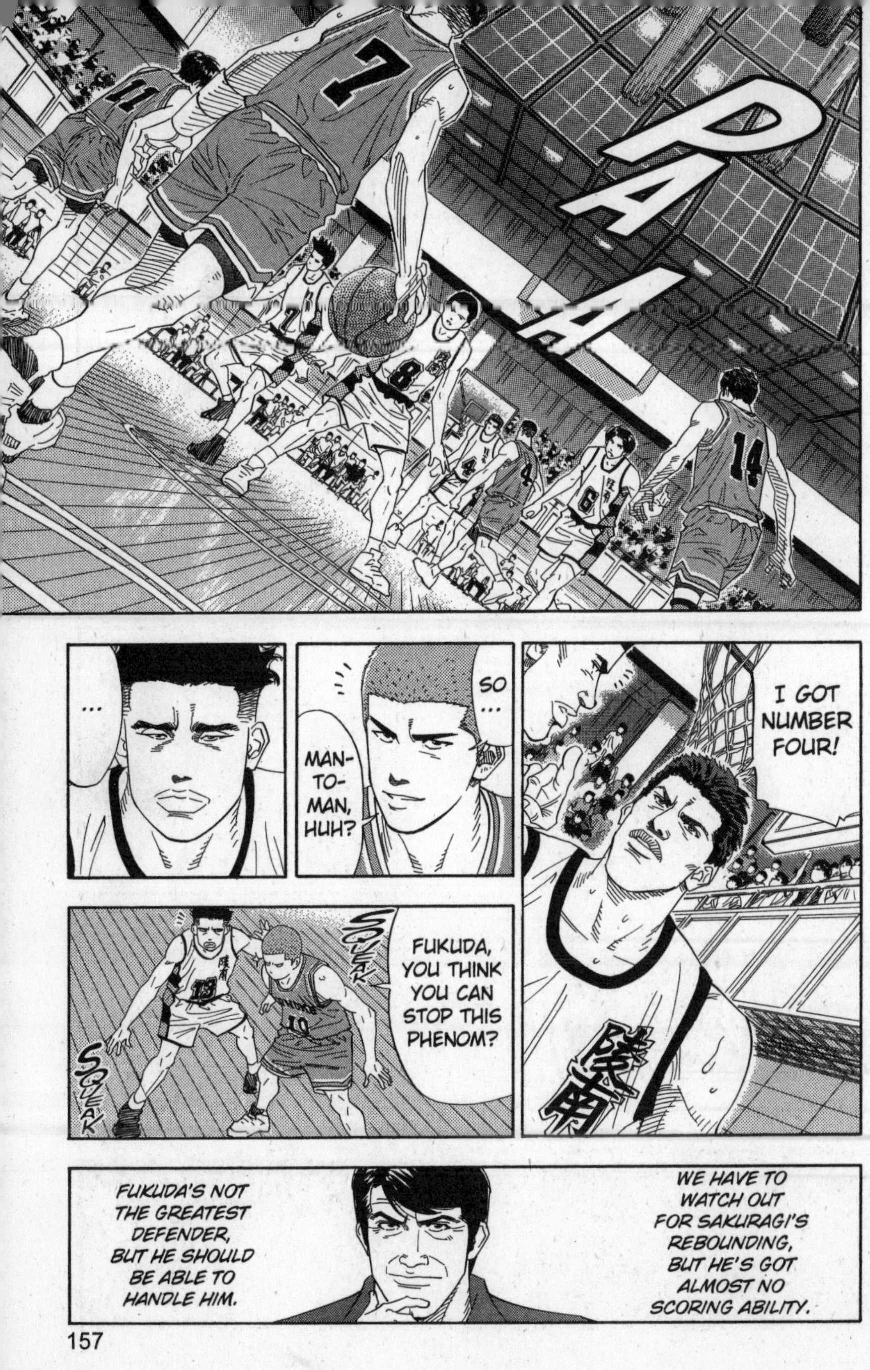
PAA
I GOT NUMBER FOUR!
SO ...
MAN-TO-MAN, HUH?
...
FUKUDA, YOU THINK YOU CAN STOP THIS PHENOM?
SQUEAK
SQUEAK
WE HAVE TO WATCH OUT FOR SAKURAGI'S REBOUNDING, BUT HE'S GOT ALMOST NO SCORING ABILITY.
FUKUDA'S NOT THE GREATEST DEFENDER, BUT HE SHOULD BE ABLE TO HANDLE HIM.

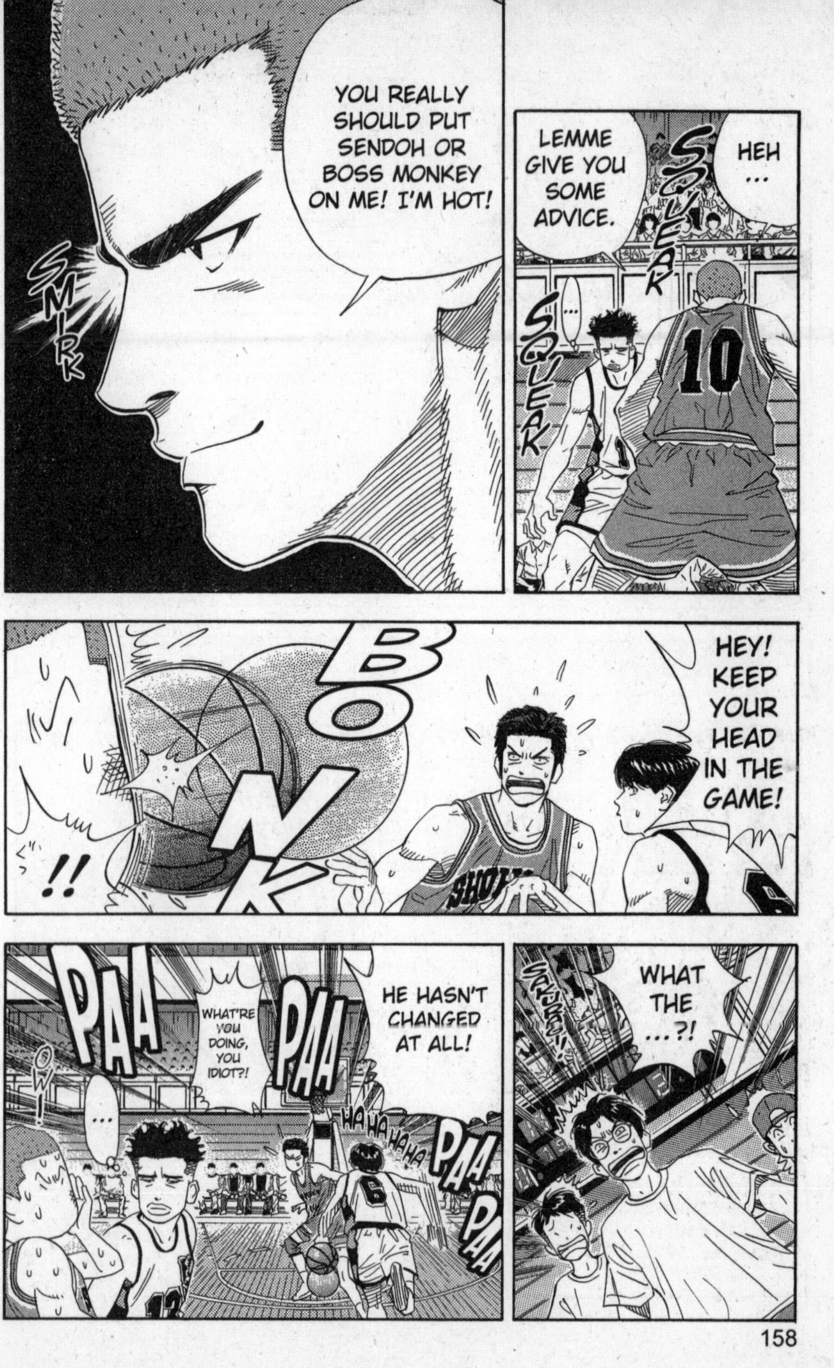
HEH ...
LEMME GIVE YOU SOME ADVICE.
SQUEAK
SQUEAK
...
YOU REALLY SHOULD PUT SENDOH OR BOSS MONKEY ON ME! I'M HOT!
SMIRK
HEY! KEEP YOUR HEAD IN THE GAME!
BONK
!!
WHAT THE ...?!
SAKURAGI!!
HE HASN'T CHANGED AT ALL!
PAA
PAA
WHAT'RE YOU DOING, YOU IDIOT?!
PAA
PAA
PAA
HA HA HA HA HA
OW!
...

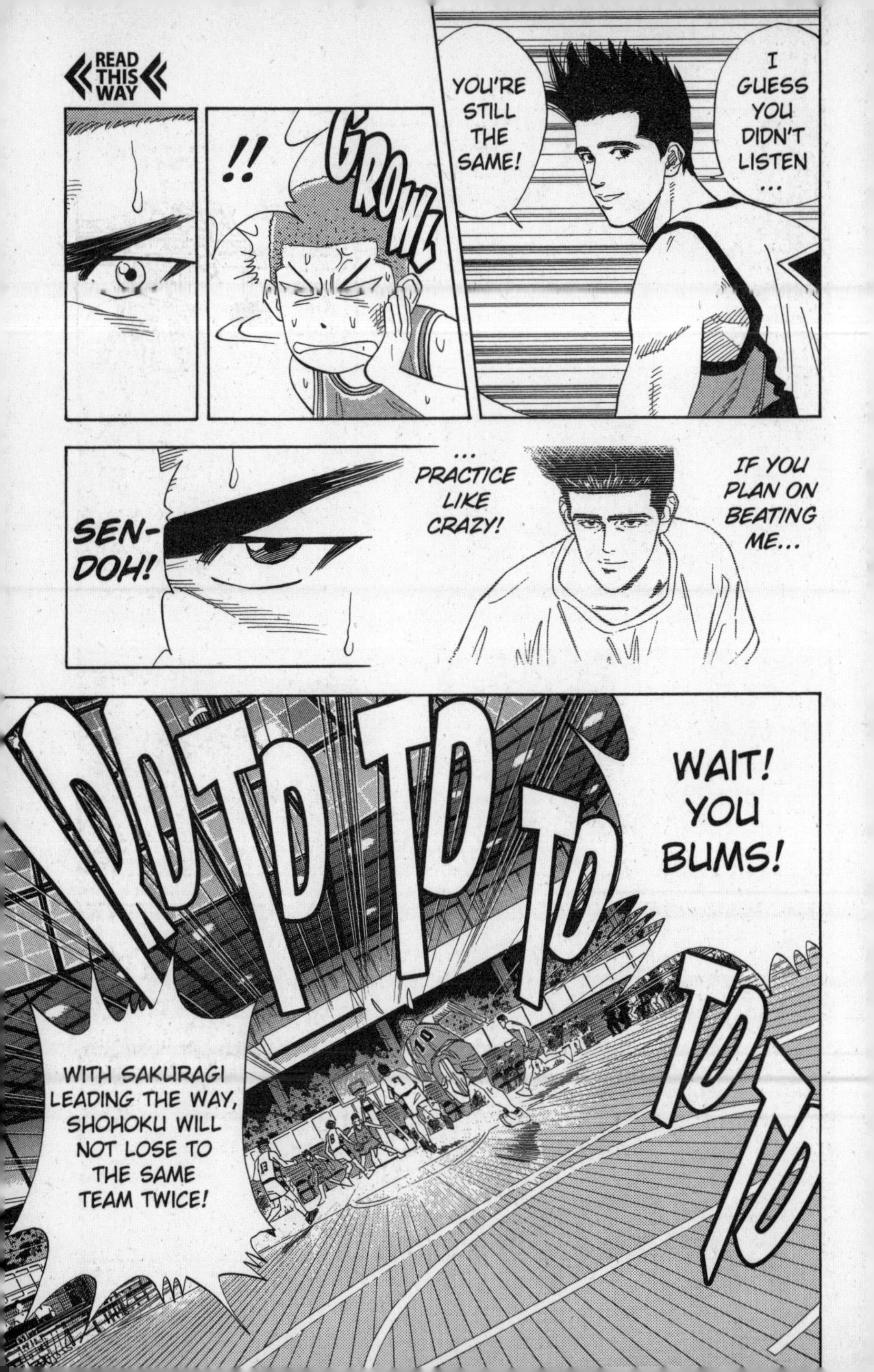
READ THIS WAY
I GUESS YOU DIDN'T LISTEN ...
YOU'RE STILL THE SAME!
!!
GROWL
IF YOU PLAN ON BEATING ME...
... PRACTICE LIKE CRAZY!
SEN-DOH!
WAIT! YOU BUMS!
WITH SAKURAGI LEADING THE WAY, SHOHOKU WILL NOT LOSE TO THE SAME TEAM TWICE!

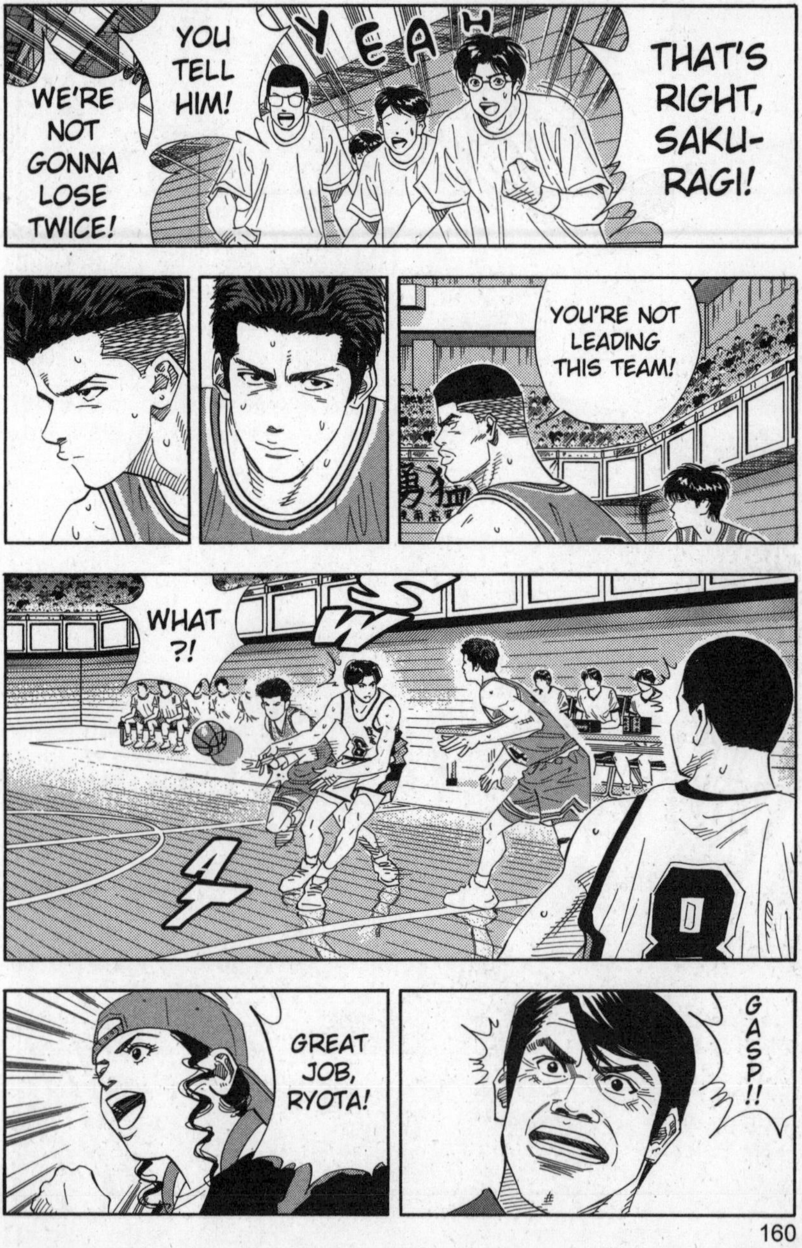
THAT'S RIGHT, SAKURAGI!
YEAH
YOU TELL HIM!
WE'RE NOT GONNA LOSE TWICE!
YOU'RE NOT LEADING THIS TEAM!
SWAT
WHAT ?!
GASP!!
GREAT JOB, RYOTA!

READ THIS WAY

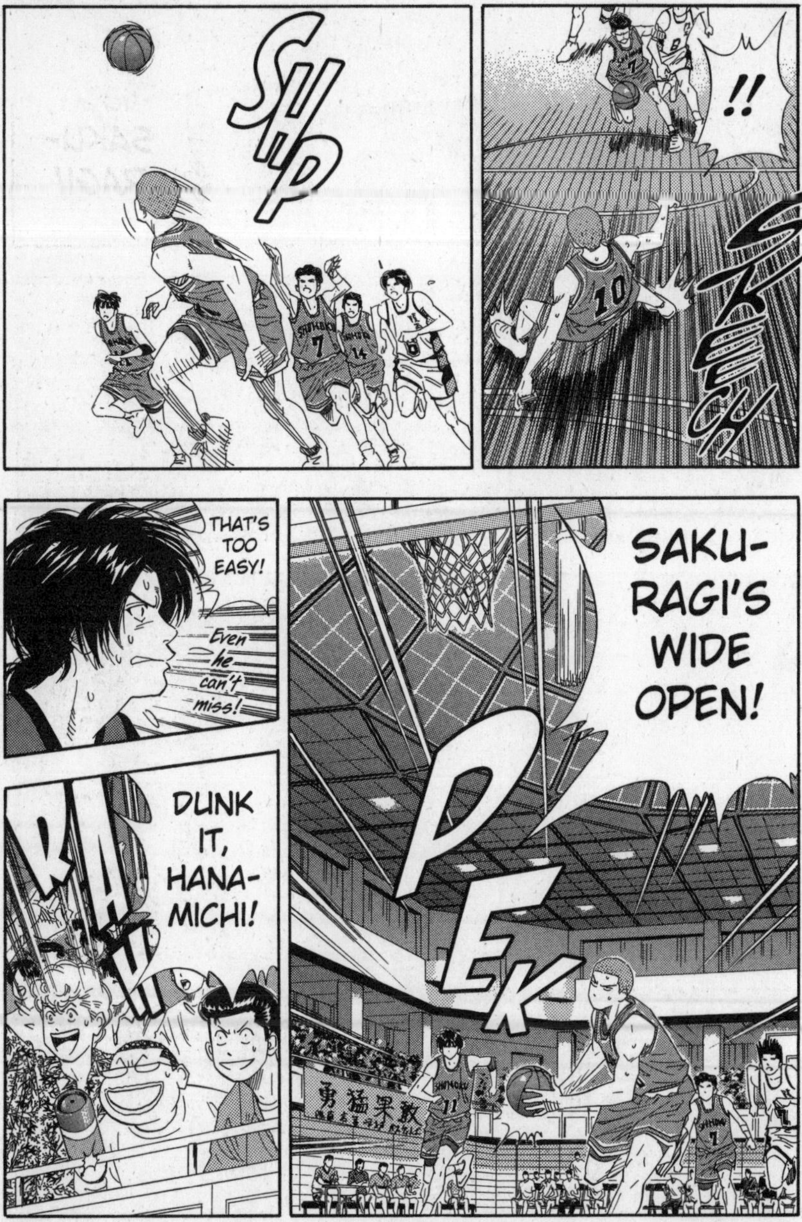
!!
SKEECH
SHP
SAKU-RAGI'S WIDE OPEN!
PEK
勇猛果敢
THAT'S TOO EASY!
Even he can't miss!
DUNK IT, HANA-MICHI!

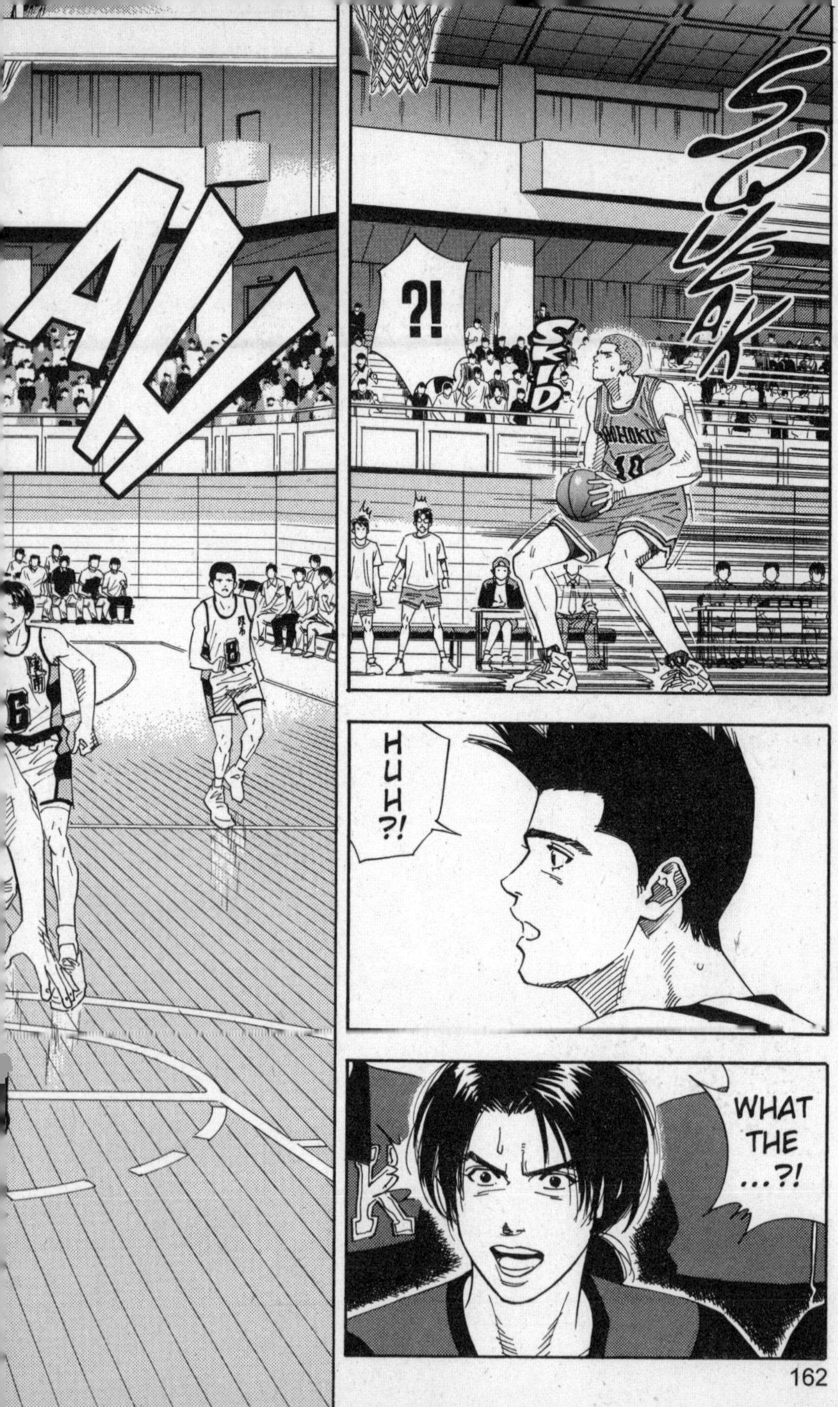
SQUEAK
SKID
?!
HUH?!
WHAT THE ...?!
AH!

READ THIS WAY

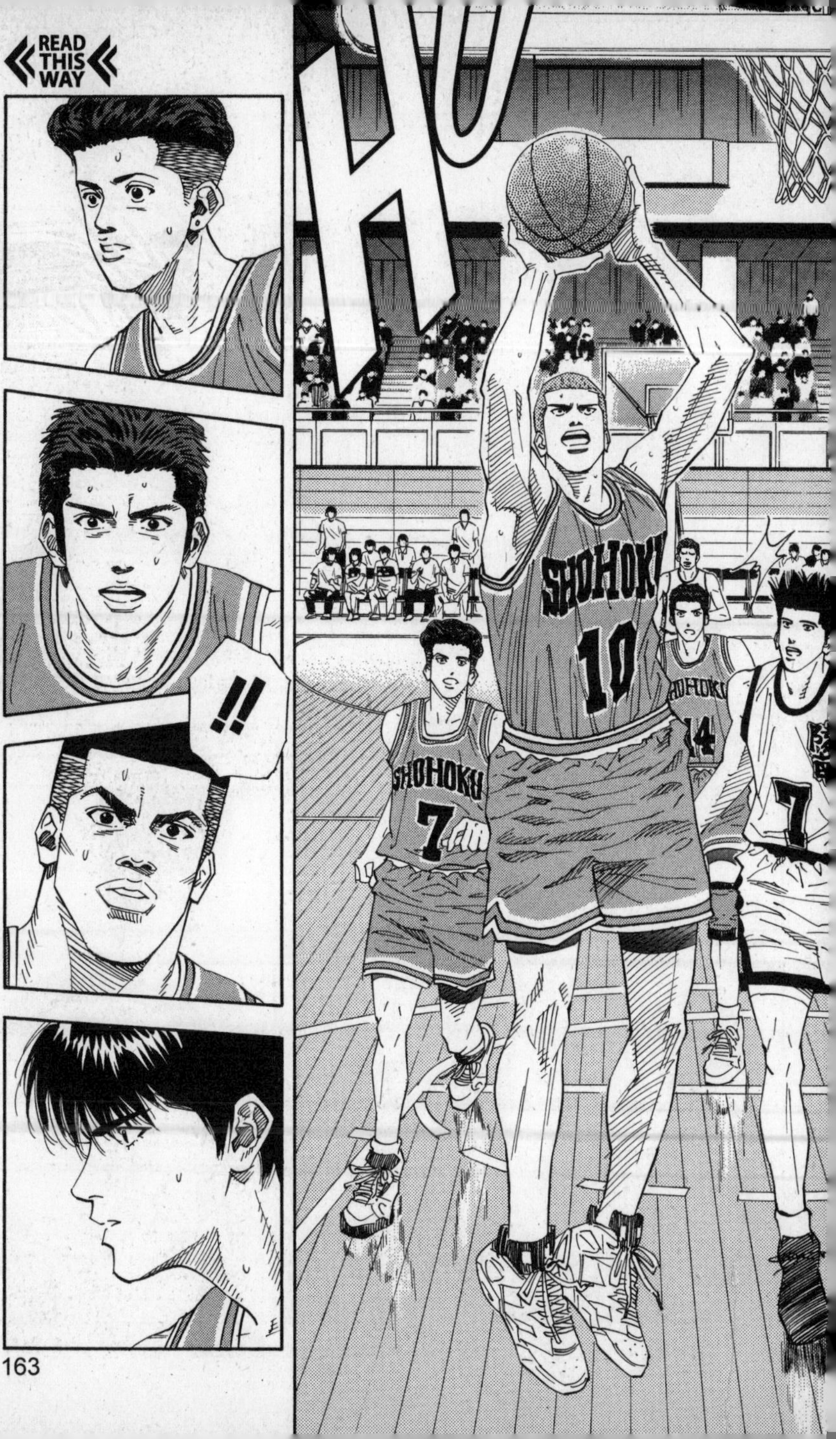
SHOHOKU
10
SHOHOKU
7
!!

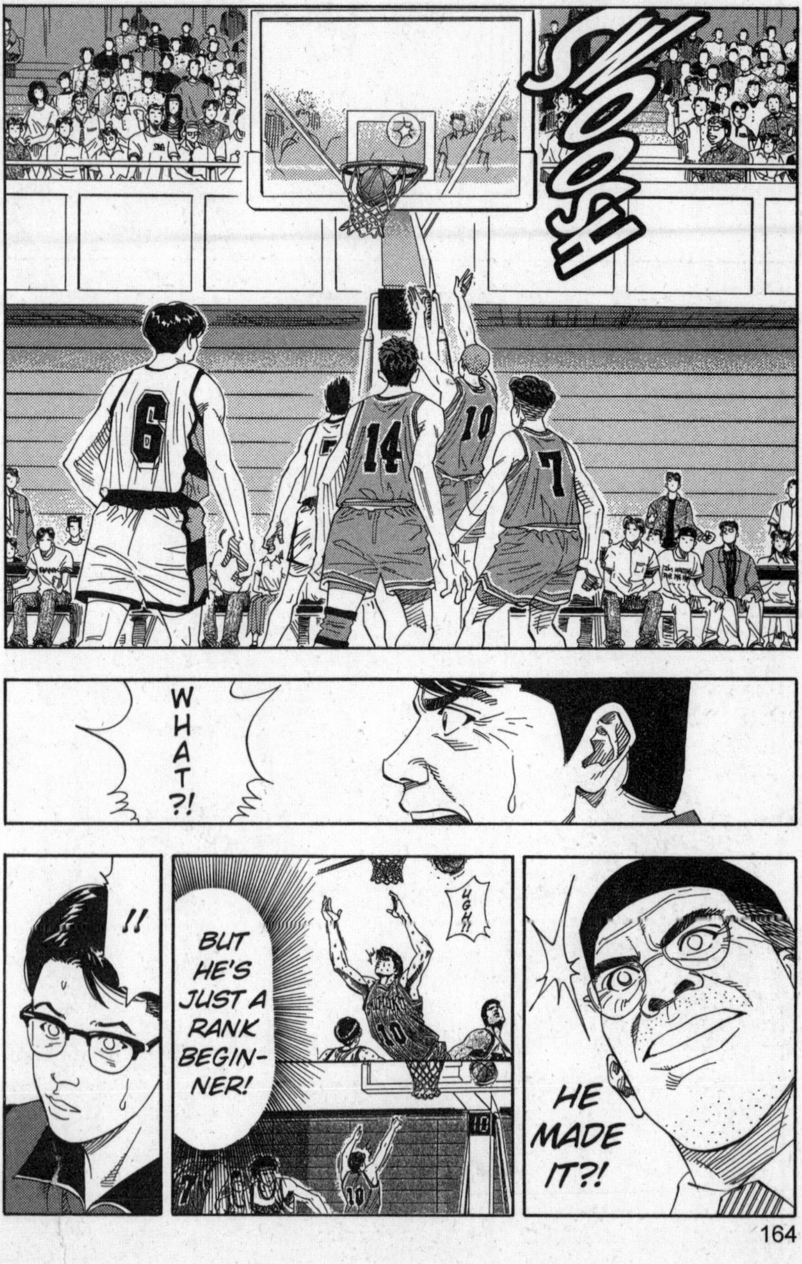
SWOOSH
WHAT?!
HE MADE IT?!
UGH!!
BUT HE'S JUST A RANK BEGINNER!
!!

READ THIS WAY

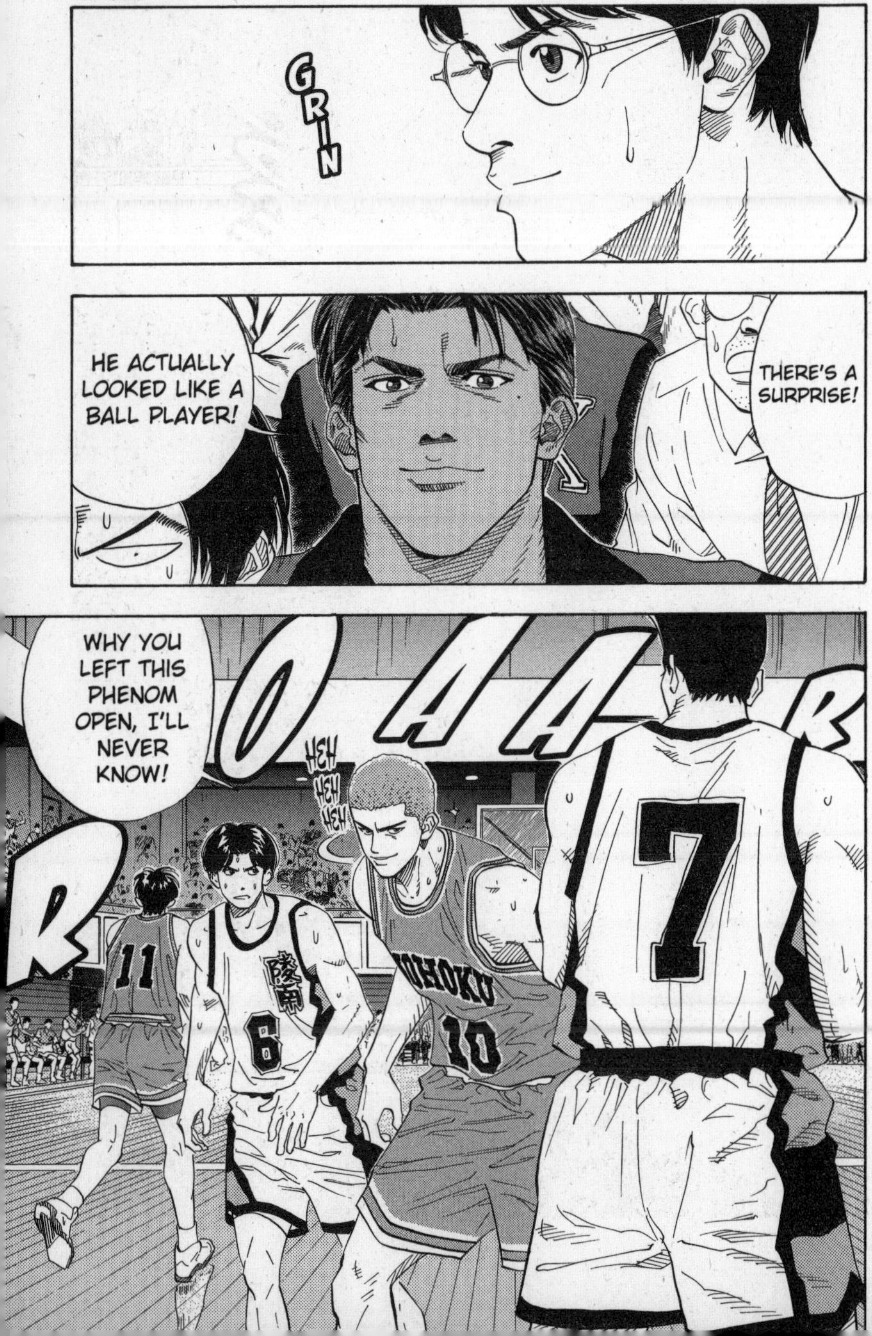
GRIN
THERE'S A SURPRISE!
HE ACTUALLY LOOKED LIKE A BALL PLAYER!
ROAAR
WHY YOU LEFT THIS PHENOM OPEN, I'LL NEVER KNOW!
HEH HEH HEH

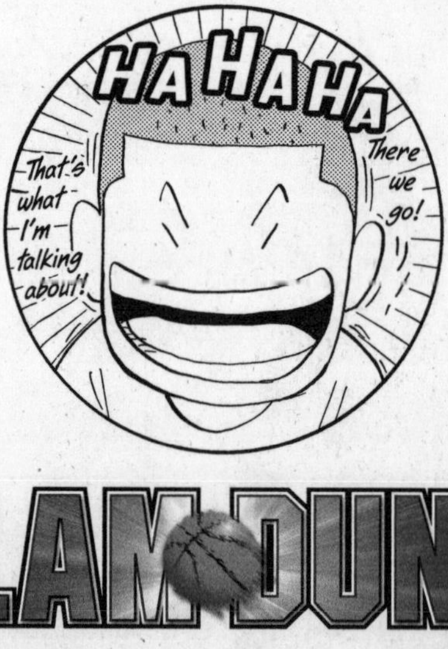
HA HA HA HA
There we go!
That's what I'm talking about!

SLAM DUNK

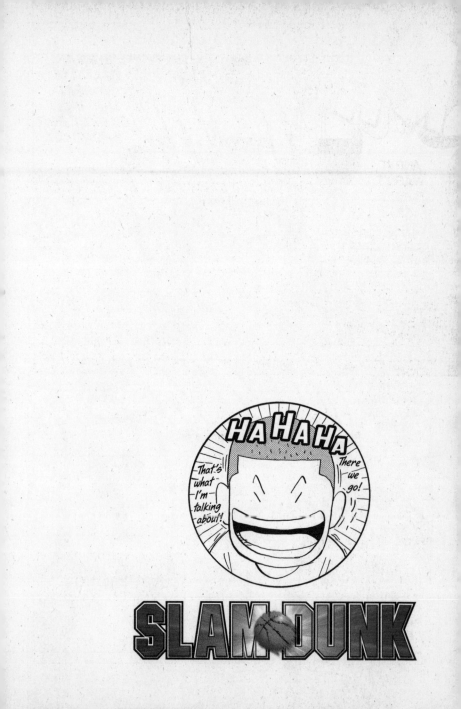

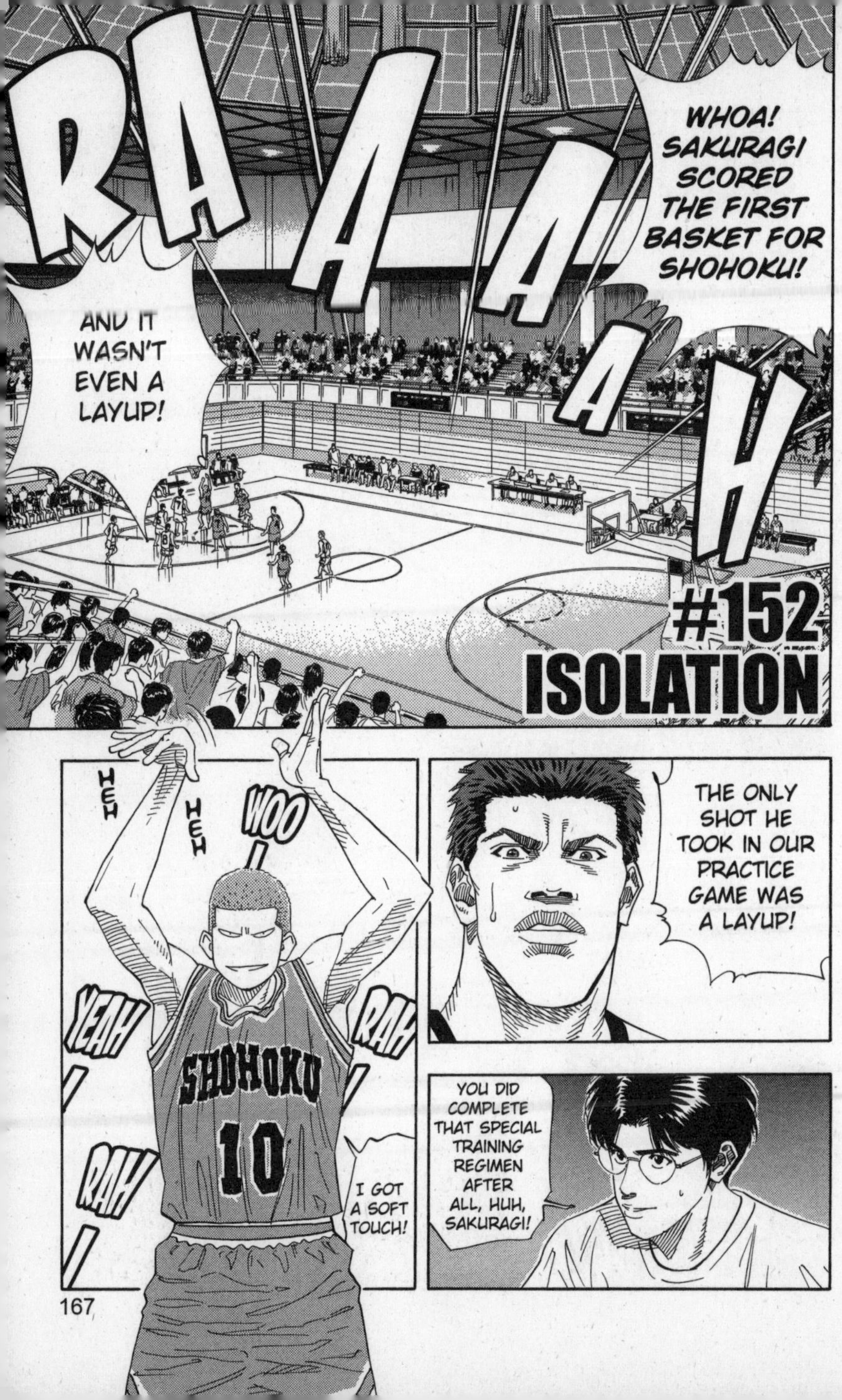
RAAAAH
WHOA! SAKURAGI SCORED THE FIRST BASKET FOR SHOHOKU!
AND IT WASN'T EVEN A LAYUP!
#152 ISOLATION
THE ONLY SHOT HE TOOK IN OUR PRACTICE GAME WAS A LAYUP!
YOU DID COMPLETE THAT SPECIAL TRAINING REGIMEN AFTER ALL, HUH, SAKURAGI!
HEH HEH
WOO
RAH
YEAH
RAH
I GOT A SOFT TOUCH!
SHOHOKU
10

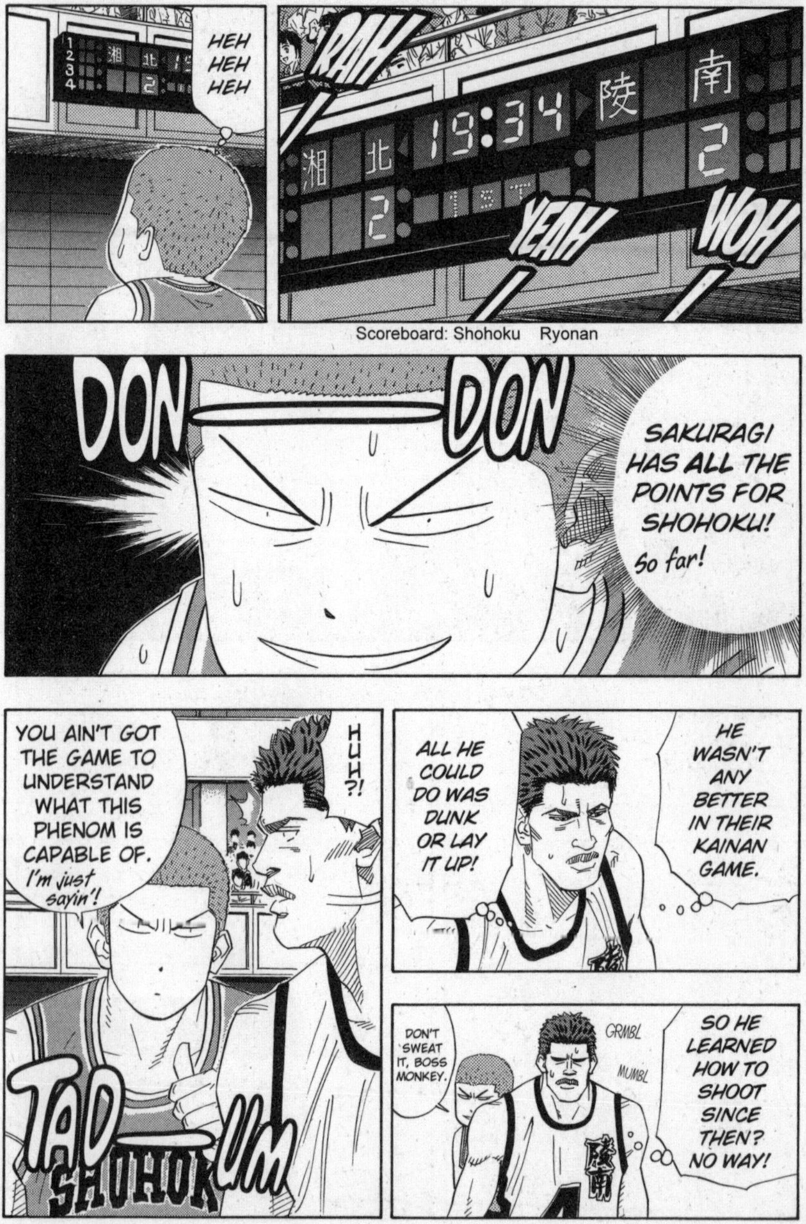
RAH
南
陵
19:34
湘
北
2
2
WOH
YEAH
HEH HEH HEH
SAKURAGI HAS ALL THE POINTS FOR SHOHOKU!
So far!
DON
DON
HE WASN'T ANY BETTER IN THEIR KAINAN GAME.
ALL HE COULD DO WAS DUNK OR LAY IT UP!
SO HE LEARNED HOW TO SHOOT SINCE THEN? NO WAY!
GRMBL
MUMBL
DON'T SWEAT IT, BOSS MONKEY.
HUH?!
YOU AIN'T GOT THE GAME TO UNDERSTAND WHAT THIS PHENOM IS CAPABLE OF.
I'm just sayin'!
TAD—UM
Scoreboard: Shohoku Ryonan

READ THIS WAY

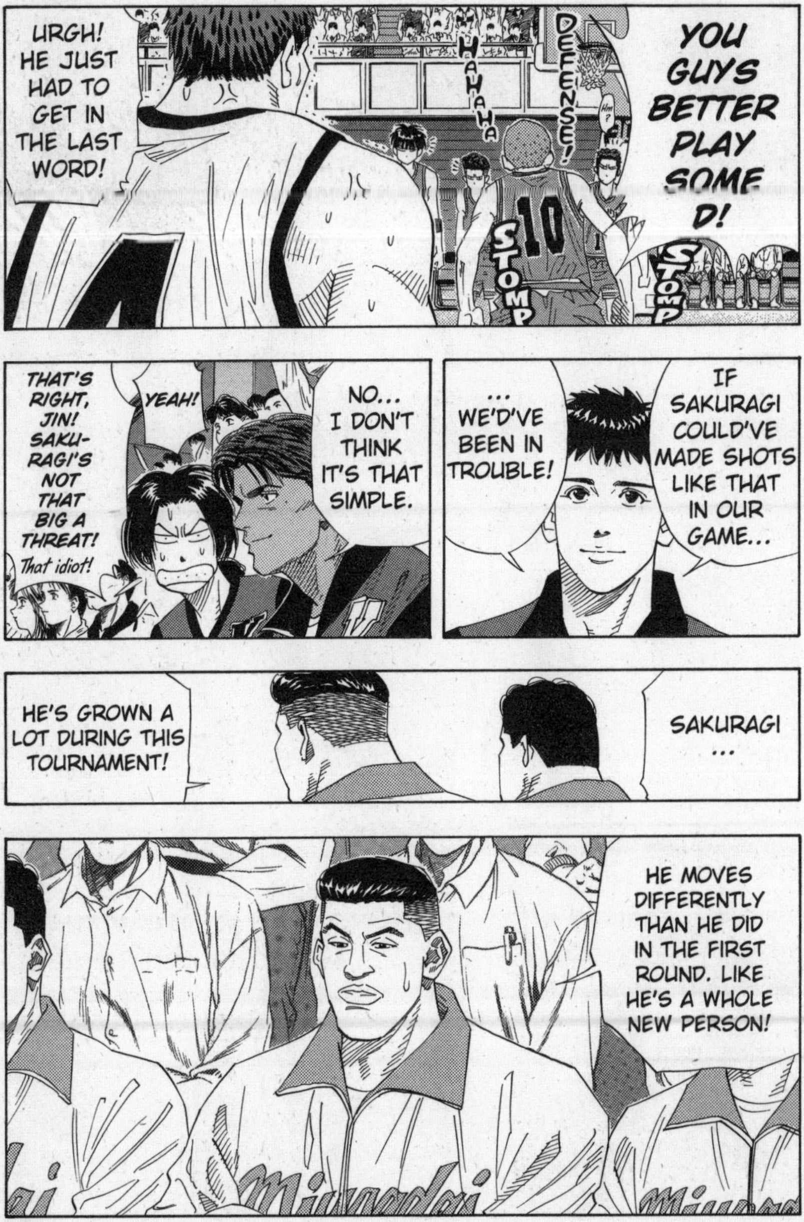

YOU GUYS BETTER PLAY SOME D!
STOMP
STOMP
DEFENSE!
HAHAHA
Hm?
URGH! HE JUST HAD TO GET IN THE LAST WORD!
IF SAKURAGI COULD'VE MADE SHOTS LIKE THAT IN OUR GAME...
... WE'D'VE BEEN IN TROUBLE!
NO... I DON'T THINK IT'S THAT SIMPLE.
YEAH!
THAT'S RIGHT, JIN! SAKURAGI'S NOT THAT BIG A THREAT!
That idiot!
SAKURAGI ...
HE'S GROWN A LOT DURING THIS TOURNAMENT!
HE MOVES DIFFERENTLY THAN HE DID IN THE FIRST ROUND. LIKE HE'S A WHOLE NEW PERSON!

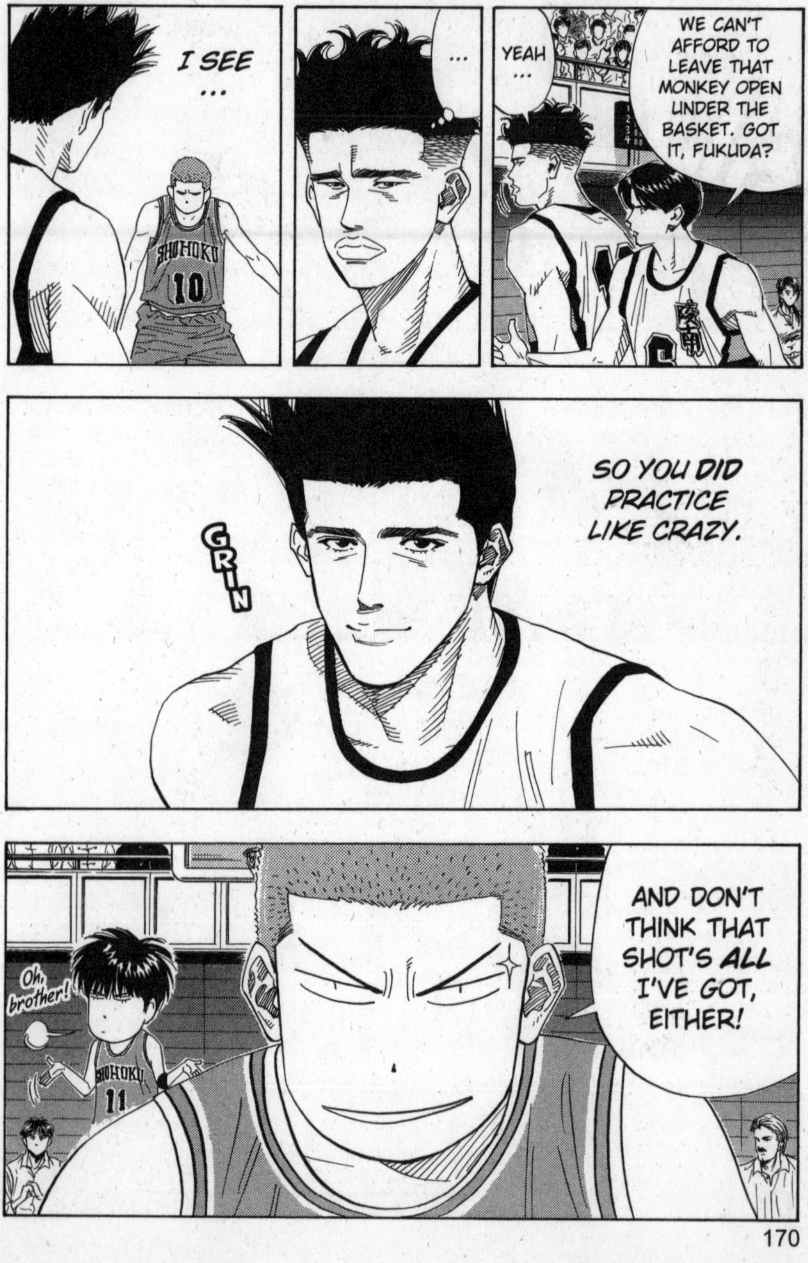
WE CAN'T AFFORD TO LEAVE THAT MONKEY OPEN UNDER THE BASKET. GOT IT, FUKUDA?
YEAH ...
...
I SEE ...
SO YOU DID PRACTICE LIKE CRAZY.
GRIN
AND DON'T THINK THAT SHOT'S ALL I'VE GOT, EITHER!
Oh, brother!

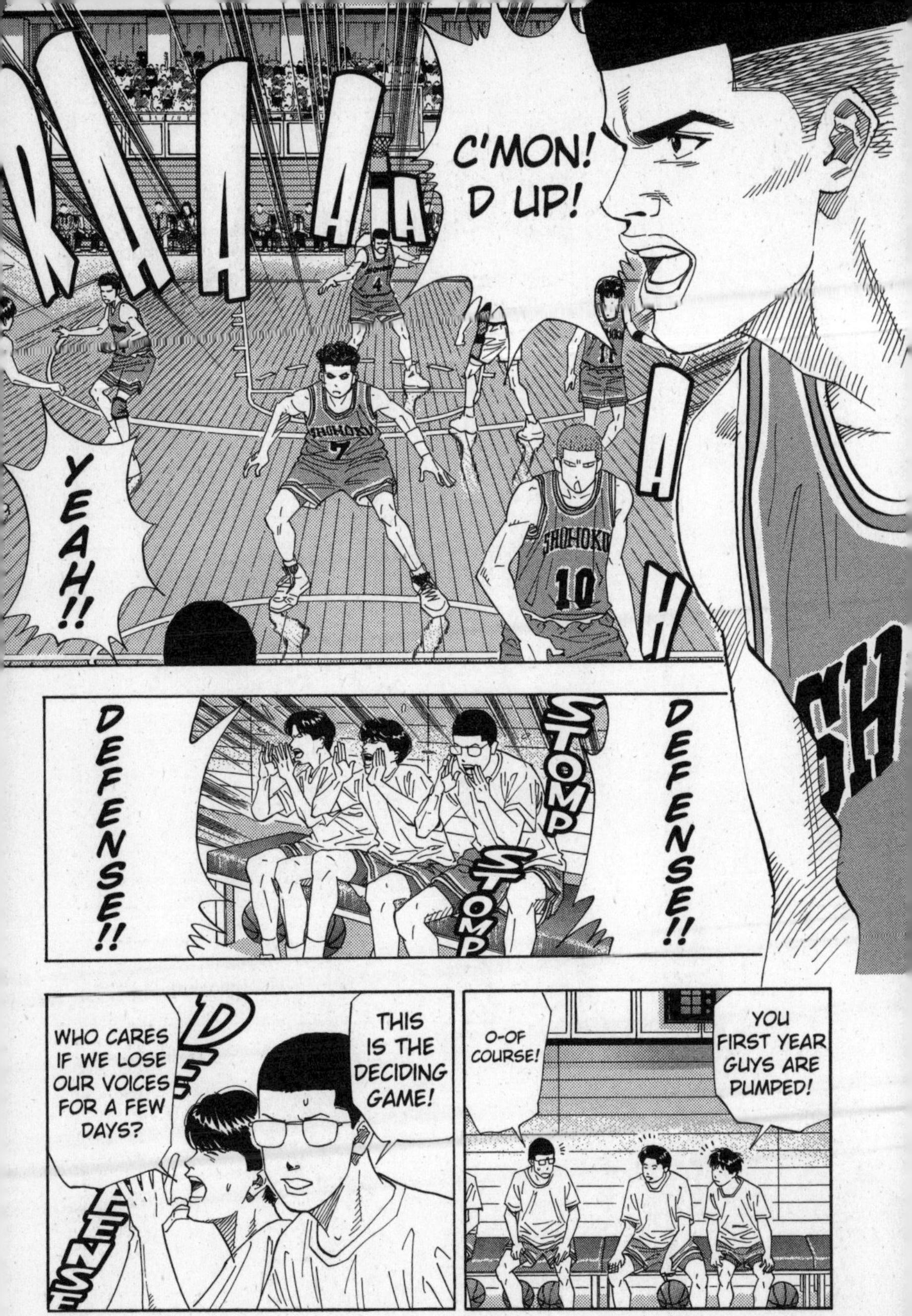
C'MON! D UP!
YEAH!!
DEFENSE!!
STOMP STOMP
DEFENSE!!
YOU FIRST YEAR GUYS ARE PUMPED!
O-OF COURSE!
THIS IS THE DECIDING GAME!
WHO CARES IF WE LOSE OUR VOICES FOR A FEW DAYS?
DEFENSE

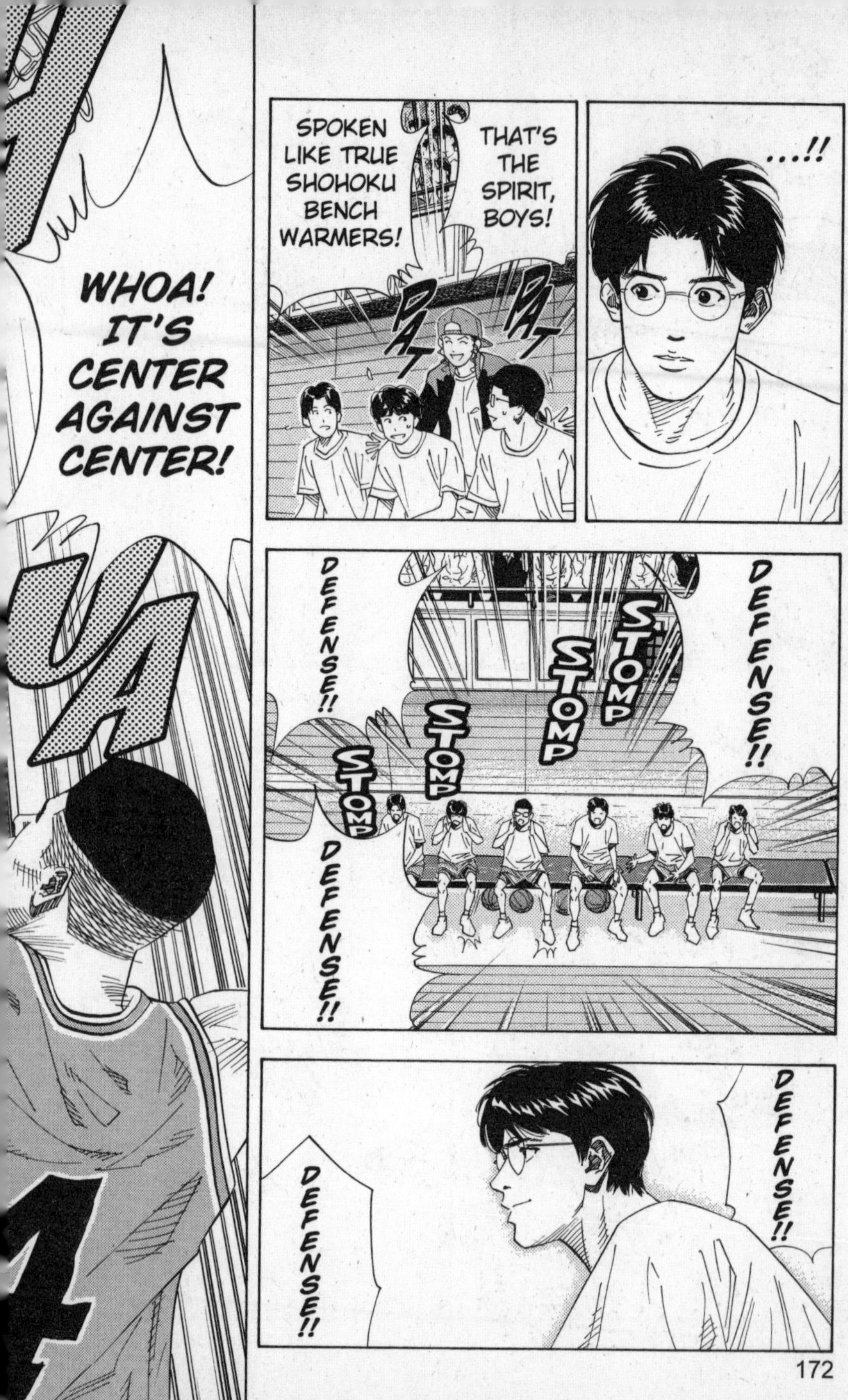
...!!
THAT'S THE SPIRIT, BOYS!
SPOKEN LIKE TRUE SHOHOKU BENCH WARMERS!
DAT
DAT
DEFENSE!!
STOMP
STOMP
STOMP
STOMP
DEFENSE!!
DEFENSE!!
DEFENSE!!
DEFENSE!!
WHOA! IT'S CENTER AGAINST CENTER!

READ THIS WAY

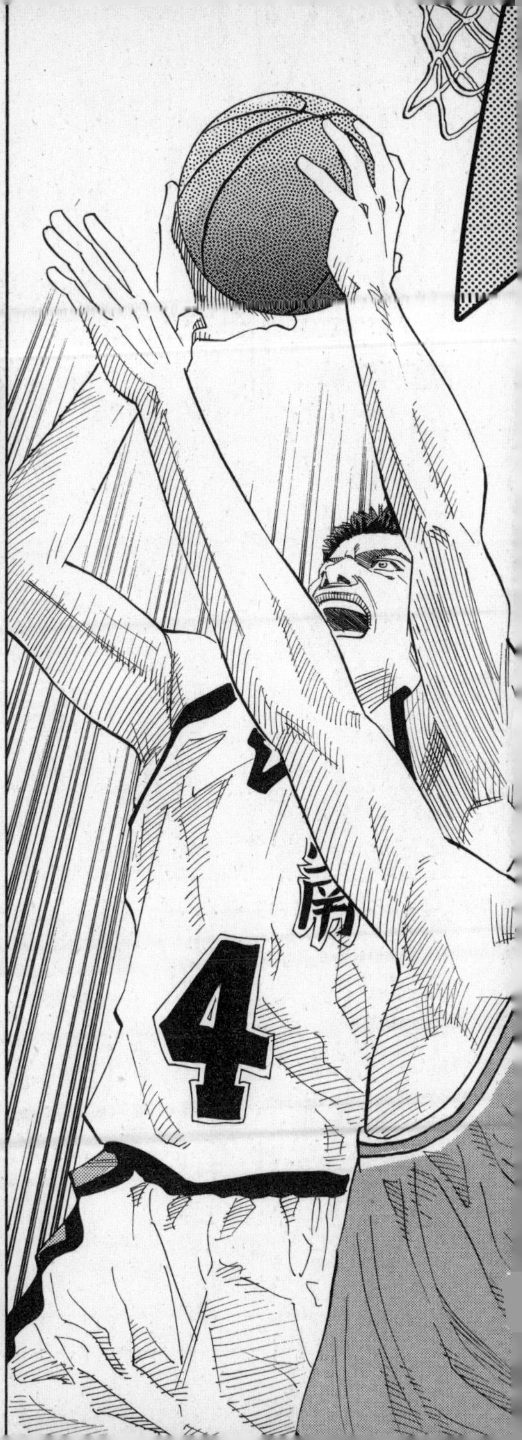

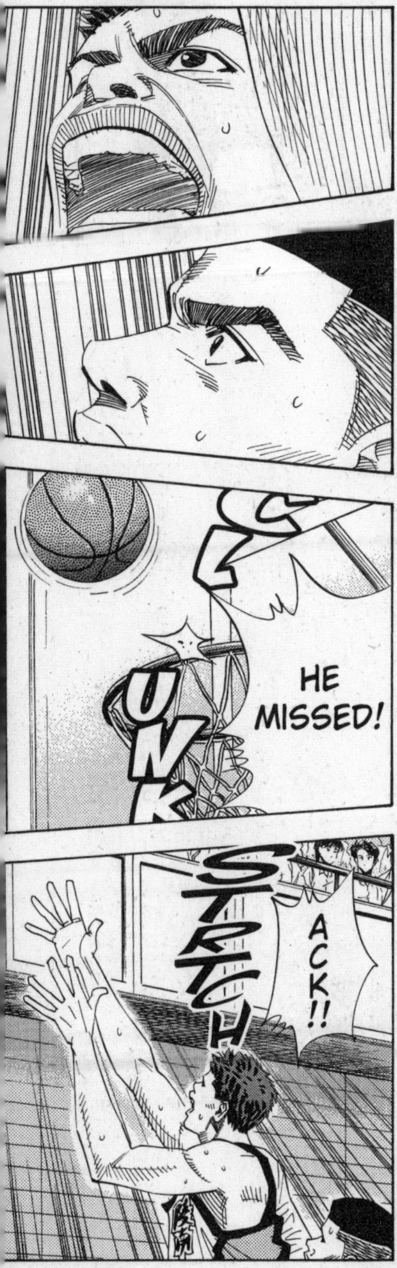
HE MISSED!
ACK!!

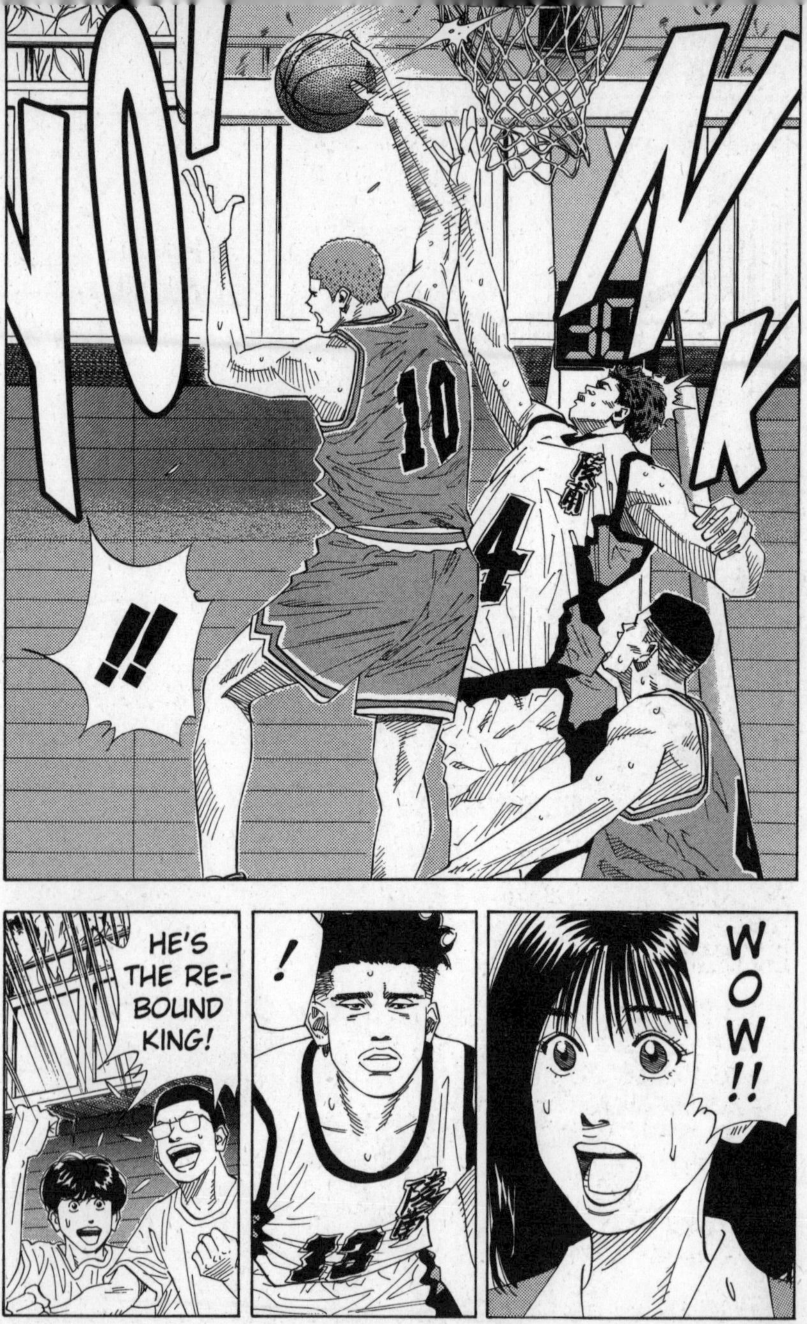
YOINK
!!
WOW!!
!
HE'S THE RE-BOUND KING!

READ THIS WAY

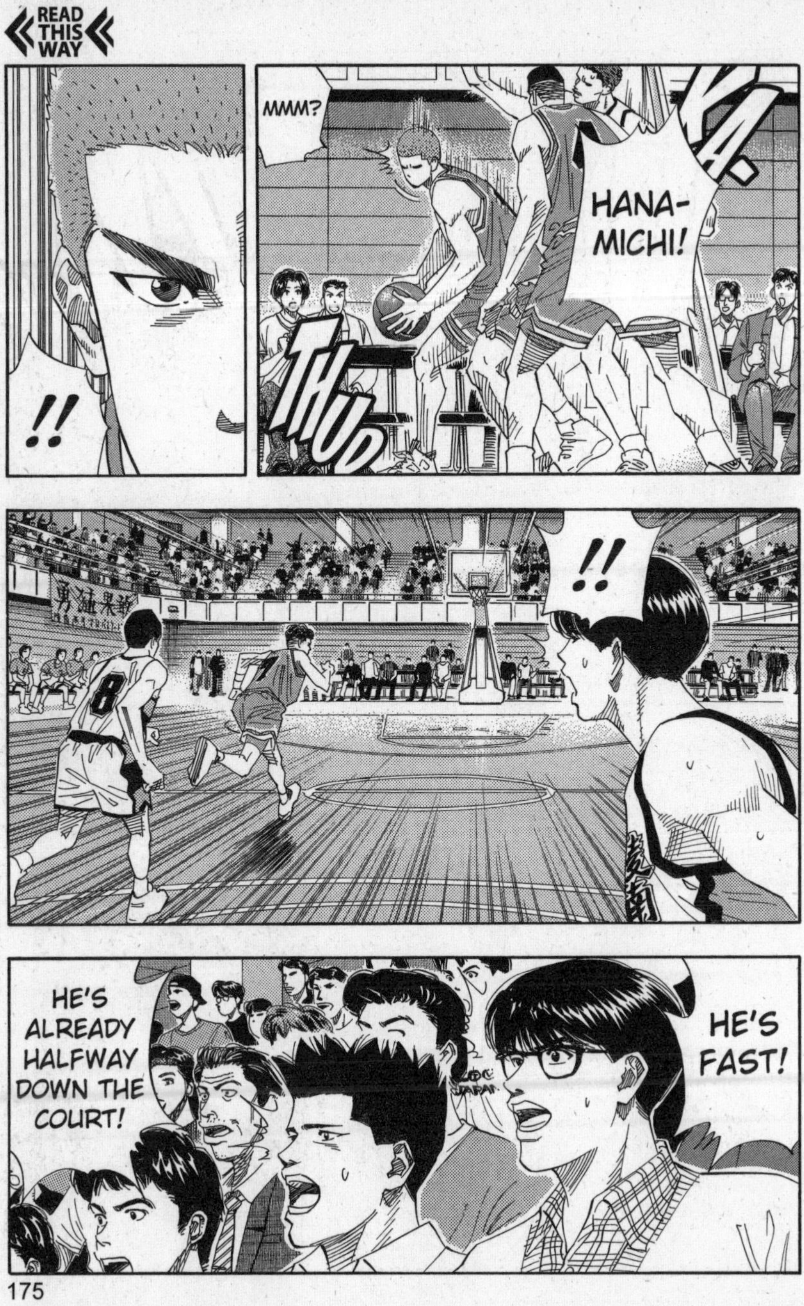
HANA-MICHI!
MMM?
THUD
!!
!!
HE'S FAST!
HE'S ALREADY HALFWAY DOWN THE COURT!

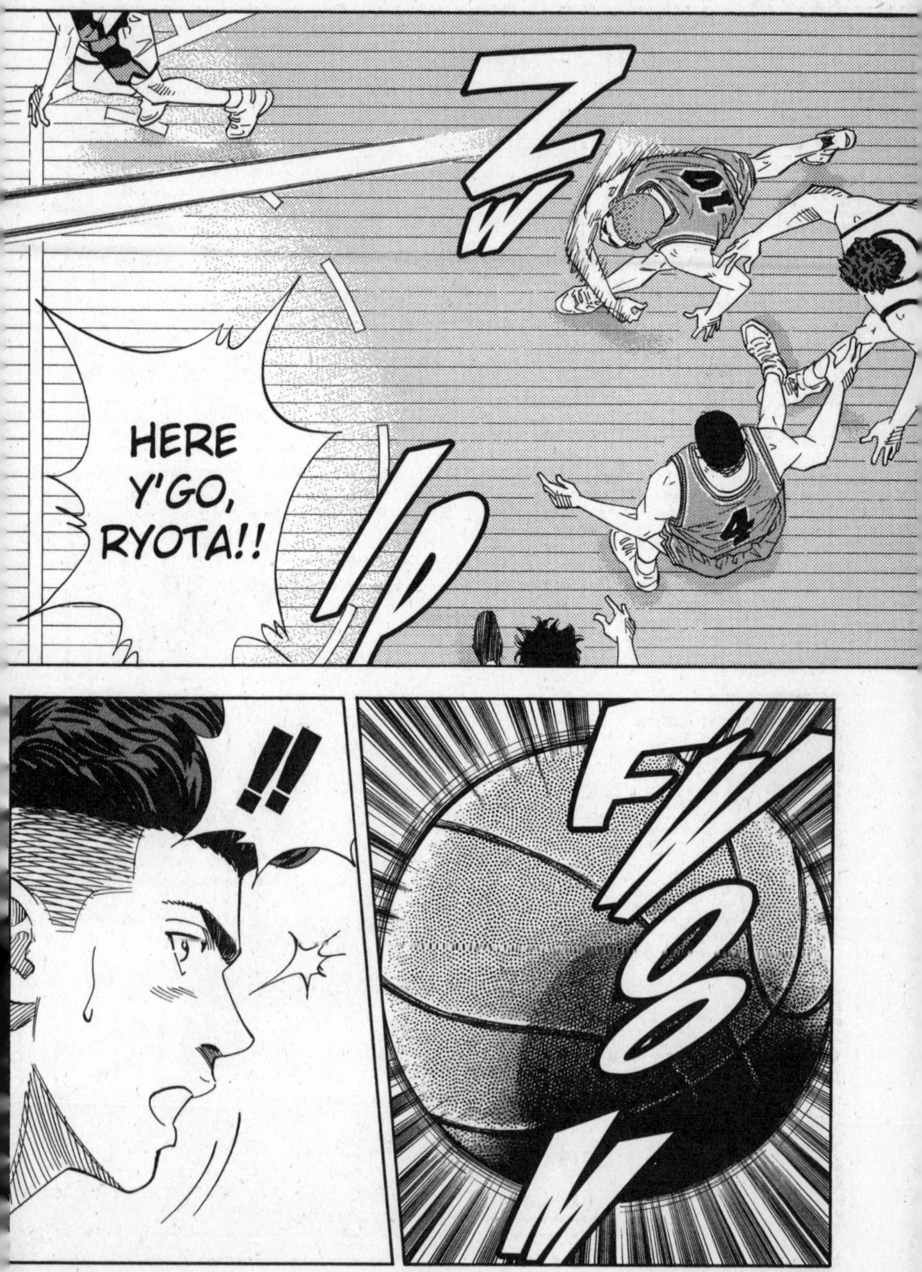
ZW
HERE Y'GO, RYOTA!!
IP
FWOOSH
!!

READ THIS WAY

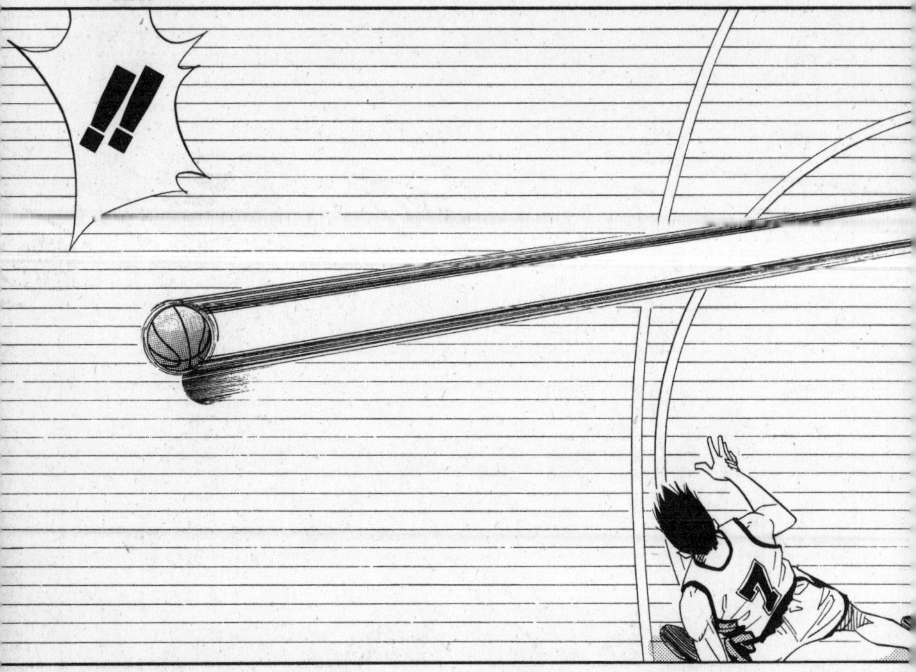
!!

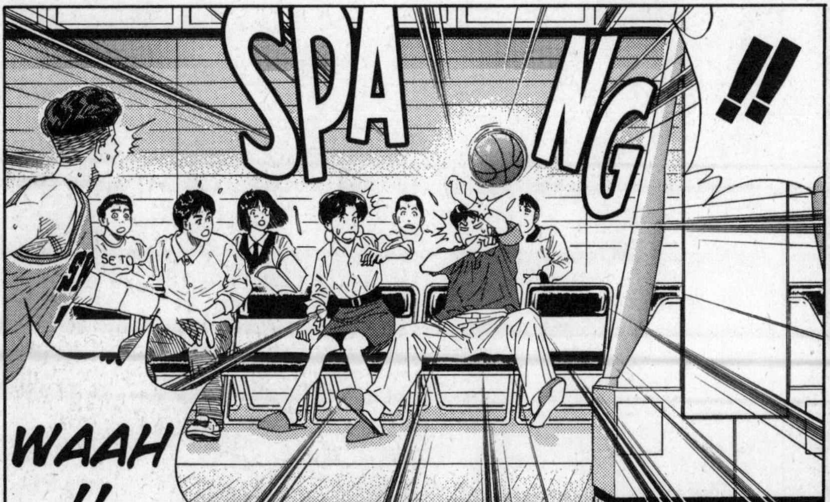
SPANG !!
SETO
WAAH !!

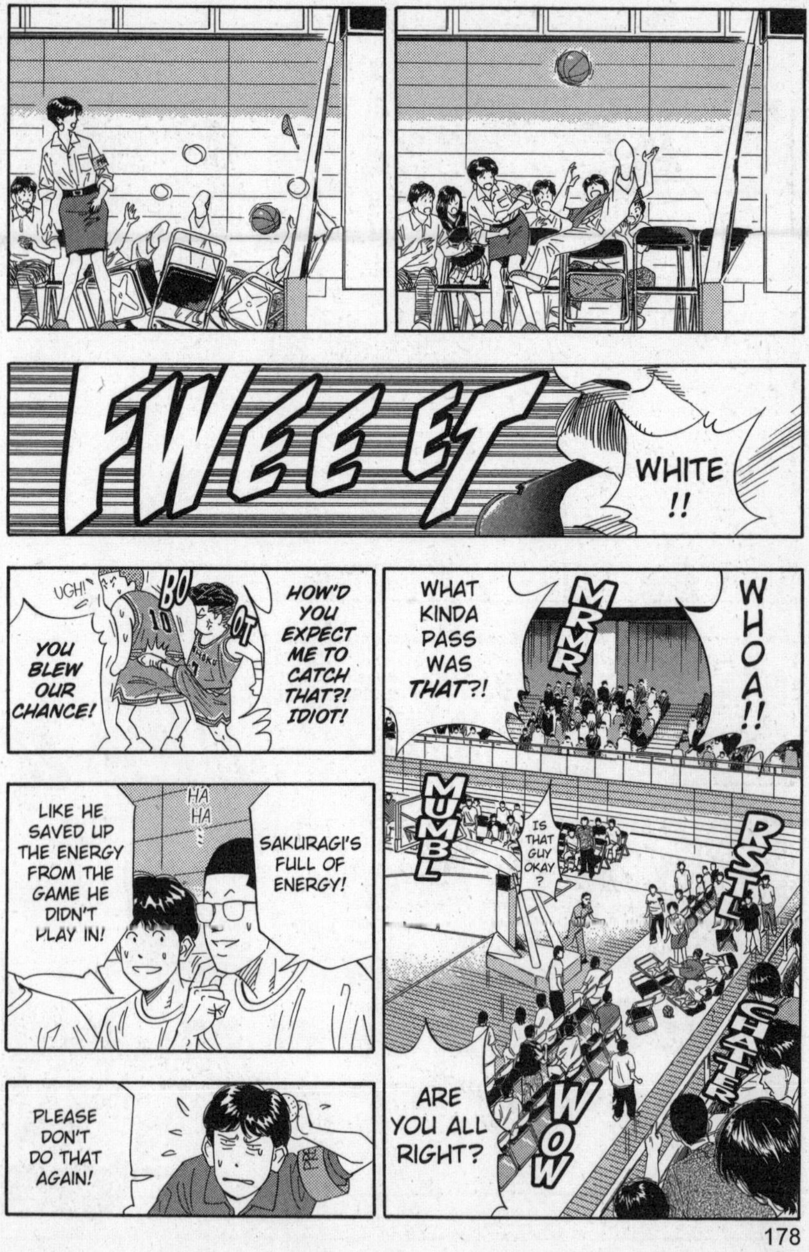

FWEEET
WHITE !!
WHOA!!
MRMR
WHAT KINDA PASS WAS THAT?!
RSTL
MUMBL
IS THAT GUY OKAY?
CHATTER
WOW
ARE YOU ALL RIGHT?
BOOT
HOW'D YOU EXPECT ME TO CATCH THAT?! IDIOT!
UGH!
YOU BLEW OUR CHANCE!
SAKURAGI'S FULL OF ENERGY!
HA HA
LIKE HE SAVED UP THE ENERGY FROM THE GAME HE DIDN'T PLAY IN!
PLEASE DON'T DO THAT AGAIN!

READ THIS WAY

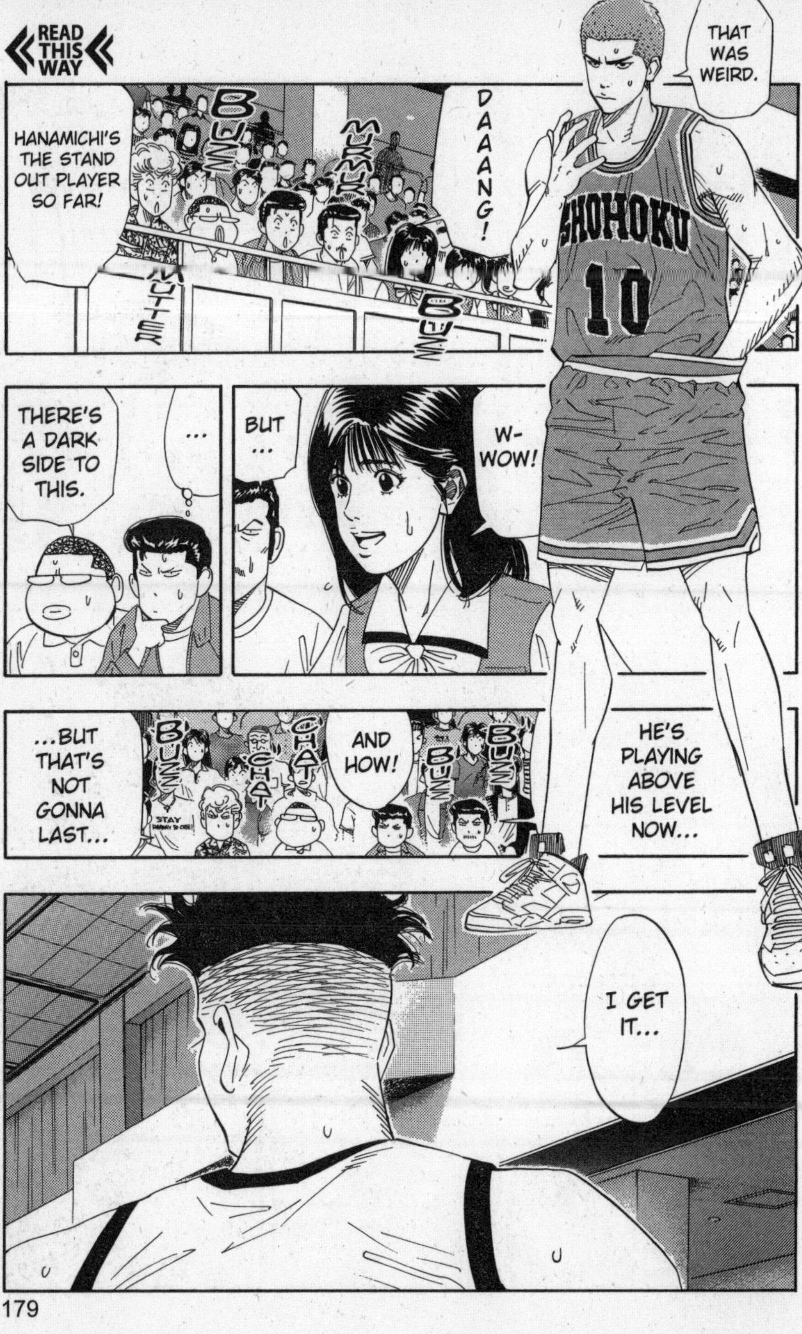
THAT WAS WEIRD.
DAAAANG!
MURMUR
BUZZ
HANAMICHI'S THE STAND OUT PLAYER SO FAR!
BUZZ
MUTTER
W-WOW!
BUT ...
...
THERE'S A DARK SIDE TO THIS.
HE'S PLAYING ABOVE HIS LEVEL NOW...
BUZZ
BUZZ
AND HOW!
CHAT
CHAT
BUZZ
...BUT THAT'S NOT GONNA LAST...
I GET IT...

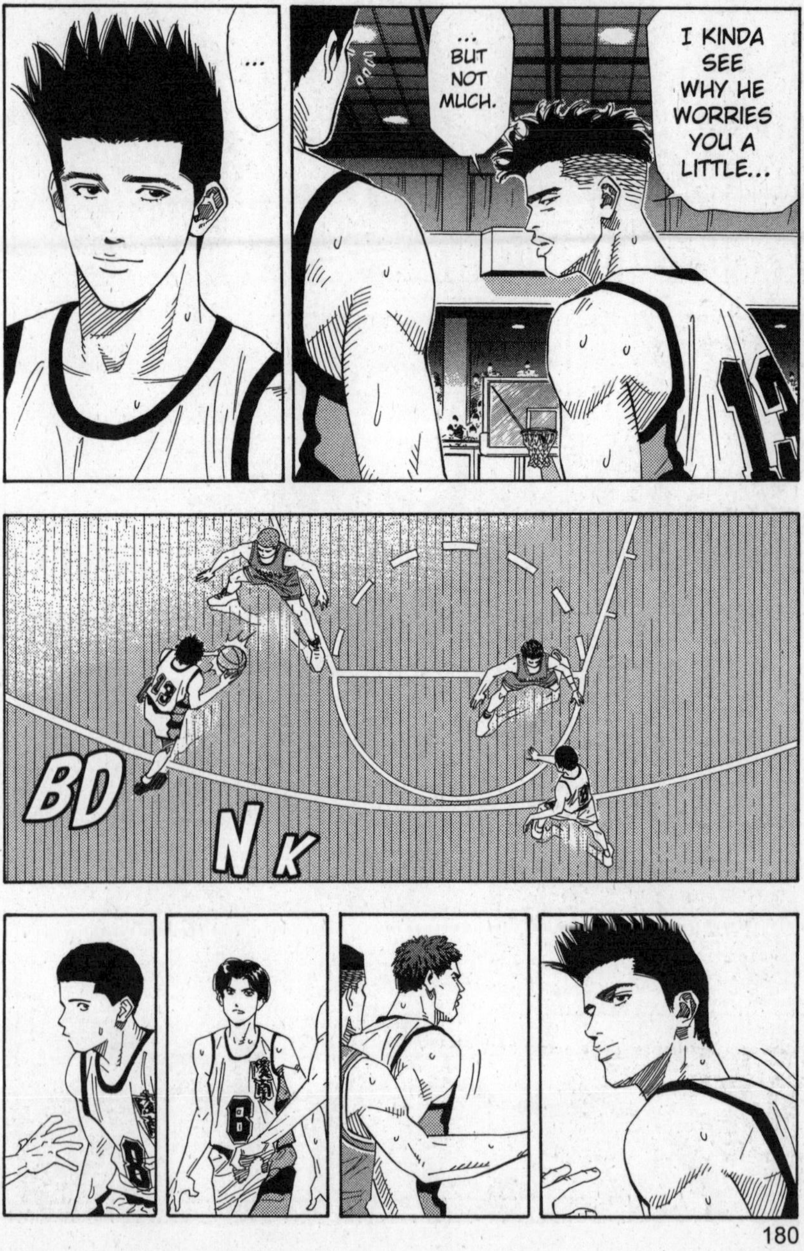
I KINDA SEE WHY HE WORRIES YOU A LITTLE...
... BUT NOT MUCH.
...
BD
N K

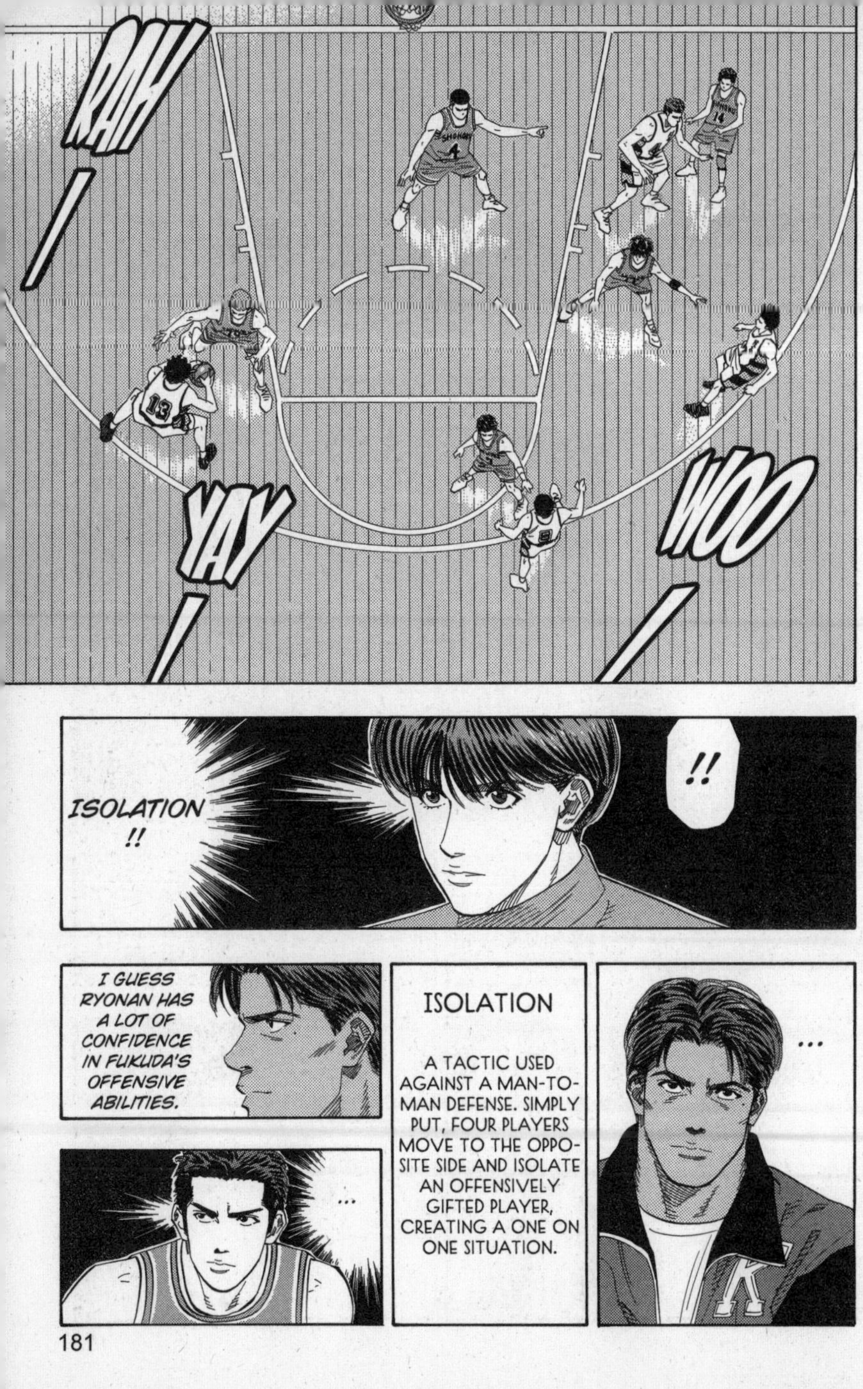
RAH—!
WOO—!
YAY—!
!!
ISOLATION !!
...
ISOLATION
A TACTIC USED AGAINST A MAN-TO-MAN DEFENSE. SIMPLY PUT, FOUR PLAYERS MOVE TO THE OPPOSITE SIDE AND ISOLATE AN OFFENSIVELY GIFTED PLAYER, CREATING A ONE ON ONE SITUATION.
I GUESS RYONAN HAS A LOT OF CONFIDENCE IN FUKUDA'S OFFENSIVE ABILITIES.
...

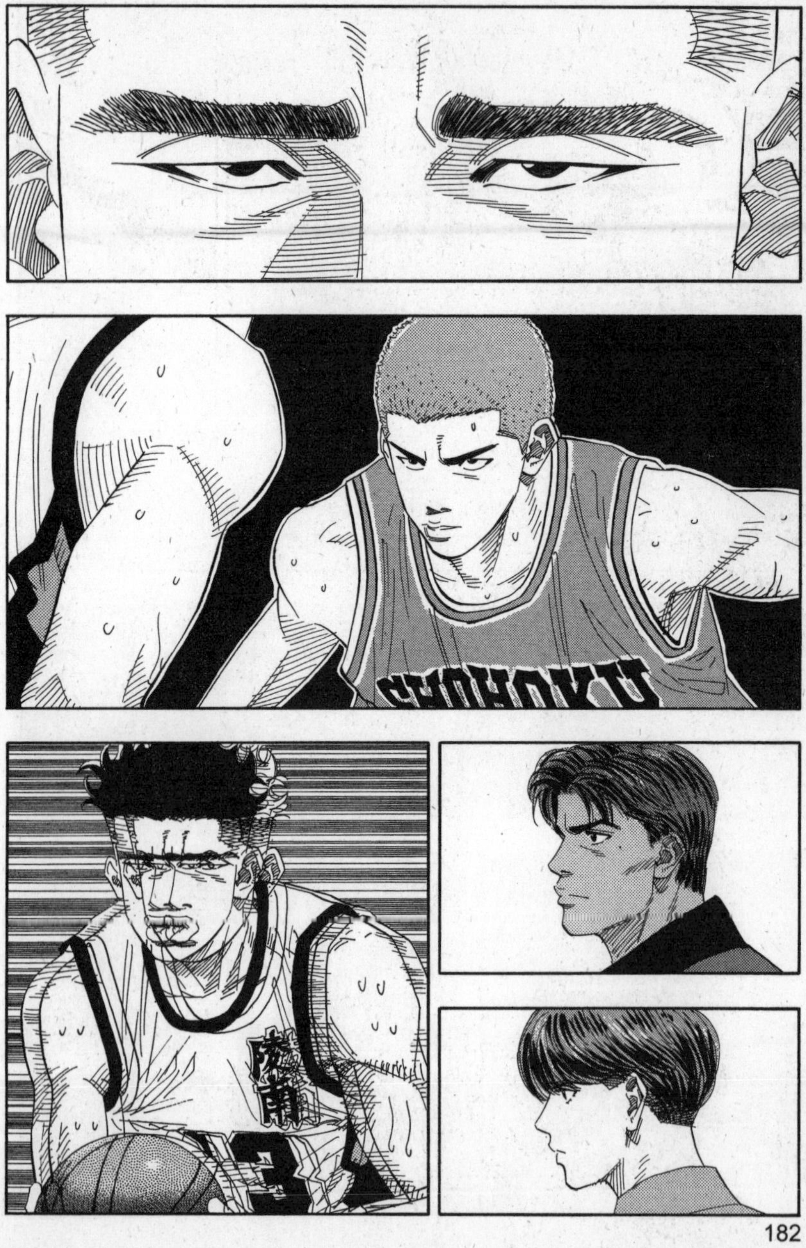
陵南

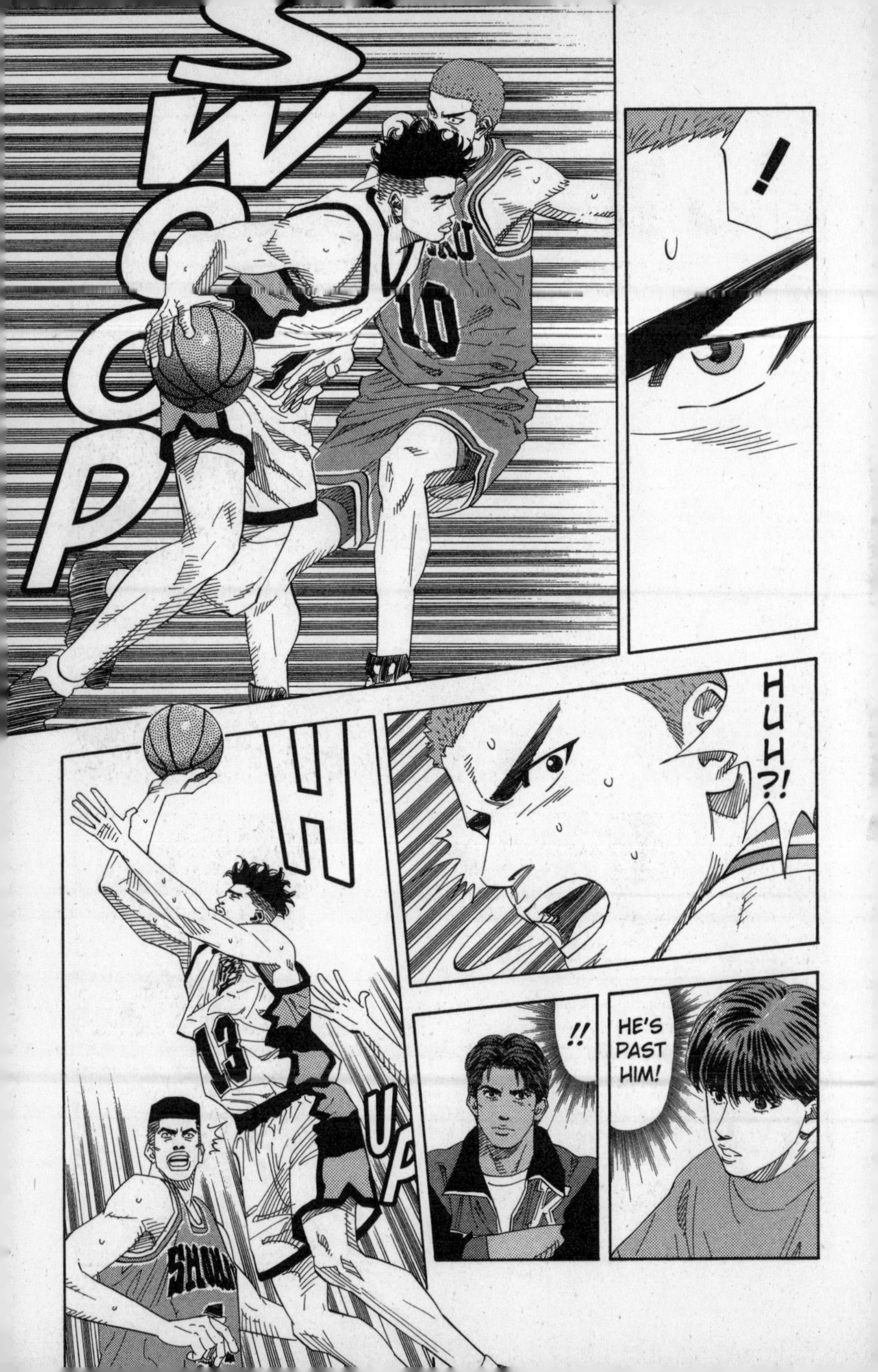
!
SWOOP
HUH?!
HE'S PAST HIM!
!!
H
UP

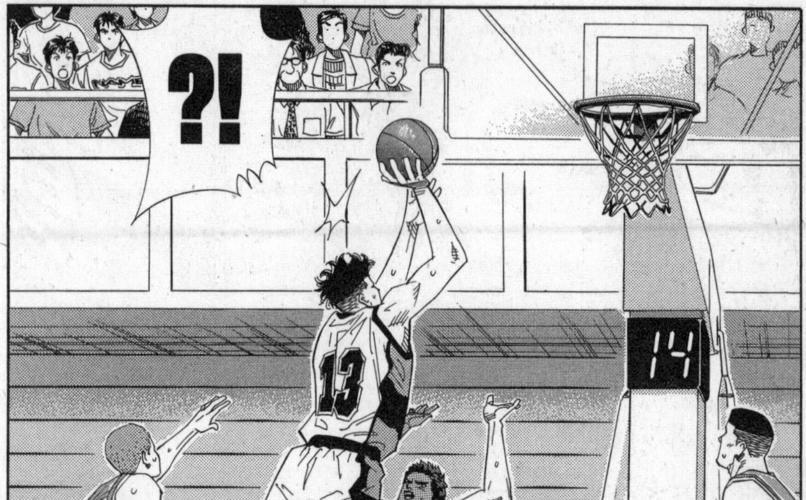
?!

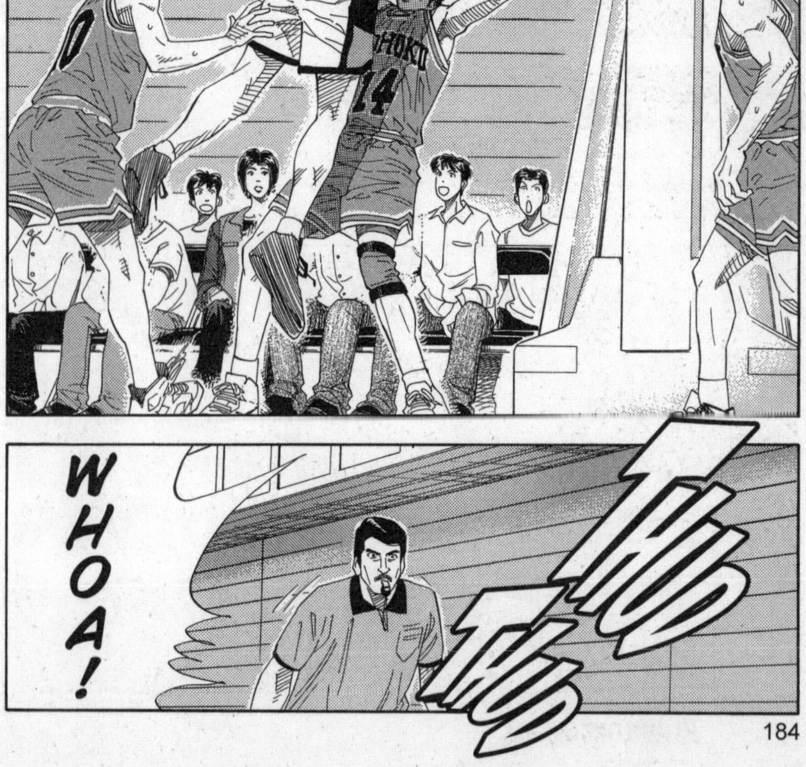
WHOA!
THUD THUD

READ THIS WAY

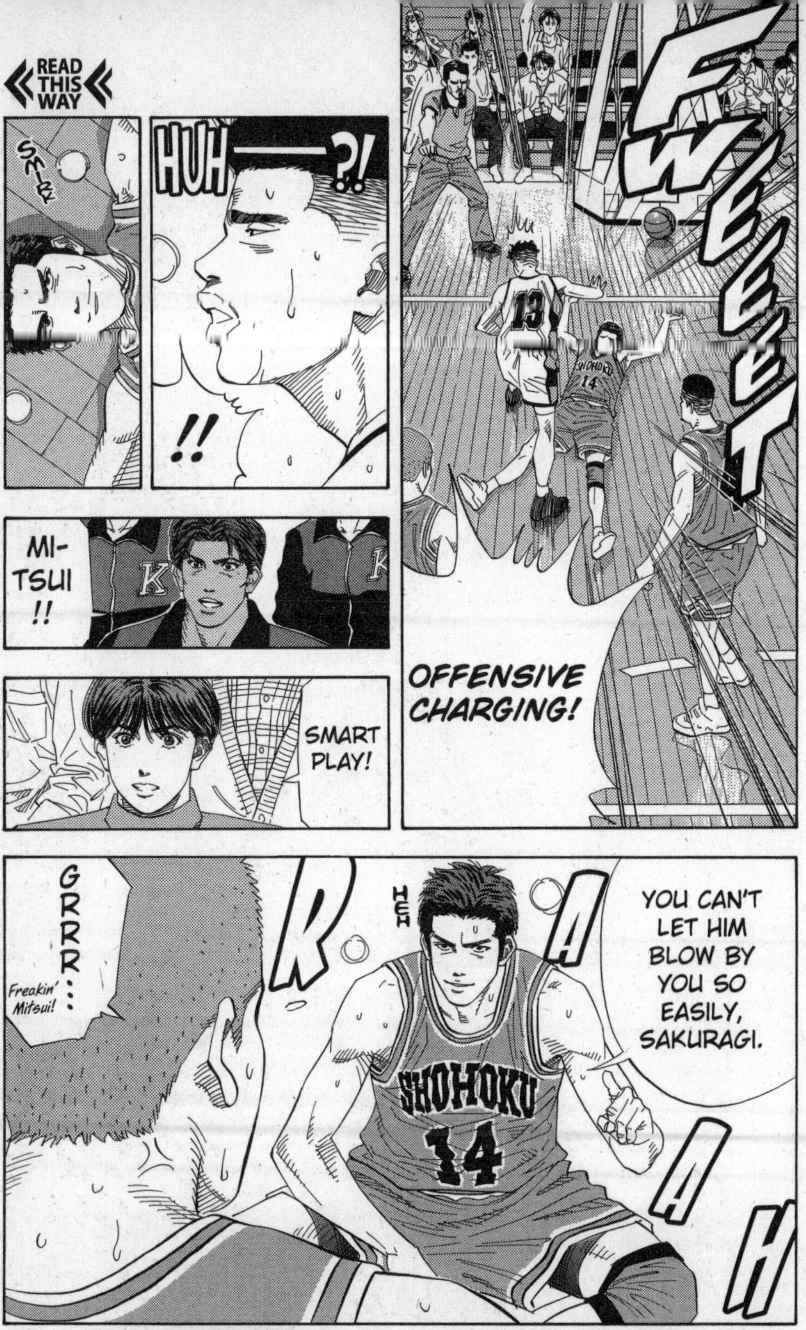
FWEEEEET
OFFENSIVE CHARGING!
HUH——?!
!!
SMIRK
MI-TSUI!!
SMART PLAY!
YOU CAN'T LET HIM BLOW BY YOU SO EASILY, SAKURAGI.
RAAAH
HEH
GRRR...
Freakin' Mitsui!

TO BE CONTINUED!

Coming Next Volume

In a white-hot competition, you need your confidence to carry you to victory. In the Shohoku vs. Ryonan game, Akagi, still recovering from an ankle injury, has his confidence shaken when Ryonan's Uozumi knocks him down. Now doubting his effectiveness, Akagi begins deferring opportunities to his teammates. Ryonan seizes the chance to pull away, leaving Shohoku wondering how they're going to get their mojo back! Sakuragi's going to have to try something unthinkable to get Akagi back on his feet and his head in the game!

ON SALE OCTOBER 2011

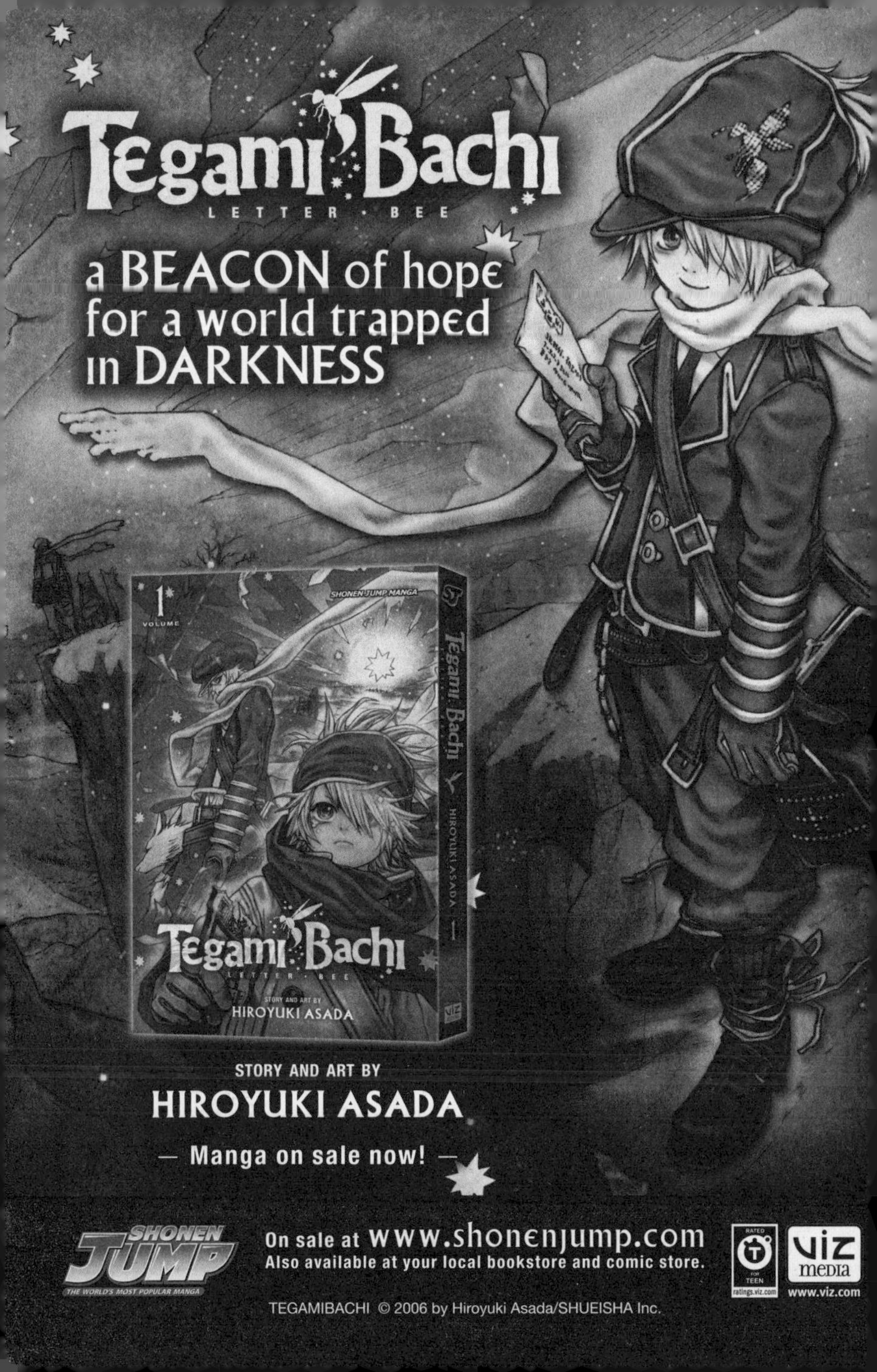
TEGAMI BACHI
LETTER · BEE
a BEACON of hope for a world trapped in DARKNESS
1 VOLUME
SHONEN JUMP MANGA
TEGAMI BACHI
LETTER · BEE
STORY AND ART BY
HIROYUKI ASADA
STORY AND ART BY
HIROYUKI ASADA
— Manga on sale now! —
SHONEN JUMP
THE WORLD'S MOST POPULAR MANGA
On sale at www.shonenjump.com
Also available at your local bookstore and comic store.
RATED T FOR TEEN
ratings.viz.com
VIZ media
www.viz.com
TEGAMIBACHI © 2006 by Hiroyuki Asada/SHUEISHA Inc.

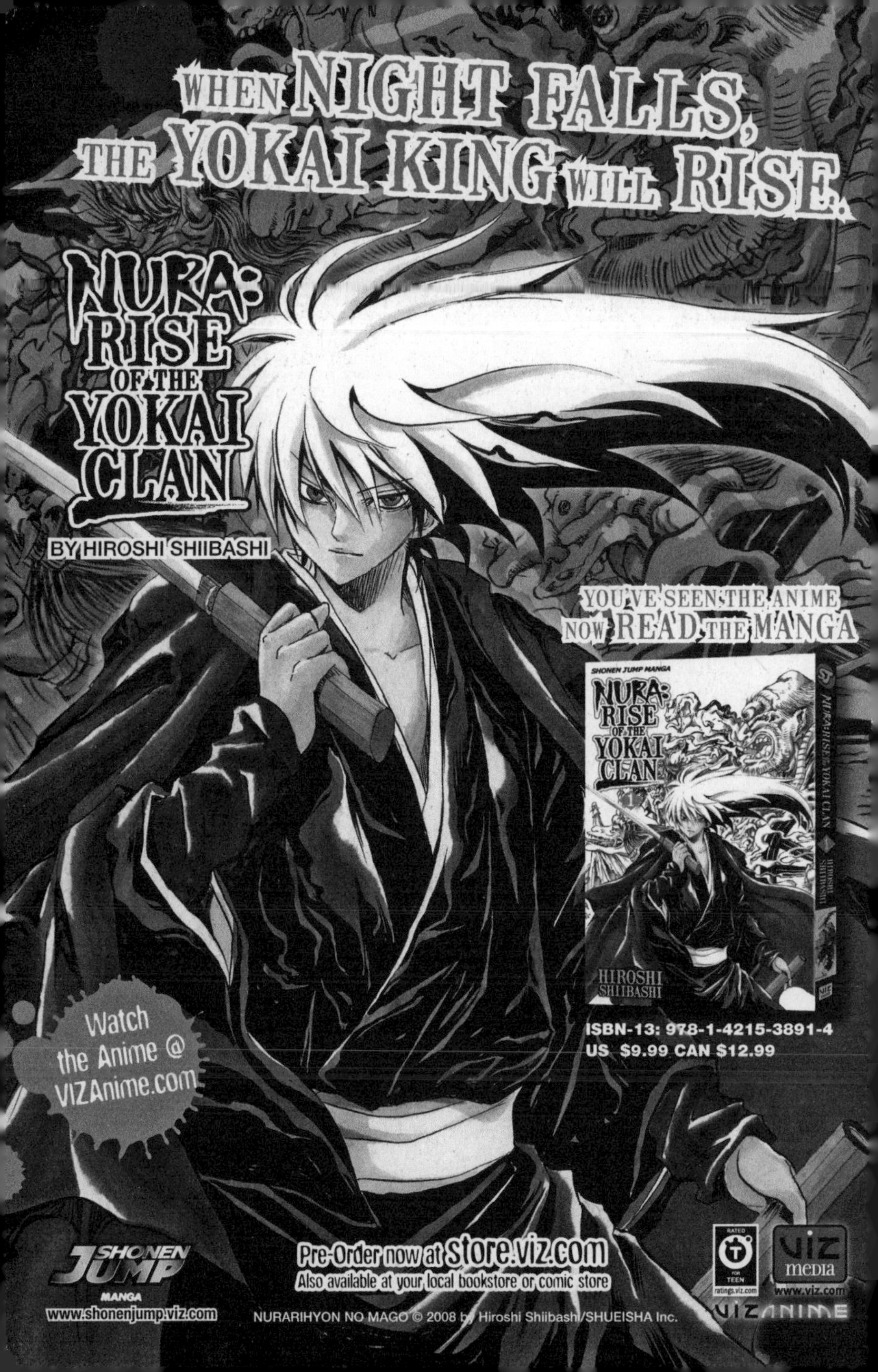

WHEN NIGHT FALLS, THE YOKAI KING WILL RISE.
NURA: RISE OF THE YOKAI CLAN
BY HIROSHI SHIIBASHI
YOU'VE SEEN THE ANIME NOW READ THE MANGA
SHONEN JUMP MANGA
NURA: RISE OF THE YOKAI CLAN
HIROSHI SHIIBASHI
ISBN-13: 978-1-4215-3891-4
US $9.99 CAN $12.99
Watch the Anime @ VIZAnime.com
SHONEN JUMP MANGA
www.shonenjump.viz.com
Pre-Order now at store.viz.com
Also available at your local bookstore or comic store
RATED T FOR TEEN
ratings.viz.com
VIZ media
www.viz.com
VIZANIME
NURARIHYON NO MAGO © 2008 by Hiroshi Shiibashi/SHUEISHA Inc.

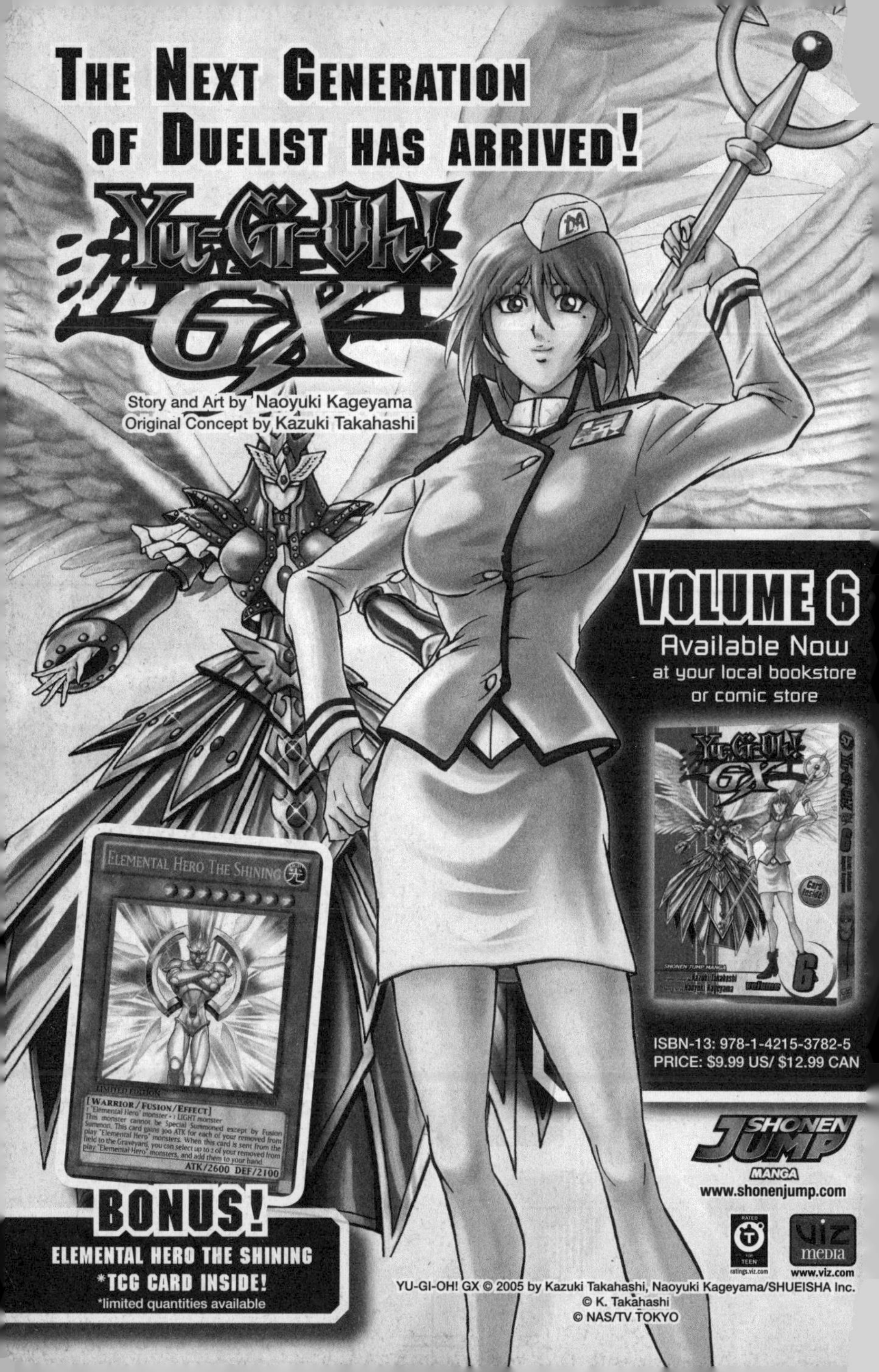
THE NEXT GENERATION OF DUELIST HAS ARRIVED!
YU-GI-OH! GX
Story and Art by Naoyuki Kageyama
Original Concept by Kazuki Takahashi
VOLUME 6
Available Now
at your local bookstore
or comic store
ISBN-13: 978-1-4215-3782-5
PRICE: $9.99 US/ $12.99 CAN
ELEMENTAL HERO THE SHINING
LIMITED EDITION
[WARRIOR / FUSION / EFFECT]
1 "Elemental Hero" monster + 1 LIGHT monster
This monster cannot be Special Summoned except by Fusion Summon. This card gains 300 ATK for each of your removed from play "Elemental Hero" monsters. When this card is sent from the field to the Graveyard, you can select up to 2 of your removed from play "Elemental Hero" monsters, and add them to your hand.
ATK/2600 DEF/2100
BONUS!
ELEMENTAL HERO THE SHINING
*TCG CARD INSIDE!
*limited quantities available
SHONEN JUMP MANGA
www.shonenjump.com
RATED T FOR TEEN
ratings.viz.com
viz media
www.viz.com
YU-GI-OH! GX © 2005 by Kazuki Takahashi, Naoyuki Kageyama/SHUEISHA Inc.
© K. Takahashi
© NAS/TV TOKYO

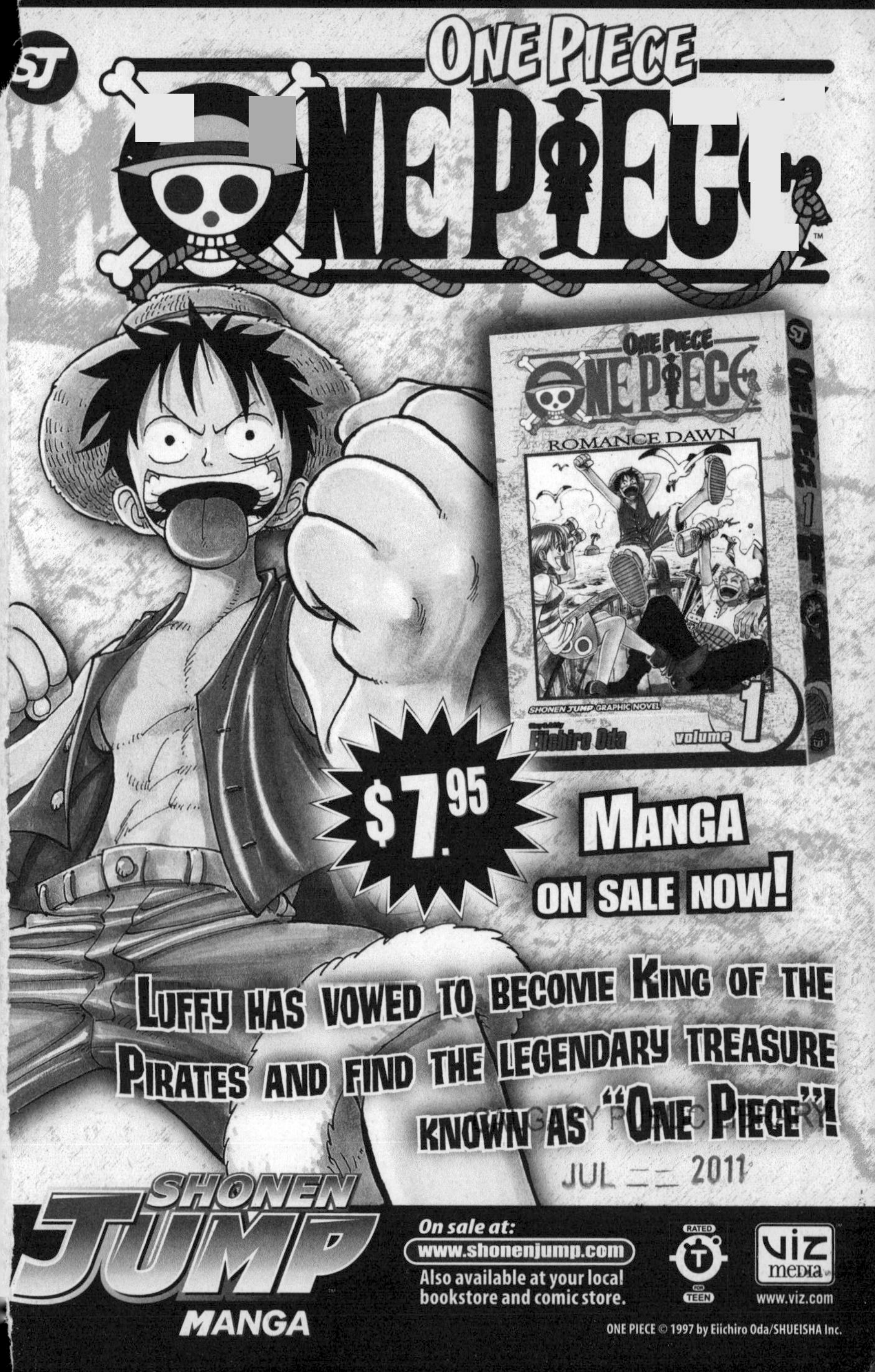
SJ
ONE PIECE
ONE PIECE
ONE PIECE
ONE PIECE
ROMANCE DAWN
SHONEN JUMP GRAPHIC NOVEL
Eiichiro Oda
volume 1
$7.95
MANGA
ON SALE NOW!
LUFFY HAS VOWED TO BECOME KING OF THE PIRATES AND FIND THE LEGENDARY TREASURE KNOWN AS "ONE PIECE"!
SHONEN JUMP MANGA
On sale at:
www.shonenjump.com
Also available at your local bookstore and comic store.
RATED T FOR TEEN
VIZ media
www.viz.com
ONE PIECE © 1997 by Eiichiro Oda/SHUEISHA Inc.

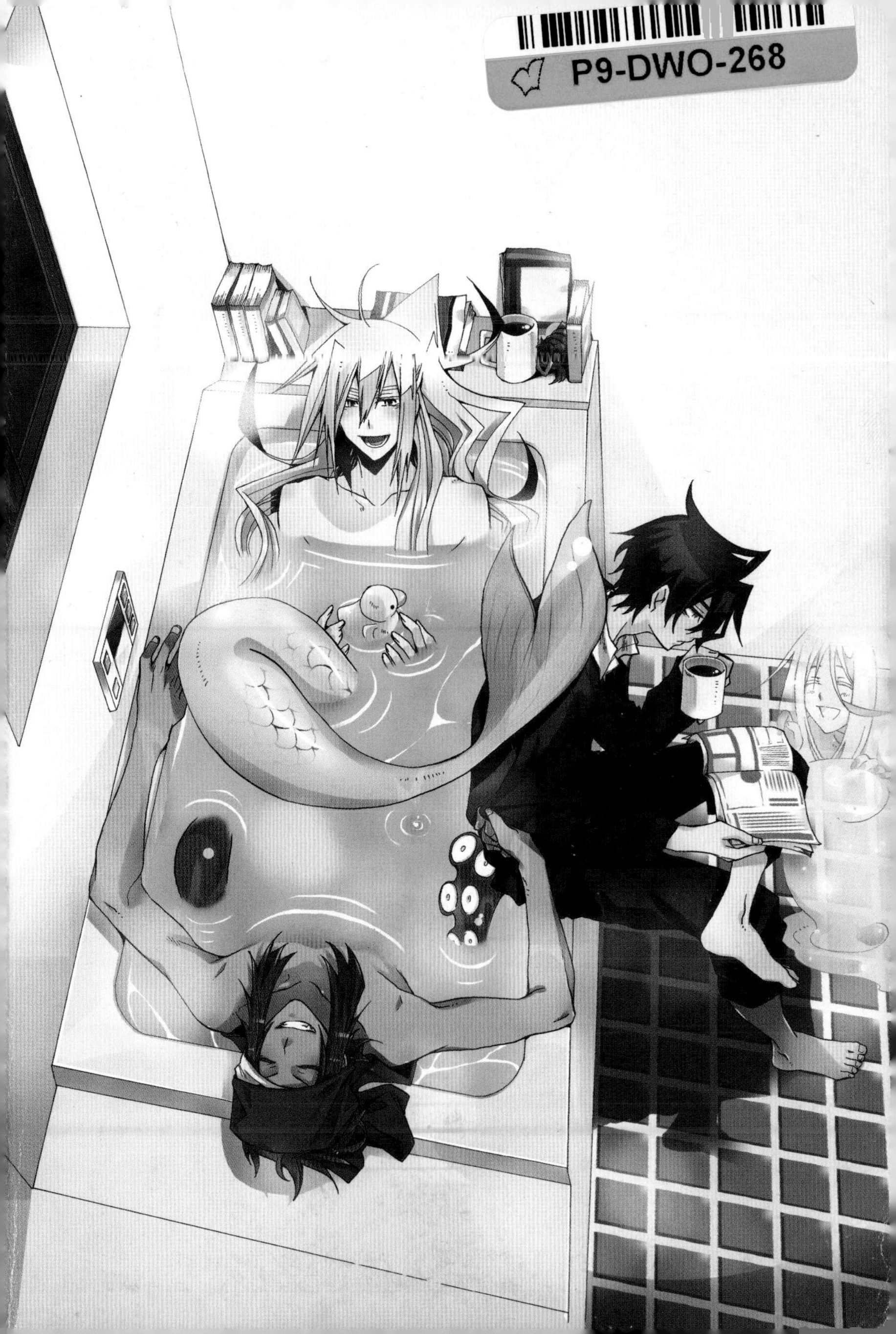

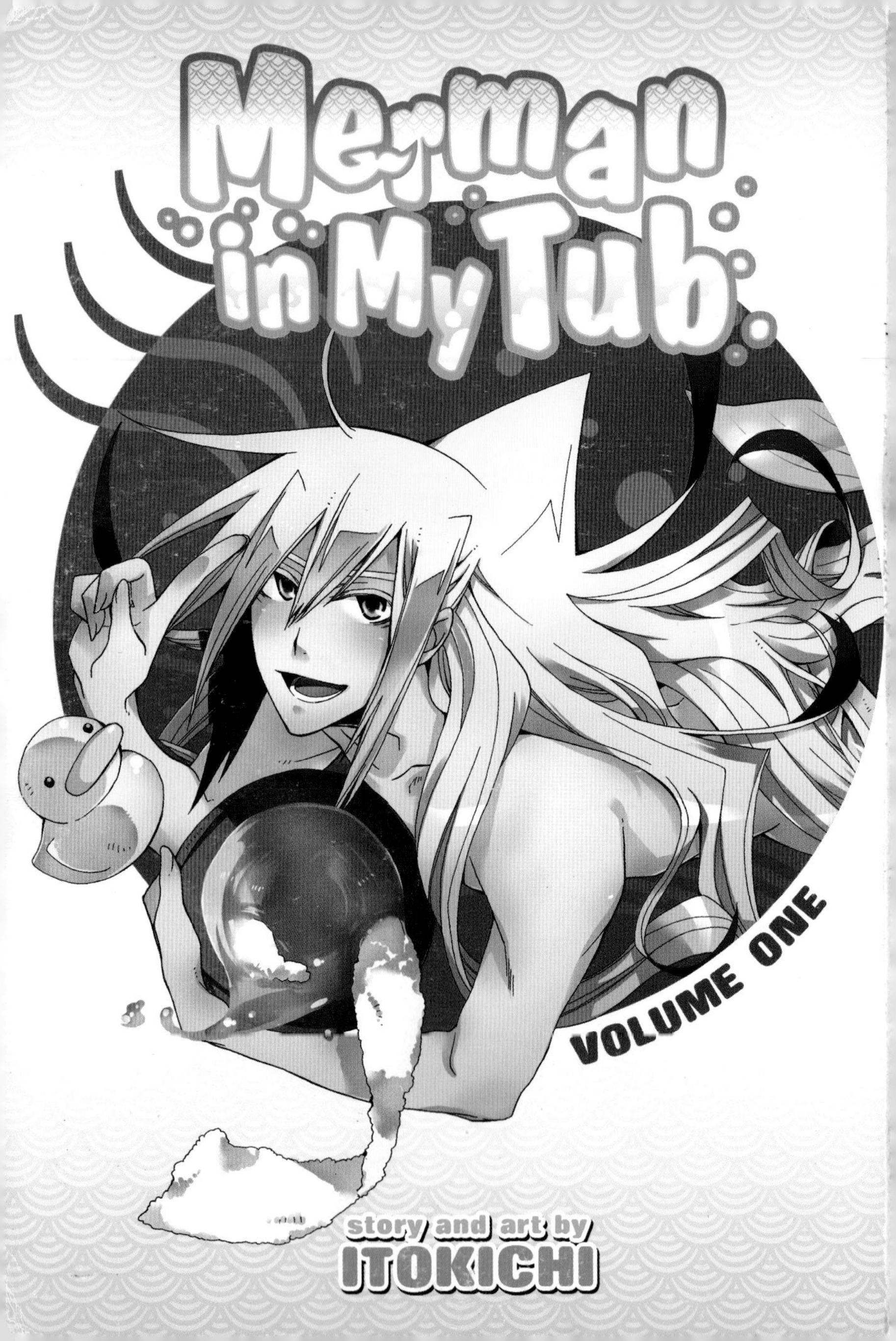
Merman in My Tub
VOLUME ONE
story and art by
ITOKICHI

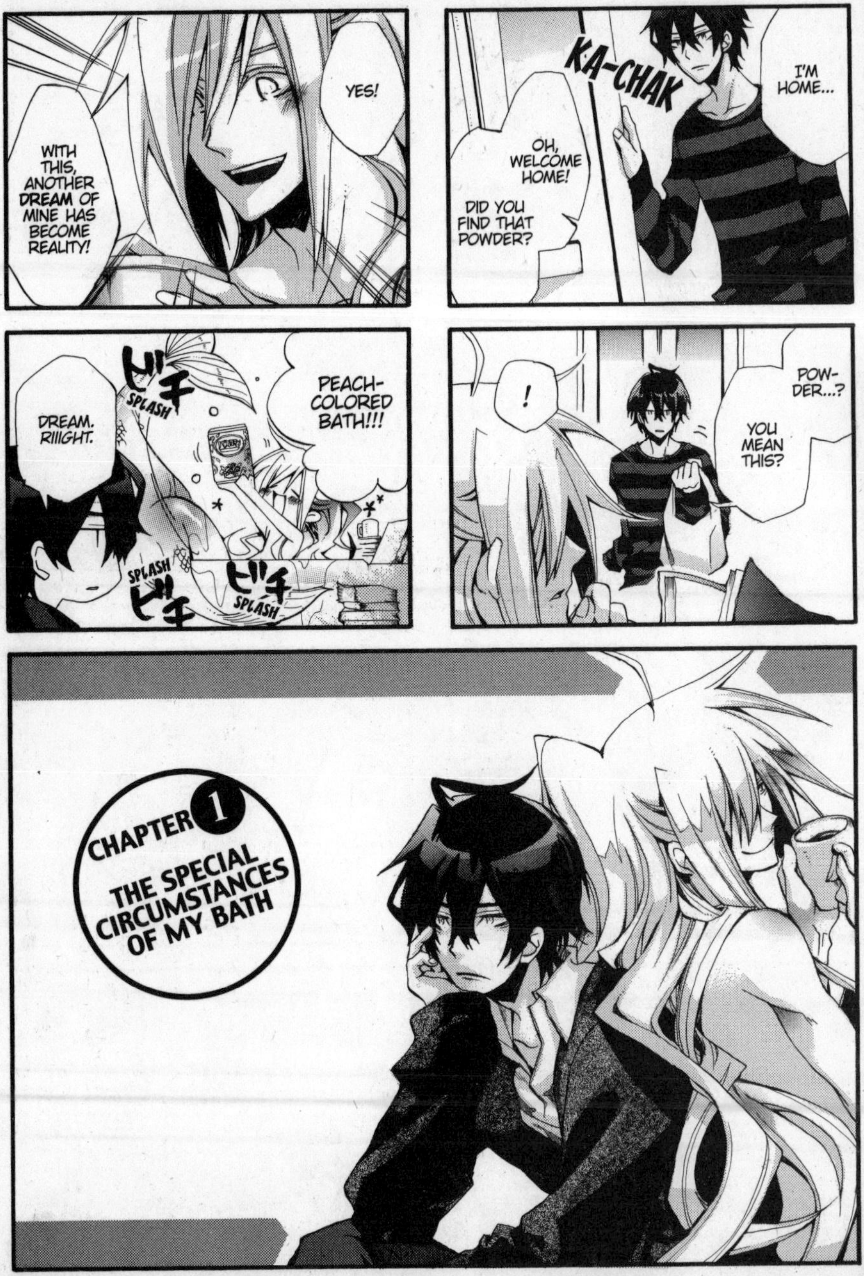
I'M HOME...
KA-CHAK
OH, WELCOME HOME!
DID YOU FIND THAT POWDER?
YES!
WITH THIS, ANOTHER DREAM OF MINE HAS BECOME REALITY!
POW-DER...?
YOU MEAN THIS?
!
PEACH-COLORED BATH!!!
ビチ SPLASH
DREAM. RIIIGHT.
ビチ SPLASH
SPLASH ビチ
CHAPTER 1
THE SPECIAL CIRCUMSTANCES OF MY BATH

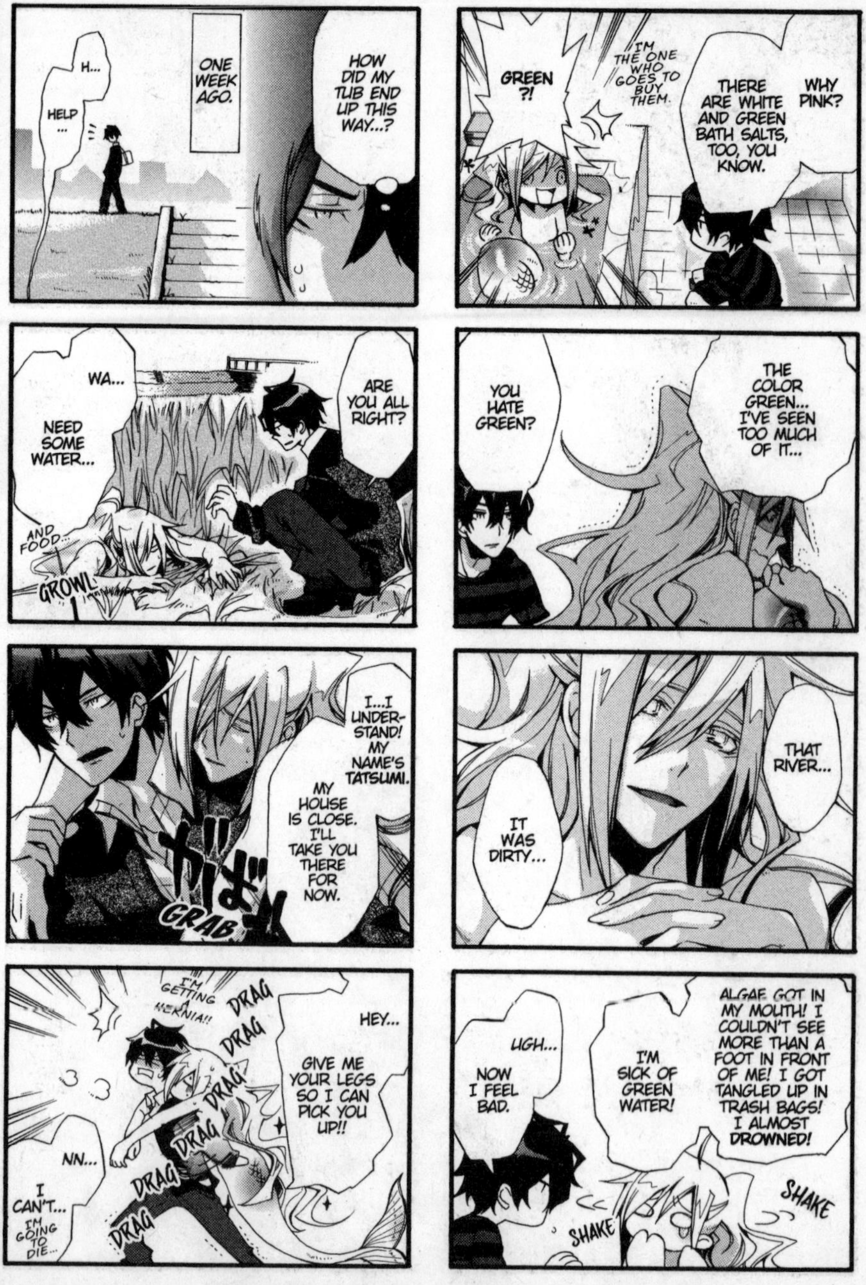
WHY PINK?
THERE ARE WHITE AND GREEN BATH SALTS, TOO, YOU KNOW.
I'M THE ONE WHO GOES TO BUY THEM.
GREEN ?!
HOW DID MY TUB END UP THIS WAY...?
ONE WEEK AGO.
H...
HELP ...
THE COLOR GREEN... I'VE SEEN TOO MUCH OF IT...
YOU HATE GREEN?
ARE YOU ALL RIGHT?
WA...
NEED SOME WATER...
AND FOOD...
GROWL
THAT RIVER...
IT WAS DIRTY...
I...I UNDER-STAND! MY NAME'S TATSUMI.
MY HOUSE IS CLOSE. I'LL TAKE YOU THERE FOR NOW.
がばっ
GRAB
ALGAE GOT IN MY MOUTH! I COULDN'T SEE MORE THAN A FOOT IN FRONT OF ME! I GOT TANGLED UP IN TRASH BAGS! I ALMOST DROWNED!
I'M SICK OF GREEN WATER!
UGH...
NOW I FEEL BAD.
SHAKE
SHAKE
HEY...
GIVE ME YOUR LEGS SO I CAN PICK YOU UP!!
I'M GETTING A HERNIA!!
DRAG DRAG DRAG DRAG DRAG DRAG DRAG
NN...
I CAN'T...
I'M GOING TO DIE...

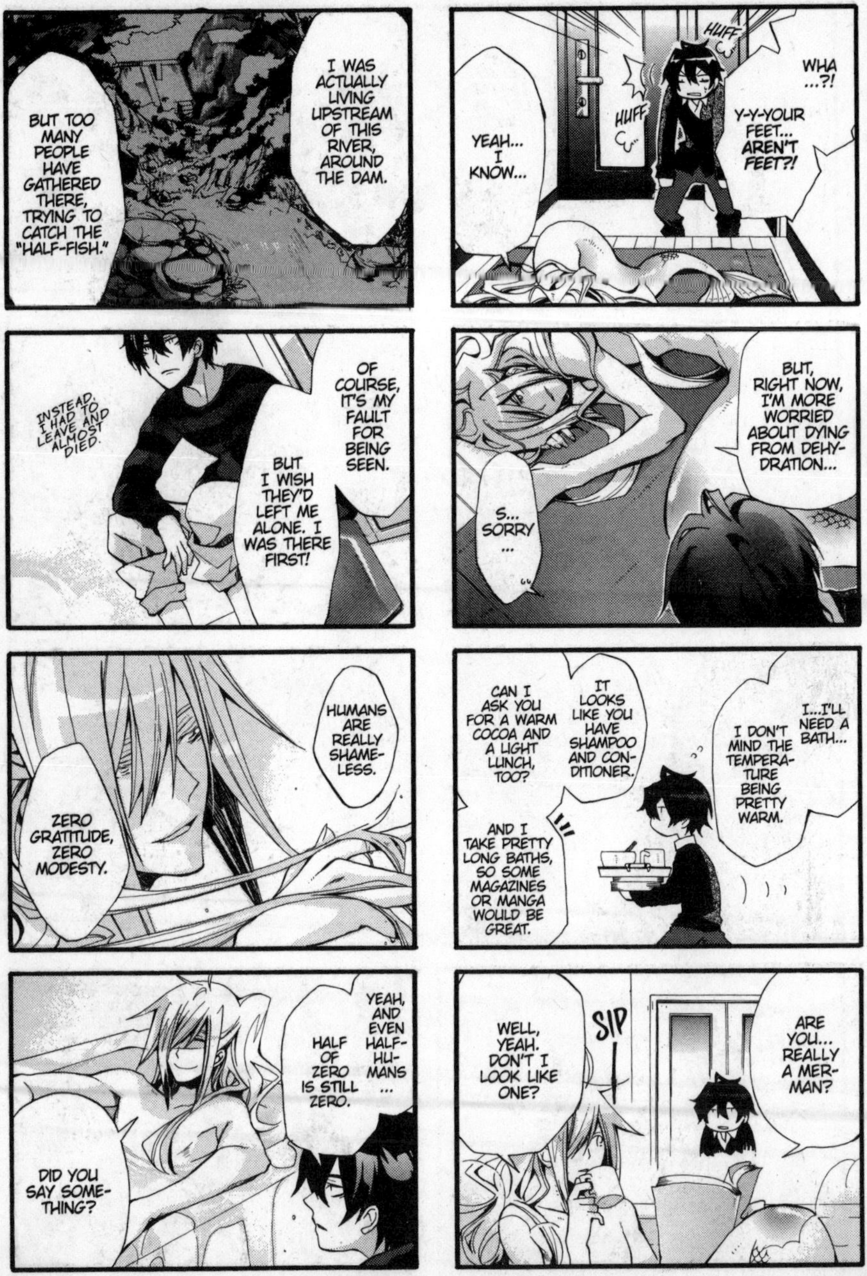
HUFF
WHA ...?!
Y-Y-YOUR FEET... AREN'T FEET?!
HUFF
YEAH... I KNOW...
I WAS ACTUALLY LIVING UPSTREAM OF THIS RIVER, AROUND THE DAM.
BUT TOO MANY PEOPLE HAVE GATHERED THERE, TRYING TO CATCH THE "HALF-FISH."
BUT, RIGHT NOW, I'M MORE WORRIED ABOUT DYING FROM DEHY-DRATION...
S... SORRY ...
OF COURSE, IT'S MY FAULT FOR BEING SEEN.
BUT I WISH THEY'D LEFT ME ALONE. I WAS THERE FIRST!
INSTEAD, I HAD TO LEAVE AND ALMOST DIED.
I...I'LL NEED A BATH...
I DON'T MIND THE TEMPERA-TURE BEING PRETTY WARM.
IT LOOKS LIKE YOU HAVE SHAMPOO AND CON-DITIONER.
CAN I ASK YOU FOR A WARM COCOA AND A LIGHT LUNCH, TOO?
AND I TAKE PRETTY LONG BATHS, SO SOME MAGAZINES OR MANGA WOULD BE GREAT.
HUMANS ARE REALLY SHAME-LESS.
ZERO GRATITUDE, ZERO MODESTY.
ARE YOU... REALLY A MER-MAN?
SIP
WELL, YEAH. DON'T I LOOK LIKE ONE?
YEAH, AND EVEN HALF-HU-MANS ...
HALF OF ZERO IS STILL ZERO.
DID YOU SAY SOME-THING?

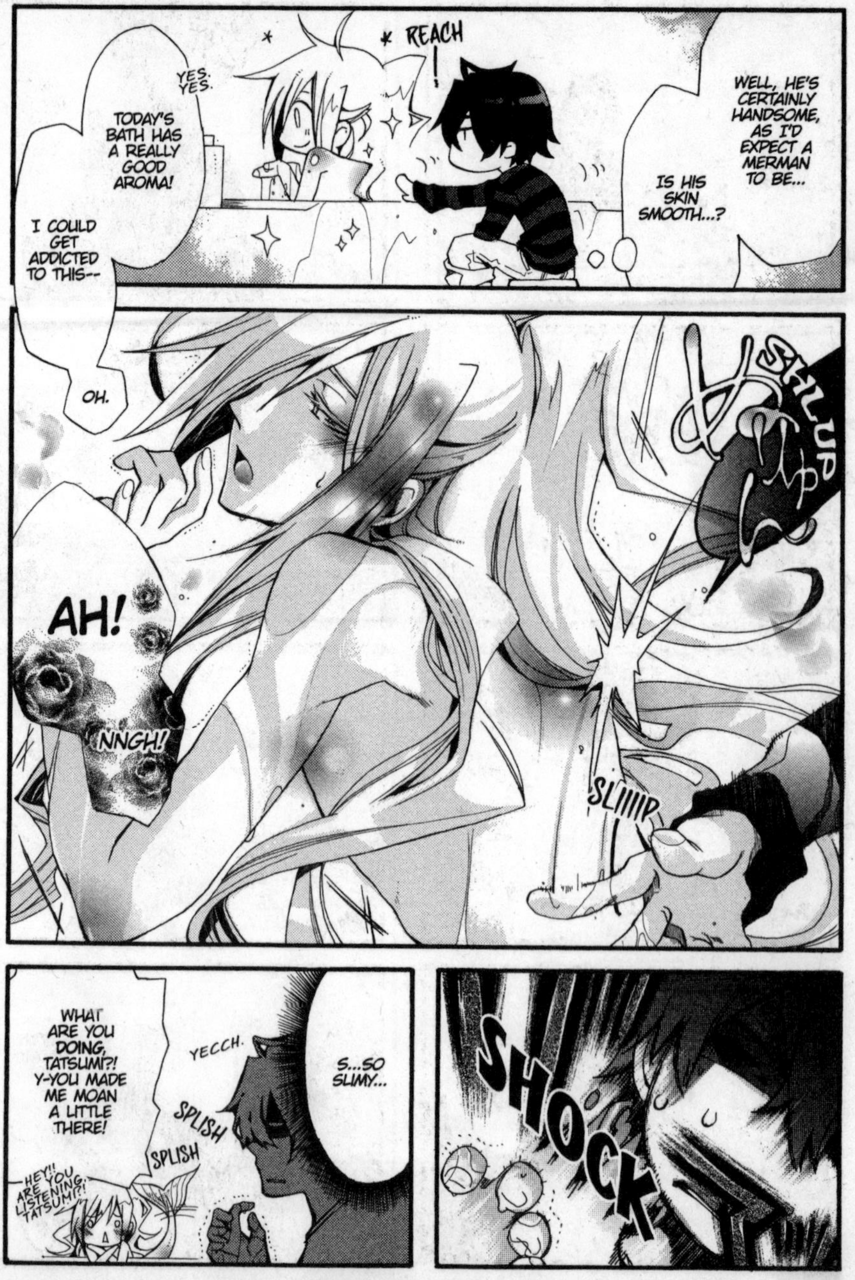
WELL, HE'S CERTAINLY HANDSOME, AS I'D EXPECT A MERMAN TO BE...
IS HIS SKIN SMOOTH...?
REACH
YES. YES.
TODAY'S BATH HAS A REALLY GOOD AROMA!
I COULD GET ADDICTED TO THIS--
SHLUP
OH.
AH!
SLIIIIP
NNGH!
SHOCK
S...SO SLIMY...
YECCH.
WHAT ARE YOU DOING, TATSUMI?! Y-YOU MADE ME MOAN A LITTLE THERE!
SPLISH
SPLISH
HEY!! ARE YOU LISTENING, TATSUMI?!

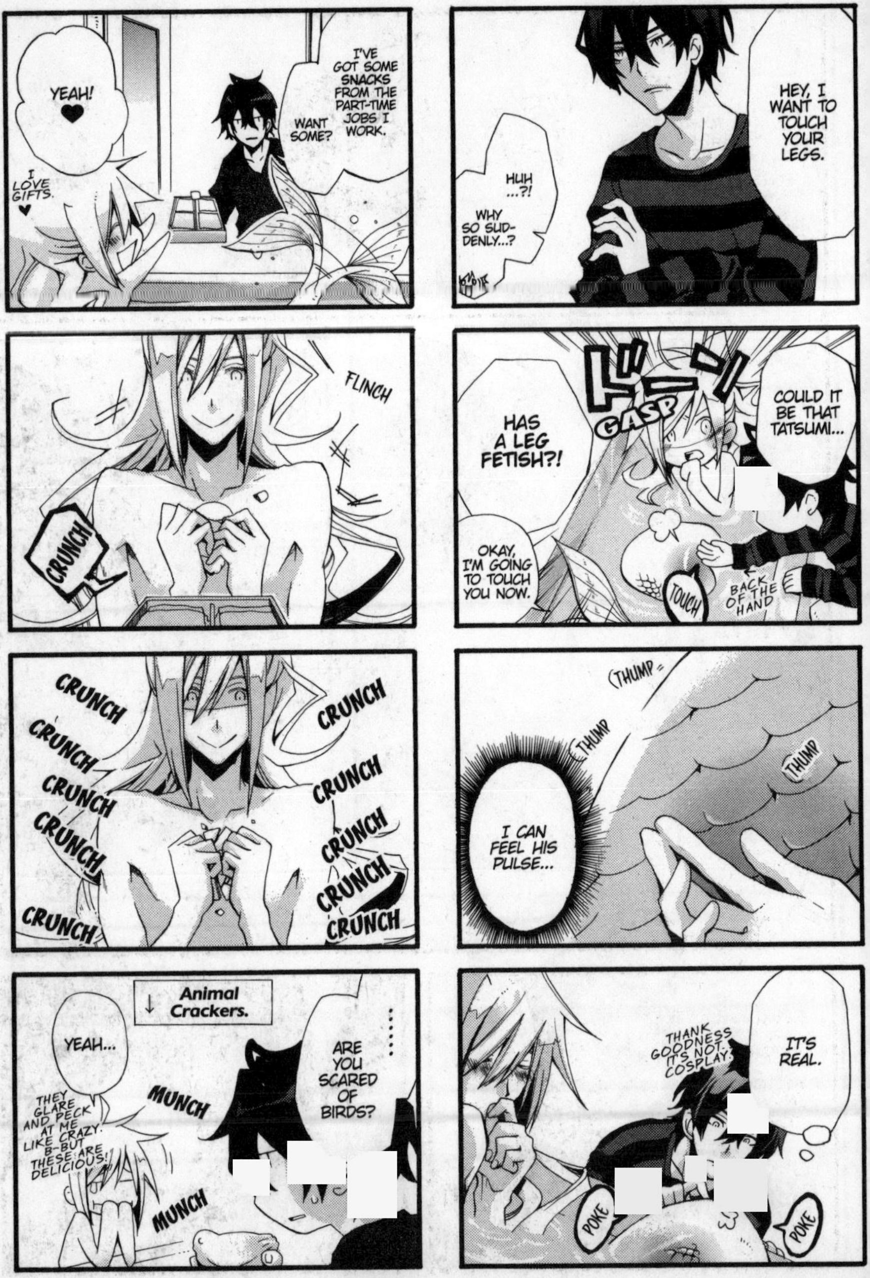
HEY, I WANT TO TOUCH YOUR LEGS.
HUH ...?!
WHY SO SUD-DENLY...?
COULD IT BE THAT TATSUMI...
GASP
HAS A LEG FETISH?!
OKAY, I'M GOING TO TOUCH YOU NOW.
TOUCH
BACK OF THE HAND
THUMP
THUMP
THUMP
I CAN FEEL HIS PULSE...
IT'S REAL.
THANK GOODNESS IT'S NOT COSPLAY.
POKE
POKE
I'VE GOT SOME SNACKS FROM THE PART-TIME JOBS I WORK.
WANT SOME?
YEAH! ♥
I LOVE GIFTS. ♥
FLINCH
CRUNCH
CRUNCH
CRUNCH
CRUNCH
CRUNCH
CRUNCH
CRUNCH
CRUNCH
CRUNCH
CRUNCH
CRUNCH
Animal Crackers.
......
ARE YOU SCARED OF BIRDS?
YEAH...
THEY GLARE AND PECK AT ME LIKE CRAZY. B-BUT THESE ARE DELICIOUS!
MUNCH
MUNCH

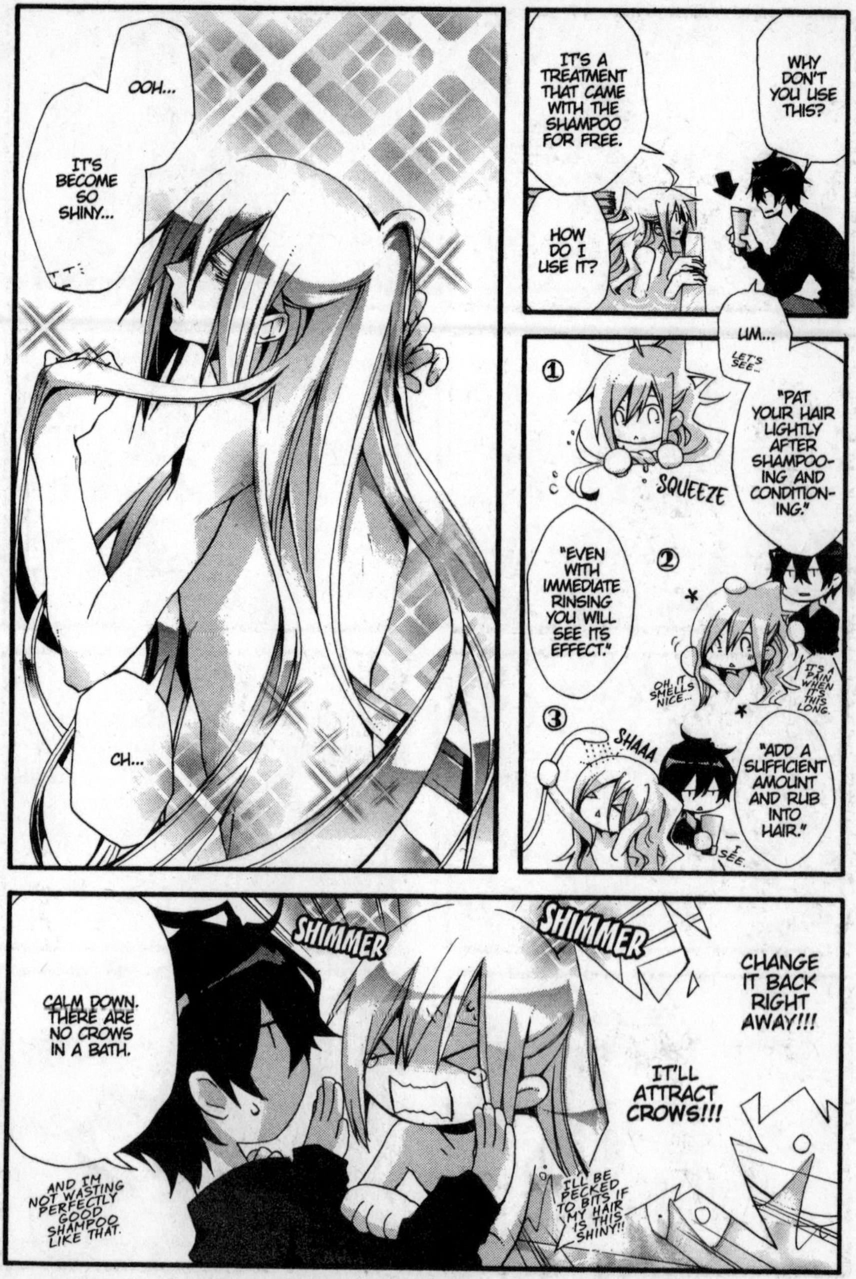
WHY DON'T YOU USE THIS?
IT'S A TREATMENT THAT CAME WITH THE SHAMPOO FOR FREE.
HOW DO I USE IT?
UM...
LET'S SEE...
"PAT YOUR HAIR LIGHTLY AFTER SHAMPOO-ING AND CONDITION-ING."
①
SQUEEZE
"EVEN WITH IMMEDIATE RINSING YOU WILL SEE ITS EFFECT."
②
IT'S A PAIN WHEN IT'S THIS LONG.
OH, IT SMELLS NICE...
"ADD A SUFFICIENT AMOUNT AND RUB INTO HAIR."
I SEE.
SHAAA
③
OOH...
IT'S BECOME SO SHINY...
CH...
SHIMMER
SHIMMER
CHANGE IT BACK RIGHT AWAY!!!
IT'LL ATTRACT CROWS!!!
I'LL BE PECKED TO BITS IF MY HAIR IS THIS SHINY!!
CALM DOWN. THERE ARE NO CROWS IN A BATH.
AND I'M NOT WASTING PERFECTLY GOOD SHAMPOO LIKE THAT.

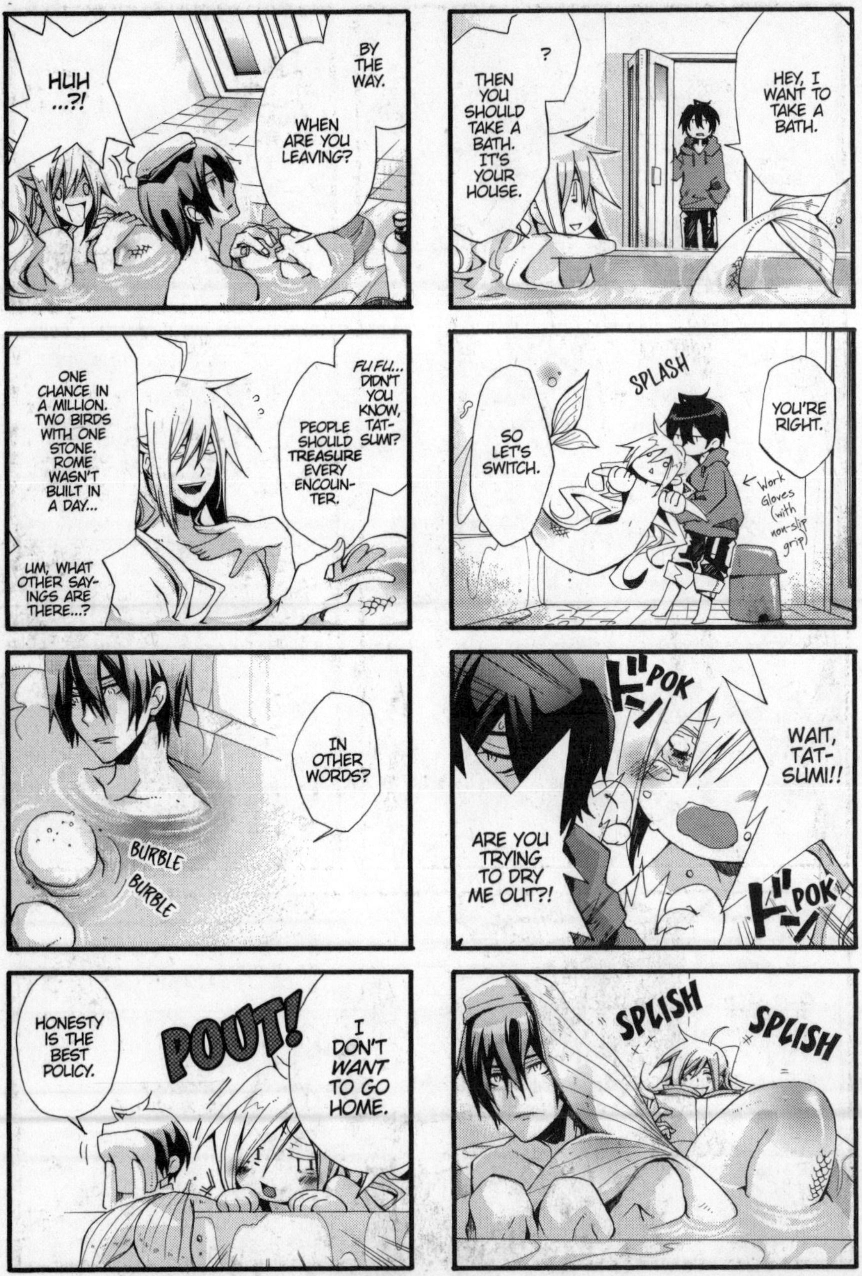
HEY, I WANT TO TAKE A BATH.
?
THEN YOU SHOULD TAKE A BATH. IT'S YOUR HOUSE.
BY THE WAY.
WHEN ARE YOU LEAVING?
HUH ...?!
YOU'RE RIGHT.
SPLASH
SO LET'S SWITCH.
Work Gloves (with non-slip grip)
FU FU... DIDN'T YOU KNOW, TATSUMI?
PEOPLE SHOULD TREASURE EVERY ENCOUNTER.
ONE CHANCE IN A MILLION. TWO BIRDS WITH ONE STONE. ROME WASN'T BUILT IN A DAY...
UM, WHAT OTHER SAYINGS ARE THERE...?
POK
WAIT, TATSUMI!!
ARE YOU TRYING TO DRY ME OUT?!
POK
IN OTHER WORDS?
BURBLE
BURBLE
SPLISH
SPLISH
I DON'T WANT TO GO HOME.
POUT!
HONESTY IS THE BEST POLICY.

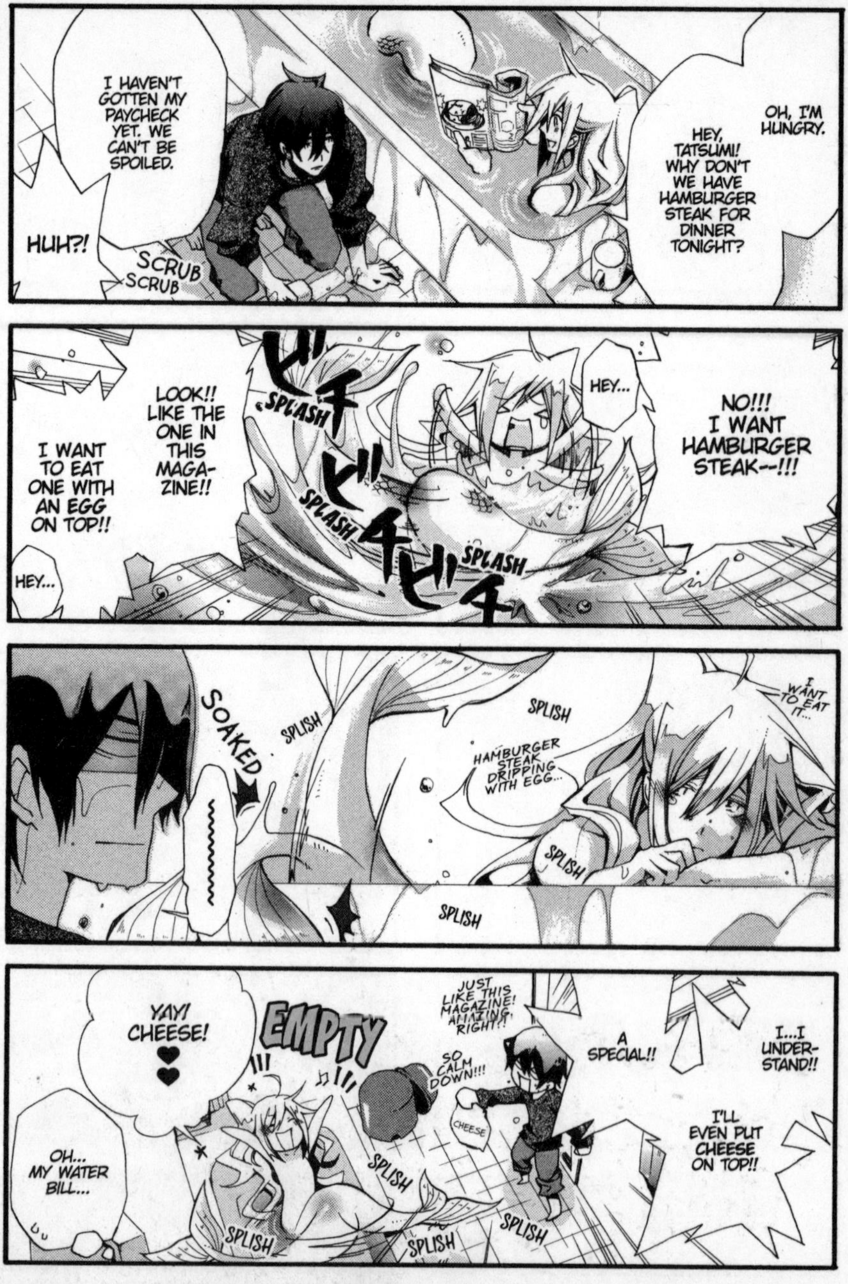

OH, I'M HUNGRY.
HEY, TATSUMI! WHY DON'T WE HAVE HAMBURGER STEAK FOR DINNER TONIGHT?
I HAVEN'T GOTTEN MY PAYCHECK YET. WE CAN'T BE SPOILED.
HUH?!
SCRUB SCRUB
NO!!! I WANT HAMBURGER STEAK--!!!
HEY...
SPLASH
SPLASH
SPLASH
LOOK!! LIKE THE ONE IN THIS MAGAZINE!!
I WANT TO EAT ONE WITH AN EGG ON TOP!!
HEY...
I WANT TO EAT IT...
SPLISH
HAMBURGER STEAK DRIPPING WITH EGG...
SPLISH
SPLISH
SOAKED
SPLISH
I...I UNDERSTAND!!
I'LL EVEN PUT CHEESE ON TOP!!
A SPECIAL!!
JUST LIKE THIS MAGAZINE! AMAZING, RIGHT?
SO CALM DOWN!!!
CHEESE
EMPTY
YAY! CHEESE! ♥♥
SPLISH
SPLISH
SPLISH
SPLISH
OH... MY WATER BILL...

Merman in My Tub

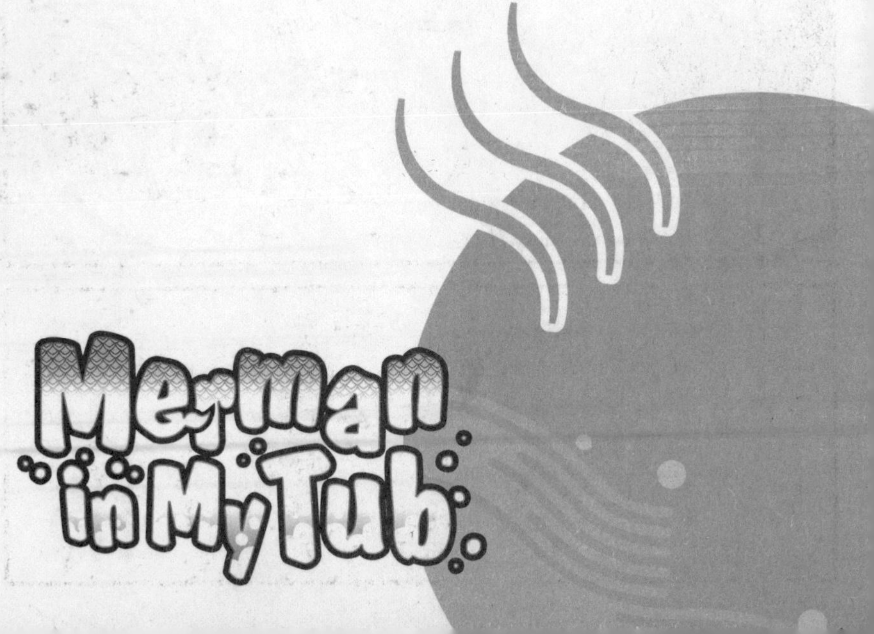

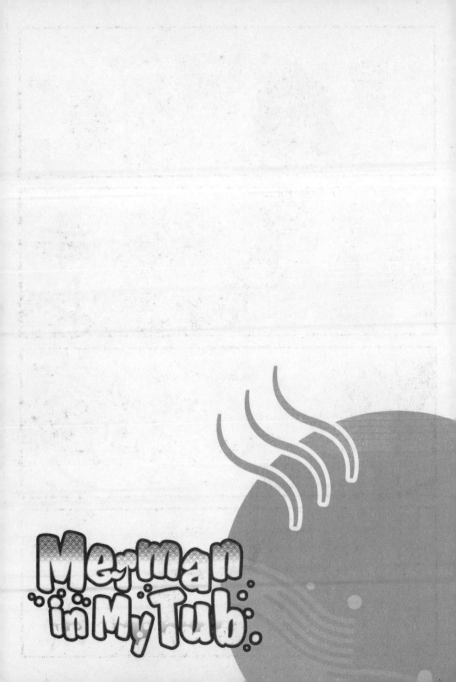

オレん家（ち）のフロ事情

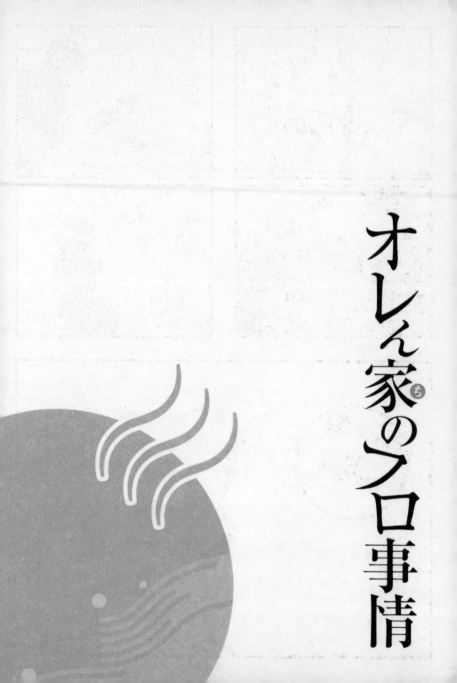

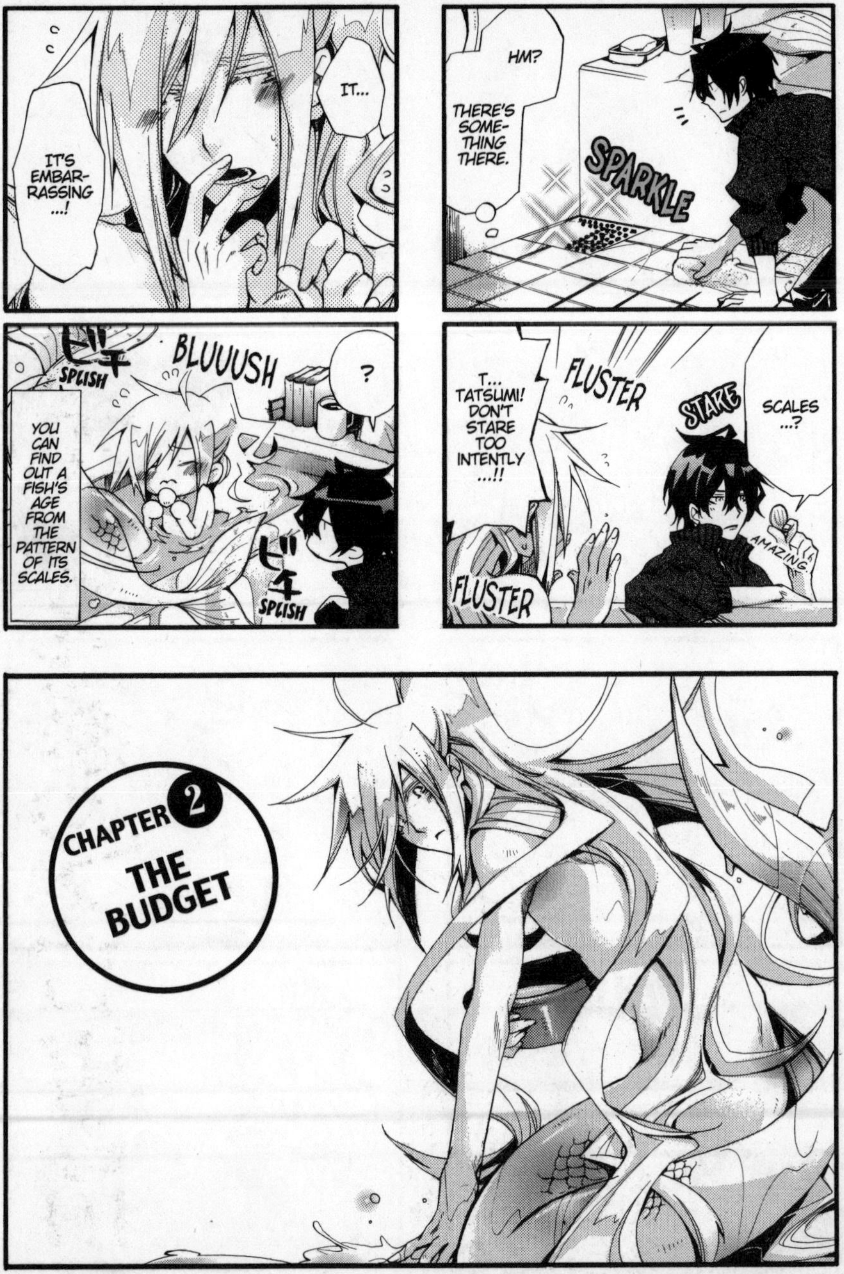
HM?
THERE'S SOME-THING THERE.
SPARKLE
IT...
IT'S EMBAR-RASSING ...!
SCALES ...?
STARE
AMAZING
T... TATSUMI! DON'T STARE TOO INTENTLY ...!!
FLUSTER
FLUSTER
?
BLUUUSH
SPLISH
YOU CAN FIND OUT A FISH'S AGE FROM THE PATTERN OF ITS SCALES.
SPLISH
CHAPTER 2
THE BUDGET

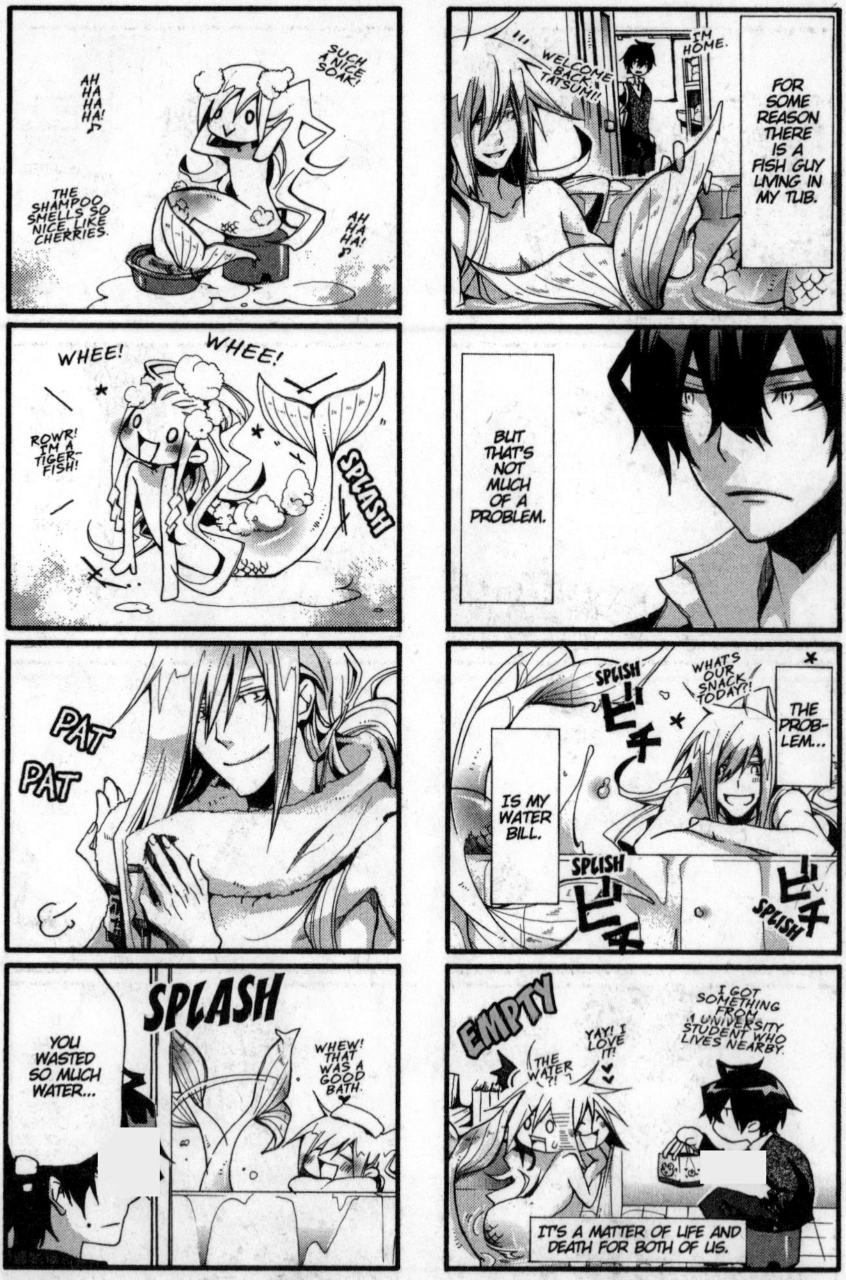
FOR SOME REASON THERE IS A FISH GUY LIVING IN MY TUB.
I'M HOME.
WELCOME BACK, TATSUMI!!
BUT THAT'S NOT MUCH OF A PROBLEM.
THE PROB-LEM...
WHAT'S OUR SNACK TODAY?!
SPLISH
IS MY WATER BILL.
SPLISH
SPLISH
I GOT SOMETHING FROM A UNIVERSITY STUDENT WHO LIVES NEARBY.
YAY! I LOVE IT!
THE WATER ?!
EMPTY
IT'S A MATTER OF LIFE AND DEATH FOR BOTH OF US.
SUCH A NICE SOAK!
AH HA HA HA!♪
THE SHAMPOO SMELLS SO NICE, LIKE CHERRIES.
AH HA HA!♪
WHEE!
WHEE!
SPLASH
ROWR! I'M A TIGER-FISH!
PAT
PAT
SPLASH
WHEW! THAT WAS A GOOD BATH.
YOU WASTED SO MUCH WATER...

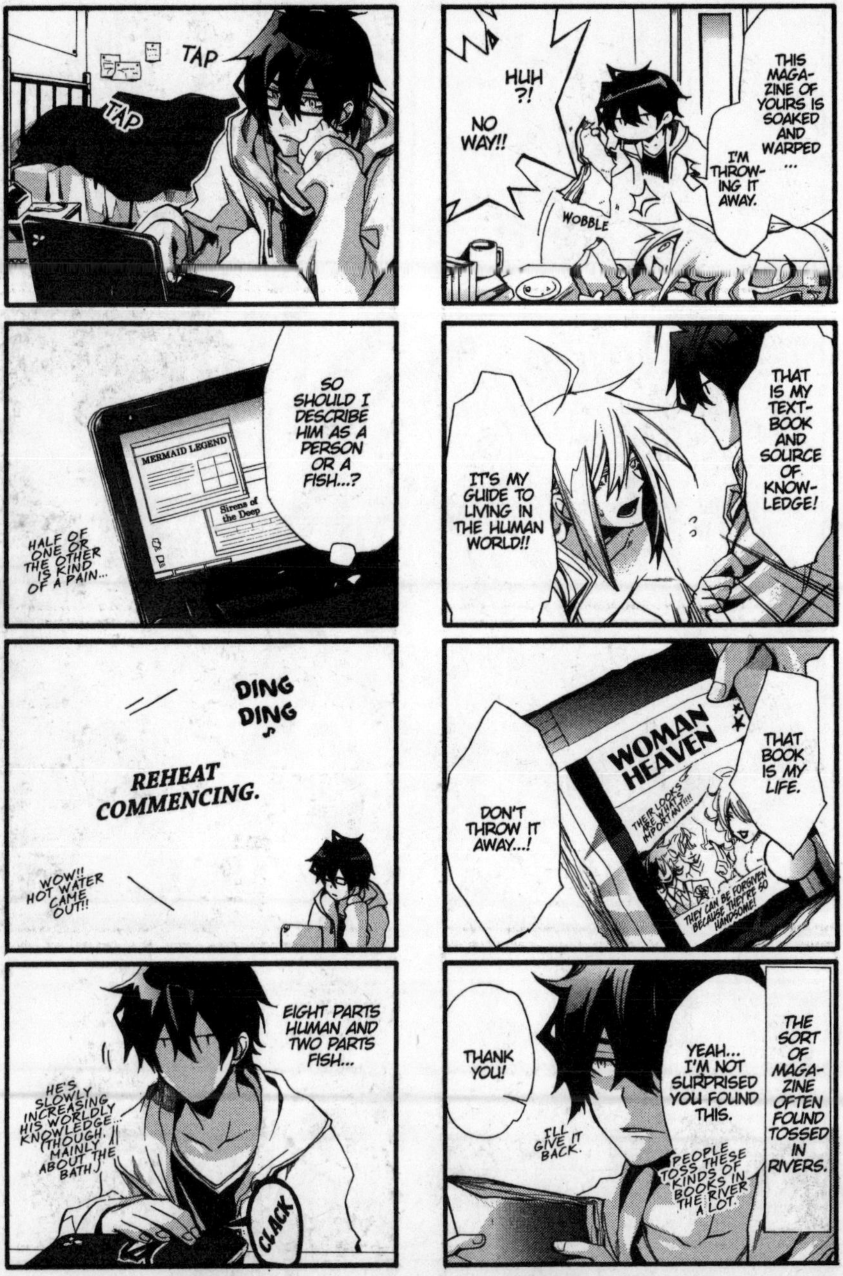
THIS MAGAZINE OF YOURS IS SOAKED AND WARPED...
I'M THROWING IT AWAY.
HUH ?!
NO WAY!!
WOBBLE
THAT IS MY TEXTBOOK AND SOURCE OF KNOWLEDGE!
IT'S MY GUIDE TO LIVING IN THE HUMAN WORLD!!
THAT BOOK IS MY LIFE.
WOMAN HEAVEN
THEIR LOOKS ARE WHAT'S IMPORTANT!!!!
THEY CAN BE FORGIVEN BECAUSE THEY'RE SO HANDSOME!
DON'T THROW IT AWAY...!
THE SORT OF MAGAZINE OFTEN FOUND TOSSED IN RIVERS.
YEAH... I'M NOT SURPRISED YOU FOUND THIS.
PEOPLE TOSS THESE KINDS OF BOOKS IN THE RIVER A LOT.
THANK YOU!
I'LL GIVE IT BACK.
TAP
TAP
SO SHOULD I DESCRIBE HIM AS A PERSON OR A FISH...?
MERMAID LEGEND
Sirens of the Deep
HALF OF ONE OR THE OTHER IS KIND OF A PAIN...
DING DING
REHEAT COMMENCING.
WOW!! HOT WATER CAME OUT!!
EIGHT PARTS HUMAN AND TWO PARTS FISH...
HE'S SLOWLY INCREASING HIS WORLDLY KNOWLEDGE... (THOUGH, MAINLY ABOUT THE BATH)
CLACK

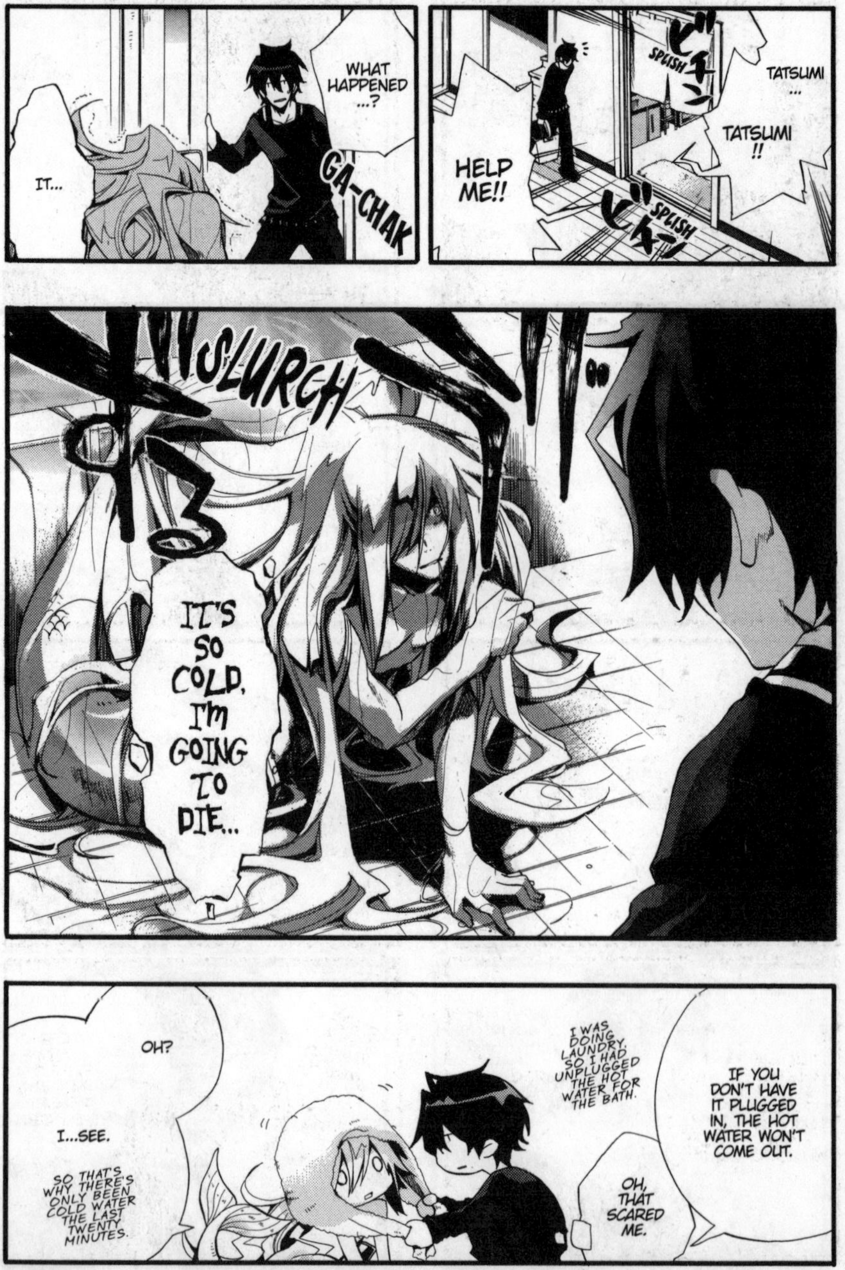
TATSUMI ...
TATSUMI !!
SPLISH
HELP ME!!
SPLISH
WHAT HAPPENED ...?
GA-CHAK
IT...
SLURCH
IT'S SO COLD, I'M GOING TO DIE...
IF YOU DON'T HAVE IT PLUGGED IN, THE HOT WATER WON'T COME OUT.
OH, THAT SCARED ME.
I WAS DOING LAUNDRY, SO I HAD UNPLUGGED THE HOT WATER FOR THE BATH.
OH?
I...SEE.
SO THAT'S WHY THERE'S ONLY BEEN COLD WATER THE LAST TWENTY MINUTES.

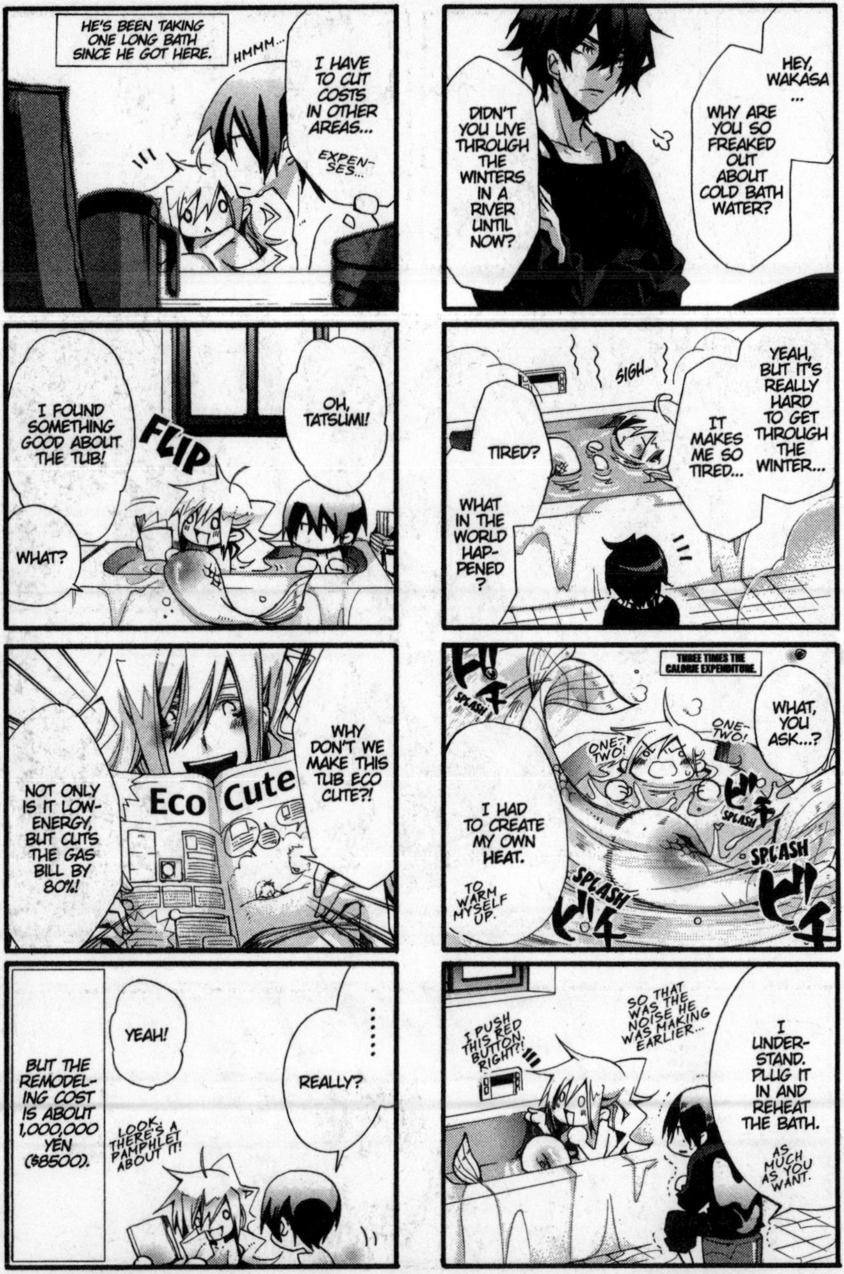
HEY, WAKASA ... WHY ARE YOU SO FREAKED OUT ABOUT COLD BATH WATER?
DIDN'T YOU LIVE THROUGH THE WINTERS IN A RIVER UNTIL NOW?
YEAH, BUT IT'S REALLY HARD TO GET THROUGH THE WINTER...
IT MAKES ME SO TIRED...
SIGH...
TIRED?
WHAT IN THE WORLD HAPPENED?
THREE TIMES THE CALORIE EXPENDITURE.
WHAT, YOU ASK...?
ONE-TWO!
ONE-TWO!
SPLASH
SPLASH
SPLASH
SPLASH
I HAD TO CREATE MY OWN HEAT.
TO WARM MYSELF UP.
I UNDERSTAND. PLUG IT IN AND REHEAT THE BATH.
AS MUCH AS YOU WANT.
SO THAT WAS THE NOISE HE WAS MAKING EARLIER...
I PUSH THIS RED BUTTON, RIGHT?!
I HAVE TO CUT COSTS IN OTHER AREAS...
HMMM...
HE'S BEEN TAKING ONE LONG BATH SINCE HE GOT HERE.
EXPENSES...
OH, TATSUMI!
FLIP
I FOUND SOMETHING GOOD ABOUT THE TUB!
WHAT?
WHY DON'T WE MAKE THIS TUB ECO CUTE?!
Eco Cute
NOT ONLY IS IT LOW-ENERGY, BUT CUTS THE GAS BILL BY 80%!
......
REALLY?
YEAH!
LOOK, THERE'S A PAMPHLET ABOUT IT!
BUT THE REMODELING COST IS ABOUT 1,000,000 YEN ($8500).

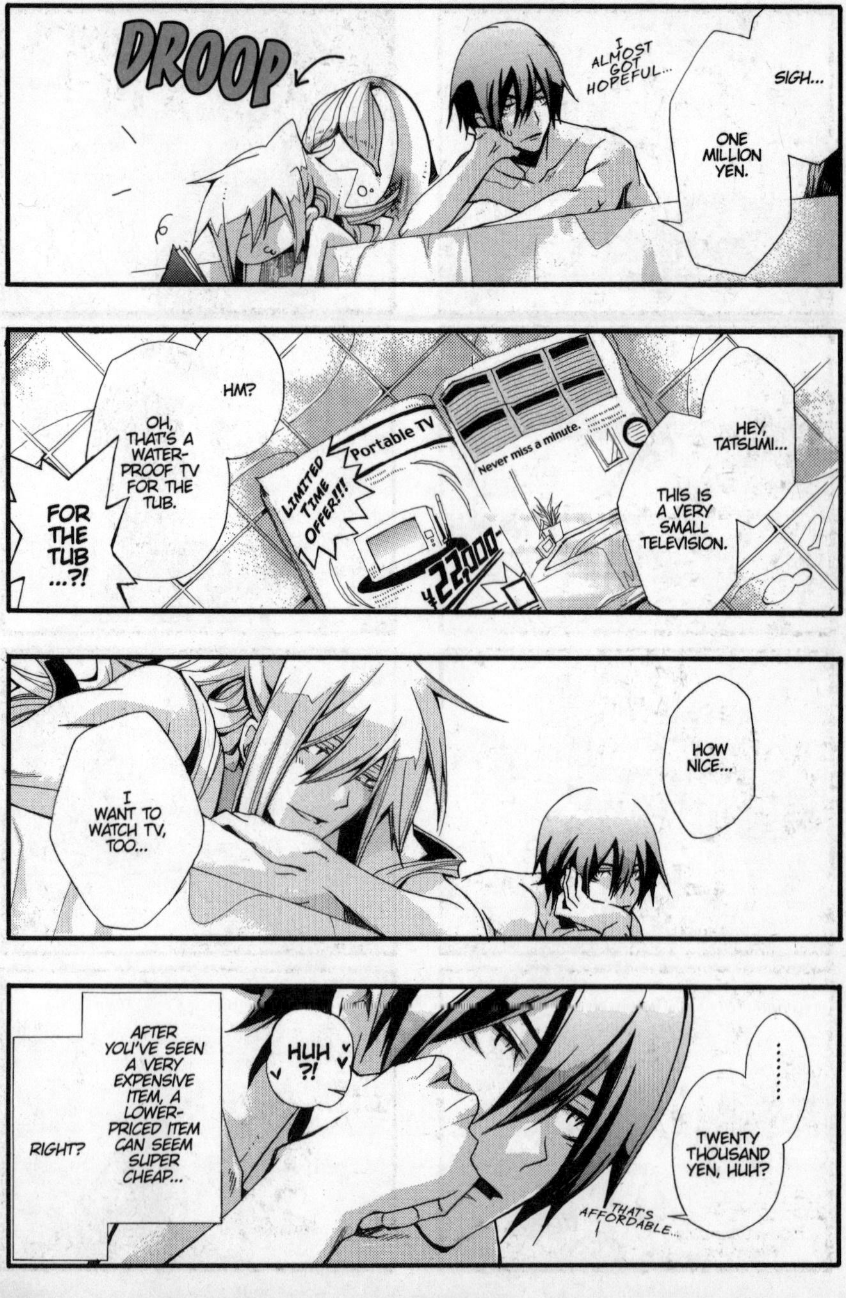
SIGH...
ONE MILLION YEN.
I ALMOST GOT HOPEFUL...
DROOP
HEY, TATSUMI...
THIS IS A VERY SMALL TELEVISION.
Never miss a minute.
Portable TV
LIMITED TIME OFFER!!!
¥22,000-
HM?
OH, THAT'S A WATER-PROOF TV FOR THE TUB.
FOR THE TUB...?!
HOW NICE...
I WANT TO WATCH TV, TOO...
......
TWENTY THOUSAND YEN, HUH?
THAT'S AFFORDABLE...
HUH?!
AFTER YOU'VE SEEN A VERY EXPENSIVE ITEM, A LOWER-PRICED ITEM CAN SEEM SUPER CHEAP...
RIGHT?

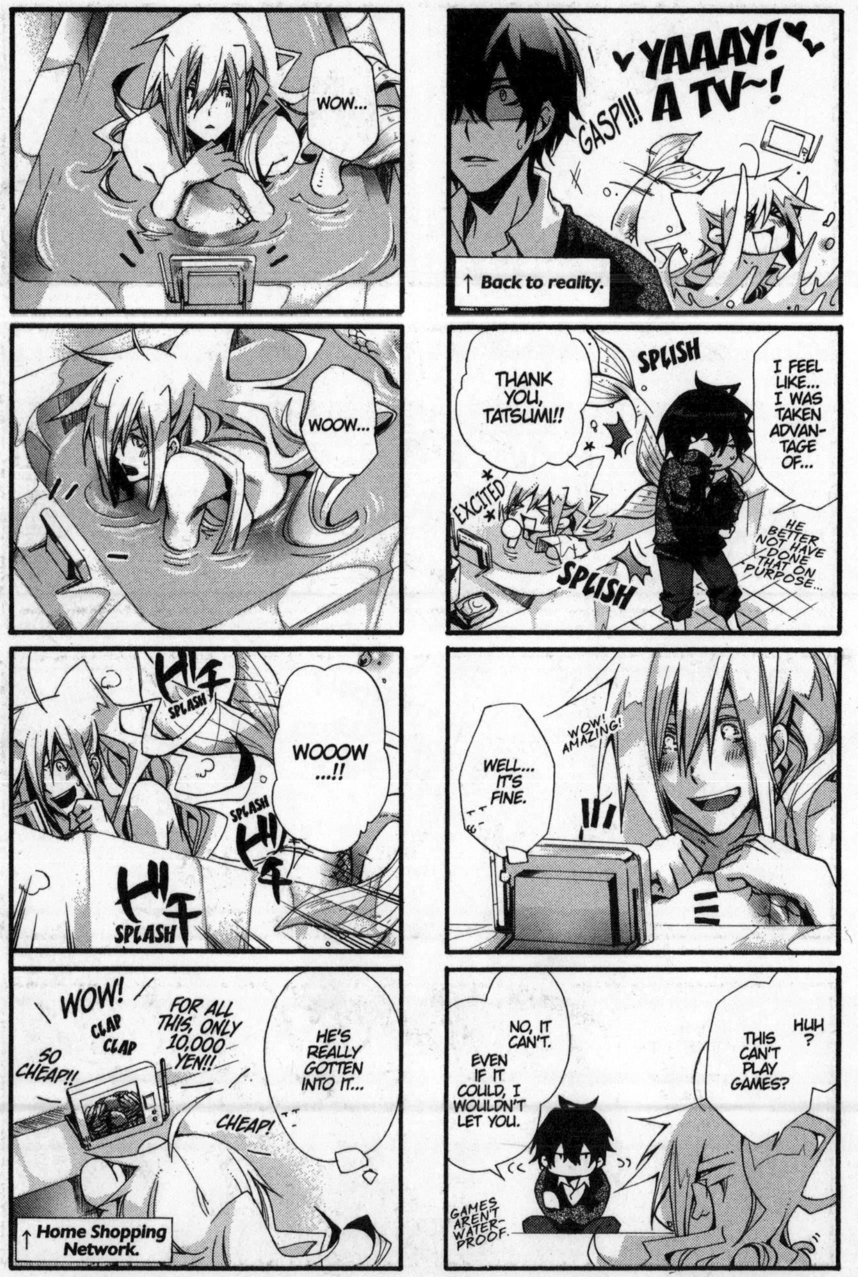
YAAAY! A TV~!
GASP!!!
↑ Back to reality.
I FEEL LIKE... I WAS TAKEN ADVANTAGE OF...
SPLISH
THANK YOU, TATSUMI!!
HE BETTER NOT HAVE DONE THAT ON PURPOSE...
EXCITED
SPLISH
WOW! AMAZING!
WELL... IT'S FINE.
HUH?
THIS CAN'T PLAY GAMES?
NO, IT CAN'T. EVEN IF IT COULD, I WOULDN'T LET YOU.
GAMES AREN'T WATERPROOF.
WOW...
WOOW...
WOOOW ...!!
SPLASH
SPLASH
SPLASH
HE'S REALLY GOTTEN INTO IT...
FOR ALL THIS, ONLY 10,000 YEN!!
WOW!
CLAP CLAP
SO CHEAP!!
CHEAP!
↑ Home Shopping Network.

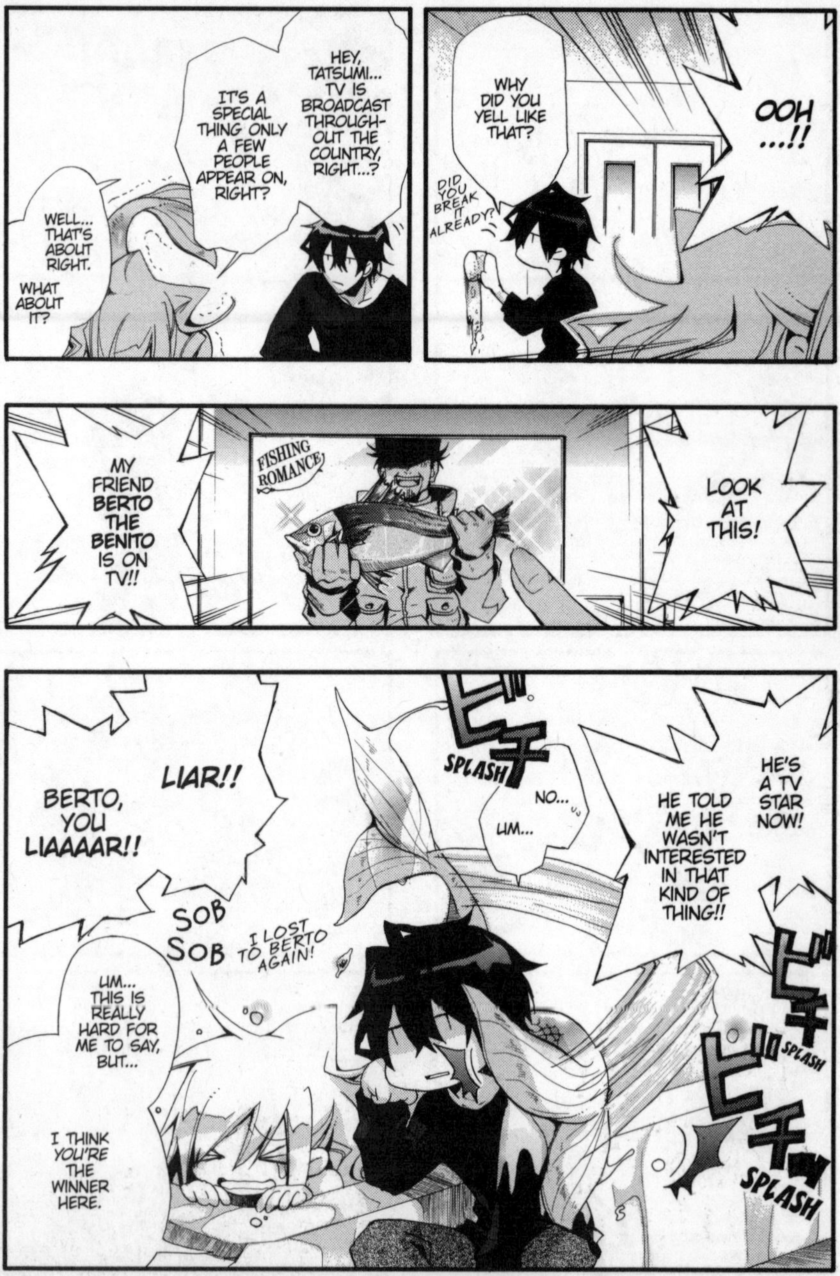
OOH ...!!
WHY DID YOU YELL LIKE THAT?
DID YOU BREAK IT ALREADY?
HEY, TATSUMI... TV IS BROADCAST THROUGH-OUT THE COUNTRY, RIGHT...?
IT'S A SPECIAL THING ONLY A FEW PEOPLE APPEAR ON, RIGHT?
WELL... THAT'S ABOUT RIGHT.
WHAT ABOUT IT?
LOOK AT THIS!
FISHING ROMANCE
MY FRIEND BERTO THE BENITO IS ON TV!!
HE'S A TV STAR NOW!
HE TOLD ME HE WASN'T INTERESTED IN THAT KIND OF THING!!
SPLASH
SPLASH
SPLASH
NO...
UM...
LIAR!!
BERTO, YOU LIAAAAR!!
SOB SOB
I LOST TO BERTO AGAIN!
UM... THIS IS REALLY HARD FOR ME TO SAY, BUT...
I THINK YOU'RE THE WINNER HERE.

Merman in My Tub

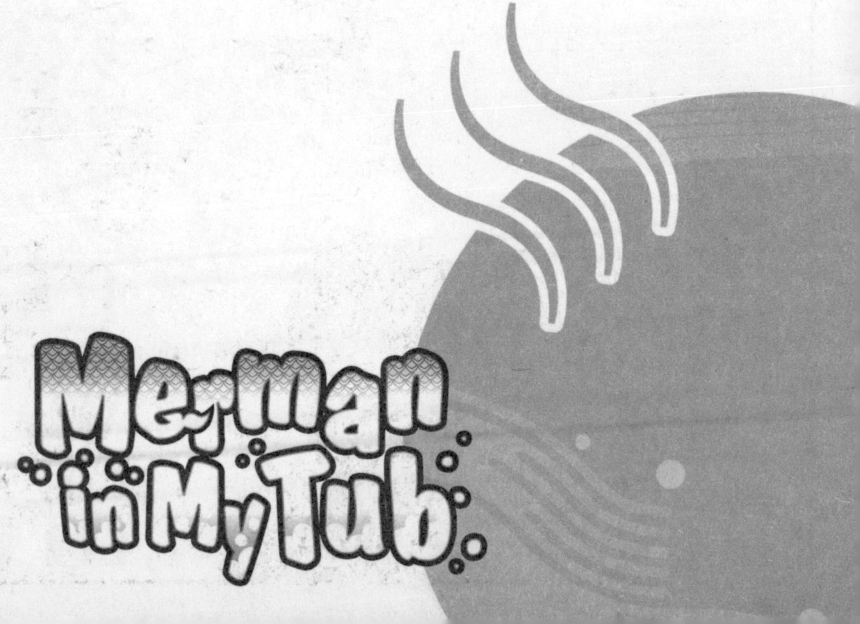

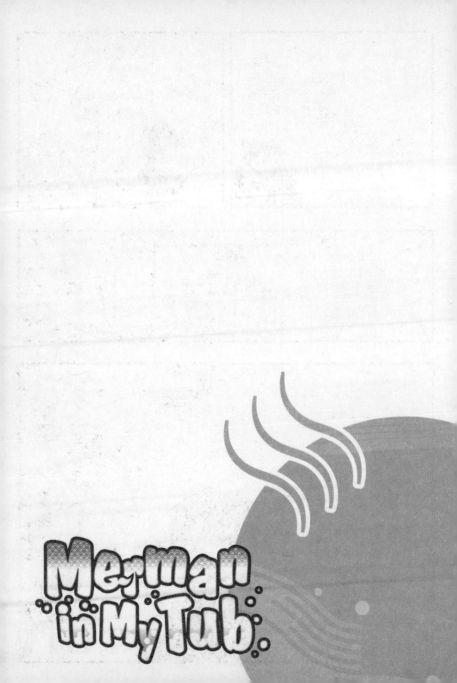

オレん家(ち)のフロ事情

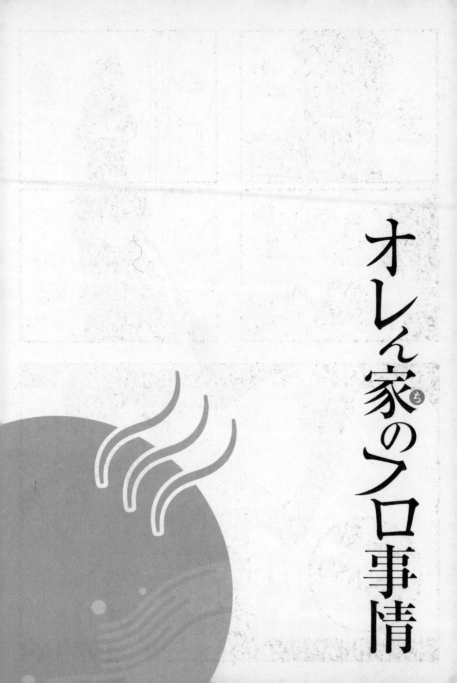

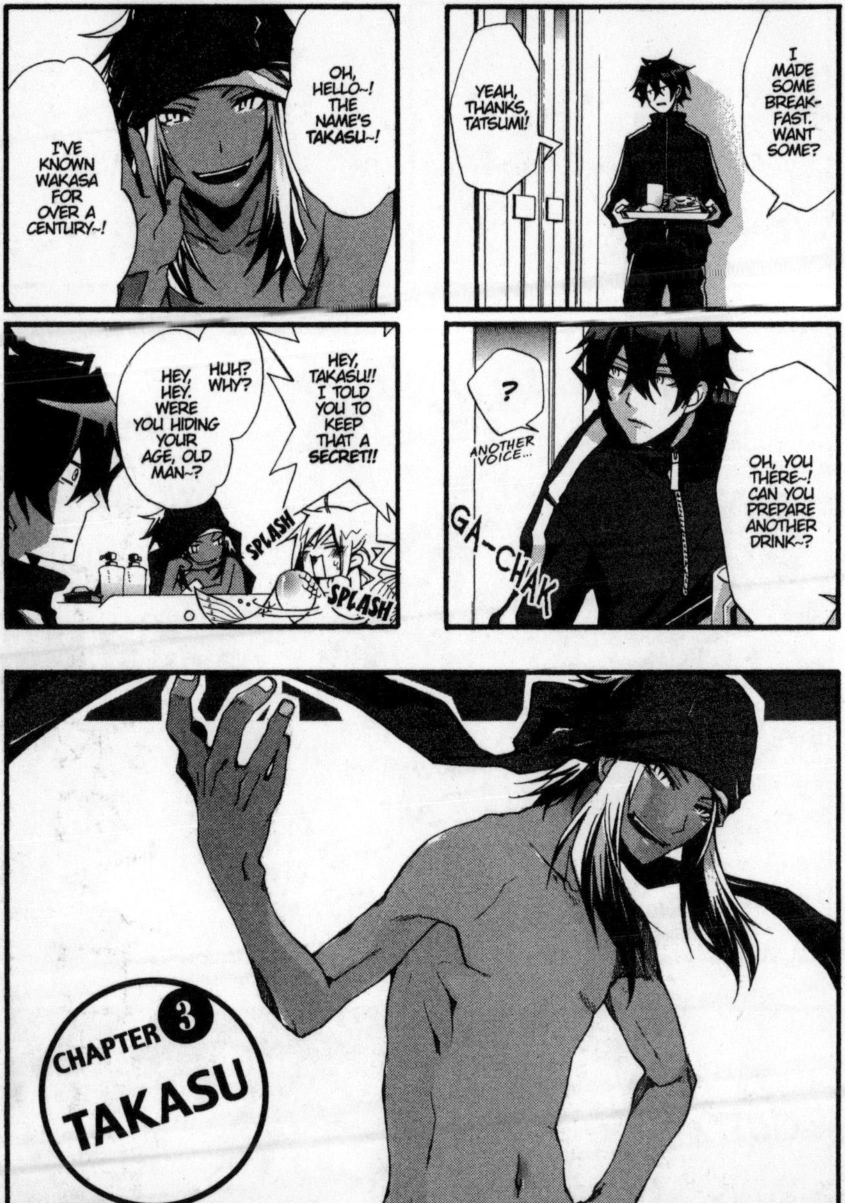
I MADE SOME BREAKFAST. WANT SOME?
YEAH, THANKS, TATSUMI!
OH, HELLO~! THE NAME'S TAKASU~!
I'VE KNOWN WAKASA FOR OVER A CENTURY~!
?
ANOTHER VOICE...
OH, YOU THERE~! CAN YOU PREPARE ANOTHER DRINK~?
GA-CHAK
HEY, TAKASU!! I TOLD YOU TO KEEP THAT A SECRET!!
HUH? WHY?
HEY, HEY. WERE YOU HIDING YOUR AGE, OLD MAN~?
SPLASH
SPLASH
CHAPTER 3
TAKASU

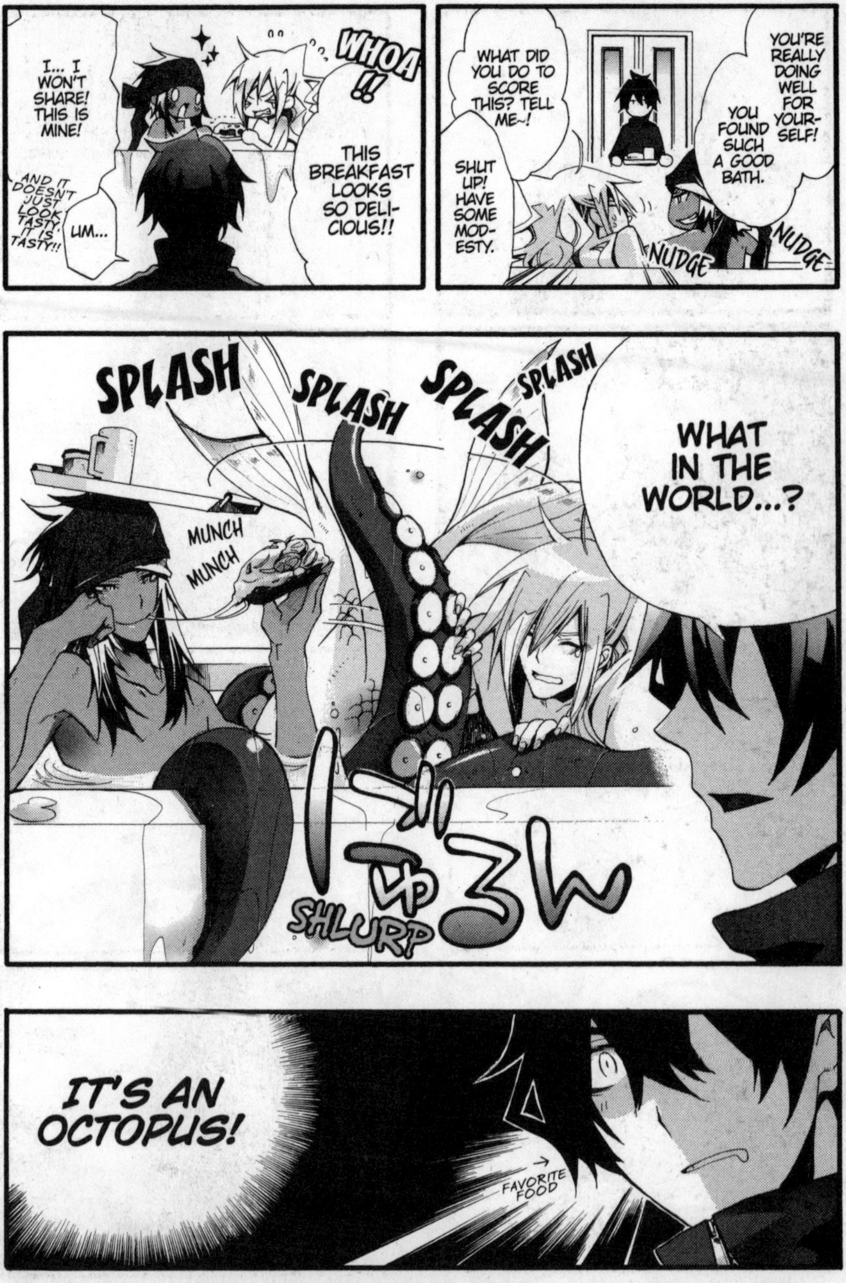
YOU'RE REALLY DOING WELL FOR YOUR-SELF!
YOU FOUND SUCH A GOOD BATH.
WHAT DID YOU DO TO SCORE THIS? TELL ME~!
SHUT UP! HAVE SOME MOD-ESTY.
NUDGE
NUDGE
WHOA!!
THIS BREAKFAST LOOKS SO DELI-CIOUS!!
I... I WON'T SHARE! THIS IS MINE!
UM...
AND IT DOESN'T JUST LOOK TASTY, IT IS TASTY!!
WHAT IN THE WORLD...?
SPLASH
SPLASH
SPLASH
SPLASH
MUNCH MUNCH
にゅるん
SHLURP
IT'S AN OCTOPUS!
FAVORITE FOOD

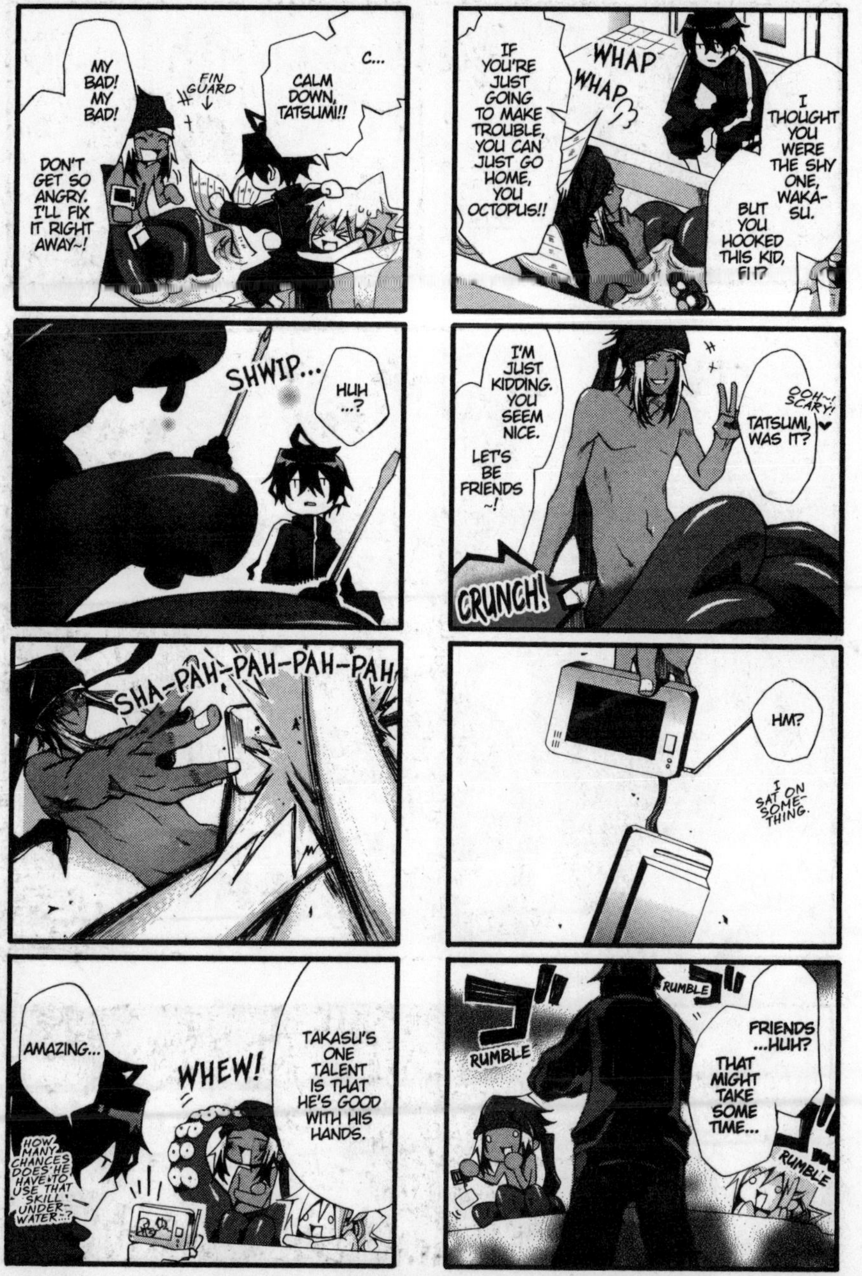
I THOUGHT YOU WERE THE SHY ONE, WAKA-SU.
BUT YOU HOOKED THIS KID, FI!?
WHAP WHAP
IF YOU'RE JUST GOING TO MAKE TROUBLE, YOU CAN JUST GO HOME, YOU OCTOPUS!!
C...
CALM DOWN, TATSUMI!!
FIN GUARD
MY BAD! MY BAD!
DON'T GET SO ANGRY. I'LL FIX IT RIGHT AWAY~!
OOH~! SCARY!
TATSUMI, WAS IT?
I'M JUST KIDDING. YOU SEEM NICE.
LET'S BE FRIENDS~!
CRUNCH!
HUH ...?
SHWIP...
HM?
I SAT ON SOME-THING.
SHA-PAH-PAH-PAH-PAH
RUMBLE
FRIENDS ...HUH?
THAT MIGHT TAKE SOME TIME...
RUMBLE
RUMBLE
TAKASU'S ONE TALENT IS THAT HE'S GOOD WITH HIS HANDS.
WHEW!
AMAZING...
HOW MANY CHANCES DOES HE HAVE TO USE THAT SKILL UNDER-WATER...?

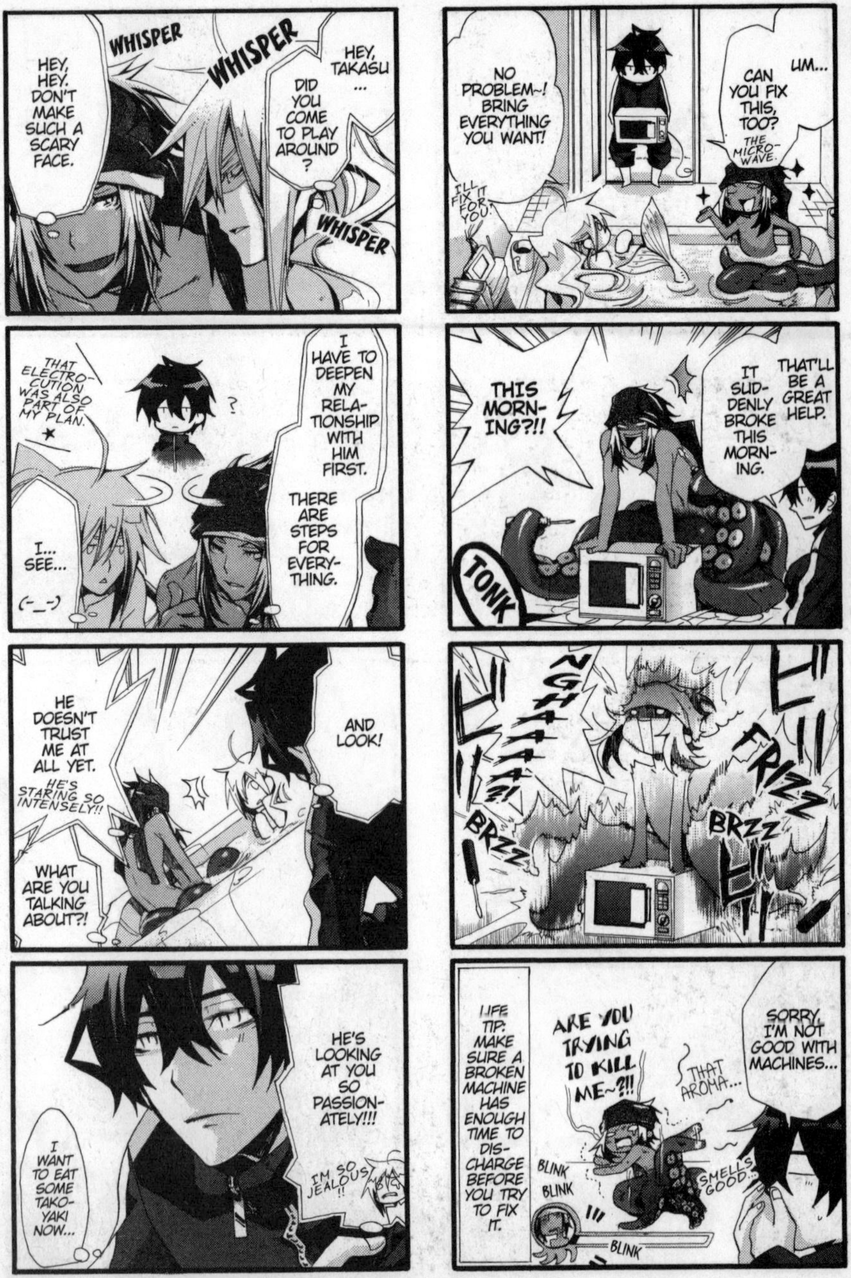
UM...
CAN YOU FIX THIS, TOO?
THE MICRO-WAVE.
NO PROBLEM~! BRING EVERYTHING YOU WANT!
I'LL FIX IT FOR YOU.
THAT'LL BE A GREAT HELP.
IT SUD-DENLY BROKE THIS MORN-ING.
THIS MORN-ING?!!
TONK
FRIZZ
BRZZ
NGHAAAAA?!
BRZZ
SORRY, I'M NOT GOOD WITH MACHINES...
SMELLS GOOD...
THAT AROMA...
ARE YOU TRYING TO KILL ME~?!!
BLINK
BLINK
BLINK
LIFE TIP: MAKE SURE A BROKEN MACHINE HAS ENOUGH TIME TO DIS-CHARGE BEFORE YOU TRY TO FIX IT.
HEY, TAKASU... DID YOU COME TO PLAY AROUND?
WHISPER
WHISPER
HEY, HEY. DON'T MAKE SUCH A SCARY FACE.
WHISPER
I HAVE TO DEEPEN MY RELA-TIONSHIP WITH HIM FIRST.
THERE ARE STEPS FOR EVERY-THING.
?
THAT ELECTRO-CUTION WAS ALSO PART OF MY PLAN. ★
I... SEE...
(-_-)
AND LOOK!
HE DOESN'T TRUST ME AT ALL YET.
HE'S STARING SO INTENSELY!!
WHAT ARE YOU TALKING ABOUT?!
HE'S LOOKING AT YOU SO PASSION-ATELY!!!
I'M SO JEALOUS!!
I WANT TO EAT SOME TAKO-YAKI NOW...

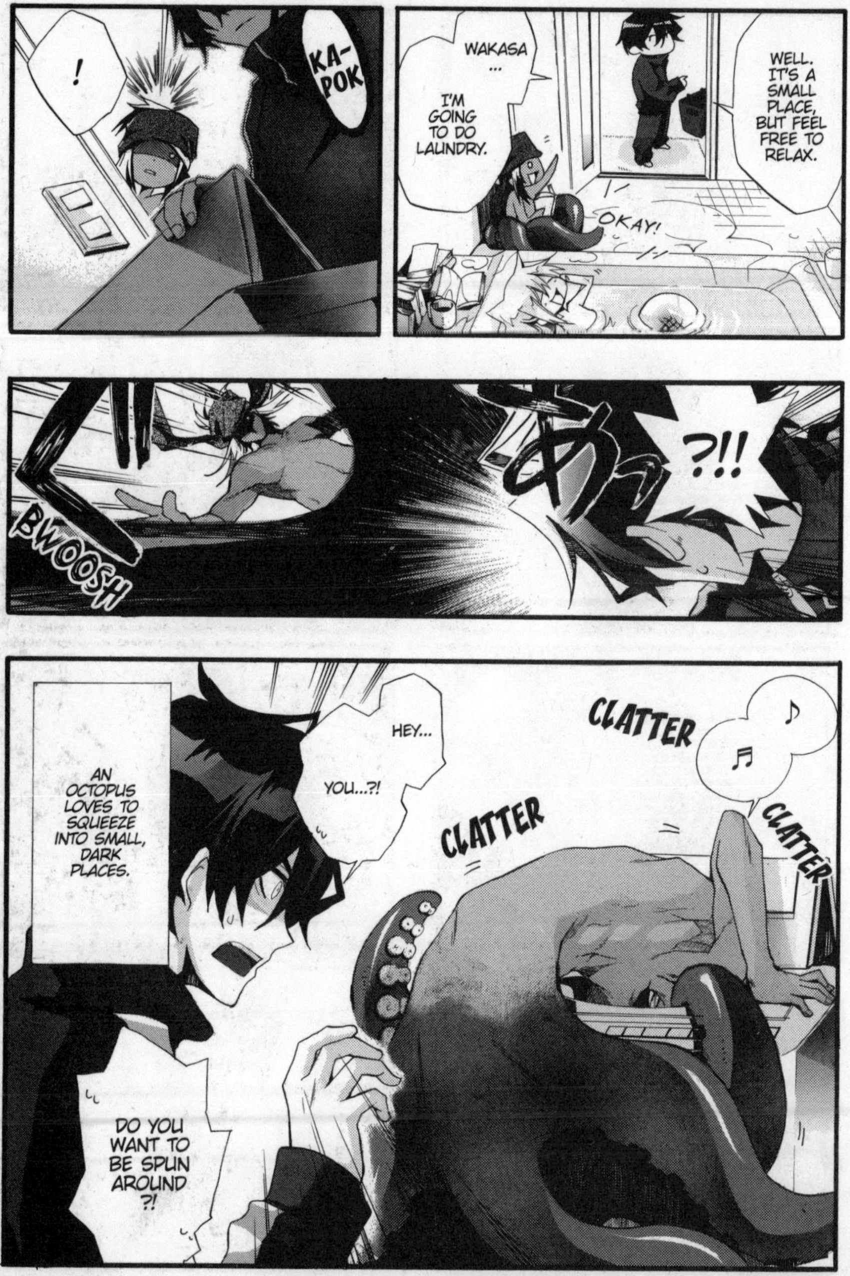
WELL. IT'S A SMALL PLACE, BUT FEEL FREE TO RELAX.
WAKASA...
I'M GOING TO DO LAUNDRY.
OKAY!
KA-POK
!
?!!
BWOOSH
♪ ♬
CLATTER
CLATTER
HEY...
YOU...?!
CLATTER
AN OCTOPUS LOVES TO SQUEEZE INTO SMALL, DARK PLACES.
DO YOU WANT TO BE SPUN AROUND?!

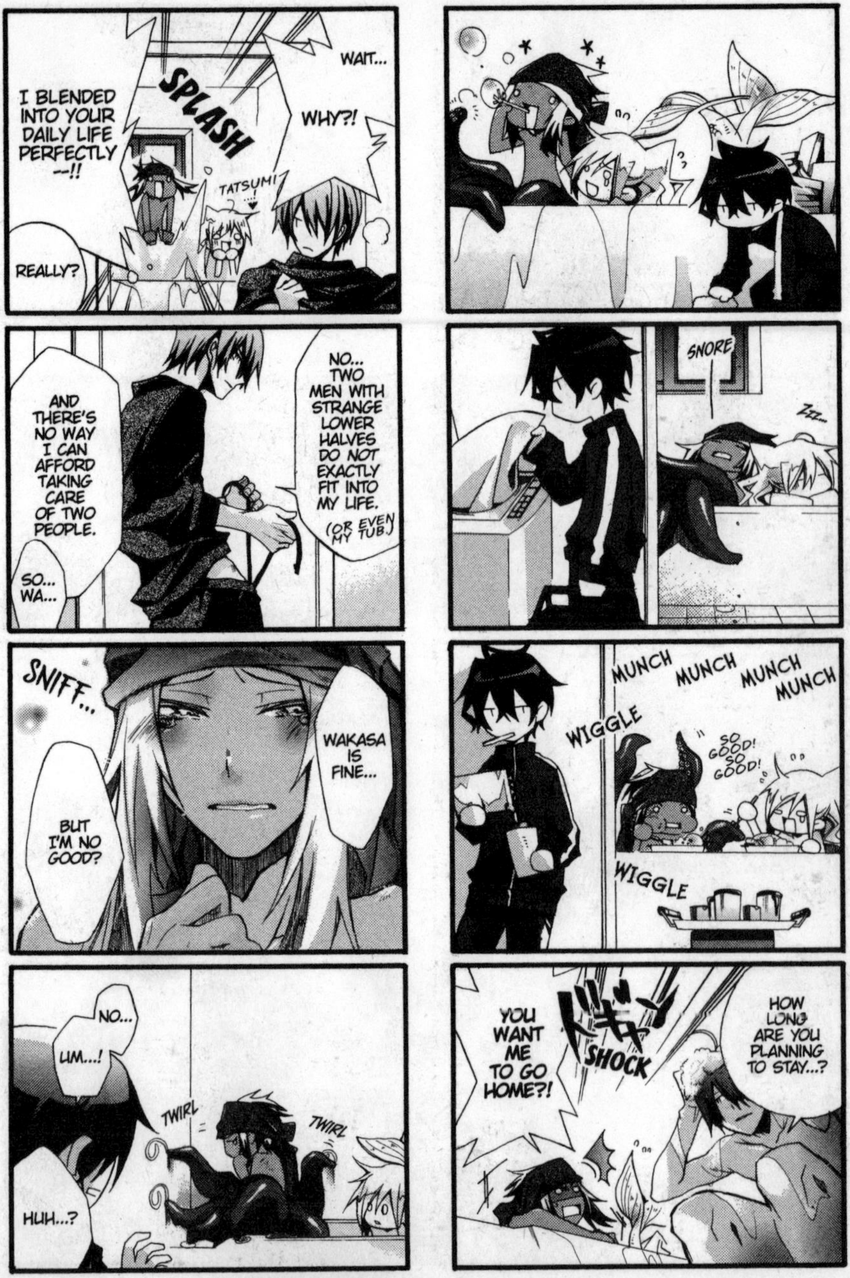
SNORE
ZZZ...
MUNCH
MUNCH
MUNCH
MUNCH
WIGGLE
SO GOOD! SO GOOD!
WIGGLE
HOW LONG ARE YOU PLANNING TO STAY...?
SHOCK
YOU WANT ME TO GO HOME?!
WAIT...
WHY?!
SPLASH
I BLENDED INTO YOUR DAILY LIFE PERFECTLY --!!
TATSUMI
REALLY?
NO... TWO MEN WITH STRANGE LOWER HALVES DO NOT EXACTLY FIT INTO MY LIFE.
(OR EVEN MY TUB.)
AND THERE'S NO WAY I CAN AFFORD TAKING CARE OF TWO PEOPLE.
SO... WA...
WAKASA IS FINE...
SNIFF...
BUT I'M NO GOOD?
NO...
UM...!
TWIRL
TWIRL
HUH...?

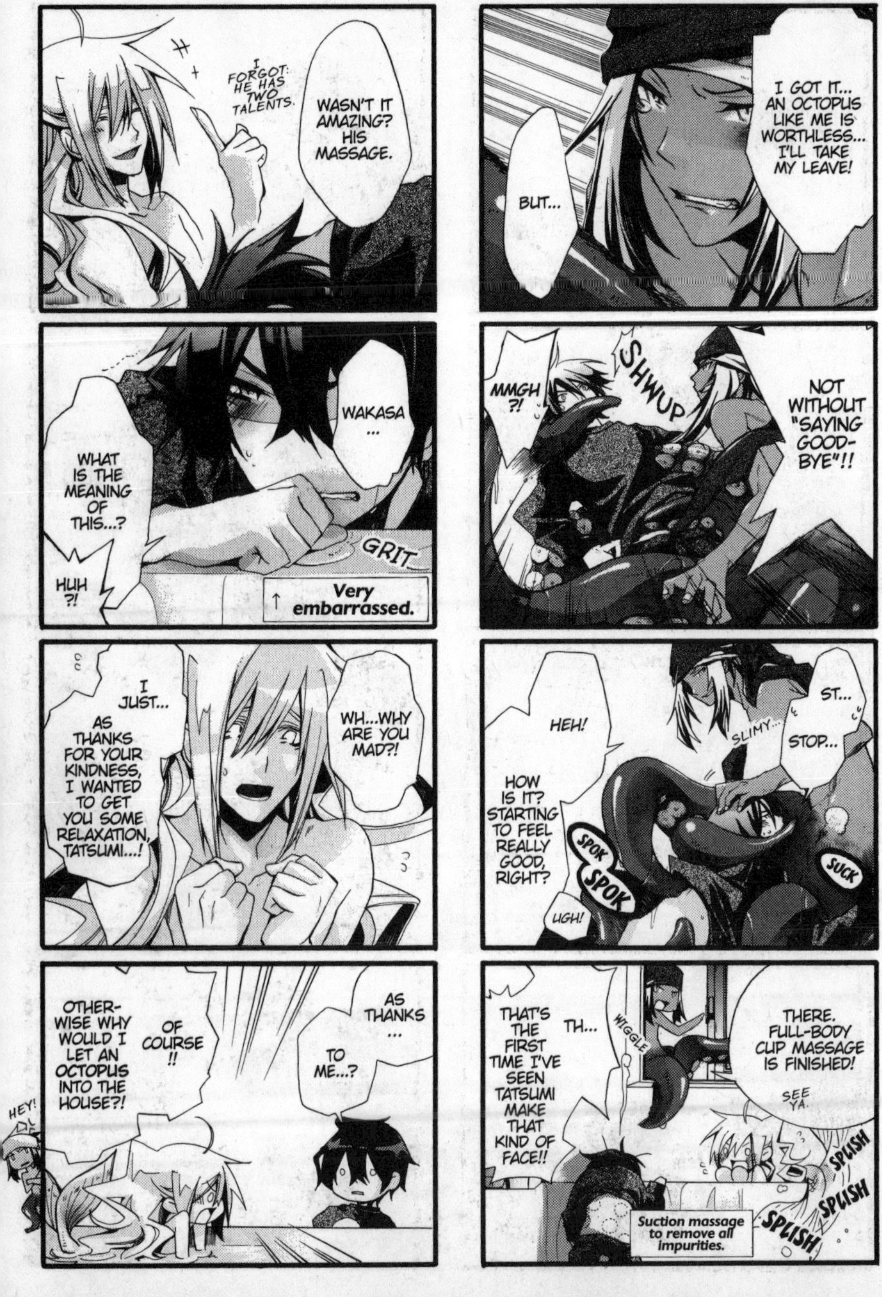
I GOT IT... AN OCTOPUS LIKE ME IS WORTHLESS... I'LL TAKE MY LEAVE!
BUT...
WASN'T IT AMAZING? HIS MASSAGE.
I FORGOT: HE HAS TWO TALENTS.
NOT WITHOUT "SAYING GOOD-BYE"!!
SHWUP
MMGH ?!
WAKASA ...
WHAT IS THE MEANING OF THIS...?
GRIT
HUH ?!
↑ Very embarrassed.
ST... STOP...
SLIMY...
HEH!
HOW IS IT? STARTING TO FEEL REALLY GOOD, RIGHT?
SUCK
SPOK SPOK
UGH!
WH...WHY ARE YOU MAD?!
I JUST... AS THANKS FOR YOUR KINDNESS, I WANTED TO GET YOU SOME RELAXATION, TATSUMI...!
THERE. FULL-BODY CUP MASSAGE IS FINISHED!
SEE YA.
SPLISH
SPLISH
SPLISH
SPLISH
TH...
THAT'S THE FIRST TIME I'VE SEEN TATSUMI MAKE THAT KIND OF FACE!!
WIGGLE
Suction massage to remove all impurities.
AS THANKS ...
TO ME...?
OF COURSE !!
OTHER-WISE WHY WOULD I LET AN OCTOPUS INTO THE HOUSE?!
HEY!

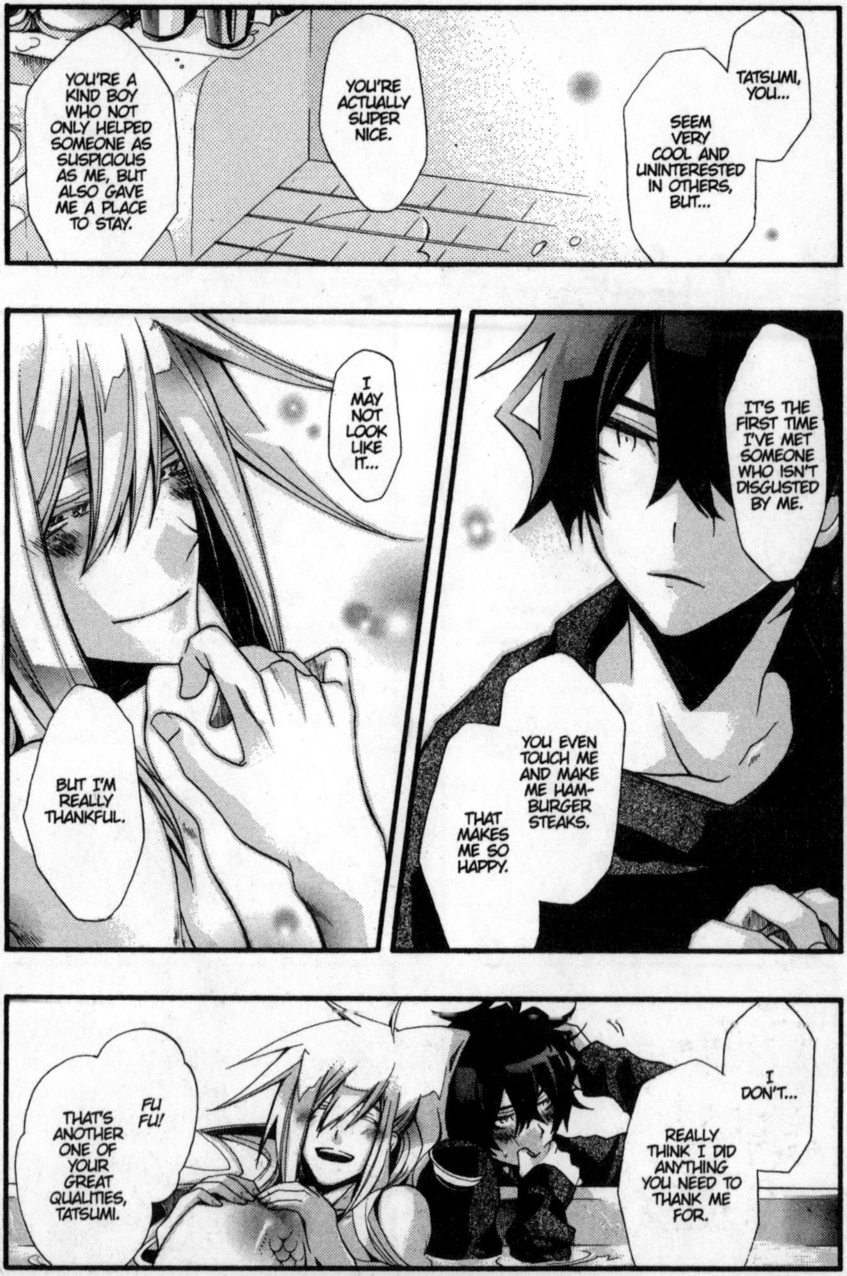
TATSUMI, YOU...
SEEM VERY COOL AND UNINTERESTED IN OTHERS, BUT...
YOU'RE ACTUALLY SUPER NICE.
YOU'RE A KIND BOY WHO NOT ONLY HELPED SOMEONE AS SUSPICIOUS AS ME, BUT ALSO GAVE ME A PLACE TO STAY.
IT'S THE FIRST TIME I'VE MET SOMEONE WHO ISN'T DISGUSTED BY ME.
YOU EVEN TOUCH ME AND MAKE ME HAM-BURGER STEAKS.
THAT MAKES ME SO HAPPY.
I MAY NOT LOOK LIKE IT...
BUT I'M REALLY THANKFUL.
I DON'T...
REALLY THINK I DID ANYTHING YOU NEED TO THANK ME FOR.
FU FU!
THAT'S ANOTHER ONE OF YOUR GREAT QUALITIES, TATSUMI.

Merman in My Tub

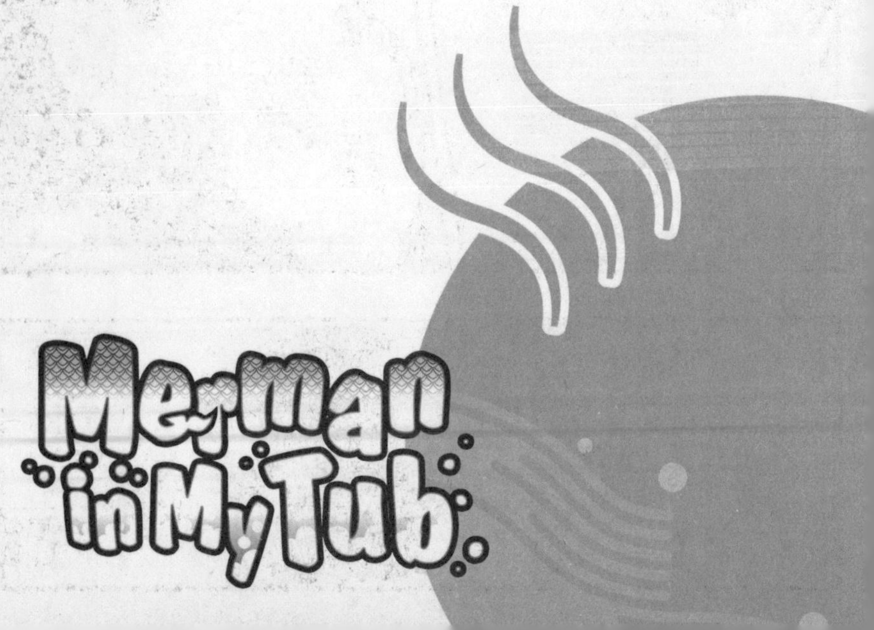

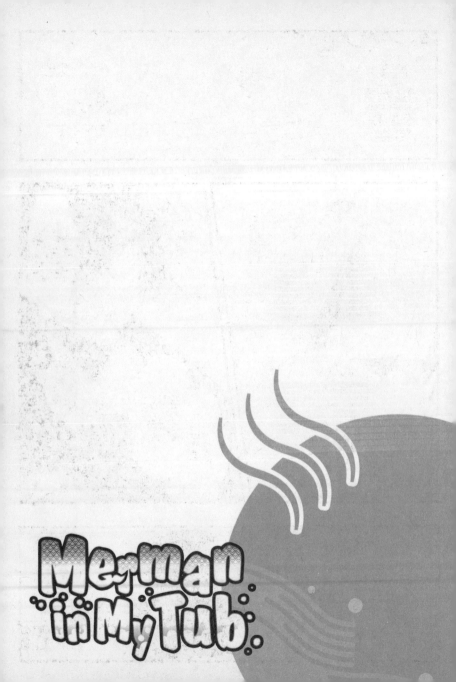

オレん家(ち)のフロ事情

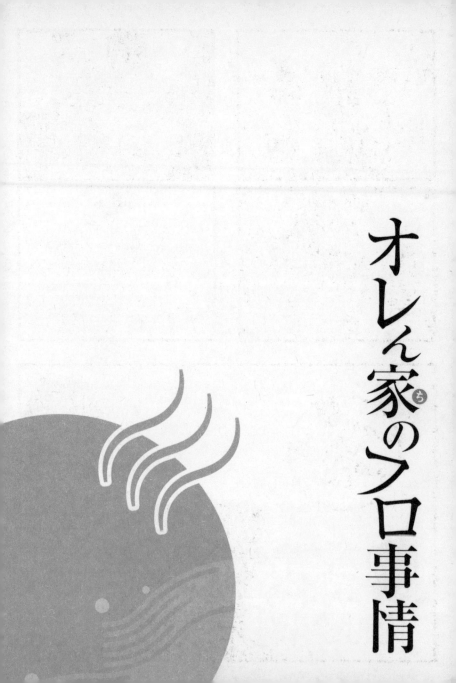

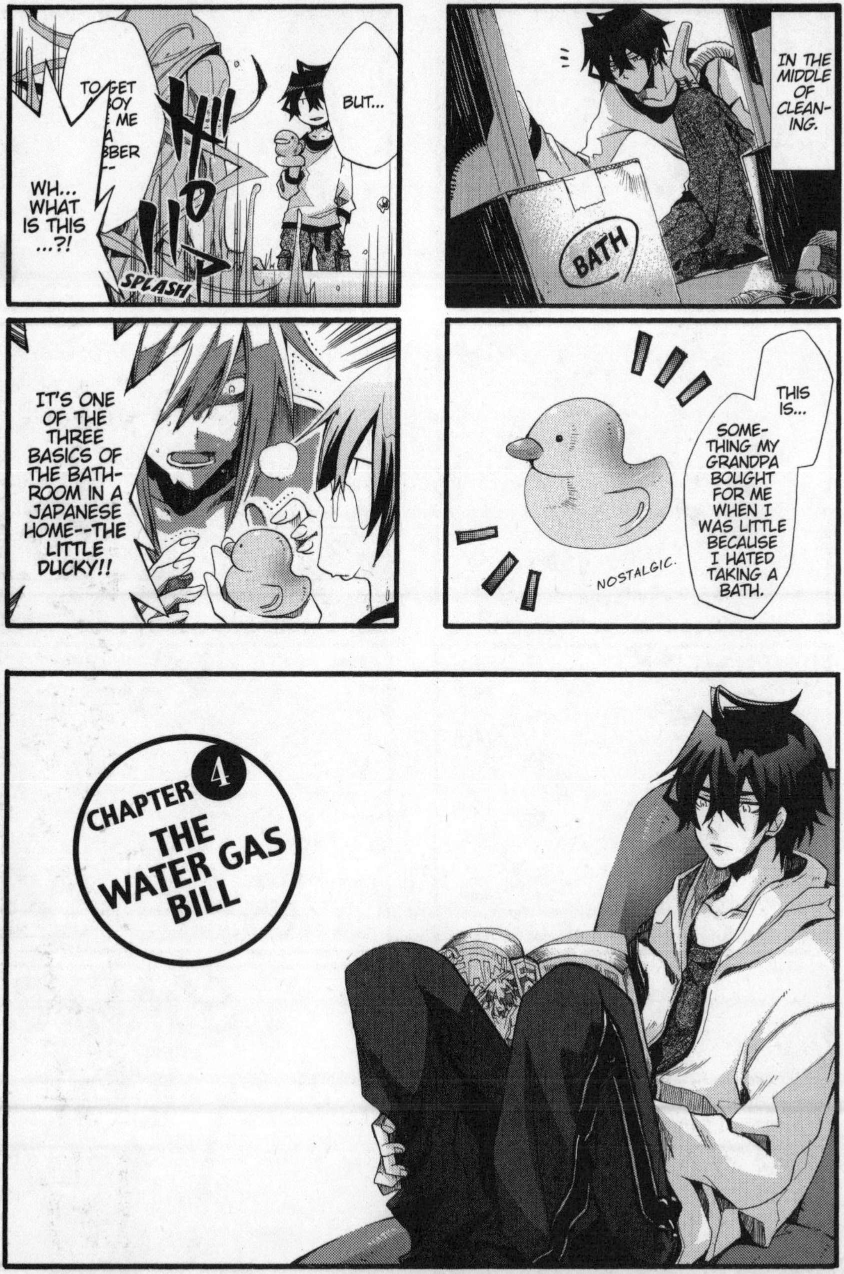
IN THE MIDDLE OF CLEANING.
BATH
BUT...
TO GET
WH... WHAT IS THIS ...?!
SPLASH
THIS IS...
SOMETHING MY GRANDPA BOUGHT FOR ME WHEN I WAS LITTLE BECAUSE I HATED TAKING A BATH.
NOSTALGIC.
IT'S ONE OF THE THREE BASICS OF THE BATHROOM IN A JAPANESE HOME--THE LITTLE DUCKY!!
CHAPTER 4
THE WATER GAS BILL

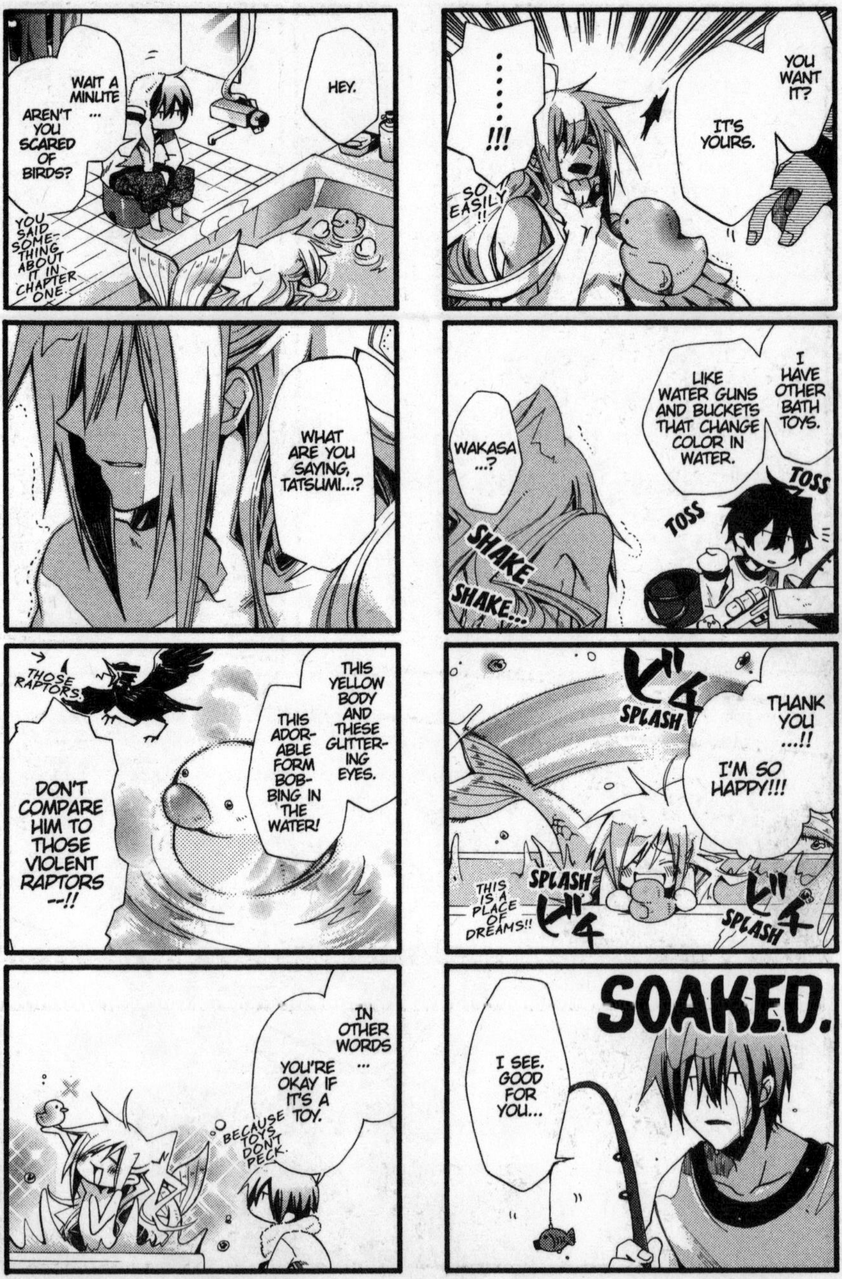
YOU WANT IT?
IT'S YOURS.
......!!!
SO EASILY!!
I HAVE OTHER BATH TOYS.
LIKE WATER GUNS AND BUCKETS THAT CHANGE COLOR IN WATER.
WAKASA ...?
TOSS
TOSS
SHAKE
SHAKE...
SPLASH
THANK YOU ...!!
I'M SO HAPPY!!!
SPLASH
SPLASH
THIS IS A PLACE OF DREAMS!!
SOAKED.
I SEE. GOOD FOR YOU...
HEY.
WAIT A MINUTE ...
AREN'T YOU SCARED OF BIRDS?
YOU SAID SOMETHING ABOUT IT IN CHAPTER ONE.
WHAT ARE YOU SAYING, TATSUMI...?
THIS YELLOW BODY AND THESE GLITTERING EYES.
THIS ADORABLE FORM BOBBING IN THE WATER!
THOSE RAPTORS.
DON'T COMPARE HIM TO THOSE VIOLENT RAPTORS--!!
IN OTHER WORDS ...
YOU'RE OKAY IF IT'S A TOY.
BECAUSE TOYS DON'T PECK.

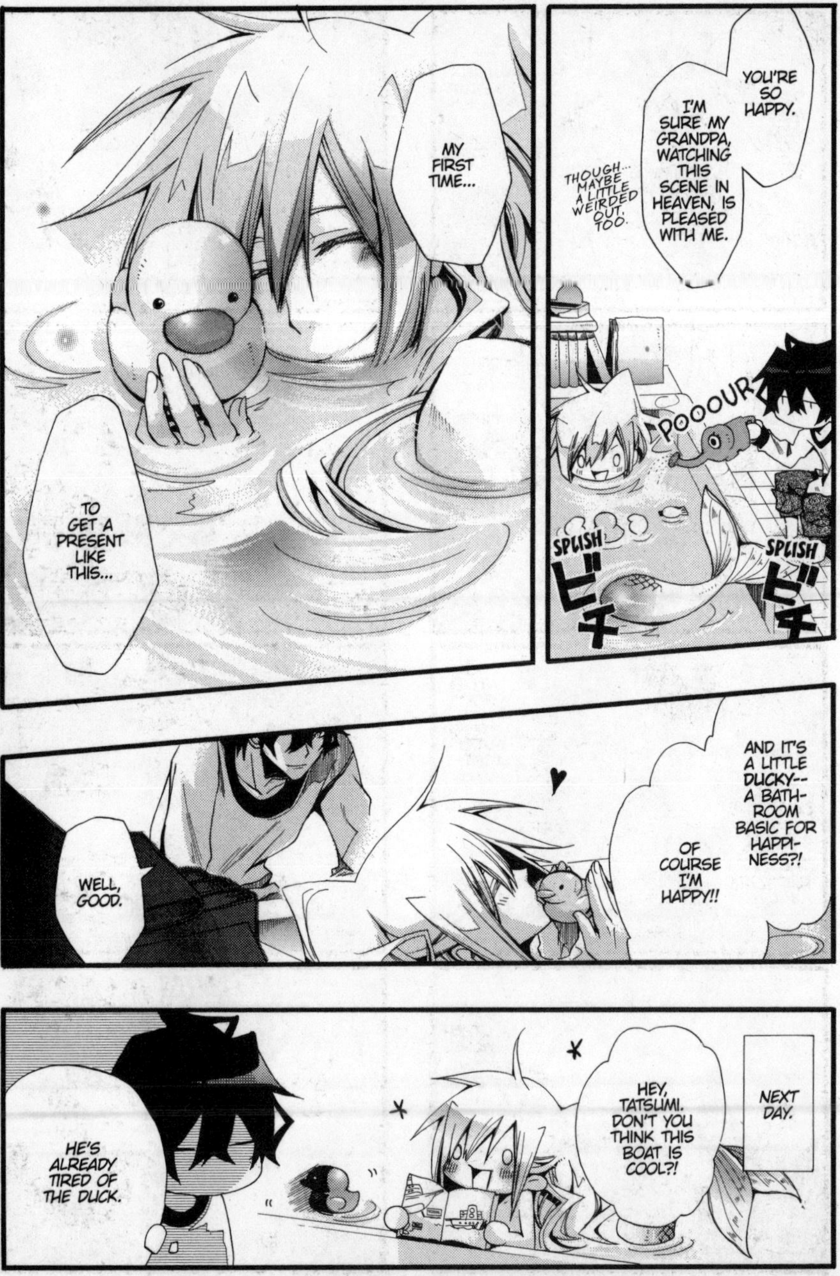
YOU'RE SO HAPPY.
I'M SURE MY GRANDPA, WATCHING THIS SCENE IN HEAVEN, IS PLEASED WITH ME.
THOUGH... MAYBE A LITTLE WEIRDED OUT, TOO.
POOOUR
SPLISH
ビチ
SPLISH
ビチ
MY FIRST TIME...
TO GET A PRESENT LIKE THIS...
AND IT'S A LITTLE DUCKY-- A BATHROOM BASIC FOR HAPPINESS?!
OF COURSE I'M HAPPY!!
WELL, GOOD.
NEXT DAY.
HEY, TATSUMI. DON'T YOU THINK THIS BOAT IS COOL?!
HE'S ALREADY TIRED OF THE DUCK.

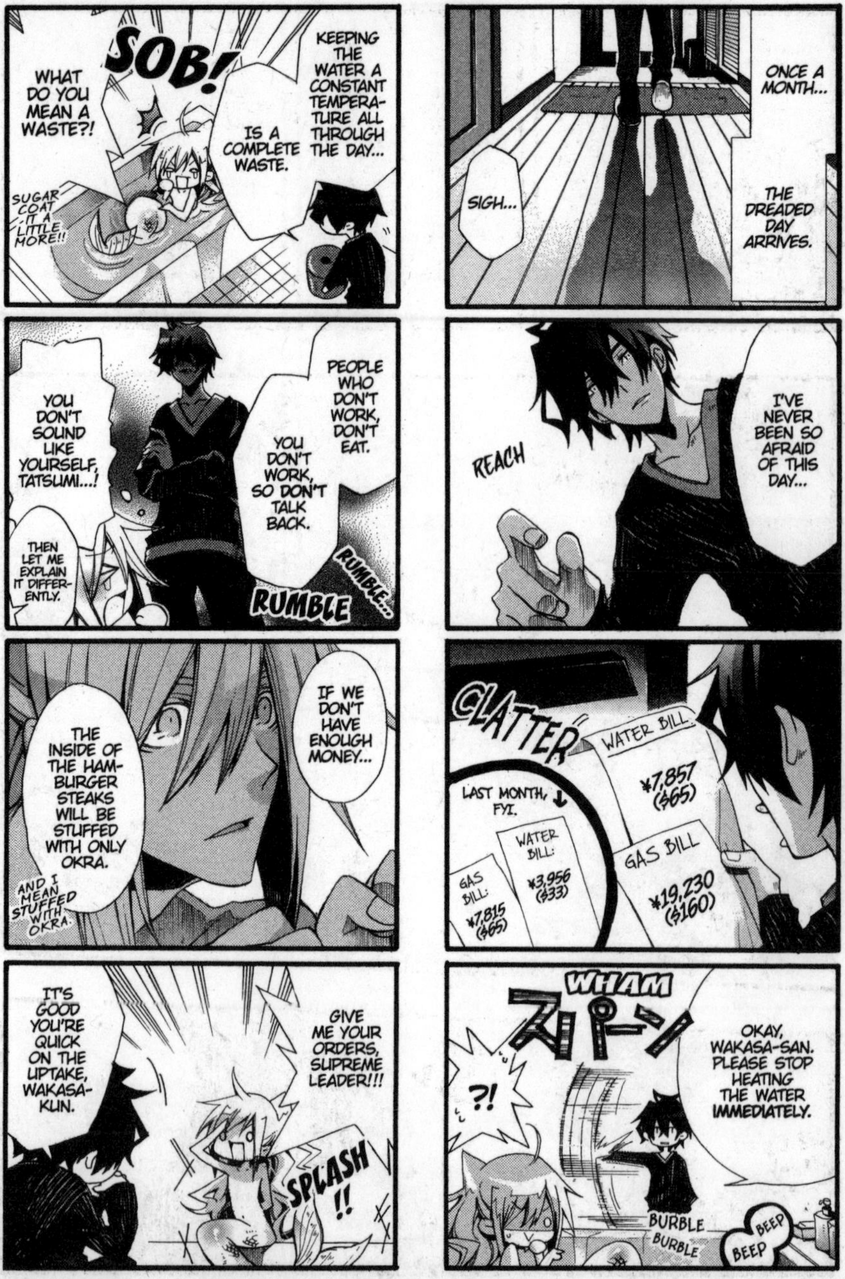
ONCE A MONTH...
THE DREADED DAY ARRIVES.
SIGH...
I'VE NEVER BEEN SO AFRAID OF THIS DAY...
REACH
CLATTER
WATER BILL ¥7,857 ($65)
GAS BILL ¥19,230 ($160)
LAST MONTH, FYI.
WATER BILL: ¥3,956 ($33)
GAS BILL: ¥7,815 ($65)
WHAM
スパーン
OKAY, WAKASA-SAN. PLEASE STOP HEATING THE WATER IMMEDIATELY.
?!
BURBLE
BURBLE
BEEP BEEP
KEEPING THE WATER A CONSTANT TEMPERA-TURE ALL THROUGH THE DAY...
IS A COMPLETE WASTE.
SOB!
WHAT DO YOU MEAN A WASTE?!
SUGAR COAT IT A LITTLE MORE!!
PEOPLE WHO DON'T WORK, DON'T EAT.
YOU DON'T WORK, SO DON'T TALK BACK.
RUMBLE...
RUMBLE
YOU DON'T SOUND LIKE YOURSELF, TATSUMI...!
THEN LET ME EXPLAIN IT DIFFER-ENTLY.
IF WE DON'T HAVE ENOUGH MONEY...
THE INSIDE OF THE HAM-BURGER STEAKS WILL BE STUFFED WITH ONLY OKRA.
AND I MEAN STUFFED WITH OKRA.
GIVE ME YOUR ORDERS, SUPREME LEADER!!!
SPLASH!!
IT'S GOOD YOU'RE QUICK ON THE UPTAKE, WAKASA-KUN.

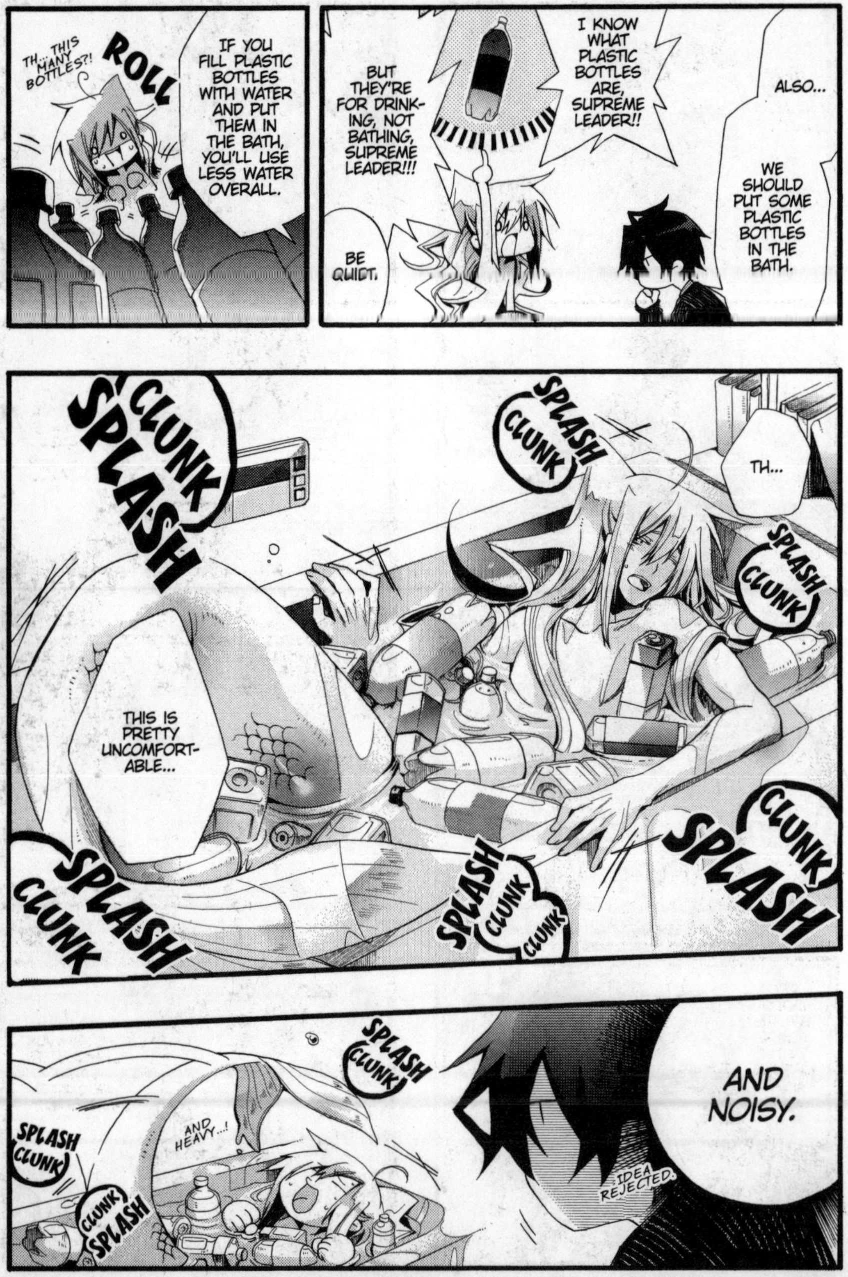
ALSO...
WE SHOULD PUT SOME PLASTIC BOTTLES IN THE BATH.
I KNOW WHAT PLASTIC BOTTLES ARE, SUPREME LEADER!!
BUT THEY'RE FOR DRINKING, NOT BATHING, SUPREME LEADER!!!
BE QUIET.
IF YOU FILL PLASTIC BOTTLES WITH WATER AND PUT THEM IN THE BATH, YOU'LL USE LESS WATER OVERALL.
ROLL
TH... THIS MANY BOTTLES?!
TH...
SPLASH CLUNK
SPLASH CLUNK
CLUNK SPLASH
THIS IS PRETTY UNCOMFORTABLE...
CLUNK SPLASH
SPLASH CLUNK CLUNK
SPLASH CLUNK
AND NOISY.
IDEA REJECTED.
SPLASH CLUNK
AND HEAVY...!
SPLASH CLUNK
CLUNK SPLASH

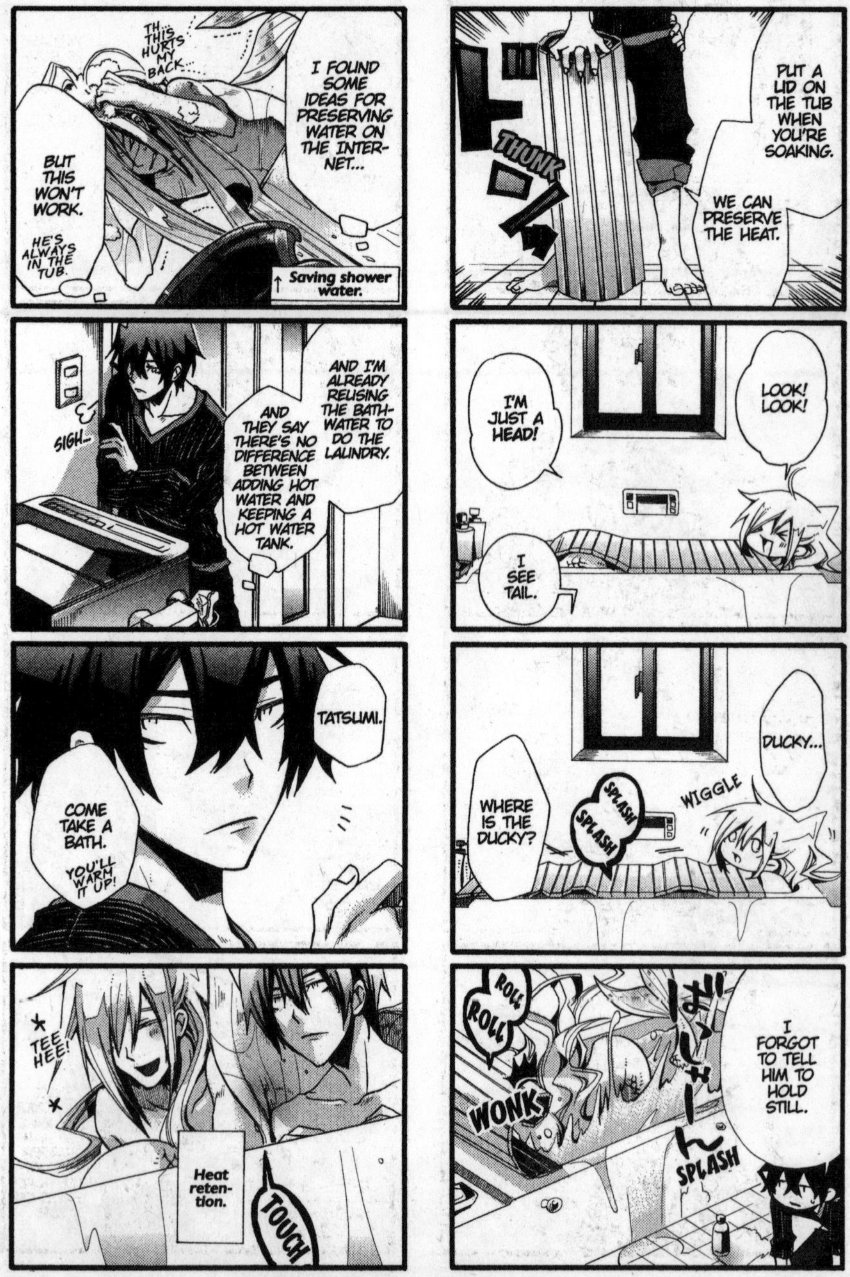
PUT A LID ON THE TUB WHEN YOU'RE SOAKING.
WE CAN PRESERVE THE HEAT.
THUNK
LOOK! LOOK!
I'M JUST A HEAD!
I SEE TAIL.
DUCKY...
WIGGLE
SPLASH SPLASH
WHERE IS THE DUCKY?
I FORGOT TO TELL HIM TO HOLD STILL.
SPLASH
WONK
ROLL ROLL
I FOUND SOME IDEAS FOR PRESERVING WATER ON THE INTERNET...
TH... THIS HURTS MY BACK...
BUT THIS WON'T WORK.
HE'S ALWAYS IN THE TUB.
↑ Saving shower water.
AND I'M ALREADY REUSING THE BATHWATER TO DO THE LAUNDRY.
AND THEY SAY THERE'S NO DIFFERENCE BETWEEN ADDING HOT WATER AND KEEPING A HOT WATER TANK.
SIGH...
TATSUMI.
COME TAKE A BATH.
YOU'LL WARM IT UP!
TEE HEE!
Heat retention.
TOUCH

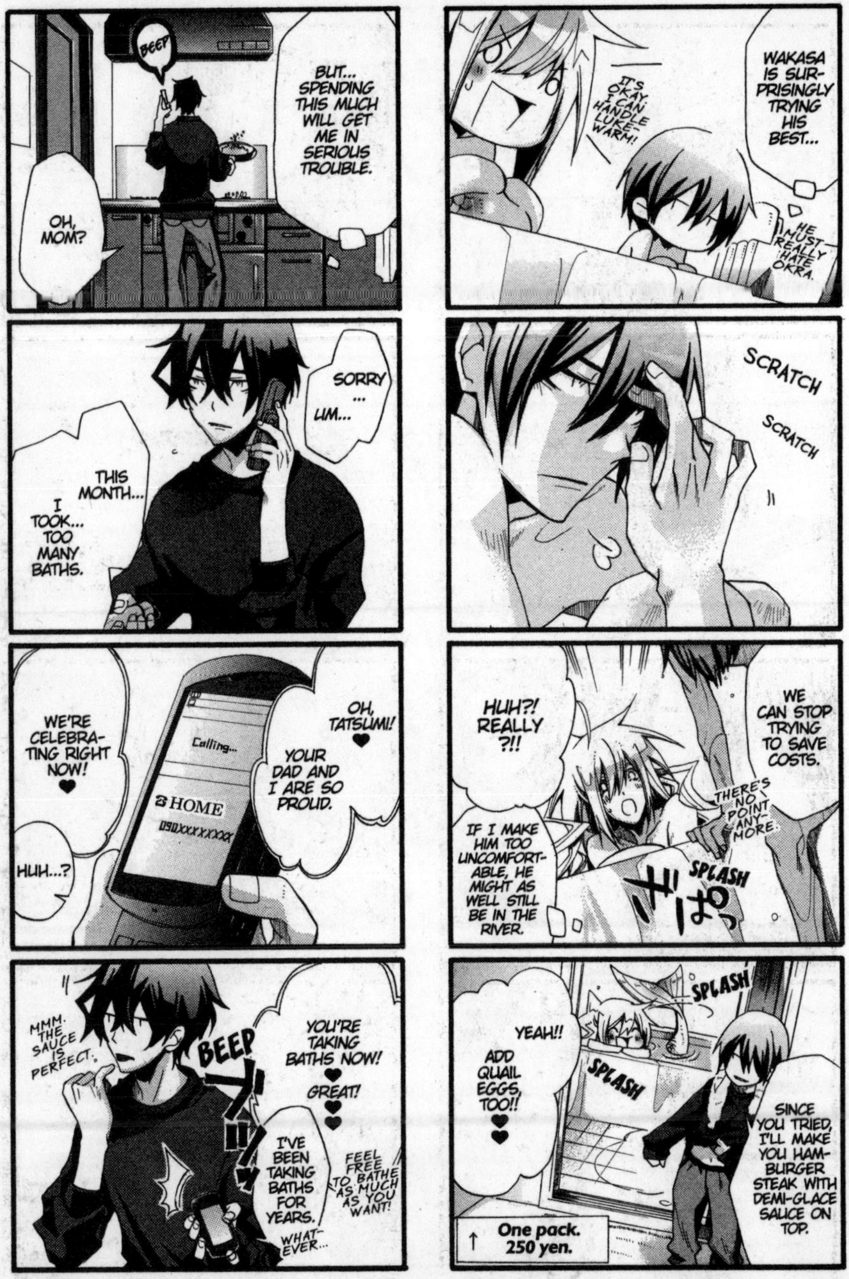
WAKASA IS SURPRISINGLY TRYING HIS BEST...
IT'S OKAY. I CAN HANDLE LUKEWARM!
HE MUST REALLY HATE OKRA.
SCRATCH
SCRATCH
WE CAN STOP TRYING TO SAVE COSTS.
THERE'S NO POINT ANYMORE.
HUH?! REALLY ?!!
IF I MAKE HIM TOO UNCOMFORTABLE, HE MIGHT AS WELL STILL BE IN THE RIVER.
SPLASH
ザぱっ
SPLASH
SINCE YOU TRIED, I'LL MAKE YOU HAMBURGER STEAK WITH DEMI-GLACE SAUCE ON TOP.
YEAH!!
ADD QUAIL EGGS, TOO!!
SPLASH
↑ One pack. 250 yen.
BUT... SPENDING THIS MUCH WILL GET ME IN SERIOUS TROUBLE.
BEEP
OH, MOM?
SORRY... UM...
THIS MONTH...
I TOOK... TOO MANY BATHS.
OH, TATSUMI!
YOUR DAD AND I ARE SO PROUD.
WE'RE CELEBRATING RIGHT NOW!
Calling...
HOME
090XXXXXXXX
HUH...?
YOU'RE TAKING BATHS NOW! GREAT!
FEEL FREE TO BATHE AS MUCH AS YOU WANT!
I'VE BEEN TAKING BATHS FOR YEARS.
BEEP
MMM. THE SAUCE IS PERFECT.
WHATEVER...

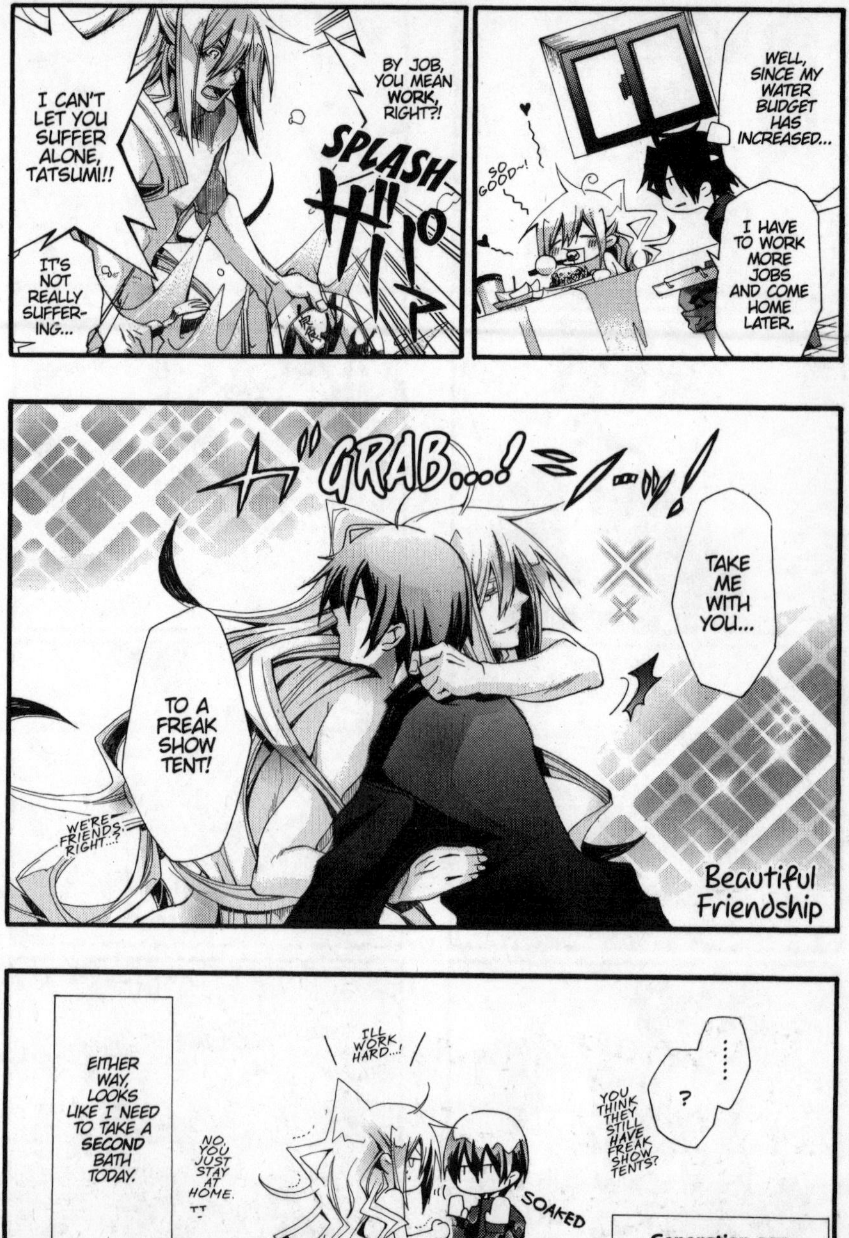
WELL, SINCE MY WATER BUDGET HAS INCREASED...
SO GOOD~!
I HAVE TO WORK MORE JOBS AND COME HOME LATER.
BY JOB, YOU MEAN WORK, RIGHT?!
SPLASH
I CAN'T LET YOU SUFFER ALONE, TATSUMI!!
IT'S NOT REALLY SUFFERING...
GRAB...!
TAKE ME WITH YOU...
TO A FREAK SHOW TENT!
WE'RE FRIENDS, RIGHT...?
Beautiful Friendship
......
?
YOU THINK THEY STILL HAVE FREAK SHOW TENTS?
SOAKED
I'LL WORK HARD...!
NO, YOU JUST STAY AT HOME.
EITHER WAY, LOOKS LIKE I NEED TO TAKE A SECOND BATH TODAY.
Generation gap.

Merman in My Tub

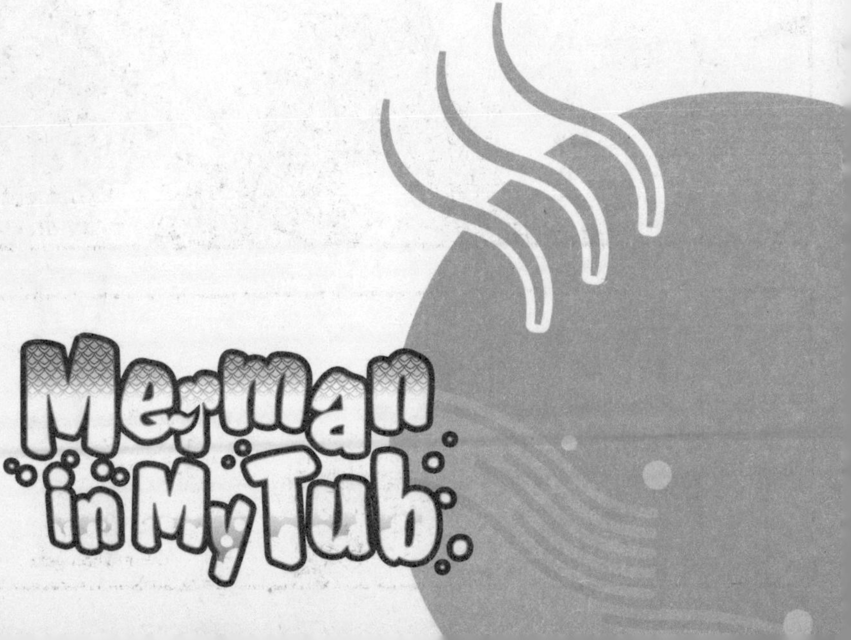

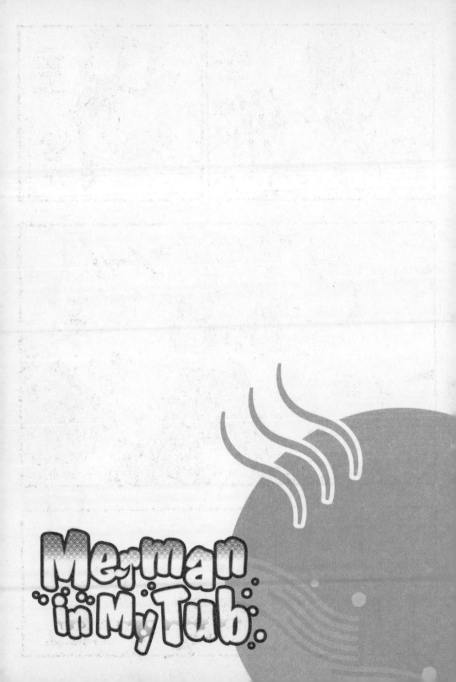

オレん家のフロ事情

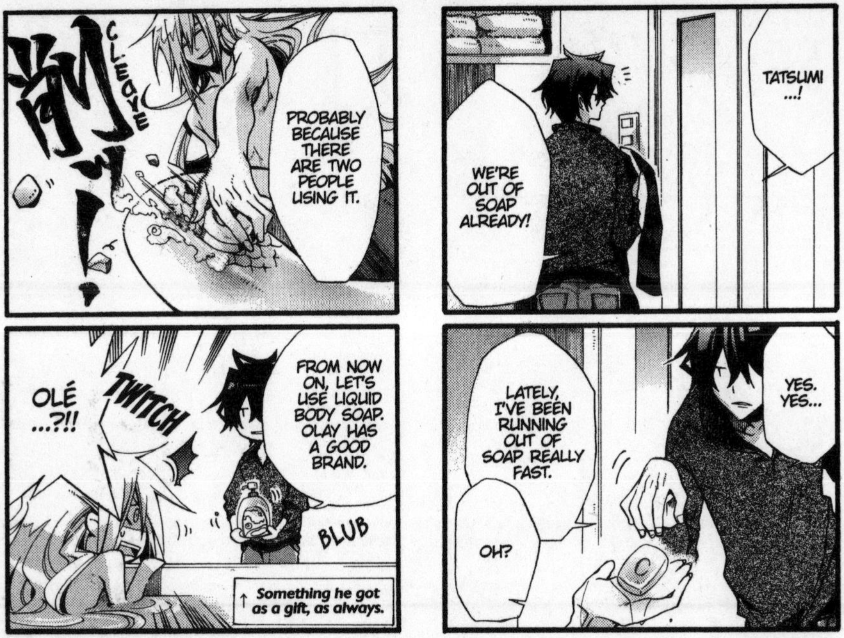
TATSUMI ...!
WE'RE OUT OF SOAP ALREADY!
PROBABLY BECAUSE THERE ARE TWO PEOPLE USING IT.
CLEAVE
YES. YES...
LATELY, I'VE BEEN RUNNING OUT OF SOAP REALLY FAST.
OH?
FROM NOW ON, LET'S USE LIQUID BODY SOAP. OLAY HAS A GOOD BRAND.
TWITCH
OLÉ ...?!!
BLUB
↑ Something he got as a gift, as always.

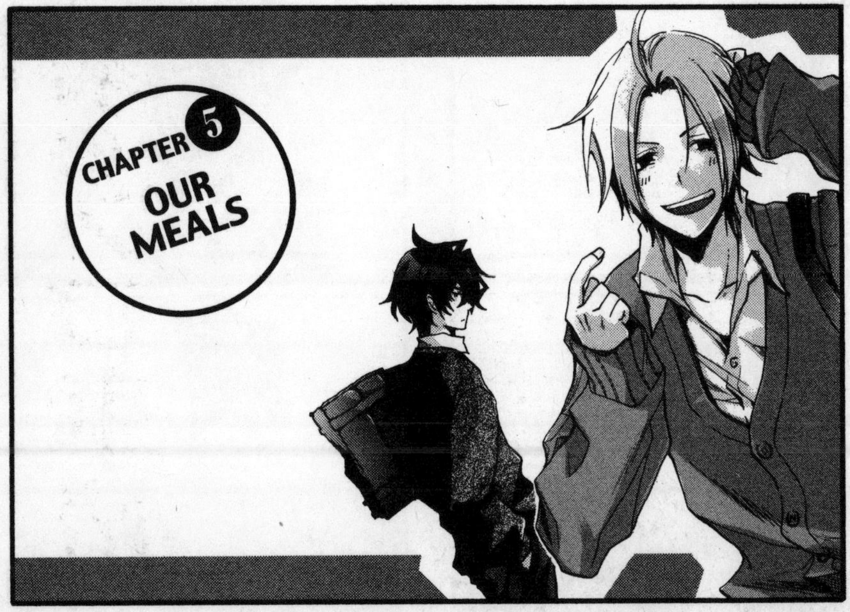
CHAPTER 5
OUR MEALS

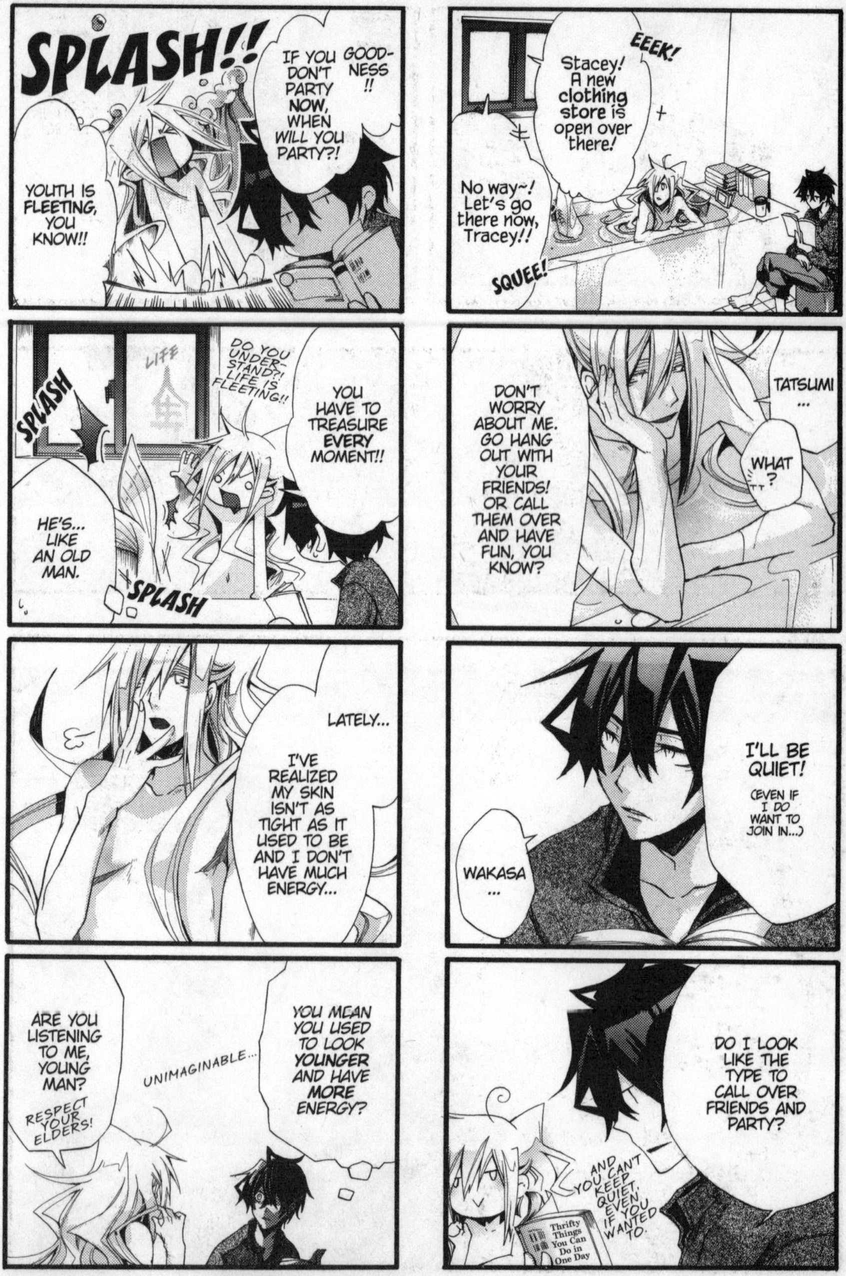

EEEK!
Stacey! A new clothing store is open over there!
No way~! Let's go there now, Tracey!!
SQUEE!
TATSUMI...
WHAT?
DON'T WORRY ABOUT ME. GO HANG OUT WITH YOUR FRIENDS! OR CALL THEM OVER AND HAVE FUN, YOU KNOW?
I'LL BE QUIET!
(EVEN IF I DO WANT TO JOIN IN...)
WAKASA...
DO I LOOK LIKE THE TYPE TO CALL OVER FRIENDS AND PARTY?
AND YOU CAN'T KEEP QUIET, EVEN IF YOU WANTED TO.
Thrifty Things You Can Do in One Day
SPLASH!!
GOODNESS!!
IF YOU DON'T PARTY NOW, WHEN WILL YOU PARTY?!
YOUTH IS FLEETING, YOU KNOW!!
YOU HAVE TO TREASURE EVERY MOMENT!!
DO YOU UNDERSTAND?! LIFE IS FLEETING!!
LIFE
SPLASH
HE'S... LIKE AN OLD MAN.
SPLASH
LATELY...
I'VE REALIZED MY SKIN ISN'T AS TIGHT AS IT USED TO BE AND I DON'T HAVE MUCH ENERGY...
YOU MEAN YOU USED TO LOOK YOUNGER AND HAVE MORE ENERGY?
UNIMAGINABLE...
ARE YOU LISTENING TO ME, YOUNG MAN?
RESPECT YOUR ELDERS!

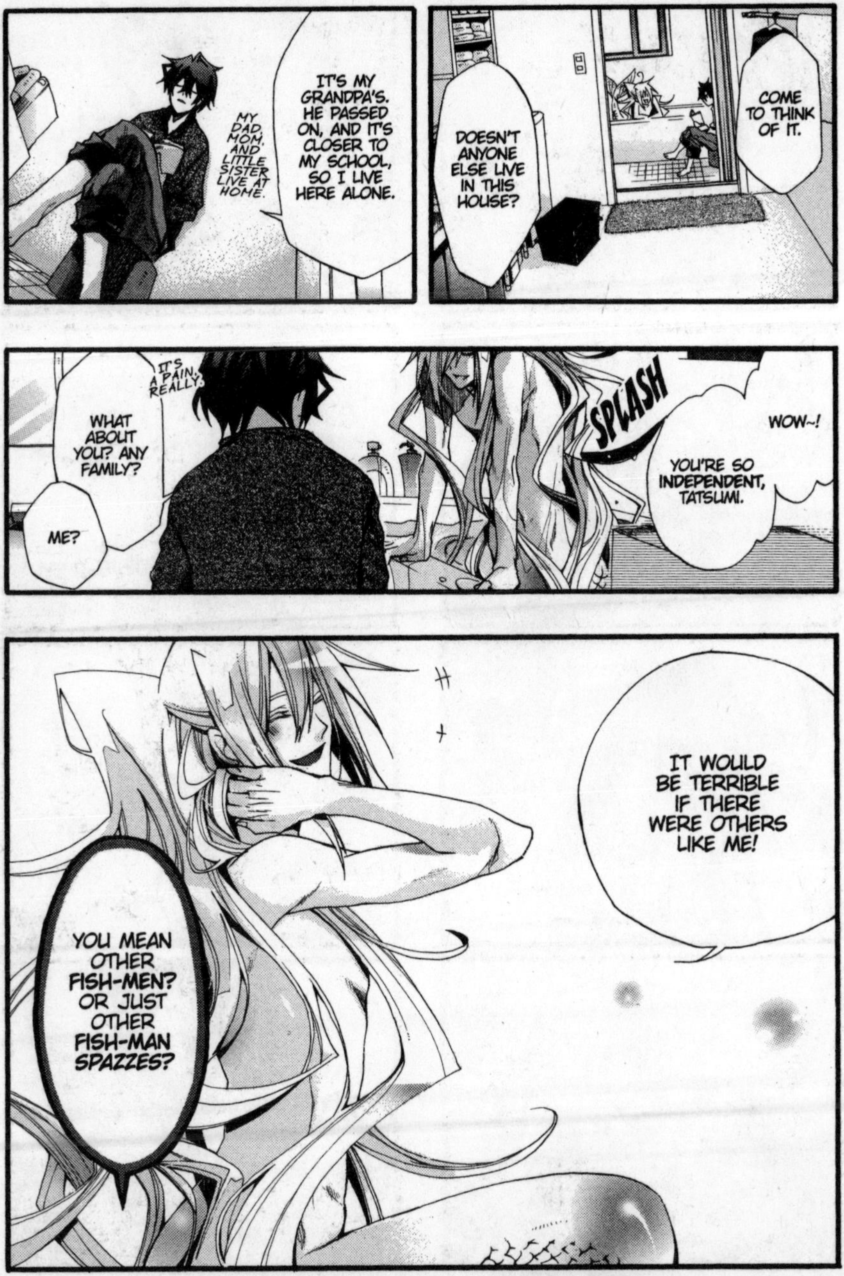
COME TO THINK OF IT.
DOESN'T ANYONE ELSE LIVE IN THIS HOUSE?
IT'S MY GRANDPA'S. HE PASSED ON, AND IT'S CLOSER TO MY SCHOOL, SO I LIVE HERE ALONE.
MY DAD, MOM, AND LITTLE SISTER LIVE AT HOME.
SPLASH
WOW~!
YOU'RE SO INDEPENDENT, TATSUMI.
IT'S A PAIN, REALLY.
WHAT ABOUT YOU? ANY FAMILY?
ME?
IT WOULD BE TERRIBLE IF THERE WERE OTHERS LIKE ME!
YOU MEAN OTHER FISH-MEN? OR JUST OTHER FISH-MAN SPAZZES?

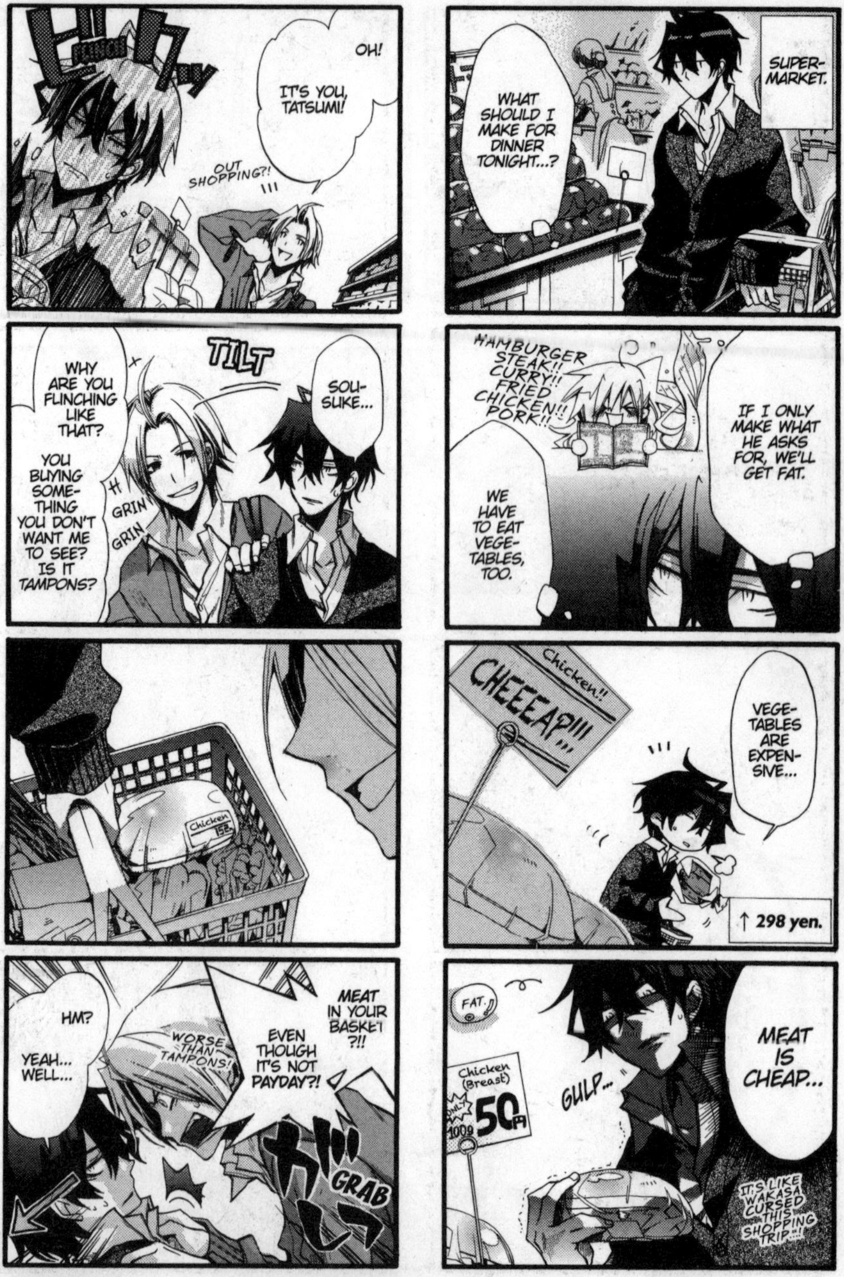
SUPER-MARKET.
WHAT SHOULD I MAKE FOR DINNER TONIGHT...?
OH!
IT'S YOU, TATSUMI!
OUT SHOPPING?!
HAMBURGER STEAK!! CURRY!! FRIED CHICKEN!! PORK!!
IF I ONLY MAKE WHAT HE ASKS FOR, WE'LL GET FAT.
WE HAVE TO EAT VEGETABLES, TOO.
SOU-SUKE...
TILT
WHY ARE YOU FLINCHING LIKE THAT?
YOU BUYING SOMETHING YOU DON'T WANT ME TO SEE? IS IT TAMPONS?
GRIN GRIN
Chicken!!
CHEEEAP!!!
VEGETABLES ARE EXPENSIVE...
↑ 298 yen.
Chicken
FAT.
Chicken (Breast)
50円
GULP...
MEAT IS CHEAP...
IT'S LIKE WAKASA CURSED THIS SHOPPING TRIP...!!
MEAT IN YOUR BASKET?!!
EVEN THOUGH IT'S NOT PAYDAY?!
HM?
WORSE THAN TAMPONS!
YEAH... WELL...
GRAB

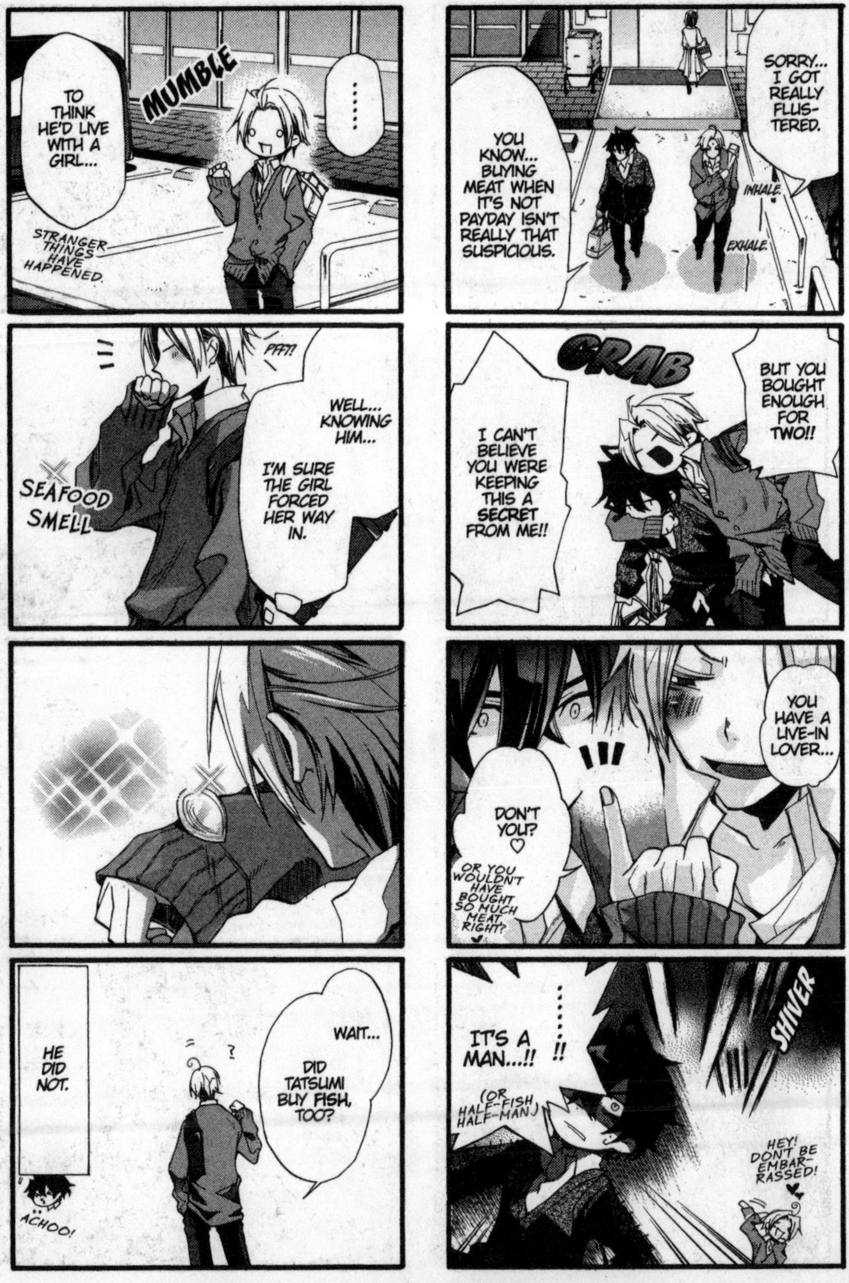
SORRY... I GOT REALLY FLUS-TERED.
INHALE.
EXHALE.
YOU KNOW... BUYING MEAT WHEN IT'S NOT PAYDAY ISN'T REALLY THAT SUSPICIOUS.
BUT YOU BOUGHT ENOUGH FOR TWO!!
GRAB
I CAN'T BELIEVE YOU WERE KEEPING THIS A SECRET FROM ME!!
YOU HAVE A LIVE-IN LOVER...
!!!
DON'T YOU? ♡
OR YOU WOULDN'T HAVE BOUGHT SO MUCH MEAT, RIGHT? ♥
SHIVER
......!!
IT'S A MAN...!!
(OR HALF-FISH HALF-MAN)
HEY! DON'T BE EMBAR-RASSED! ♥
......
MUMBLE
TO THINK HE'D LIVE WITH A GIRL...
STRANGER THINGS HAVE HAPPENED.
PFFT!
WELL... KNOWING HIM...
I'M SURE THE GIRL FORCED HER WAY IN.
SEAFOOD SMELL
WAIT...
DID TATSUMI BUY FISH, TOO?
HE DID NOT.
ACHOO!

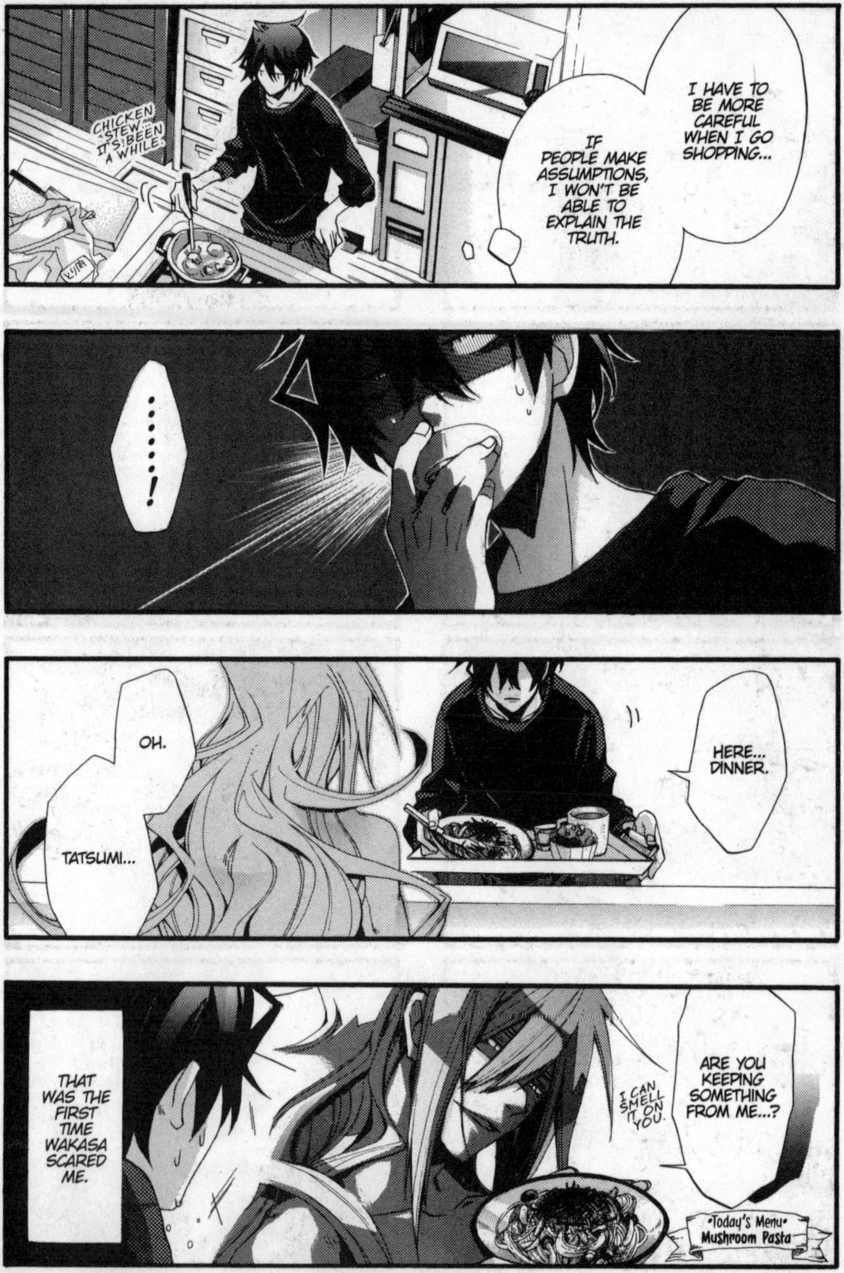
I HAVE TO BE MORE CAREFUL WHEN I GO SHOPPING...
IF PEOPLE MAKE ASSUMPTIONS, I WON'T BE ABLE TO EXPLAIN THE TRUTH.
CHICKEN STEW... IT'S BEEN A WHILE.
......!
HERE... DINNER.
OH.
TATSUMI...
ARE YOU KEEPING SOMETHING FROM ME...?
I CAN SMELL IT ON YOU.
THAT WAS THE FIRST TIME WAKASA SCARED ME.
•Today's Menu•
Mushroom Pasta

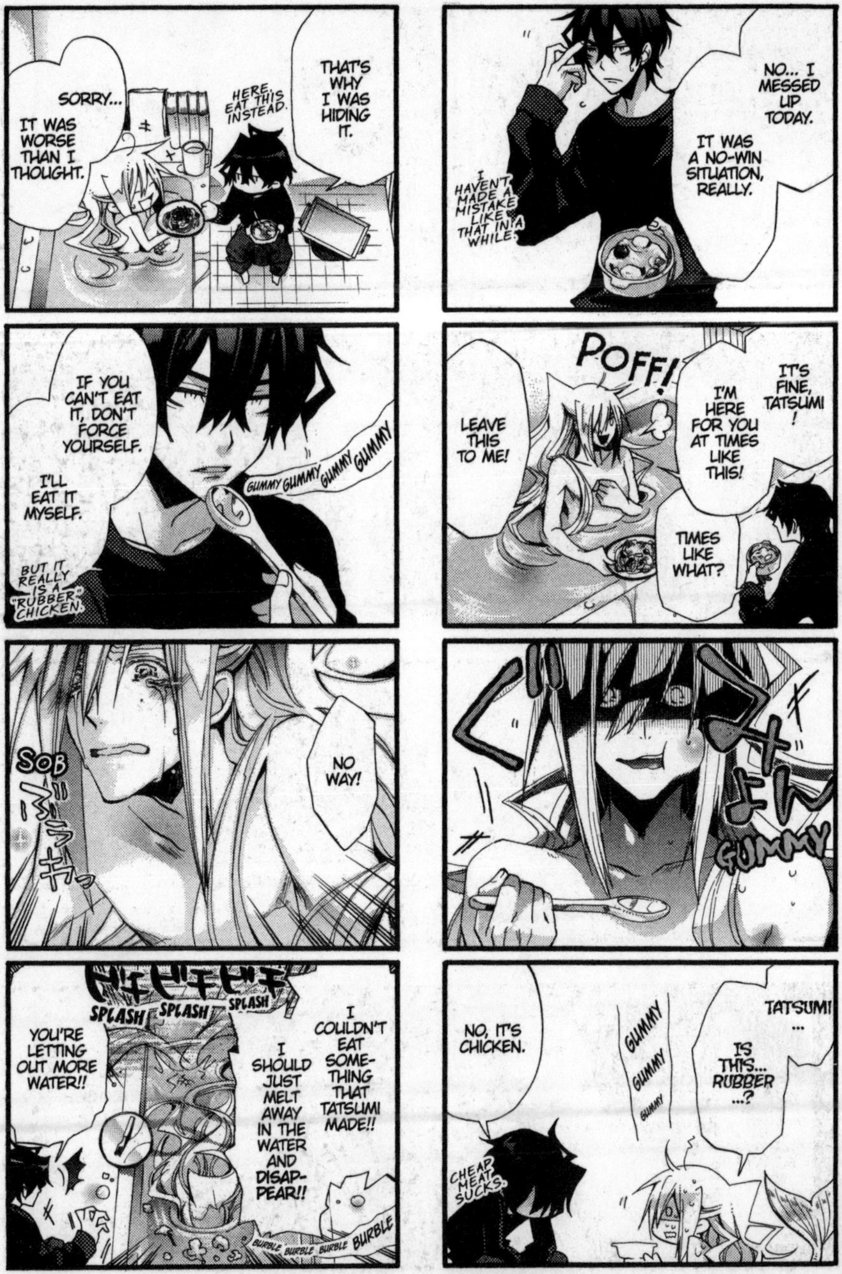
NO... I MESSED UP TODAY.
IT WAS A NO-WIN SITUATION, REALLY.
I HAVEN'T MADE A MISTAKE LIKE THAT IN A WHILE.
THAT'S WHY I WAS HIDING IT.
HERE, EAT THIS INSTEAD.
SORRY... IT WAS WORSE THAN I THOUGHT.
POFF!
IT'S FINE, TATSUMI!
I'M HERE FOR YOU AT TIMES LIKE THIS!
LEAVE THIS TO ME!
TIMES LIKE WHAT?
IF YOU CAN'T EAT IT, DON'T FORCE YOURSELF.
I'LL EAT IT MYSELF.
GUMMY GUMMY GUMMY GUMMY
BUT IT REALLY IS A "RUBBER" CHICKEN.
GUMMY
NO WAY!
SOB
TATSUMI... IS THIS... RUBBER...?
GUMMY GUMMY GUMMY
NO, IT'S CHICKEN.
CHEAP MEAT SUCKS.
I COULDN'T EAT SOMETHING THAT TATSUMI MADE!!
I SHOULD JUST MELT AWAY IN THE WATER AND DISAPPEAR!!
SPLASH SPLASH SPLASH
YOU'RE LETTING OUT MORE WATER!!
BURBLE BURBLE BURBLE BURBLE

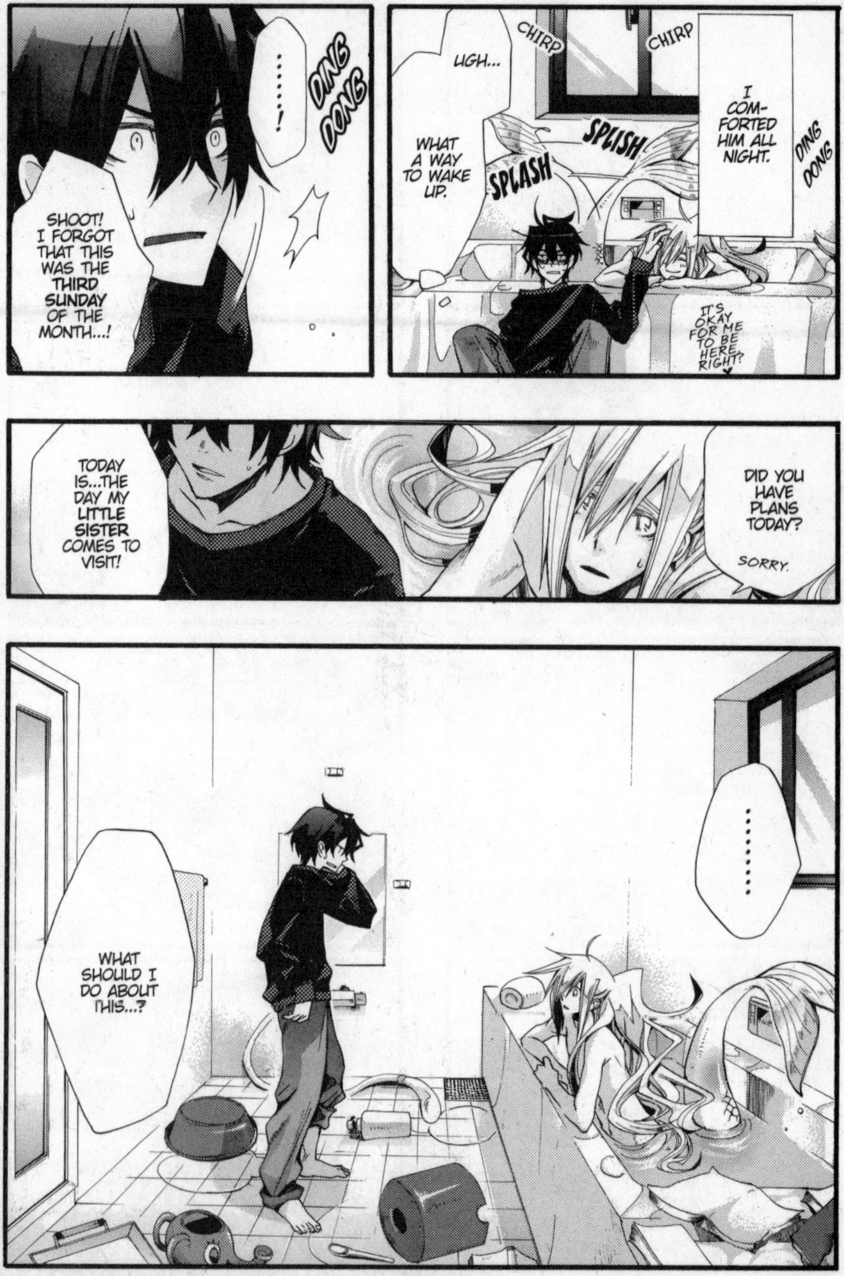
I COM-FORTED HIM ALL NIGHT.
CHIRP
CHIRP
UGH...
DING DONG
SPLISH
WHAT A WAY TO WAKE UP.
SPLASH
IT'S OKAY FOR ME TO BE HERE, RIGHT?
DING DONG
......!
SHOOT! I FORGOT THAT THIS WAS THE THIRD SUNDAY OF THE MONTH...!
DID YOU HAVE PLANS TODAY?
SORRY.
TODAY IS...THE DAY MY LITTLE SISTER COMES TO VISIT!
....
WHAT SHOULD I DO ABOUT THIS...?

Merman in My Tub

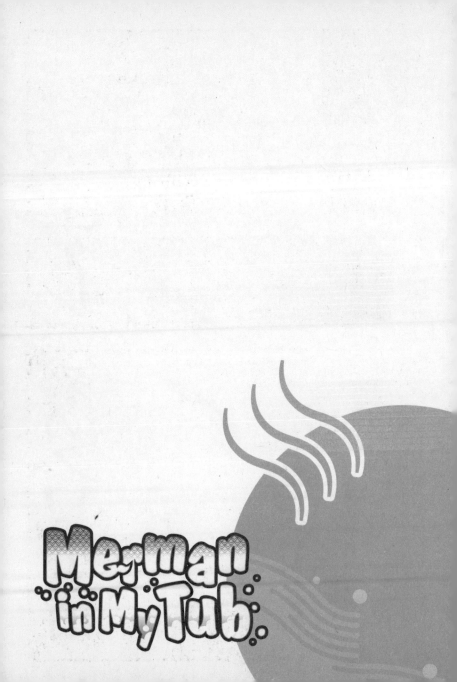

オレん家のフロ事情

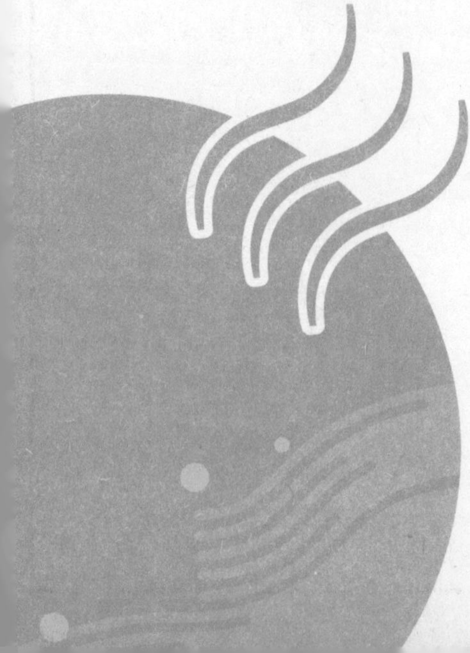

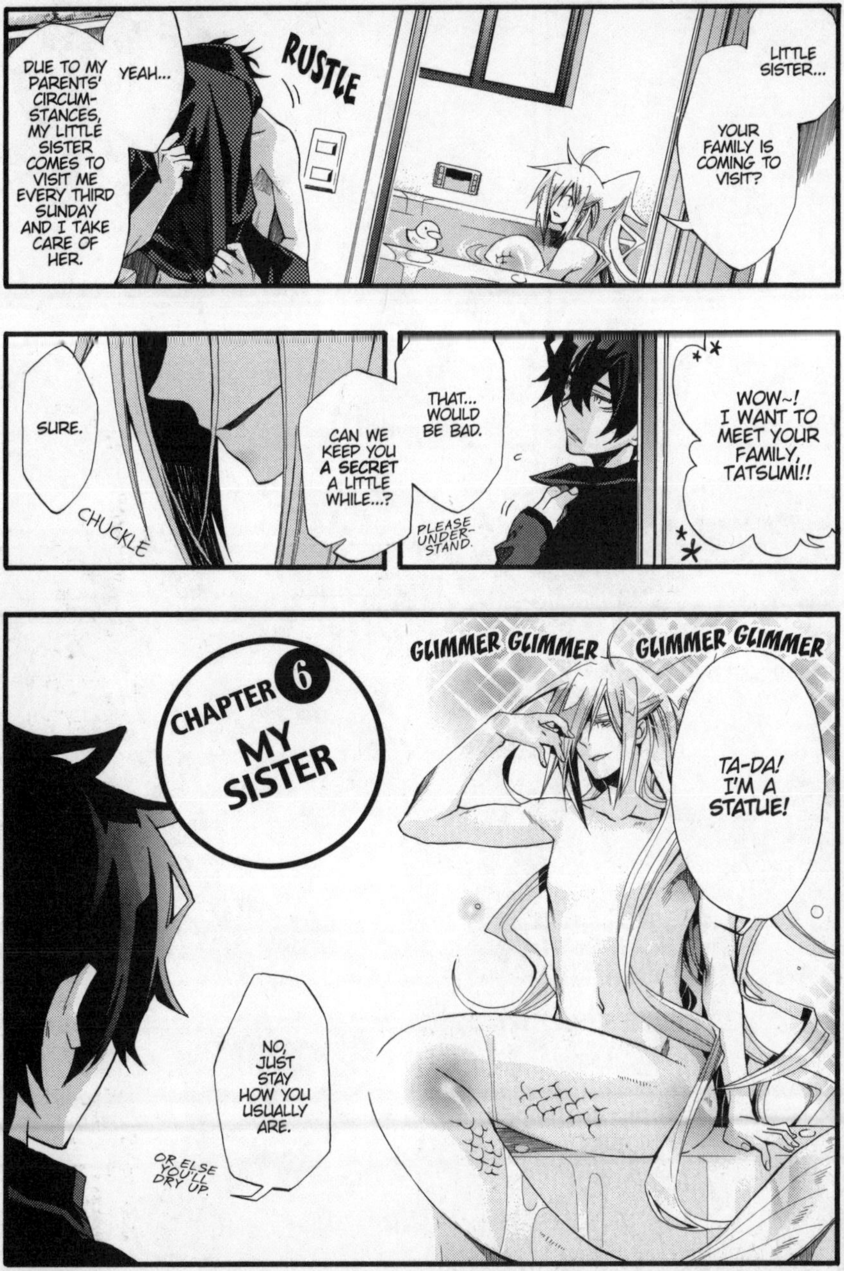
LITTLE SISTER...
YOUR FAMILY IS COMING TO VISIT?
RUSTLE
YEAH...
DUE TO MY PARENTS' CIRCUM-STANCES, MY LITTLE SISTER COMES TO VISIT ME EVERY THIRD SUNDAY AND I TAKE CARE OF HER.
WOW~! I WANT TO MEET YOUR FAMILY, TATSUMI!!
THAT... WOULD BE BAD.
PLEASE UNDER-STAND.
CAN WE KEEP YOU A SECRET A LITTLE WHILE...?
SURE.
CHUCKLE
GLIMMER GLIMMER
GLIMMER GLIMMER
TA-DA! I'M A STATUE!
CHAPTER 6
MY SISTER
NO, JUST STAY HOW YOU USUALLY ARE.
OR ELSE YOU'LL DRY UP.

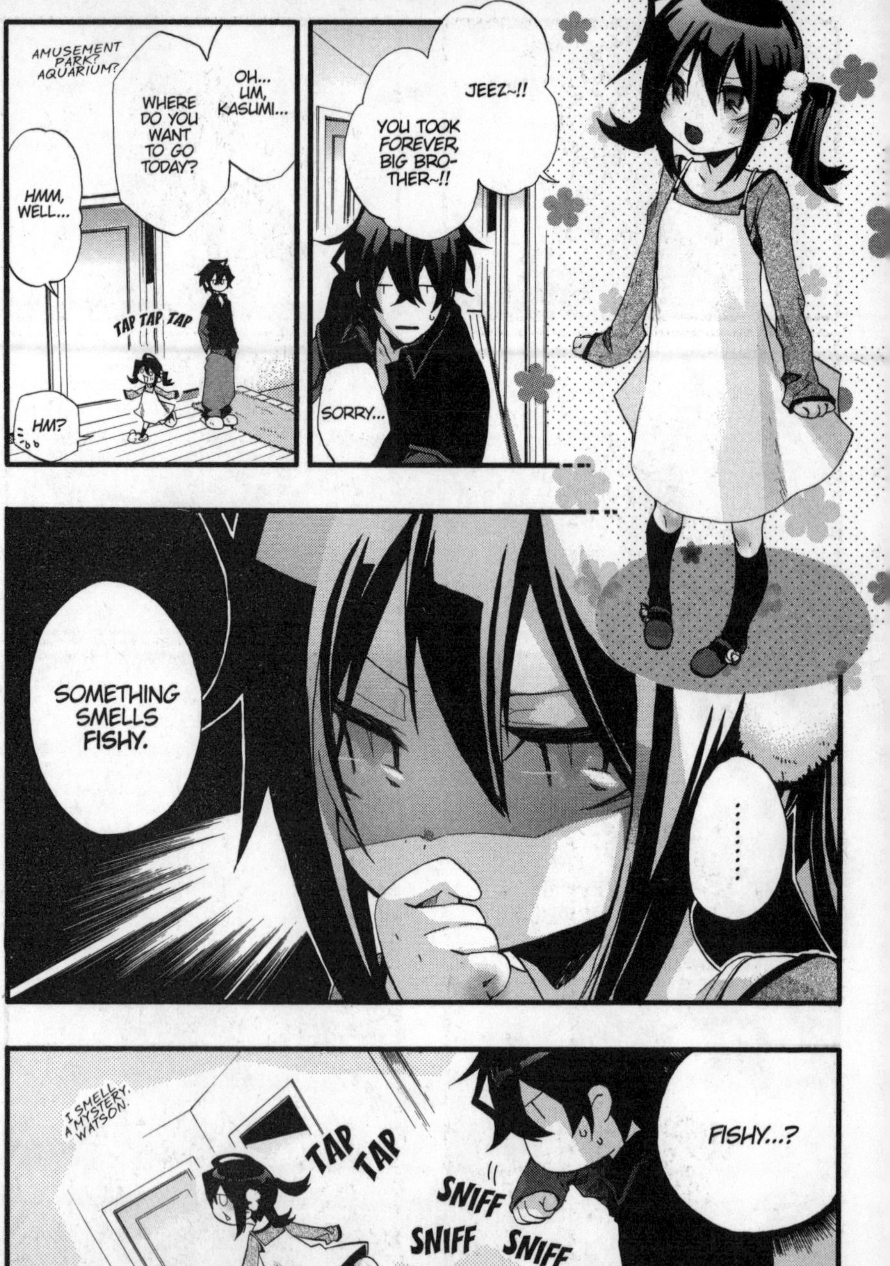
JEEZ~!!
YOU TOOK FOREVER, BIG BROTHER~!!
SORRY...
OH... UM, KASUMI...
WHERE DO YOU WANT TO GO TODAY?
AMUSEMENT PARK? AQUARIUM?
HMM, WELL...
TAP TAP TAP
HM?
......
SOMETHING SMELLS FISHY.
FISHY...?
SNIFF SNIFF SNIFF
TAP TAP
I SMELL A MYSTERY, WATSON.

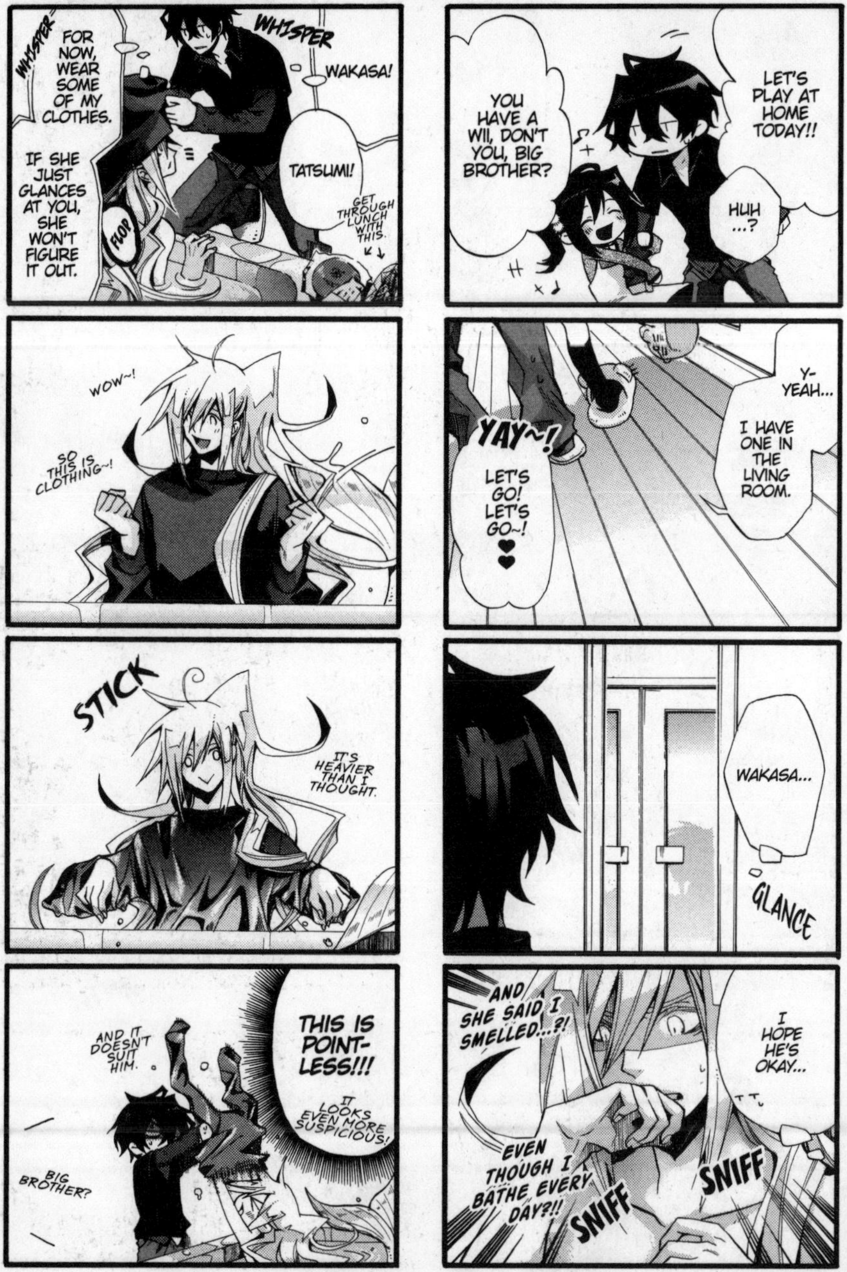
LET'S PLAY AT HOME TODAY!!
YOU HAVE A WII, DON'T YOU, BIG BROTHER?
HUH ...?
Y- YEAH... I HAVE ONE IN THE LIVING ROOM.
YAY~!
LET'S GO! LET'S GO~! ❤❤
WAKASA...
GLANCE
I HOPE HE'S OKAY...
AND SHE SAID I SMELLED...?!
SNIFF
EVEN THOUGH I BATHE EVERY DAY?!!
SNIFF
WHISPER
WAKASA!
TATSUMI!
WHISPER
FOR NOW, WEAR SOME OF MY CLOTHES.
IF SHE JUST GLANCES AT YOU, SHE WON'T FIGURE IT OUT.
GET THROUGH LUNCH WITH THIS.
FLOP
WOW~!
SO THIS IS CLOTHING~!
STICK
IT'S HEAVIER THAN I THOUGHT.
THIS IS POINTLESS!!!
IT LOOKS EVEN MORE SUSPICIOUS!
AND IT DOESN'T SUIT HIM.
BIG BROTHER?

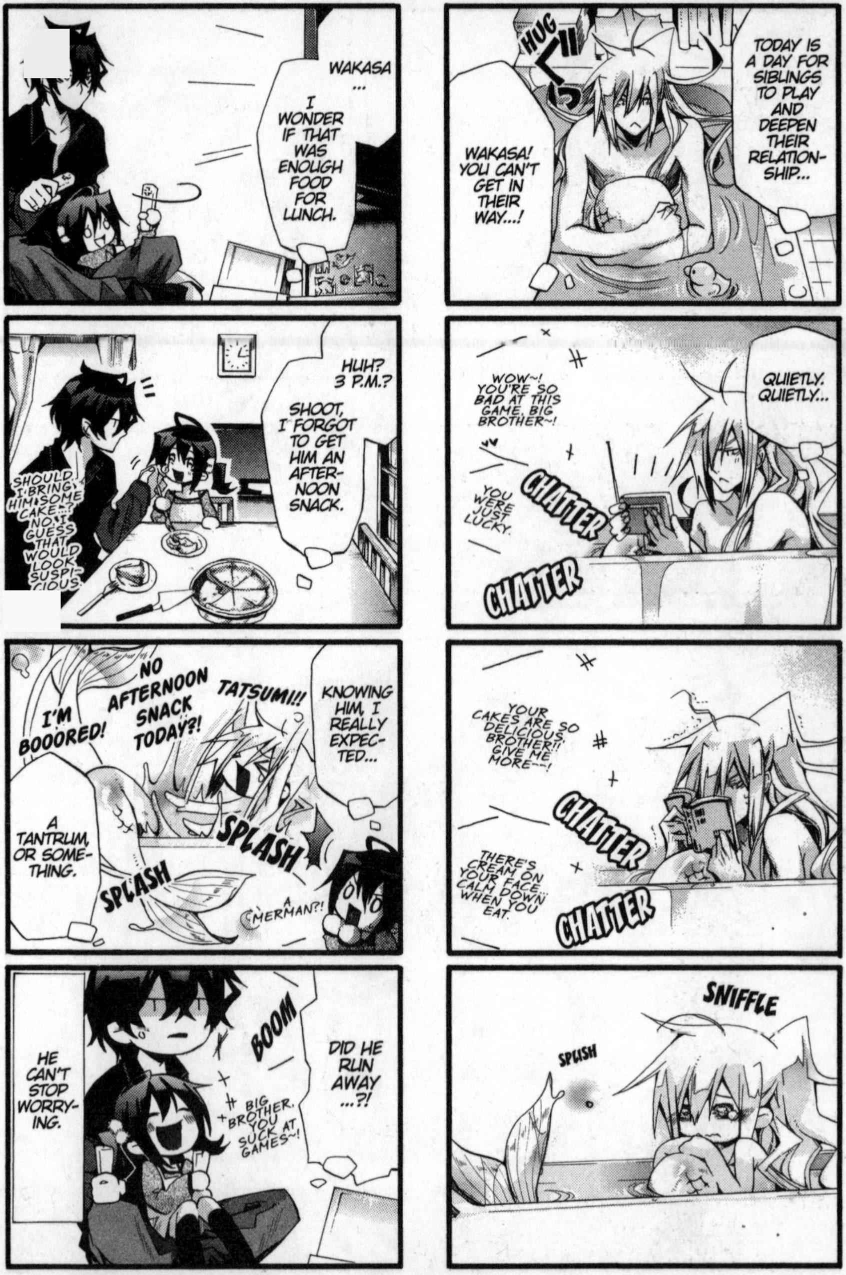
HUG
TODAY IS A DAY FOR SIBLINGS TO PLAY AND DEEPEN THEIR RELATIONSHIP...
WAKASA! YOU CAN'T GET IN THEIR WAY...!
QUIETLY. QUIETLY...
WOW~! YOU'RE SO BAD AT THIS GAME, BIG BROTHER~!
CHATTER
YOU WERE JUST LUCKY.
CHATTER
YOUR CAKES ARE SO DELICIOUS, BROTHER!! GIVE ME MORE~~!
CHATTER
THERE'S CREAM ON YOUR FACE... CALM DOWN WHEN YOU EAT.
CHATTER
SNIFFLE
SPLISH
WAKASA... I WONDER IF THAT WAS ENOUGH FOOD FOR LUNCH.
HUH? 3 P.M.? SHOOT, I FORGOT TO GET HIM AN AFTERNOON SNACK.
SHOULD I BRING HIM SOME CAKE...? NO, I GUESS THAT WOULD LOOK SUSPICIOUS.
KNOWING HIM, I REALLY EXPECTED...
TATSUMI!!
NO AFTERNOON SNACK TODAY?!
I'M BOOORED!
SPLASH
A TANTRUM, OR SOMETHING.
SPLASH
A MERMAN?!
DID HE RUN AWAY...?!
BOOM
BIG BROTHER, YOU SUCK AT GAMES~!
HE CAN'T STOP WORRYING.

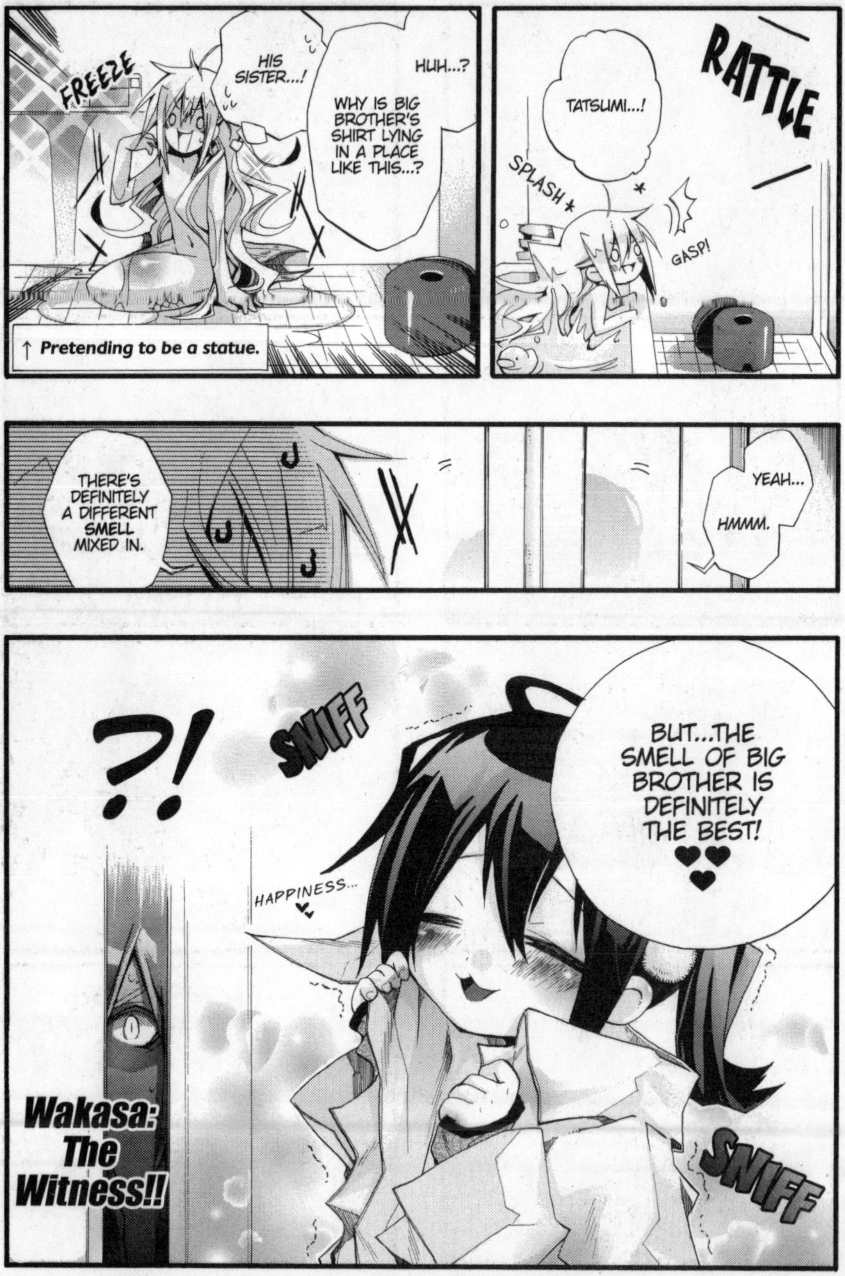
RATTLE
TATSUMI...!
SPLASH
GASP!
HUH...?
WHY IS BIG BROTHER'S SHIRT LYING IN A PLACE LIKE THIS...?
HIS SISTER...!
FREEZE
↑ Pretending to be a statue.
YEAH...
HMMM.
THERE'S DEFINITELY A DIFFERENT SMELL MIXED IN.
BUT...THE SMELL OF BIG BROTHER IS DEFINITELY THE BEST!
SNIFF
?!
HAPPINESS...
Wakasa: The Witness!!
SNIFF

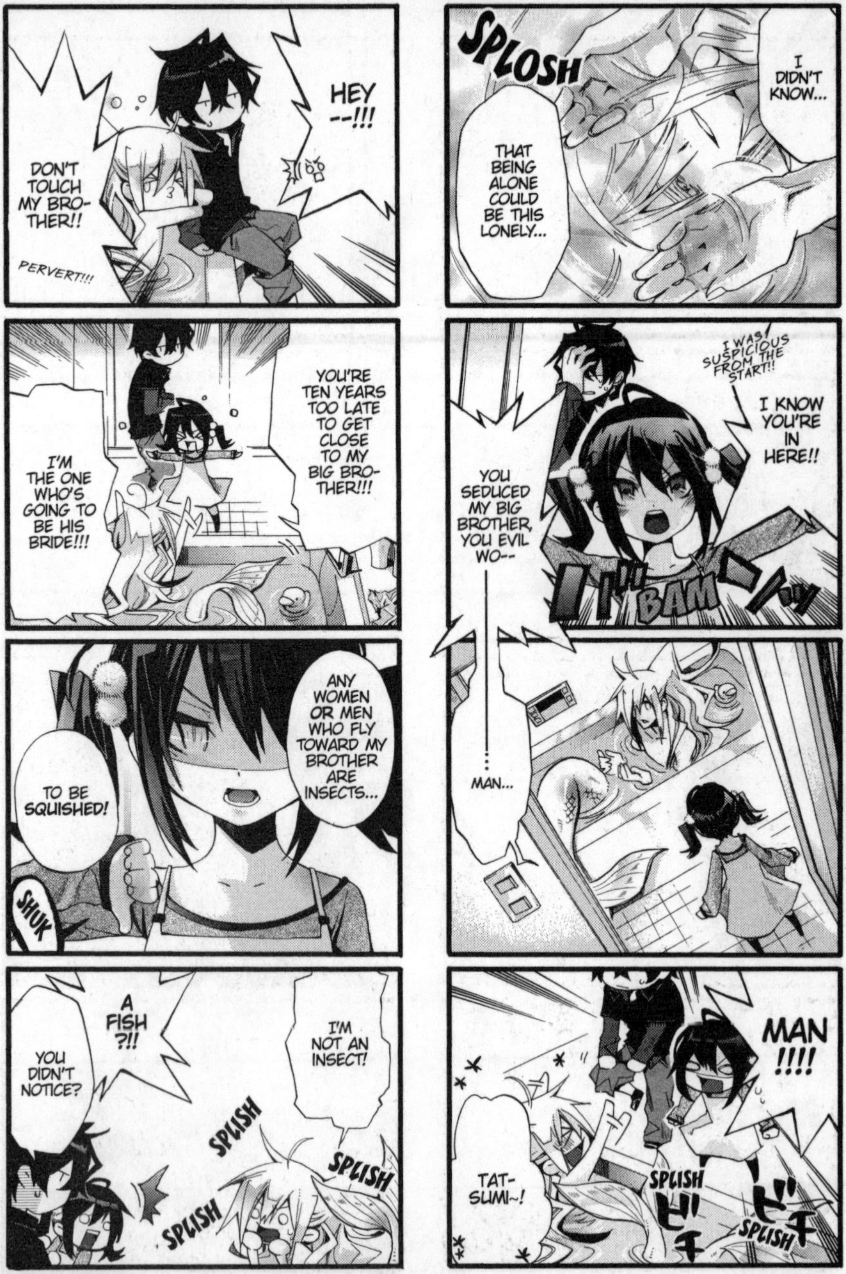
SPLOSH
I DIDN'T KNOW...
THAT BEING ALONE COULD BE THIS LONELY...
I WAS SUSPICIOUS FROM THE START!!
I KNOW YOU'RE IN HERE!!
YOU SEDUCED MY BIG BROTHER, YOU EVIL WO--
BAM
...MAN...
MAN!!!!
TAT-SUMI~!
SPLISH
SPLISH
HEY--!!!
DON'T TOUCH MY BRO-THER!!
PERVERT!!!
YOU'RE TEN YEARS TOO LATE TO GET CLOSE TO MY BIG BRO-THER!!!
I'M THE ONE WHO'S GOING TO BE HIS BRIDE!!!
ANY WOMEN OR MEN WHO FLY TOWARD MY BROTHER ARE INSECTS...
TO BE SQUISHED!
SHUK
I'M NOT AN INSECT!
A FISH?!!
YOU DIDN'T NOTICE?
SPLISH
SPLISH
SPLISH

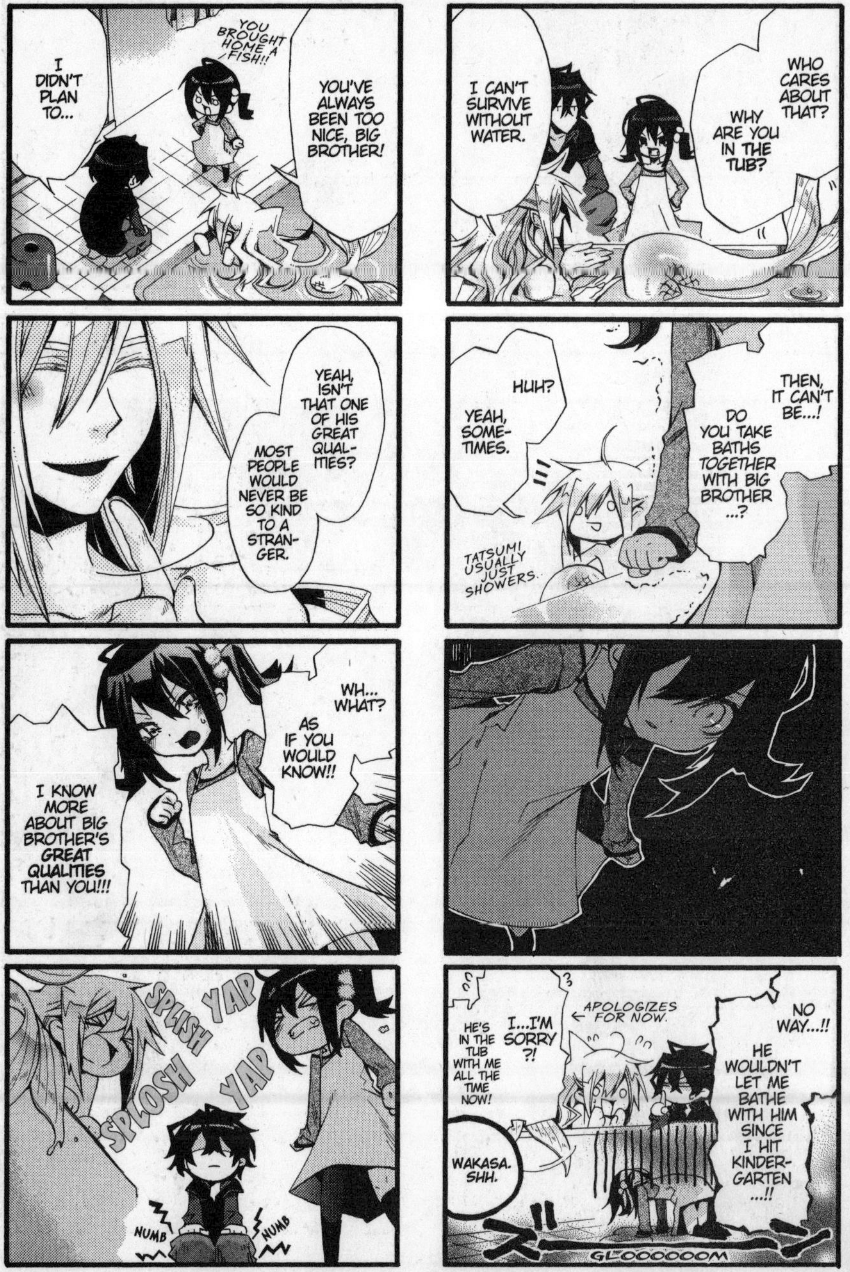
WHO CARES ABOUT THAT?
WHY ARE YOU IN THE TUB?
I CAN'T SURVIVE WITHOUT WATER.
THEN, IT CAN'T BE...!
DO YOU TAKE BATHS TOGETHER WITH BIG BROTHER ...?
HUH?
YEAH, SOMETIMES.
TATSUMI USUALLY JUST SHOWERS.
NO WAY...!!
HE WOULDN'T LET ME BATHE WITH HIM SINCE I HIT KINDERGARTEN ...!!
APOLOGIZES FOR NOW.
I...I'M SORRY ?!
HE'S IN THE TUB WITH ME ALL THE TIME NOW!
WAKASA. SHH.
GLOOOOOOM
YOU BROUGHT HOME A FISH!!
YOU'VE ALWAYS BEEN TOO NICE, BIG BROTHER!
I DIDN'T PLAN TO...
YEAH, ISN'T THAT ONE OF HIS GREAT QUALITIES?
MOST PEOPLE WOULD NEVER BE SO KIND TO A STRANGER.
WH... WHAT?
AS IF YOU WOULD KNOW!!
I KNOW MORE ABOUT BIG BROTHER'S GREAT QUALITIES THAN YOU!!!
YAP
YAP
SPLISH
SPLOSH
NUMB
NUMB

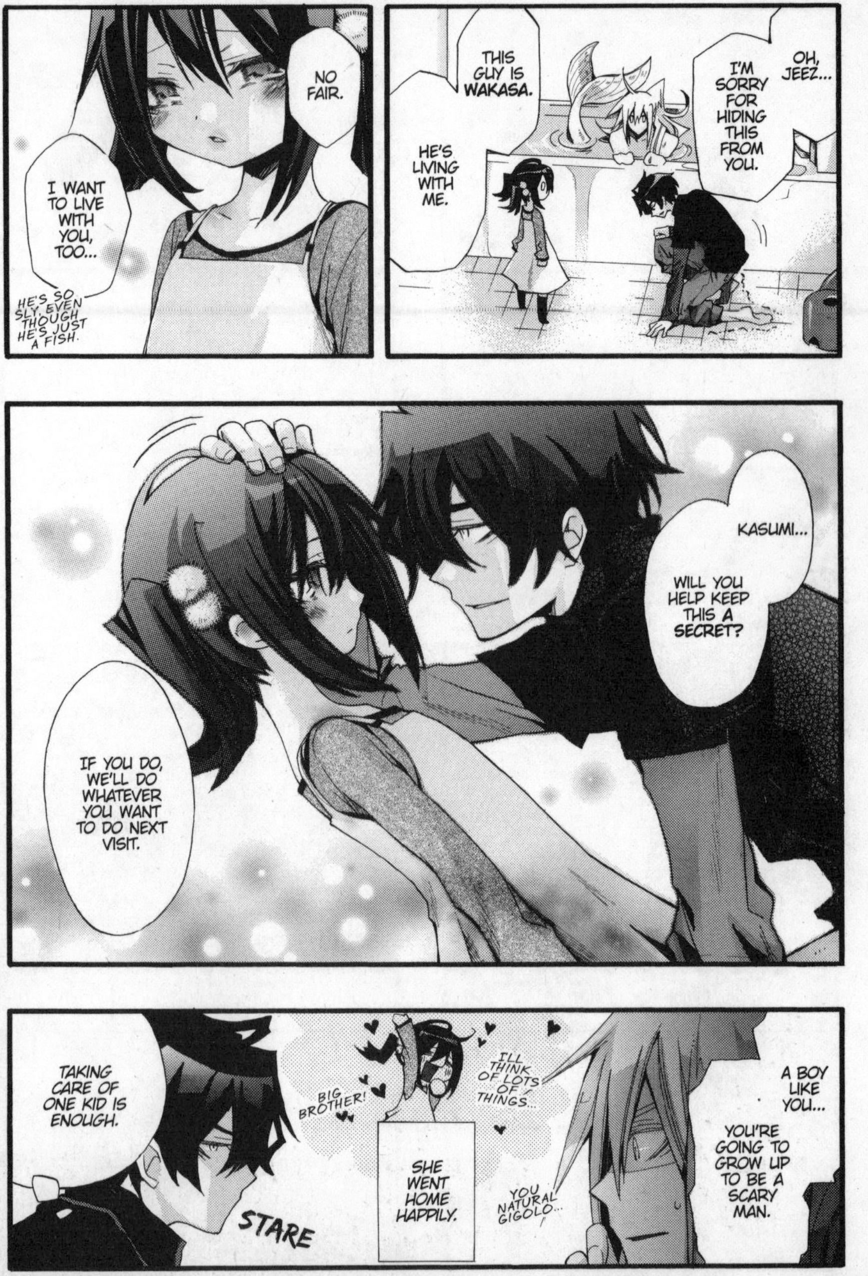
OH, JEEZ...
I'M SORRY FOR HIDING THIS FROM YOU.
THIS GUY IS WAKASA.
HE'S LIVING WITH ME.
NO FAIR.
I WANT TO LIVE WITH YOU, TOO...
HE'S SO SLY, EVEN THOUGH HE'S JUST A FISH.
KASUMI...
WILL YOU HELP KEEP THIS A SECRET?
IF YOU DO, WE'LL DO WHATEVER YOU WANT TO DO NEXT VISIT.
A BOY LIKE YOU...
YOU'RE GOING TO GROW UP TO BE A SCARY MAN.
YOU NATURAL GIGOLO...
I'LL THINK OF LOTS OF THINGS...
BIG BROTHER!
SHE WENT HOME HAPPILY.
TAKING CARE OF ONE KID IS ENOUGH.
STARE

Merman in My Tub

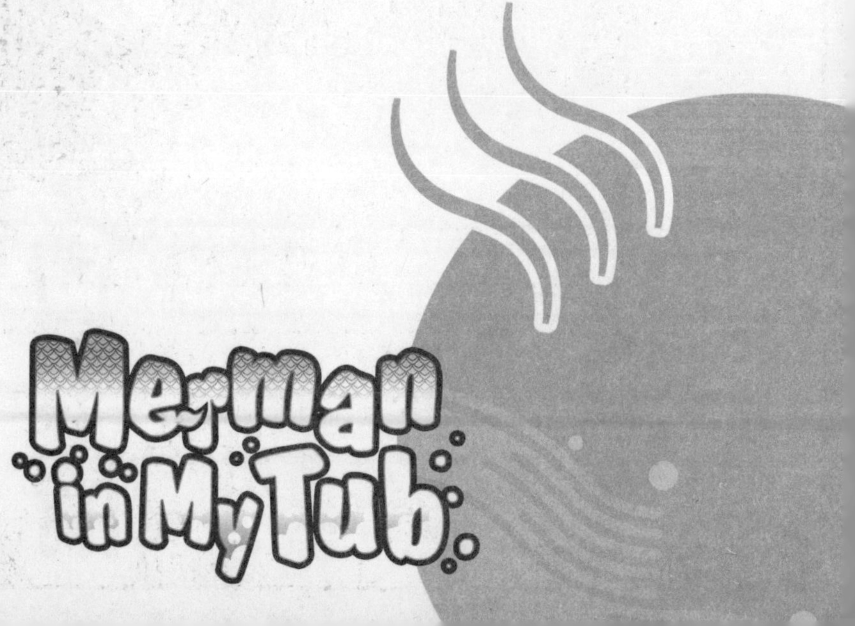

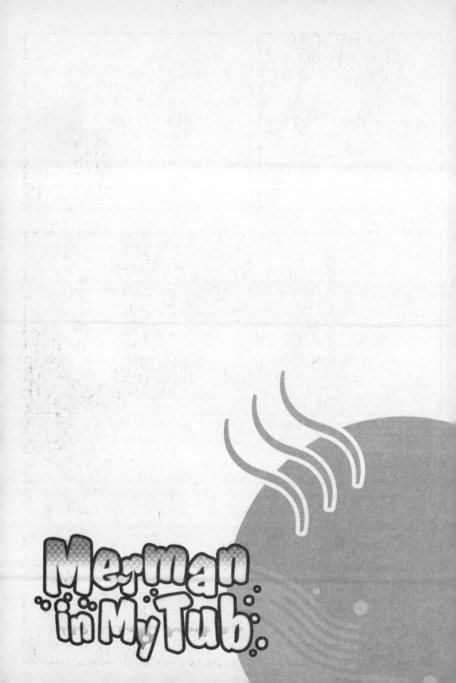

オレん家（ち）のフロ事情

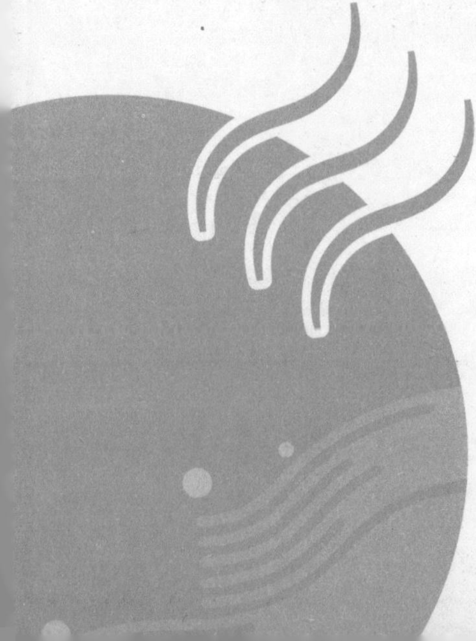

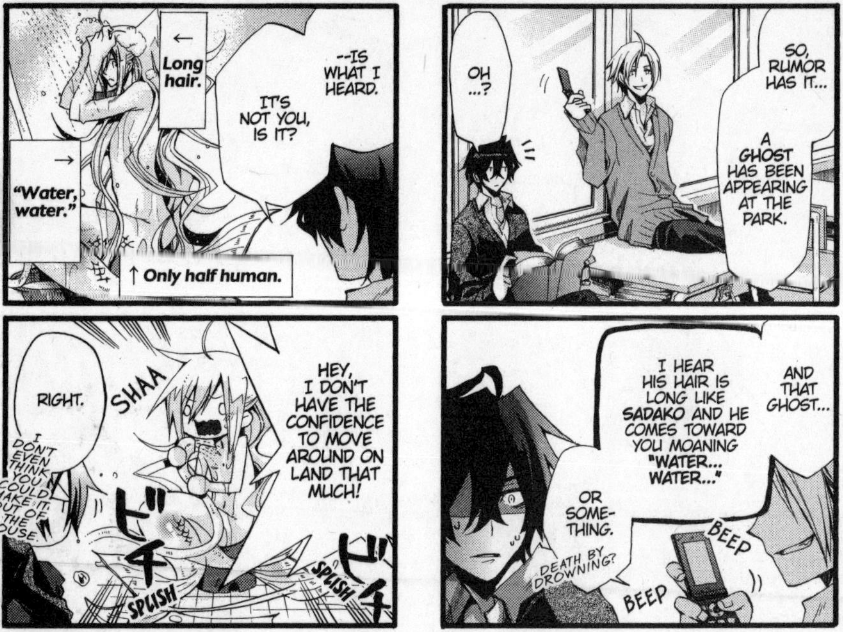
SO, RUMOR HAS IT...
A GHOST HAS BEEN APPEARING AT THE PARK.
OH ...?
--IS WHAT I HEARD.
IT'S NOT YOU, IS IT?
← Long hair.
→ "Water, water."
↑ Only half human.
AND THAT GHOST...
I HEAR HIS HAIR IS LONG LIKE SADAKO AND HE COMES TOWARD YOU MOANING "WATER... WATER..."
OR SOME-THING.
BEEP
DEATH BY DROWNING?
BEEP
HEY, I DON'T HAVE THE CONFIDENCE TO MOVE AROUND ON LAND THAT MUCH!
SHAA
RIGHT.
I DON'T EVEN THINK YOU COULD MAKE IT OUT OF THE HOUSE.
SPLISH
SPLISH
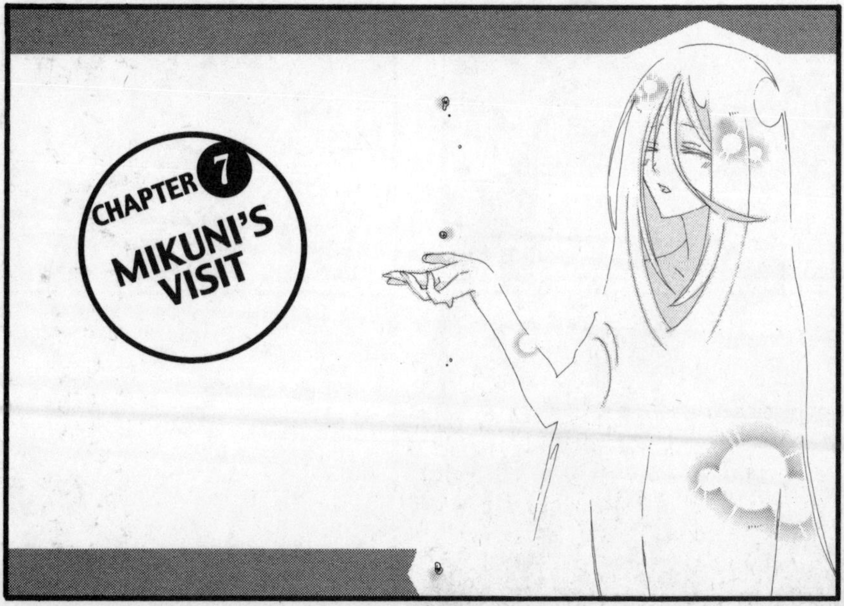
CHAPTER 7
MIKUNI'S VISIT

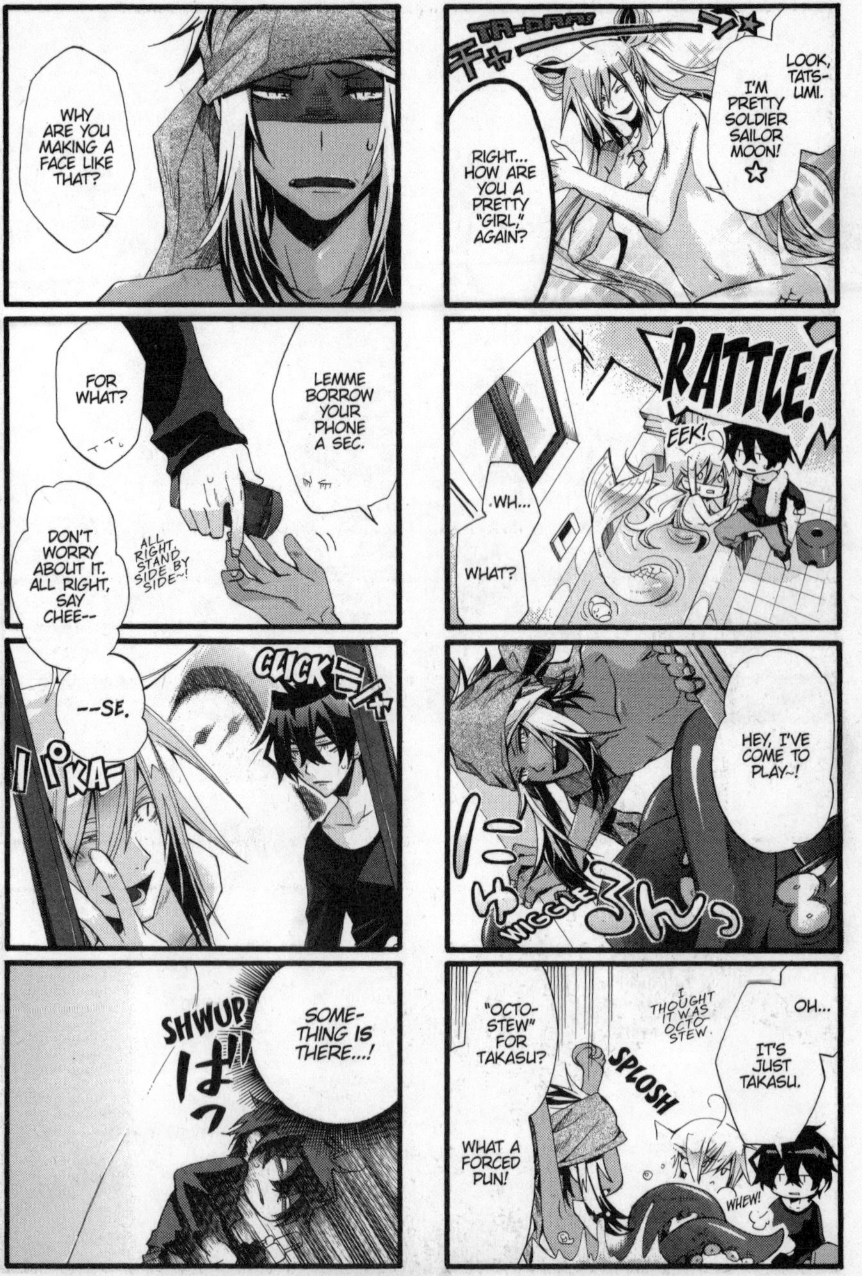
TA-DAA!
LOOK, TATSUMI.
I'M PRETTY SOLDIER SAILOR MOON! ☆
RIGHT... HOW ARE YOU A PRETTY "GIRL," AGAIN?
RATTLE!
EEK!
WH...
WHAT?
HEY, I'VE COME TO PLAY~!
WIGGLE
OH...
IT'S JUST TAKASU.
I THOUGHT IT WAS OCTO STEW.
"OCTO-STEW" FOR TAKASU?
SPLOSH
WHAT A FORCED PUN!
WHEW!
WHY ARE YOU MAKING A FACE LIKE THAT?
LEMME BORROW YOUR PHONE A SEC.
FOR WHAT?
ALL RIGHT, STAND SIDE BY SIDE~!
DON'T WORRY ABOUT IT. ALL RIGHT, SAY CHEE--
CLICK
--SE.
PKA
SOME-THING IS THERE...!
SHWUP

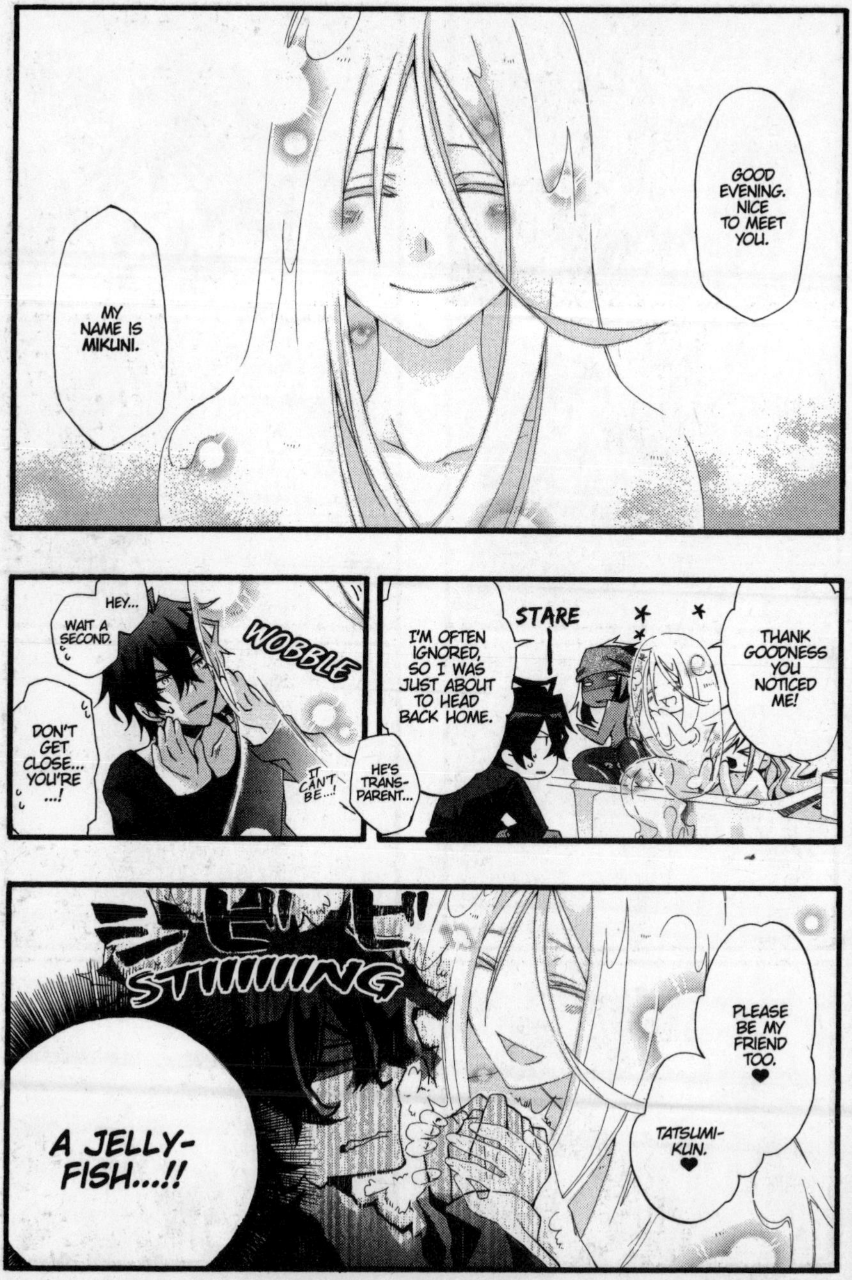
GOOD EVENING. NICE TO MEET YOU.
MY NAME IS MIKUNI.
THANK GOODNESS YOU NOTICED ME!
STARE
I'M OFTEN IGNORED, SO I WAS JUST ABOUT TO HEAD BACK HOME.
HE'S TRANS-PARENT...
IT CAN'T BE...!
WOBBLE
HEY... WAIT A SECOND.
DON'T GET CLOSE... YOU'RE ...!
PLEASE BE MY FRIEND TOO. ♥
TATSUMI-KUN. ♥
STIIIIIIING
A JELLY-FISH...!!

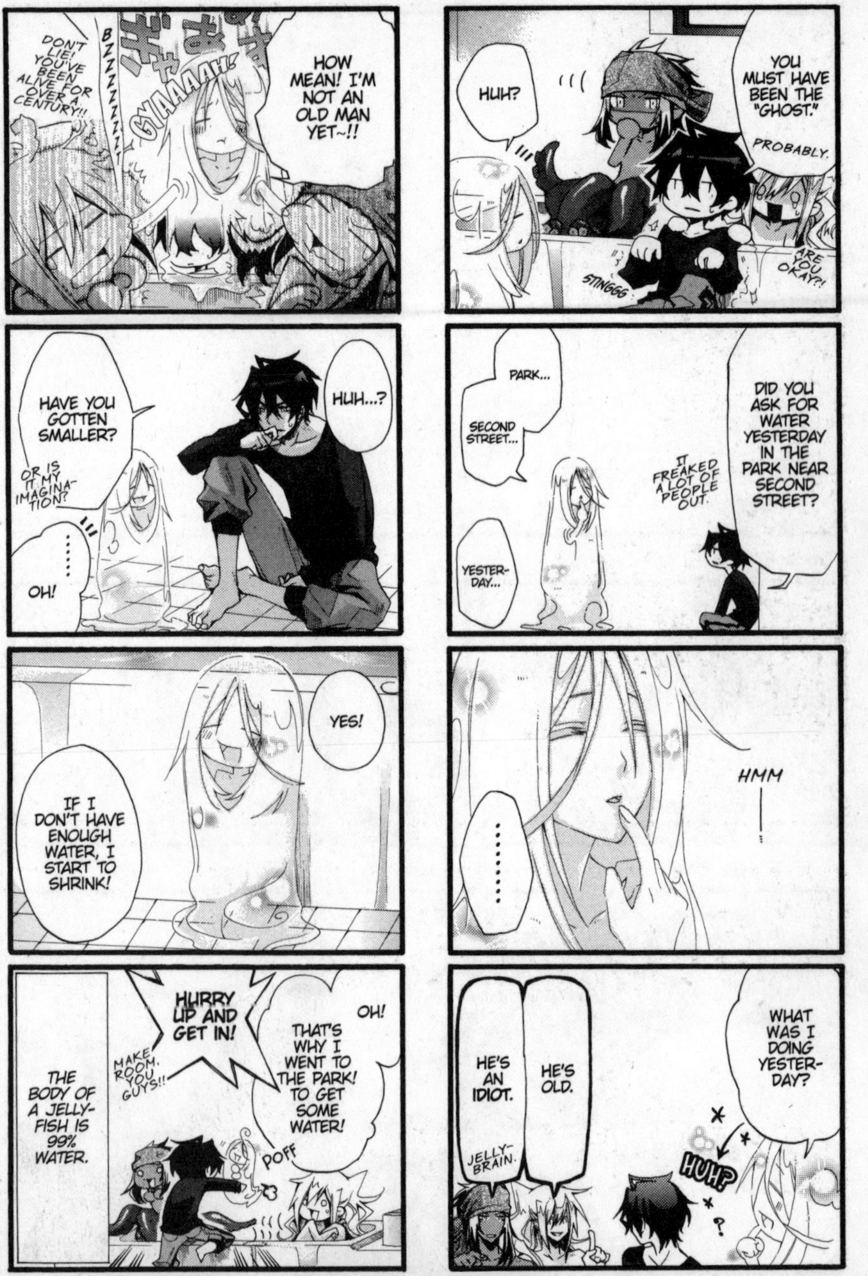
YOU MUST HAVE BEEN THE "GHOST."
PROBABLY.
HUH?
ARE YOU OKAY?!
STINGGG
HOW MEAN! I'M NOT AN OLD MAN YET~!!
GYAAAAH!
BZZZZZZZ
DON'T LIE! YOU'VE BEEN ALIVE FOR OVER A CENTURY!!
DID YOU ASK FOR WATER YESTERDAY IN THE PARK NEAR SECOND STREET?
IT FREAKED A LOT OF PEOPLE OUT.
PARK...
SECOND STREET...
YESTER-DAY...
HUH...?
HAVE YOU GOTTEN SMALLER?
OR IS IT MY IMAGINATION?
......
OH!
HMM
......
YES!
IF I DON'T HAVE ENOUGH WATER, I START TO SHRINK!
WHAT WAS I DOING YESTER-DAY?
HUH?
HE'S OLD.
HE'S AN IDIOT.
JELLY-BRAIN.
OH!
THAT'S WHY I WENT TO THE PARK! TO GET SOME WATER!
HURRY UP AND GET IN!
MAKE ROOM, YOU GUYS!!
POFF
THE BODY OF A JELLY-FISH IS 99% WATER.

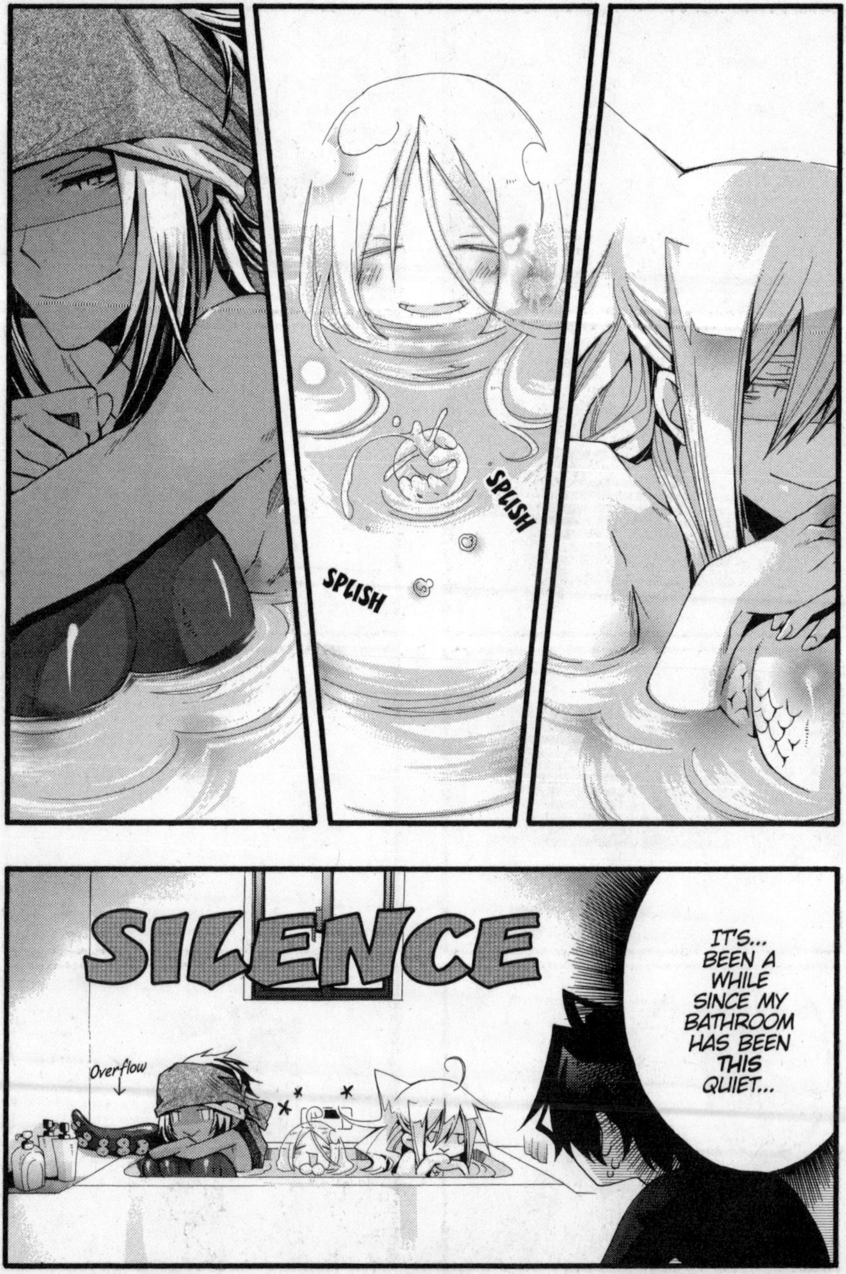

SPLISH
SPLISH
IT'S... BEEN A WHILE SINCE MY BATHROOM HAS BEEN THIS QUIET...
SILENCE
Overflow

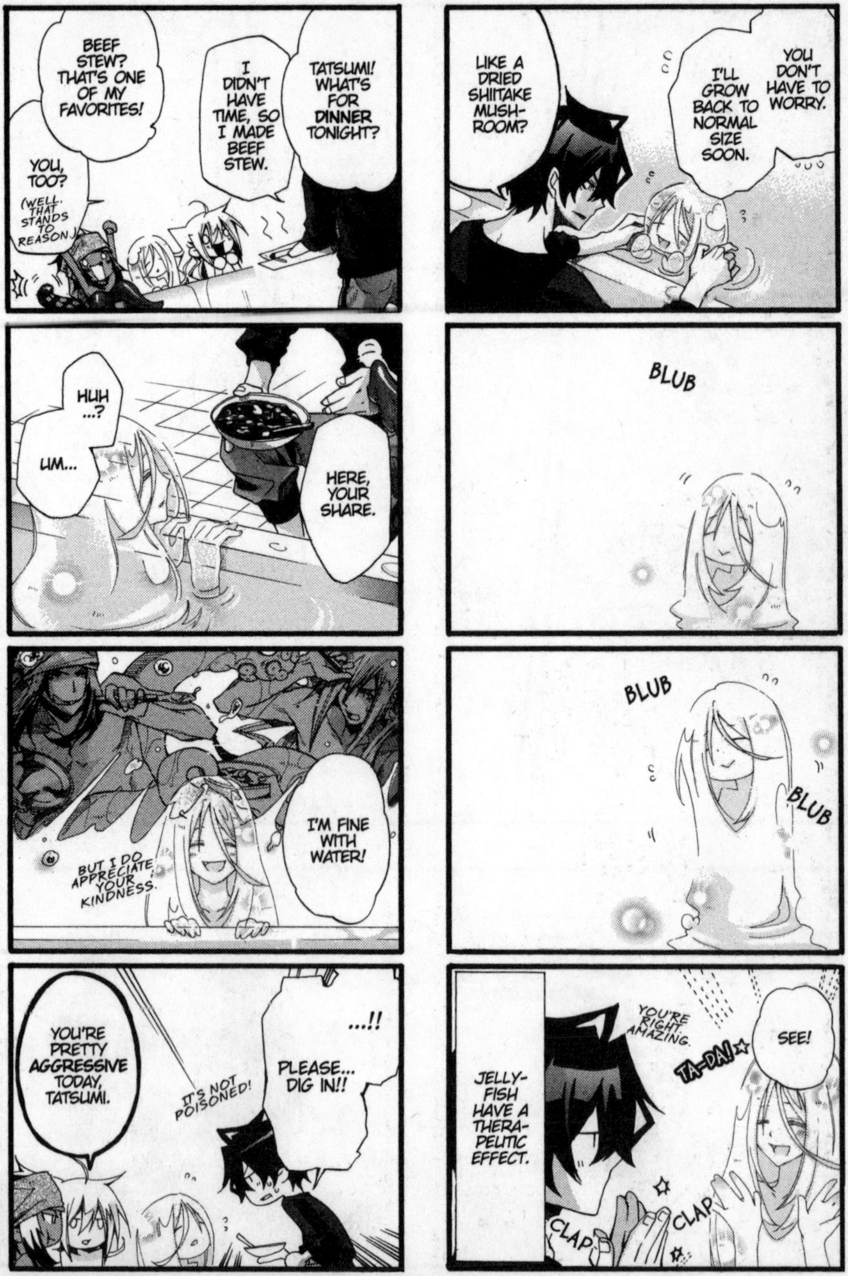
YOU DON'T HAVE TO WORRY.
I'LL GROW BACK TO NORMAL SIZE SOON.
LIKE A DRIED SHIITAKE MUSH-ROOM?
BLUB
BLUB
BLUB
SEE!
TA-DA!☆
YOU'RE RIGHT. AMAZING.
JELLY-FISH HAVE A THERA-PEUTIC EFFECT.
CLAP
CLAP
TATSUMI! WHAT'S FOR DINNER TONIGHT?
I DIDN'T HAVE TIME, SO I MADE BEEF STEW.
BEEF STEW? THAT'S ONE OF MY FAVORITES!
YOU, TOO?
(WELL, THAT STANDS TO REASON.)
HERE, YOUR SHARE.
HUH ...?
UM...
I'M FINE WITH WATER!
BUT I DO APPRECIATE YOUR KINDNESS.
...!!
PLEASE... DIG IN!!
IT'S NOT POISONED!
YOU'RE PRETTY AGGRESSIVE TODAY, TATSUMI.

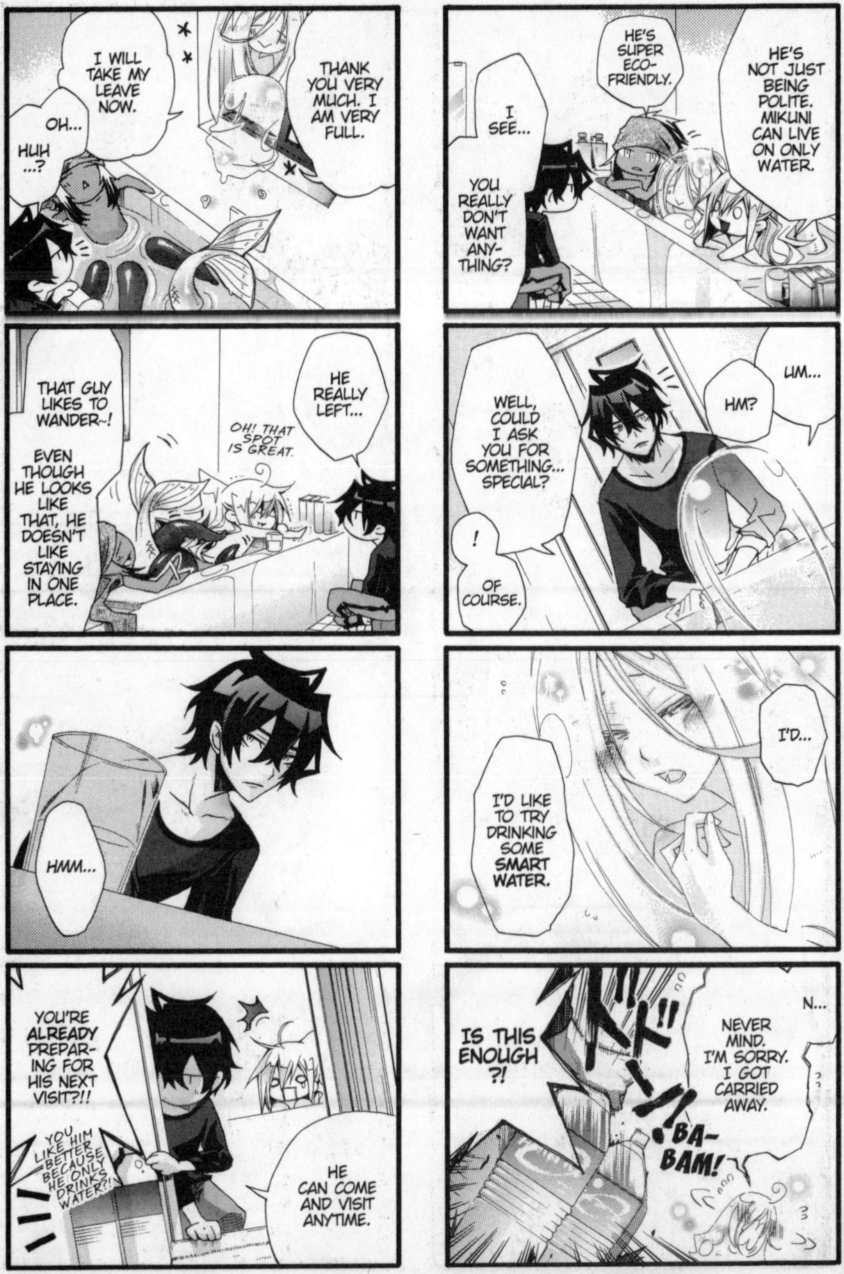
HE'S NOT JUST BEING POLITE. MIKUNI CAN LIVE ON ONLY WATER.
HE'S SUPER ECO-FRIENDLY.
I SEE...
YOU REALLY DON'T WANT ANYTHING?
THANK YOU VERY MUCH. I AM VERY FULL.
I WILL TAKE MY LEAVE NOW.
OH...
HUH ...?
UM...
HM?
WELL, COULD I ASK YOU FOR SOMETHING... SPECIAL?
!
OF COURSE.
HE REALLY LEFT...
OH! THAT SPOT IS GREAT.
THAT GUY LIKES TO WANDER~!
EVEN THOUGH HE LOOKS LIKE THAT, HE DOESN'T LIKE STAYING IN ONE PLACE.
I'D...
I'D LIKE TO TRY DRINKING SOME SMART WATER.
HMM...
N...
NEVER MIND. I'M SORRY. I GOT CARRIED AWAY.
BA-BAM!
IS THIS ENOUGH ?!
HE CAN COME AND VISIT ANYTIME.
YOU'RE ALREADY PREPARING FOR HIS NEXT VISIT?!!
YOU LIKE HIM BETTER BECAUSE HE ONLY DRINKS WATER?!

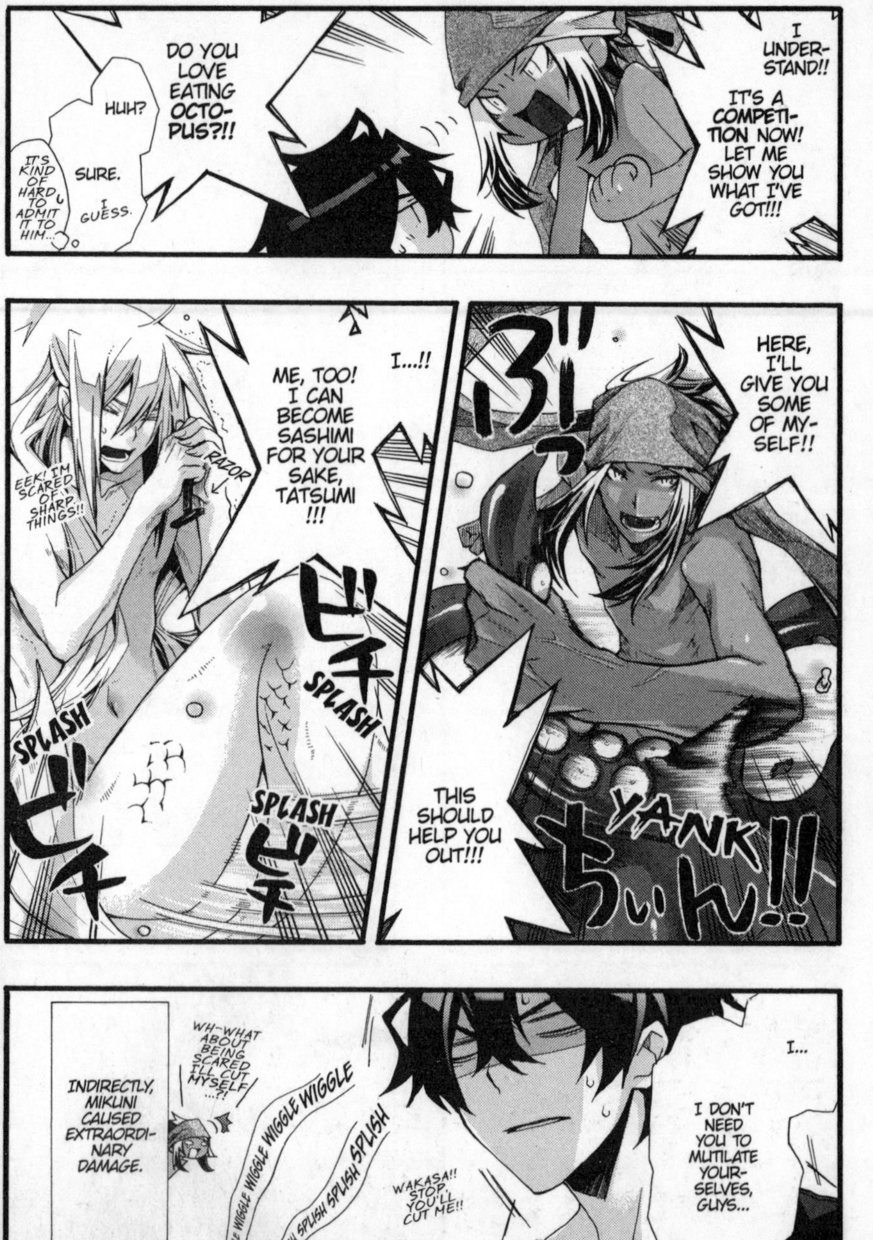
I UNDERSTAND!!
IT'S A COMPETITION NOW! LET ME SHOW YOU WHAT I'VE GOT!!!
DO YOU LOVE EATING OCTOPUS?!!
HUH?
SURE.
I GUESS.
IT'S KIND OF HARD TO ADMIT IT TO HIM...
HERE, I'LL GIVE YOU SOME OF MYSELF!!
ぶりっ
THIS SHOULD HELP YOU OUT!!!
YANK
ちぃん!!
I...!!
ME, TOO! I CAN BECOME SASHIMI FOR YOUR SAKE, TATSUMI!!!
RAZOR
EEK! I'M SCARED OF SHARP THINGS!!
ビチ
SPLASH
SPLASH
ビチ
SPLASH
ビチ
I...
I DON'T NEED YOU TO MUTILATE YOURSELVES, GUYS...
WAKASA!! STOP. YOU'LL CUT ME!!
SPLISH SPLISH SPLISH SPLISH
WIGGLE WIGGLE WIGGLE WIGGLE
WH-WHAT ABOUT BEING SCARED I'LL CUT MYSELF...?!
INDIRECTLY, MIKUNI CAUSED EXTRAORDINARY DAMAGE.

Merman in My Tub

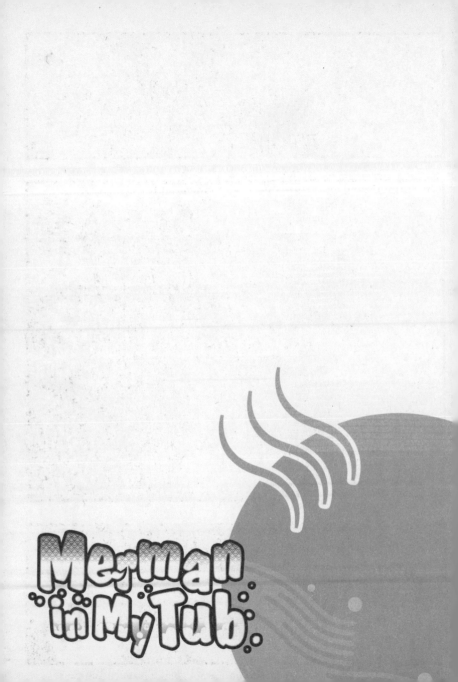

オレん家（ち）のフロ事情

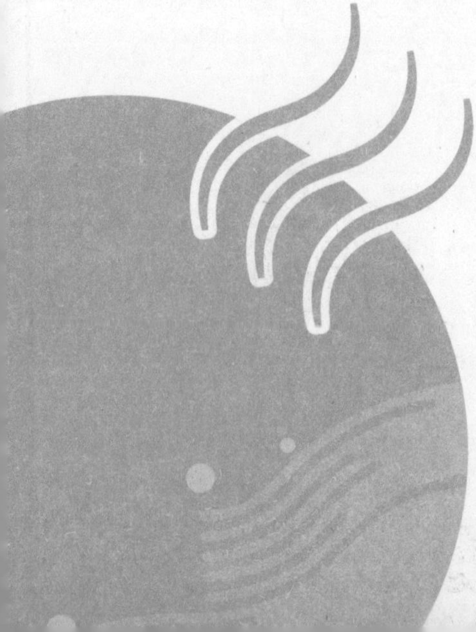

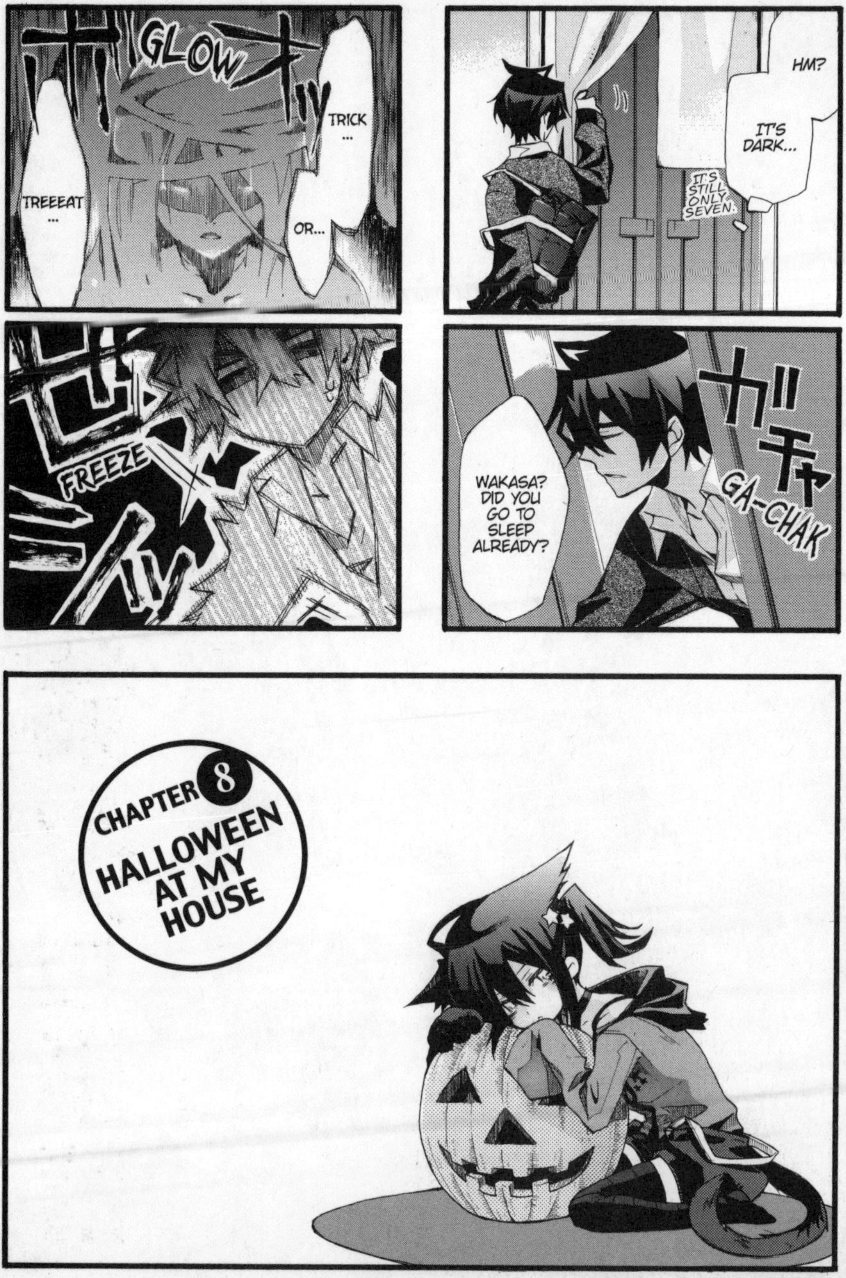
HM?
IT'S DARK...
IT'S STILL ONLY SEVEN.
GLOW
TRICK ...
OR...
TREEEAT ...
GA-CHAK
WAKASA? DID YOU GO TO SLEEP ALREADY?
FREEZE
CHAPTER 8
HALLOWEEN AT MY HOUSE

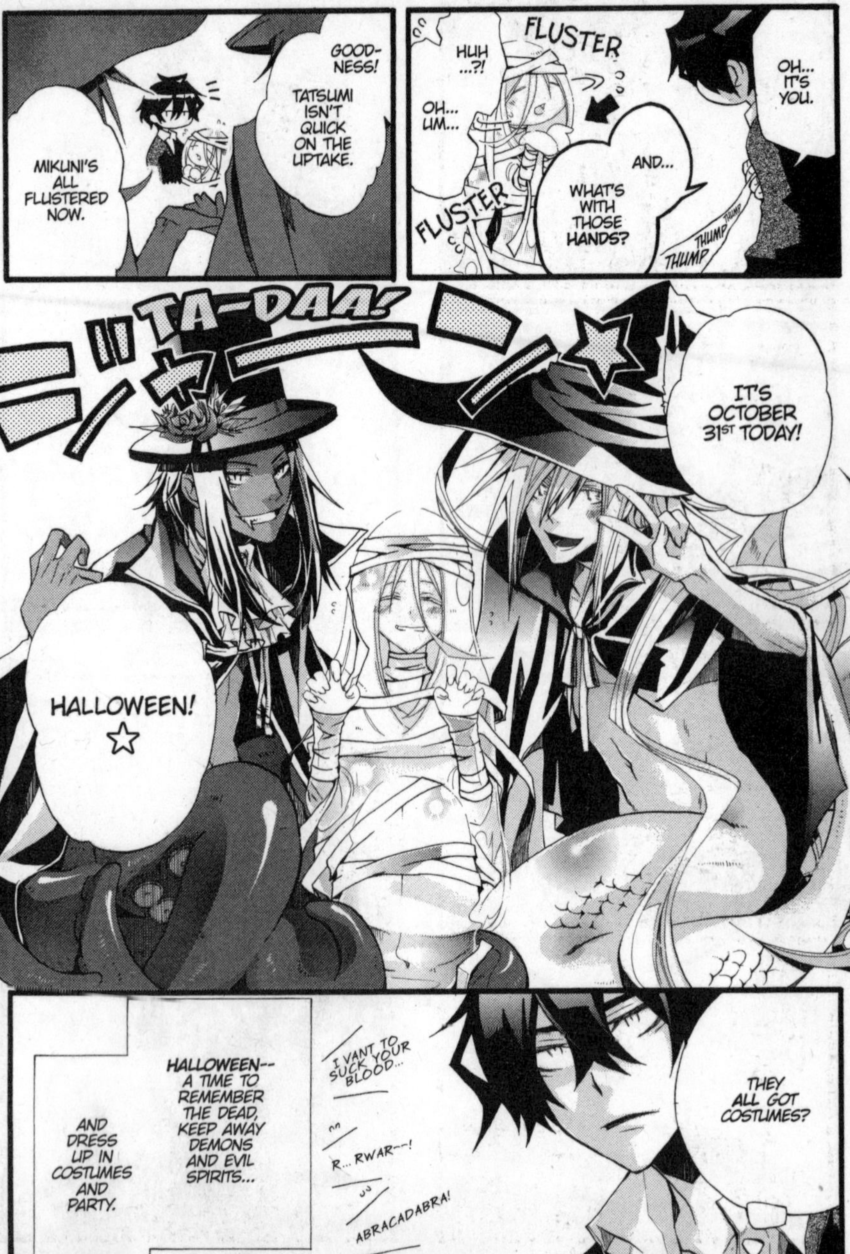
OH... IT'S YOU.
FLUSTER
HUH ...?!
OH... UM...
AND... WHAT'S WITH THOSE HANDS?
FLUSTER
THUMP THUMP THUMP
GOODNESS! TATSUMI ISN'T QUICK ON THE UPTAKE.
MIKUNI'S ALL FLUSTERED NOW.
IT'S OCTOBER 31ST TODAY!
TA-DAA!
HALLOWEEN! ☆
THEY ALL GOT COSTUMES?
I VANT TO SUCK YOUR BLOOD...
R... RWAR--!
ABRACADABRA!
HALLOWEEN-- A TIME TO REMEMBER THE DEAD, KEEP AWAY DEMONS AND EVIL SPIRITS...
AND DRESS UP IN COSTUMES AND PARTY.

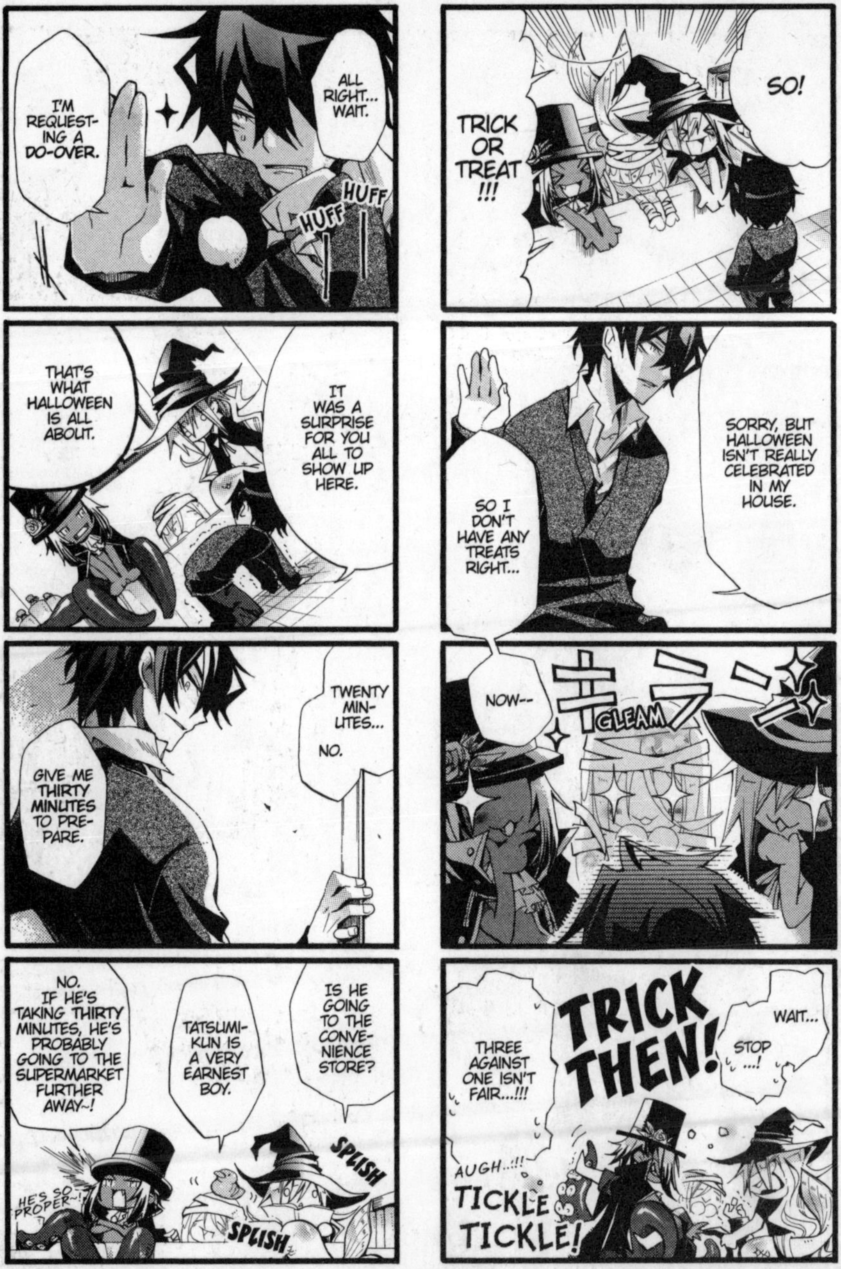
SO!
TRICK OR TREAT !!!
ALL RIGHT... WAIT.
HUFF
HUFF
I'M REQUESTING A DO-OVER.
SORRY, BUT HALLOWEEN ISN'T REALLY CELEBRATED IN MY HOUSE.
SO I DON'T HAVE ANY TREATS RIGHT...
IT WAS A SURPRISE FOR YOU ALL TO SHOW UP HERE.
THAT'S WHAT HALLOWEEN IS ALL ABOUT.
NOW--
GLEAM
TWENTY MINUTES...
NO.
GIVE ME THIRTY MINUTES TO PREPARE.
WAIT...
STOP ...!
TRICK THEN!
THREE AGAINST ONE ISN'T FAIR...!!!
AUGH..!!!
TICKLE TICKLE!
IS HE GOING TO THE CONVENIENCE STORE?
SPLISH
TATSUMI-KUN IS A VERY EARNEST BOY.
NO. IF HE'S TAKING THIRTY MINUTES, HE'S PROBABLY GOING TO THE SUPERMARKET FURTHER AWAY~!
SPLISH
HE'S SO PROPER~!

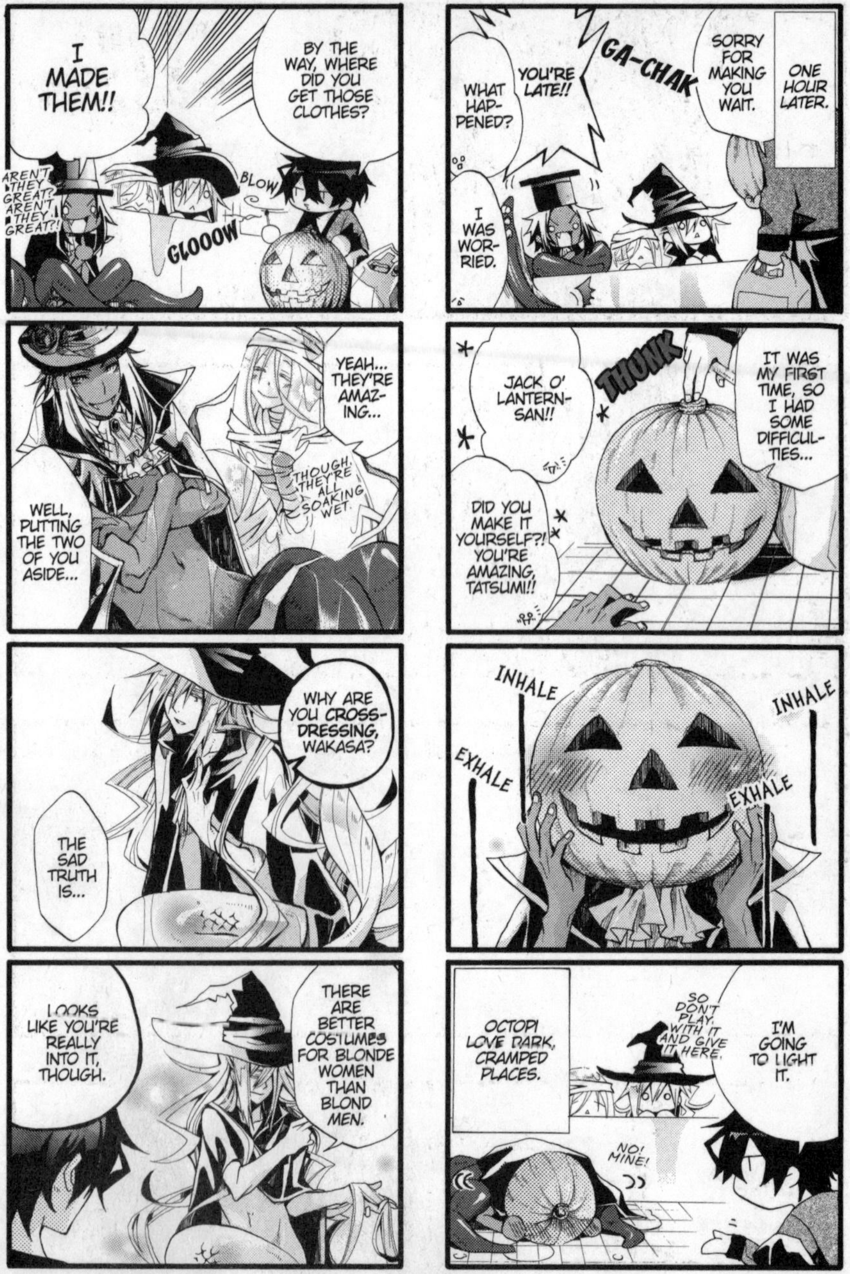
ONE HOUR LATER.
SORRY FOR MAKING YOU WAIT.
GA-CHAK
YOU'RE LATE!!
WHAT HAPPENED?
I WAS WORRIED.
IT WAS MY FIRST TIME, SO I HAD SOME DIFFICULTIES...
THUNK
JACK O' LANTERN-SAN!!
DID YOU MAKE IT YOURSELF?! YOU'RE AMAZING, TATSUMI!!
INHALE
INHALE
EXHALE
EXHALE
I'M GOING TO LIGHT IT.
SO DON'T PLAY WITH IT AND GIVE IT HERE.
OCTOPI LOVE DARK, CRAMPED PLACES.
NO! MINE!
BY THE WAY, WHERE DID YOU GET THOSE CLOTHES?
I MADE THEM!!
BLOW
AREN'T THEY GREAT? AREN'T THEY GREAT?!
GLOOOW
YEAH... THEY'RE AMAZING...
THOUGH, THEY'RE ALL SOAKING WET.
WELL, PUTTING THE TWO OF YOU ASIDE...
WHY ARE YOU CROSS-DRESSING, WAKASA?
THE SAD TRUTH IS...
THERE ARE BETTER COSTUMES FOR BLONDE WOMEN THAN BLOND MEN.
LOOKS LIKE YOU'RE REALLY INTO IT, THOUGH.

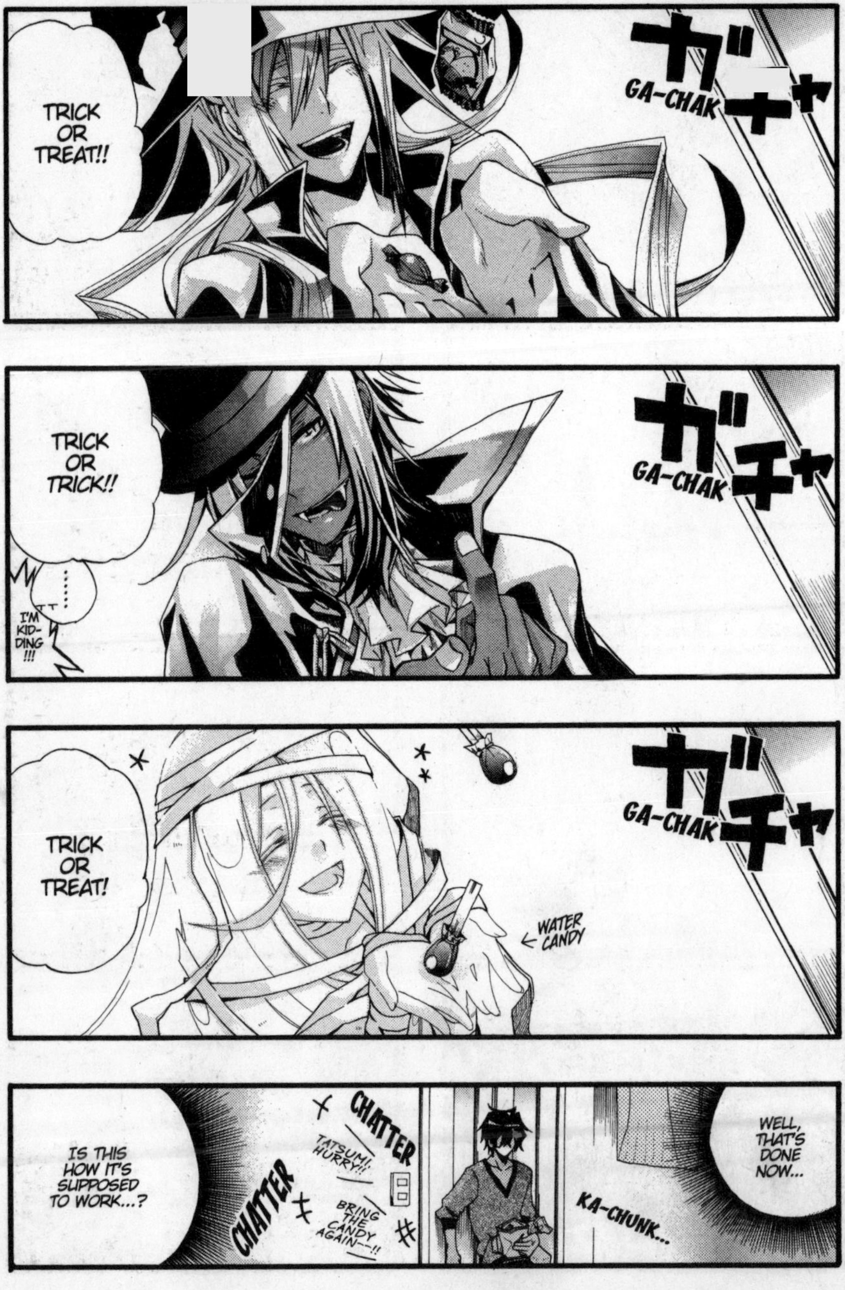
GA-CHAK
TRICK OR TREAT!!
ガチャ
GA-CHAK
TRICK OR TRICK!!
......
I'M KID-DING!!!
ガチャ
GA-CHAK
WATER CANDY
TRICK OR TREAT!
WELL, THAT'S DONE NOW...
KA-CHUNK...
CHATTER
TATSUMI, HURRY!!
BRING THE CANDY AGAIN--!!
CHATTER
IS THIS HOW IT'S SUPPOSED TO WORK...?

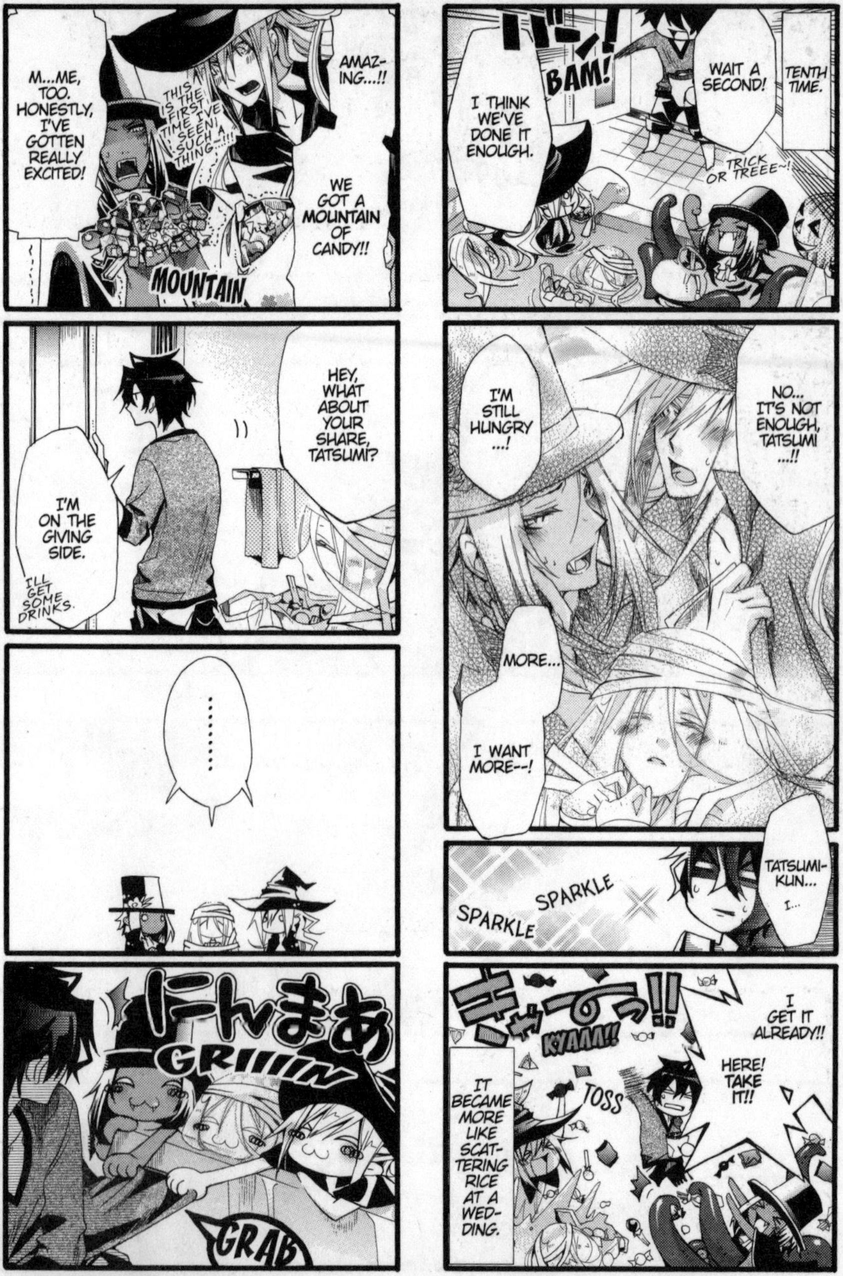
BAM!
TENTH TIME.
WAIT A SECOND!
TRICK OR TREEE~!
I THINK WE'VE DONE IT ENOUGH.
NO... IT'S NOT ENOUGH, TATSUMI...!!
I'M STILL HUNGRY...!
MORE...
I WANT MORE--!
TATSUMI-KUN... I...
SPARKLE
SPARKLE
I GET IT ALREADY!!
HERE! TAKE IT!!
きゃーっ!!
KYAAA!!
TOSS
IT BECAME MORE LIKE SCATTERING RICE AT A WEDDING.
AMAZING...!!
THIS IS THE FIRST TIME I'VE SEEN SUCH A THING--!!!
M...ME, TOO. HONESTLY, I'VE GOTTEN REALLY EXCITED!
WE GOT A MOUNTAIN OF CANDY!!
MOUNTAIN
HEY, WHAT ABOUT YOUR SHARE, TATSUMI?
I'M ON THE GIVING SIDE.
I'LL GET SOME DRINKS.
......
にんまあ
GRIIIIN
GRAB

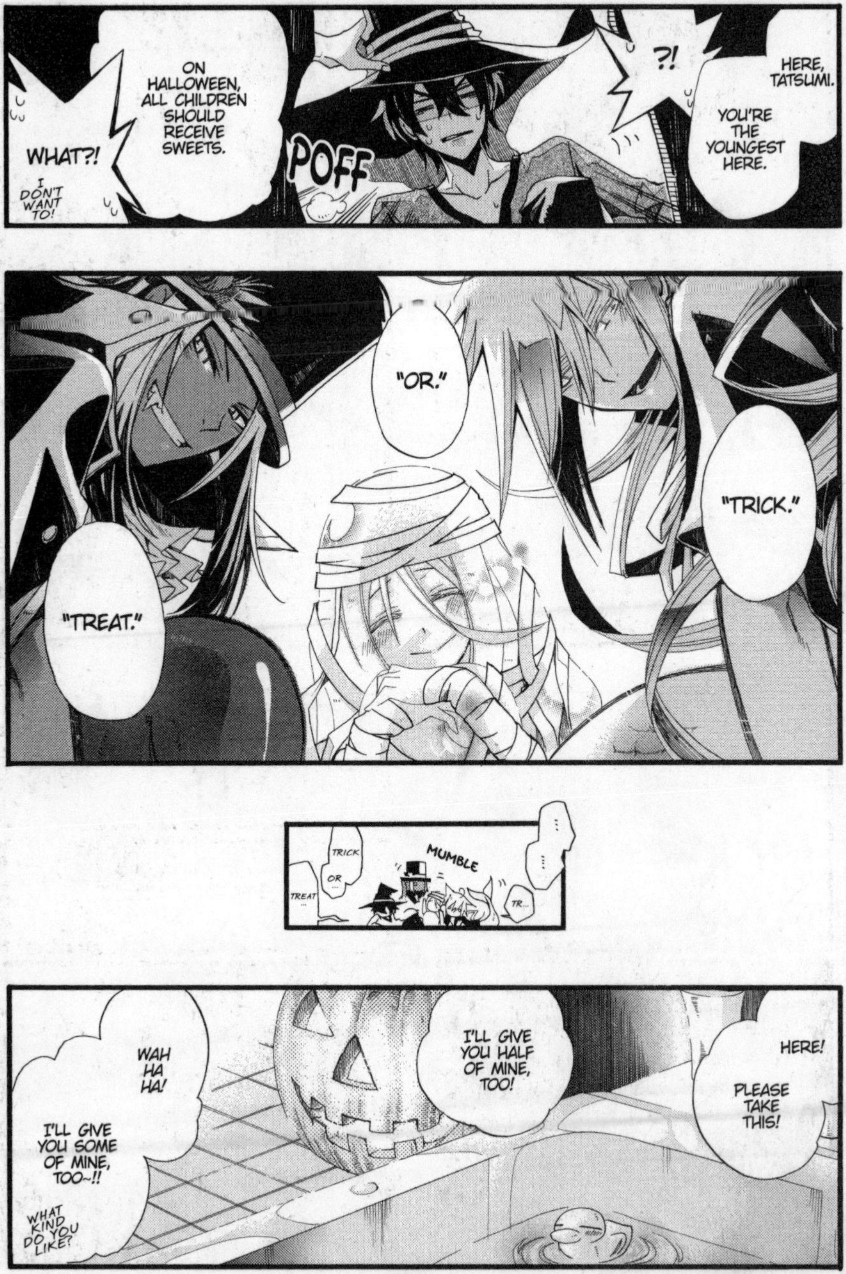
HERE, TATSUMI.
YOU'RE THE YOUNGEST HERE.
?!
POFF
ON HALLOWEEN, ALL CHILDREN SHOULD RECEIVE SWEETS.
WHAT?!
I DON'T WANT TO!
"TRICK."
"OR."
"TREAT."
...
...
TR...
MUMBLE
TRICK
OR ...
TREAT ...
HERE!
PLEASE TAKE THIS!
I'LL GIVE YOU HALF OF MINE, TOO!
WAH HA HA!
I'LL GIVE YOU SOME OF MINE, TOO~!!
WHAT KIND DO YOU LIKE?

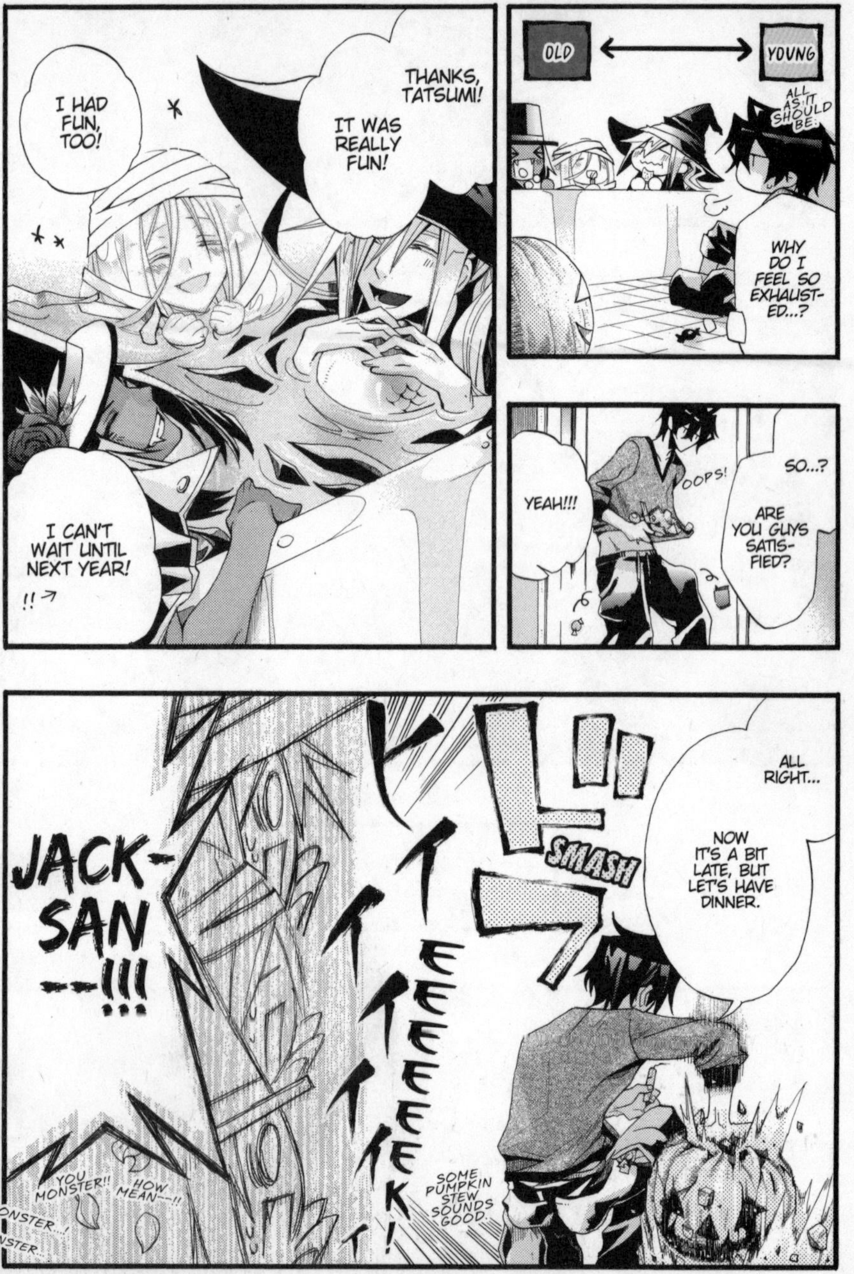
OLD
YOUNG
ALL AS IT SHOULD BE.
WHY DO I FEEL SO EXHAUSTED...?
SO...?
ARE YOU GUYS SATISFIED?
OOPS!
YEAH!!!
THANKS, TATSUMI!
IT WAS REALLY FUN!
I HAD FUN, TOO!
I CAN'T WAIT UNTIL NEXT YEAR!
!!
ALL RIGHT...
NOW IT'S A BIT LATE, BUT LET'S HAVE DINNER.
SMASH
SOME PUMPKIN STEW SOUNDS GOOD.
EEEEEEEK!
JACK-SAN---!!!
HOW MEAN--!!
YOU MONSTER!!
MONSTER...!

Merman in My Tub

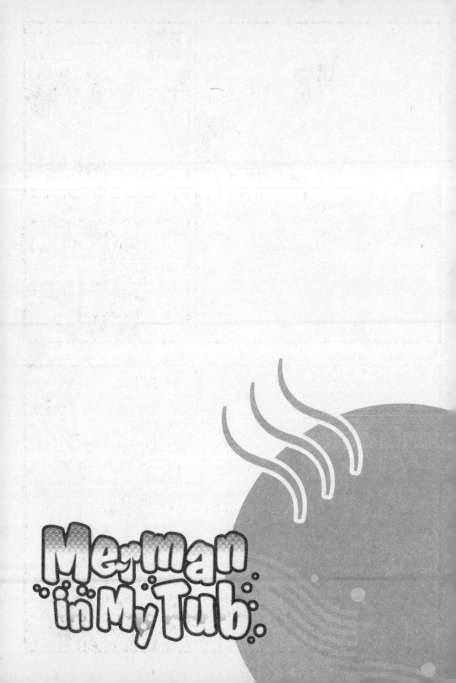

オレん家（ち）のフロ事情

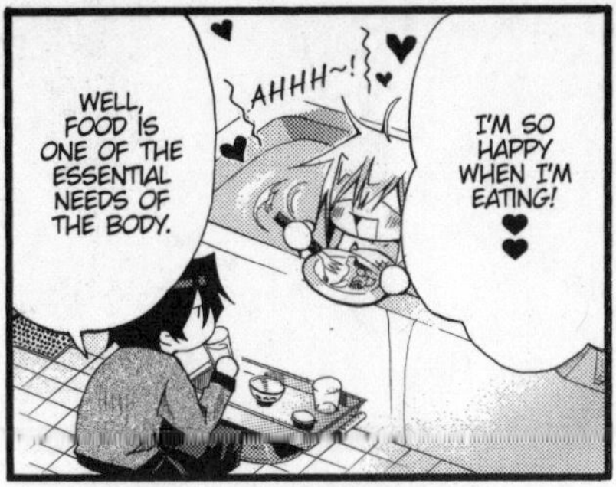
I'M SO HAPPY WHEN I'M EATING!
AHHH~!
WELL, FOOD IS ONE OF THE ESSENTIAL NEEDS OF THE BODY.

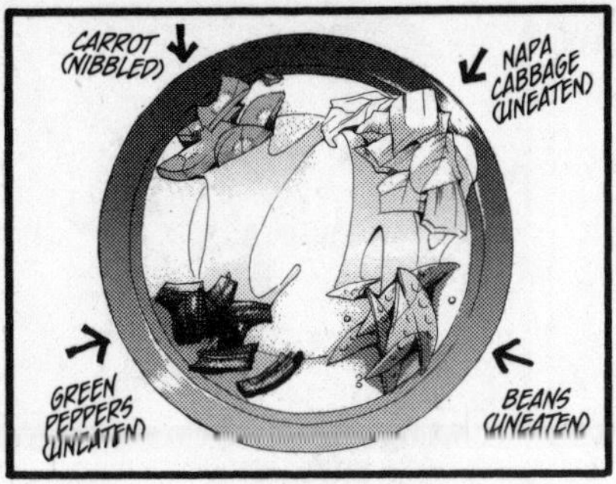
NAPA CABBAGE (UNEATEN)
CARROT (NIBBLED)
BEANS (UNEATEN)
GREEN PEPPERS (UNEATEN)

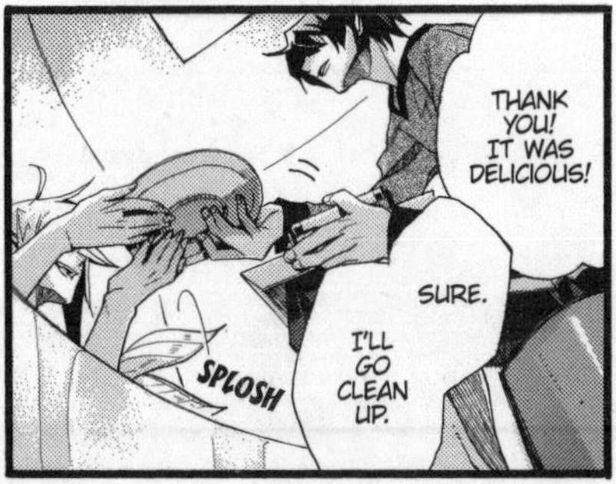
THANK YOU! IT WAS DELICIOUS!
SURE.
I'LL GO CLEAN UP.
SPLOSH

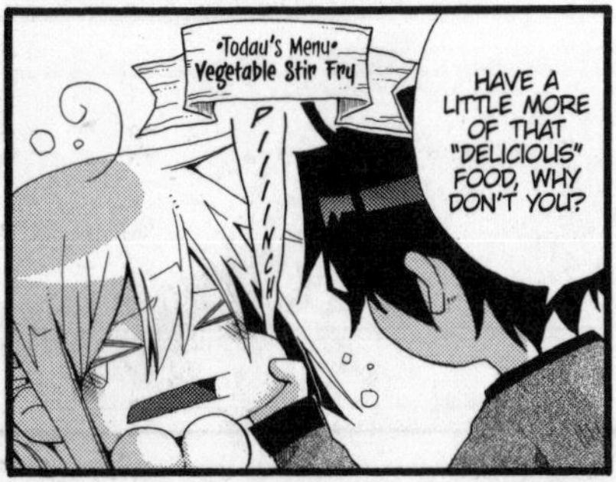
HAVE A LITTLE MORE OF THAT "DELICIOUS" FOOD, WHY DON'T YOU?
•Todau's Menu• Vegetable Stir Fry
PIIIINCH

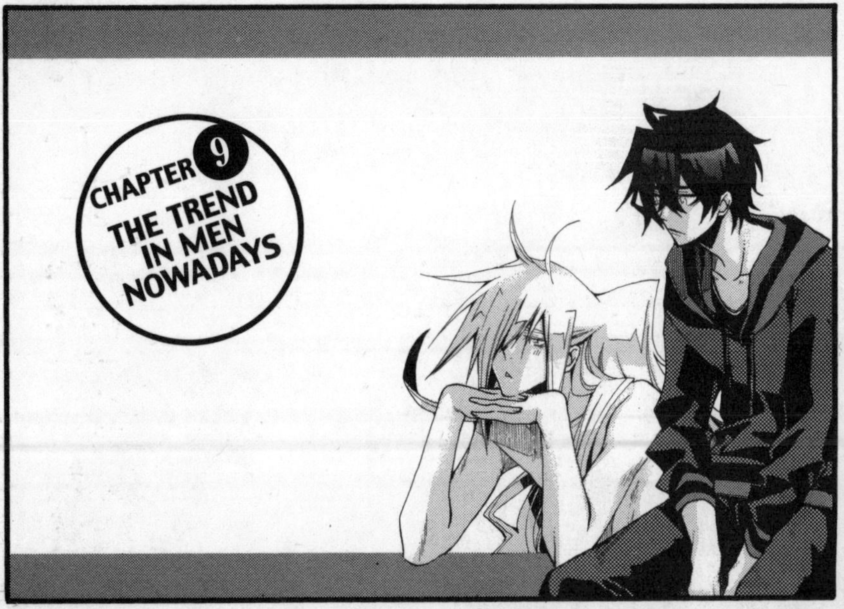
CHAPTER 9
THE TREND IN MEN NOWADAYS

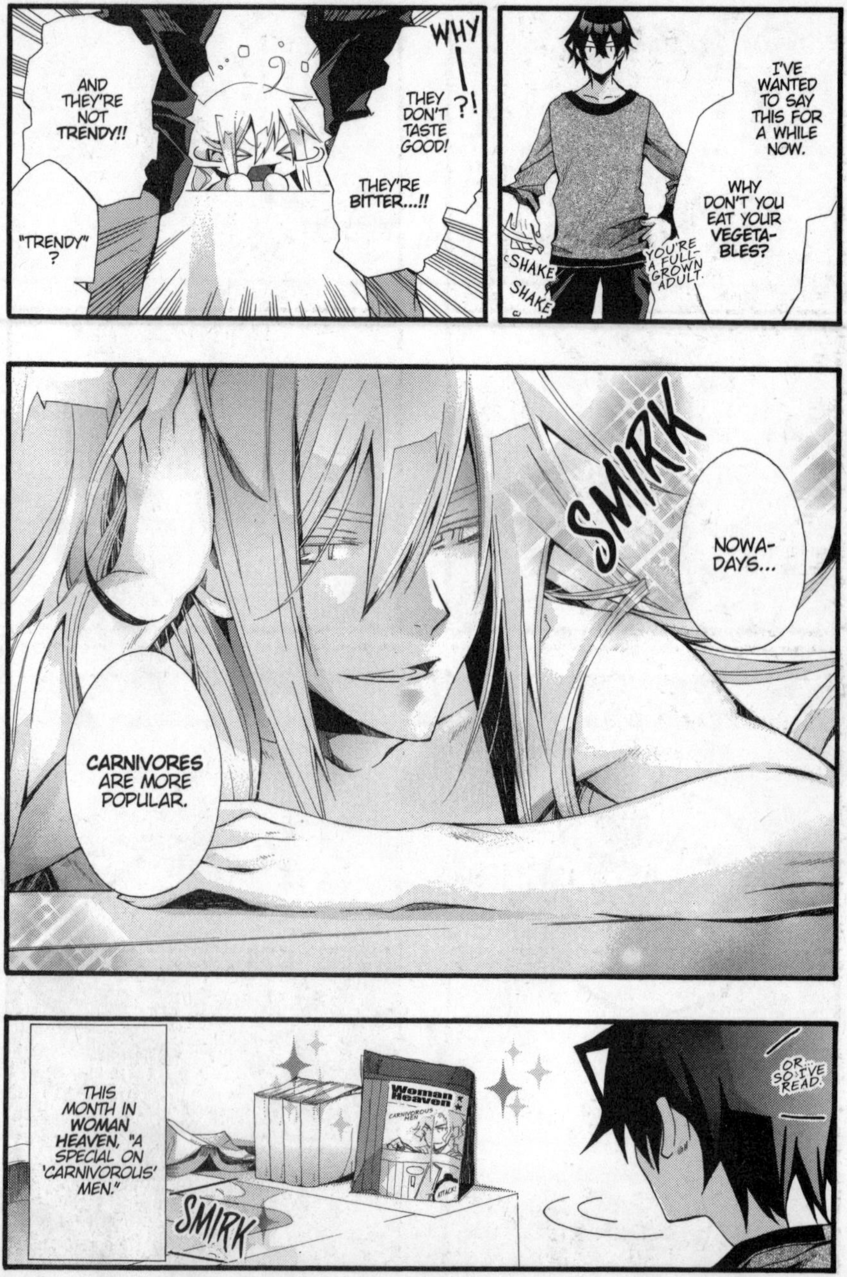
I'VE WANTED TO SAY THIS FOR A WHILE NOW.
WHY DON'T YOU EAT YOUR VEGETA-BLES?
YOU'RE A FULL-GROWN ADULT.
SHAKE
SHAKE
WHY!?!
THEY DON'T TASTE GOOD!
THEY'RE BITTER...!!
AND THEY'RE NOT TRENDY!!
"TRENDY"?
SMIRK
NOWA-DAYS...
CARNIVORES ARE MORE POPULAR.
OR... SO I'VE READ.
Woman Heaven
CARNIVOROUS MEN
ATTACK!
THIS MONTH IN WOMAN HEAVEN, "A SPECIAL ON 'CARNIVOROUS' MEN."
SMIRK

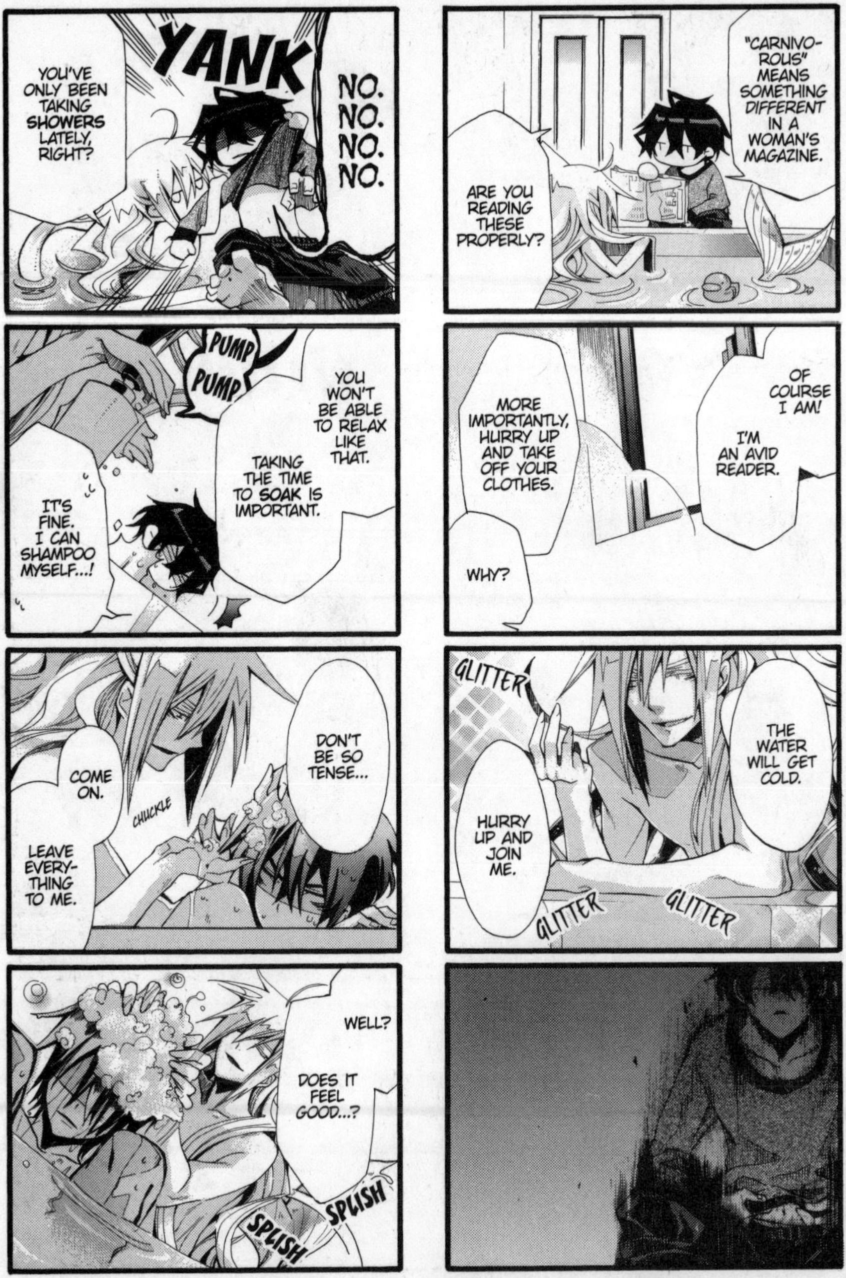
"CARNIVO-ROUS" MEANS SOMETHING DIFFERENT IN A WOMAN'S MAGAZINE.
ARE YOU READING THESE PROPERLY?
OF COURSE I AM!
I'M AN AVID READER.
MORE IMPORTANTLY, HURRY UP AND TAKE OFF YOUR CLOTHES.
WHY?
GLITTER
THE WATER WILL GET COLD.
HURRY UP AND JOIN ME.
GLITTER
GLITTER
YANK
YOU'VE ONLY BEEN TAKING SHOWERS LATELY, RIGHT?
NO. NO. NO. NO.
PUMP
PUMP
YOU WON'T BE ABLE TO RELAX LIKE THAT.
TAKING THE TIME TO SOAK IS IMPORTANT.
IT'S FINE. I CAN SHAMPOO MYSELF...!
DON'T BE SO TENSE...
COME ON.
CHUCKLE
LEAVE EVERY-THING TO ME.
WELL?
DOES IT FEEL GOOD...?
SPLISH
SPLISH

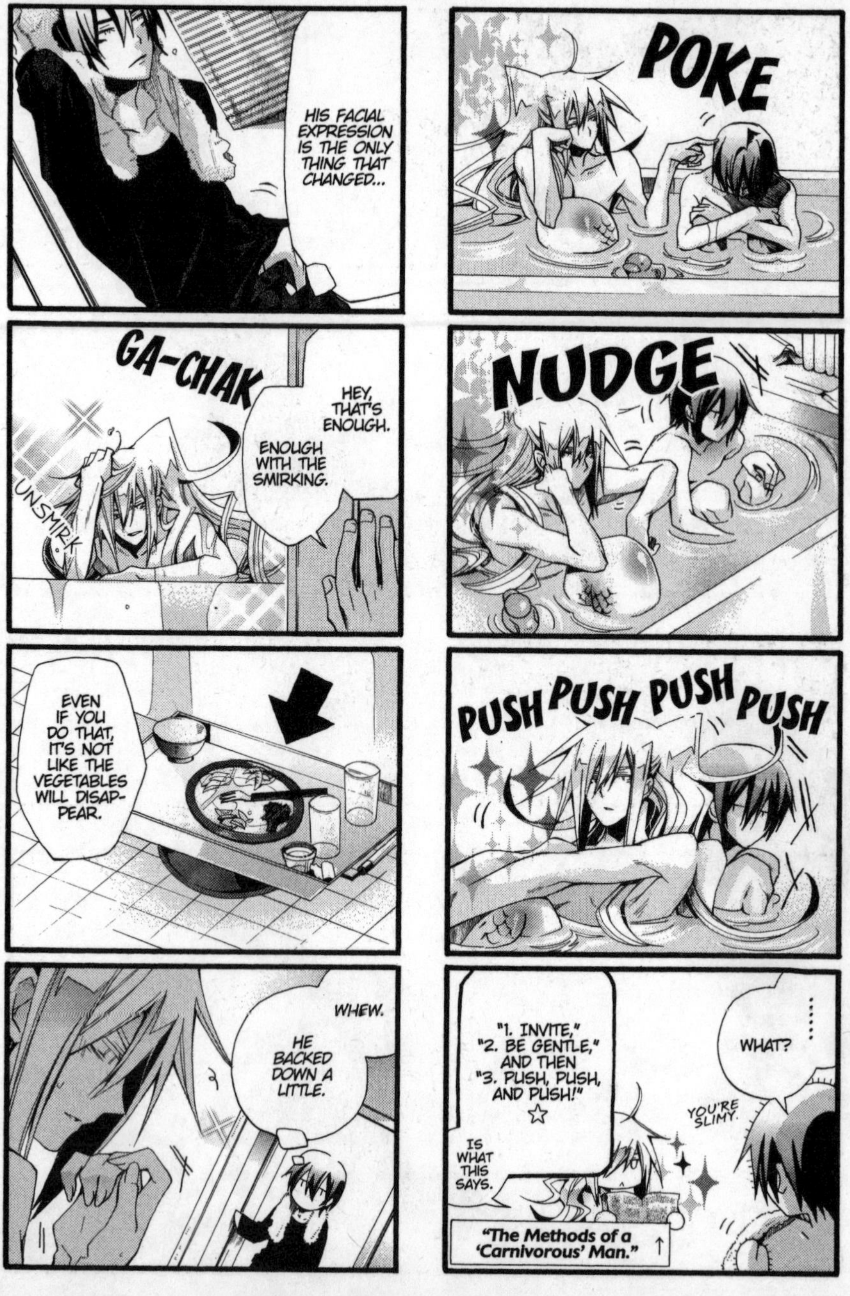
POKE
NUDGE
PUSH PUSH PUSH PUSH
......
WHAT?
"1. INVITE," "2. BE GENTLE," AND THEN "3. PUSH, PUSH, AND PUSH!" ☆
YOU'RE SLIMY.
IS WHAT THIS SAYS.
"The Methods of a 'Carnivorous' Man." ↑
HIS FACIAL EXPRESSION IS THE ONLY THING THAT CHANGED...
GA-CHAK
HEY, THAT'S ENOUGH.
ENOUGH WITH THE SMIRKING.
UNSMIRK
EVEN IF YOU DO THAT, IT'S NOT LIKE THE VEGETABLES WILL DISAP-PEAR.
WHEW.
HE BACKED DOWN A LITTLE.

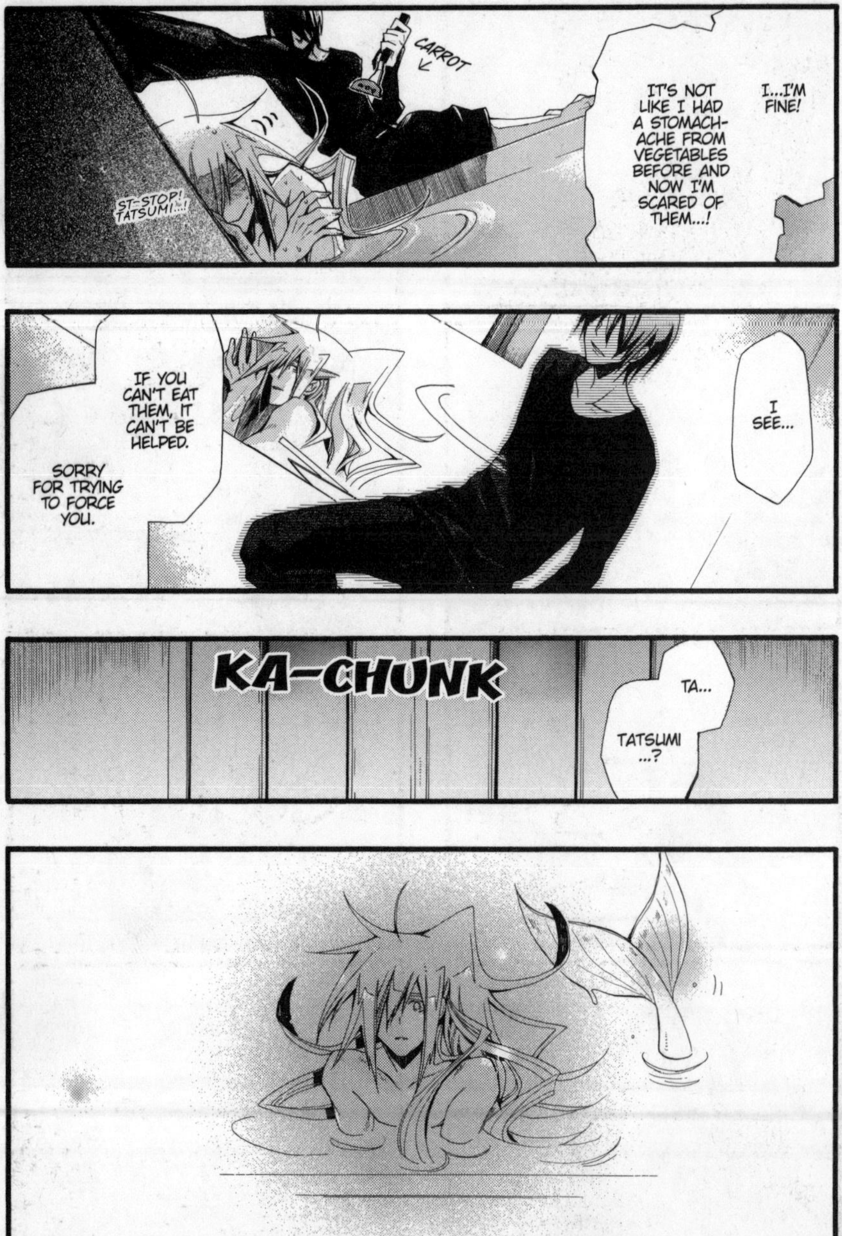
I...I'M FINE!
IT'S NOT LIKE I HAD A STOMACH-ACHE FROM VEGETABLES BEFORE AND NOW I'M SCARED OF THEM...!
CARROT
ST-STOP! TATSUMI...!
I SEE...
IF YOU CAN'T EAT THEM, IT CAN'T BE HELPED.
SORRY FOR TRYING TO FORCE YOU.
KA-CHUNK
TA...
TATSUMI ...?

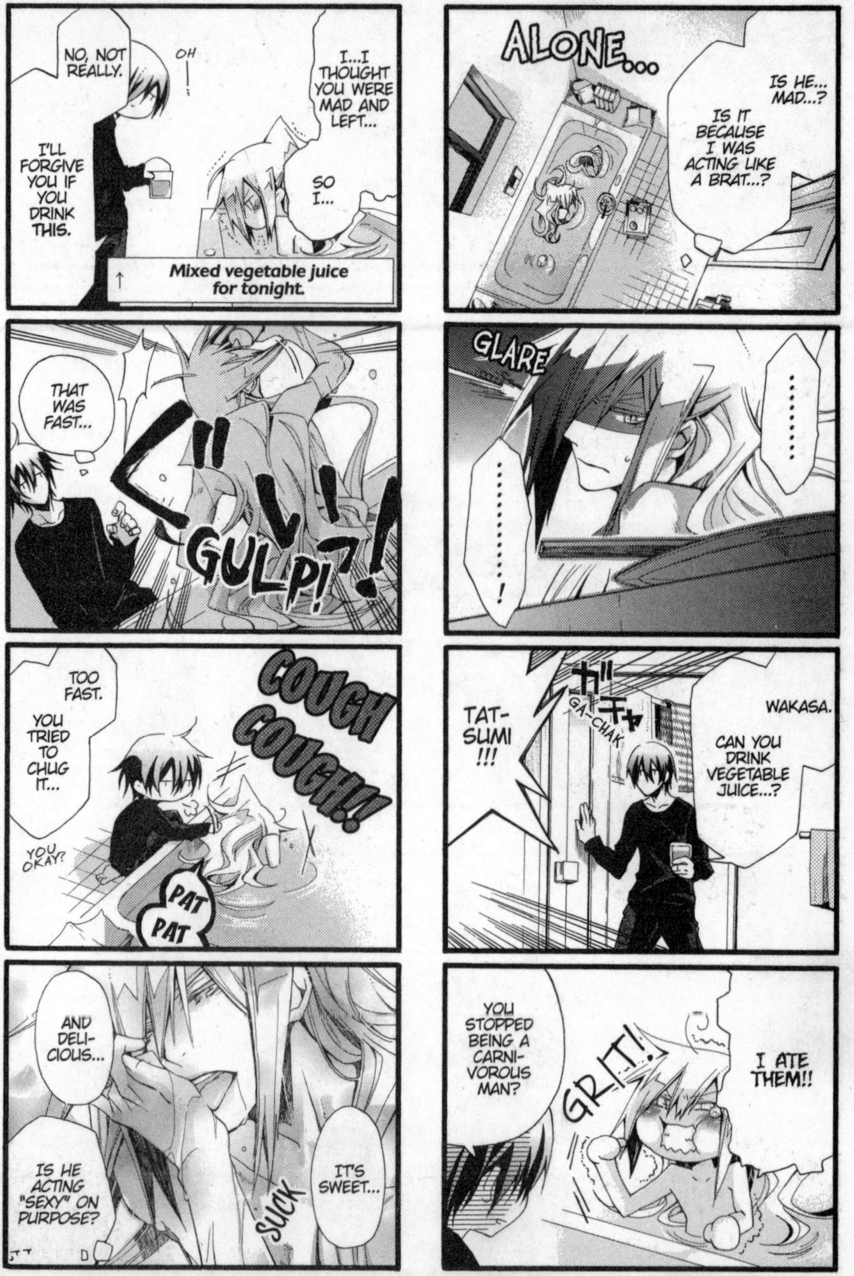
ALONE...
IS HE... MAD...?
IS IT BECAUSE I WAS ACTING LIKE A BRAT...?
I...I THOUGHT YOU WERE MAD AND LEFT...
SO I...
OH
!
NO, NOT REALLY.
I'LL FORGIVE YOU IF YOU DRINK THIS.
↑ Mixed vegetable juice for tonight.
GLARE
......
......!
GULP!
THAT WAS FAST...
ガチャ
GA-CHAK
WAKASA.
CAN YOU DRINK VEGETABLE JUICE...?
TAT-SUMI!!!
COUGH COUGH!!
TOO FAST.
YOU TRIED TO CHUG IT...
YOU OKAY?
PAT PAT
I ATE THEM!!
GRIT!
YOU STOPPED BEING A CARNIVOROUS MAN?
AND DELICIOUS...
IT'S SWEET...
SUCK
IS HE ACTING "SEXY" ON PURPOSE?

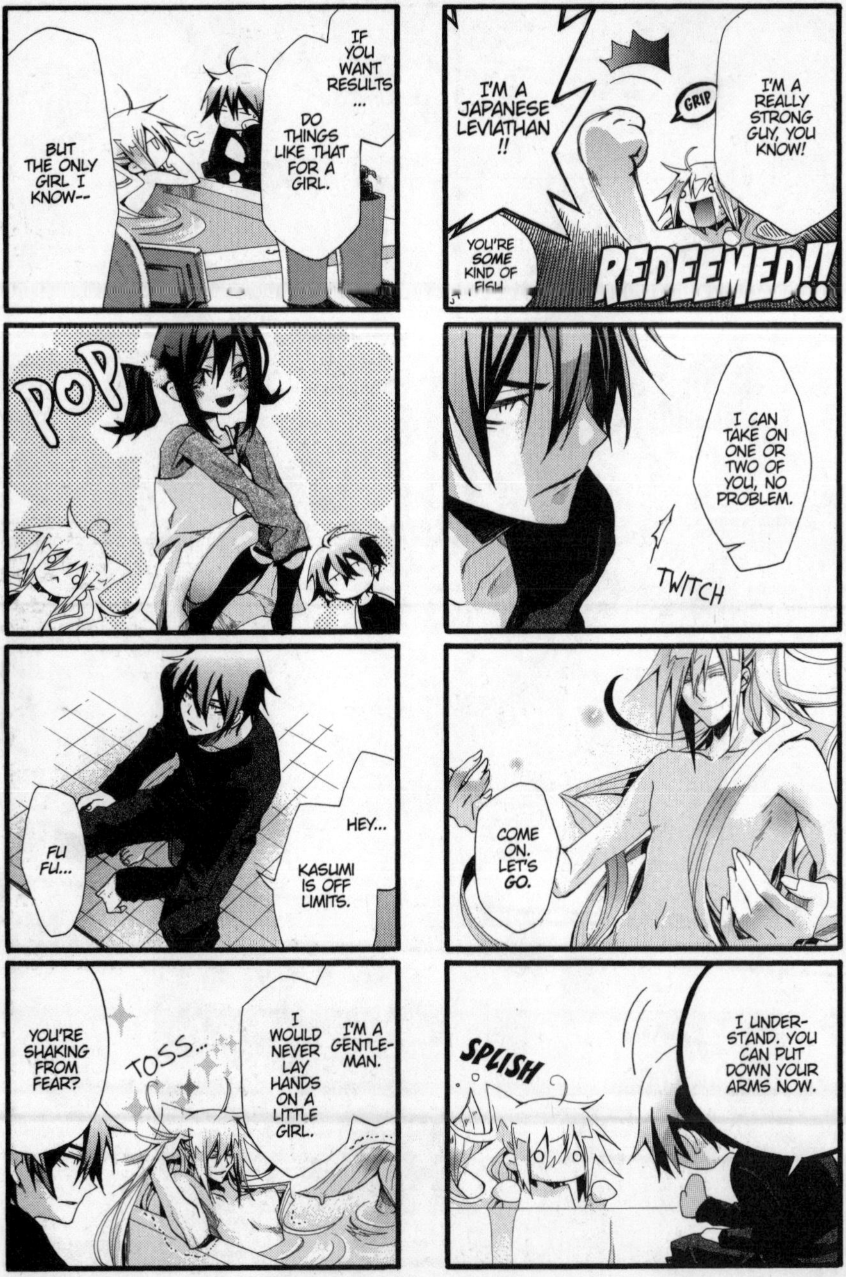
I'M A REALLY STRONG GUY, YOU KNOW!
GRIP
I'M A JAPANESE LEVIATHAN !!
YOU'RE SOME KIND OF FISH
REDEEMED!!
IF YOU WANT RESULTS ...
DO THINGS LIKE THAT FOR A GIRL.
BUT THE ONLY GIRL I KNOW--
I CAN TAKE ON ONE OR TWO OF YOU, NO PROBLEM.
TWITCH
POP
COME ON. LET'S GO.
HEY...
KASUMI IS OFF LIMITS.
FU FU...
I UNDER-STAND. YOU CAN PUT DOWN YOUR ARMS NOW.
SPLISH
I'M A GENTLE-MAN.
I WOULD NEVER LAY HANDS ON A LITTLE GIRL.
TOSS...
YOU'RE SHAKING FROM FEAR?

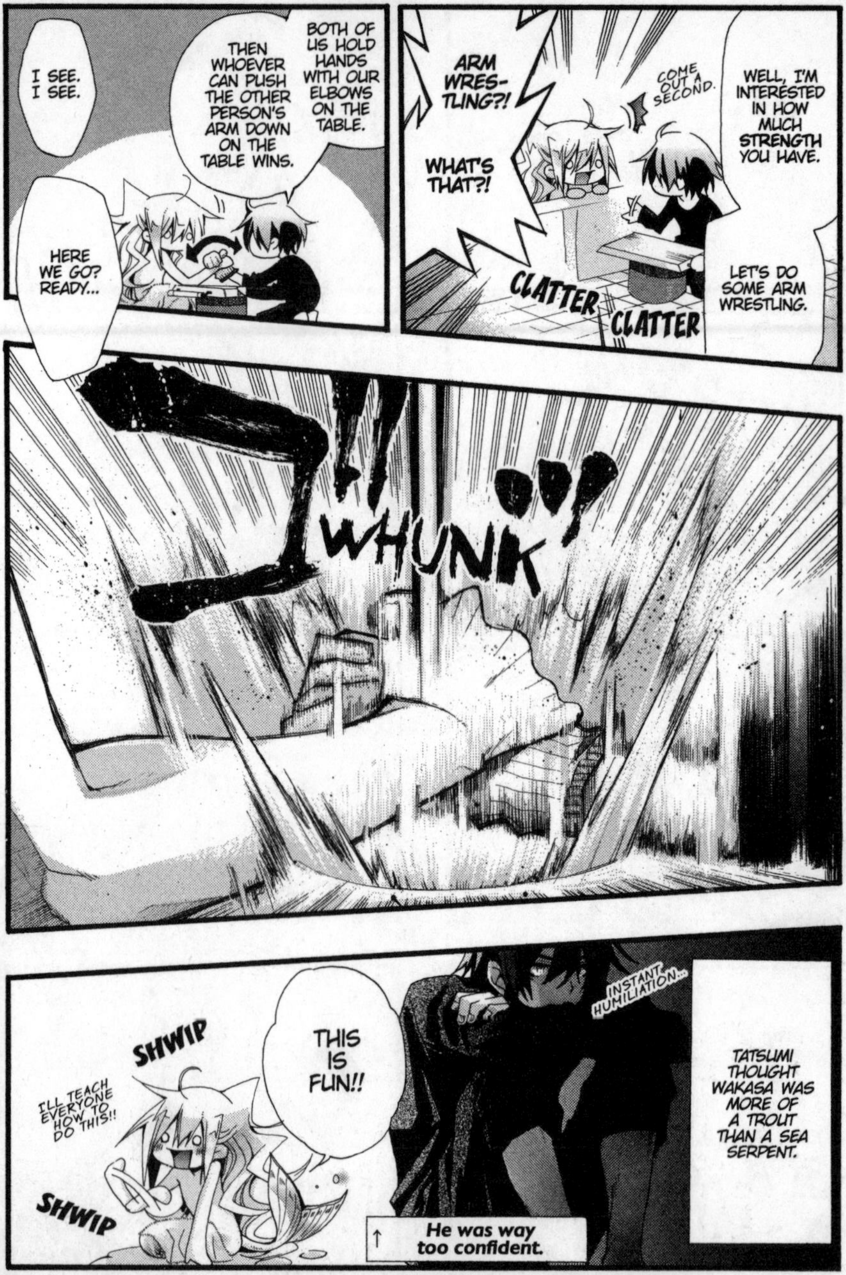
WELL, I'M INTERESTED IN HOW MUCH STRENGTH YOU HAVE.
COME OUT A SECOND.
LET'S DO SOME ARM WRESTLING.
ARM WRES-TLING?!
WHAT'S THAT?!
CLATTER
CLATTER
BOTH OF US HOLD HANDS WITH OUR ELBOWS ON THE TABLE.
THEN WHOEVER CAN PUSH THE OTHER PERSON'S ARM DOWN ON THE TABLE WINS.
I SEE. I SEE.
HERE WE GO? READY...
WHUNK
TATSUMI THOUGHT WAKASA WAS MORE OF A TROUT THAN A SEA SERPENT.
INSTANT HUMILIATION...
THIS IS FUN!!
SHWIP
I'LL TEACH EVERYONE HOW TO DO THIS!!
SHWIP
↑ He was way too confident.

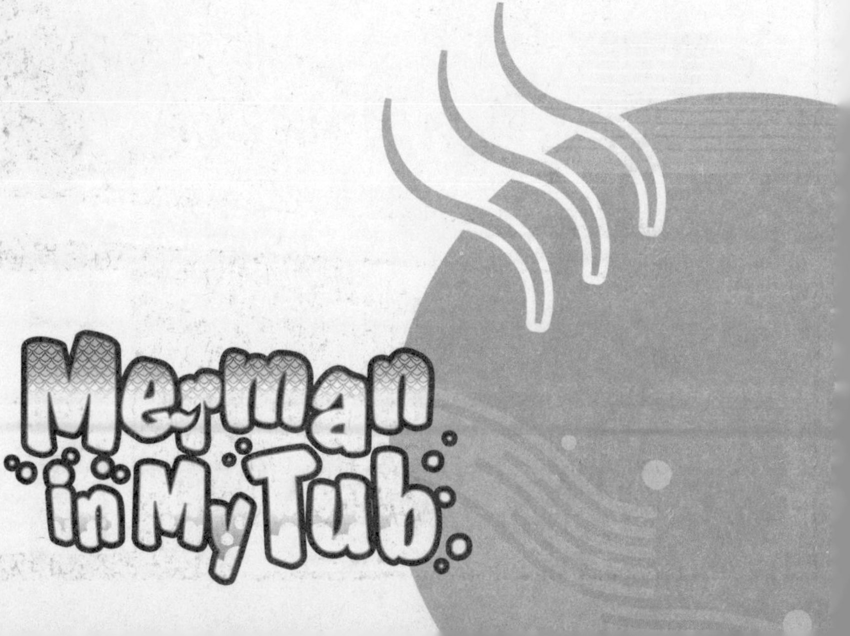

Merman in My Tub

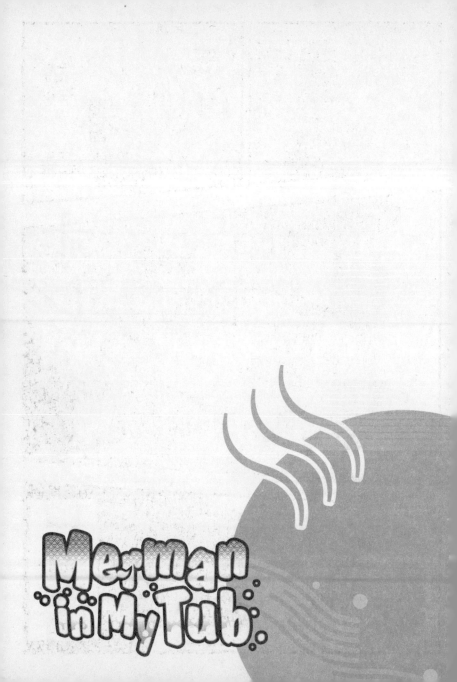

オレん家のフロ事情

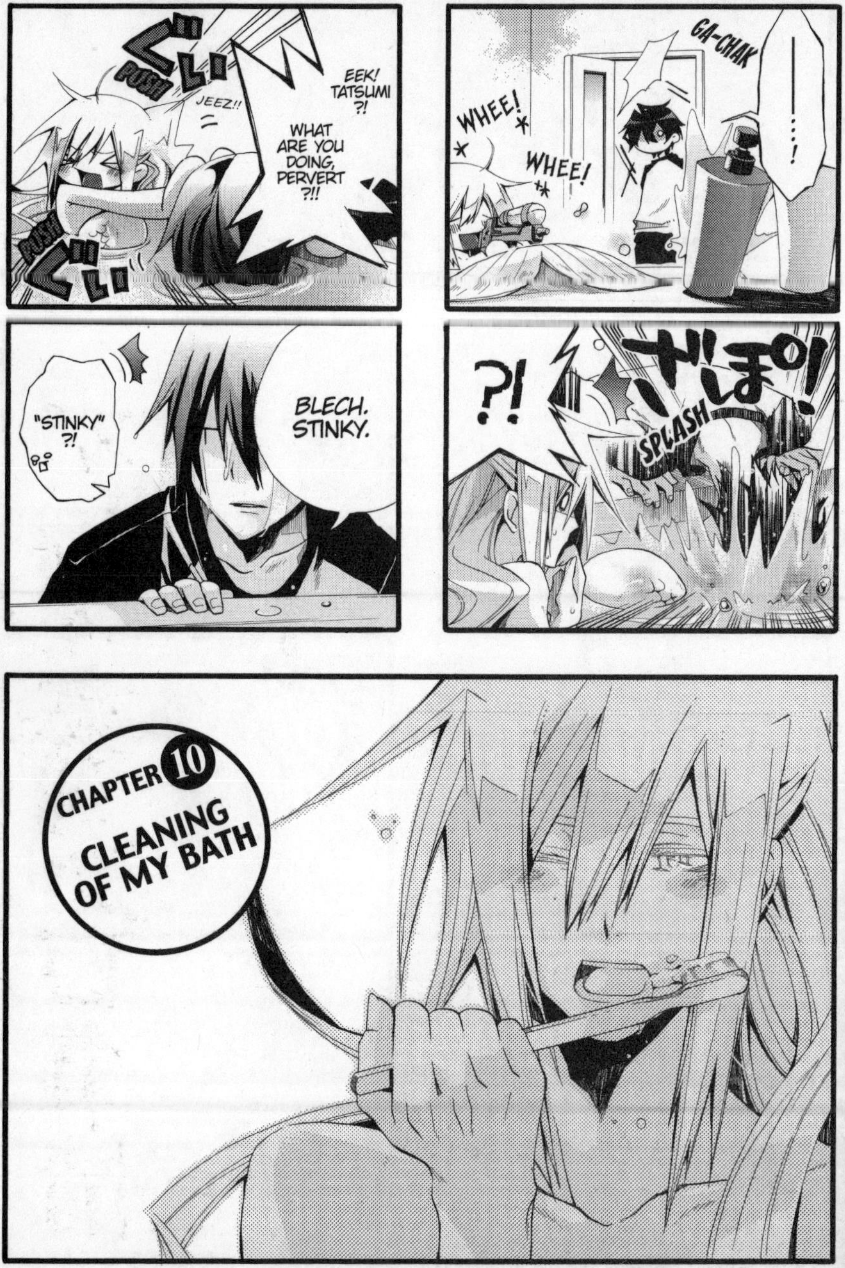
GA-CHAK
WHEE!
WHEE!
EEK! TATSUMI ?!
WHAT ARE YOU DOING, PERVERT ?!!
JEEZ!!
PUSH
PUSH
?!
SPLASH
BLECH. STINKY.
"STINKY" ?!
CHAPTER 10
CLEANING OF MY BATH

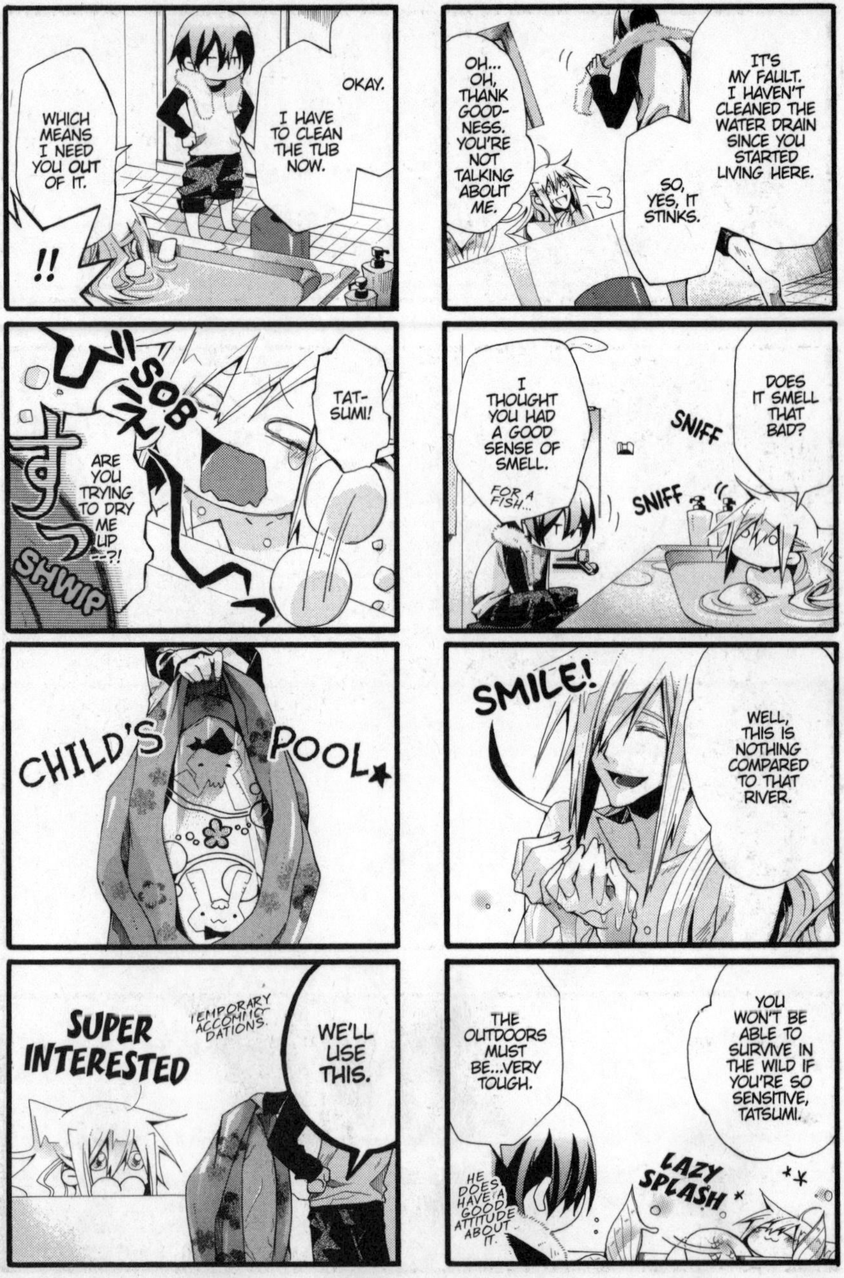
IT'S MY FAULT. I HAVEN'T CLEANED THE WATER DRAIN SINCE YOU STARTED LIVING HERE.
SO, YES, IT STINKS.
OH... OH, THANK GOODNESS. YOU'RE NOT TALKING ABOUT ME.
OKAY.
I HAVE TO CLEAN THE TUB NOW.
WHICH MEANS I NEED YOU OUT OF IT.
!!
DOES IT SMELL THAT BAD?
SNIFF
SNIFF
I THOUGHT YOU HAD A GOOD SENSE OF SMELL.
FOR A FISH...
TAT-SUMI!
SOB
ARE YOU TRYING TO DRY ME UP--?!
SHWIP
WELL, THIS IS NOTHING COMPARED TO THAT RIVER.
SMILE!
CHILD'S POOL★
YOU WON'T BE ABLE TO SURVIVE IN THE WILD IF YOU'RE SO SENSITIVE, TATSUMI.
THE OUTDOORS MUST BE...VERY TOUGH.
LAZY SPLASH
HE DOES HAVE A GOOD ATTITUDE ABOUT IT.
WE'LL USE THIS.
TEMPORARY ACCOMODATIONS.
SUPER INTERESTED

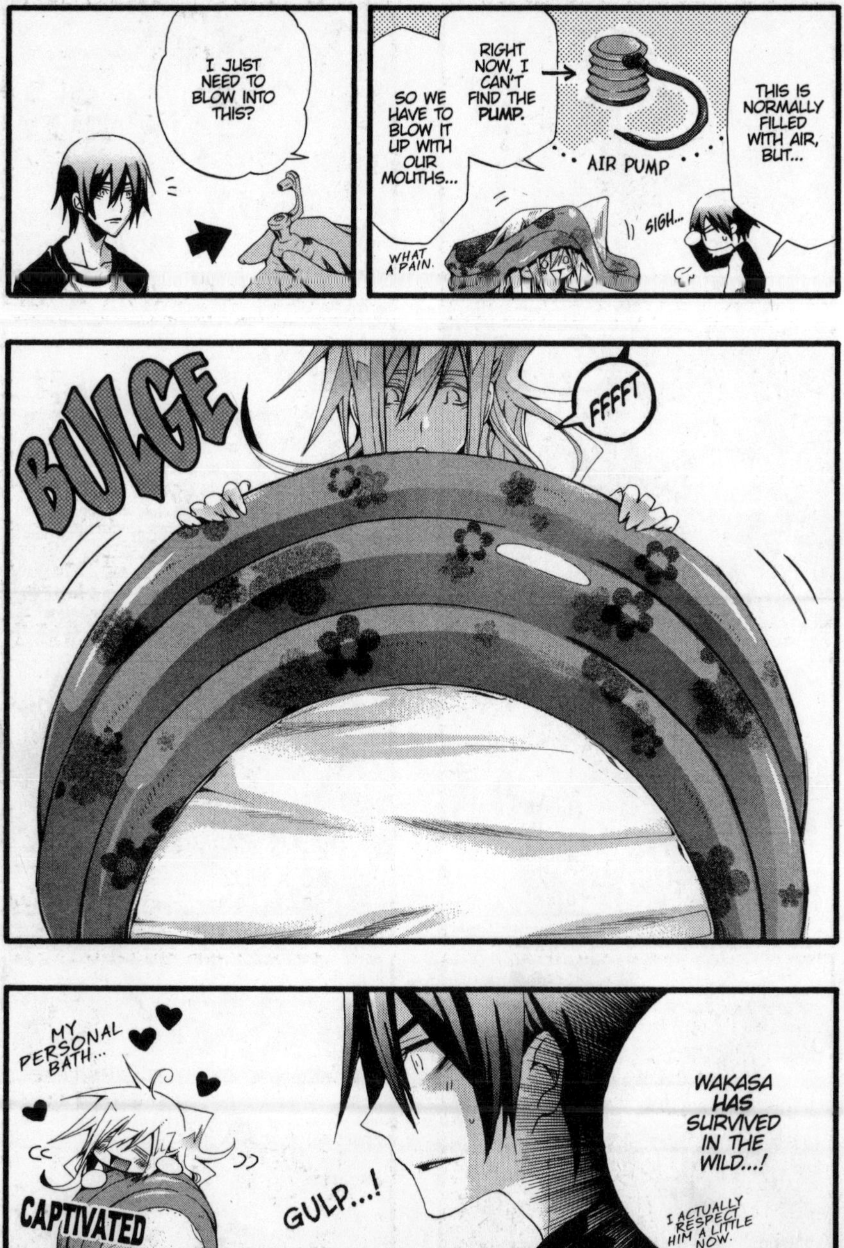
THIS IS NORMALLY FILLED WITH AIR, BUT...
SIGH...
AIR PUMP
RIGHT NOW, I CAN'T FIND THE PUMP.
SO WE HAVE TO BLOW IT UP WITH OUR MOUTHS...
WHAT A PAIN.
I JUST NEED TO BLOW INTO THIS?
FFFFT
BULGE
WAKASA HAS SURVIVED IN THE WILD...!
I ACTUALLY RESPECT HIM A LITTLE NOW.
GULP...!
MY PERSONAL BATH...
CAPTIVATED

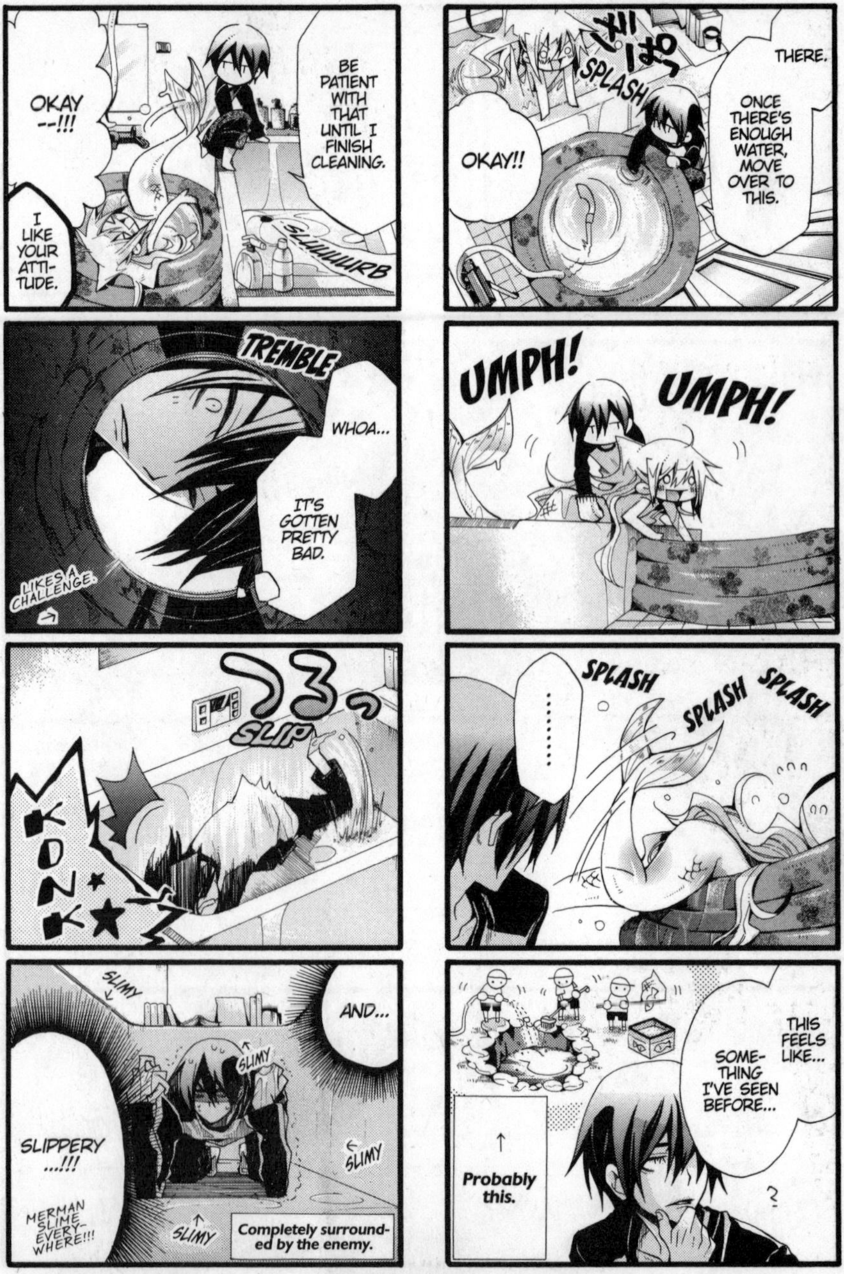
ざぱっ
SPLASH
THERE.
ONCE THERE'S ENOUGH WATER, MOVE OVER TO THIS.
OKAY!!
UMPH!
UMPH!
SPLASH
SPLASH
SPLASH
......
THIS FEELS LIKE...
SOMETHING I'VE SEEN BEFORE...
?
↑ Probably this.
BE PATIENT WITH THAT UNTIL I FINISH CLEANING.
OKAY--!!!
I LIKE YOUR ATTITUDE.
SLUUUUURB
TREMBLE
WHOA...
IT'S GOTTEN PRETTY BAD.
LIKES A CHALLENGE. →
つるっ
SLIP
KONK
AND...
SLIMY
SLIMY
SLIPPERY ...!!!
SLIMY
SLIMY
MERMAN SLIME EVERYWHERE!!!
Completely surrounded by the enemy.

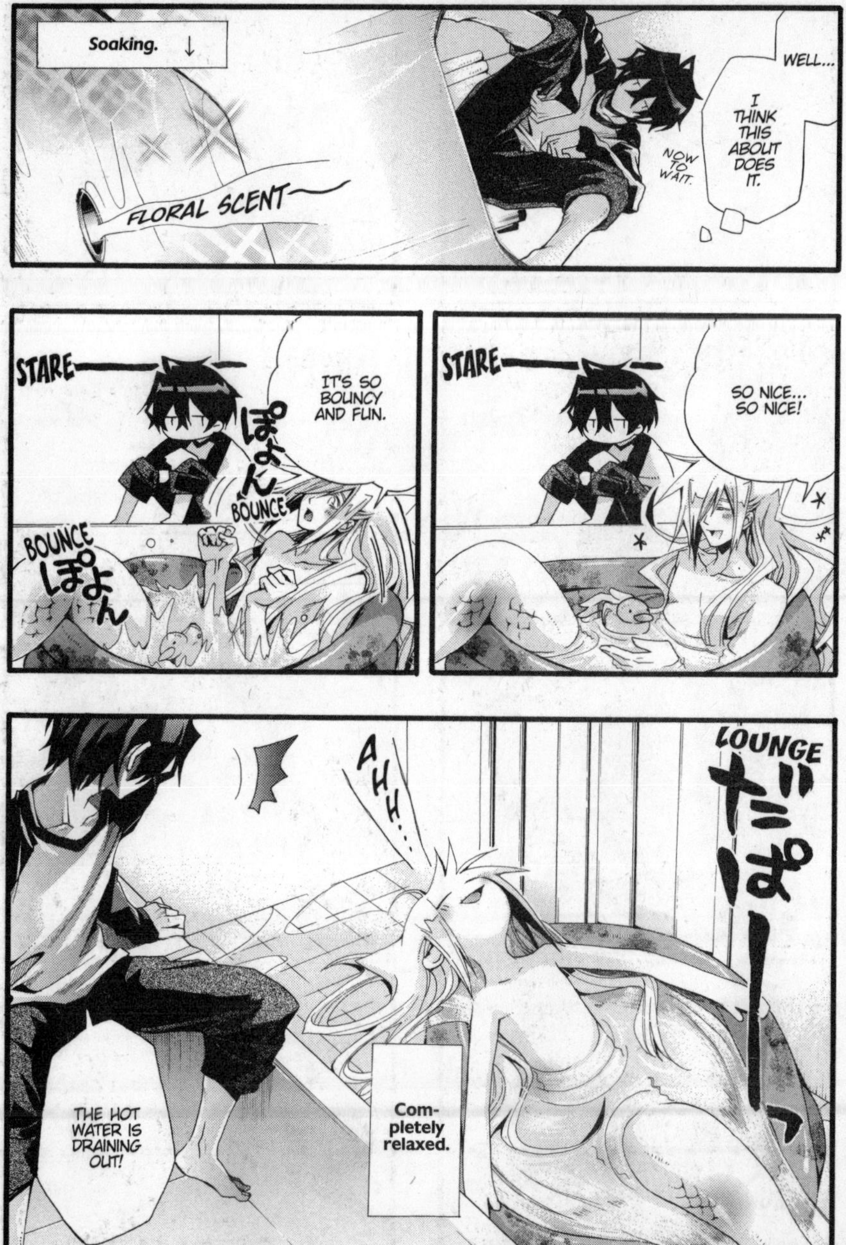
WELL... I THINK THIS ABOUT DOES IT.
NOW TO WAIT.
FLORAL SCENT
Soaking. ↓
STARE
SO NICE... SO NICE!
IT'S SO BOUNCY AND FUN.
STARE
ぽよん BOUNCE
BOUNCE ぽよん
LOUNGE だぱー
AHH...
Com-pletely relaxed.
THE HOT WATER IS DRAINING OUT!

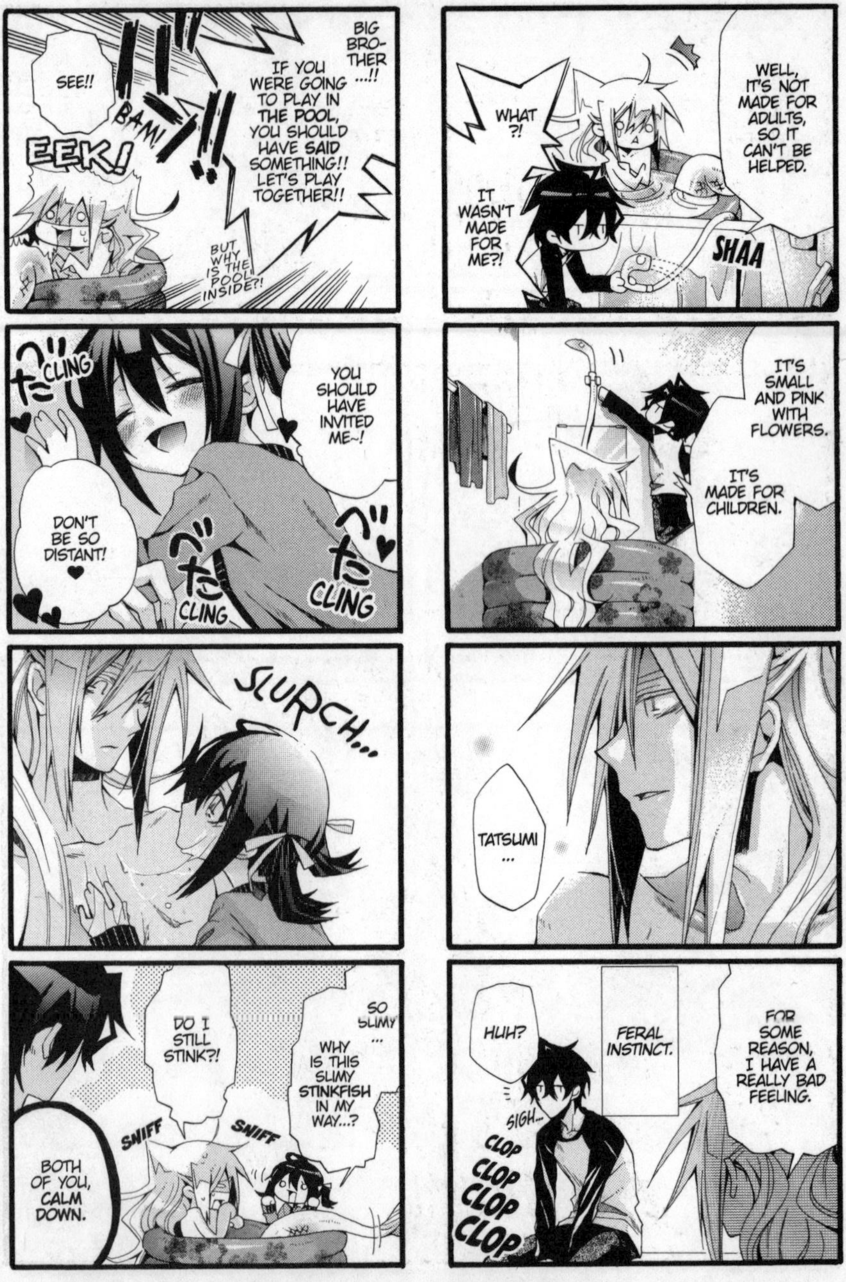
WELL, IT'S NOT MADE FOR ADULTS, SO IT CAN'T BE HELPED.
WHAT ?!
IT WASN'T MADE FOR ME?!
SHAA
BIG BRO-THER ...!!
IF YOU WERE GOING TO PLAY IN THE POOL, YOU SHOULD HAVE SAID SOMETHING!! LET'S PLAY TOGETHER!!
SEE!!
BAM!
EEK!
BUT WHY IS THE POOL INSIDE?!
IT'S SMALL AND PINK WITH FLOWERS.
IT'S MADE FOR CHILDREN.
YOU SHOULD HAVE INVITED ME~!
べた CLING
べた CLING
DON'T BE SO DISTANT! ♥
べた CLING
TATSUMI ...
SLURCH...
FOR SOME REASON, I HAVE A REALLY BAD FEELING.
FERAL INSTINCT.
HUH?
SIGH...
CLOP CLOP CLOP CLOP
SO SLIMY ...
WHY IS THIS SLIMY STINKFISH IN MY WAY...?
DO I STILL STINK?!
SNIFF
SNIFF
BOTH OF YOU, CALM DOWN.

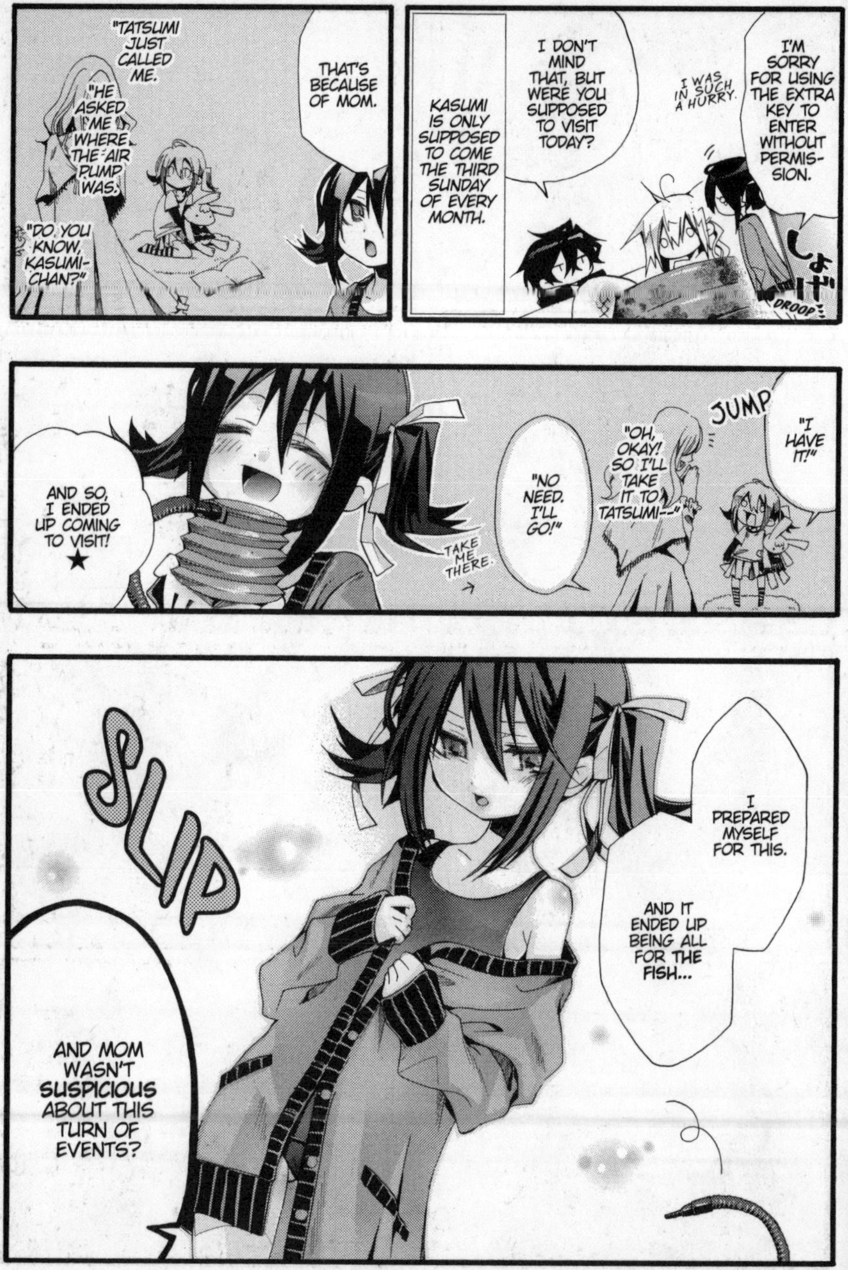
I'M SORRY FOR USING THE EXTRA KEY TO ENTER WITHOUT PERMISSION.
I WAS IN SUCH A HURRY.
しょげ
DROOP
I DON'T MIND THAT, BUT WERE YOU SUPPOSED TO VISIT TODAY?
KASUMI IS ONLY SUPPOSED TO COME THE THIRD SUNDAY OF EVERY MONTH.
THAT'S BECAUSE OF MOM.
"TATSUMI JUST CALLED ME.
"HE ASKED ME WHERE THE AIR PUMP WAS.
"DO YOU KNOW, KASUMI-CHAN?"
"I HAVE IT!"
JUMP
"OH, OKAY! SO I'LL TAKE IT TO TATSUMI--"
"NO NEED. I'LL GO!"
TAKE ME THERE.
AND SO, I ENDED UP COMING TO VISIT! ★
I PREPARED MYSELF FOR THIS.
AND IT ENDED UP BEING ALL FOR THE FISH...
SLIP
AND MOM WASN'T SUSPICIOUS ABOUT THIS TURN OF EVENTS?

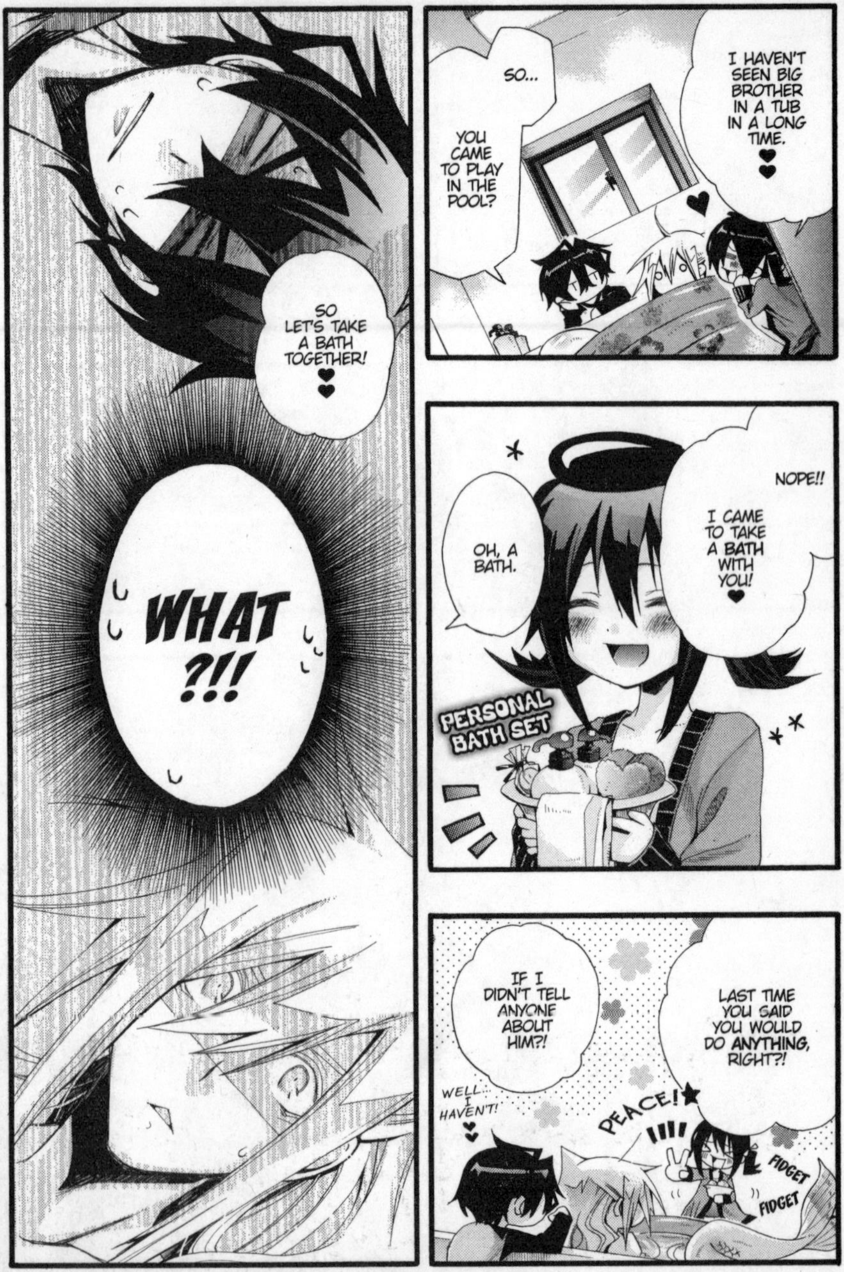
I HAVEN'T SEEN BIG BROTHER IN A TUB IN A LONG TIME. ♥♥
SO...
YOU CAME TO PLAY IN THE POOL?
NOPE!!
I CAME TO TAKE A BATH WITH YOU! ♥
OH, A BATH.
PERSONAL BATH SET
LAST TIME YOU SAID YOU WOULD DO ANYTHING, RIGHT?!
IF I DIDN'T TELL ANYONE ABOUT HIM?!
PEACE!★
FIDGET FIDGET
WELL... I HAVEN'T! ♥
SO LET'S TAKE A BATH TOGETHER! ♥♥
WHAT ?!!

Merman in My Tub

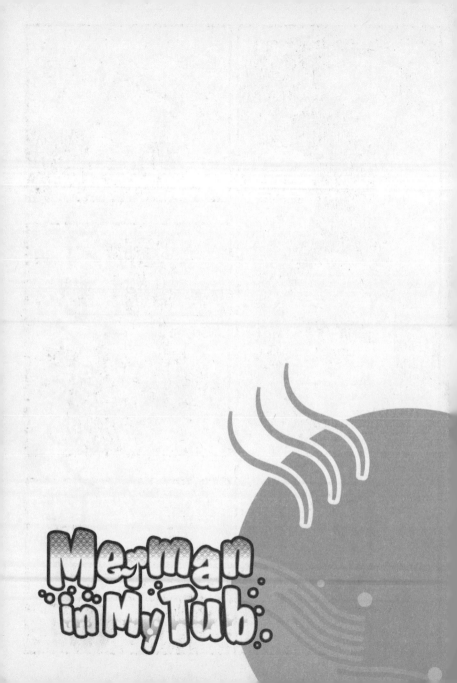

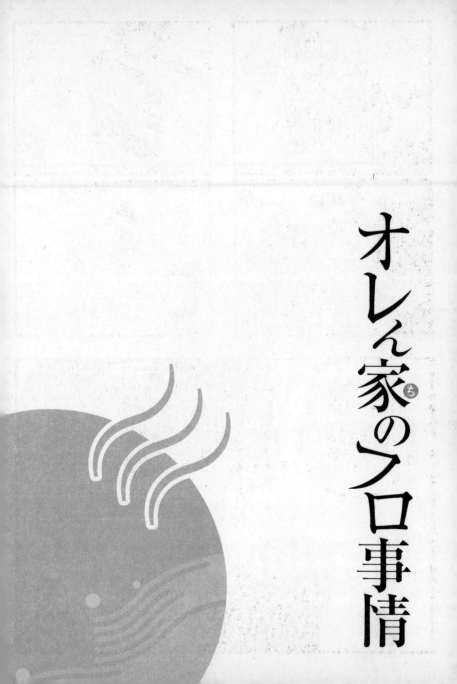

オレん家のフロ事情

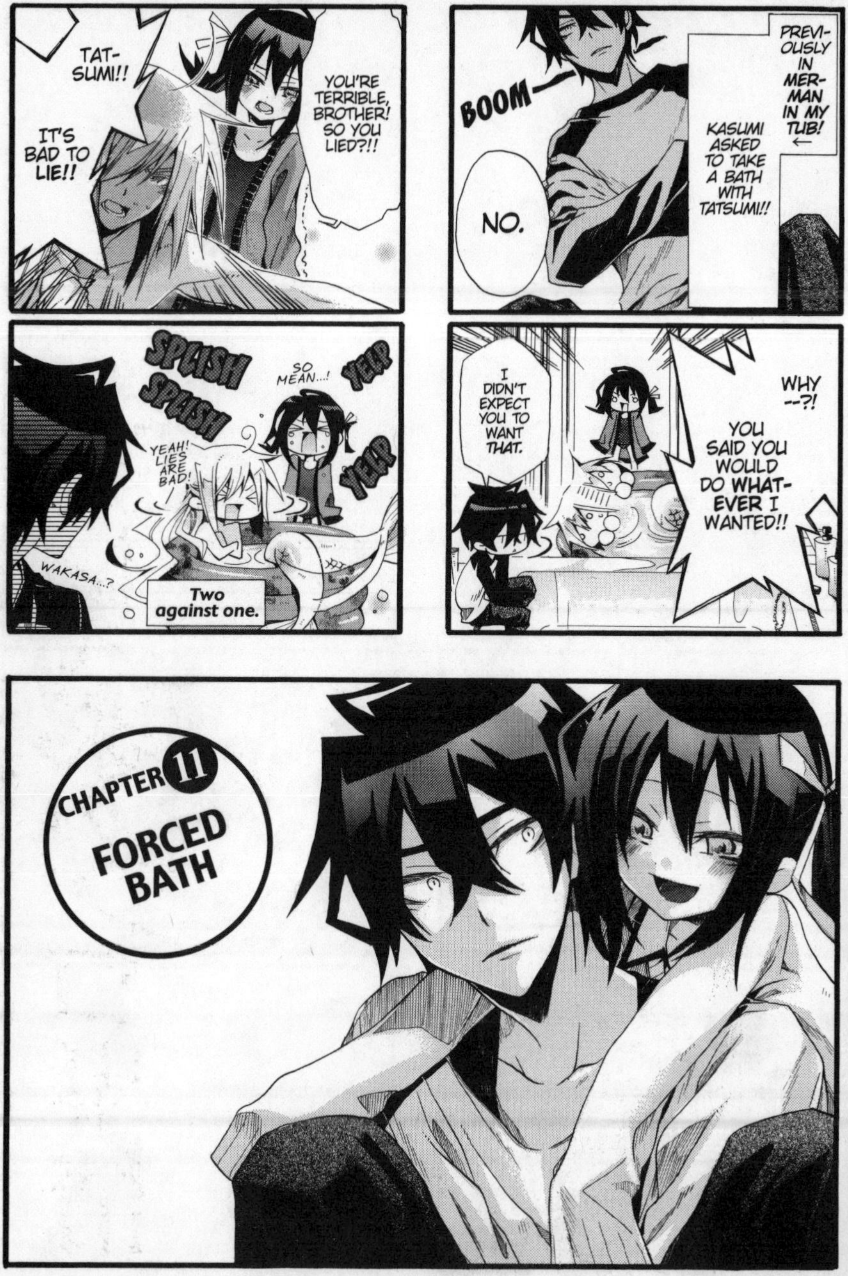
PREVIOUSLY IN MERMAN IN MY TUB! ←
KASUMI ASKED TO TAKE A BATH WITH TATSUMI!!
BOOM—
NO.
YOU'RE TERRIBLE, BROTHER! SO YOU LIED?!!
TAT-SUMI!!
IT'S BAD TO LIE!!
WHY --?!
YOU SAID YOU WOULD DO WHAT-EVER I WANTED!!
I DIDN'T EXPECT YOU TO WANT THAT.
YEAP
YEAP
SO MEAN...!
SPLISH SPLASH
YEAH! LIES ARE BAD!
WAKASA...?
Two against one.
CHAPTER 11
FORCED BATH

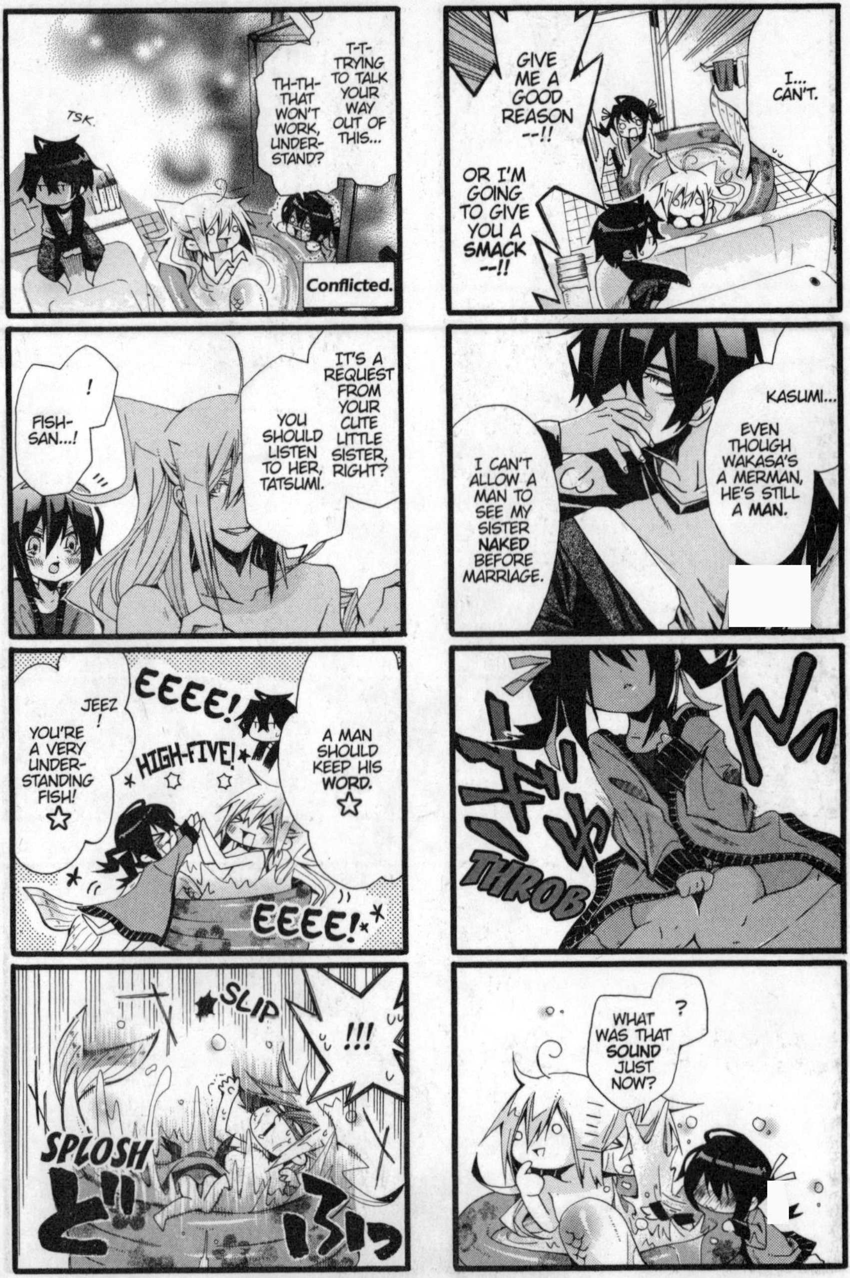
GIVE ME A GOOD REASON --!!
OR I'M GOING TO GIVE YOU A SMACK --!!
I... CAN'T.
KASUMI...
EVEN THOUGH WAKASA'S A MERMAN, HE'S STILL A MAN.
I CAN'T ALLOW A MAN TO SEE MY SISTER NAKED BEFORE MARRIAGE.
THROB
?
WHAT WAS THAT SOUND JUST NOW?
T-T-TRYING TO TALK YOUR WAY OUT OF THIS...
TH-TH-THAT WON'T WORK, UNDERSTAND?
TSK.
Conflicted.
IT'S A REQUEST FROM YOUR CUTE LITTLE SISTER, RIGHT?
YOU SHOULD LISTEN TO HER, TATSUMI.
!
FISH-SAN...!
A MAN SHOULD KEEP HIS WORD. ☆
EEEE!
HIGH-FIVE!
JEEZ! YOU'RE A VERY UNDERSTANDING FISH! ☆
EEEE!
SLIP
!!!
SPLOSH

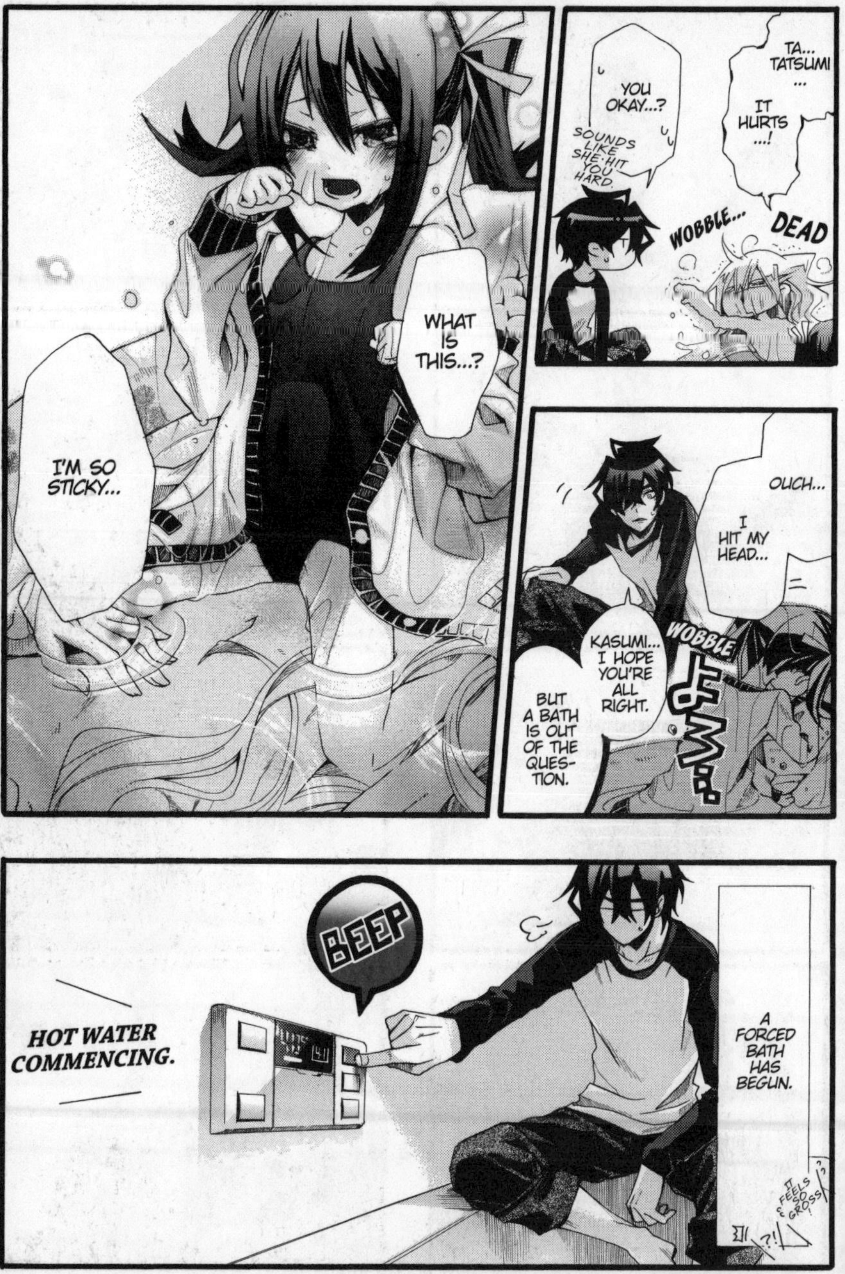
TA... TATSUMI ... IT HURTS ...!
YOU OKAY...?
SOUNDS LIKE SHE HIT YOU HARD.
DEAD
WOBBLE...
OUCH... I HIT MY HEAD...
WOBBLE
よろ..
KASUMI... I HOPE YOU'RE ALL RIGHT.
BUT A BATH IS OUT OF THE QUES-TION.
WHAT IS THIS...?
I'M SO STICKY...
A FORCED BATH HAS BEGUN.
IT FEELS SO GROSS!
?!
BEEP
41
HOT WATER COMMENCING.

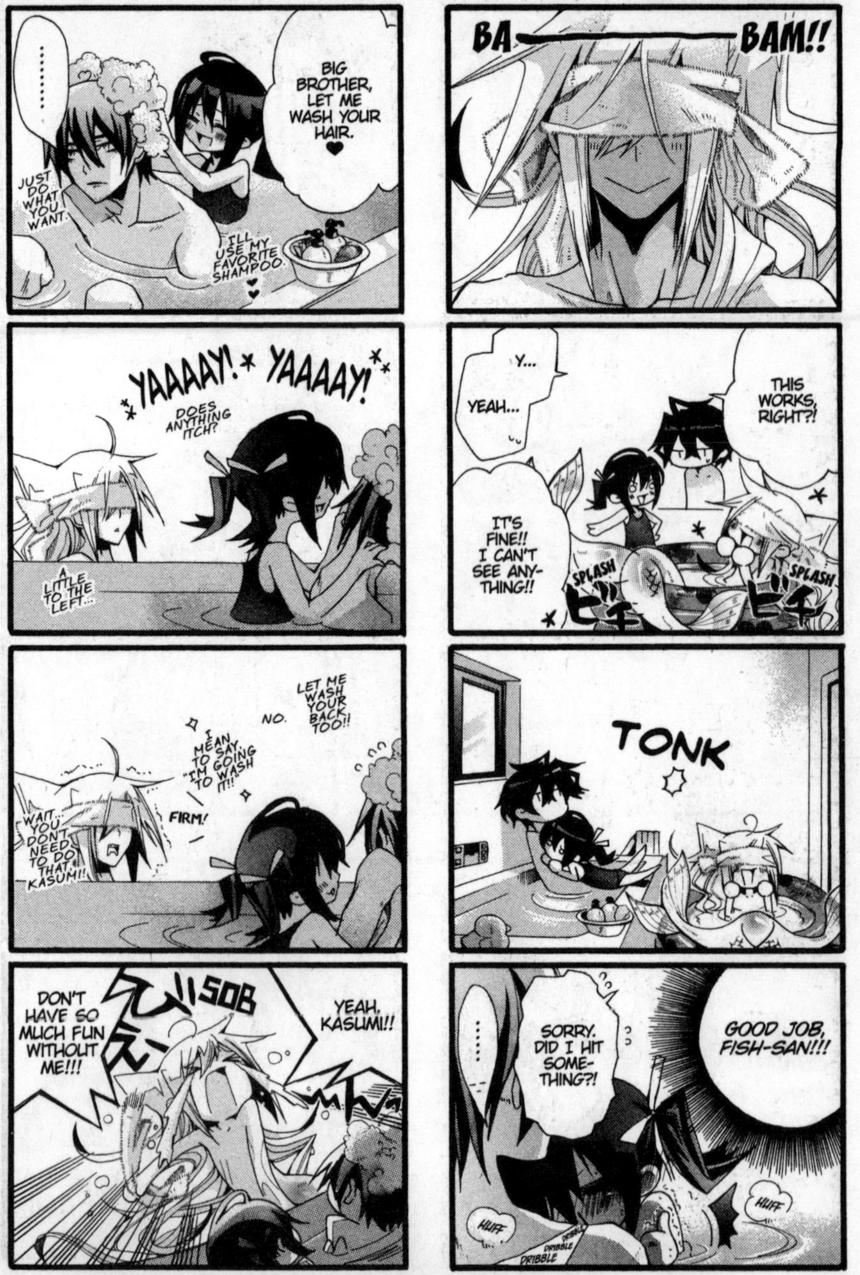
BA——BAM!!
......
BIG BROTHER, LET ME WASH YOUR HAIR.
JUST DO WHAT YOU WANT.
I'LL USE MY FAVORITE SHAMPOO.
THIS WORKS, RIGHT?!
Y... YEAH...
IT'S FINE!! I CAN'T SEE ANYTHING!!
SPLASH
ビチ
SPLASH
ビチ
YAAAAY! YAAAAY!
DOES ANYTHING ITCH?
A LITTLE TO THE LEFT...
TONK
LET ME WASH YOUR BACK TOO!!
NO.
I MEAN TO SAY, "I'M GOING TO WASH IT!!"
FIRM!
WAIT... YOU DON'T NEED TO DO THAT, KASUMI!!
GOOD JOB, FISH-SAN!!!
SORRY. DID I HIT SOMETHING?!
......
HUFF
HUFF
DRIBBLE DRIBBLE
YEAH, KASUMI!!
SOB
DON'T HAVE SO MUCH FUN WITHOUT ME!!!

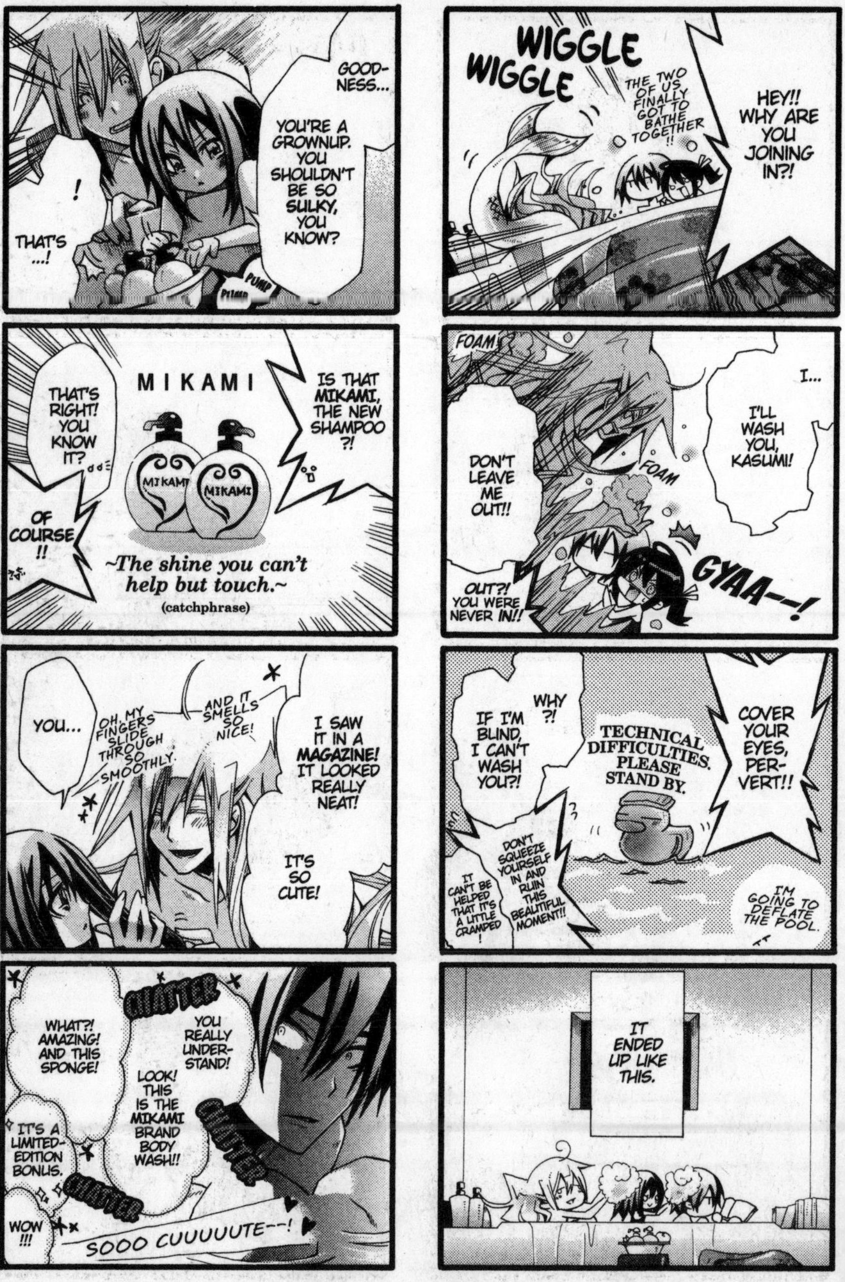
HEY!! WHY ARE YOU JOINING IN?!
THE TWO OF US FINALLY GOT TO BATHE TOGETHER!!
WIGGLE WIGGLE
FOAM
I...
I'LL WASH YOU, KASUMI!
FOAM
DON'T LEAVE ME OUT!!
GYAA--!
OUT?! YOU WERE NEVER IN!!
COVER YOUR EYES, PERVERT!!
TECHNICAL DIFFICULTIES. PLEASE STAND BY.
WHY?!
IF I'M BLIND, I CAN'T WASH YOU?!
I'M GOING TO DEFLATE THE POOL.
DON'T SQUEEZE YOURSELF IN AND RUIN THIS BEAUTIFUL MOMENT!!
IT CAN'T BE HELPED THAT IT'S A LITTLE CRAMPED!
IT ENDED UP LIKE THIS.
GOODNESS...
YOU'RE A GROWNUP. YOU SHOULDN'T BE SO SULKY, YOU KNOW?
PUMP
PUMP
!
THAT'S...!
IS THAT MIKAMI, THE NEW SHAMPOO?!
MIKAMI
MIKAMI
MIKAMI
~The shine you can't help but touch.~
(catchphrase)
THAT'S RIGHT! YOU KNOW IT?
OF COURSE!!
I SAW IT IN A MAGAZINE! IT LOOKED REALLY NEAT!
IT'S SO CUTE!
AND IT SMELLS SO NICE!
OH, MY FINGERS SLIDE THROUGH SO SMOOTHLY.
YOU...
CHATTER
YOU REALLY UNDERSTAND!
LOOK! THIS IS THE MIKAMI BRAND BODY WASH!!
WHAT?! AMAZING! AND THIS SPONGE!
CHATTER
IT'S A LIMITED-EDITION BONUS.
CHATTER
WOW!!!
SOOO CUUUUTE--!

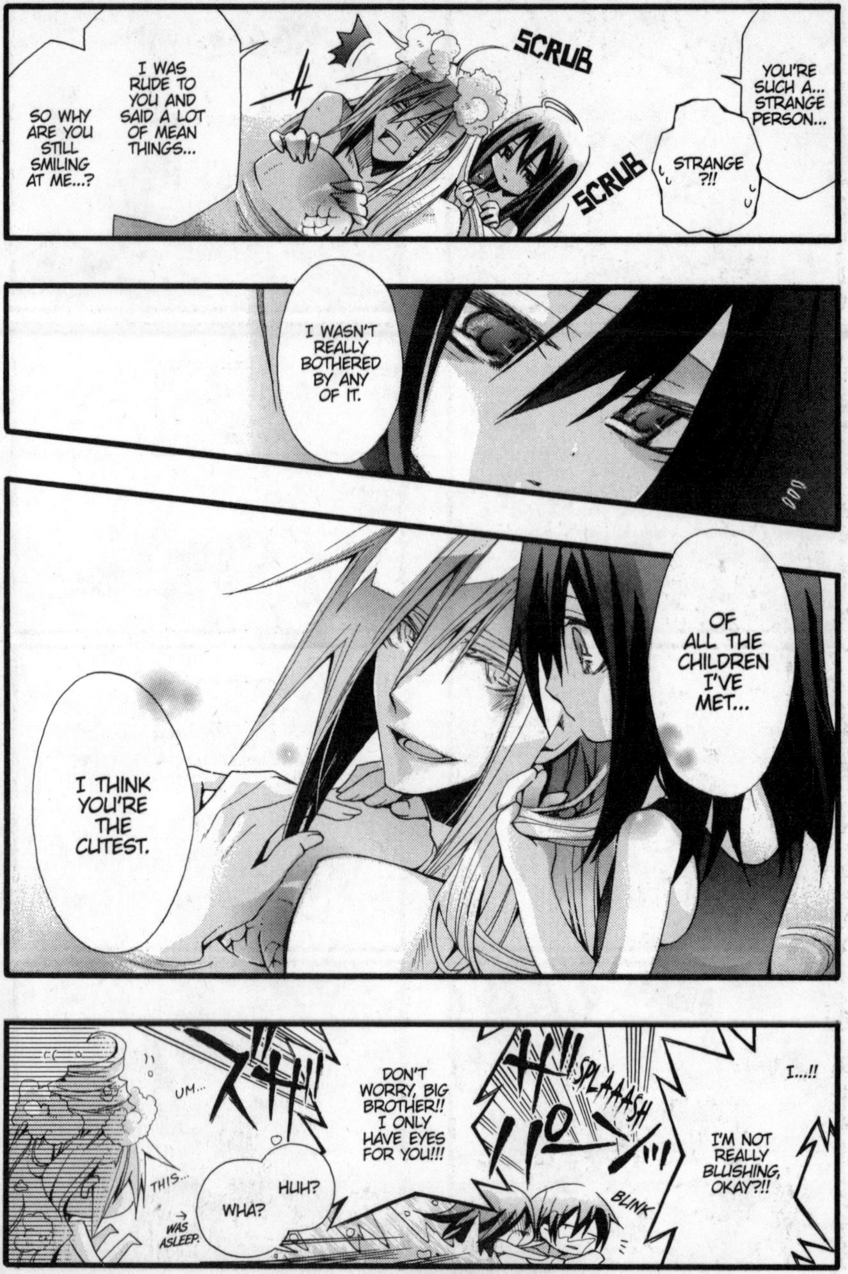
YOU'RE SUCH A... STRANGE PERSON...
STRANGE ?!!
SCRUB
SCRUB
I WAS RUDE TO YOU AND SAID A LOT OF MEAN THINGS...
SO WHY ARE YOU STILL SMILING AT ME...?
I WASN'T REALLY BOTHERED BY ANY OF IT.
OF ALL THE CHILDREN I'VE MET...
I THINK YOU'RE THE CUTEST.
I...!!
I'M NOT REALLY BLUSHING, OKAY?!!
BLINK
SPLAAASH
DON'T WORRY, BIG BROTHER!! I ONLY HAVE EYES FOR YOU!!!
HUH?
WHA?
UM...
THIS...
WAS ASLEEP.

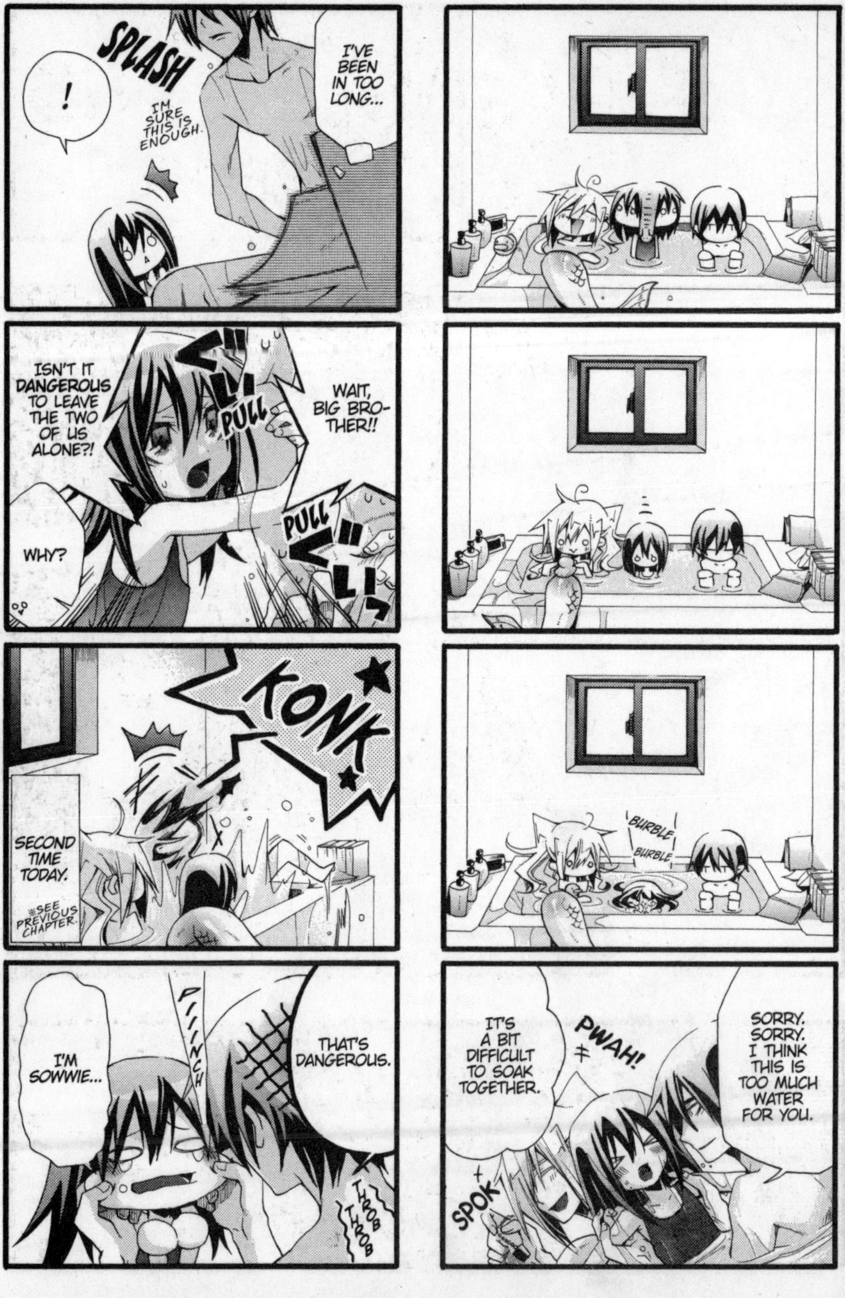
BURBLE
BURBLE
SORRY. SORRY. I THINK THIS IS TOO MUCH WATER FOR YOU.
PWAH!
IT'S A BIT DIFFICULT TO SOAK TOGETHER.
SPOK
I'VE BEEN IN TOO LONG...
SPLASH
I'M SURE THIS IS ENOUGH.
!
WAIT, BIG BRO-THER!!
PULL
ISN'T IT DANGEROUS TO LEAVE THE TWO OF US ALONE?!
PULL
WHY?
KONK
SECOND TIME TODAY.
※SEE PREVIOUS CHAPTER.
THAT'S DANGEROUS.
PIIIINCH
THROB THROB
I'M SOWWIE...

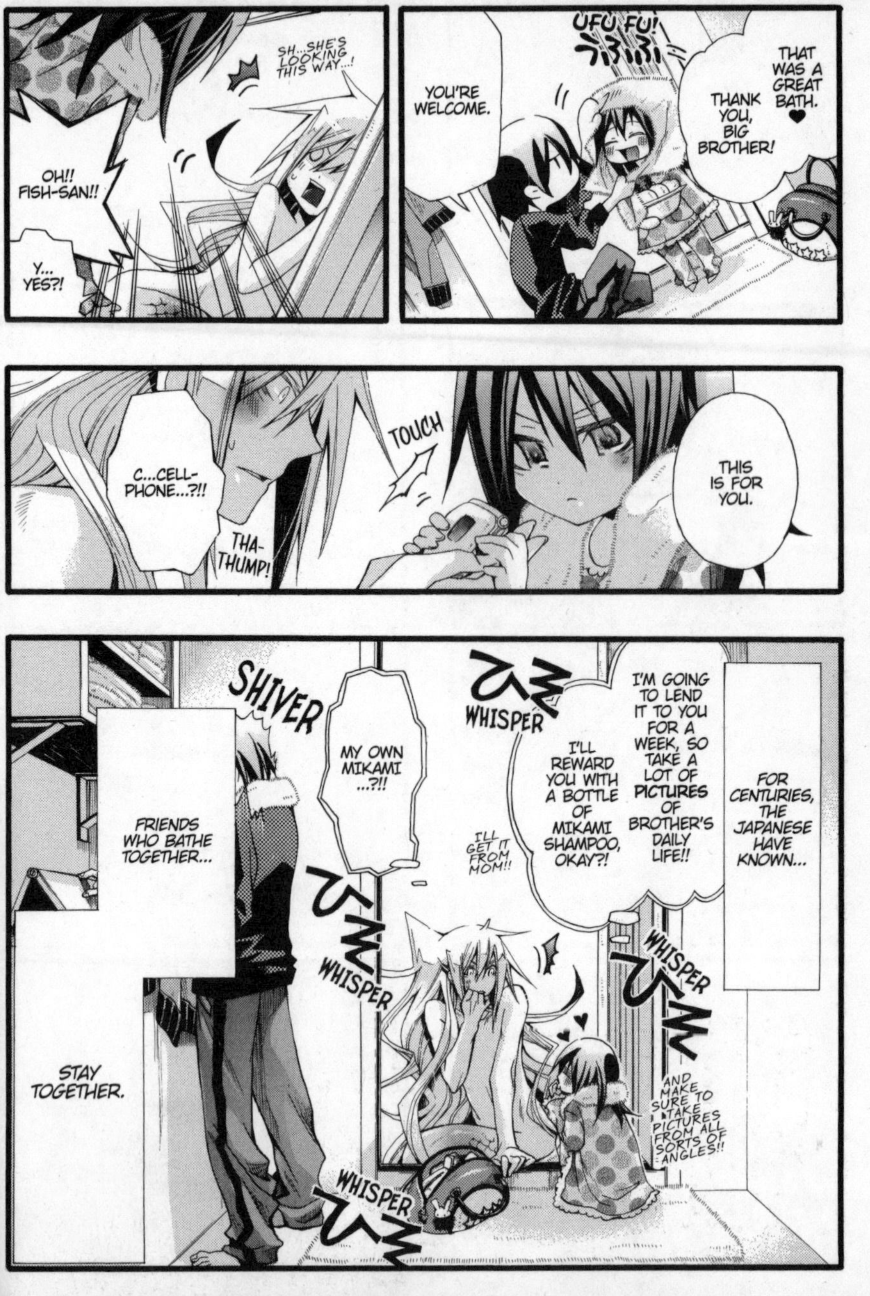
UFU FU!
うふふ
THAT WAS A GREAT BATH. ♥
THANK YOU, BIG BROTHER!
YOU'RE WELCOME.
SH...SHE'S LOOKING THIS WAY...!
OH!! FISH-SAN!!
Y... YES?!
THIS IS FOR YOU.
TOUCH
C...CELL-PHONE...?!!
THA-THUMP!
FOR CENTURIES, THE JAPANESE HAVE KNOWN...
I'M GOING TO LEND IT TO YOU FOR A WEEK, SO TAKE A LOT OF PICTURES OF BROTHER'S DAILY LIFE!!
ひそ
WHISPER
I'LL REWARD YOU WITH A BOTTLE OF MIKAMI SHAMPOO, OKAY?!
I'LL GET IT FROM MOM!!
WHISPER
ひそ
MY OWN MIKAMI ...?!!
SHIVER
FRIENDS WHO BATHE TOGETHER...
ひそ
WHISPER
AND MAKE SURE TO TAKE PICTURES FROM ALL SORTS OF ANGLES!!
WHISPER
ひそ
STAY TOGETHER.

Merman in My Tub

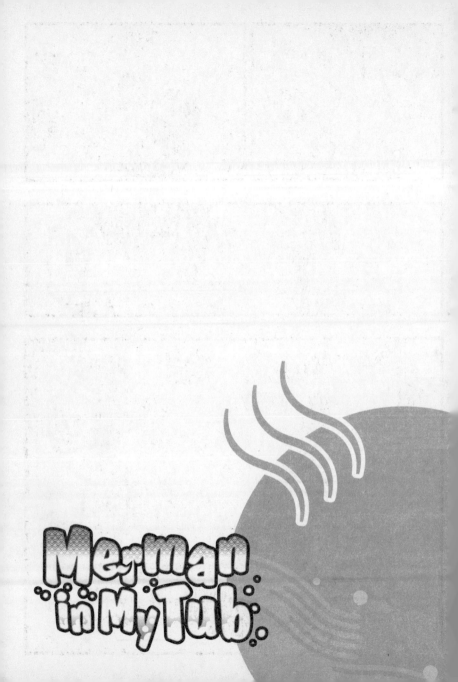

オレん家のフロ事情

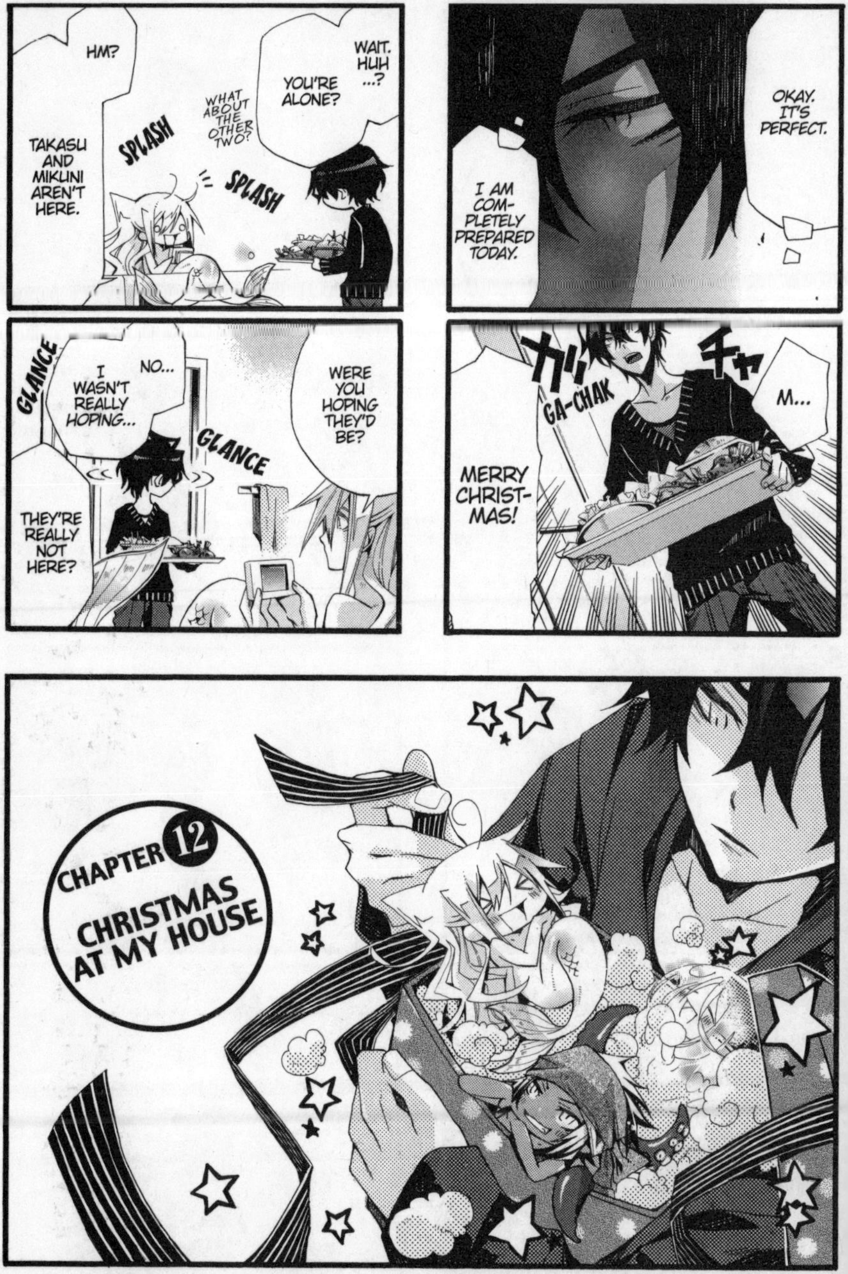

OKAY. IT'S PERFECT.
I AM COM-PLETELY PREPARED TODAY.
WAIT. HUH ...?
YOU'RE ALONE?
WHAT ABOUT THE OTHER TWO?
HM?
SPLASH
SPLASH
TAKASU AND MIKUNI AREN'T HERE.
ガッ
チャ
GA-CHAK
M...
MERRY CHRIST-MAS!
WERE YOU HOPING THEY'D BE?
GLANCE
NO...
I WASN'T REALLY HOPING...
GLANCE
THEY'RE REALLY NOT HERE?
CHAPTER 12
CHRISTMAS AT MY HOUSE

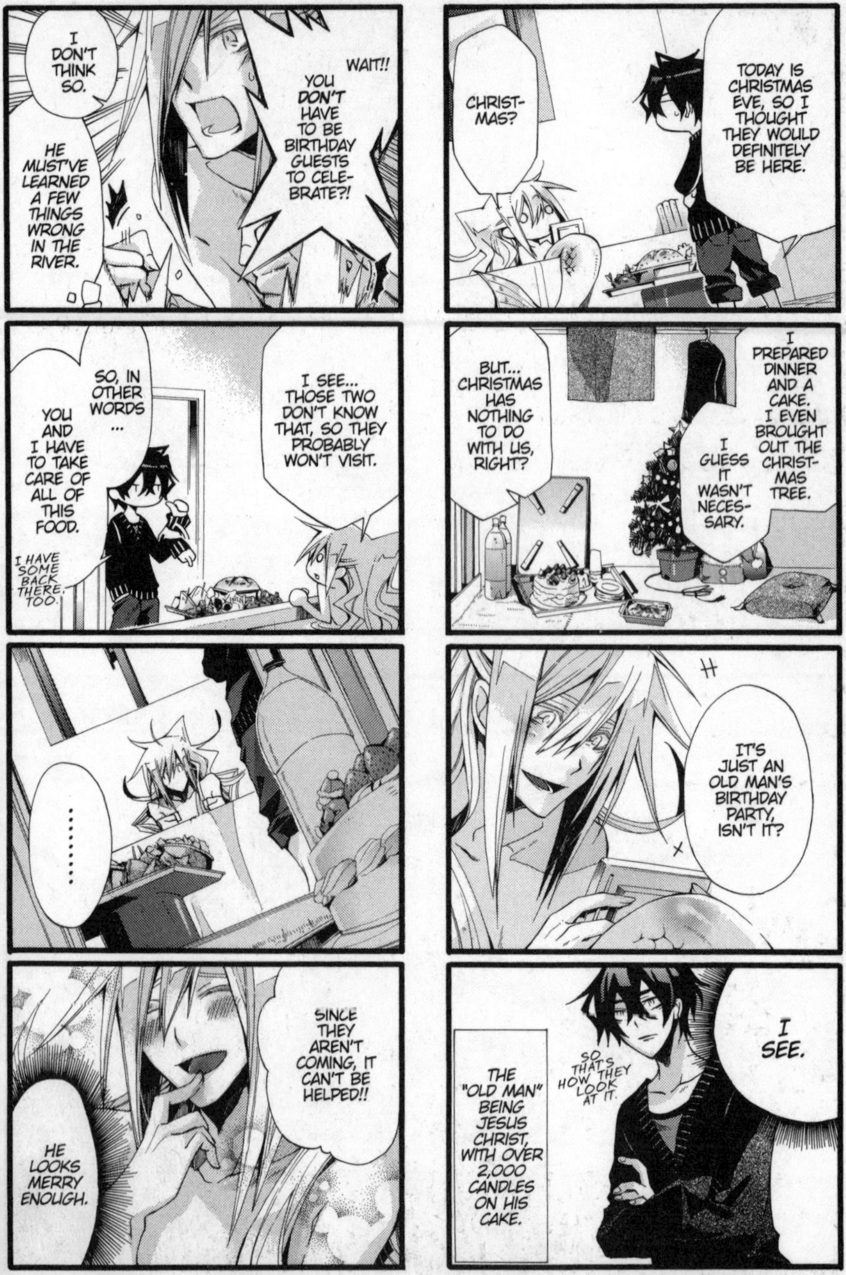
TODAY IS CHRISTMAS EVE, SO I THOUGHT THEY WOULD DEFINITELY BE HERE.
CHRIST-MAS?
WAIT!!
YOU DON'T HAVE TO BE BIRTHDAY GUESTS TO CELE-BRATE?!
I DON'T THINK SO.
HE MUST'VE LEARNED A FEW THINGS WRONG IN THE RIVER.
I PREPARED DINNER AND A CAKE. I EVEN BROUGHT OUT THE CHRIST-MAS TREE.
I GUESS IT WASN'T NECES-SARY.
BUT... CHRISTMAS HAS NOTHING TO DO WITH US, RIGHT?
I SEE... THOSE TWO DON'T KNOW THAT, SO THEY PROBABLY WON'T VISIT.
SO, IN OTHER WORDS ...
YOU AND I HAVE TO TAKE CARE OF ALL OF THIS FOOD.
I HAVE SOME BACK THERE, TOO.
IT'S JUST AN OLD MAN'S BIRTHDAY PARTY, ISN'T IT?
....
I SEE.
SO THAT'S HOW THEY LOOK AT IT.
THE "OLD MAN" BEING JESUS CHRIST, WITH OVER 2,000 CANDLES ON HIS CAKE.
SINCE THEY AREN'T COMING, IT CAN'T BE HELPED!!
HE LOOKS MERRY ENOUGH.

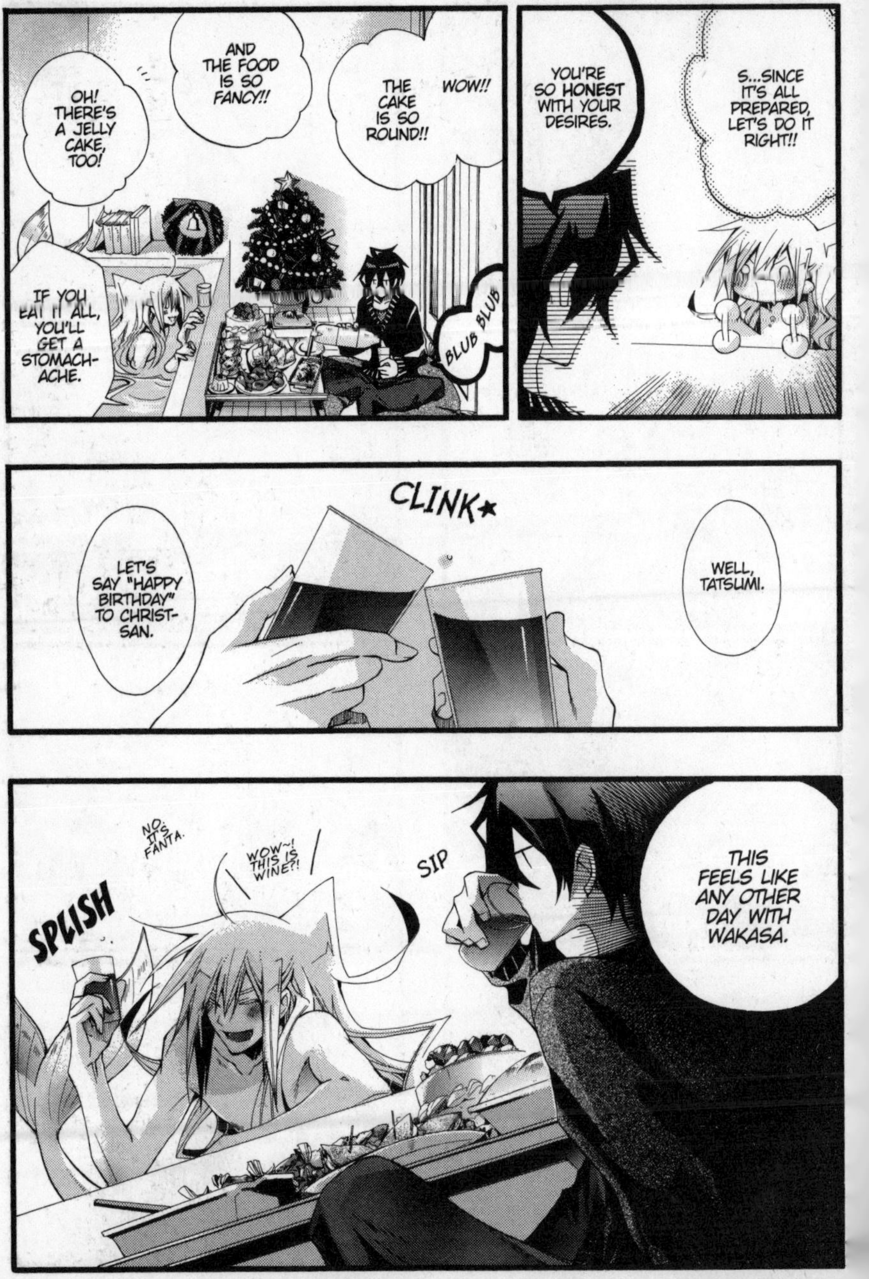
S...SINCE IT'S ALL PREPARED, LET'S DO IT RIGHT!!
YOU'RE SO HONEST WITH YOUR DESIRES.
WOW!!
THE CAKE IS SO ROUND!!
AND THE FOOD IS SO FANCY!!
OH! THERE'S A JELLY CAKE, TOO!
BLUB BLUB
IF YOU EAT IT ALL, YOU'LL GET A STOMACH-ACHE.
WELL, TATSUMI.
CLINK★
LET'S SAY "HAPPY BIRTHDAY" TO CHRIST-SAN.
THIS FEELS LIKE ANY OTHER DAY WITH WAKASA.
SIP
WOW~! THIS IS WINE?!
NO, IT'S FANTA.
SPLISH

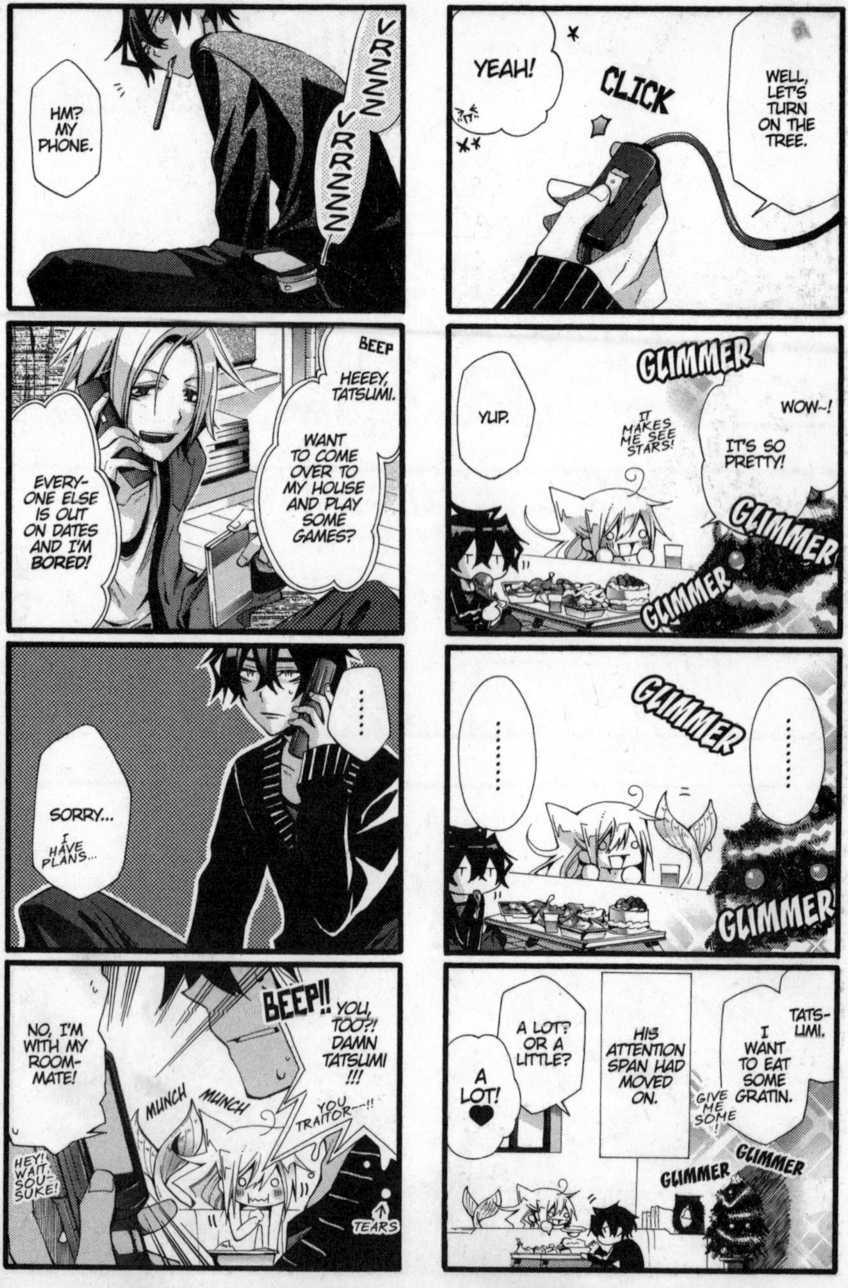

WELL, LET'S TURN ON THE TREE.
CLICK
YEAH!
GLIMMER
WOW~!
IT'S SO PRETTY!
IT MAKES ME SEE STARS!
YUP.
GLIMMER
GLIMMER
GLIMMER
......
GLIMMER
......
GLIMMER
TATSU-MI.
I WANT TO EAT SOME GRATIN.
GIVE ME SOME!
HIS ATTENTION SPAN HAD MOVED ON.
A LOT? OR A LITTLE?
A LOT! ♥
GLIMMER
GLIMMER
VRZZZ
VRRZZZ
HM? MY PHONE.
BEEP
HEEEY, TATSUMI.
WANT TO COME OVER TO MY HOUSE AND PLAY SOME GAMES?
EVERY-ONE ELSE IS OUT ON DATES AND I'M BORED!
......
SORRY...
I HAVE PLANS...
BEEP!!
YOU, TOO?! DAMN TATSUMI!!!
YOU TRAITOR--!!
NO, I'M WITH MY ROOM-MATE!
MUNCH
MUNCH
HEY! WAIT. SOU-SUKE!
TEARS

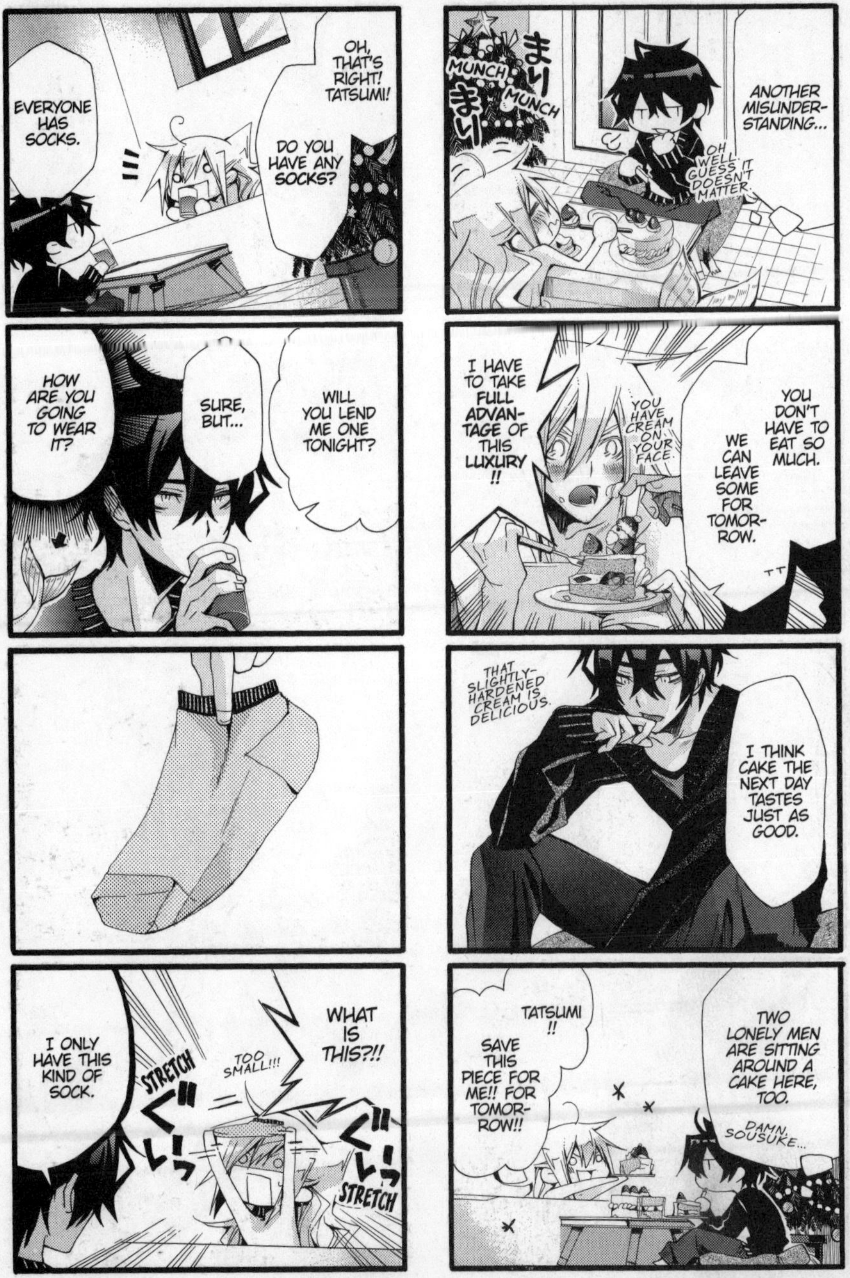
ANOTHER MISUNDER-STANDING...
OH WELL GUESS IT DOESN'T MATTER.
まり MUNCH
まり MUNCH
YOU DON'T HAVE TO EAT SO MUCH.
WE CAN LEAVE SOME FOR TOMOR-ROW.
YOU HAVE CREAM ON YOUR FACE.
I HAVE TO TAKE FULL ADVAN-TAGE OF THIS LUXURY !!
I THINK CAKE THE NEXT DAY TASTES JUST AS GOOD.
THAT SLIGHTLY-HARDENED CREAM IS DELICIOUS.
TWO LONELY MEN ARE SITTING AROUND A CAKE HERE, TOO.
DAMN, SOUSUKE...
TATSUMI !!
SAVE THIS PIECE FOR ME!! FOR TOMOR-ROW!!
OH, THAT'S RIGHT! TATSUMI!
DO YOU HAVE ANY SOCKS?
EVERYONE HAS SOCKS.
WILL YOU LEND ME ONE TONIGHT?
SURE, BUT...
HOW ARE YOU GOING TO WEAR IT?
WHAT IS THIS?!!
TOO SMALL!!!
ぐいっ STRETCH
ぐいっ STRETCH
I ONLY HAVE THIS KIND OF SOCK.

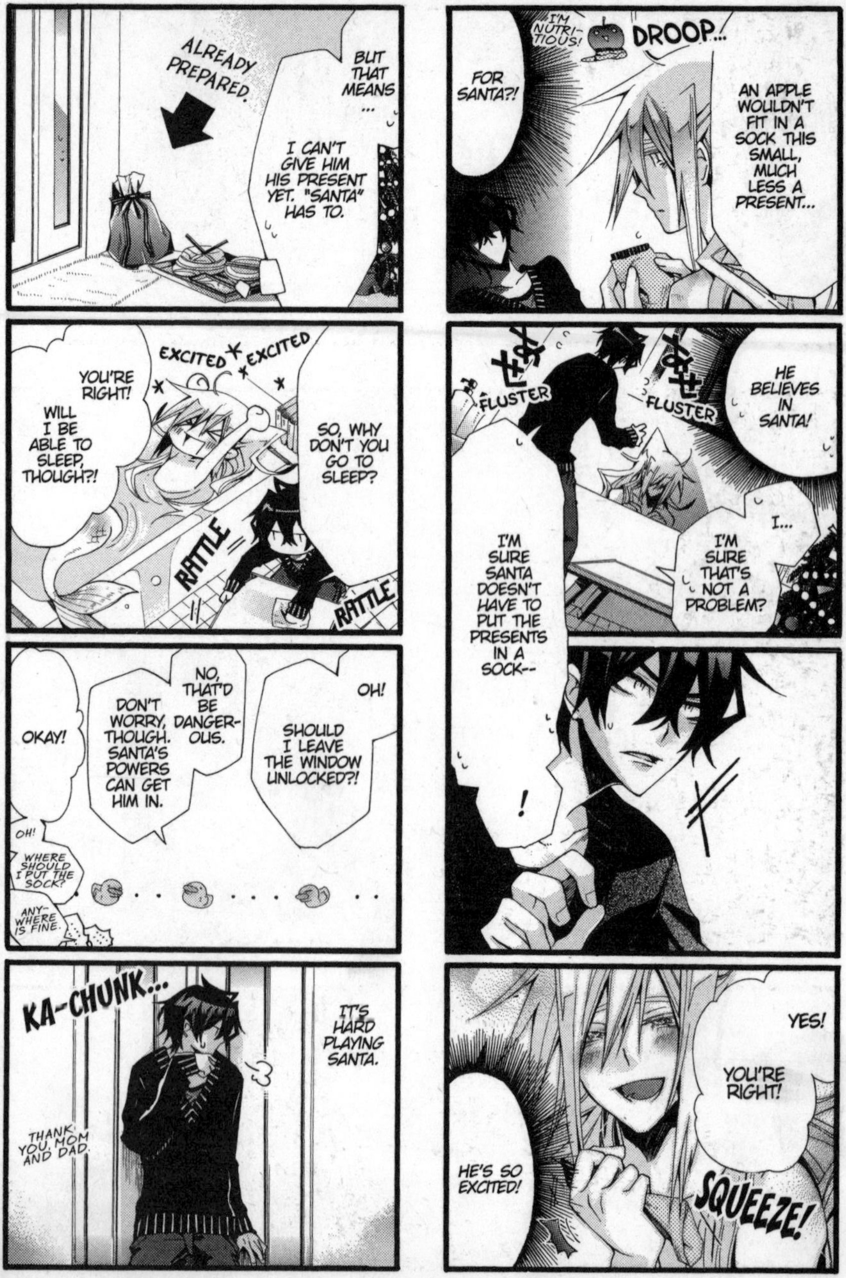
DROOP...
I'M NUTRITIOUS!
AN APPLE WOULDN'T FIT IN A SOCK THIS SMALL, MUCH LESS A PRESENT...
FOR SANTA?!
HE BELIEVES IN SANTA!
FLUSTER
FLUSTER
I...
I'M SURE THAT'S NOT A PROBLEM?
I'M SURE SANTA DOESN'T HAVE TO PUT THE PRESENTS IN A SOCK--
YES!
YOU'RE RIGHT!
HE'S SO EXCITED!
SQUEEZE!
BUT THAT MEANS ...
I CAN'T GIVE HIM HIS PRESENT YET. "SANTA" HAS TO.
ALREADY PREPARED.
SO, WHY DON'T YOU GO TO SLEEP?
EXCITED EXCITED
YOU'RE RIGHT!
WILL I BE ABLE TO SLEEP, THOUGH?!
RATTLE
RATTLE
OH!
SHOULD I LEAVE THE WINDOW UNLOCKED?!
NO, THAT'D BE DANGEROUS.
DON'T WORRY, THOUGH. SANTA'S POWERS CAN GET HIM IN.
OKAY!
OH!
WHERE SHOULD I PUT THE SOCK?
ANYWHERE IS FINE.
IT'S HARD PLAYING SANTA.
KA-CHUNK...
THANK YOU, MOM AND DAD.

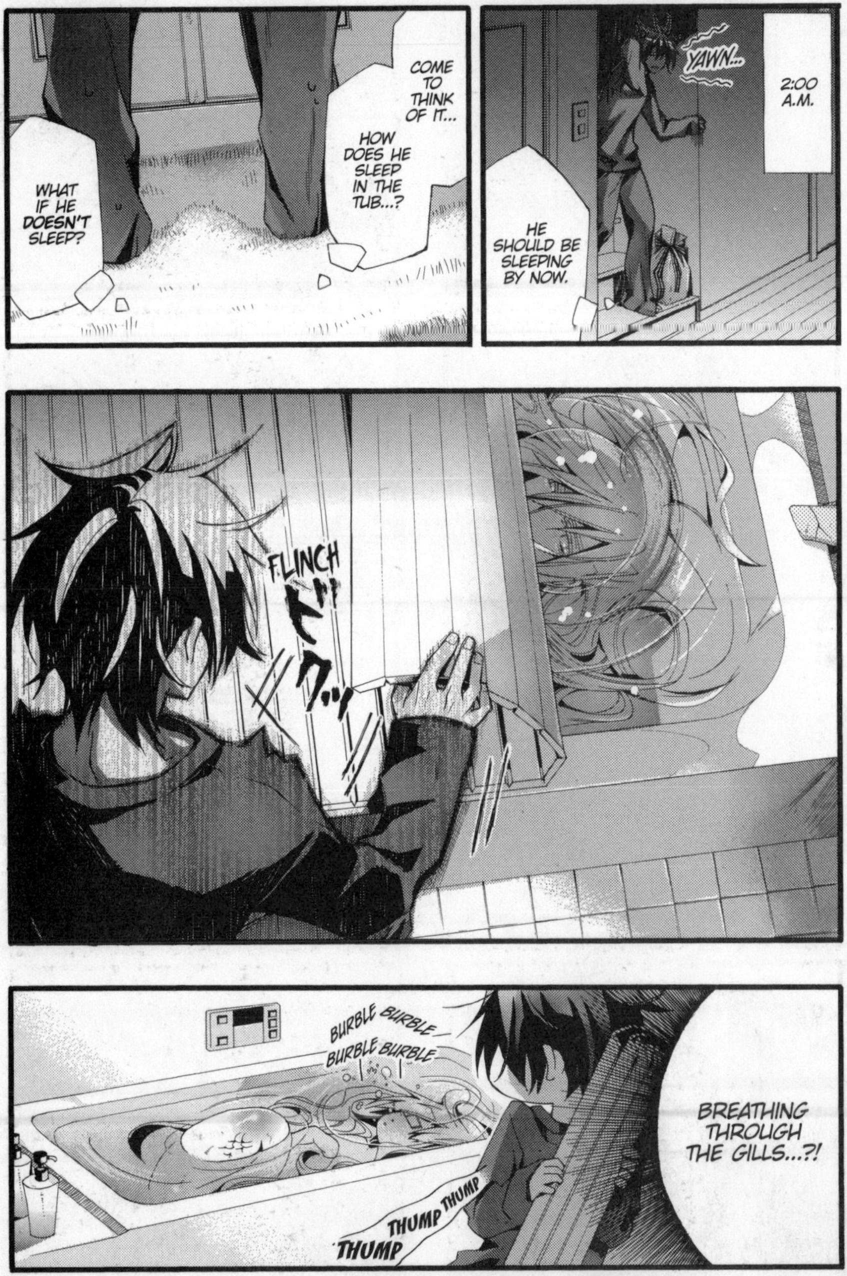
2:00 A.M.
YAWN...
HE SHOULD BE SLEEPING BY NOW.
COME TO THINK OF IT...
HOW DOES HE SLEEP IN THE TUB...?
WHAT IF HE DOESN'T SLEEP?
FLINCH
BREATHING THROUGH THE GILLS...?!
BURBLE BURBLE
BURBLE BURBLE
THUMP THUMP
THUMP THUMP

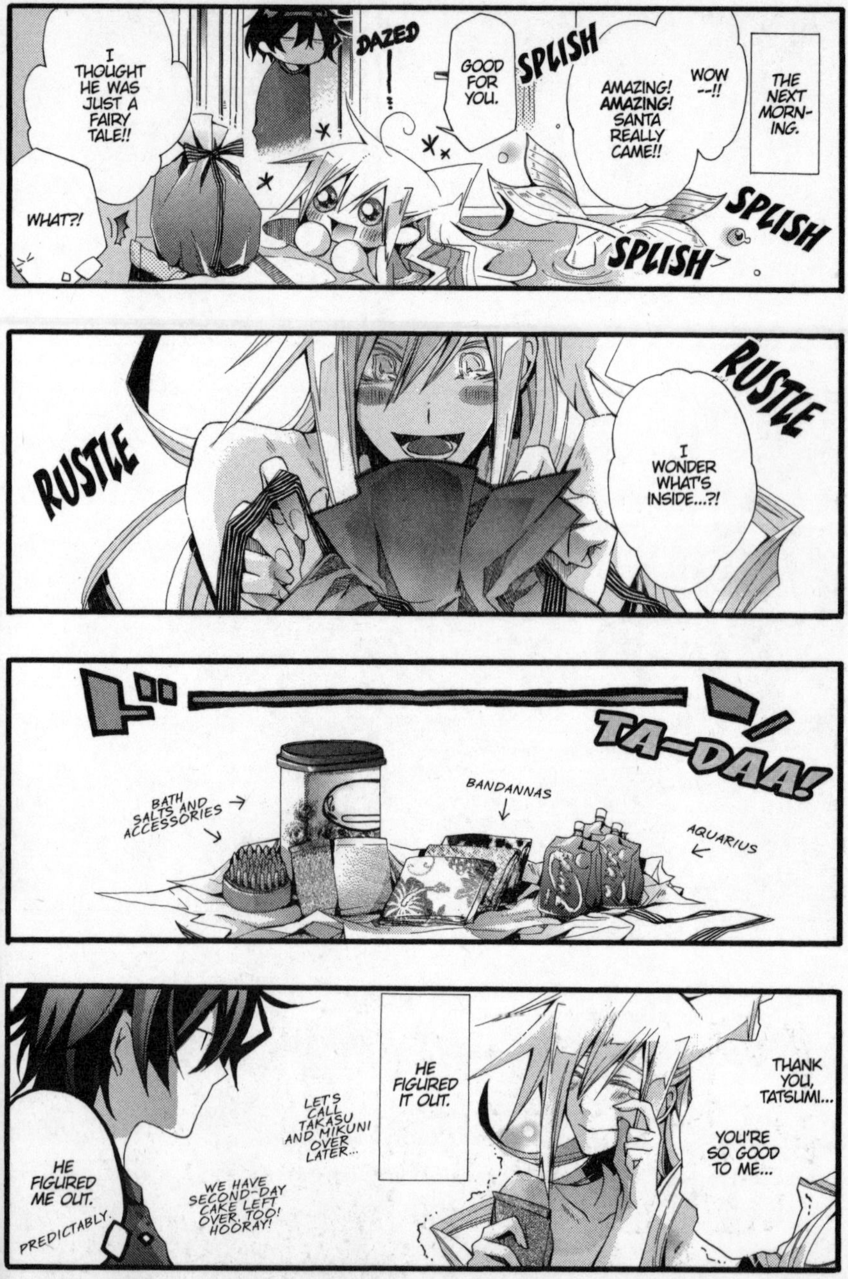
THE NEXT MORNING.
WOW--!!
AMAZING! AMAZING! SANTA REALLY CAME!!
SPLISH
SPLISH
SPLISH
GOOD FOR YOU.
DAZED
I THOUGHT HE WAS JUST A FAIRY TALE!!
WHAT?!
RUSTLE
I WONDER WHAT'S INSIDE...?!
RUSTLE
TA-DAA!
AQUARIUS
BANDANNAS
BATH SALTS AND ACCESSORIES
THANK YOU, TATSUMI...
YOU'RE SO GOOD TO ME...
HE FIGURED IT OUT.
LET'S CALL TAKASU AND MIKUNI OVER LATER...
WE HAVE SECOND-DAY CAKE LEFT OVER, TOO! HOORAY!
HE FIGURED ME OUT.
PREDICTABLY.

Merman in My Tub

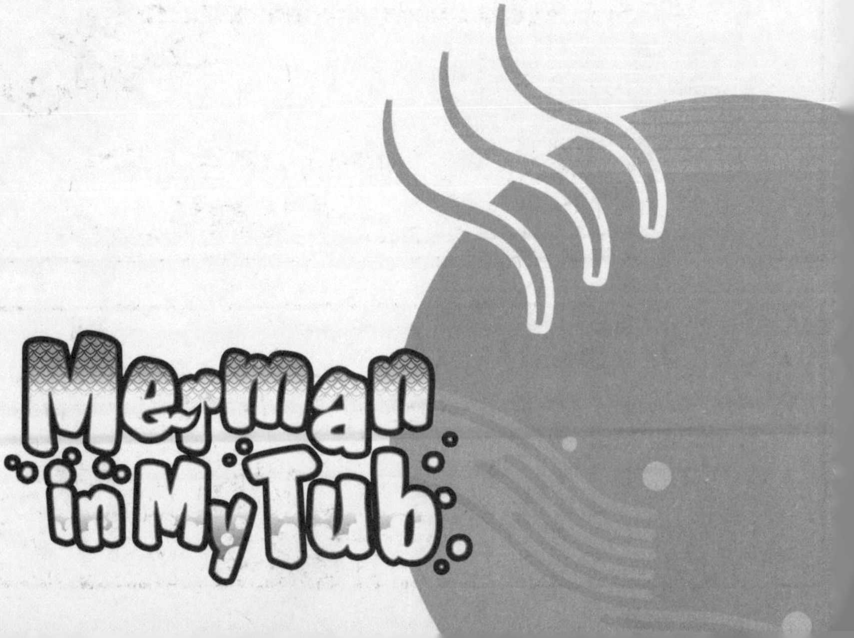

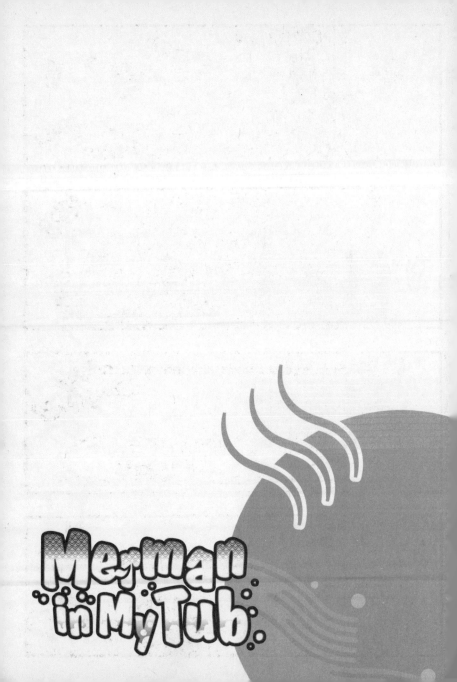

オレん家のフロ事情

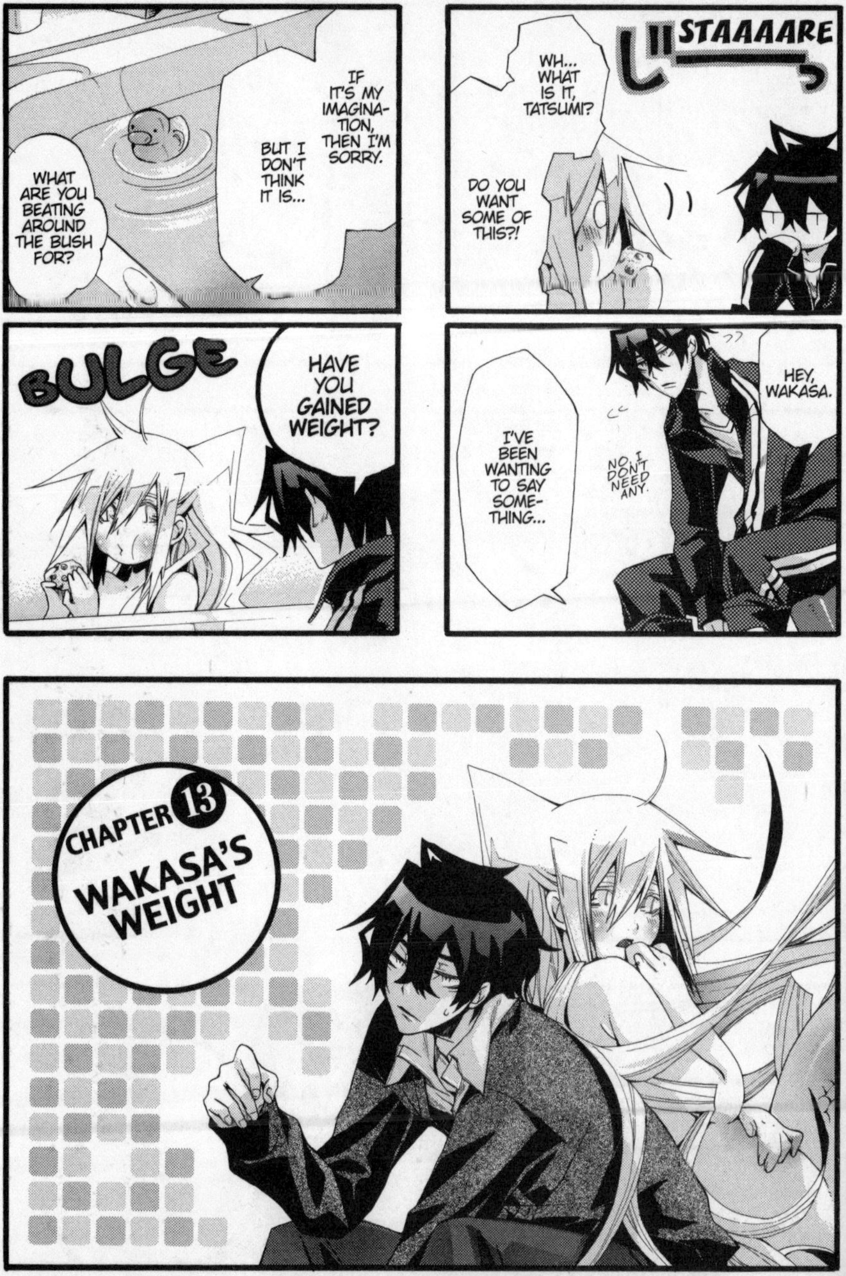
STAAAARE
WH... WHAT IS IT, TATSUMI?
DO YOU WANT SOME OF THIS?!
HEY, WAKASA.
I'VE BEEN WANTING TO SAY SOMETHING...
NO, I DON'T NEED ANY.
IF IT'S MY IMAGINATION, THEN I'M SORRY.
BUT I DON'T THINK IT IS...
WHAT ARE YOU BEATING AROUND THE BUSH FOR?
HAVE YOU GAINED WEIGHT?
BULGE
CHAPTER 13
WAKASA'S WEIGHT

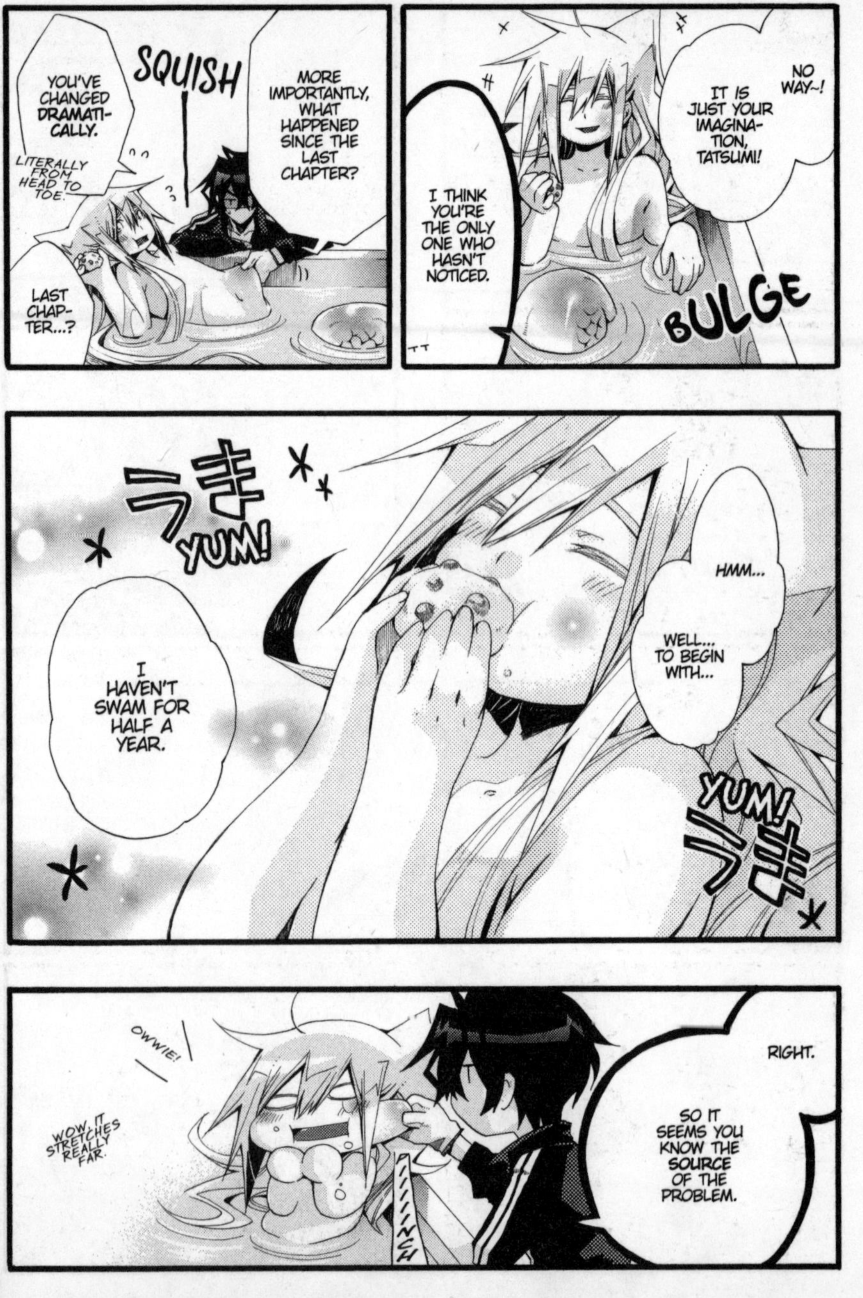
NO WAY~!
IT IS JUST YOUR IMAGINATION, TATSUMI!
I THINK YOU'RE THE ONLY ONE WHO HASN'T NOTICED.
BULGE
MORE IMPORTANTLY, WHAT HAPPENED SINCE THE LAST CHAPTER?
SQUISH
YOU'VE CHANGED DRAMATICALLY.
LITERALLY FROM HEAD TO TOE.
LAST CHAPTER...?
HMM...
WELL... TO BEGIN WITH...
YUM! うま
YUM! うま
I HAVEN'T SWAM FOR HALF A YEAR.
RIGHT.
SO IT SEEMS YOU KNOW THE SOURCE OF THE PROBLEM.
PIIIIINCH
OWWIE!
WOW, IT STRETCHES REALLY FAR.

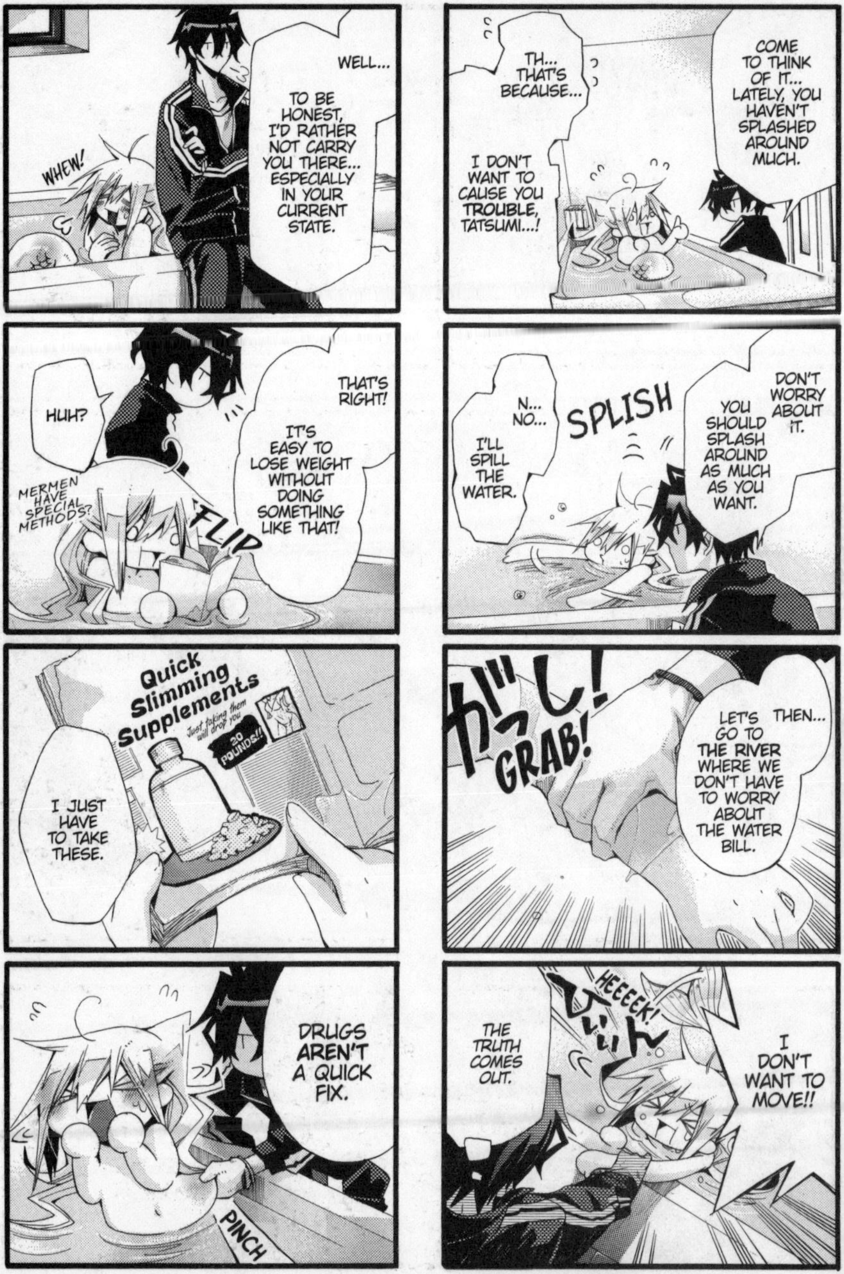
COME TO THINK OF IT... LATELY, YOU HAVEN'T SPLASHED AROUND MUCH.
TH... THAT'S BECAUSE...
I DON'T WANT TO CAUSE YOU TROUBLE, TATSUMI...!
WELL...
TO BE HONEST, I'D RATHER NOT CARRY YOU THERE... ESPECIALLY IN YOUR CURRENT STATE.
WHEW!
DON'T WORRY ABOUT IT.
YOU SHOULD SPLASH AROUND AS MUCH AS YOU WANT.
SPLISH
N... NO...
I'LL SPILL THE WATER.
THAT'S RIGHT!
IT'S EASY TO LOSE WEIGHT WITHOUT DOING SOMETHING LIKE THAT!
HUH?
MERMEN HAVE SPECIAL METHODS?
FLIP
THEN...
LET'S GO TO THE RIVER WHERE WE DON'T HAVE TO WORRY ABOUT THE WATER BILL.
がっし!
GRAB!
Quick Slimming Supplements
Just taking them will drop you
20 POUNDS!!
I JUST HAVE TO TAKE THESE.
I DON'T WANT TO MOVE!!
HEEEEK!
ひぃぃん
THE TRUTH COMES OUT.
DRUGS AREN'T A QUICK FIX.
PINCH

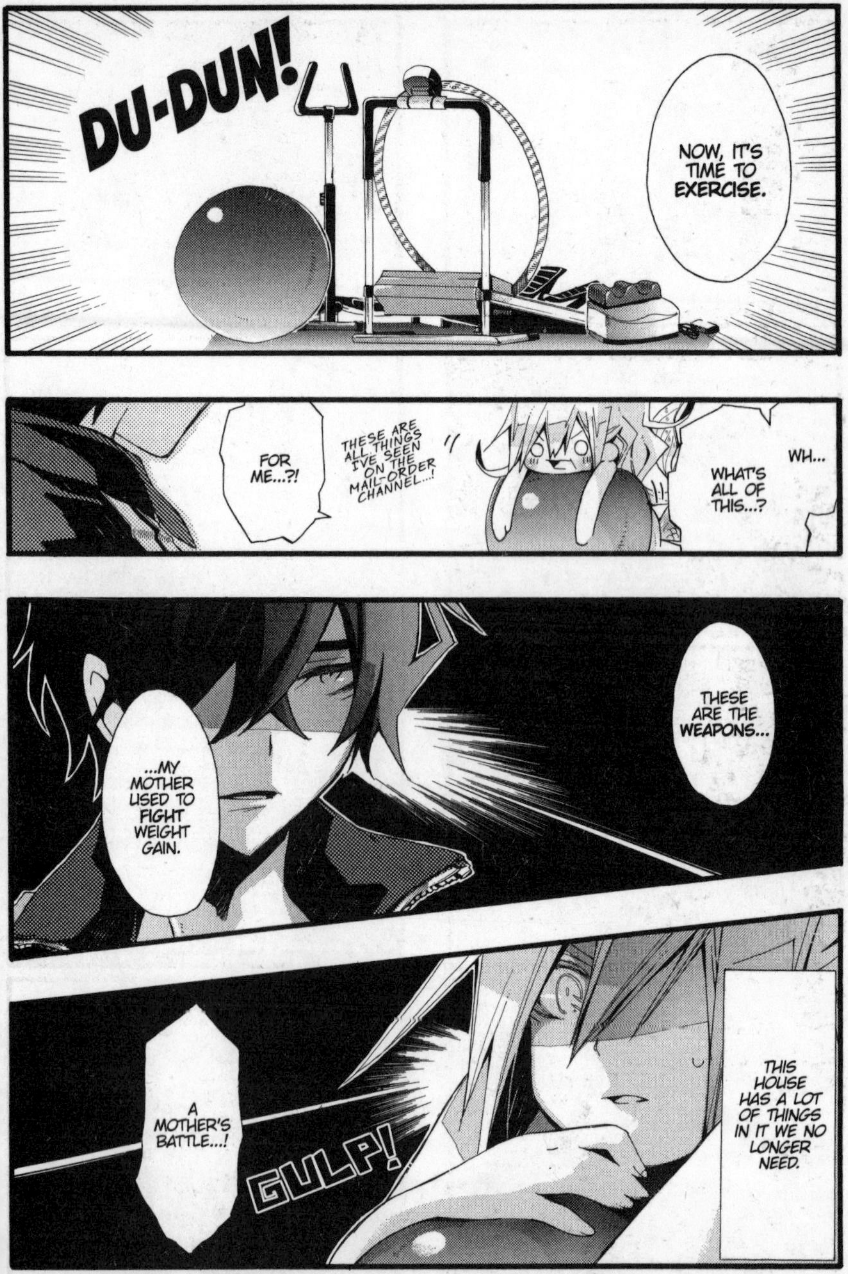
NOW, IT'S TIME TO EXERCISE.
DU-DUN!
WH...
WHAT'S ALL OF THIS...?
THESE ARE ALL THINGS I'VE SEEN ON THE MAIL-ORDER CHANNEL...!
FOR ME...?!
THESE ARE THE WEAPONS...
...MY MOTHER USED TO FIGHT WEIGHT GAIN.
THIS HOUSE HAS A LOT OF THINGS IN IT WE NO LONGER NEED.
GULP!
A MOTHER'S BATTLE...!

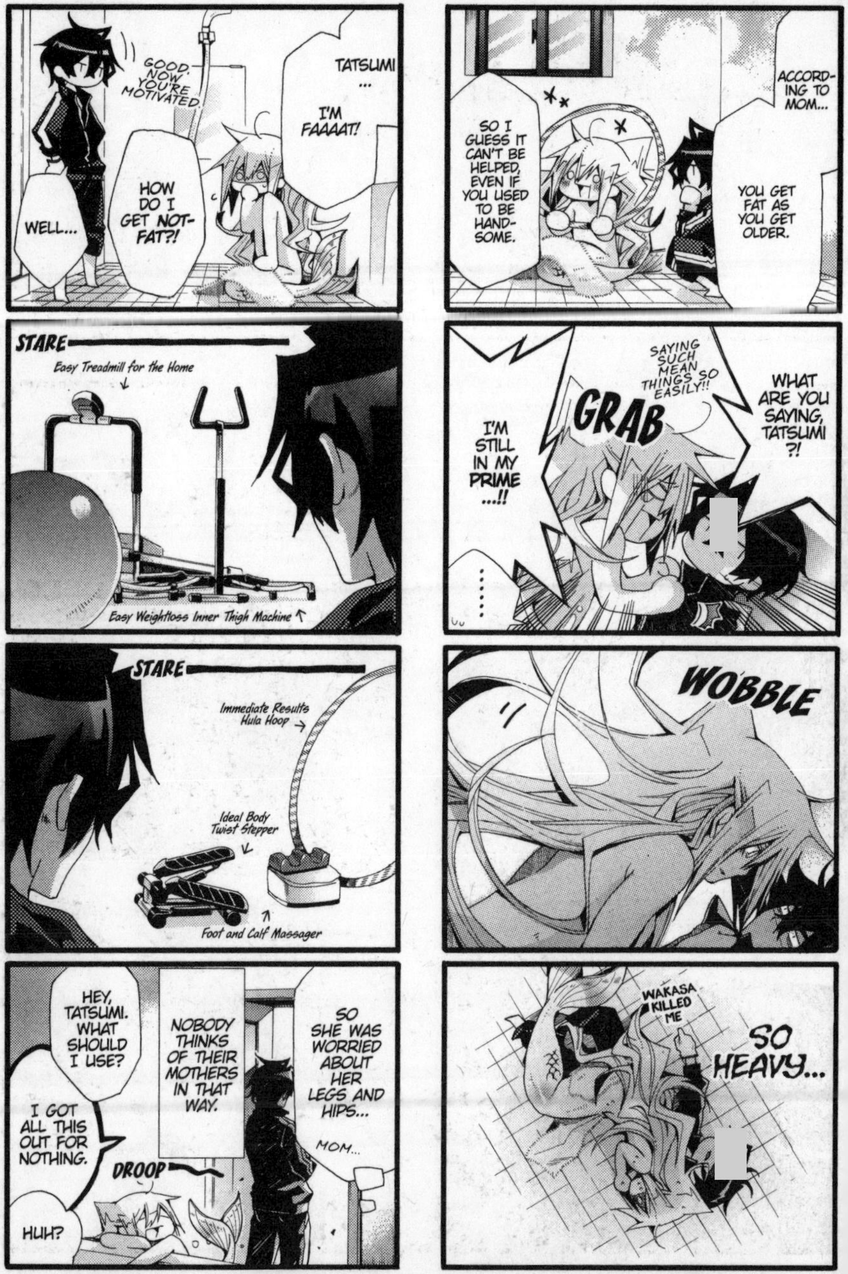
ACCORD-ING TO MOM...
YOU GET FAT AS YOU GET OLDER.
SO I GUESS IT CAN'T BE HELPED, EVEN IF YOU USED TO BE HAND-SOME.
WHAT ARE YOU SAYING, TATSUMI?!
SAYING SUCH MEAN THINGS SO EASILY!!
GRAB
I'M STILL IN MY PRIME...!!
......
WOBBLE
SO HEAVY...
WAKASA KILLED ME
TATSUMI ... I'M FAAAAT!
GOOD. NOW YOU'RE MOTIVATED.
HOW DO I GET NOT-FAT?!
WELL...
STARE
Easy Treadmill for the Home
Easy Weightloss Inner Thigh Machine
STARE
Immediate Results Hula Hoop
Ideal Body Twist Stepper
Foot and Calf Massager
SO SHE WAS WORRIED ABOUT HER LEGS AND HIPS...
MOM...
NOBODY THINKS OF THEIR MOTHERS IN THAT WAY.
HEY, TATSUMI. WHAT SHOULD I USE?
I GOT ALL THIS OUT FOR NOTHING.
DROOP
HUH?

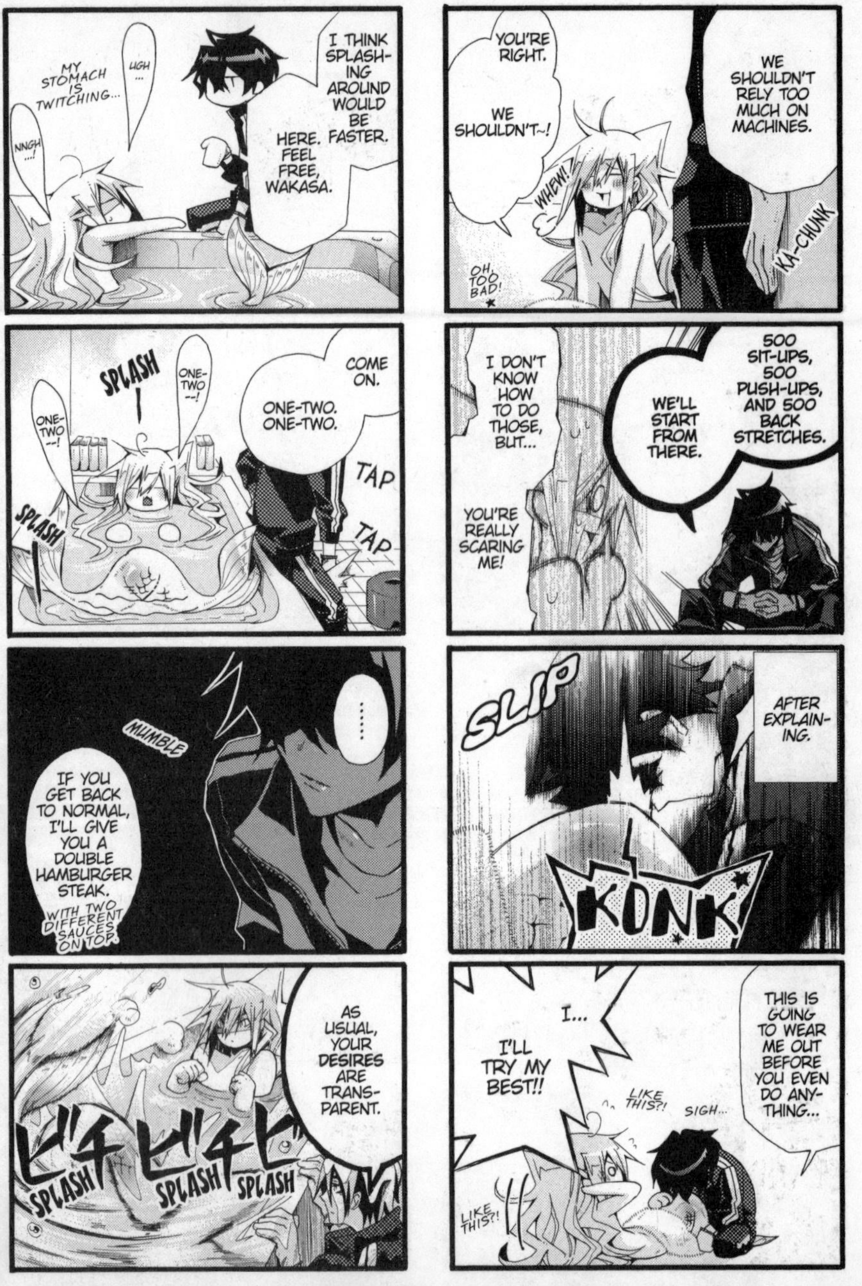
WE SHOULDN'T RELY TOO MUCH ON MACHINES.
KA-CHUNK
YOU'RE RIGHT.
WE SHOULDN'T~!
WHEW!
OH, TOO BAD!
I THINK SPLASHING AROUND WOULD BE FASTER.
HERE. FEEL FREE, WAKASA.
UGH...
MY STOMACH IS TWITCHING...
NNGH...!
500 SIT-UPS, 500 PUSH-UPS, AND 500 BACK STRETCHES.
WE'LL START FROM THERE.
I DON'T KNOW HOW TO DO THOSE, BUT...
YOU'RE REALLY SCARING ME!
COME ON.
ONE-TWO. ONE-TWO.
TAP
TAP
ONE-TWO--!
SPLASH
ONE-TWO--!
SPLASH
AFTER EXPLAINING.
SLIP
KONK
......
MUMBLE
IF YOU GET BACK TO NORMAL, I'LL GIVE YOU A DOUBLE HAMBURGER STEAK.
WITH TWO DIFFERENT SAUCES ON TOP.
THIS IS GOING TO WEAR ME OUT BEFORE YOU EVEN DO ANYTHING...
SIGH...
I...
I'LL TRY MY BEST!!
LIKE THIS?!
LIKE THIS?!
AS USUAL, YOUR DESIRES ARE TRANSPARENT.
ビチ
SPLASH
ビチ
SPLASH
ビ
SPLASH

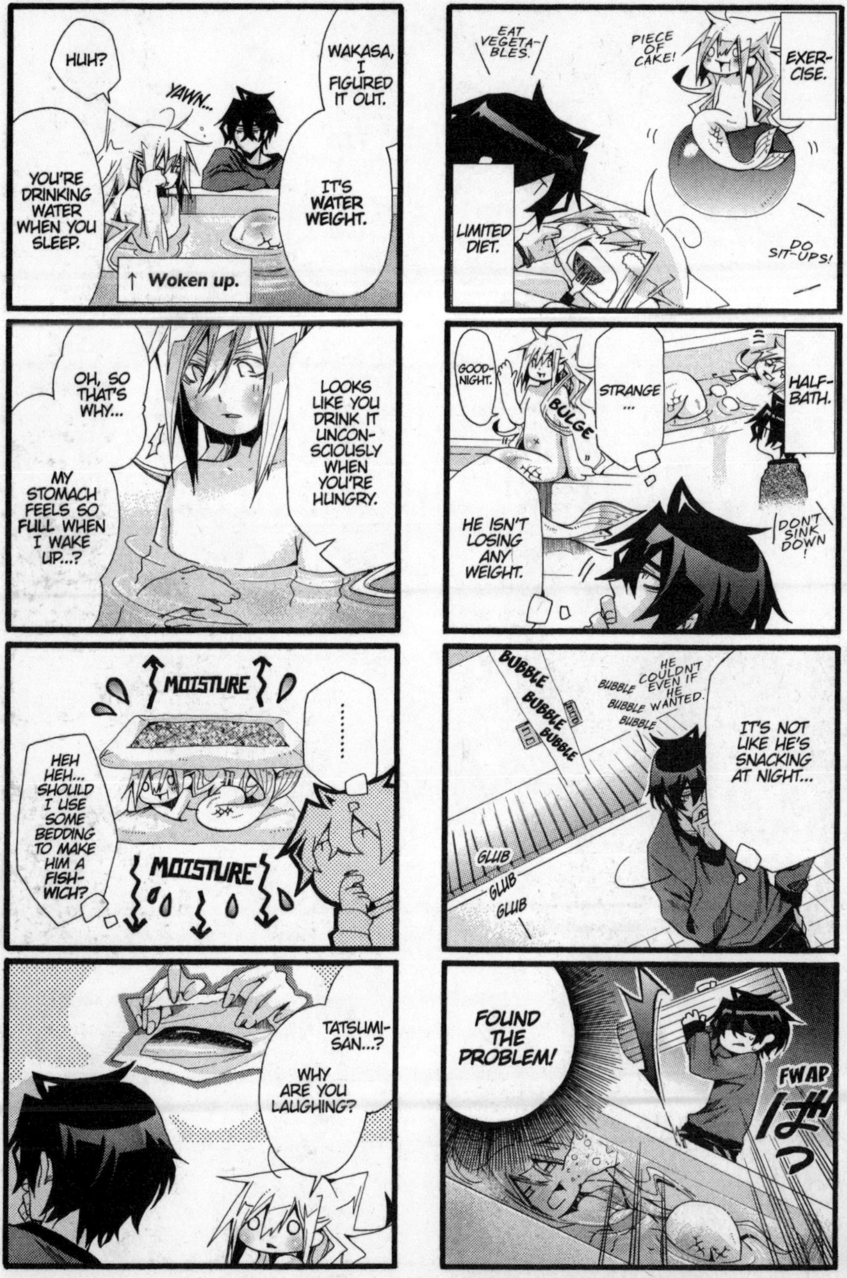
EXERCISE.
PIECE OF CAKE!
EAT VEGETABLES.
DO SIT-UPS!
LIMITED DIET.
HALF-BATH.
DON'T SINK DOWN!
STRANGE...
GOOD-NIGHT.
BULGE
HE ISN'T LOSING ANY WEIGHT.
IT'S NOT LIKE HE'S SNACKING AT NIGHT...
HE COULDN'T EVEN IF HE WANTED.
BUBBLE BUBBLE BUBBLE BUBBLE
BUBBLE BUBBLE BUBBLE
GLUB GLUB GLUB
FWAP ぱっ
FOUND THE PROBLEM!
WAKASA, I FIGURED IT OUT.
IT'S WATER WEIGHT.
YAWN...
HUH?
YOU'RE DRINKING WATER WHEN YOU SLEEP.
↑ Woken up.
LOOKS LIKE YOU DRINK IT UNCONSCIOUSLY WHEN YOU'RE HUNGRY.
OH, SO THAT'S WHY...
MY STOMACH FEELS SO FULL WHEN I WAKE UP...?
......
MOISTURE
HEH HEH... SHOULD I USE SOME BEDDING TO MAKE HIM A FISH-WICH?
MOISTURE
TATSUMI-SAN...?
WHY ARE YOU LAUGHING?

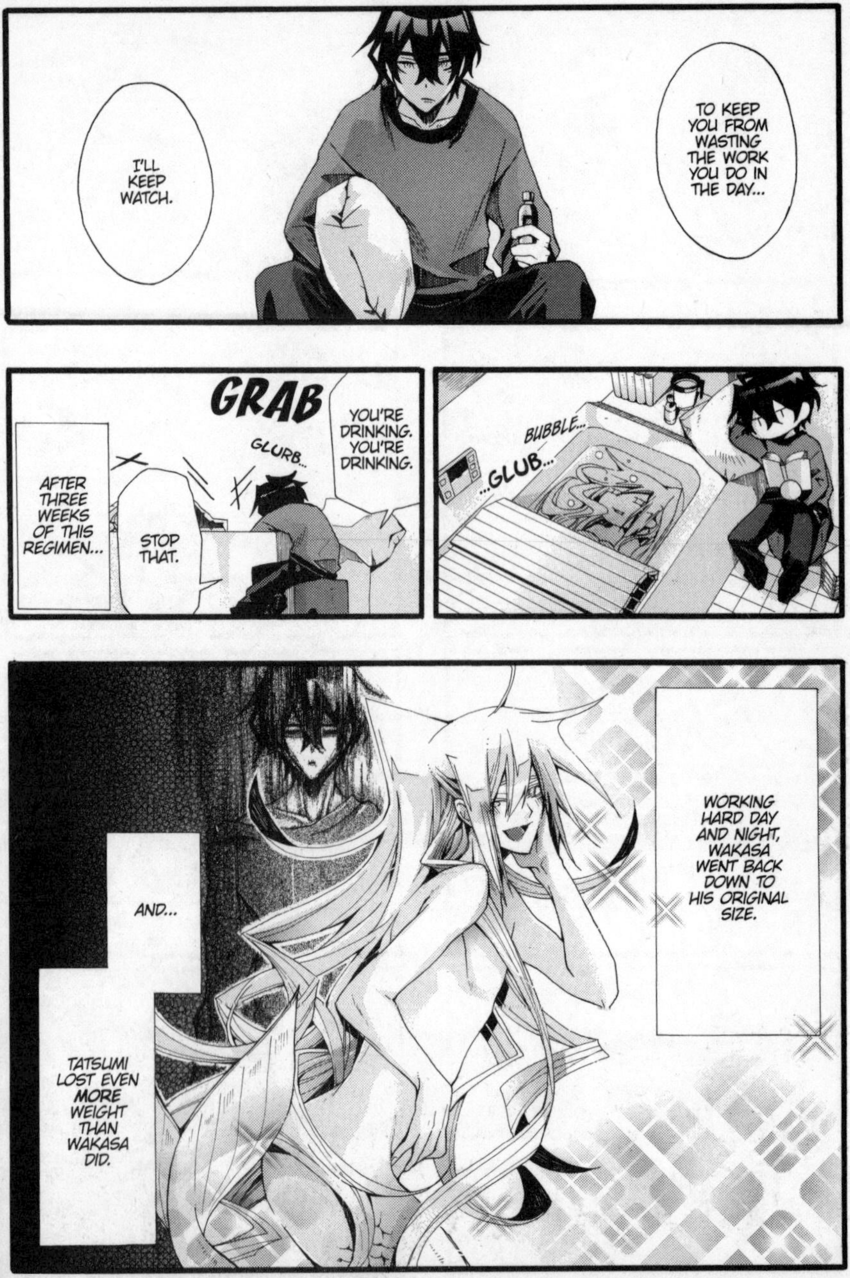
TO KEEP YOU FROM WASTING THE WORK YOU DO IN THE DAY...
I'LL KEEP WATCH.
BUBBLE...
...GLUB...
YOU'RE DRINKING. YOU'RE DRINKING.
GRAB
GLURB...
STOP THAT.
AFTER THREE WEEKS OF THIS REGIMEN...
WORKING HARD DAY AND NIGHT, WAKASA WENT BACK DOWN TO HIS ORIGINAL SIZE.
AND...
TATSUMI LOST EVEN MORE WEIGHT THAN WAKASA DID.

Merman in My Tub

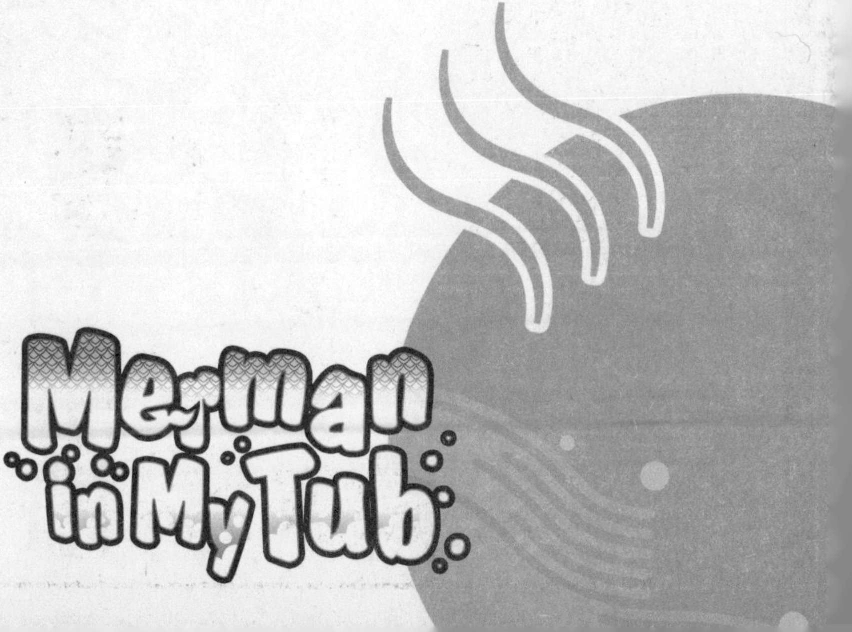

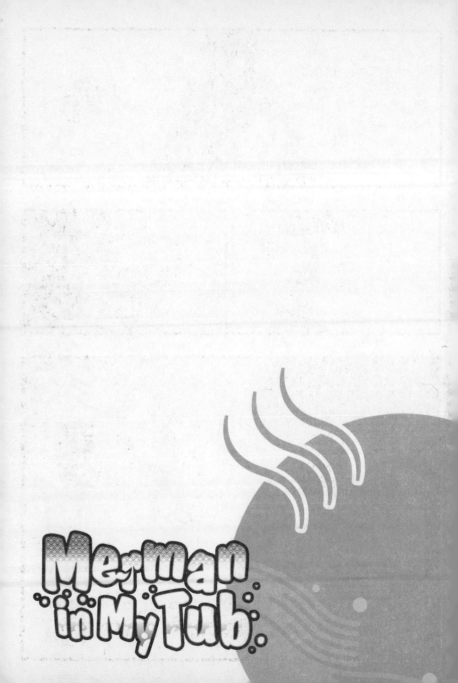

オレん家(ち)のフロ事情

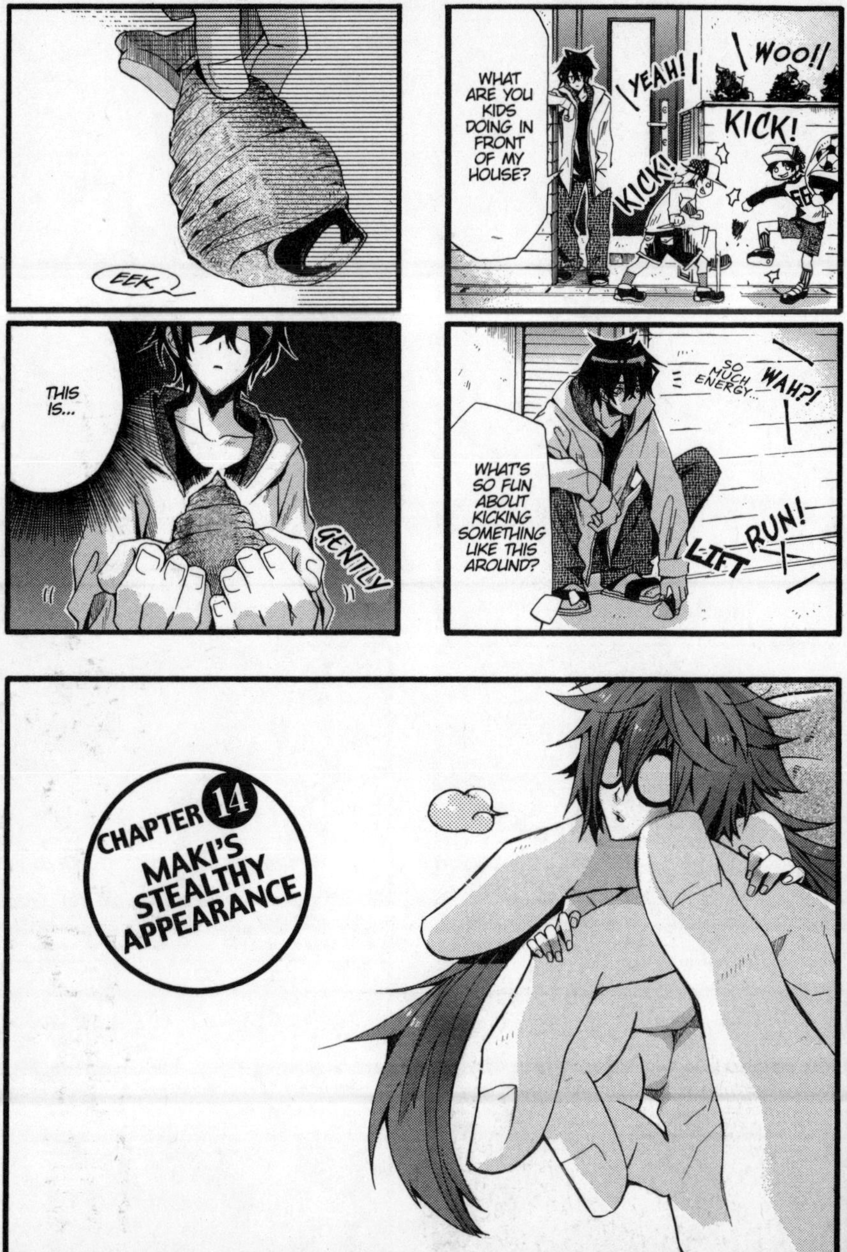
WHAT ARE YOU KIDS DOING IN FRONT OF MY HOUSE?
YEAH!
WOO!!
KICK!
KICK!
EEK.
SO MUCH ENERGY...
WAH?!
WHAT'S SO FUN ABOUT KICKING SOMETHING LIKE THIS AROUND?
RUN!
LIFT
THIS IS...
GENTLY
CHAPTER 14
MAKI'S STEALTHY APPEARANCE

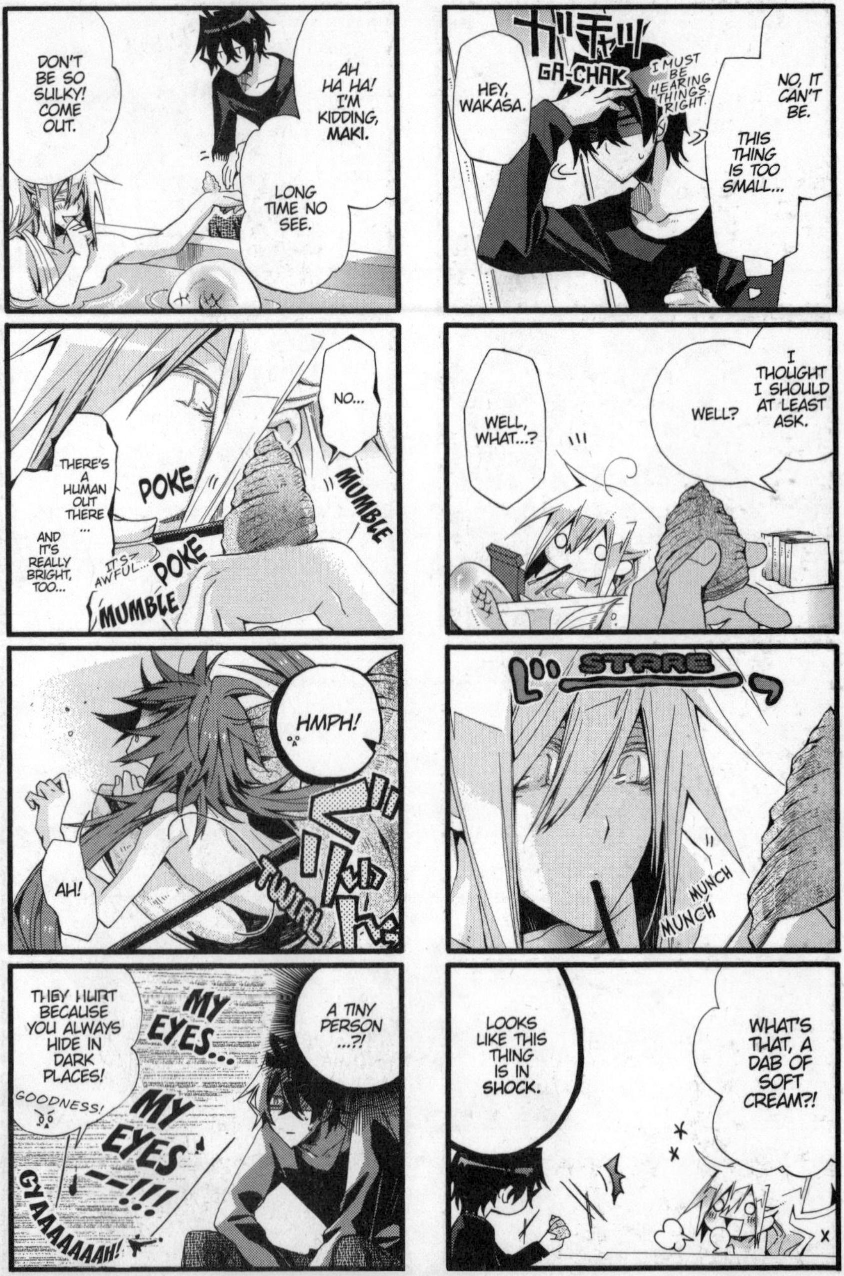
GA-CHAK
NO, IT CAN'T BE.
THIS THING IS TOO SMALL...
I MUST BE HEARING THINGS. RIGHT.
HEY, WAKASA.
AH HA HA! I'M KIDDING, MAKI.
LONG TIME NO SEE.
DON'T BE SO SULKY! COME OUT.
I THOUGHT I SHOULD AT LEAST ASK.
WELL?
WELL, WHAT...?
NO...
MUMBLE
POKE
THERE'S A HUMAN OUT THERE ...
AND IT'S REALLY BRIGHT, TOO...
IT'S AWFUL...
POKE
MUMBLE
STARE
MUNCH
MUNCH
HMPH!
TWIRL
AH!
WHAT'S THAT, A DAB OF SOFT CREAM?!
LOOKS LIKE THIS THING IS IN SHOCK.
A TINY PERSON ...?!
MY EYES...
MY EYES---!!!
THEY HURT BECAUSE YOU ALWAYS HIDE IN DARK PLACES!
GOODNESS!
GYAAAAAAAH!

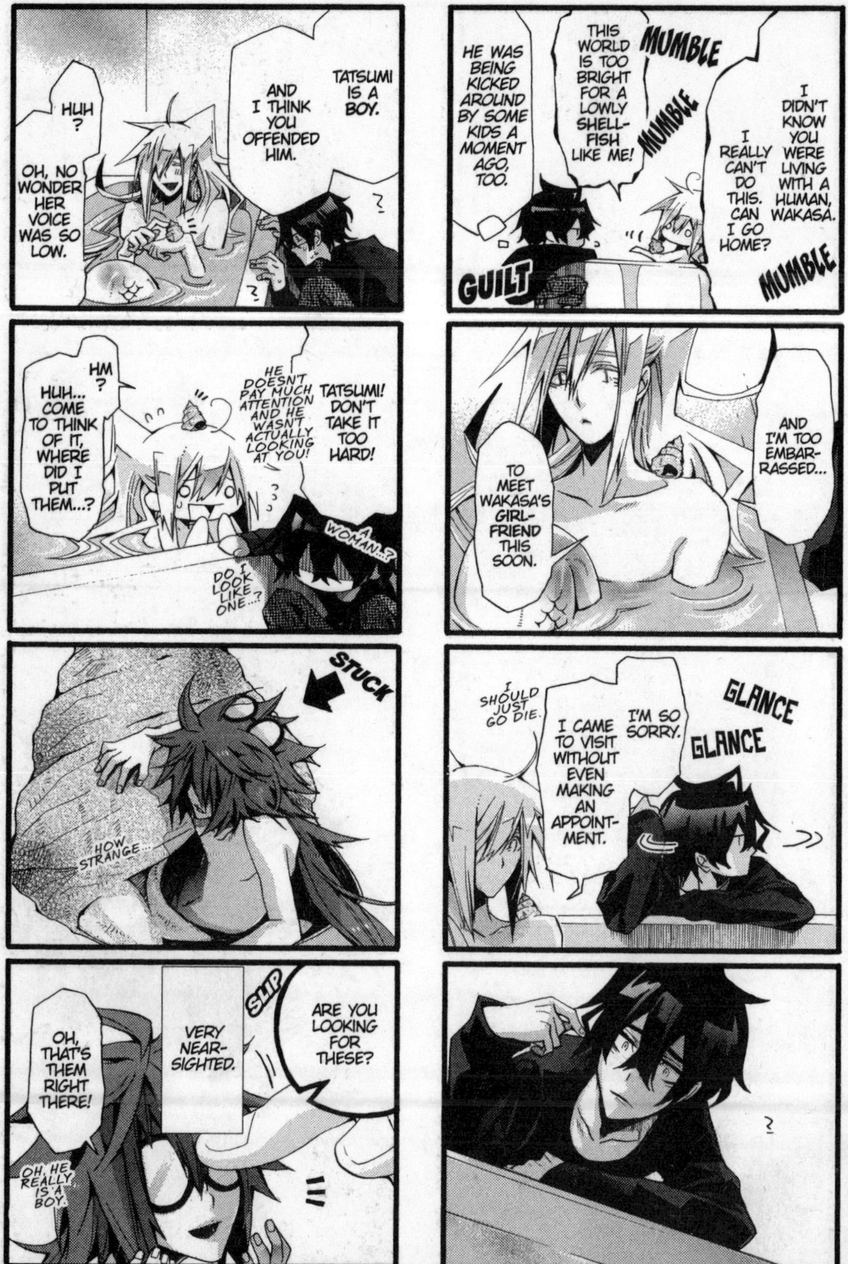
MUMBLE
MUMBLE
I DIDN'T KNOW YOU WERE LIVING WITH A HUMAN, WAKASA.
I REALLY CAN'T DO THIS. CAN I GO HOME?
THIS WORLD IS TOO BRIGHT FOR A LOWLY SHELL-FISH LIKE ME!
HE WAS BEING KICKED AROUND BY SOME KIDS A MOMENT AGO, TOO.
MUMBLE
GUILT
AND I'M TOO EMBAR-RASSED...
TO MEET WAKASA'S GIRL-FRIEND THIS SOON.
GLANCE
GLANCE
I'M SO SORRY.
I CAME TO VISIT WITHOUT EVEN MAKING AN APPOINT-MENT.
I SHOULD JUST GO DIE.
TATSUMI IS A BOY.
AND I THINK YOU OFFENDED HIM.
HUH?
OH, NO WONDER HER VOICE WAS SO LOW.
TATSUMI! DON'T TAKE IT TOO HARD!
HE DOESN'T PAY MUCH ATTENTION AND HE WASN'T ACTUALLY LOOKING AT YOU!
HM?
HUH... COME TO THINK OF IT, WHERE DID I PUT THEM...?
A WOMAN...?
DO I LOOK LIKE ONE...?
STUCK
HOW STRANGE...
ARE YOU LOOKING FOR THESE?
SLIP
VERY NEAR-SIGHTED.
OH, THAT'S THEM RIGHT THERE!
OH, HE REALLY IS A BOY.

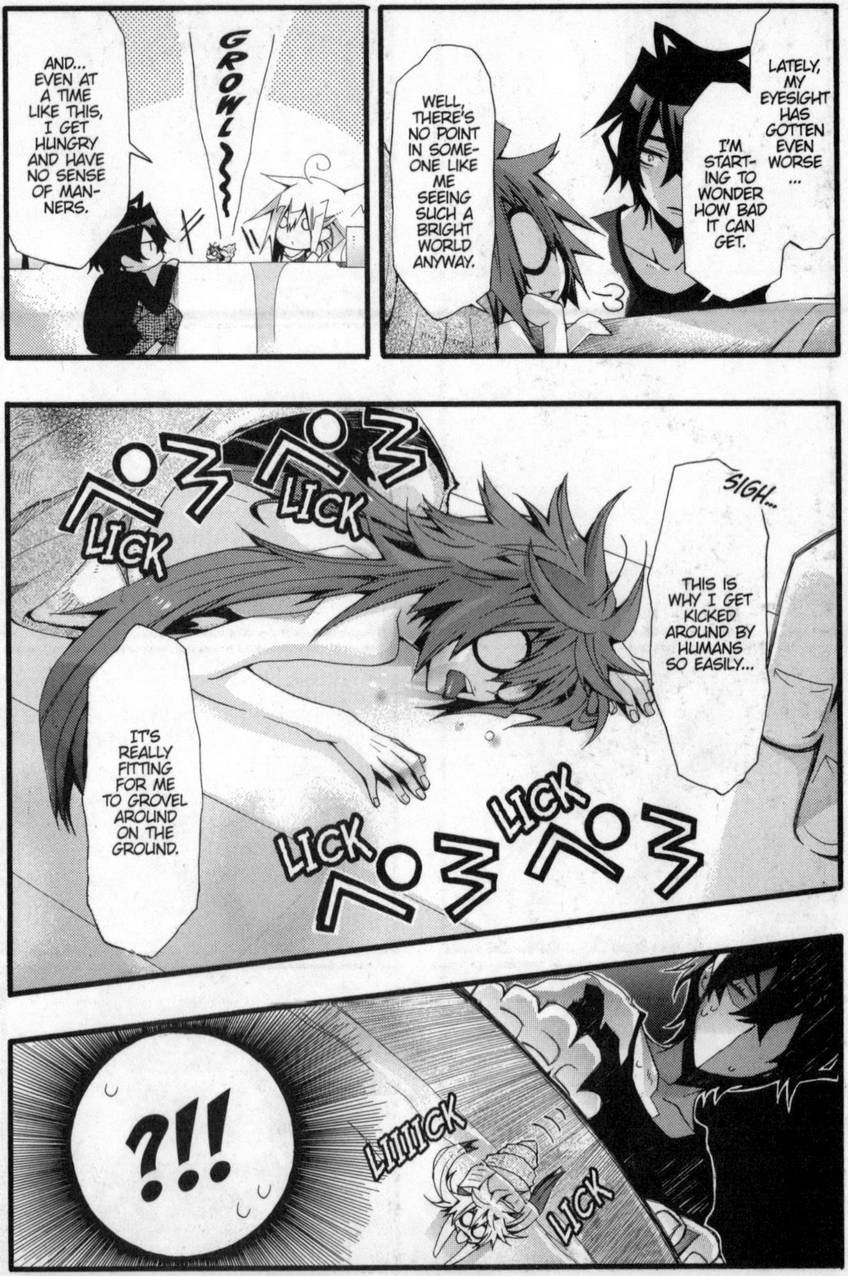
LATELY, MY EYESIGHT HAS GOTTEN EVEN WORSE...
I'M STARTING TO WONDER HOW BAD IT CAN GET.
WELL, THERE'S NO POINT IN SOMEONE LIKE ME SEEING SUCH A BRIGHT WORLD ANYWAY.
AND... EVEN AT A TIME LIKE THIS, I GET HUNGRY AND HAVE NO SENSE OF MANNERS.
GROWL~~~
SIGH...
THIS IS WHY I GET KICKED AROUND BY HUMANS SO EASILY...
ぺろ LICK
ぺろ LICK
IT'S REALLY FITTING FOR ME TO GROVEL AROUND ON THE GROUND.
ぺろ LICK
ぺろ LICK
LIIIICK
LICK
?!!

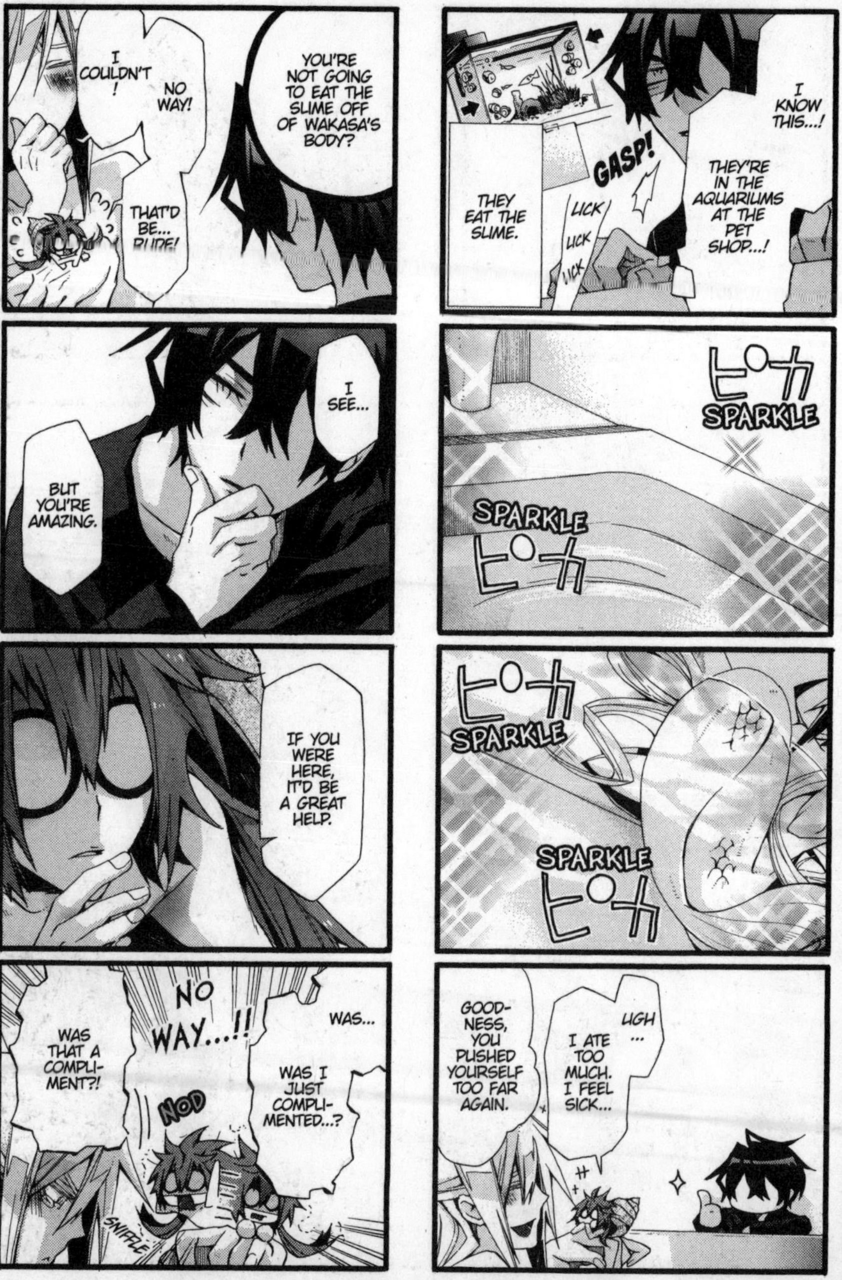
I KNOW THIS...!
THEY'RE IN THE AQUARIUMS AT THE PET SHOP...!
GASP!
THEY EAT THE SLIME.
LICK LICK LICK
SPARKLE
SPARKLE
SPARKLE
SPARKLE
UGH ...
I ATE TOO MUCH. I FEEL SICK...
GOODNESS, YOU PUSHED YOURSELF TOO FAR AGAIN.
YOU'RE NOT GOING TO EAT THE SLIME OFF OF WAKASA'S BODY?
NO WAY!
THAT'D BE... RUDE!
I COULDN'T!
I SEE...
BUT YOU'RE AMAZING.
IF YOU WERE HERE, IT'D BE A GREAT HELP.
WAS...
WAS I JUST COMPLIMENTED...?
NO WAY...!!
NOD
WAS THAT A COMPLIMENT?!
SNIFFLE

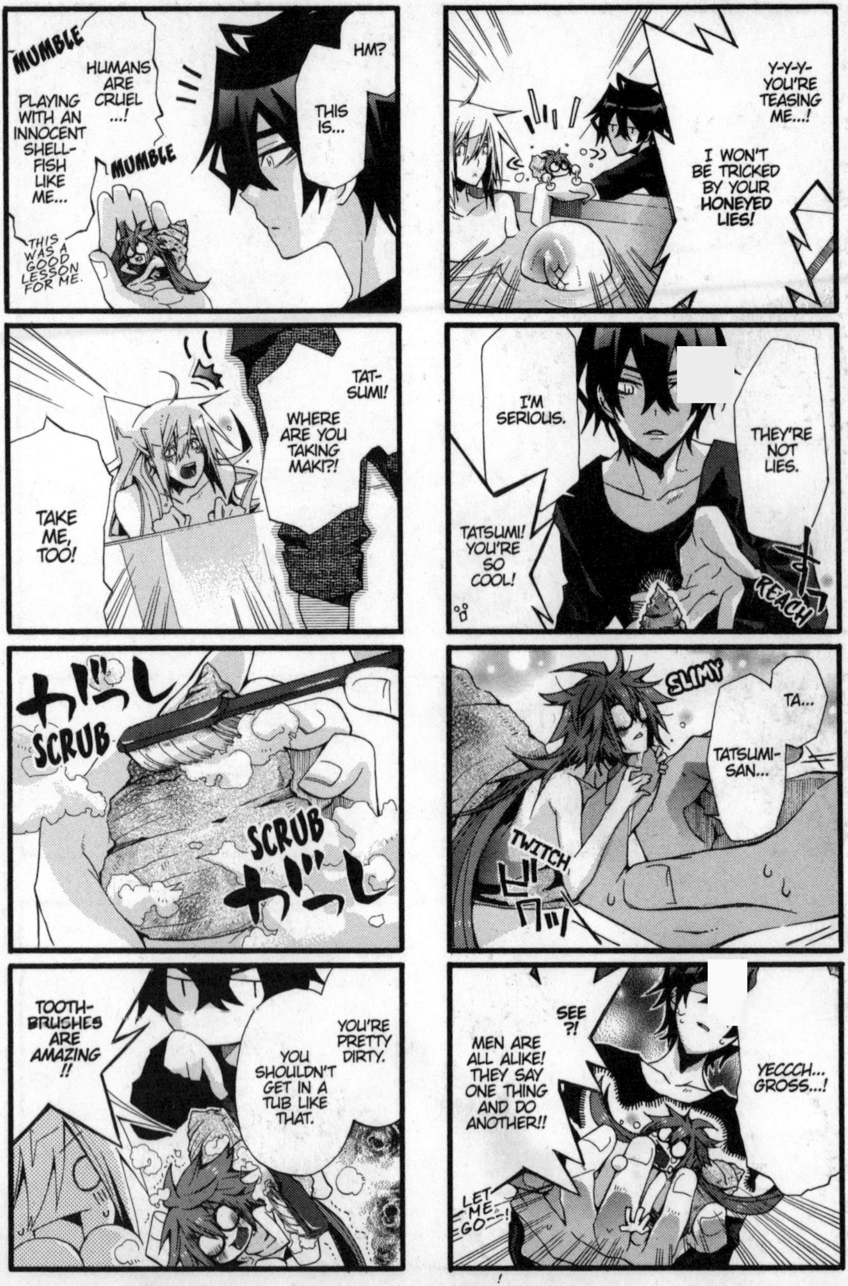
Y-Y-Y-YOU'RE TEASING ME...!
I WON'T BE TRICKED BY YOUR HONEYED LIES!
I'M SERIOUS.
THEY'RE NOT LIES.
TATSUMI! YOU'RE SO COOL!
REACH
SLIMY
TA...
TATSUMI-SAN...
TWITCH
ビクッ
YECCCH... GROSS...!
SEE?!
MEN ARE ALL ALIKE! THEY SAY ONE THING AND DO ANOTHER!!
LET ME GO--!
HM?
THIS IS...
HUMANS ARE CRUEL...!
MUMBLE
PLAYING WITH AN INNOCENT SHELLFISH LIKE ME...
MUMBLE
THIS WAS A GOOD LESSON FOR ME.
TAT-SUMI!
WHERE ARE YOU TAKING MAKI?!
TAKE ME, TOO!
SCRUB
SCRUB
YOU'RE PRETTY DIRTY.
YOU SHOULDN'T GET IN A TUB LIKE THAT.
TOOTH-BRUSHES ARE AMAZING!!

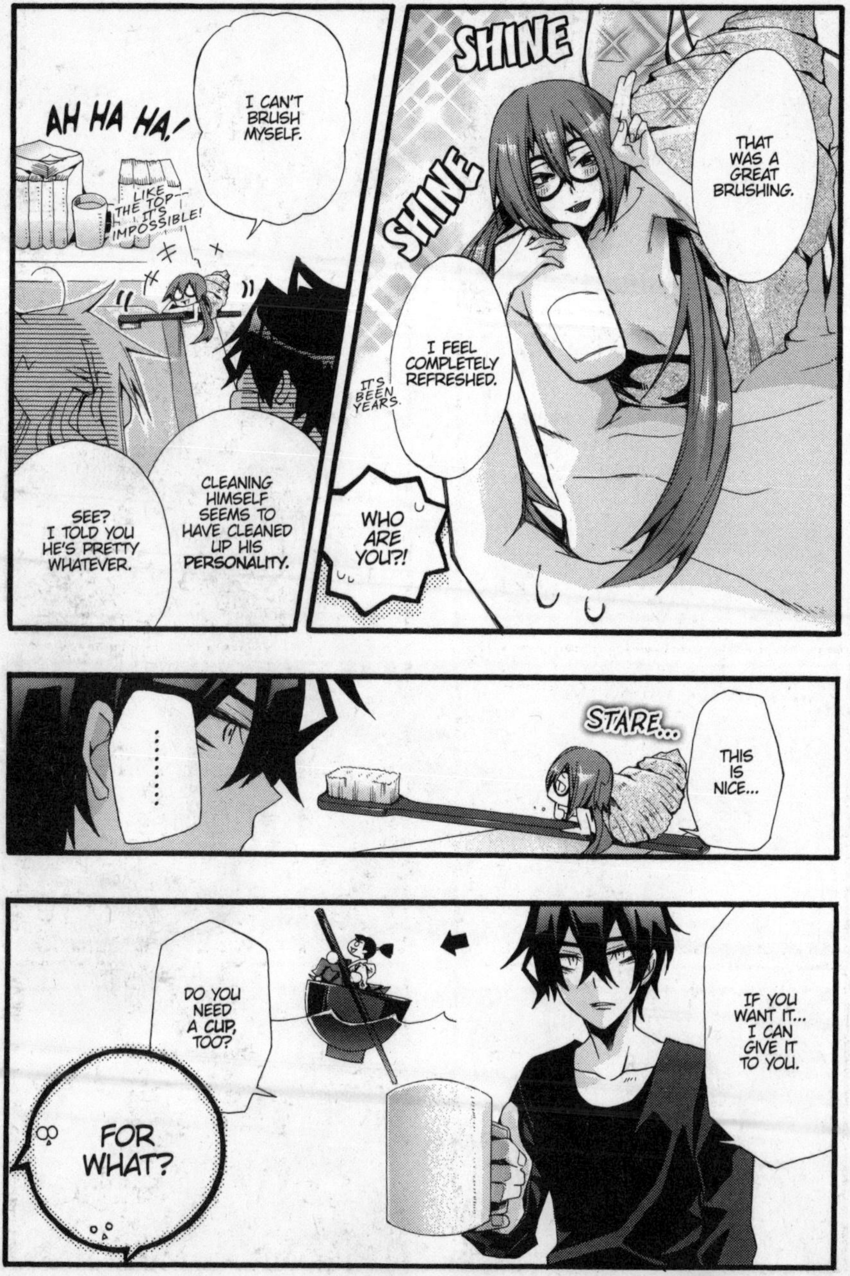
SHINE
SHINE
THAT WAS A GREAT BRUSHING.
I FEEL COMPLETELY REFRESHED.
IT'S BEEN YEARS.
WHO ARE YOU?!
I CAN'T BRUSH MYSELF.
AH HA HA!
LIKE THE TOP-- IT'S IMPOSSIBLE!
CLEANING HIMSELF SEEMS TO HAVE CLEANED UP HIS PERSONALITY.
SEE? I TOLD YOU HE'S PRETTY WHATEVER.
STARE...
THIS IS NICE...
....
IF YOU WANT IT... I CAN GIVE IT TO YOU.
DO YOU NEED A CUP, TOO?
FOR WHAT?

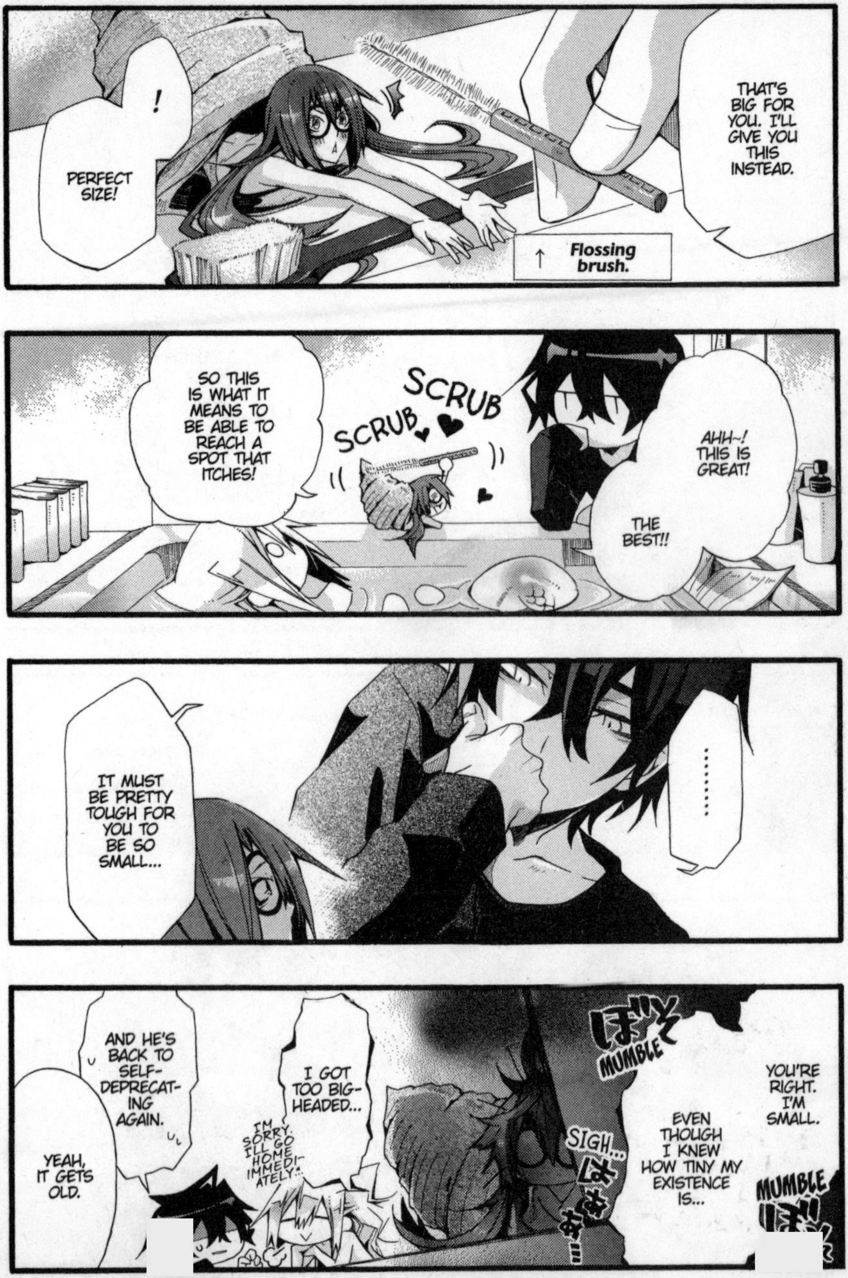
THAT'S BIG FOR YOU. I'LL GIVE YOU THIS INSTEAD.
↑ Flossing brush.
!
PERFECT SIZE!
AHH~! THIS IS GREAT!
THE BEST!!
SCRUB
SCRUB
SO THIS IS WHAT IT MEANS TO BE ABLE TO REACH A SPOT THAT ITCHES!
......
IT MUST BE PRETTY TOUGH FOR YOU TO BE SO SMALL...
YOU'RE RIGHT. I'M SMALL.
MUMBLE
MUMBLE
EVEN THOUGH I KNEW HOW TINY MY EXISTENCE IS...
SIGH...
I GOT TOO BIG-HEADED...
I'M SORRY. I'LL GO HOME IMMEDIATELY...
AND HE'S BACK TO SELF-DEPRECATING AGAIN.
YEAH, IT GETS OLD.

Merman in My Tub

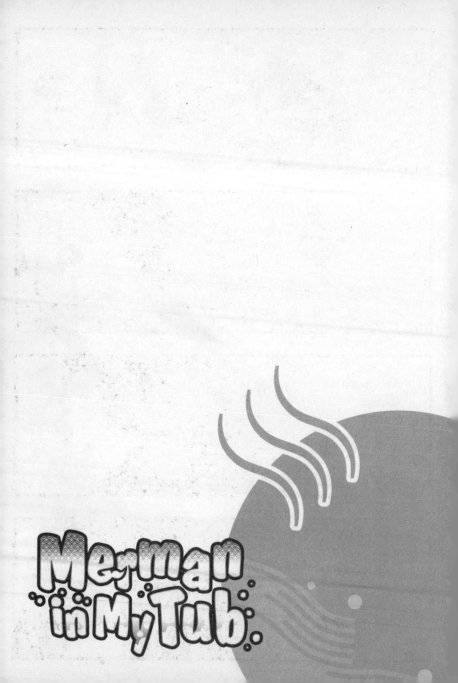

オレん家(ち)のフロ事情

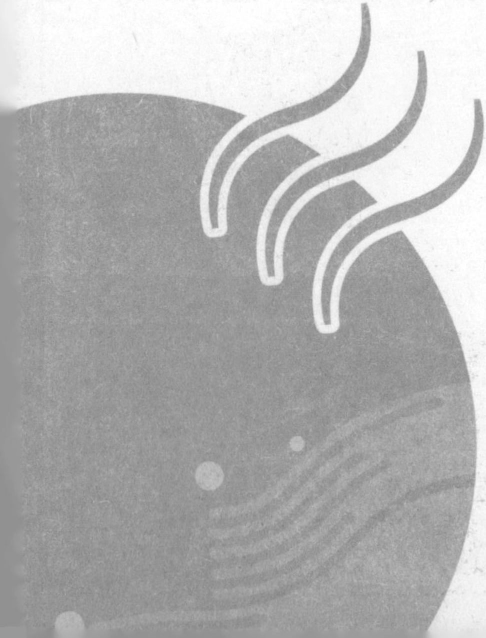

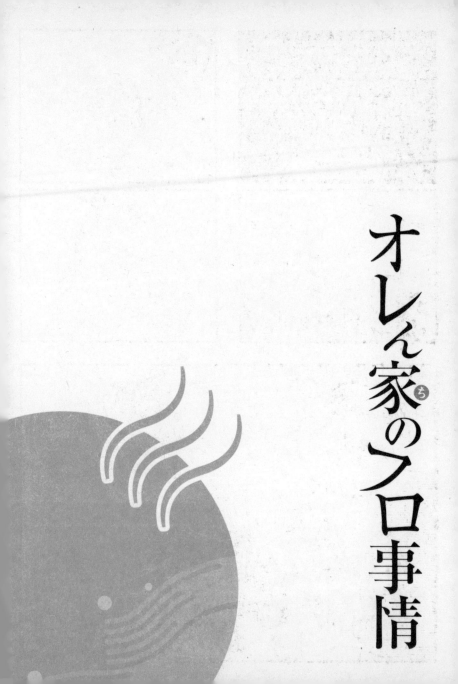

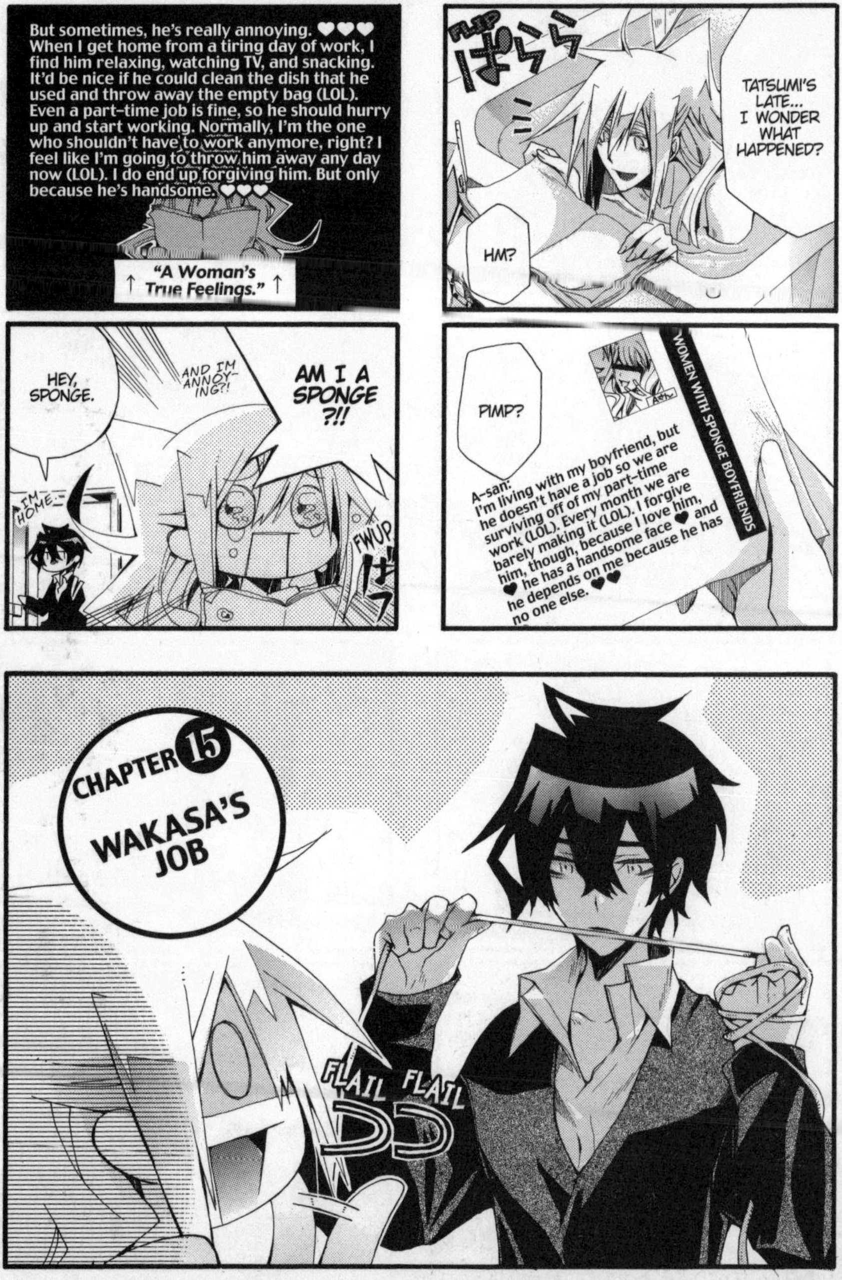
FLIP
TATSUMI'S LATE... I WONDER WHAT HAPPENED?
HM?
But sometimes, he's really annoying. ❤❤❤ When I get home from a tiring day of work, I find him relaxing, watching TV, and snacking. It'd be nice if he could clean the dish that he used and throw away the empty bag (LOL). Even a part-time job is fine, so he should hurry up and start working. Normally, I'm the one who shouldn't have to work anymore, right? I feel like I'm going to throw him away any day now (LOL). I do end up forgiving him. But only because he's handsome. ❤❤❤
↑ "A Woman's True Feelings." ↑
WOMEN WITH SPONGE BOYFRIENDS
A-san: I'm living with my boyfriend, but he doesn't have a job so we are surviving off of my part-time work (LOL). Every month we are barely making it (LOL). I forgive him, though, because I love him, ❤ he has a handsome face ❤ and he depends on me because he has no one else. ❤❤
PIMP?
AM I A SPONGE ?!!
AND I'M ANNOY-ING?!
HEY, SPONGE.
I'M HOME.
FWUP
CHAPTER 15
WAKASA'S JOB
FLAIL FLAIL

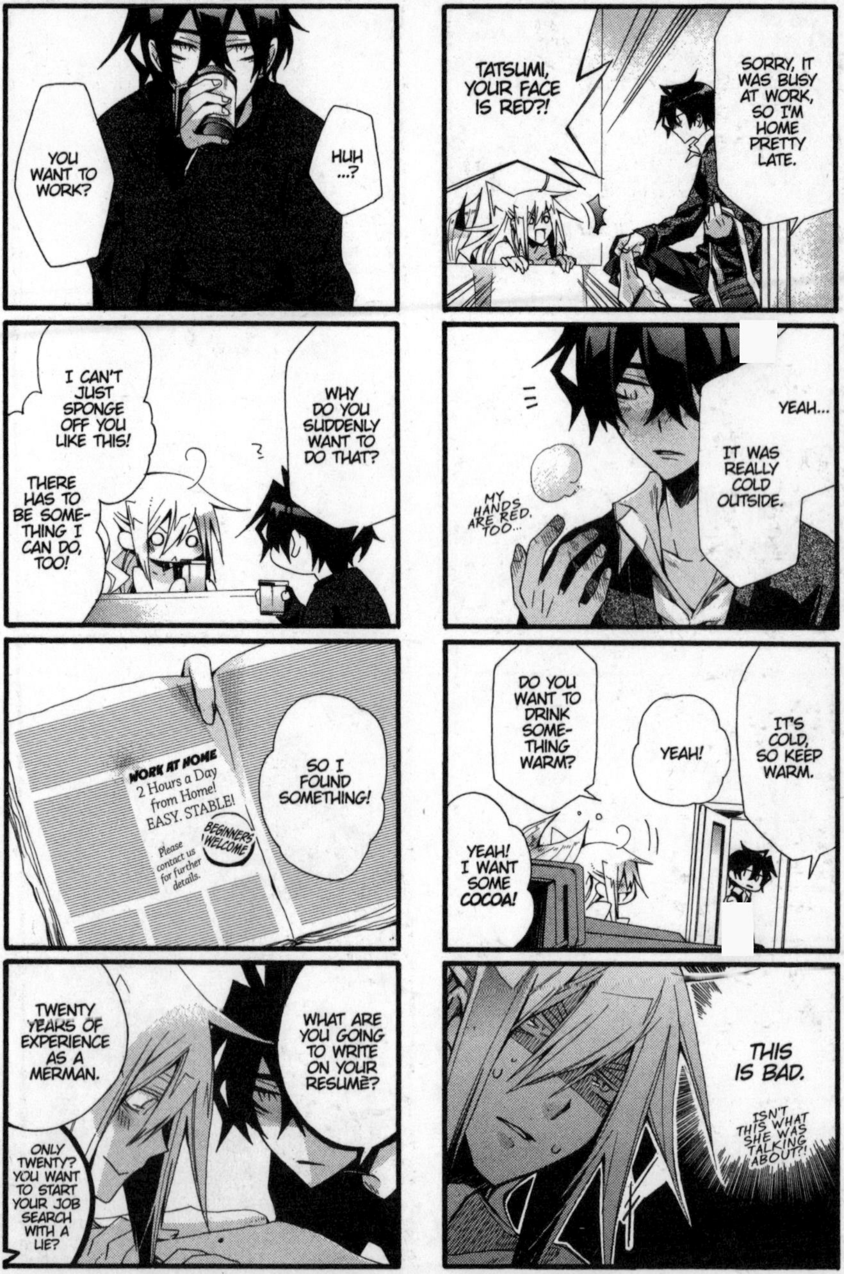
SORRY, IT WAS BUSY AT WORK, SO I'M HOME PRETTY LATE.
TATSUMI, YOUR FACE IS RED?!
YEAH...
IT WAS REALLY COLD OUTSIDE.
MY HANDS ARE RED, TOO...
IT'S COLD, SO KEEP WARM.
YEAH!
DO YOU WANT TO DRINK SOME-THING WARM?
YEAH! I WANT SOME COCOA!
THIS IS BAD.
ISN'T THIS WHAT SHE WAS TALKING ABOUT?!
HUH ...?
YOU WANT TO WORK?
WHY DO YOU SUDDENLY WANT TO DO THAT?
I CAN'T JUST SPONGE OFF YOU LIKE THIS!
THERE HAS TO BE SOME-THING I CAN DO, TOO!
SO I FOUND SOMETHING!
WORK AT HOME
2 Hours a Day from Home! EASY. STABLE!
BEGINNERS' WELCOME
Please contact us for further details.
WHAT ARE YOU GOING TO WRITE ON YOUR RESUMÉ?
TWENTY YEARS OF EXPERIENCE AS A MERMAN.
ONLY TWENTY? YOU WANT TO START YOUR JOB SEARCH WITH A LIE?

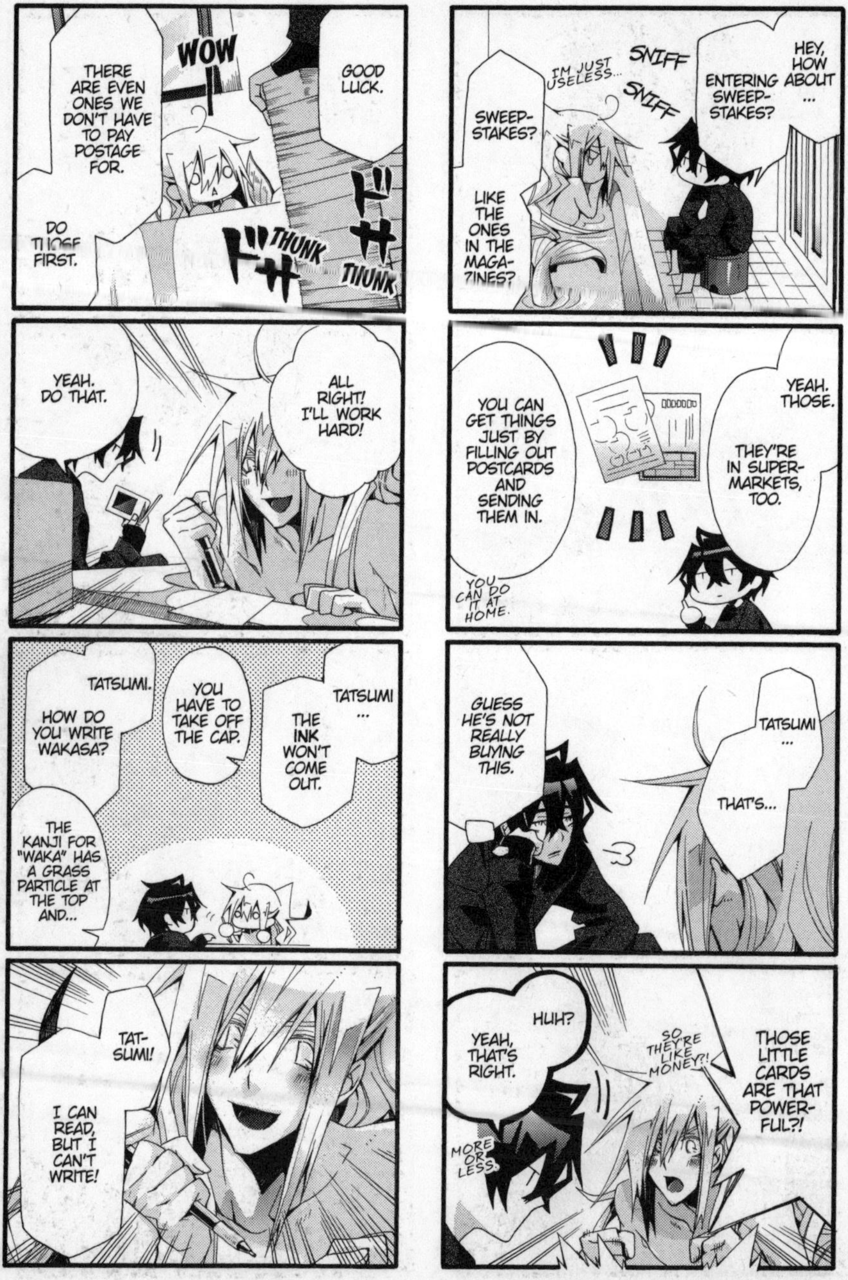
HEY, HOW ABOUT ... ENTERING SWEEP-STAKES?
SNIFF
SNIFF
I'M JUST USELESS...
SWEEP-STAKES?
LIKE THE ONES IN THE MAGAZINES?
YEAH. THOSE.
THEY'RE IN SUPER-MARKETS, TOO.
YOU CAN GET THINGS JUST BY FILLING OUT POSTCARDS AND SENDING THEM IN.
YOU CAN DO IT AT HOME.
TATSUMI ...
THAT'S...
GUESS HE'S NOT REALLY BUYING THIS.
THOSE LITTLE CARDS ARE THAT POWER-FUL?!
SO THEY'RE LIKE MONEY?!
HUH?
YEAH, THAT'S RIGHT.
MORE OR LESS.
GOOD LUCK.
WOW
THUNK
THUNK
THERE ARE EVEN ONES WE DON'T HAVE TO PAY POSTAGE FOR.
DO THOSE FIRST.
ALL RIGHT! I'LL WORK HARD!
YEAH. DO THAT.
TATSUMI ...
THE INK WON'T COME OUT.
YOU HAVE TO TAKE OFF THE CAP.
TATSUMI.
HOW DO YOU WRITE WAKASA?
THE KANJI FOR "WAKA" HAS A GRASS PARTICLE AT THE TOP AND...
TAT-SUMI!
I CAN READ, BUT I CAN'T WRITE!

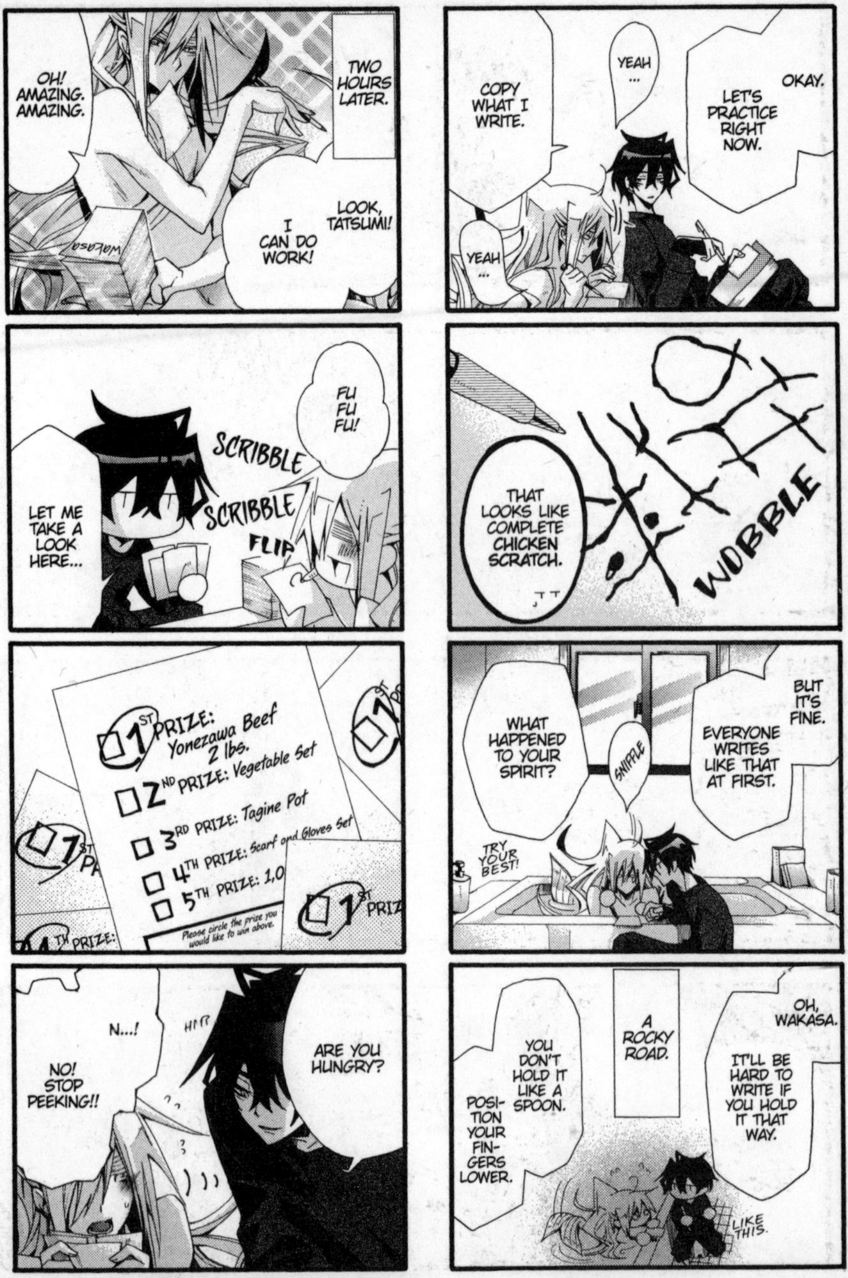
OKAY.
LET'S PRACTICE RIGHT NOW.
YEAH...
COPY WHAT I WRITE.
YEAH...
THAT LOOKS LIKE COMPLETE CHICKEN SCRATCH.
WOBBLE
BUT IT'S FINE.
EVERYONE WRITES LIKE THAT AT FIRST.
SNIFFLE
WHAT HAPPENED TO YOUR SPIRIT?
TRY YOUR BEST!
OH, WAKASA.
IT'LL BE HARD TO WRITE IF YOU HOLD IT THAT WAY.
A ROCKY ROAD.
YOU DON'T HOLD IT LIKE A SPOON.
POSI- TION YOUR FIN- GERS LOWER.
LIKE THIS.
TWO HOURS LATER.
LOOK, TATSUMI!
I CAN DO WORK!
OH! AMAZING. AMAZING.
FU FU FU!
SCRIBBLE
SCRIBBLE
FLIP
LET ME TAKE A LOOK HERE...
1ST PRIZE: Yonezawa Beef 2 lbs.
2ND PRIZE: Vegetable Set
3RD PRIZE: Tagine Pot
4TH PRIZE: Scarf and Gloves Set
5TH PRIZE: 1,0
Please circle the prize you would like to win above.
ARE YOU HUNGRY?
HM?
N...!
NO! STOP PEEKING!!

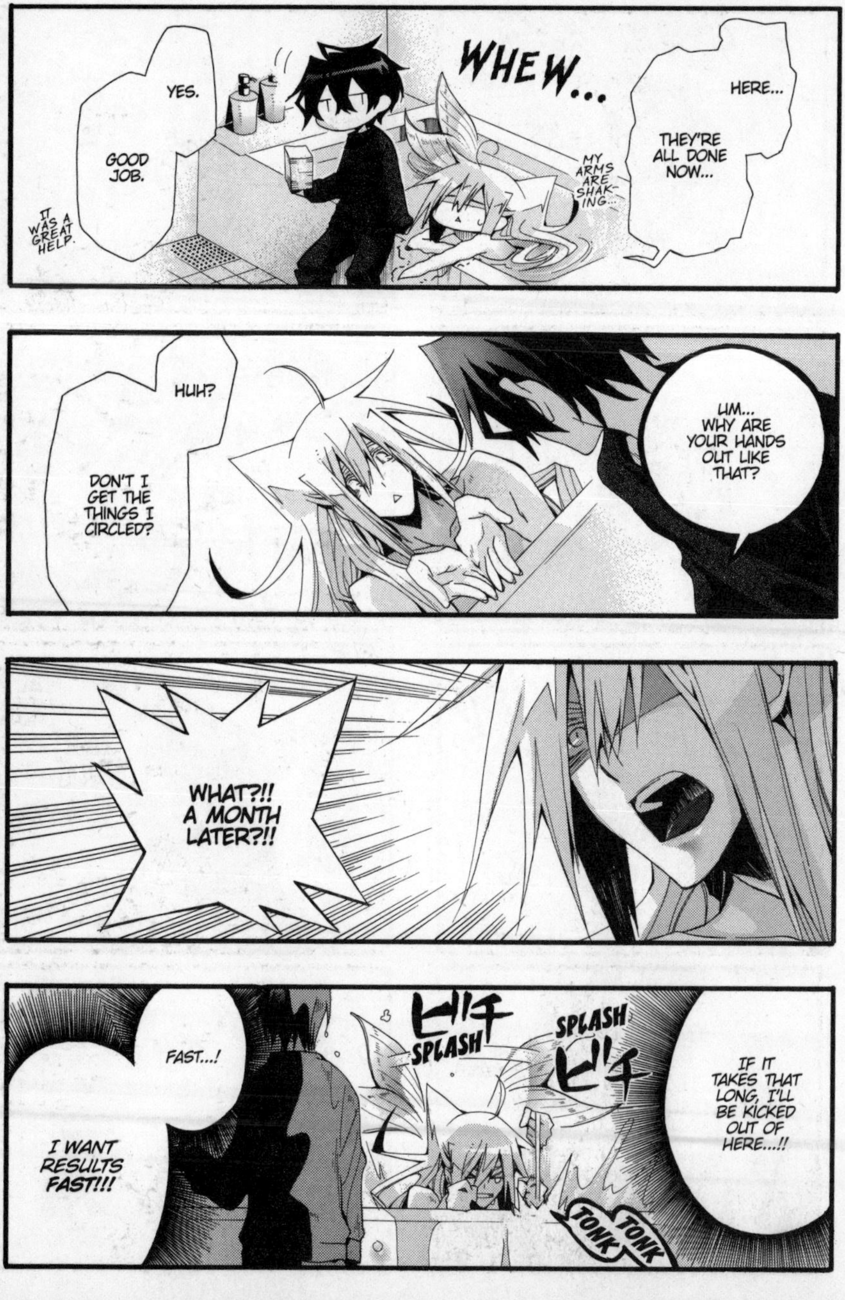
HERE... THEY'RE ALL DONE NOW...
MY ARMS ARE SHAKING...
WHEW...
YES. GOOD JOB.
IT WAS A GREAT HELP.
UM... WHY ARE YOUR HANDS OUT LIKE THAT?
HUH? DON'T I GET THE THINGS I CIRCLED?
WHAT?!! A MONTH LATER?!!
IF IT TAKES THAT LONG, I'LL BE KICKED OUT OF HERE...!!
SPLASH
ビチ
SPLASH
ビチ
TONK
TONK
FAST...!
I WANT RESULTS FAST!!!

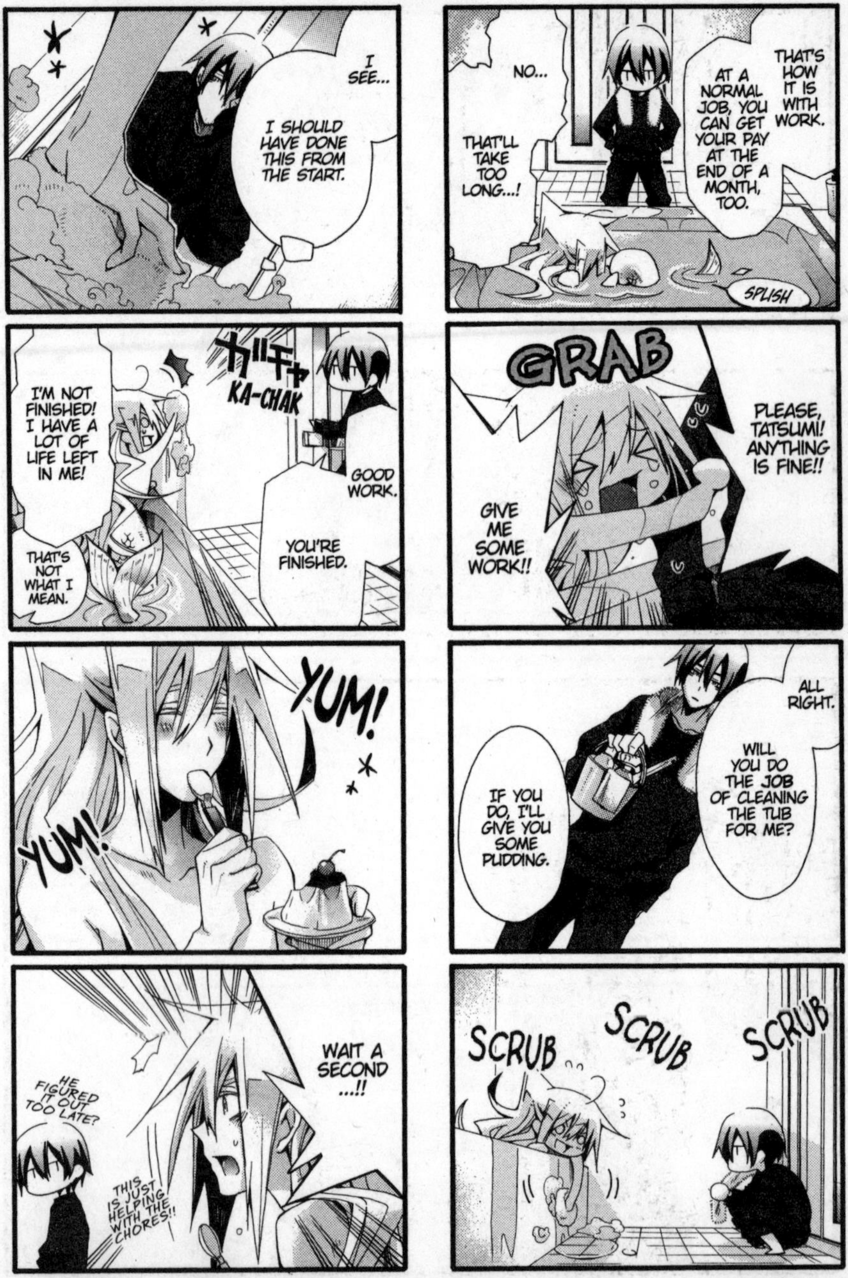
THAT'S HOW IT IS WITH WORK.
AT A NORMAL JOB, YOU CAN GET YOUR PAY AT THE END OF A MONTH, TOO.
NO...
THAT'LL TAKE TOO LONG...!
SPLISH
GRAB
PLEASE, TATSUMI! ANYTHING IS FINE!!
GIVE ME SOME WORK!!
ALL RIGHT.
WILL YOU DO THE JOB OF CLEANING THE TUB FOR ME?
IF YOU DO, I'LL GIVE YOU SOME PUDDING.
SCRUB
SCRUB
SCRUB
I SEE...
I SHOULD HAVE DONE THIS FROM THE START.
ガチャ
KA-CHAK
GOOD WORK.
YOU'RE FINISHED.
I'M NOT FINISHED! I HAVE A LOT OF LIFE LEFT IN ME!
THAT'S NOT WHAT I MEAN.
YUM!
YUM!
WAIT A SECOND...!!
THIS IS JUST HELPING WITH THE CHORES!!
HE FIGURED IT OUT TOO LATE?

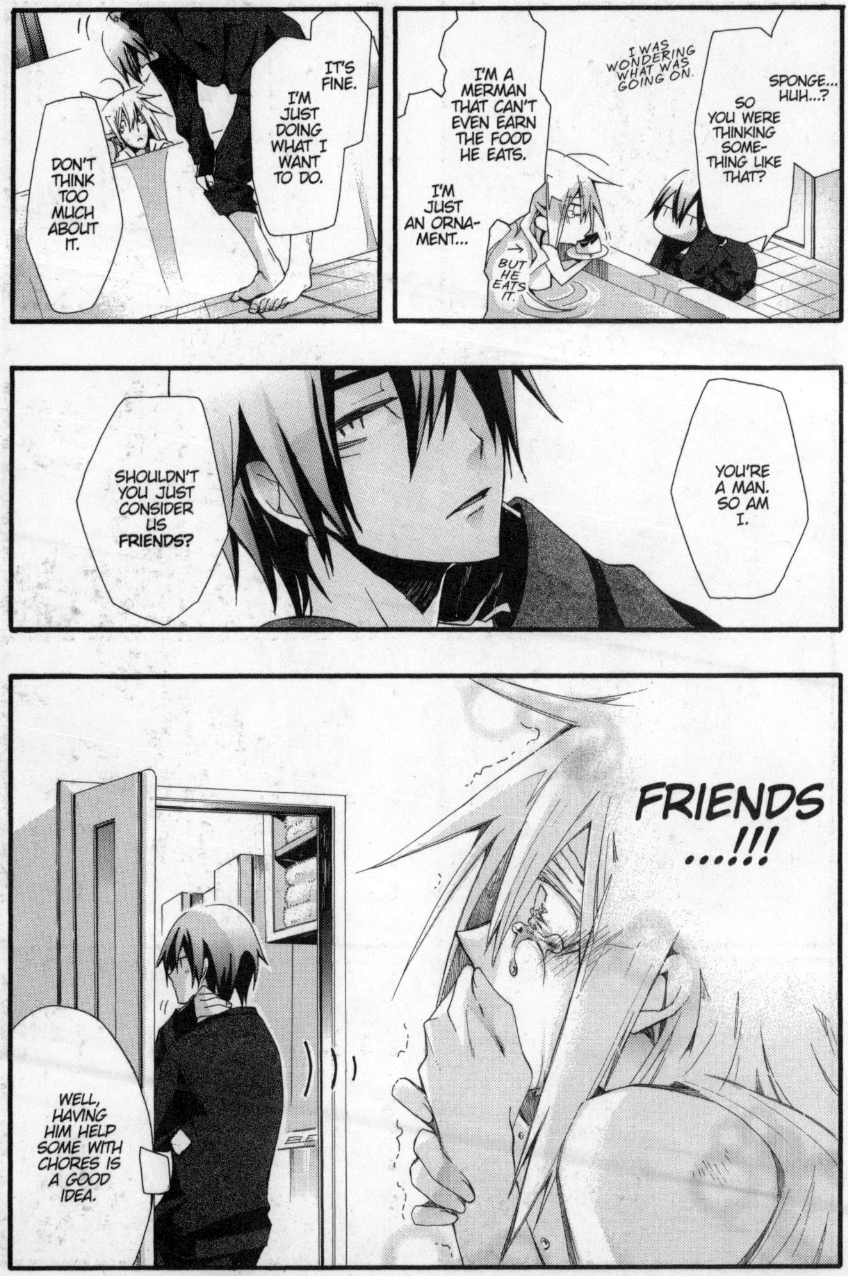
SPONGE... HUH...?
SO YOU WERE THINKING SOME-THING LIKE THAT?
I WAS WONDERING WHAT WAS GOING ON.
I'M A MERMAN THAT CAN'T EVEN EARN THE FOOD HE EATS.
I'M JUST AN ORNA-MENT...
→ BUT HE EATS IT.
IT'S FINE.
I'M JUST DOING WHAT I WANT TO DO.
DON'T THINK TOO MUCH ABOUT IT.
YOU'RE A MAN. SO AM I.
SHOULDN'T YOU JUST CONSIDER US FRIENDS?
FRIENDS ...!!!
WELL, HAVING HIM HELP SOME WITH CHORES IS A GOOD IDEA.

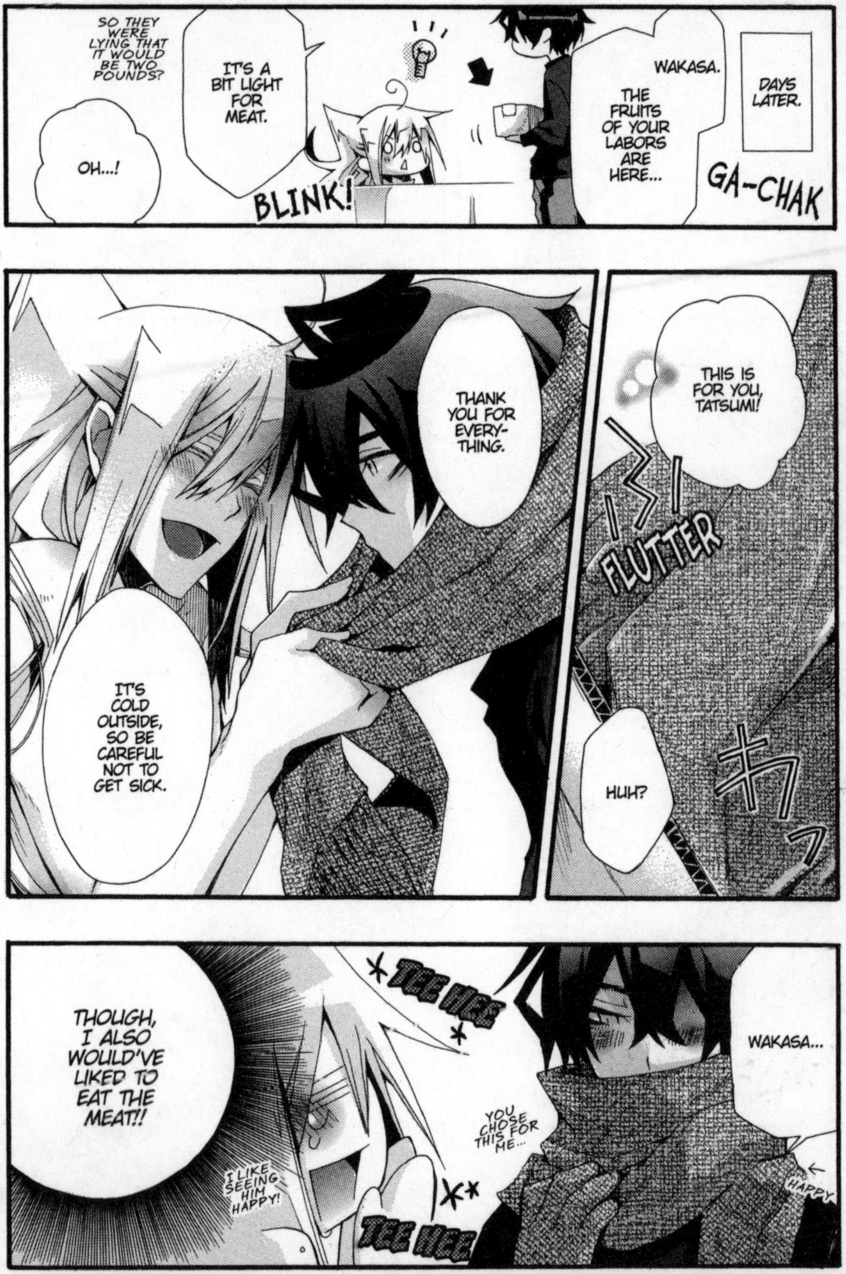
DAYS LATER.
GA-CHAK
WAKASA.
THE FRUITS OF YOUR LABORS ARE HERE...
IT'S A BIT LIGHT FOR MEAT.
BLINK!
SO THEY WERE LYING THAT IT WOULD BE TWO POUNDS?
OH...!
THIS IS FOR YOU, TATSUMI!
FLUTTER
HUH?
THANK YOU FOR EVERYTHING.
IT'S COLD OUTSIDE, SO BE CAREFUL NOT TO GET SICK.
WAKASA...
HAPPY
YOU CHOSE THIS FOR ME...
TEE HEE
TEE HEE
I LIKE SEEING HIM HAPPY!
THOUGH, I ALSO WOULD'VE LIKED TO EAT THE MEAT!!

TO BE CONTINUED
IN VOLUME 2!

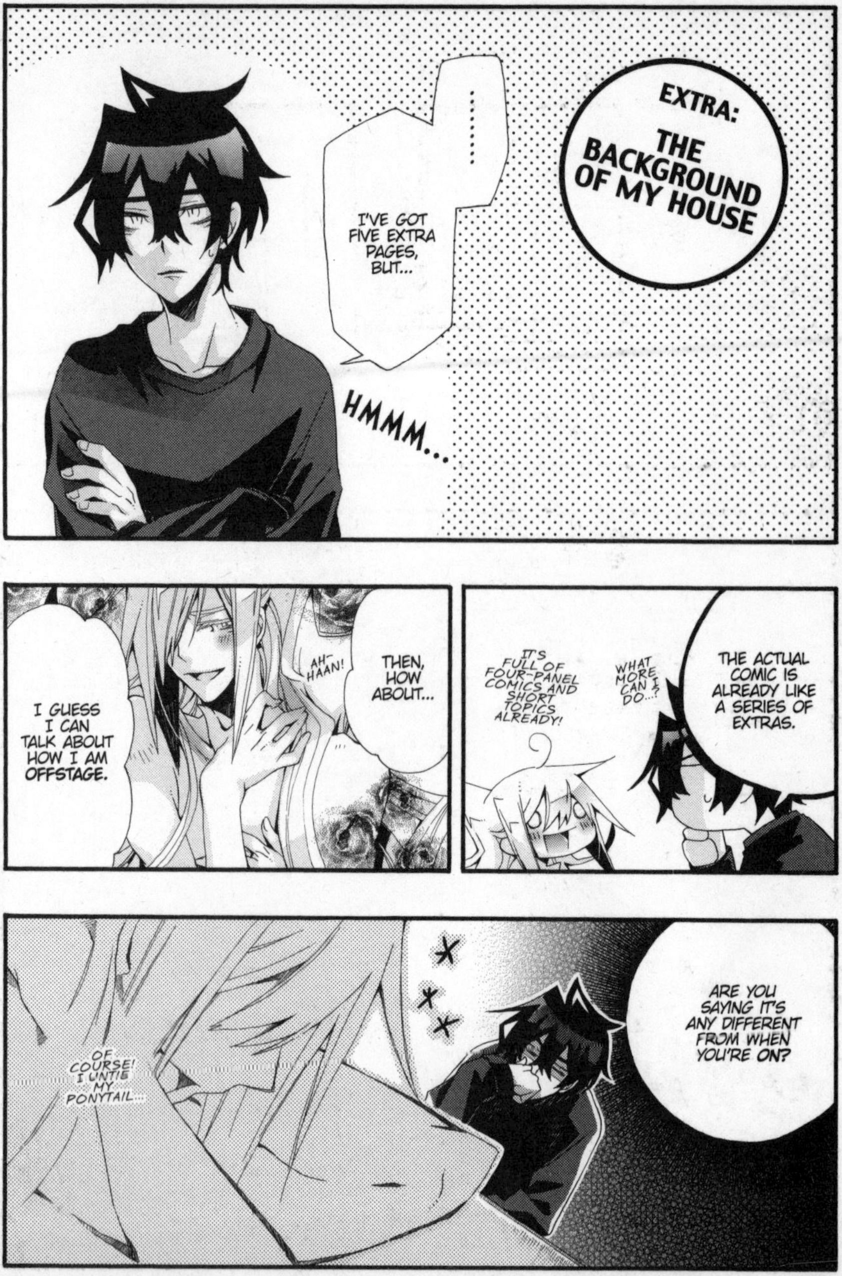
EXTRA: THE BACKGROUND OF MY HOUSE
......
I'VE GOT FIVE EXTRA PAGES, BUT...
HMMM...
THE ACTUAL COMIC IS ALREADY LIKE A SERIES OF EXTRAS.
WHAT MORE CAN I DO...?
IT'S FULL OF FOUR-PANEL COMICS AND SHORT TOPICS ALREADY!
THEN, HOW ABOUT...
AH-HAAN!
I GUESS I CAN TALK ABOUT HOW I AM OFFSTAGE.
ARE YOU SAYING IT'S ANY DIFFERENT FROM WHEN YOU'RE ON?
OF COURSE! I UNTIE MY PONYTAIL...

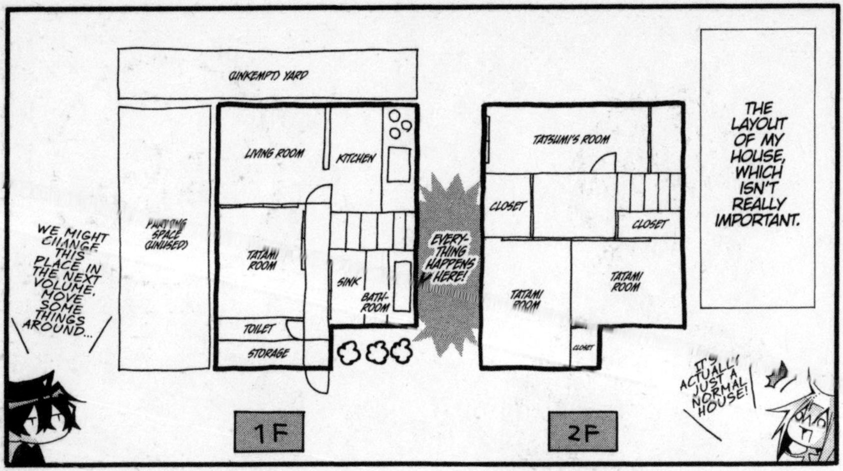
THE LAYOUT OF MY HOUSE, WHICH ISN'T REALLY IMPORTANT.
2F
TATSUMI'S ROOM
CLOSET
CLOSET
TATAMI ROOM
TATAMI ROOM
CLOSET
IT'S ACTUALLY JUST A NORMAL HOUSE!
EVERYTHING HAPPENS HERE!
1F
(UNKEMPT) YARD
LIVING ROOM
KITCHEN
TATAMI ROOM
SINK
BATHROOM
TOILET
STORAGE
PARKING SPACE (UNUSED)
WE MIGHT CHANGE THIS PLACE IN THE NEXT VOLUME. MOVE SOME THINGS AROUND...

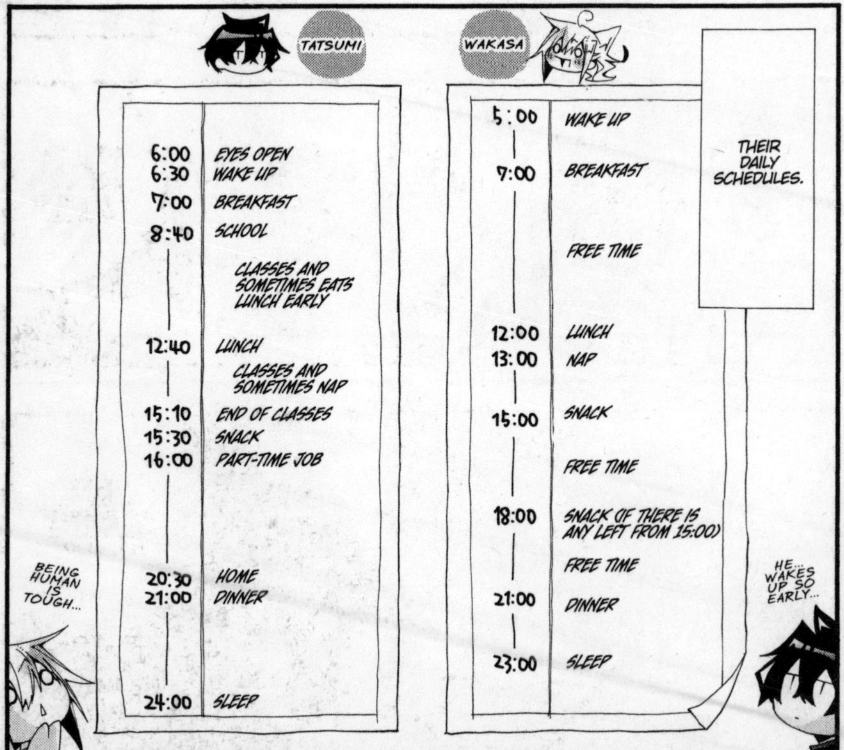
THEIR DAILY SCHEDULES.
WAKASA
5:00 WAKE UP
7:00 BREAKFAST
FREE TIME
12:00 LUNCH
13:00 NAP
15:00 SNACK
FREE TIME
18:00 SNACK (IF THERE IS ANY LEFT FROM 15:00)
FREE TIME
21:00 DINNER
23:00 SLEEP
HE... WAKES UP SO EARLY...
TATSUMI
6:00 EYES OPEN
6:30 WAKE UP
7:00 BREAKFAST
8:40 SCHOOL
CLASSES AND SOMETIMES EATS LUNCH EARLY
12:40 LUNCH
CLASSES AND SOMETIMES NAP
15:10 END OF CLASSES
15:30 SNACK
16:00 PART-TIME JOB
20:30 HOME
21:00 DINNER
24:00 SLEEP
BEING HUMAN IS TOUGH...

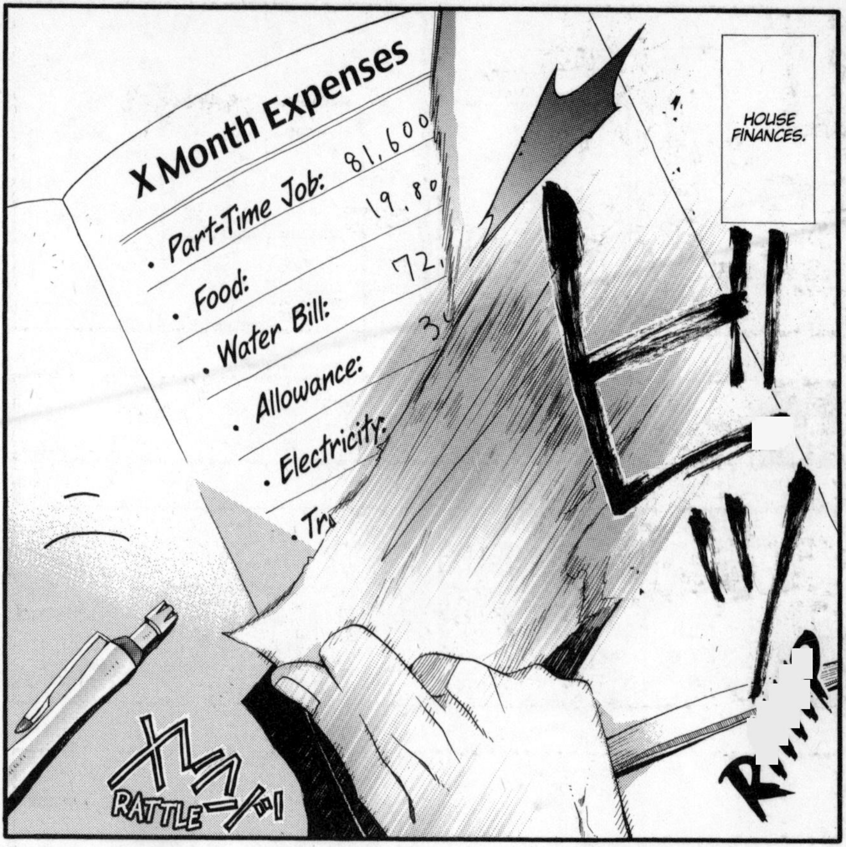
HOUSE FINANCES.
X Month Expenses
• Part-Time Job: 81,600
• Food: 19,80
• Water Bill: 72,
• Allowance: 3
• Electricity:
• Tr
RATTLE

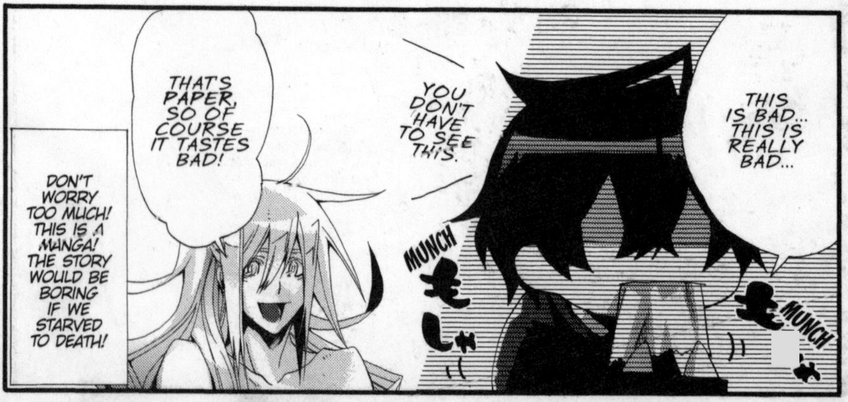
THIS IS BAD... THIS IS REALLY BAD...
MUNCH
YOU DON'T HAVE TO SEE THIS.
MUNCH
THAT'S PAPER, SO OF COURSE IT TASTES BAD!
DON'T WORRY TOO MUCH! THIS IS A MANGA! THE STORY WOULD BE BORING IF WE STARVED TO DEATH!

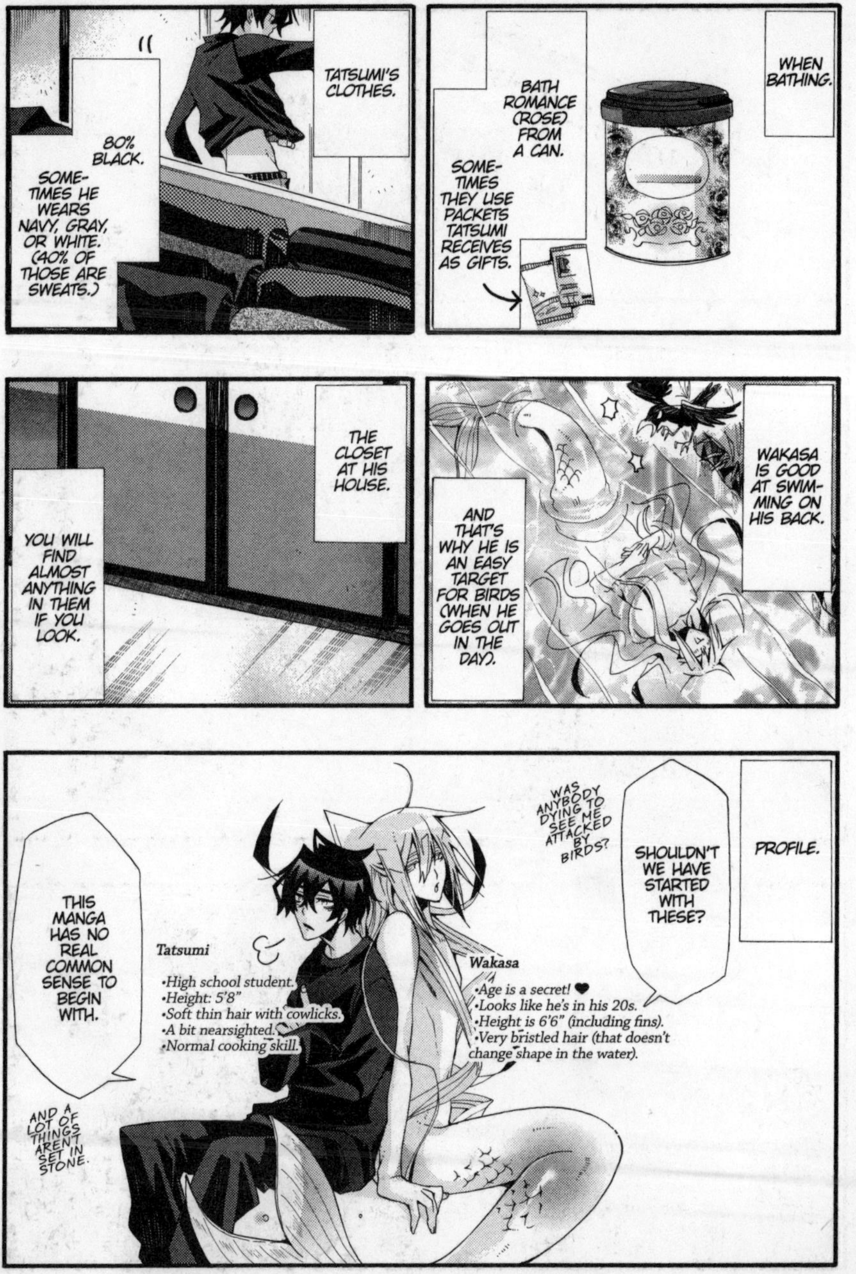
WHEN BATHING.
BATH ROMANCE (ROSE) FROM A CAN.
SOMETIMES THEY USE PACKETS TATSUMI RECEIVES AS GIFTS.
TATSUMI'S CLOTHES.
80% BLACK.
SOMETIMES HE WEARS NAVY, GRAY, OR WHITE. (40% OF THOSE ARE SWEATS.)
WAKASA IS GOOD AT SWIMMING ON HIS BACK.
AND THAT'S WHY HE IS AN EASY TARGET FOR BIRDS (WHEN HE GOES OUT IN THE DAY).
THE CLOSET AT HIS HOUSE.
YOU WILL FIND ALMOST ANYTHING IN THEM IF YOU LOOK.
PROFILE.
SHOULDN'T WE HAVE STARTED WITH THESE?
WAS ANYBODY DYING TO SEE ME ATTACKED BY BIRDS?
Wakasa
•Age is a secret! ❤
•Looks like he's in his 20s.
•Height is 6'6" (including fins).
•Very bristled hair (that doesn't change shape in the water).
Tatsumi
•High school student.
•Height: 5'8"
•Soft thin hair with cowlicks.
•A bit nearsighted.
•Normal cooking skill.
THIS MANGA HAS NO REAL COMMON SENSE TO BEGIN WITH.
AND A LOT OF THINGS AREN'T SET IN STONE.

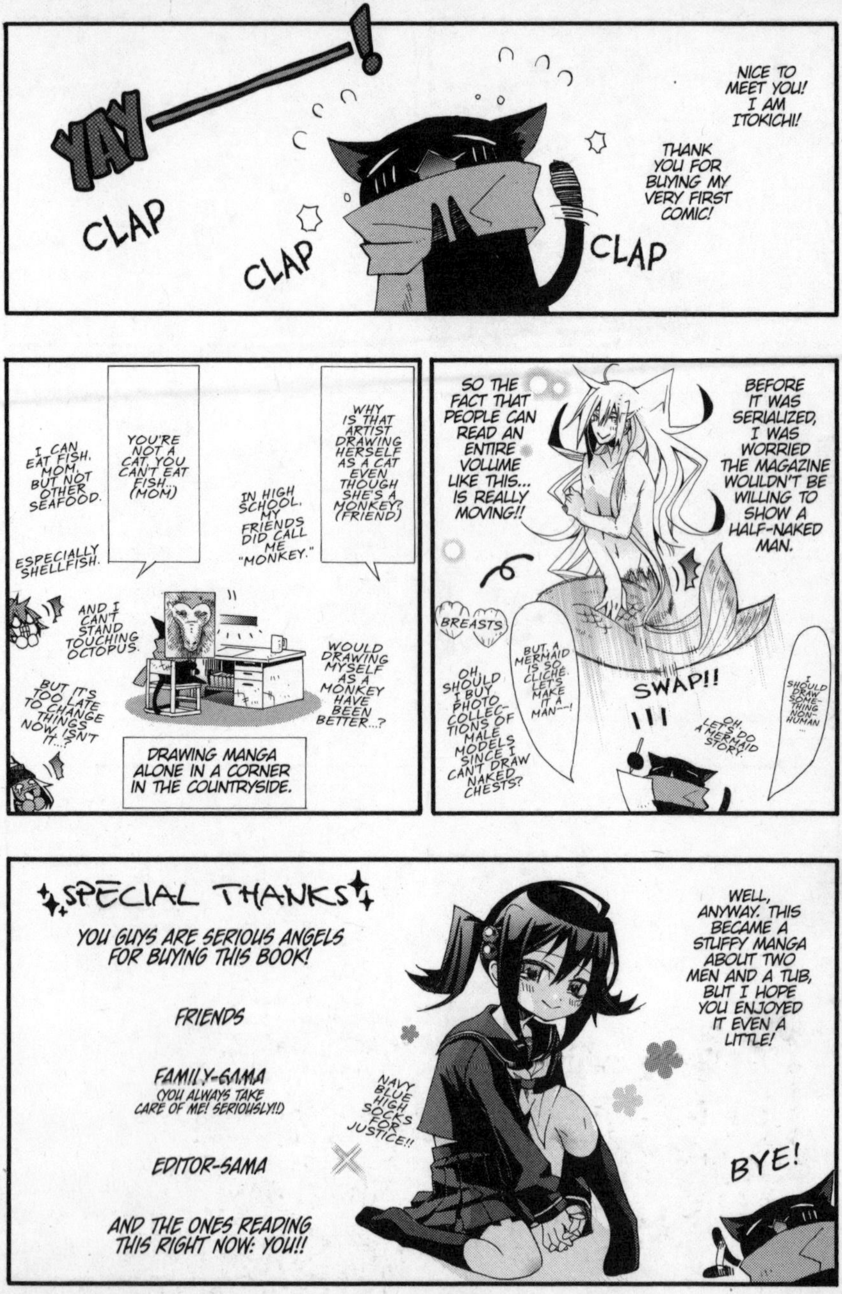
NICE TO MEET YOU! I AM ITOKICHI!
THANK YOU FOR BUYING MY VERY FIRST COMIC!
CLAP
CLAP
CLAP
YAY
BEFORE IT WAS SERIALIZED, I WAS WORRIED THE MAGAZINE WOULDN'T BE WILLING TO SHOW A HALF-NAKED MAN.
SO THE FACT THAT PEOPLE CAN READ AN ENTIRE VOLUME LIKE THIS... IS REALLY MOVING!!
I SHOULD DRAW SOMETHING NON-HUMAN...
OH, LET'S DO A MERMAID STORY!
BUT, A MERMAID IS SO CLICHE. LET'S MAKE IT A MAN---!
SWAP!!
BREASTS
OH, SHOULD I BUY PHOTO COLLECTIONS OF MALE MODELS SINCE I CAN'T DRAW NAKED CHESTS?
WHY IS THAT ARTIST DRAWING HERSELF AS A CAT EVEN THOUGH SHE'S A MONKEY? (FRIEND)
IN HIGH SCHOOL, MY FRIENDS DID CALL ME "MONKEY."
YOU'RE NOT A CAT, YOU CAN'T EAT FISH. (MOM)
I CAN EAT FISH, MOM, BUT NOT OTHER SEAFOOD.
ESPECIALLY SHELLFISH.
AND I CAN'T STAND TOUCHING OCTOPUS.
WOULD DRAWING MYSELF AS A MONKEY HAVE BEEN BETTER...?
BUT IT'S TOO LATE TO CHANGE THINGS NOW, ISN'T IT...?
DRAWING MANGA ALONE IN A CORNER IN THE COUNTRYSIDE.
WELL, ANYWAY. THIS BECAME A STUFFY MANGA ABOUT TWO MEN AND A TUB, BUT I HOPE YOU ENJOYED IT EVEN A LITTLE!
SPECIAL THANKS
YOU GUYS ARE SERIOUS ANGELS FOR BUYING THIS BOOK!
FRIENDS
FAMILY-SAMA
(YOU ALWAYS TAKE CARE OF ME! SERIOUSLY!!)
EDITOR-SAMA
AND THE ONES READING THIS RIGHT NOW: YOU!!
NAVY BLUE HIGH SOCKS FOR JUSTICE!!
BYE!

Merman in My Tub

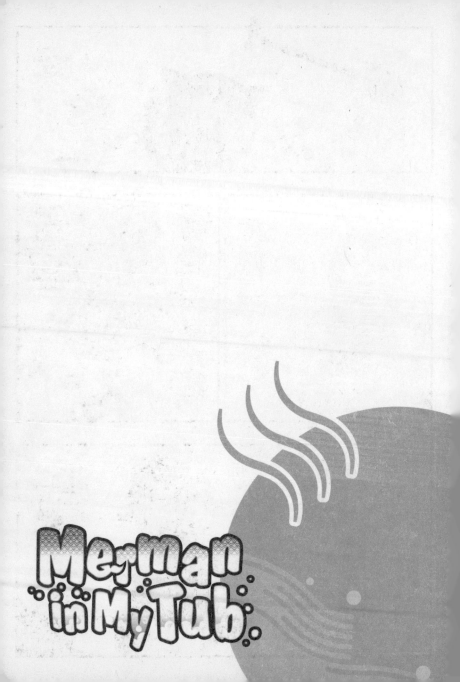

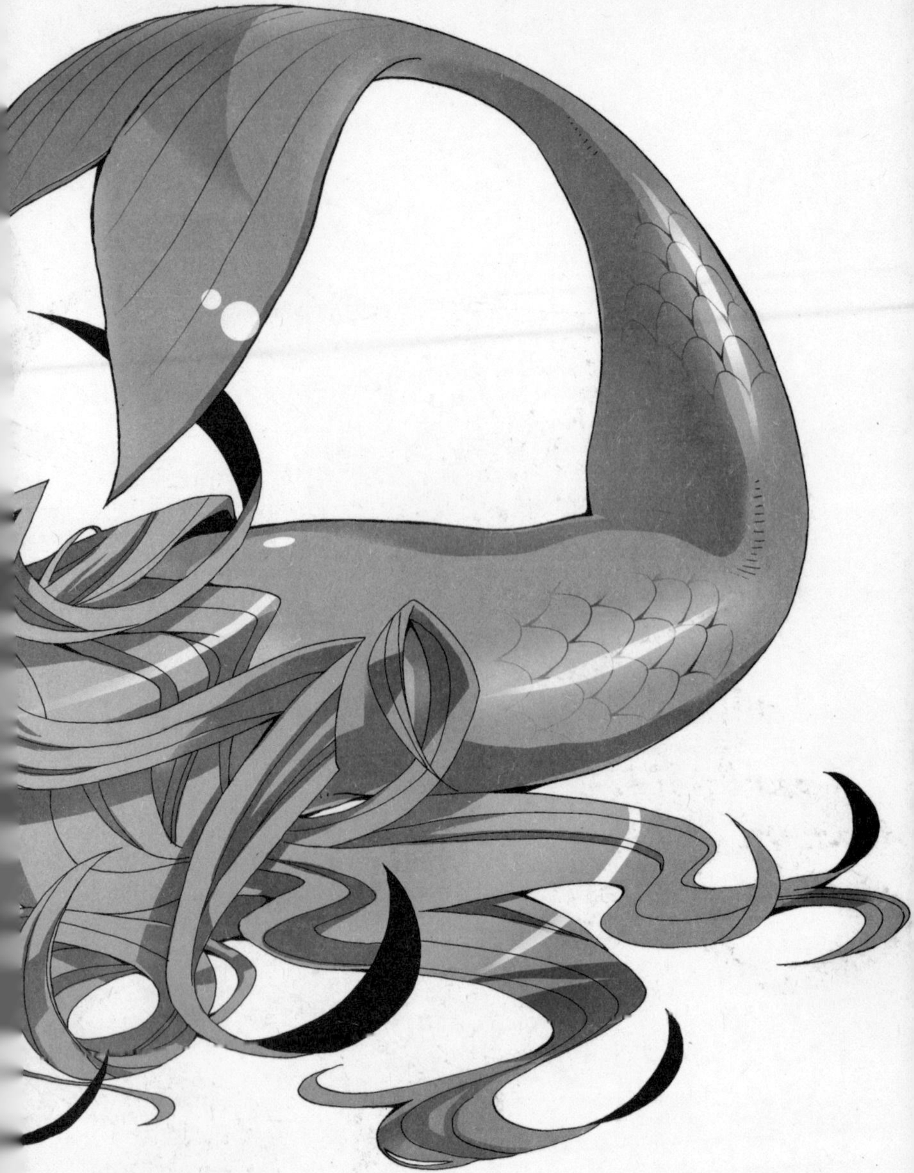

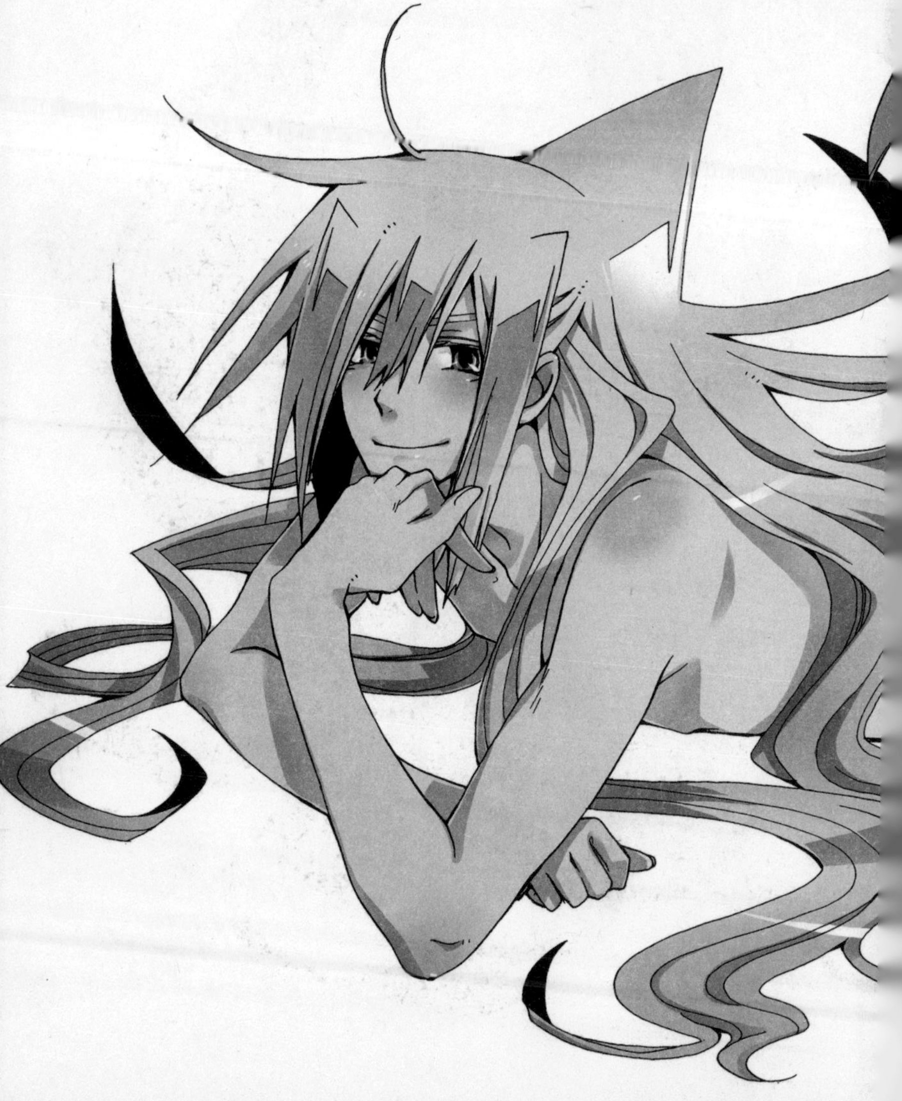

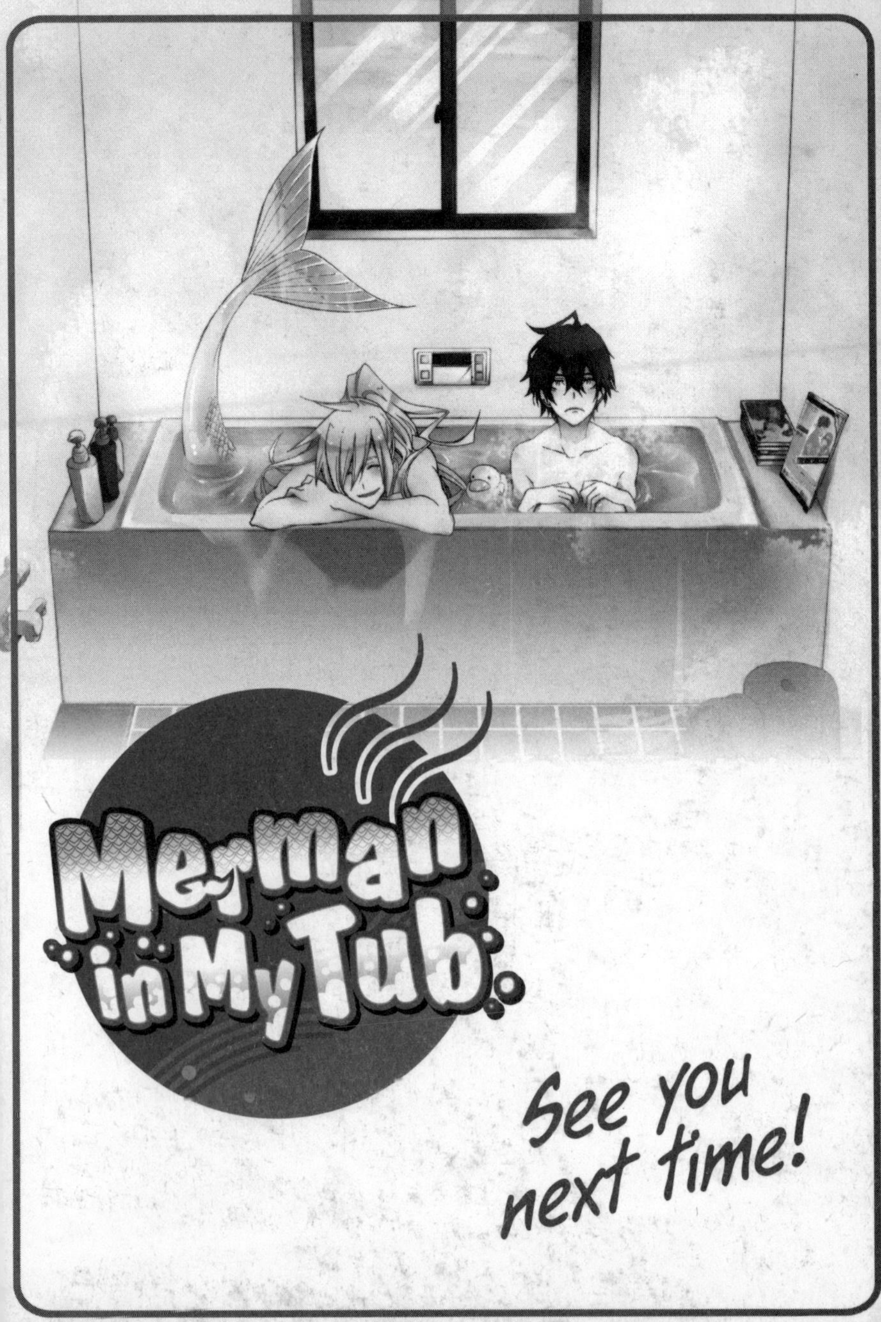
Merman in My Tub
See you next time!

SEVEN SEAS ENTERTAINMENT PRESENTS

Merman in My Tub

story and art by ITOKICHI

volume 1

TRANSLATION
Angela Liu

ADAPTATION
T Campbell

LETTERING AND LAYOUT
Laura Scoville

LOGO DESIGN
Meaghan Tucker

COVER DESIGN
Nicky Lim

PROOFREADER
Patrick King
Danielle King

ASSISTANT EDITOR
Lissa Pattillo

MANAGING EDITOR
Adam Arnold

PUBLISHER
Jason DeAngelis

MERMAN IN MY TUB VOL. 1

Edited by MEDIA FACTORY.
First published in Japan in 2012 by KADOKAWA CORPORATION, Tokyo.
English translation rights reserved by Seven Seas Entertainment, LLC.
under the license from KADOKAWA CORPORATION, Tokyo.

ISBN: 978-1-626922-26-6

Printed in Canada

First Printing: October 2015

10 9 8 7 6 5 4 3 2 1

FOLLOW US ONLINE: ***www.gomanga.com***

READING DIRECTIONS

This book reads from ***right to left***, Japanese style. If this is your first time reading manga, you start reading from the top right panel on each page and take it from there. If you get lost, just follow the numbered diagram here. It may seem backwards at first, but you'll get the hang of it! Have fun!!

1
2
3
4
5
6
7
8
9

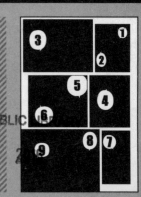